D1202515

The Writer's Harbrace Handbook

Baylor University Edition

Cheryl Glenn and Loretta Gray

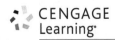
CENGAGE
Learning·

Australia • Brazil • Japan • Korea • Mexico • Singapore • Spain • United Kingdom • United States

CENGAGE
Learning·

The Writer's Harbrace Handbook: Baylor University Edition

The Writer's Harbrace Handbook, 5th Edition
Cheryl Glenn, Loretta Gray

© 2013 Cengage Learning. All rights reserved.

Market Development Manager:

Linda deStefano

Market Development Manager:

Heather Kramer

Senior Production/ Manufacturing Manager:

Donna M. Brown

Production Editorial Manager:

Kim Fry

Sr. Rights Acquisition Account Manager:

Todd Osborne

For product information and technology assistance, contact us at
Cengage Learning Customer & Sales Support, 1-800-354-9706

For permission to use material from this text or product,
submit all requests online at **cengage.com/permissions**
Further permissions questions can be emailed to
permissionrequest@cengage.com

This book contains select works from existing Cengage Learning resources and was produced by Cengage Learning Custom Solutions for collegiate use. As such, those adopting and/or contributing to this work are responsible for editorial content accuracy, continuity and completeness.

Compilation © 2013 Cengage Learning.

ISBN-13:   978-1-285-87953-6

ISBN-10:   1-285-87953-8

Cengage Learning
5191 Natorp Boulevard
Mason, Ohio 45040
USA

Cengage Learning is a leading provider of customized learning solutions with office locations around the globe, including Singapore, the United Kingdom, Australia, Mexico, Brazil, and Japan. Locate your local office at:
international.cengage.com/region.

Cengage Learning products are represented in Canada by Nelson Education, Ltd.
For your lifelong learning solutions, visit **www.cengage.com/custom.**
Visit our corporate website at **www.cengage.com.**

Printed in the United States of America

Guide for Freshman Composition:
English 1302 and 1304

Freshman composition is a general education requirement for all students who expect to graduate with a baccalaureate degree under any curriculum at Baylor University. Students should enroll in English 1302 and 1304 as early as possible in their college careers. They may wish to take English 1302 and 1304 to develop their writing skills even though appropriate test scores can exempt them from 1302, though test scores do not exempt students from 1304. English 1302 and 1304 are prerequisites for English 2301, 2304, and 2306.

English 1302
Thinking and Writing

Course Objectives:
English 1302 is designed to help students develop the rhetorical knowledge and practical habits of successful college writers. Students will learn to use the concepts of purpose, audience, and genre as they develop their own documents; to generate claims, ideas, supporting details, and evidence; to use appropriate expository structures; to produce drafts and to revise their work as they develop a final product; to produce a prose style that is readable, effective, and free from error; and to develop critical skills through an analysis of good expository writing.

Textbooks:
Reid, *The Essential Guide for College Writing,* custom edition for Baylor University
Glenn, Miller, & Webb, *The Writer's Harbrace Handbook,* 5th ed.

*Note: An instructor may use an alternate or additional text when approved by the Freshman English Committee.

Assignments:
Students in English 1302 write a minimum of six essays, including the final exam, a departmental in-class essay. The major essay assignments of the course reflect the following emphasis: Reading and Responding, Explaining, Analyzing and Evaluating, Problem Solving and Arguing, Writing the In-Class Essay, and the final exam. Drafting, revising, and editing will be included in all course units.

English 1302 assignments present writing as a recursive process in which students complete a series of both in-class and out-of-class assignments as they work toward creating the final essay document. Reading and writing assignments address a variety of rhetorical aims and patterns in writing as students develop skills of focusing on interesting topics, providing adequate and appropriate support for assertions, writing clearly and coherently, and organizing material in an effective and efficient manner. Stylistic issues such as precise diction and effective and varied sentence patterns are also addressed. Both in-class and out-of-class assignments help prepare students for writing requirements in other university courses as well as in English 1304.

Final Examination:
The final examination is departmental, given at a time set by the university, and requires students to write an essay within a two-hour period. During this time, students should demonstrate the ability to choose a topic, present a clearly-worded thesis supported by appropriate examples, and effectively organize the arrangement of their claims. Writing style on the final exam should be precise and effective and also reflect standard conventions of usage as presented in course texts.

Final Grade for English 1302:
Instructors base the final grade upon the following approximate percentages: essays—75%; writing process assignments, tests and other daily work—15%; final examination—10%.

English 1304
Thinking, Writing, and Research

Prerequisite for English 1304: In order to receive credit for English 1304, a student must have credit for English 1302.

Course Objectives:
While continuing to build on the knowledge and skills developed in English 1302, English 1304 focuses on the relationship between critical reading and writing in an academic context. Assignments require students to read sources carefully and critically and to evaluate information and arguments; to represent their reading accurately and fairly through summary, paraphrase, and quotation; and to use sources appropriately in their own writing. Students learn to use an academic library and appropriate research tools. These reading, writing, and research skills will be presented in the context of preparing critical analyses and arguments, including a formal research paper.

Textbooks:
Wood, *Perspective on Argument,* 7th ed.
Glenn, Miller & Webb, *The Writer's Harbrace Handbook,* 5th ed.

Optional text:
MLA Handbook.

*Note: An instructor may use an alternate or additional text when approved by the Freshman English Committee.

Assignments:
Students in English 1304 complete work within four major categories: Analysis and Response to Argument; Construction and Presentation of Rogerian and Toulmin Argument; Survey and Annotation of Academic Resources; Academic Research Essay. As part of these units of focus, students will complete a minimum of six assignments,

including an Annotated Bibliography and Preliminary Draft for the Research Paper. The final research paper must reflect genuine research with the assimilation of a number of appropriate sources and meet all standards of writing and research presented in class.

Final Examination:
Each instructor composes a final examination, to be given at the scheduled time during the finals period. The examination tests critical and argumentative skills and includes questions or topics requiring well-developed, articulate responses.

Research in English 1304:
Research in English 1304 requires students to survey and report on a representative sampling of others' arguments on a subject worthy of academic interest. The writer then uses this survey of information and arguments to support his or her own conclusions on the subject. This paper may focus on causal relationships, evaluation of evidence, or further development of a previously established argument.

The final paper must reflect a thoroughly researched, fair, and accurate review of arguments from credible sources and reach a logical and insightful conclusion based on thorough academic research.

Instructors establish individual guidelines for the completion of the research process and final paper. In all classes, students are required to demonstrate adequate knowledge of documentation and manuscript form as well as thorough research of their topics.

Final Grade for English 1304:
A student cannot earn credit for English 1304 if the research paper receives the grade of "F." A failing grade on the research paper may result from incomplete assignments, inadequate research, inadequately developed and/or poorly organized content, unsubstantiated claims, incorrect documentation, any violation of Baylor's Honor Code, and/or failure to meet instructor's assignments and complete work in a timely manner.

This emphasis is placed on the research paper grade because English 1304 is designed so that the research paper is a culmination of work completed and skills developed in English 1302 and 1304. Understanding and applying the basic principles of academic research and documentation are essential skills for success in other university courses and, often, in professional pursuits; and the emphasis placed upon academic integrity reflects Baylor's mission to "develop ethical and capable scholars and practitioners who contribute to their academic disciplines, professional fields, and society."

Instructors base the final grade upon the following approximate percentages: essays and final examination—60%; a passing research paper—25%; writing process assignments, tests and other daily work—15%.

General Policies
For English 1302 and 1304

Grades:

Instructors consider all essays and other assigned work when giving students final grades. Students must achieve a passing average on the final four essays in order to receive credit for English 1302 or 1304. Students must complete all essay assignments in order to pass the course. *Plagiarism on any assignment warrants failure in the course.*

Essay Evaluation:

Instructors will inform students of grading standards and expectations, often presenting a specialized rubric for each major assignment. Students should ask for clarification of any assignment expectations before the assignment is due.

Instructors will evaluate essays in the following categories: overall meeting of criteria specific to assignment; a title indicating the focus and tone of the essay; an introduction engaging the reader's interest and providing clear direction for the essay; an easily identifiable thesis; clear and logical organization; thorough development of ideas; careful and thoughtful reading of sources; correct presentation and documentation of sources; logical and analytical thinking in response to sources and in development of ideas; appropriate supportive detail for ideas and arguments; unity and coherence throughout the essay; effective transitions within and between paragraphs; a satisfactory conclusion; clear and concise sentences with varied and effective structure; consistently precise diction appropriate for audience and subject; conventional special, grammar, and punctuation usage.

An **A** essay demonstrates excellence in fulfilling the specific assignment and in the majority of listed criteria. The **B** essay also fulfills the assignment and presents a thorough treatment of the subject but may lack the mastery of all writing skills as demonstrated by the A essay. The **C** essay reflects writing competency in addressing the assignment but may offer superficial development of content, weakness in meeting several criteria, or contain mechanical and grammatical errors that obscure content. The **D** essay marginally fulfills the assignment but fails to demonstrate competency in a number of areas. The **F** essay does not fulfill the assignment and/or is so deficient in areas of content and mechanical proficiency that it fails to communicate ideas clearly and coherently.

Returning of Essays: Instructors will return graded essays to students. Students will return all graded essays to their instructors who retain hard copies of all essays for one semester after the course ends.

Class Attendance: Students are expected to attend all classes. In keeping with the College of Arts and Sciences and English Department's attendance policy, any student who fails to attend at least 75% of all classes will fail automatically. Instructors set their own policies regarding excused absences and penalties for unexcused absences.

Make-up Work:
An instructor will allow a student full credit for a make-up essay only if the student has an excused absence and completes the work within two weeks. Make-up work or late essay assignments for unexcused absences will be penalized according to the instructor's policies. Students should assume responsibility for keeping up with assignments missed during an absence and for contacting the instructor to make up any material missed during an absence.

Incomplete Grade for the Course:
Only emergencies qualify students for the grade of "I." Such emergencies would include the sudden onset of physical illness, hospitalization, prolonged health or family issues requiring a student to be away from school. All emergency situations must be verified by the appropriate offices on campus such as the Vice-Provost of Student Life or the Chaplain's Office.

Plagiarism

Students in English 1302 and 1304 are expected to be familiar with the Baylor University Honor Code and the Policies and Procedures of the Office of Academic Integrity. Information is available at http://www.baylor.edu/honorcode/ . All students should read all Academic Integrity documents available through this page.

The Honor Code states that "Baylor University students and faculty shall act in academic matters with the utmost honesty and integrity." Students violate the honor code if they engage in dishonorable conduct in an academic matter.
Among the types of dishonorable conduct defined in the Honor Code, the following are particularly relevant to a writing course:

1. "Offering for course credit as one's own work, in whole or in part, the work of another."

2. "Incorporating into one's work offered for course credit passages taken either word for word or in substance from a work or another, unless the student credits the original author and identifies the original author's work with quotation marks, footnotes, or another appropriate written explanation."

3. "Offering for course credit one's own work, but work that one has previously offered for course credit in another course, unless one secures permission to do so prior to submission from the instructor in whose course the work is being offered." *This includes work submitted for credit in high school, a community college, or another university.

4. "Offering for course credit work prepared in collaboration with another, unless the student secures the instructor's permission in advance of

submission.
A student does not prepare work in collaboration with another if he or she merely discusses with another a matter relevant to the work in question."
*Work with tutor in the English Department Writing Centers does not constitute dishonest collaboration.

Plagiarism on any work in English 1302 and English 1304 warrants failure in the course. Students should avoid the intellectual theft of plagiarism by (1) using quotation marks and documentation of the original source for any word-for-word copying of any part of another's work, (2) documenting the source of any partially quoted or paraphrased passage from a source, and (3) documenting the source of any completely paraphrased passage. Students are expected to follow the MLA documentation forms presented by their instructors.

Instructors of English 1302 and English 1304 will provide detailed instruction and examples to guide students in the appropriate use of source materials. Textbook and online resources are also available as is tutoring in the English Department Writing Centers. Students are expected to follow the instructors' guidelines and to seek help whenever in doubt about appropriate source use. Misuse or misrepresentation of sources as well as undocumented source use warrants failure in a course and a referral to the Office of Judicial Affairs. Students should take this issue seriously and always seek direction and guidance from their instructors.

Writing Center: The English Department's Writing Center is located on the ground level of Carroll Science Building in G06. The Center is staffed by English Department Graduate Students with training in tutoring student writers. Tutoring services are available at no extra cost for any student enrolled in any course at Baylor. Tutors will not proofread or edit papers for students, but instead will work with students in all stages of the writing process and answer specific questions from students about their work. Faculty may make specific referrals or students may sign up for tutoring sessions on their own. Students should schedule appointments in advance to reserve tutoring time. Sign-up sheets are located at the front desk; students may also make appointments by calling the Center at 710-4849.

Revised May 2013

CONTENTS

iv   Contents

G   **PART 4** GRAMMAR

S   PART 5   EFFECTIVE SENTENCES

M   PART 8   MECHANICS

PART 9 ADVICE FOR MULTILINGUAL WRITERS

PREFACE

Welcome to *The Writer's Harbrace Handbook,* Fifth Edition. The book in your hands is part of a long tradition that started with *The Hodges Harbrace Handbook*, which celebrated its seventieth birthday in 2011. Because each edition of *The Writer's Harbrace Handbook* changes in response to current studies in composition and linguistics, students can depend on the research-based guidance offered in this book. Each edition is also class-tested. In this book, just as in our classrooms, we strive to show, rather than just tell, students how to write. Our goal is to provide them with the advice they need, explained in language they can understand. To that end, we use visuals, checklists, tip boxes, charts, examples, and annotated student papers that emphasize information discussed in the text. Skimming through the chapters will show you what we mean.

The Fifth Edition both introduces the new and keeps the best of the old. Our focus on the rhetorical demands of writing remains strong. Whether students are working with pen and paper or with keyboard and screen, they will find practical suggestions for successfully completing their assignments. We also continue to prepare students to write successfully in a range of academic disciplines. Students will find not only guidelines for writing in the arts, humanities, sciences, and business but also fully annotated, full-length examples of many kinds of papers.

As in previous editions, early chapters support writing assignments that are general in nature, requiring limited or no use of secondary sources. These initial chapters are followed by three chapters on finding, evaluating, and integrating source material. Because of our emphasis on cross-disciplinary writing, we include nine chapters devoted to the conventions and documentation guides that will help students write for a range of classes. The second half of the book comprises chapters on grammar, usage, sentence style, punctuation, and other mechanical concerns.

How Have We Revised This Edition to Address "Framework for Success in Postsecondary Writing"?

Since the last edition of this handbook was published, the Council of Writing Program Administrators (CWPA), the National Council of Teachers of English (NCTE), and the National Writing Project (NWP) have jointly published "Framework for Success in Postsecondary Writing." This document stresses the need to help students develop their (1) rhetorical knowledge, (2) critical thinking, (3) understanding of the writing process, (4) knowledge of conventions, and (5) ability to craft prose in a range of contexts, including those that call for the use of technology. We have revised this edition of *The Writer's Harbrace Handbook* to ensure that each of these areas is fully covered.

Rhetorical knowledge

- Chapter 1, "Reading, Writing, and the Rhetorical Situation," introduces students to the elements of the rhetorical situation and to the steps for reading and writing rhetorically. The explanations of the rhetorical situation in this chapter (and in the rest of the book) have been simplified for easier understanding and application.
- Chapter 6, "Composing with Visuals," presents rhetorical principles for interpreting and producing visuals on paper and in electronic communications.
- Chapter 10, "Integrating Sources and Avoiding Plagiarism," asks students to consider their rhetorical situation as they do research.
- In Part 3, "Disciplines and Documentation Styles," Chapters 11, 13, 15, 17, and 19 cover the discipline-specific rhetorical knowledge that students need for informed research and successful writing.
- In Part 4, "Grammar," Chapters 20 through 26 invite students to think rhetorically about grammar.

Critical thinking

- Chapter 4, "Managing Academic Writing," introduces strategies for developing ideas at various levels of intellectual complexity (according to Bloom's Taxonomy of Learning Domains), especially when writing under time constraints.

- Chapter 7, "Writing Arguments," demonstrates ways to analyze a text, reason logically, avoid rhetorical fallacies, incorporate evidence, and compose several types of arguments.
- Chapter 10, "Integrating Sources and Avoiding Plagiarism," provides students with the strategies and language they need to demonstrate proficiency at the levels of intellectual complexity noted in Bloom's Taxonomy. Boxes provide students with sentence frames, or templates, that employ phraseology that is frequently used to summarize, synthesize, and respond to sources.

Writing process

- Chapter 2, "Planning and Drafting Essays," helps students generate ideas for topics and organize the message of their essays.
- Chapter 3, "Revising and Editing Essays," introduces strategies for recursive writing, editing, and proofreading.
- Chapter 4, "Managing Academic Writing," demonstrates ways students can compress the writing process and develop persuasive portfolios.

Knowledge of conventions

- In Part 3, "Disciplines and Documentation Styles," Chapters 12, 14, 16, and 18 present the citation and documentation guidelines for various disciplines—MLA, APA, CMS, and CSE, respectively.
- In Part 7, "Punctuation," Chapters 35–39 explain the conventions of punctuation.
- In Part 8, "Mechanics," Chapters 40–43 include guidelines for other mechanical issues: spelling, capitalization, and the use of italics, abbreviations, acronyms, and numbers.

Writing in multiple contexts

- Chapter 4, "Managing Academic Writing," introduces strategies for writing under pressure.
- Chapter 5, "Online Writing," presents the skills for creating various types of online documents that may be called for in school or work environments.
- Chapter 6, "Composing with Visuals," guides students in the effective use of visuals in their essays and publications.

- Chapter 13, "Writing in the Social Sciences," includes a consent form in its sample student paper to draw attention to the federal government's requirement that students (or faculty members) who conduct research involving human participants must use such a form and have their study approved by their school's institutional review board.
- In Part 3, "Disciplines and Documentation Styles," Chapters 11, 13, 15, 17, and 19 describe discipline-specific expectations for written work.

What Is New to This Edition?

Based on our observations of the ever-changing student population, we have added new material to address current issues and challenges.

New Part 9, Advice for Multilingual Writers

- Chapter 45, "Determiners, Nouns, and Adjectives," helps students decide when (and when not) to use determiners (such as articles) before nouns and adjectives.
- Chapter 46, "Verbs and Verb Forms," provides detailed information on verb tenses, modal auxiliaries, phrasal and prepositional verbs, and participles used as adjectives.
- Chapter 47, "Word Order," focuses on the ordering of adverbs and adjectives as well as on word order in embedded questions and in adjectival clauses.

New, fully annotated student papers from across the disciplines

- Chapter 3, "Revising and Editing Essays," includes a process-analysis essay that discusses the steps taken by student-athletes as they select a college. The writer conducted primary research in the form of interviews.
- Chapter 11, "Writing about Literature," presents a literary interpretation of the short story "The Yellow Wallpaper" from a feminist perspective.
- Chapter 13, "Writing in the Social Sciences," includes a laboratory report that investigates the role gender plays in assigning status to occupations.
- Chapter 16, "CMS Documentation," offers a research paper that examines the economic implications of South Africa's difficulties in providing electricity to its poorer citizens.

- Chapter 17, "Writing in the Natural Sciences," presents a field report on the relationship between tree trunk height and lichen distribution.
- Chapter 18, "CSE Documentation," includes a research report on the environmental damage caused by the tsunami that devastated the coastal areas of Thailand in 2004.

Exercises

- One-third of the handbook's exercises have been replaced to introduce fresh topics or to test newly introduced concepts.

The History

The Harbrace family of handbooks has the longest history of any set of handbooks in the United States. First published in 1941 by University of Tennessee English professor John C. Hodges, *The Harbrace Handbook of English* was a product of Hodges's classroom experience and his federally funded research, which comprised an analysis of twenty thousand student papers. Sixteen English professors from various regions of the United States marked those papers; they found a number of common mistakes, including (1) misplaced commas, (2) misspelling, (3) inexact language, (4) lack of subject-verb agreement, (5) superfluous commas, (6) shifts in tense, (7) misused apostrophes, (8) omission of words, (9) wordiness, and (10) lack of standard usage.

After collecting these data, Hodges worked with a cadre of graduate students to create a taxonomy of writing issues (from punctuation and grammar to style and usage) that would organize the first writing manual for American college students and teachers. This taxonomy still underpins the overall design and organization of nearly every handbook on the market today. Hodges's original handbook evolved into *The Writer's Harbrace Handbook*, Fifth Edition, which continues to respond to the needs of students and writing instructors alike.

How to Use This Handbook

The Writer's Harbrace Handbook routinely receives praise for its comprehensive treatment of a wide range of topics. Whether you have a question about drafting or revising a paper, using visuals, understanding the logic of arguments, identifying a complete sentence, capitalizing a word, punctuating a sentence (or any other question related to reading and writing rhetorically), the answer is at your fingertips.

Brief Table of Contents

If you have a topic in mind, such as writing a thesis statement or using commas correctly, check the contents list inside the front cover. With each topic is a number-and-letter combination (2c or 20d, for example) that corresponds to the number and letter at the top of the relevant right-hand page(s) in the book.

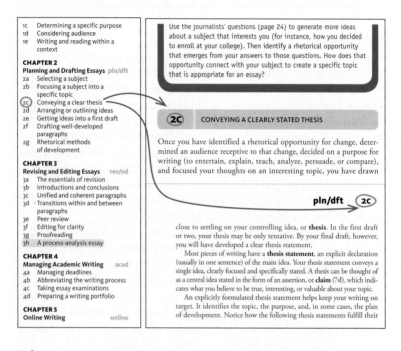

Use the journalists' questions (page 24) to generate more ideas about a subject that interests you (for instance, how you decided to enroll at your college). Then identify a rhetorical opportunity that emerges from your answers to those questions. How does that opportunity connect with your subject to create a specific topic that is appropriate for an essay?

2c   CONVEYING A CLEARLY STATED THESIS

Once you have identified a rhetorical opportunity for change, determined an audience receptive to that change, decided on a purpose for writing (to entertain, explain, teach, analyze, persuade, or compare), and focused your thoughts on an interesting topic, you have drawn

pln/dft   **2c**

close to settling on your controlling idea, or **thesis**. In the first draft or two, your thesis may be only tentative. By your final draft, however, you will have developed a clear thesis statement.

Most pieces of writing have a **thesis statement**, an explicit declaration (usually in one sentence) of the main idea. Your thesis statement conveys a single idea, clearly focused and specifically stated. A thesis can be thought of as a central idea stated in the form of an assertion, or **claim** (7d), which indicates what you believe to be true, interesting, or valuable about your topic.

An explicitly formulated thesis statement helps keep your writing on target. It identifies the topic, the purpose, and, in some cases, the plan of development. Notice how the following thesis statements fulfill their

Tabs

Colored tabs, which correspond to the distinctive colors of Parts 1 through 9 and the four documentation chapters, are staggered down the outside edges of the book's pages. These tabs help orient you to the section of the handbook you are in as you look up information.

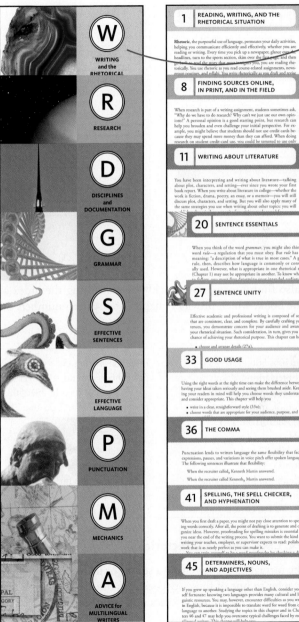

W

WRITING
and the
RHETORICAL

1 **READING, WRITING, AND THE RHETORICAL SITUATION**

Rhetoric, the purposeful use of language, permeates your daily activities, helping you communicate efficiently and effectively, whether you are reading or writing. Every time you pick up a newspaper, glance over the headlines, turn to the sports section, skim over the listings, and then look to read the story that most interests you, you are reading rhetorically. You use rhetoric as you read course-related assignments, newsgroup postings, and syllabi. You write rhetorically as you draft and revise

R

RESEARCH

8 **FINDING SOURCES ONLINE, IN PRINT, AND IN THE FIELD**

When research is part of a writing assignment, students sometimes ask, "Why do we have to do research? Why can't we just use our own opinions?" A personal opinion is a good starting point, but research can help you broaden and even challenge your initial perspective. For example, you might believe that students should not use credit cards because they may spend more money than they can afford. When doing research on student credit-card use, you could be tempted to use only

D

DISCIPLINES
and
DOCUMENTATION

11 **WRITING ABOUT LITERATURE**

You have been interpreting and writing about literature—talking about plot, characters, and setting—ever since you wrote your first book report. When you write about literature in college—whether the work is fiction, drama, poetry, an essay, or a memoir—you will still discuss plot, characters, and setting. But you will also apply many of the same strategies you use when writing about other topics: you will

G

GRAMMAR

20 **SENTENCE ESSENTIALS**

When you think of the word *grammar*, you might also think of the word *rule*—a regulation that you must obey. But *rule* has another meaning: "a description of what is true in most cases." A grammar rule, then, describes how language is commonly or conventionally used. However, what is appropriate in one rhetorical situation (Chapter 1) may not be appropriate in another. To know which rules to follow, you must first determine your intended audience, your

S

EFFECTIVE
SENTENCES

27 **SENTENCE UNITY**

Effective academic and professional writing is composed of sentences that are consistent, clear, and complete. By carefully crafting your sentences, you demonstrate concern for your audience and awareness of your rhetorical situation. Such consideration, in turn, gives you a better chance of achieving your rhetorical purpose. This chapter can help you

- choose and arrange details (27a),

L

EFFECTIVE
LANGUAGE

33 **GOOD USAGE**

Using the right words at the right time can make the difference between having your ideas taken seriously and seeing them brushed aside. Keeping your readers in mind will help you choose words they understand and consider appropriate. This chapter will help you

- write in a clear, straightforward style (33a);
- choose words that are appropriate for your audience, purpose, and

P

PUNCTUATION

36 **THE COMMA**

Punctuation lends to written language the same flexibility that facial expressions, pauses, and variations in voice pitch offer spoken language. The following sentences illustrate that flexibility:

When the recruiter called, Kenneth Martin answered.

When the recruiter called Kenneth, Martin answered.

M

MECHANICS

41 **SPELLING, THE SPELL CHECKER, AND HYPHENATION**

When you first draft a paper, you might not pay close attention to spelling words correctly. After all, the point of drafting is to generate and organize ideas. However, proofreading for spelling mistakes is essential as you near the end of the writing process. You want to submit the kind of writing your teacher, employer, or supervisor expects to read: polished work that is as nearly perfect as you can make it.

A

ADVICE for
MULTILINGUAL
WRITERS

45 **DETERMINERS, NOUNS, AND ADJECTIVES**

If you grew up speaking a language other than English, consider yourself fortunate: knowing two languages provides many cultural and linguistic resources. You may, however, encounter difficulties as you write in English, because it is impossible to translate word for word from one language to another. Studying the topics in this chapter and in Chapters 46 and 47 may help you overcome typical challenges faced by multilingual writers. This chapter will help you

Index

You can also find information quickly by consulting the index at the back of the book, which provides chapter and section numbers as well as page numbers.

MLA, APA, CMS, and CSE Directories

To find the format to use for citing a source or listing a source in a bibliography, refer to one of these style-specific directories. If you use one of these directories often, put a sticky note on it so that you can locate it in an instant.

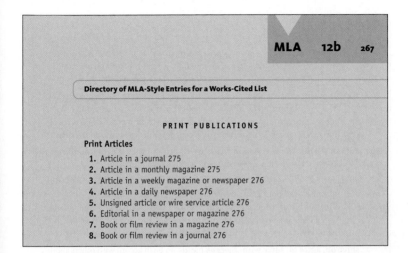

Directory of MLA-Style Entries for a Works-Cited List

PRINT PUBLICATIONS

Print Articles

1. Article in a journal 275
2. Article in a monthly magazine 275
3. Article in a weekly magazine or newspaper 276
4. Article in a daily newspaper 276
5. Unsigned article or wire service article 276
6. Editorial in a newspaper or magazine 276
7. Book or film review in a magazine 276
8. Book or film review in a journal 276

Revision Symbols

Inside the back cover of the book is a list of revision symbols. The symbols can be used to provide feedback on papers, and the list identifies chapters or sections where pertinent rules, guidelines, or strategies are discussed in more detail.

coh		Coherence	" "	39	Quotation mark
	26d	modifiers	red	35a(1)	Redundant
	3c	paragraphs	ref	25d	Reference
:	37b	Colon	rep	31d, 35a	Repetition
,	36a–f	Comma	rev	3a–g	Revision
cs	23b–c	Comma splice	;	37a	Semicolon
con	35	Conciseness	sg		Singular
cst		Consistency	/	40h	Slash
	28a	verb tense	sp	41a–e	Spelling
	28b	point of view	sub	29a, 29c	Subordination
coor	29b–c	Coordination	[ ]	40f	Square brackets
—	40d	Dash	t	24b	Tense
ɘ		Delete	trans	3d	Transition
dev		Development	∩∪		Transpose
			u		Unity

Glossary of Usage

This glossary includes definitions of words that are commonly confused or misused (such as *accept* and *except*). Organized like a dictionary, it provides not only common meanings for the words but also example sentences demonstrating usage.

a lot of *A lot of* is conversational for *many, much,* or *a great deal of:* They do not have ~~a lot of~~ much time. *A lot* is sometimes misspelled as *alot.*

a while, awhile *A while* means "a period of time." It is often used with the prepositions *after, for,* and *in:* We rested for **a while.** *Awhile* means "a short time." It is not preceded by a preposition: We rested **awhile.**

accept, except The verb *accept* means "to receive": I **accept** your apology. The verb *except* means "to exclude": The policy was to have everyone wait in line, but parents with mothers and small children were **excepted.** The preposition *except* means "other than": All **except** Joe will attend the conference.

advice, advise *Advice* is a noun: They asked their attorney for **advice.** *Advise* is a verb: The attorney **advised** us to save all relevant documents.

affect, effect *Affect* is a verb that means "to influence": The lobbyist's pleas did not **affect** the politician's decision. The noun *effect* means "a result": The **effect** of his decision on the staff's morale was positive and long lasting. When used as a verb, *effect* means "to produce" or "to cause": The activists believed that they could **effect** real political change.

agree on, agree to, agree with *Agree on* means "to be in accord with others about something": We **agreed on** a date for the conference. *Agree to* means "to accept something" or "to consent to do something": The customer **agreed to** our terms. The negotiators **agreed to** conclude talks by midnight. *Agree with*

Teaching and Learning Resources

Enhanced InSite™ for *The Writer's Harbrace Handbook*

Printed Access Card (two semester): 978-1-133-43388-0
Instant Access Code (two semester): 978-1-133-43383-5

This easy-to-navigate site allows users (you and your students) to manage the flow of papers online, check for originality, and conduct peer reviews. Students can access the interactive eBook for a text-specific workbook, private tutoring options, and writing resources that include tutorials for avoiding plagiarism and downloadable grammar podcasts. Enhanced InSite provides the tools and resources you and your students need *plus* the training and support you want. Learn more at **www.cengage.com/insite**. *(Access card/code is required.)*

Multimedia eBook

Printed Access Card: 978-1-133-43389-7
Instant Access Code: 978-1-133-43384-2

The Writer's Harbrace Handbook is available as a multimedia eBook. Now students can do all of their reading online or use the eBook as a handy reference while they are completing other coursework. The eBook includes the full text of the print version with interactive exercises and an integrated text-specific workbook; it also provides user-friendly navigation, search, and highlighting tools and links to videos that enhance the handbook content. *(Access card/code is required.)*

Online College Workbook

A great companion to the handbook, the Online College Workbook covers grammar, punctuation, usage, style, and writing. Also included are exercises with clear examples and explanations that supplement the exercises found in the handbook. The workbook is available as part of the multimedia eBook (described above) or as a password-protected, downloadable PDF for instructors at the handbook's companion website. The Answer Key is included in the Online Instructor's Resource Manual.

Online Instructor's Resource Manual

Available for easy download at the handbook's companion website, the password-protected Online Instructor's Resource Manual is designed to give instructors maximum flexibility in planning and customizing a course. The manual includes a variety of pedagogical questions (and possible solutions) relevant to those teaching a course with the handbook, sample syllabi with possible assignments for a semester-long course and for a quarter-long course, sample in-class collaborative learning activities, technology-oriented activities, and critical thinking and writing activities.

English Composition CourseMate

The Writer's Harbrace Handbook is complemented by English Composition CourseMate, which includes the following:
- an interactive eBook
- interactive teaching and learning tools, including quizzes, flashcards, videos, a workbook, and more
- Engagement Tracker, a first-of-its-kind tool that monitors student engagement in the course

Go to **login.cengage.com** and look for the icon ⁇CourseMate, which denotes a resource available within CourseMate.

WebTutor™

Blackboard® Printed Access Card: 978-1-133-43605-8
Instant Access Code: 978-1-133-43601-0

WebCT™ Printed Access Card: 978-1-133-43606-5
Instant Access Code: 978-1-133-43602-7

You can customize your course with text-specific content using this flexible course management system. It makes it easy to blend, add, edit, or delete content, media assets, quizzes, web links, discussion topics, interactive games and exercises, and more. For web-enabling a class or putting an entire course online, WebTutor delivers!

Personal Tutor

Printed Access Card: 978-1-133-43390-3
Instant Access Code: 978-1-133-43387-3

Access to Personal Tutor provides students with private tutoring as they write their papers. With this valuable resource, students gain access to multiple sessions in which they can either request tutoring services or submit a paper for review—whichever they need most.

InfoTrac® College Edition with InfoMarks™

Printed Access Card: 978-0-534-55853-6

This online research and learning center offers over twenty million full-text articles from nearly six thousand scholarly and popular periodicals. The articles cover a broad spectrum of disciplines and topics—providing an ideal resource for every type of research. Learn more at **www .cengage.com/infotrac**. *(Access code/card is required.)*

Turnitin®

Printed Access Card (1 semester): 978-1-4130-3018-1
Printed Access Card (2 semester): 978-1-4130-3019-8

This proven, online plagiarism-prevention tool promotes fairness in the classroom by helping students learn to cite sources correctly and allowing instructors to check for originality before reading and grading papers. *(Access code/card is required.)*

Additional Resources

Merriam-Webster's Collegiate® Dictionary, 11th Edition

Casebound: 978-0-8777-9809-5 *Not available separately.*

Merriam-Webster's Dictionary, 2nd Edition

Paperbound: 978-0-8777-9930-6 *Not available separately.*

Merriam-Webster's Dictionary/Thesaurus

Paperbound: 978-0-8777-9851-4 *Not available separately.*

Acknowledgments

The question was where to begin—so many people deserve thanks for their work on this book. We decided to start with our colleagues who reviewed previous editions and provided us with ideas for improving this edition. Their comments, questions, and occasional jokes made us see our work anew. We hope they will approve of the results of their feedback in these pages.

Jesse Airaudi, Rachel Webster, and Jared Wheeler, *Baylor University*
Elizabeth Aydelott, *Northwest Christian University*
Rachel Byrd, *Southern Adventist University*
James Crooks, *Shasta College*
Betty Davis, *Morgan State University*
Yasmin DeGout, *Howard University*
Cecile Anne de Rocher, *Dalton State College*
Jane Gamber, *Hutchinson Community College*
Bernadette Gambino, *University of North Florida*
Jan Geyer, *Hudson Valley Community College*
BJ Keeton and Eric Stalions, *Martin Methodist College*
Donna Kilgore, *Texas Southern University*
Larry Martin, *Hinds Community College*

James Mayo, *Jackson State Community College*
Patricia McLaughlin, *St. Ambrose University*
Richard Moye, *Lyndon State College*
Sherry Rosenthal, *College of Southern Nevada*
Blaine Wall, *Pensacola Junior College*
Ronald Wheeler, *Johnson Bible College*
Stephen Whited, *Piedmont College*

As we drafted (and revised), we depended on the assistance of our students. Penn State University PhD candidate Heather Brook Adams embodies grace, intelligence, and drive, making her the optimal traffic controller for large parts of this project; her tasks ranged from supervising the undergraduate contributions to composing the PowerPoint images. Another PhD candidate, Michael Faris, provided us with a screenshot from his course blog, for which we are grateful. In addition, we received help from a number of undergraduates: Josephine Lee provided her comments from a course blog. Research interns Jordan Clapper, Kristin Ford, Ian Morgan, Jeremy Popkin, Salvia Sim, and Robert Turchick helped by researching and proofreading portions of the manuscript. Finally, several undergraduate students provided samples of their written work and enriched our understanding of the writing process. To Danielle Dezell, Kayla Berg, Alyssa Jergens, Kristin Ford, Mary LeNoir, and Cristian Núñez, we give our heartfelt thanks. Without such students, where would we instructors be?

The successful completion of this project would have been impossible without the members of the Cengage Learning/Wadsworth staff, whose patience, good humor, and innovative ideas kept us moving in the right direction. Tops on our thank-you list are PJ Boardman, Editor-in-Chief; Lyn Uhl, Senior Publisher; and Kate Derrick, Acquiring Sponsoring Editor. We are truly amazed by how they can make meetings so enjoyable and productive. For the scrupulous work that occurred after the project went into production, we are grateful to Rosemary Winfield, Senior Content Project Manager, and Jane Hoover, production and copy editor; for the striking interior design, we thank Anne Carter; and for helping us bring our work to you, we extend gratitude to Melissa Holt, Marketing Manager, and Stacey Purviance, Executive Marketing Manager.

Michell Phifer, Senior Development Editor and friend, deserves a paragraph of thanks all her own. She has been a member of our team for four editions, always there to figure out our schedules, respond to our drafts with insightful feedback, and give us encouragement as we desperately try to balance our teaching with our research and writing deadlines—and she does it all with generosity, brilliance, and her own touch of elegance. We cannot imagine producing this handbook without her editorial expertise and abiding friendship.

To all our friends and family members, we owe as much gratitude as a book could hold—at least a pageful for each day of our research and writing that they made possible. We know that they often changed their plans or sacrificed their own time so that we could complete this project. For their support, we are forever grateful.

Cheryl Glenn
Loretta Gray
October 2011

The

Writer's
Harbrace
Handbook

godrick/Veer

WRITING
and the
RHETORICAL
SITUATION

1 | READING, WRITING, AND THE RHETORICAL SITUATION

Rhetoric, the purposeful use of language, permeates your daily activities, helping you communicate efficiently and effectively, whether you are reading or writing. Every time you pick up a newspaper, glance over the headlines, turn to the sports section, skim over the first page, and then go back to read the story that most intrigues you, you are reading rhetorically. You use rhetoric as you read course-related assignments, newsgroup postings, and syllabi. You write rhetorically as you draft and revise a message—aimed at a specific audience—that you hope will help resolve some problem or create some change. Thus, you use rhetoric when you complete written course assignments and compose in-class essays, lecture or study notes, and text messages. In fact, you have been reading and writing rhetorically—participating in rhetorical situations—for most of your life and are probably already knowledgeable about using rhetoric. So, you can build on what you know and go from there.

In this chapter, you will see how reading and writing rhetorically are processes, each a series of sometimes overlapping steps. The chapter will help you

- understand the elements of any rhetorical situation (**1a**),
- recognize a rhetorical opportunity (**1b**),
- determine a purpose for a message (**1c**),
- consider the intended audience (**1d**), and
- think about the rhetorical effects of context (**1e**).

This chapter will also help you see exactly how reading and writing rhetorically can help you succeed with a variety of class assignments, some of which are discussed in this handbook:

- an essay from personal experience (**3h**),
- a web page for an organization (**5d**, **5e**),
- an argument from personal experience and research (**7j**),
- an argument based on research (Chapters **8–10**),
- an interpretation of a literary text (**11b**),
- a field report and a lab report (**17d**), and
- a business letter and a résumé (**19b**, **19d**).

1a   UNDERSTANDING THE RHETORICAL SITUATION

When you hear the word *rhetoric,* you might think of language used to persuade. However, if you remember that rhetoric is the *purposeful* use of language, you will soon realize that persuading is not the only reason for using language. Other reasons include explaining concepts, describing experiences, and informing others about important ideas. The best way to establish a purpose for using language is to examine the **rhetorical situation** (Figure 1.1), which is composed of the writer (or speaker), the audience, the opportunity, the message, and the context. Any assignment that asks you to read or write rhetorically will be easier and more enjoyable if you keep the rhetorical situation in mind.

Writers (or speakers) enter a rhetorical situation when they identify an **opportunity** to propose change through the effective use of language. They may want to change other people's behavior or attitude or just help them notice something new. Once writers have identified a rhetorical opportunity, they prepare a **message** (using words and sometimes images) for a specific **audience**. Successful writers always link their purpose to their audience. The audience receives a writer's message within a specific **context** that includes what others have already said about the topic and how that topic was presented. Your primary role as a writer is to take into account all the elements of the rhetorical situation.

In your role as a rhetorical or critical reader, you also follow a series of steps, previewing an entire text—maybe jumping from the title to the table of contents and the author biography, then to the visuals, the final chapter, and the index—to see how much time and expertise reading the text will require. Often you preview a text **chronologically** (in order of occurrence), reading for content and responding with comments and questions, and then reread the text **recursively** (alternating between moving forward and looping back), maybe taking time to talk with

Figure 1.1. The rhetorical situation.

your peers about their understanding of the content. Previewing a text means staying alert for the author's major points, for transitional words that reveal sequence (**3d**), and for developmental structures (or other clues) that indicate summary, causation, repetition, exemplification, or intensification. You may want to respond to those important points, as though you were carrying on a conversation with the author. To do so, you can use a pen, sticky notes, or online highlighting to underline, highlight, annotate, or question passages that interest or confuse you.

Thus, reading rhetorically helps you determine what you already know about a topic and what you are likely to learn from the text; it also helps you gauge the expertise and credibility of the writer and the intended audience, purpose, and context of the text. In addition, learning to read rhetorically will help you distinguish between actual content and your personal response to that content and prepare you to handle the heavy academic reading load you experience in college. The following checklist will help you read rhetorically.

✓ CHECKLIST for Reading Rhetorically

- What is your purpose for reading the text—pleasure, research, fulfillment of a course requirement, problem solving, inspiration?

- What is the author's purpose for writing? What do you know about this author's credibility, use of reliable (or unreliable) sources, experience, and biases?

- What knowledge or experience does the reading demand? Does your knowledge or experience meet that demand?

- What are the key parts of the text? How do those parts relate to your purpose for reading? What specific information from this text will help you achieve your purpose?

- What is your strategy for previewing, reading, and rereading? Are you reading online or on paper? How will you respond to the text?

- With which passages do you agree or disagree, and why?

- As you read, what do you understand clearly? What do you want to know more about?

- What questions do you have for your instructor or peers? What questions—and answers—might they have for you?

Reading and writing rhetorically allow you to consider each of the elements of the rhetorical situation separately as well as in combination. In addition, when you read or write rhetorically, you consider how information is or should be delivered. You evaluate the thesis statement (2c), the key points of the message, and the support provided for each point, as well as identifying what needs to be said and what is purposefully left unsaid. When you *read* rhetorically, you read more effectively and thus are able to speak or write knowledgeably about what you have read. When you *write* rhetorically, you generate new ideas and communicate them clearly and concisely to your audience (Chapters 2 and 3)—and you improve your understanding of what you have read.

1b   RESPONDING TO A RHETORICAL OPPORTUNITY

A rhetorical situation offers you an opportunity to make a difference, often by solving a specific problem or addressing an issue for a specific audience. A speeding ticket, an engagement, a college application, a price discrepancy—these are all circumstances that invite you to speak or write, opportunities for you to use words to address the problem of protesting a fine, planning a wedding, being accepted by a college, or negotiating a fair price. Once you engage the rhetorical opportunity—the reason that impels you to speak or write—you will be better able to gauge all the elements of your message (from word choice to organizational pattern) in terms of your intended audience and your purpose.

As a rhetorical reader, you need to determine the author's reason for writing. Is the author writing to answer a question, solve a problem, address an issue, or entertain you? The title of the text, the summary, or the abstract may provide that information. The cover of science writer Rebecca Skloot's book *The Immortal Life of Henrietta Lacks* (Figure 1.2) reveals that the book is the medical biography of an unwitting cell donor, whose harvested cells became the most commonly used line in biomedical research. Skloot addresses the complicated issue of patient consent in medical research.

Figure 1.2. Cover of *The Immortal Life of Henrietta Lacks.*

❓ THINKING RHETORICALLY

OPPORTUNITY TO ADDRESS AN ISSUE

Historical events often serve as rhetorical opportunities. In 2010, for example, thirty-three Chilean miners were trapped nearly a mile underground for sixty-nine days, a tragic and near-fatal event that could have been prevented had the mining industry initially heeded the miners' warnings about unsafe conditions. The whole world watched—but also embraced the opportunity to advise, petition, and report—while Chilean officials planned the miners' successful rescue. During the same year, a British Petroleum (BP) offshore drilling rig exploded, releasing 5.2 million barrels of crude oil into the Gulf of Mexico for eighty-seven days before it was capped. The BP oil

(continued on page 8)

(continued from page 7)

spill was an unprecedented ecological disaster with undetermined financial consequences; it created issues that politicians, engineers, fishing industry workers, humanitarian groups, celebrities, and local individuals have continued to address. When Sarah Palin stole the national campaign spotlight in 2007 and then used her continuing popular appeal to start the Tea Party movement, political analysts raised their collective voices—written and spoken—to examine the underpinnings of her enormous popularity and extraordinary influence.

1C   DETERMINING A SPECIFIC PURPOSE

Once you realize that your words can stimulate change, modify a situation, address a need, or resolve a problem, you can determine your specific purpose. Writers choose their words carefully in order to clarify their purpose, always aligning that purpose with the potential to influence the thinking of their intended audience. The audience (whether listeners or readers) should be influenced according to that purpose— whether the writer wants to evoke emotions or challenge beliefs about a topic, amuse or entertain, report information, explain or evaluate the significance of information, analyze a situation, clarify a point, invite the audience to consider alternative points of view, or argue for or against a course of action.

Writers need to identify their overall purpose in terms of their intended audience, knowing that they can achieve that purpose using various methods of development (such as narration, description, and cause-and-consequence analysis; see **2g**). As a writer, your goal should be to compose a message that responds to an opportunity to make a change. You should also strive to provide your audience with a clear plan for effecting that change.

Readers need to identify the writer's purpose as well, assessing it to determine what audience response the writer expects. If you can identify specific words or passages that convey the writer's purpose, you can discern whether the writer wants you to be entertained, informed, or persuaded. For example, the purpose of Rebecca Skloot's book is not clear from its title, but the blurb on the front cover provides helpful

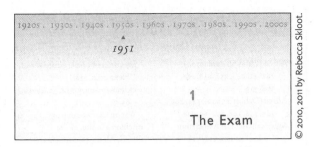

Figure 1.3. Visuals on chapter-opening pages in *The Immortal Life of Henrietta Lacks* reveal the chronology of events.

information: "Doctors took her cells without asking. Those cells never died. They launched a medical revolution and a multimillion-dollar industry. More than twenty years later, her children found out. *Their lives would never be the same.*" Skloot's purpose is to inform.

Often, visuals help direct you to a writer's purpose, as do the time-lines running across the tops of the opening pages of the chapters in Skloot's book (Figure 1.3). Each timeline orients the reader to the chronology of the events described in that chapter: for example, when Lacks's cells were removed from her (Chapter 1, "The Exam") and when her husband and children finally learned from Skloot what their family member had contributed to scientific research (Chapter 6, "Lady's on the Phone").

You can also look at a book's index to help orient yourself to the content and the writer's purpose. For example, the index of Skloot's book includes these entries, among others (Figure 1.4): "*A Conspiracy of Cells*," "Cell Culture Collection Committee," "cervical cancer," and "HeLa [or Henrietta Lacks] cells." Thus, you might be able to tell from the index whether the book contains the information you need to conduct research or satisfy your curiosity about African American medical history, cancer research, cell culture, or another related topic you are interested in.

Readers also need to establish their purpose for reading: to summarize what they are learning, apply this information to solve a problem, analyze the constituent parts of the text, make a decision, support a position, or combine the information in an original way. In Figure 1.5, you can see how one reader responded to a passage in the text of Skloot's book.

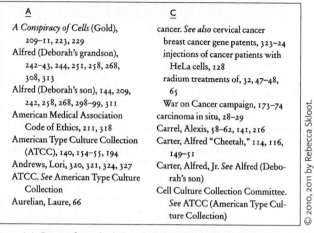

Figure 1.4. Excerpt from the index of *The Immortal Life of Henrietta Lacks*.

"Henrietta's cells have now been living outside her body far longer than they ever lived inside it," Defler said. If we went to almost any cell culture lab in the world and opened its freezers, he told us, we'd probably find millions—if not billions—of Henrietta's cells in small vials on ice. *Wouldn't ice damage cells?*

Research what these are.

Her cells were part of research into the genes that cause cancer and (those that suppress it;) they helped develop drugs for treating herpes, leukemia, influenza, hemophilia, and Parkinson's disease; and they've been used to study lactose digestion, sexually transmitted diseases, appendicitis, human longevity, mosquito mating, and the negative cellular effects of working in sewers. Their chromosomes and proteins have been studied with such detail and precision that scientists know their every quirk. Like guinea pigs and mice, Henrietta's cells have become the standard laboratory workhorse.

Then why haven't I heard of them?

Figure 1.5. Annotated excerpt from *The Immortal Life of Henrietta Lacks*.

Your challenge as a reader is to grasp the meaning the author wants to convey to you within the particular rhetorical situation. As a writer, your challenge is to make the purpose of your writing clear to your intended readers. Successful academic readers and writers always take time to talk with their instructor (and check the assignment sheet) to review the rhetorical opportunity, purpose, audience, context, and message of each reading and writing assignment (4a). They also talk about their reading and writing with their peers, to make sure they are on the right track. So, ask questions, listen to the answers, and try to answer the questions of your peers as you all work together to establish what is most significant, maybe even memorable, about the writing and reading you are assigned.

✓ CHECKLIST *for Assessing Purpose*

- How is the rhetorical purpose of the text linked to its intended audience? How might that audience help the writer fulfill the purpose of addressing an issue or resolving a problem?

- What purpose does the writer want the message to fulfill: to evoke emotion, to entertain or inspire, to convey information, or to argue for or against a course of action or an attitude? Does the writer have more than one purpose?

- How well do the topic and the audience connect to the rhetorical purpose? What examples or choice of words help fulfill that purpose?

Depending on the writer's overall purpose, writing can be classified as expressive, expository, or argumentative. Any of these types of writing can help a writer fulfill an overall purpose.

(1) Expressive writing

Expressive writing emphasizes the writer's feelings and reactions to people, objects, events, or ideas. Personal letters and journals are often expressive, as are many essays and short stories. As you read paragraph 1, which comes from a memoir, notice how philosopher Kathleen Dean Moore conveys her thoughts about what it takes to be happy. (For ease of reference, sample paragraphs in this chapter are numbered.)

1   So many people are telling me what should make me happy. Buy a cute car. Be thin. Get promoted or honored or given a raise. Travel: Baja! Belize! Finish the laundry. The voices may or may not be my own; they are so insistent that I can't distinguish them from the ringing in my ears. Maybe they are the voices of my mother and father, long dead and well intended, wanting only that I would be happy. Or my husband Frank, fully alive

but ditto in all other respects. My colleagues. Maybe they're the voices of advertisers, popular songwriters, even the president. Most of the time, I don't even think about making choices, plowing through my life as if I were pulled by a mule. —**KATHLEEN DEAN MOORE**, "The Happy Basket"

(2) Expository writing

Much of the academic material you read—textbooks, news accounts, reports, books (such as the one by Rebecca Skloot featured in this chapter), and journal articles—is expository, as are most of the essays you will be asked to write in college. Expository writing focuses more on objects, events, or ideas than on the writer's feelings about them. Any time you report, explain, analyze, or assess, you are practicing exposition. Paragraph 2, an excerpt from Nina Jablonski's book, *Skin*, explains why the covering on our bodies varies.

2   [A] distinctive attribute of human skin is that it comes naturally in a wide range of colors, from the darkest brown, nearly black, to the palest ivory, nearly white. This exquisite sepia rainbow shades from darkest near the equator to lightest near the poles. This range forms a natural cline, or gradient, that is related primarily to the intensity of the ultraviolet radiation (UVR) that falls on the different latitudes of the earth's surface. Skin color is one of the ways in which evolution has fine-tuned our bodies to the environment, uniting humanity through a palette of adaptation. Unfortunately, skin color has also divided humanity because of its damaging association with concepts of race. The spurious connections made between skin color and social position have riven peoples and countries for centuries. —**NINA G. JABLONSKI**, *Skin*

(3) Argumentative writing

Argumentative writing is intended to influence the reader's attitudes and actions. Most writing is to some extent an argument. Even something as apparently straightforward as a résumé can be seen as an argument for a job interview. However, writing is usually called argumentative if it clearly supports a specific position (Chapter 7). As you read paragraph 3, note how Rebecca Skloot demonstrates that Henrietta Lacks's story became an integral and ongoing part of Skloot's life.

3   I couldn't have imagined it then, but that phone call [an attempt to locate Lacks's husband] would mark the beginning of a decadelong

adventure through scientific laboratories, hospitals, and mental institutions, with a cast of characters that would include Nobel laureates, grocery store clerks, convicted felons, and a professional con artist. While trying to make sense of the history of cell culture and the complicated ethical debate surrounding the use of human tissues in research, I'd be accused of conspiracy and slammed into a wall both physically and metaphorically, and I'd eventually find myself on the receiving end of something that looked a lot like an exorcism. I did eventually meet Deborah [Lacks's daughter], who would turn out to be one of the strongest and most resilient women I'd ever known. We'd form a deep personal bond, and slowly, without realizing it, I'd become a character in her story, and she in mine.   —REBECCA SKLOOT, *The Immortal Life of Henrietta Lacks*

Exercise 1

Write two paragraphs that begin to develop an expressive, expository, or argumentative essay on one of the following subjects.

1. your physical health
2. paying for college
3. your career goals
4. volunteer work
5. academic pressures

6. the key(s) to happiness
7. a good teacher
8. your computer expertise
9. your living situation
10. an admirable friend or relative

1d   CONSIDERING AUDIENCE

A clear understanding of the audience—its values, concerns, knowledge, and capabilities—helps writers convey their purpose through their message and helps readers orient themselves to that message. Writers fashion a message by considering quality and quantity of details, choice of words, and inclusion of effective examples and supporting details. Of course, the audience is anyone who reads a text, but the rhetorical, or intended, audience consists of those people whom the author considers capable of being influenced by the words or who are capable of bringing about change.

When you read rhetorically, you may become a member of the writer's rhetorical audience, someone who reads purposefully, often recording notes and questions, identifying important evidence within the text, forging connections among relevant passages, and evaluating the quality of the supporting details and evidence. As part of that audience, you also consider how you can apply the text to a problem you want to solve or a decision you want to make. The better you understand the text, the better able you will be to synthesize the information it provides with what you already know to create an original idea.

As a writer, you need to think clearly about who exactly will be reading (or might end up reading) what you write and ask yourself whether your word choices and examples are appropriate for that audience, especially if it is an unintended audience. As a reader, you want to use those same criteria to determine if an author has intentionally included you in (or excluded you from) the audience. You can weigh the author's purpose, opinions, assertions, word choices, and examples in order to make such a determination.

There are three general kinds of audience. A **specialized audience** has demonstrated interest or expertise in the subject and can help resolve the issue (even if only by understanding the author's message). Someone who has an interest in scientific research, the rights of patients, African American medical history, or a related topic is most likely to read *The Immortal Life of Henrietta Lacks*. A **diverse audience** consists of readers with differing levels of expertise and varying interest in the subject. When you are in a doctor's waiting room, reading whatever magazines are available, you might find yourself becoming part of a diverse audience. **Multiple audiences** are composed of a primary target audience of intended readers and a secondary audience who has access to and may read the text. When you communicate online, you need to stay alert to the likelihood that you are writing for multiple audiences: although you have composed your message for your primary audience, your e-mail messages or posts to a chat room can be forwarded to and easily accessed by others—and not always with your permission.

(1) A specialized audience

A specialized audience has a demonstrated interest in the subject. If your sister is a Title I teacher, she might be interested in helping her colleagues build the school-district infrastructure necessary for implementing the No Child Left Behind (NCLB) Act of 2001. She would be part of the audience for paragraph 4.

4   Of course, the vast majority of districts . . . will be scrambling to find staff who can assume responsibility for NCLB. . . . Deciding how to assign new responsibilities for NCLB and how to restructure other duties should be predicated upon fully developed plans that identify the tasks that need to be accomplished. It may be a small comfort, but recognizing the trade-offs of different assignment decisions can help administrators and their staffs cope with them. Wherever NCLB coordination responsibility is housed, it is important to inform all district staff of where that is. Parents may contact the district at different entry points. They need to be directed efficiently to the NCLB authority.

—**OFFICE OF INNOVATION AND IMPROVEMENT,**
US DEPARTMENT OF EDUCATION,
"Innovations in Education: Creating Strong District School Choice Programs"

Although you can probably read every word in the preceding excerpt, the specialized terms and ideas might not be clear to you. A specialized audience has both interest in and knowledge of the topic under consideration.

Many of the essays you will be assigned to write in college—in the sciences, history, economics, English, and psychology, for example—will be aimed at your instructor, who comprises a specialized audience. Your job as an academic writer, then, is to weigh what your instructor knows against the specific information she or he needs and then determine how best to develop the needed information. Most of the materials you will be required to read in college are also aimed at a specialized audience. As part of such an audience, you will want to preview the text to assess what it demands of you in terms of time, effort, and knowledge. You will also want to review the directories within the text (table of contents, index, and bibliography) and the visual aids to orient yourself to the text and its context. You may also have to refer to a dictionary, an encyclopedia, or other resource as you read.

(2) A diverse audience

A diverse audience consists of readers with differing levels of expertise and varying interest in the subject at hand. Paragraph 5 is taken from physician Atul Gawande's essay on blushing, which explains this universal human behavior.

5   Why we have such a reflex is perplexing. One theory is that the blush exists to show embarrassment, just as the smile exists to show happiness. This would explain why the reaction appears only in the visible regions of the body (the face, the neck, and the upper chest). But then why do dark-skinned people blush? Surveys find that nearly everyone blushes, regardless of skin color, despite the fact that in many people it is nearly invisible. And you don't need to turn red in order for people to recognize that you're embarrassed. Studies show that people detect embarrassment *before* you blush. Apparently, blushing takes between fifteen and twenty seconds to reach its peak, yet most people need less than five seconds to recognize that someone is embarrassed—they pick it up from the almost immediate shift in gaze, usually down and to the left, or from the sheepish, self-conscious grin that follows a half second to a second later. So there's reason to doubt that the purpose of blushing is entirely expressive.

—**ATUL GAWANDE**, "Crimson Tide"

As a writer, you can easily imagine a diverse audience if you think of thoughtful, receptive, educated adults, with whom you may share some common ground. As a reader, you may often find yourself as a member of a diverse audience, one likely to include people with different beliefs, knowledge, and experience (7e(2)). Rarely will you write for or read something by someone who is exactly like you (33c), so remember that connections between writers and readers are made through the choice of language (Chapters 33–35), details, and examples (2f), which either invite readers into or exclude them from a written work.

(3) Multiple audiences

Writers often need to consider multiple audiences, a task related to—yet different from—addressing a diverse audience. When you address a diverse audience, you try to reach everyone. When you consider multiple audiences, you gauge your choice of words and tone according to your primary audience, knowing that a secondary audience might have access to your text. For peer reviews, for example, your primary audience is the peer whose writing you are reviewing. Knowing that your instructor (the secondary audience) will also be reading your commentary, you may respond to your peer's writing with more thoughtfulness and tact than you would otherwise. When you know that your rhetorical situation includes multiple audiences, you can better adjust your words and edit your information. And when you consciously read as a member of either a primary or a secondary audience, you can better evaluate your responses.

When writing essays in college, you will regularly find yourself addressing multiple audiences. You may use research you have done in history class as the starting point for developing an essay for an economics class or compose an essay for a general (secondary) audience and submit it to an instructor who is a specialist in the subject (and therefore your primary audience).

The following checklist may help you assess an audience, whether you are doing so as the writer or the reader.

✓ CHECKLIST *for Assessing Audience*

- Who is the intended audience for this writing? Who else might read it? Has the writer identified the primary audience while also accommodating a secondary audience? What passages indicate that the writer has addressed the primary audience and also recognized the expectations of a secondary audience?

- What do you know about the backgrounds, values, and characteristics of the members of the intended audience? What do the audience members have in common? How are they different?

- What background, values, and characteristics do you (as either the writer or a reader) share with the members of the intended audience? How do you differ from them?

- How open are the members of this audience to views that are different from their own?

- What do you not know about this audience? In other words, what assumptions about its members might be risky to make?

- What kind of language, examples, and details are most appropriate (or inappropriate) for the members of this audience?

- What does this audience already know about the topic under consideration?

- What level of expertise will this audience expect from the writer?

Exercise 2

In both an introductory textbook and an advanced textbook in a discipline of your choice, locate a passage devoted to the same issue or concept and photocopy these passages. Prepare a class presentation in which you explain how each passage addresses the needs and expectations of a specific audience.

1e   WRITING AND READING A MESSAGE WITHIN A CONTEXT

Context includes the time and place in which a message is read or written, the writer and the intended audience, and the medium of delivery (print, online, spoken, or visual); in other words, context comprises the set of circumstances under which the writer and reader (or speaker and listener) communicate. Social, political, religious, and other cultural factors as well as attitudes and beliefs influence context by helping or hindering successful communication. All of these factors serve as constraints (obstacles) or resources (positive influences) in any rhetorical situation.

Whatever you read, write, or speak is always influenced (positively or negatively) by the context. Writers who consider the factors influencing the context in which they are writing are more likely to convey their ideas effectively to their audience and thus achieve their purpose. Readers who consider the overall context of a text constitute a more insightful and attuned rhetorical audience.

The medium of delivery is also part of the context. Writing material for a web page, for example, requires you to consider additional features of organization, design, and style related to onscreen presentation of material. Reading online also requires an adjustment to visual and audio elements that can enhance (or distract from) your experience. An online method of delivery, then, requires you to make different kinds of rhetorical decisions than you make for a text in a wholly static print medium (Chapter 5).

When you read the work of other writers, you will sometimes find the context for the work explicitly stated in a preface or an introduction. Often, however, the context must be inferred. Whether or not the context is announced, it is important that writers and readers identify and consider it.

> ## ✔ **CHECKLIST** *for Assessing Context*
>
> ■ What are the factors influencing the context in which you are writing: the time and place, the intended audience, and the medium of delivery (print, online, spoken, or visual)?
>
> ■ What other events (personal, local, or global) are influencing the context for writing?
>
> ■ What are the expectations concerning the length of this written message? If a length has not been specified, what seems appropriate in terms of purpose and audience?
>
> ■ What document design (Chapter 6) is appropriate, given the context?
>
> ■ Under what circumstances will this piece of writing be read? How can you help the intended audience quickly see the purpose of the text within these circumstances?

2 ‖ PLANNING AND DRAFTING ESSAYS

As an experienced writer, you already understand that writing is a process. Think of all the writing you do outside of school; when you compose an e-mail message, for instance, you are responding to a rhetorical opportunity while considering your intended audience, the medium of delivery, and your overall purpose. Even though you write and revise your e-mail message quickly, you often cut and paste or delete in order to clarify the meaning or adjust the tone—just as you do when you are writing more slowly to fulfill an academic assignment. Whether you are writing in or out of school, you revise and edit in light of your rhetorical opportunity, purpose, audience, and context (**1c–e**).

This chapter will help you understand your writing process by showing you how to

- recognize suitable topics (**2a**),
- focus your ideas (**2b**),
- write a clear thesis statement (**2c**),
- organize your ideas (**2d**),
- express your ideas in multiple drafts (**2e**), and
- use various strategies to develop effective paragraphs (**2f**) and essays (**2g**).

Most experienced writers break down their writing process into a series of (sometimes overlapping and even repetitive) steps that include generating, organizing, developing, and clarifying ideas, often polishing their prose along the way. Because the writing process is **recursive**, you may find yourself returning to a specific activity (generating ideas or editing, for instance) several times as you plan and draft a piece of writing. During drafting, you may realize that you need to go back and generate more supporting ideas, modify your thesis, or even start over with a new thesis. As you become more conscious of your writing process, you will begin to recognize how revisiting passages in need of further improvement often yields new ideas.

Despite the infinite variations of the writing process, it usually involves four basic, recursive stages, described in the following box.

STAGES OF THE WRITING PROCESS

■ **Prewriting** is the initial stage of the writing process. As you begin thinking about a specific writing task, you consider the rhetorical opportunity (what interests you about it and how you can use words to respond to it), the audience and purpose, the context (including the expectations for this piece of writing), and the medium of delivery. Then you start exploring your topic by talking with others working on the same assignment, keeping a journal, freewriting, asking questions, or conducting preliminary research. By now, you may already know the best ways to energize your thinking and jump-start your writing.

■ **Drafting** involves writing down your ideas quickly, writing as much as you can, without worrying about being perfect or staying on topic. Some writers like to cluster their ideas and supporting material, creating a preliminary arrangement for a piece; others just write, write, write. After all, the more ideas you get down on paper (whether they are organized or not), the more options you will have as you begin to clarify your thesis, compose your first draft, and revise. Progress is your goal at this stage, not perfection.

■ **Revising** offers you the opportunity to focus your purpose in terms of your audience, establish a clear thesis statement that conveys your main idea (2c), and organize your ideas toward those ends (2d). Now is the time to stabilize the overall arrangement of your piece, develop the individual paragraphs (2f and 3c), and reconsider your introduction and conclusion (3b). Revising is not the end, though; revising produces yet another draft meriting further revision and editing.

■ **Editing** focuses on surface features: punctuation, spelling, word choice, grammar, sentence structure, and all the rest of the details of Standardized English (3f). As you prepare your work for final submission, you may want to read it aloud to discover which sentence structures and word choices could be improved. You may even catch a few spelling errors in the process.

2a   SELECTING A SUBJECT

If you are not assigned a subject and are free to choose your own, you can start by identifying a problem that your words can address or resolve. You can think about what you already know—or would like to learn—about the problem as well as what is likely to interest your intended audience (**1d**). Your most successful writing will often emerge from your knowledge of or interest in politics, cultural groups, pastimes, sports, jobs, or even places, especially when you write for an appropriate audience with a clear purpose and use well-chosen details and examples (**1c** and **2f**).

In college, though, you will be asked to write about subjects that are outside your personal experience but directly related to your academic coursework. If, for instance, you are assigned to write an essay for a course in ancient Roman history, you may be permitted to choose a subject that interests you, as long as it relates directly to the course. To find a subject that meets both those criteria, you might start by looking through your textbook (particularly in the section on suggestions for further reading) as well as by reviewing your lecture notes or any marginal annotations you have made in your textbook. Ask yourself whether any details of the subject have surprised, annoyed, or intrigued you—if you have discovered an opportunity for entering the scholarly conversation by explaining or arguing a point, supplying additional information, or overturning a traditional belief. When you discover a subject you want to explore further, you can combine your need to know more with the opportunity to deliver that new information to your audience.

(1) Keeping a journal to explore subjects

Many experienced writers use journals to explore various subjects. Whether private or public, electronic or handwritten, a journal is a convenient place to record your thoughts, which will often reveal subjects that interest you. In a **personal journal**, you can reflect on your experiences and inner life or focus on external events (such as political campaigns, natural disasters, sporting events, and new books and films), writing for your own benefit. Some writers prefer to keep a **reading journal**, where they record quotations, observations, and other material that they might use in their own writing. Whatever type of journal you keep, allow yourself to write in it quickly, without worrying about spelling or grammar.

(2) Freewriting as a risk-free way to explore a subject

When **freewriting**, writers record whatever comes to mind about a subject, writing without stopping for a limited period of time—often no more than ten minutes. When they repeat themselves or get off track, writers keep going in order to generate ideas, make connections, and bring information and memories to the surface. Some writers use colored markers (or change the font or color in their word-processing program) to identify different subjects and make connections as well as to generate a tentative organization.

When Mary LeNoir's English instructor asked her to write for five minutes about how she chose a college, Mary produced the following freewriting as the first step toward her final essay (which appears in Chapter 3).

I'm an athlete. I've always been an athlete. But being an athlete won't be my job when I graduate from college. So when I was thinking about which school to attend, I tried hard not to let high school athletics and the college recruiting process cloud my decision making. I also tried not to listen to all the people who seem to think that "money" is how we student-athletes make our decision. That's not true. In fact, many athletes place the athletic factor above the academic one, as though to say, "I'm going to X school to play Y sport and I'll take classes while I'm there." But play time is not the only factor that takes over the decision-making process. Some athletes commit to their school for reasons they haven't really thought through: they make their decision based on their emotions, on how much they like the school (whatever that means) or like the coach or like the other players. They can end up in a school located halfway across the country from home, a school with rigorous academics and a huge party scene. Sometimes, they don't find out until too late that they cannot balance the academics with the athletics, not to mention the parties and big classes. And they're too far from home to get the support they need. If they're not partiers (or if they party too much) or if they need a small class and don't have that, then, they're out of luck. I'm also aware of athletes choosing a school based on potential for a professional career, even though the majority of them will move on from their sport, unless they venture into coaching or play it with friends. I know I'm throwing out a lot of things here and will need to narrow it down to one focus and come up with a thesis and an outline.

Mary's freewriting generated a number of possibilities for developing an essay about why she chose the college she did: she cites academics, emotional responses, and athletics as strong reasons. She was responding to the opportunity to explain the selection process, especially to people who believe that student-athletes think only of how much money they will receive if they attend a particular college. Notice, however, that her freewriting leads her to describe other athletes, not herself, and that she realizes she needs to think about what comes next in her writing process.

(3) Questioning to push the boundaries of a subject

You can also explore a subject by asking yourself some questions. The simplest questioning strategy for exploring a subject comes from journalism. **Journalists' questions**—*Who? What? When? Where? Why?* and *How?*—are easy to use and can help you generate ideas about any subject. Using journalists' questions to explore how a student-athlete chooses a college could lead you to the following: *Who* qualifies as a student-athlete? *What* criteria do and should student-athletes use in choosing a college? *When* should student-athletes expect to give up their sports? *Where* can student-athletes best succeed? *Why* is financial aid not the only or even the most important selection criterion? *How* might a student-athlete make the best decision, given his or her characteristics and circumstances?

2b	FOCUSING A SUBJECT INTO A SPECIFIC TOPIC

By exploring a subject, you can discover productive strategies for development as well as a specific focus for your topic. As you prewrite, you will decide that some ideas seem worth pursuing while others seem inappropriate for the rhetorical opportunity to which you are responding, your intended audience, or the context. During the process of exploring, some ideas will fall away as new ones arise and your topic comes into sharper focus.

After generating ideas through strategies such as freewriting and questioning, you can use various rhetorical methods for developing the ideas (**2g**). In responding to a rhetorical opportunity to explain how student-athletes choose (or should choose) a college, Mary LeNoir needed to focus this fairly broad subject into a more narrow (and manageable) topic. Therefore, she considered how she might use each of the rhetorical methods of development to sharpen her focus:

- *Narration.* What is a typical story about a student-athlete deciding on a college?

- *Description.* How do colleges distinguish themselves in terms of size, course offerings, location, and cost? How do student-athletes differ? What distinctive characteristics of college and student produce the best matches?
- *Process analysis.* What steps do student-athletes take as they choose a college? What are the most and least useful of those steps?
- *Cause-and-consequence analysis.* What considerations lead to the best choice of a college? What are the considerations that too many student-athletes overlook? What are the consequences of making the right choice? Of making the wrong one?
- *Comparison and contrast.* How does the process of choosing a college differ for a student-athlete and a nonathlete? How does the process differ for a student whose goal is to be only a college athlete and a student whose goal is to be a professional athlete?
- *Classification and division.* How might student-athletes' college-related needs and expectations be classified? How might colleges be categorized based on what they offer student-athletes?
- *Definition.* How can the "best" college be defined? What are the best reasons for choosing a college? Are these reasons defined by immediate or long-term benefits?

A combination of strategies soon led Mary to a tentative focus:

> After interviewing five student-athletes about their personal goals and circumstances and considering my own situation, I discovered that despite our differences, we all used three basic criteria in choosing our college: the overall atmosphere of the school, the potential for our athletic development, and the material conditions associated with attending the college (costs and geographic location).

Because some of Mary's friends believed that student-athletes choose a college on the basis of the financial aid offered, she wanted to explain how she and her fellow athletes actually made their decisions.

Whatever rhetorical method you use to bring a topic into focus, your final topic should be determined not only by the rhetorical opportunity that is engaging you but also by your intended audience, the way that audience connects with your purpose, and the context in which you are writing (the constraints and resources of time, place, and medium of delivery). Because writing is a form of thinking and discovering, your focus might not emerge until after you have written a draft or two.

The following checklist may help you assess your topic.

✅ CHECKLIST for Assessing a Topic

- What unresolved problem or issue related to this topic captures your interest? How can you use words to address this rhetorical opportunity for change?
- What audience might be interested in this topic?
- What is your purpose in writing about this topic for this audience?
- Can you address the topic in the time and space (page length) available to you? Or should you narrow or expand the topic in order to accommodate a time constraint or length expectations?
- Do you have the information you need to address this topic? If not, how will you acquire additional information?
- Are you willing to take the time to learn more about the topic in order to engage the rhetorical opportunity?

Exercise 1

Use the journalists' questions (page 24) to generate more ideas about a subject that interests you (for instance, how you decided to enroll at your college). Then identify a rhetorical opportunity that emerges from your answers to those questions. How does that opportunity connect with your subject to create a specific topic that is appropriate for an essay?

| 2C | CONVEYING A CLEARLY STATED THESIS |

Once you have identified a rhetorical opportunity for change, determined an audience receptive to that change, decided on a purpose for writing (to entertain, explain, teach, analyze, persuade, or compare), and focused your thoughts on an interesting topic, you have drawn close to settling on your controlling idea, or **thesis**. In the first draft or two, your thesis may be only tentative. By your final draft, however, you will have developed a clear thesis statement.

Most pieces of writing have a **thesis statement**, an explicit declaration (usually in one sentence) of the main idea. Your thesis statement conveys a single idea, clearly focused and specifically stated. A thesis can be thought of as a central idea stated in the form of an assertion, or **claim** (7d), which indicates what you believe to be true, interesting, or valuable about your topic.

An explicitly formulated thesis statement helps keep your writing on target. It identifies the topic, the purpose, and, in some cases, the plan of development. Notice how the following thesis statements fulfill their purpose. The first is from a descriptive essay.

> If Lynne Truss were Catholic, I'd nominate her for sainthood.
>
> —FRANK McCOURT, Foreword, *Eats, Shoots & Leaves*

With this simple statement, McCourt establishes that the topic is Lynne Truss and indicates that he will describe why she should be a saint. He conveys enthusiasm and admiration for Truss's work.

The following thesis statement for a cause-and-consequence analysis sets the stage for the series of incidents that unfolded after surgeon and writer Richard Selzer was granted refuge in an Italian monastery when he had no hotel reservations:

> Wanderers know it—beggars, runaways, exiles, fugitives, the homeless, all of the dispossessed—that if you knock at the door of a monastery seeking shelter you will be taken in.
>
> —RICHARD SELZER, "Diary of an Infidel: Notes from a Monastery"

The main idea in an argumentative essay usually conveys a strong point of view, as in the following, which unmistakably argues for a specific course of action:

> Amnesty International opposes the death penalty in all cases without exception.
>
> —AMNESTY INTERNATIONAL, "The Death Penalty: Questions and Answers"

The following are possible thesis statements that Mary LeNoir might have based on two of the rhetorical methods of development (2g). This sentence suggests a focus on comparison and contrast:

> Student-athletes who want to play only college sports and those who want to go pro should employ different criteria for selecting a college.

The following sentence focuses on cause and consequence:

> By establishing exactly what I wanted from my college experience, I was able to choose the best college for me.

It is just as important to allow your thesis statement to remain tentative in the early stages of writing as it is to allow your essay to remain flexible through the initial drafts. Rather than sticking with your original thesis, which you might have to struggle to support because it was not well conceived, you want to let your final thesis statement evolve as you think, explore, draft, and revise. The following tips might help you develop a thesis statement that is neither too obvious nor too general.

TIPS FOR DEVELOPING A THESIS STATEMENT

- Decide which feature of the topic opens up a rhetorical opportunity—a problem your words might resolve or a change they might bring about.
- Write down your opinion about that feature.
- Mark the passages in your freewriting, journal, or rough draft that support your opinion.
- Draft a thesis statement that connects the rhetorical opportunity with your rhetorical purpose and intended audience.
- After completing a draft, ask yourself whether your thesis is too broad or too narrow. Revise either your thesis or your draft accordingly.
- If you are unhappy with the results, start again with the first tip, and be even more specific.

A clear, precise thesis statement helps unify your message so that it is appropriate for your audience and your rhetorical purpose, accurately reflects the material you generate, and directs your readers through the writing that follows. Therefore, as you continue to write and revise, check your thesis statement frequently to make sure that all your supporting material (your assertions, examples, and details) remain anchored to that thesis. Your thesis should influence your decisions about which details to keep and which to eliminate as well as guide your search for appropriate additional information to support your assertions.

A thesis statement is usually a declarative sentence with a single main clause—that is, either a simple or a complex sentence (**21c**). If your thesis statement presents two or more related ideas, as a compound sentence does (**21c**), be sure that it allows for a single direction and focus. For example, the following thesis statement, composed of two sentences, coordinates two ideas, indicating a discussion that will contrast men's and women's use of language:

> Male students are more likely to be comfortable attacking the readings and might find the inclusion of personal anecdotes irrelevant and "soft." Women are more likely to resist discussion they perceive as hostile, and, indeed, it is women in my classes who are most likely to offer personal anecdotes.
>
> —**DEBORAH TANNEN**, "How Male and Female Students Use Language Differently"

If you wish to sharpen a thesis statement by adding information that qualifies or supports it, subordinate such material to the main idea:

> In elementary school, I had noticed the mean-spiritedness of some kids, part of it directed at me and my siblings.
>
> —**MARY PIPHER**, "Growing Our Souls"

As you develop your thesis statement, resist using such vague qualifiers as *interesting, important,* and *unusual,* which can signal that the topic lacks focus. For example, in the thesis statement "My education has been very unusual," the word *unusual* conveys very little. It might indicate that the writer's topic is weak and unfocused—or it might be masking an idea of real interest and audience appeal that simply needs to be made more specific: "After my parents decided to teach me at home, I pursued educational avenues I didn't know existed." The following examples show how vague thesis statements can be improved:

Vague thesis	It is hard to balance work with school.
Better thesis	Hardworking students who balance a part-time job with academic success can gain maturity and self-confidence.
Vague thesis	Genetically modified foods are highly controversial.
Better thesis	Developed responsibly, genetically modified foods may be able to ameliorate current worldwide food shortages.

Vague thesis	Student-athletes choose a college for a number of reasons.
Better thesis	No matter what their sport or their professional aspirations, student-athletes usually use the same criteria in choosing a college: opportunity to play the sport, geographic location, financial aid, and emotional connection with the school.

The thesis statement most often appears in the first paragraph of an essay, although you can put yours wherever it best furthers your overall purpose (perhaps somewhere later in the introduction or even in the conclusion). The advantage of putting the thesis statement in the first paragraph is that readers know from the beginning what your essay is about, to whom you are writing, why you are writing, and how the essay is likely to take shape. This technique has proved to be especially effective in academic writing. If the thesis statement begins the opening paragraph, the rest of the sentences in the paragraph support or clarify it, as is the case in paragraph 1. (For ease of reference, each of the sample paragraphs in this chapter is numbered.)

1   *The cafeteria was a dreadful place in the basement.* Hundreds of kids at a time ate there, kids who'd spent all morning having to be quiet and sit still. Because of the room's low ceilings and hard surfaces, the sound bounced all over the place, creating a din, a roar so deafening you had to scream to be heard. It was a madhouse, the Hades of the school, a place where the Furies all ran wild.   —SAM SWOPE, "The Animal in Miguel"

If the thesis statement is the last sentence of the opening paragraph, the preceding sentences build toward it, as in paragraph 2.

2   The story of zero is an ancient one. Its roots stretch back to the dawn of mathematics, in the time thousands of years before the first civilization, long before humans could read and write. But as natural as zero seems to us today, for ancient peoples zero was a foreign—and frightening—idea. An Eastern concept, born in the Fertile Crescent a few centuries before the birth of Christ, zero not only evoked images of a primal void, it also had dangerous mathematical properties. *Within zero there is the power to shatter the framework of logic.*   —CHARLES SEIFE, *Zero: The Biography of a Dangerous Idea*

Keep in mind that most academic writing features an easy-to-locate thesis statement. The following checklist may help you assess a thesis.

✔ CHECKLIST *for Assessing a Thesis*

- Does your thesis respond to a rhetorical opportunity to create a change (in action, thinking, perception, or opinion) or to address a problem?
- Does your thesis accurately reflect your point of view about your topic?
- How does your thesis relate to the interests of the intended audience? To your purpose? To the context in which you are writing?
- Where is your thesis located? Would your readers benefit from having it stated earlier or later?
- Does your thesis reflect your overall purpose? Does it clarify your focus and indicate your coverage of the topic?
- What are the two strongest assertions you can make to support your thesis?
- What specific examples, details, or experiences support your assertions?

2d	ARRANGING OR OUTLINING IDEAS

Most writers benefit from a provisional organizational plan that helps them order their ideas and manage their writing. You can simplify your organizational plan if you base it on Aristotle's claim that every speech needs "a beginning, a middle, and an end." Even the simplest outline offers an essay a structure, much like the basic framework of a house. And, like the framework of a house, a simple outline can quickly become more elaborate and detailed.

Some writers compose informal lists of ideas and then examine them for overlap, pertinence, and potential. While some ideas will surely be discarded, others can lead to a thesis statement, a provocative introduction, a reasonable conclusion, or a supporting example. Considered together, the items on such a list of ideas might reveal the traces of an overall organizational plan. Other writers rely on more formal outlines, in which main points form the major headings and supporting ideas form the subheadings. Either method (list or outline) can provide a visual map of your thinking, which is particularly valuable when you are writing a lengthy paper or writing under time constraints (**4a**). Whatever method you choose for arranging your ideas, remember that you can always alter your arrangement to accommodate any changes your thinking undergoes as you proceed.

An outline of Mary LeNoir's essay might look something like the following:

TENTATIVE THESIS STATEMENT: No matter what their sport, student-athletes tend to choose a college using three criteria: (1) how much play time they will have; (2) material considerations, mainly geographic location and financial aid; and (3) emotional connection with the school.

I. Many student-athletes begin by dreaming about going pro after college, even though few will.

   A. They anticipate how much playing time they will have on the college field.

   B. They consider schools with the strongest teams.

II. Then, they consider the material reasons for attending a school.

   A. They consider the geographic location of the school.

   B. They try to negotiate the best financial aid package available to a student-athlete of their caliber.

III. Many student-athletes ultimately base their decision on an emotional connection with the school.

   A. They always dreamed about playing their sport at a particular college.

   B. They fell in love with the campus or the city—or really liked the coach or the other players.

IV. How I worked through these criteria toward my decision

V. The consequences (positive and negative) of my decision

Notice that the last main points of Mary's outline are less well developed than the others. However, she is already beginning to organize her ideas from her freewriting, and she is developing her topic within the boundaries stated in her tentative thesis. Still, as she begins to draft, she may discover that her essay does not follow her outline exactly. She may find herself moving ideas around, deleting some, or adding others. An outline is a tool to help a writer get started—it is not an inflexible framework.

2e   GETTING IDEAS INTO A FIRST DRAFT

When writing a first draft, get your ideas down quickly. Spelling, punctuation, and correct usage are not important in the first draft—ideas are. Experienced writers know that the most important thing about a first draft is to have done it, for it is something to work on—and against. If you are not sure how to begin, look over some of the journal writing, listing, or outlining you have already done, and try to identify a rhetorical opportunity and a tentative thesis that responds to that opportunity. Then write down some main points you might like to develop, along with some supporting information for that development. Keep your overall plan in mind as you draft. If you find yourself losing track of where you want to go, stop writing and reread what you have already done. Talk with someone working on the same assignment, write in your journal, or imagine talking directly to your intended audience. You will probably need to revise your plan and rethink your topic as you write and revise. Experienced writers anticipate such changes.

If you become stalled while attempting to write an early section of your essay, simply move to a later section, which might allow you to "restart your engine" by writing (rather than worrying about being stalled). Or work on something that seems easier to write, such as sentences that develop another supporting idea, an introduction, or a conclusion. Just keep writing, pursuing whatever path of thought interests you. Later, during revision, you can experiment with ways of polishing, integrating, or deleting these passages (3f). What is important at this stage is to begin, remembering that writing is a form of discovering and understanding. Be sure to save your early drafts so that you can refer to them as you revise (Chapter 3).

2f   DRAFTING WELL-DEVELOPED PARAGRAPHS

You compose a draft by developing paragraphs. If you are working from an informal list (2d), you will have a sense of where you want to take your ideas but may be uncertain about the number and nature of the paragraphs you will need. If you are working from an outline (2d), you can anticipate the number of paragraphs you will probably write and what you hope to accomplish in each paragraph. In the first case, you enjoy the freedom to pursue new ideas that occur as you draft. In the second, you enjoy the security of starting off with a clear direction. In both cases, however, your goal is to develop each paragraph fully and then ask yourself what additional paragraphs (or additional supporting information within any single paragraph) would further support your thesis statement and enhance your overall message in terms of your rhetorical opportunity, intended audience, and purpose.

Paragraphs have no set length. Typically, they range from 50 to 250 words, and paragraphs in books are usually longer than those in newspapers and magazines. There are certainly times when a long paragraph provides rich reading, as well as times when a long paragraph exhausts a single minor point, combines too many points, or becomes repetitive. On the other hand, short, one-sentence paragraphs can be used effectively to add emphasis (Chapter **31**) or to establish transition (**3d**). Short paragraphs can also, however, indicate inadequate development. You can sometimes combine two or more short paragraphs (Chapter **3**) or expand a single one into a well-developed, well-supported, longer paragraph. Think of revising and developing your paragraphs as a luxury, an opportunity to articulate exactly what you want to say without anyone interrupting you—or changing the subject.

(1) Developing a paragraph with details

A good paragraph developed with details brings an idea to life. Consider the following well-developed paragraph by Brenda Jo Brueggemann:

3   *This reminds me of how I learned to drive growing up in western Kansas: my parents and grandparents turned me loose behind the wheel of grandpa's old blue Ford pickup in the big, open cow pasture behind their farm house, gave me some basic instructions on gears, clutches, brakes, accelerator—and then let me go.* It was exhilarating to get the feel of the thing, bumping along over gopher holes with dried cow patties flying behind me, creating a little dust cloud to mark the path I had taken, and not worrying about which way I should turn or go next. And I learned well the basics of the machine and its movement by driving this way. But soon I wanted more: a road to travel, a radio that actually worked, a destination and goal, a more finely tuned knowledge of navigation involving blinkers, lights, different driving conditions, and—most of all—the ability to travel and negotiate with others also on the road.

—**BRENDA JO BRUEGGEMANN**, "American Sign Language and the Academy"

Notice how the series of details in paragraph 3 supports the main idea, or topic sentence (3c), which has been italicized to highlight it. Readers can easily see how one sentence leads into the next, creating a clear picture of the experience being described.

(2) Developing a paragraph with examples

Like details, examples contribute to paragraph development by making specific what otherwise might seem general and hard to grasp. **Details** describe a person, place, or thing; **examples** illustrate an idea with information that can come from different times and places. Both details and examples support the main idea of a paragraph.

The author of paragraph 4 uses several closely related examples (as well as details) to support the main idea with which she begins.

4   *It began with coveting our neighbor's chickens.* Lily would volunteer to collect the eggs, and then she offered to move in with them. Not the neighbors, the chickens. She said if she could have some of her own, she would be the happiest girl on earth. What parent could resist this bait? Our lifestyle could accommodate a laying flock; my husband and I had kept poultry before, so we knew it was a project we could manage, and a responsibility Lily could handle largely by herself. I understood how much that meant to her when I heard her tell her grandmother, "They're going to be just *my chickens*, grandma. Not even one of them will be my sister's." To be five years old and have some other life form entirely under your control—not counting goldfish or parents—is a majestic state of affairs.   —**BARBARA KINGSOLVER, "Lily's Chickens"**

Exercise 2

Examine some of your own writing—such as a recent draft of an essay, e-mail messages still on file, or entries in your journal— and select one paragraph that holds potential interest. Write out (by hand) the original paragraph. Then rewrite it, enriching and expanding it with additional details or examples.

2g   EMPLOYING RHETORICAL METHODS OF DEVELOPMENT

When drafting an essay, you can develop a variety of paragraphs using **rhetorical methods**, approaches to writing that help you address and resolve various types of rhetorical opportunities. Using rhetorical methods can help you establish boundaries (definition); investigate similarities or differences (comparison or contrast); make sense of a person, place, or event (description and narration); organize concepts (classification and division), think critically about a process (process analysis or cause-and-consequence analysis); or convince someone (argumentation—see Chapter 7). The strategies used for generating ideas, focusing a topic (**2b**), developing paragraphs and essays, and arranging ideas are already second nature to you. Every day, you use one or more of them to define a concept, narrate a significant incident, supply examples for an assertion, classify or divide information, compare two or more things, analyze a process, or identify a cause or consequence. As you draft, you may realize that you need to define a term or explain a process before you can take your readers further into your topic. Writers have the option of employing one, two, or several rhetorical methods to fulfill their overall purpose, which might be to explain, entertain, argue, or evaluate.

(1) Narration

A **narrative** discusses a sequence of events, normally in **chronological order** (the order in which they occur), to develop a particular point or set a mood. It often includes a setting, characters, dialogue, and description and usually makes use of transition words or phrases such as *first, then, later, that evening, the following week*, and so forth to guide readers from one incident to the next. Whatever its length, a narrative must remain focused on the main idea. The narrative in paragraph 5 traces the history of the *Beaver*, a replica of the original Boston Tea Party ship:

5   In 1972, three Boston businessmen got the idea of sailing a ship across the Atlantic for the tea party's bicentennial. They bought a Baltic schooner, built in Denmark in 1908, and had her rerigged as an English brig, powered by an anachronistic engine that was, unfortunately, put in backwards and caught fire on the way over. Still, she made it to Boston in time for the

hoopla. After that, the bicentennial *Beaver* was anchored at the Congress Street Bridge, next to what became the Boston Children's Museum. For years, it was a popular attraction. In 2001, though, the site was struck by lightning and closed for repairs. A renovation was planned. But that was stalled by the Big Dig, the excavation of three and a half miles of tunnel designed to rescue the city from the blight of Interstate 93, an elevated expressway that, since the 1950s, had made it almost impossible to see the ocean, and this in a city whose earliest maps were inked with names like Flounder Lane, Sea Street, and Dock Square. . . . In 2007, welders working on the Congress Street Bridge accidentally started another fire, although by then, the *Beaver* had already been towed, by tugboat, twenty-eight miles to Gloucester, where she'd been ever since, bereft, abandoned, and all but forgotten.

—JILL LEPORE, "Prologue: Party Like It's 1773"

(2) Description

By describing a person, place, object, or sensation, you can make your writing come alive. Often descriptions are predominantly visual, but even visual descriptions can include the details of what you hear, smell, taste, or touch; that is, descriptions appeal to the senses.

Image Courtesy of the Advertising Archives

The description of the candy and the appetizing image appeal to the reader's sense of taste.

Description should align with your rhetorical opportunity as well as with your purpose and audience. In paragraph 6, Ishmael Beah employs vivid descriptive details to convey what he saw and heard as he walked through a small town in Sierra Leone that had been devastated by rebels.

6   I am pushing a rusty wheelbarrow in a town where the air smells of blood and burnt flesh. The breeze brings the faint cries of those whose last breaths are leaving their mangled bodies. I walk past them. Their arms and legs are missing; their intestines spill out through the bullet holes in their

stomachs; brain matter comes out of their noses and ears. The flies are so excited and intoxicated that they fall on the pools of blood and die. The eyes of the nearly dead are redder than the blood that comes out of them, and it seems that their bones will tear through the skin of their taut faces at any minute. I turn my face to the ground to look at my feet. My tattered *crapes* [sneakers] are soaked with blood, which seems to be running down my army shorts. I feel no physical pain, so I am not sure whether I've been wounded. I can feel the warmth of my AK-47's barrel on my back; I don't remember when I last fired it. It feels as if needles have been hammered into my brain, and it is hard to be sure whether it is day or night. The wheelbarrow in front of me contains a dead body wrapped in white bedsheets. I do not know why I am taking this particular body to the cemetery.   —ISHMAEL BEAH, *A Long Way Gone: Memoirs of a Boy Soldier*

(3) Process analysis

Process paragraphs, in explaining how something is done or made, often use both description and narration. You might describe the items used in a process and then narrate the steps of the process chronologically. By adding an explanation of a process to a draft, you could illustrate a concept that might otherwise be hard for your audience to grasp. In paragraph 7, Sam Swope explains the process by which an elementary school assistant principal tried (unsuccessfully) to intimidate students into identifying a fellow student who stole report cards.

7   Later that day, a frowning assistant principal appeared in the doorway, and the room went hush. Everyone knew why he was there. I'd known Mr. Ziegler only as a friendly, mild-mannered fellow with a comb-over, so I was shocked to see him play the heavy. His performance began calmly, reasonably, solemnly. He told the class that the administration was deeply disappointed, that this theft betrayed the trust of family, teachers, school, and country. Then he told the children it was their

Time & Life Pictures/Getty Images

Sam Swope worked as an elementary school teacher in Queens, New York, for three years, interacting with children like these.

duty to report anything they'd seen or heard. When no one responded, he added a touch of anger to his voice, told the kids no stone would go unturned, the truth would out; he vowed he'd find the culprit—it was only a question of time! When this brought no one forward, he pumped up the volume. His face turned red, the veins on his neck bulged, and he wagged a finger in the air and shouted, "I'm not through with this investigation, not by a long shot! And if any of you know anything, you better come tell me, privately, in private, because they're going to be in a lot of trouble, *a lot of trouble!*"   —SAM SWOPE, "The Case of the Missing Report Cards"

(4) Cause-and-consequence analysis

Writers who analyze cause and consequence raise the question *Why?* and must answer it to the satisfaction of their audience, often differentiating the **primary cause** (the most important one) from **contributory causes** (which add to but do not directly cause an event or situation) and the **primary consequence** (the most important result) from **secondary consequences** (which are less important than the primary consequence). Writers who analyze cause and consequence usually link a sequence of events along a timeline. Always keep in mind, though, that just because one event occurs before—or after—another event does not necessarily make it a cause—or a consequence—of that event. In paragraph 8, journalist Christopher Hitchens analyzes the consequences of his chemotherapy.

8   It's quite something, this chemo-poison. It has caused me to lose about 14 pounds, though without making me feel any lighter. It has cleared up a vicious rash on my shins that no doctor could ever name, let alone cure. . . . Let it please be this mean and ruthless with the alien and its spreading dead-zone colonies. But as against that, the death-dealing stuff and life-preserving stuff have also made me strangely neuter. I was fairly reconciled to the loss of my hair, which began to come out in the shower in the first two weeks of treatment, and which I saved in a plastic bag so that it could help fill a floating dam in the Gulf of Mexico. But I wasn't quite prepared for the way that my razorblade would suddenly go slipping pointlessly down my face, meeting no stubble. Or for the way that my newly smooth upper lip would begin to look as if it had undergone electrolysis, causing me to look a bit too much like somebody's maiden auntie. (The chest hair that was once the toast of two continents hasn't yet wilted, but so much of it was shaved off for various hospital incisions that it's a rather patchy affair.) I feel upsettingly de-natured. If Penélope Cruz were one of my nurses, I wouldn't even notice. In the war against

Thanatos, if we must term it a war, the immediate loss of Eros is a huge initial sacrifice.   —**CHRISTOPHER HITCHENS**, "Topic of Cancer"

© 2010. Reprinted by permission.

Writers also catalogue consequences, as Mark Orwoll does in paragraph 9, listing the results of a recent ruling in favor of air-passenger rights.

9   The turning point [in air-passenger rights] came last April when a new Department of Transportation (DOT) rule went into effect prohibiting lengthy tarmac delays on domestic flights at large and midsize hub airports. It requires that airlines provide food, water, and working toilets within two hours of delaying a plane on the ground and, after three hours, that passengers be allowed to safely leave the plane.

—**MARK ORWOLL**, "Revolution in the Skies"

(5) Comparison and contrast

A **comparison** points out similarities, and a **contrast** points out differences. When drafting, consider whether a comparison might help your readers see a relationship they might otherwise miss or whether a contrast might help them establish useful distinctions in order to better understand an issue or make a decision. Thus, paragraphs—or essays—that compare or contrast establish a relationship between two things (rather than simply listing all the points of comparison or contrast for one followed by all of them for the other). In paragraph 10, Robert D. Putnam and David E. Campbell use descriptive details to compare two Catholic presidential candidates.

10   In 1960, presidential candidate John F. Kennedy had to reassure Protestants that they could safely vote for a Catholic. (At the time 30 percent of Americans freely told pollsters that they would not vote for a Catholic as president.) At the same time, Kennedy won overwhelming support from his fellow Catholics, even though he explicitly disagreed with his church on a number of public issues. In 2004, America had another Catholic presidential candidate—also a Democratic senator from Massachusetts, also a highly decorated veteran, and also with the initials JFK. Like Kennedy, John (Forbes) Kerry also publicly disagreed with his church on at least one prominent issue—in this case, abortion. But unlike Kennedy, Kerry split the Catholic vote with his Republican opponent, and lost handily among Catholics who frequently attend church. Kennedy would likely

have found it inexplicable that Kerry not only lost to a Protestant, but to George W. Bush, an evangelical Protestant at that. . . . In 1960, religion's role in politics was mostly a matter of something akin to tribal loyalty—Catholics and Protestants each supported their own. In order to win, Kennedy had to shatter the stained glass ceiling that had kept Catholics out of national elective office in a Protestant-majority nation. By the 2000s, how religious a person is had become more important as a political dividing line than which denomination he or she belonged to. Church-attending evangelicals and Catholics (and other religious groups too) have found common political cause. Voters who are not religious have also found common cause with one another, but on the opposite end of the political spectrum.

www.loriferber.com

Even though John Kerry shares many characteristics with John F. Kennedy, he was not able to win the presidency.

—ROBERT PUTNAM AND DAVID E. CAMPBELL,
"Religious Polarization and Pluralism in America"

© 2010. Reprinted by permission.

(6) Classification and division

To classify is to place things into groups based on shared characteristics. **Classification** is a way to understand or explain something by establishing how it fits within a category or group. For example, a book reviewer might classify a new novel as a mystery—leading readers to expect a plot based on suspense. **Division**, in contrast, separates something into component parts and examines the relationships among them. A novel can be discussed in terms of its components, such as plot, setting, and theme (Chapter 11).

Classification and division represent two different perspectives: ideas can be put into groups (classification) or split into subclasses (division). As strategies for organizing (or developing) an idea, classification and division often work together. In paragraph 11, for example, both classification and division are used to differentiate the two versions of the cowboy icon. Like many paragraphs, this one mixes rhetorical methods; the writer uses description, comparison and contrast, and classification to make her point.

KINGDOM	Animalia
PHYLUM	Arthropoda
CLASS	Insecta
ORDER	Hymenoptera
FAMILY	Apidae
GENUS	*Apis*
SPECIES	*mellifera*

© Scott T. Smith/Corbis

The scientific identification of the honeybee (*Apis mellifera*) requires a classification in the genus *Apis* and a division within that genus, the species *mellifera*.

11   First, and perhaps most fundamentally, the cowboy icon has two basic incarnations: the cowboy hero and the cowboy villain. Cowboy heroes often appear in roles such as sheriff, leader of a cattle drive, or what I'll call a "wandering hero," such as the Lone Ranger, who appears much like a frontier Superman wherever and whenever help is needed. Writers and producers most commonly place cowboy heroes in conflict either with "Indians" or with the cowboy villain. In contrast to the other classic bad guys of the Western genre, cowboy villains pose a special challenge because they are essentially the alter ego of the cowboy hero; the cowboy villain shares the hero's skill with a gun, his horse-riding maneuvers, and his knowledge of the land. What distinguishes the two, of course, is character: the cowboy hero is essentially good, while the cowboy villain is essentially evil.

—JODY M. ROY, "The Case of the Cowboy"

(7) Definition

By defining a concept or a term, you efficiently clarify your meaning and so develop an idea. By defining a word for your readers, you immediately connect with them; they know what you are and are not talking about. Definitions are usually constructed in a two-step process: the first step locates a term by placing it in a class; the second step differentiates this particular term from other terms in the same class. For instance, "A concerto [the term] is a symphonic piece [the class] consisting of three movements performed by one or more solo instruments accompanied at times by an orchestra [the difference]." A symphony belongs to the same basic class as a concerto; it too is a symphonic piece. However, a symphony can be differentiated from a concerto in two specific ways: a symphony consists of four movements, and its performance involves the entire orchestra.

Paragraph 12 defines volcanoes by putting them into a class ("landforms") and by distinguishing them ("built of molten material") from other members of that class. The definition is then clarified by examples.

12   Volcanoes are landforms built of molten material that has spewed out onto the earth's surface. Such molten rock is called lava. Volcanoes may be no larger than small hills, or thousands of feet high. All have a characteristic cone shape. Some well-known mountains are actually volcanoes. Examples are Mt. Fuji (Japan), Mt. Lassen (California), Mt. Hood (Oregon), Mt. Etna and Mt. Vesuvius (Italy), and Paricutín (Mexico). The Hawaiian Islands are all immense volcanoes whose summits rise above the ocean, and these volcanoes are still quite active.   —JOEL AREM, *Rocks and Minerals*

Using definition and the other rhetorical methods just described will make your writing more understandable to your audience, because all of us—writers and readers, speakers and listeners—employ these rhetorical methods to help us make sense of the world around us. Even though these methods are familiar, however, you need to make sure that you use the one(s) best suited to your rhetorical situation, to supporting your thesis and making your purpose clear to your intended audience. As you draft and revise, you can easily check to see whether the rhetorical method employed in each paragraph keeps your essay anchored to its thesis statement and helps you address your rhetorical opportunity. You may need to expand, condense, or delete paragraphs accordingly (3c and 3f).

3 ‖ REVISING AND EDITING ESSAYS

Revising, which literally means "seeing again," lies at the heart of all successful writing. When you are revising your writing, you resee it in the role of reader rather than writer. Revising involves considering a number of global issues: how successfully you have responded to the rhetorical opportunity, how clearly you have stated your thesis, how successfully you have communicated your purpose to your audience, how effectively you have arranged your information, and how thoroughly you have developed your assertions. **Editing**, on the other hand, focuses on local issues, which are smaller in scale. When you are editing, you polish your writing: you choose words more precisely (Chapter **34**), shape prose more distinctly (Chapter **35**), and structure sentences more effectively (Chapters **27–32**). While you are editing, you are also **proofreading**, focusing even more sharply to eliminate surface errors in grammar, punctuation, and mechanics. Revising and editing often overlap (just as drafting and revising do), and peer review can be helpful throughout these stages of the writing process. Usually revising occurs before editing, but not always. Edited passages may be redrafted, rearranged, and even cut as writers revise further.

As you revise and edit your essays, this chapter will help you

- consider your work as a whole (**3a(1)** and **3a(2)**),
- evaluate your tone (**3a(3)**),
- compose an effective introduction and conclusion (**3b**),
- strengthen the unity and coherence of paragraphs (**3c**),
- improve transitions (**3d**),
- benefit from a reviewer's comments (**3e**),
- edit to improve style (**3f**),
- proofread to eliminate surface errors (**3g**), and
- submit a final draft (**3h**).

3a   THE ESSENTIALS OF REVISION

In truth, you are revising throughout the planning and drafting stages of the writing process, whether at the word, phrase, sentence, or paragraph level. But no matter how much you may have revised during those stages of the writing process, you will still do most of your revising after you have completed a draft. You may then rewrite specific sentences and paragraphs as well as reconsider the draft as a whole. A few writers prefer to start revising immediately after drafting, while their minds are still fully engaged by their topic. But most writers like to let a draft "cool off," so that when they return to it, they can assess it more objectively, with fresh eyes. Even an overnight cooling-off period will give you more objectivity as a reader and will reveal more options to you as a writer.

◉ TECH SAVVY

Most word-processing programs enable you to track your revisions easily using a feature like Microsoft Word's Track Changes. Tracking changes is especially useful if your instructor requires you to submit all your drafts or if one or more peers are reviewing your drafts. If your word-processing program does not have this function, simply save and date each version of your work. You can open and compare these different versions as you write, and then submit all of them, if required.

(1) Revising purposefully

As you reread a draft, you need to keep in mind your audience, your purpose, and your thesis. Does your purpose come through clearly in every paragraph? Which paragraphs demonstrate your thesis? Which ones repeat or contradict what has come before? Which ones digress (3c)?

Revision should enhance the development of your thesis while strengthening the connection between your rhetorical purpose and your intended audience (1d). In order to meet the needs, the expectations, and even the resistance of those in your audience, try to anticipate their responses (understanding, acceptance, or opposition) to your thesis statement, to each of your assertions, to the supporting examples and details you employ, and to the language you choose. In other words, revising successfully requires that you reread your work as both a writer and a reader. As a writer, ask yourself whether your words accurately reflect your intention and meaning. As a reader, ask yourself whether what seems clear and logical to you will also be clear to others.

(2) Adding essential information

Writers are always aware of what they have put on the page—but they seldom spend enough time considering what they may have left out. In order to ensure that you have provided all the information necessary for a reader to understand your points, consider the following questions: How might your audience be interested in addressing or resolving the rhetorical opportunity for change? What does your audience already know about this topic or issue? What information might your audience be expecting or be surprised by? What information might strengthen your thesis?

Keep in mind that your best ideas will not always surface in your first draft; you will sometimes come up with an important idea only after you have finished that draft, let it cool off, and then looked at it again. No matter how complete a draft seems, you can use questioning strategies to check whether anything is missing (**2a(3)**), whether some explanation, description, or example could be added that would enhance your message and strengthen your connection with your audience. Or you might share your draft with a peer who is working on the same assignment, asking that person to mark confusing, unclear, or provocative passages (**3e**).

(3) Creating the right tone

Tone reflects a writer's attitude toward a subject, so you will want to make sure that your tone is appropriate to your purpose, audience, and context (**1a**). Decide what you intend your tone to be (how you want to sound in order to engage your intended audience and achieve your purpose), and then read your draft aloud to see if it has that tone. Whether you are writing for school, work, or personal reasons, you want to control the tone so that it reflects your confidence, your preparation, your fair-mindedness, and, perhaps most of all, your willingness to engage with your audience. You want all your words as well as your sentence structures to convey your intended tone. If any of the passages in your draft sound defensive, self-centered, or apologetic to you or to a peer reviewer, revise them. You want to ensure that your tone helps elicit from your readers the desired response—to you as well as to the information you are presenting.

Consider the tone in paragraph 1, in which Dorothy Allison describes some of the positive and negative things she remembers about growing up in South Carolina. (For ease of reference, each of the sample paragraphs in this chapter is numbered.)

1   Where I was born—Greenville, South Carolina—smelled like nowhere else I've ever been. Cut wet grass, split green apples, baby shit and beer bottles, cheap makeup and motor oil. Everything was ripe, everything was rotting. Hound dogs butted my calves. People shouted in the distance; crickets boomed in my ears. That country was beautiful, I swear to you, the most beautiful place I've ever been. Beautiful and terrible. It is the country of my dreams and the country of my nightmares: a pure pink and blue sky, red dirt, white clay, and all that endless green—willows and dogwood and firs going on for miles.

     —**DOROTHY ALLISON,** *Two or Three Things I Know for Sure*

Exercise 1

Establishing a distinctive tone, create a paragraph about the place where you grew up. Identify specific words and phrases from paragraph 1 that helped you with your version. Be prepared to share your list of words and phrases with the class.

When Mary LeNoir revised the first draft reprinted later in this chapter (pages 69–72), she decided to adjust her tone because she thought it seemed too dry and academic. Of course, Mary wanted to sound like she had a lot of knowledge and insight about her topic. But she also wanted to connect immediately with her audience, helping them recognize that her essay could help clear up the question of how student-athletes actually choose a college. To meet her goals, she would have to revise her introduction, striking a more natural and inviting tone that better aligned with her rhetorical opportunity (**1a**).

> **⊙ TECH SAVVY**
>
> The thesaurus in your word-processing program may give you advice that can affect the tone of your writing. This tool is easy to use; however, only you can make the word choices that will achieve the appropriate tone. For example, a thesaurus may suggest a synonym for a word that you have been intentionally repeating in order to establish a rhythm. Give careful consideration to the suggestions a thesaurus makes, weighing those suggestions in terms of your rhetorical opportunity as you revise.

3b   GUIDING READERS WITH THE INTRODUCTION AND THE CONCLUSION

Your introduction and conclusion orient your readers to the purpose of your essay as a whole. In fact, readers intentionally read these two sections for guidance and clarification.

(1) An effective introduction

Experienced writers know that the opening paragraph is their best chance to arouse the reader's interest with provocative information; establish the rhetorical opportunity, topic, and writer as worthy of consideration; and set the overall tone. An effective introduction makes the intended audience want to read on. In paragraph 2, herpetologist Rick Roth introduces himself to a diverse audience, readers of *Sierra* magazine.

2   A lot of people know me as "Snake Man" now and don't know my real name. I've always been a critter person. My mother was never afraid of anything, and I used to actually get to keep snakes in the house. I'm 58, so this was a long time ago, when *nobody* got to keep snakes in the house. I've got 75 or so now at home—and a really cool landlord.

—RICK ROTH, "Snake Charmer"

Roth's friendly introduction immediately grabs readers' attention with his down-home language and unusual partiality for snakes. He then moves quickly to his childhood fascination with butterflies and dragonflies (thereby establishing common ground with those of his readers who are agitated by snakes) and goes on to explain his current occupation as the executive director of the Cape Ann Vernal Pond Team.

Introductions have no set length; they can be as brief as a couple of sentences or as long as two or more paragraphs, sometimes even longer. Although introductions always appear first, they are often drafted and revised after other parts of an essay. Just like the thesis statements they often include, introductions evolve during the drafting and revising stages, as the material is shaped, focused, and developed toward fulfilling the writer's overall purpose. Most writers experiment with several different introductions to determine which one is most effective.

You can arouse the interest of your audience by writing introductions in a number of ways.

(a) Opening with an unusual fact or statistic

3   Americans aren't just reading fewer books, but are reading less and less of everything, in any medium. That's the doleful conclusion of "To Read or Not to Read," a report released last week by the National Endowment for the Arts.

—JENNIFER HOWARD, **"Americans Are Closing the Book on Reading, Study Finds"**

Reading, Over Time

Among all 8- to 18-year-olds, average amount of time spent using each type of print media in a typical day, over time:

HOURS   ☐ 1999 ☐ 2004 ■ 2009

Books: :21 :23 :25
Magazines: :15 :14 :09
Newspapers: :07 :06 :03

Source: Kaiser Family Foundation, Generation M²: Media in the Lives of 8- to 18-Year-Olds, 2010.

"Generation M2: Media in the Lives of 8- to 18-Year-Olds," (#8010) The Henry J. Kaiser Family Foundation, January 2010

Opening with a thought-provoking statistic can be an effective introduction.

(b) Opening with an intriguing statement

4   I belong to a Clan of One-Breasted Women. My mother, my grand-mothers, and six aunts have all had mastectomies. Seven are dead. The two who survive have just completed rounds of chemotherapy and radiation.

—TERRY TEMPEST WILLIAMS, "The Clan of One-Breasted Women"

(c) Opening with an anecdote or example

5   When I used to ask my mother which we were, rich or poor, she refused to tell me. I was then nine years old and of course what I was dying to hear was that we were poor. I was reading a book called *Five Little Peppers* and my heart was set on baking a cake for my mother in a stove with a hole in it. Some version of rich, crusty old Mr. King—up till that time not living on our street—was sure to come down the hill in his wheelchair and rescue me if anything went wrong. But before I could start a cake at all I had to find out if we were rich or poor, and poor *enough*; and my mother wouldn't tell me, she said she was too busy. I couldn't wait too long; I had to go on reading and soon Polly Pepper got into more trouble, some that was a little harder on her and easier on me.   —EUDORA WELTY, "A Sweet Devouring"

(d) Opening with a question

6   Fellow-Citizens—pardon me, and allow me to ask, why am I called upon to speak here today? What have I, or those I represent, to do with your national independence? Are the great principles of political freedom and of natural justice, embodied in that Declaration of Independence, extended to us? and am I, therefore, called upon to bring our humble offering to the national altar, and to confess the benefits, and express devout gratitude for the blessings, resulting from your independence to us?

—FREDERICK DOUGLASS, "What to the Slave Is the Fourth of July?"

(e) Opening with an appropriate quotation

7   "My wife and I like the kind of trouble you've been stirring, Miss Williams," he said, with a smile and a challenge. He had an avuncular, wizardy twinkle, very Albus Dumbledore. It made me feel feisty and smart, like Hermione Granger. They *liked* my kind of trouble. But let this be a lesson: When a woman of my great dignity and years loses her sanity and starts imagining she's one of Harry Potter's magical little friends, you can be sure that the cosmic gyroscope is wobbling off its center . . . .

—PATRICIA J. WILLIAMS, *Open House: Of Family, Friends, Food, Piano Lessons, and the Search for a Room of My Own*

(f) Opening with general information or background about the topic

8   Scientists have long touted the benefits of the Mediterranean diet for heart health. But now researchers are finding more and more evidence that the diet can keep you healthy in other ways, too, including lowering the risk of certain cancers and easing the pain and stiffness of arthritis.

—MELISSA GOTTHARDT, "The Miracle Diet"

(g) Opening with a thesis statement

9   When America first met her in 1992, Hillary Rodham Clinton looked like what she was: a working mother. She had recently chucked her Coke-bottle glasses but still sported headbands and weird amounts of ineptly applied makeup. Why should it have been otherwise? Clinton was a busy woman when her husband ran for president. Mind-bogglingly, she would be the first first lady in American history to have maintained a full-time career outside her husband's political life prior to his presidency. In short, Clinton was the first candidate for the job of first lady to have a life that reflected [America after the feminist movement of the 1970s] and the many working women who made their careers and raised their families here.

—REBECCA TRAISTER, *Big Girls Don't Cry*

However you open your essay, use your introduction to specify your topic, engage your readers' attention, initiate an appropriate tone, and establish your credibility (7f(1)).

(2) An effective conclusion

Just as a good introduction tantalizes readers, a good conclusion satisfies them. It helps readers recognize the important points of your essay and the significance of those points while, at the same time, wrapping up the essay in a meaningful, thought-provoking way. As you draft and revise, you may want to keep a list of ideas for your conclusion. Some suggestions for writing effective conclusions follow, beginning with the reliable method of simply restating the thesis and main points. This kind of conclusion can be effective for a long essay that includes several important points that the writer wants the reader to recall.

(a) Rephrasing the thesis and summarizing the main points

10   The Endangered Species Act should not take into account economic considerations. Economics doesn't know how to value a species or a forest. Its logic drives people to exploit resources to the point of extinction. The Endangered Species Act tells us that extinction is morally unacceptable.

It was enacted by a Congress and president in a wise mood, to express a higher value than a bottom line.

—DONELLA MEADOWS, "Not Seeing the Forest for the Dollar Bills"

(b) Calling attention to larger issues

11   If tough breaks have not soured me, neither have my glory-moments caused me to build any altars to myself where I can burn incense before God's best job of work. My sense of humor will always stand in the way of my seeing myself, my family, my race or my nation as the whole intent of the universe. When I see what we really are like, I know that God is too great an artist for we folks on my side of the creek to be all of His best works. Some of His finest touches are among us, without doubt, but some more of His masterpieces are among those folks who live over the creek.

—ZORA NEALE HURSTON, *Dust Tracks on a Road: An Autobiography*

(c) Calling for a change in action or attitude

12   Although [Anna Julia] Cooper published *A Voice* in 1892, its political implications remain relevant to twenty-first-century scholars and activists. As our society grows increasingly multicultural, and the borders between colors and countries grow ever more porous, the strategies for organizing communities of resistance must necessarily follow suit. Academics and activists engaged in efforts to transform inequitable social relations benefit from thinking not only about what separates but also what unites humanity.

—KATHY L. GLASS, "Tending to the Roots"

(d) Concluding with a vivid image

13   At just past 10 A.M., farm workers and scrap-yard laborers in Somerset County looked up to see a large commercial airliner dipping and lunging as it swooped low over the hill country of southern Pennsylvania, near the town of Shanksville. A man driving a coal truck on Route 30 said he saw the jet tilt violently from side to side, then suddenly plummet "straight down." It hit nose first on the grassy face of a reclaimed strip mine at approximately 10:05 Eastern Daylight Time and exploded into a fireball, shattering windowpanes a half-mile away. The seventy-two-year-old man who was closest to the point of impact saw what looked to him like the yellow mushroom cloud of an atomic blast. Twenty-eight-year-old Eric Peterson was one of the first on the scene. He arrived to discover a flaming crater fifty feet deep. Shredded clothing hung from the trees, and smoldering airplane parts littered the ground. It did not look much like the site of a great American victory, but it was.   —RANDALL SULLIVAN, "Flight 93"

(e) Connecting with the introduction

The introduction

14   Peterson Yazzie (Navajo) may be only 26, but this young contemporary painter from Greasewood Springs, Arizona has already garnered impressive accolades and is considered one of the rising stars of the Native art realm.

In the essay that follows this introduction, Debra Utacia Krol provides a brief biographical sketch of the artist's life and education, followed by an enthusiastic assessment of his art.

The conclusion

15   Among other honors amassed over his meteoric career, Yazzie took home the best of class ribbon in painting from the Heard Museum Guild Indian Fair & Market in 2006, and looks forward to returning again this year as he continues to delve even further into expressing his worldview through art.   —DEBRA UTACIA KROL, "Peterson Yazzie"

Whatever technique you choose for your conclusion, provide readers with a sense of closure. Bear in mind that they may be wondering, "So what? Why have you told me all this?" Your conclusion gives you an opportunity to address that concern. If there is any chance that readers may not understand your purpose, use your conclusion to clarify why you think they needed to read what they have just read.

Exercise 2

Thumb through a magazine you enjoy, skimming the introductions of all the articles. Select two introductions that catch your attention. Consider the reasons *why* they interest you. What specific techniques for an introduction did the authors use? Next, look through the same or another magazine for two effective conclusions. Analyze their effectiveness as well. Be prepared to share your findings with the rest of the class.

3c   REVISING FOR UNIFIED AND COHERENT PARAGRAPHS

When revising the body of an essay, writers are likely to find opportunities for further development within each paragraph (2f and 2g) and to discover ways to make each paragraph more unified by relating every sentence within the paragraph to a single main idea (3c(2)), which might appear in a topic sentence. After weeding out unrelated sentences, writers concentrate on coherence, ordering the sentences so that ideas progress logically and smoothly from one sentence to the next. A successful paragraph is well developed, unified, and coherent.

(1) Expressing the main idea in a topic sentence

Much like the thesis statement of an essay, a **topic sentence** states the main idea of a paragraph and comments on that main idea. Although the topic sentence is usually the first sentence in a paragraph, it can appear in any position within the paragraph, even as the closing sentence. Sometimes, paragraphs build up to the final, topic sentence; other times, all the sentences together imply an unstated topic sentence. If you want to ensure that your paragraphs are unified and coherent, you might want to place the topic sentence at the beginning of each paragraph. A topic sentence in that location will both remind you of your focus and be obvious to your readers, who will recognize and then follow your main idea immediately. More experienced writers often add interest to their writing by varying the placement of their topic sentences within different paragraphs.

When you announce your general topic in a topic sentence and then provide specific support for it, you are writing **deductively**. Your topic sentence appears first, like the one in italics in paragraph 16, which indicates that the author will offer evidence as to why we are suspicious of rapid cognition.

16   *I think we are innately suspicious of . . . rapid cognition.* We live in a world that assumes that the quality of a decision is directly related to the time and effort that went into making it. When doctors are faced with a difficult diagnosis, they order more tests, and when we are uncertain about what we hear, we ask for a second opinion. And what do we tell our children? Haste makes waste. Look before you leap. Stop and *think*. Don't judge a book by its cover. We believe that we are always better off gathering

as much information as possible and spending as much time as possible in deliberation. We really only trust conscious decision making. But there are moments, particularly in times of stress, when haste does not make waste, when our snap judgments and first impressions can offer a much better means of making sense of the world.   —MALCOLM GLADWELL, *Blink*

If you want to emphasize the main idea of a paragraph or give its organization some extra support, you can begin and conclude the paragraph with two versions of the same idea. This strategy is particularly useful for long paragraphs because it gives readers whose attention may have wandered a second chance to grasp the main idea. In paragraph 17, both the first sentence and the last convey the idea that the English language has become a global language.

17   *English is the most widely spoken language in the history of our planet, used in some way by at least one out of every seven human beings around the globe.* Half of the world's books are written in English, and the majority of international telephone calls are made in English. English is the language of over sixty percent of the world's radio programs, many of them beamed, ironically, by the Russians, who know that to win friends and influence nations, they're best off using English. More than seventy percent of international mail is written and addressed in English, and eighty percent of all computer text is stored in English. *English has acquired the largest vocabulary of all the world's languages, perhaps as many as two million words, and has generated one of the noblest bodies of literature in the annals of the human race.*   —RICHARD LEDERER, "English Is a Crazy Language"

As you prepare to revise a draft, try underlining the topic sentences you can identify. If you cannot find a topic sentence in one of your paragraphs, add a sentence stating the main idea of that paragraph. If you find that you open every paragraph with a topic sentence, you might try experimenting with another pattern, revising a paragraph so that the topic sentence appears at the end, as in paragraph 18.

18   The first time I visited Texas, I wore a beige polyester-blend lab coat with reinforced slits for pocket access and mechanical-pencil storage. I was attending a local booksellers' convention, having just co-written a pseudo-scientific book . . . , and my publicist suggested that the doctor getup would attract attention. It did. Everyone thought I was the janitor. Lesson No. 1: When in Texas, do not dress down.   —PATRICIA MARX, "Dressin' Texan"

Placing the topic sentence at the end of the paragraph works well when you are moving from specific supporting details to a generalization about those ideas—that is, when you are writing **inductively**. Effective writers try to meet the expectations of their readers, which often include the anticipation that the first sentence will be the topic sentence; however, writers and readers alike enjoy an occasional departure from the expected. And writers need to adjust paragraph structure to reflect the rhetorical purpose of each paragraph.

(2) Creating unified paragraphs

Paragraphs are **unified** when every sentence relates to the main idea; unity is violated when something unrelated to the rest of the material appears. Consider the obvious violation in paragraph 19.

19   The Marion, Ohio of my childhood offered lots of opportunities for making memories. The summers were particularly rich in those occasions. Often, I'd make the one-hour walk to the library and spend the afternoon browsing or reading, either in the children's library in the dark, cool basement or in the adult library, which was sunnier and warmer. On the way home, I would stop by Isaly's Dairy and buy a skyscraper ice cream cone for twenty-five cents. Sometimes, I'd make plans to meet up with my cousin Babs to walk downtown for a movie matinée and a grilled-cheese sandwich at Woolworth's lunch counter. Her parents, Aunt Agnes and Uncle Jack, both worked downtown, she at JC Penney and he at Jim Dugan's Menswear, so Babs and I would include visiting both of them at work in our day's activities. *Funny, now that I think back on those good summer afternoons, I think about how I haven't seen Babs since her mother's funeral, ten years ago.* On the days I didn't walk downtown, I usually swam in our neighborhood swimming pool, Fair Park pool, where all of us kids played freely and safely, often without any parents around but usually with our younger siblings trailing after us (including my own). Or we Fair Park kids might take a city bus out to the roller rink or, if something big was going on, walk out to the fairgrounds, sneaking under the fence, to see what was going on.

Easy to delete, the italicized sentence about not having seen Babs for ten years violates the unity of a paragraph devoted to childhood activities in a small town. But if the essay included a comparison of what the two cousins did when they were together as children and what they do now as adults, the writer could develop the sentence into a separate paragraph.

As you revise your paragraphs for unity, the following tips may help you.

TIPS FOR IMPROVING PARAGRAPH UNITY

- **Identify.** Identify the topic sentence for each paragraph. Where is each located? Why is each one located where it is?

- **Relate.** Read each sentence in a paragraph and determine how (and if) it relates directly to or develops the topic sentence.

- **Eliminate.** Any sentence that does not relate to the topic sentence violates the unity of the paragraph—cut it or save it to use elsewhere.

- **Clarify.** If a sentence "almost" relates to the topic sentence, either revise it or delete it. As you revise, you might clarify details or add information or a transitional word or phrase to make the relationship clear.

- **Rewrite.** If more than one idea is being conveyed in a single paragraph, either rewrite the topic sentence so that it includes both ideas and establishes a relationship between them or split the single paragraph into two paragraphs, dividing up the information accordingly.

---

(3) Arranging ideas into coherent paragraphs

Some paragraphs are unified (**3c(2)**) but not coherent. In a unified paragraph, every sentence relates to the main idea of the paragraph. In a **coherent** paragraph, the relationship among the ideas is clear and meaningful, and the progression from one sentence to the next is easy for readers to follow. Paragraph 20 has unity but lacks coherence.

Lacks coherence

20   The land was beautiful, gently rolling hills, an old orchard with fruit-bearing potential, a small clear stream—over eleven acres. But the house itself was another story. It had sat empty for years. Perhaps not empty, though that's what the realtor told us. There were macaroni and cheese boxes, how-to-play the mandolin books and videos, extra countertops, a kitchen sink, single socks looking for their mates, a ten-year-old pan of refried beans, and all sorts of random stuff strewn all through the house. Had the owner stayed there until he gave up on remodeling it? Had homeless people squatted there? Or had it been a hangout for teenagers—until the hole in the roof got too big for comfort? Who had been living there, and what kind of damage had they brought to the house? *We looked at the house with an eye toward buying it.* The price was right: very low, just what we could afford. And the location and acreage were perfect, too. But the house itself was a wreck. It needed a new roof, but it also needed a kitchen,

flooring, drywall, updated plumbing and electricity—and a great big dumpster. We didn't know if we had the energy, let alone the know-how, to fix it up. Plus it wasn't like it was just the two of us we had to think about. We had three children to consider. If we bought it, where would we start working to make it inhabitable?

Although every sentence in this paragraph has to do with the writer's reaction to a house offered for sale, the sentences themselves are not arranged coherently; they are not in any logical order. First, the italicized topic sentence could be moved to the beginning of the paragraph, where it could control the meaningful flow of ideas. Then, the other sentences could be clustered according to subtopic: the land, the condition of the house, and the potential advantages and disadvantages of the purchase.

Revised for coherence

21   *We looked at the house with an eye toward buying it.* The land was beautiful, gently rolling hills, an old orchard with fruit-bearing potential, a small clear stream—over eleven acres. But the house itself was another story. It had sat empty for years. Perhaps not empty, though that's what the realtor told us. There were macaroni and cheese boxes, how-to-play the mandolin books and videos, extra countertops, a kitchen sink, single socks looking for their mates, a ten-year-old pan of refried beans, and all sorts of random stuff strewn all through the house. Had the owner stayed there until he gave up on remodeling it? Had homeless people squatted there? Or had it been a hangout for teenagers—until the hole in the roof got too big for comfort? By now, the house needed a new roof as well as a kitchen, flooring, drywall, updated plumbing and electricity—and a great big dumpster. We didn't know if we had the energy, let alone the know-how, to fix it up. Plus it wasn't like it was just the two of us we had to think about. We had three children to consider. Still, the price was right: very low, just what we could afford. And the location and acreage were perfect, too.

Paragraph 21 is coherent as well as unified.

To achieve coherence as well as unity in your paragraphs, study the following patterns of organization (chronological, spatial, emphatic, and logical), and consider which ones you might use in your own writing.

(a) Using chronological order

When you use **chronological order**, you arrange ideas according to the order in which things happened. This organizational pattern is particularly useful for narration.

22   The years following the Civil War laid the foundation for the division in the narrative. The war initially raised the hope that citizenship might replace race as the sole basis for American identity, but the realities of Reconstruction and its aftermath forced African Americans to redefine their collective history. . . . This memory of hope and sacrifice was given credence and promoted in the latter part of the nineteenth century through black-owned newspapers and black ministers, who reminded their audiences of the experiences and hopes of the past in connection with the struggles of the present. The journey, so filled with false promises and unrealized dreams, suggested greater rewards. The outline of this collective memory carried over into the twentieth century via slave narratives, autobiographies and adventure literature catering to the rising literacy rate for African Americans.

—K. BINDAS, "Re-remembering a Segregated Past: Race in American Memory"

© 2010. Reprinted by permission.

(b) Using spatial order

When you arrange ideas according to **spatial order**, you orient the reader's focus from right to left, near to far, top to bottom, and so on. This organizational pattern is particularly effective in descriptions. Often the organization is so obvious that the writer can forgo a topic sentence, as in paragraph 23.

23   I went to see a prospective student, Steve, up on the North Branch Road. His mother, Tammi, told me to look for the blue trailer with cars in the yard. There were *lots* of junk cars—rusted, hoods up, and wheels off, a Toyota truck filled with bags of trash. The yard was littered with transmission parts, hubcaps, empty soda bottles, Tonka trucks, deflated soccer balls, retired chain saws and piles of seasoned firewood hidden in the overgrowth of jewelweed. A pen held an assortment of bedraggled, rain-soaked chickens and a belligerent, menacing turkey. A small garden of red and yellow snapdragons marked the way to the door.

—TAL BIRDSEY, *A Room for Learning: The Making of a School in Vermont*

(c) Using emphatic order

When you use **emphatic order**, you arrange information in order of importance, usually from least to most important. Emphatic order is especially useful in expository and persuasive writing, both of which involve helping readers understand logical relationships (such as what caused something to happen or what kinds of priorities should be established). The information in paragraph 24 leads up to the writer's conclusion—that rats raised in enriched environments are smarter rats.

24   Raising animals in a rich environment can result in increased brain tissue and improved performance on memory tests. Much of this work has been done with rats. The "rich" rat environment involved raising rats in social groups in large cages with exercise wheels, toys, and climbing terrain. Control "poor" rats were raised individually in standard laboratory cages without the stimulating objects the rich rats had. Both the rich and poor rats were kept clean and given sufficient food and water. Results of these studies were striking: Rich rats had substantially thicker cerebral cortex, the highest region of the brain and the substrate of cognition, with many more synaptic connections, than the poor rats. They also learned to run mazes better.

> —RICHARD F. THOMPSON AND STEPHEN A. MADIGAN,
> *Memory: The Key to Consciousness*

(d) Using logical order

Sometimes the movement within a paragraph follows a **logical order**, from specific to general or from general to specific. A paragraph may begin with a series of details and conclude with a summarizing statement, as paragraphs 18 and 25 do, or it may begin with a general statement or idea, which is then supported by particular details, as in paragraphs 21 and 26.

25   Whether one reads for work or for pleasure, comprehension is the goal. Comprehension is an active process; readers must interact and be engaged with a text. To accomplish this, proficient readers use strategies or conscious plans of action. Less proficient readers often lack awareness of comprehension strategies, however, and cannot develop them on their own. For adult literacy learners in particular, integrating and synthesizing information from any but the simplest texts can pose difficulties.

> —MARY E. CURTIS AND JOHN R. KRUIDENIER, "Teaching Adults to Read"

26   It was not the only disappointment my mother felt in me. In the years that followed, I failed her so many times, each time asserting my own will, my right to fall short of expectations. I didn't get straight As. I didn't become class president. I didn't get into Stanford. I dropped out of college.

> —AMY TAN, "Two Kinds"

Exercise 3

Working with a classmate, skim through your personal reading materials (things you are reading for courses or for pleasure) and together, select a paragraph that lacks coherence and unity. Each of you should revise that paragraph and then compare your revisions. Next, collaborate on an improved joint revision that you can share with the rest of the class. As you revise (alone and together), consider the paragraph's topic sentence and the other sentences as well, adding and deleting supporting information as you see fit. If you reorder the sentences within the paragraph, make a conscious decision to use chronological, spatial, emphatic, or logical order. Explain your choice of order to the rest of the class.

3d   TRANSITIONS WITHIN AND BETWEEN PARAGRAPHS

Even if its sentences are arranged in a seemingly clear sequence, a single paragraph may lack internal coherence, and a series of paragraphs may lack overall coherence if transitions are abrupt or nonexistent. When revising, you can improve coherence by using pronouns, repetition, or conjunctions and transitional words or phrases (23c(5)).

(1) Using pronouns to establish links between sentences

In paragraph 27, the writer enumerates the similarities of identical twins raised separately. She mentions their names only once, but uses the pronouns *both, their,* and *they* to keep the references to the twins always clear.

27   Jim Springer and Jim Lewis were adopted as infants into working-class Ohio families. **Both** liked math and did not like spelling in school. **Both** had law enforcement training and worked part-time as deputy sheriffs. **Both** vacationed in Florida, **both** drove Chevrolets. Much has been made of the fact that **their** lives are marked by a trail of similar names. **Both** married and divorced women named Linda and had second marriages with women named Betty. **They** named **their** sons James Allan and James Alan,

respectively. **Both** like mechanical drawing and carpentry. **They** have almost identical drinking and smoking patterns. **Both** chew **their** fingernails down to the nubs.   —CONSTANCE HOLDEN, "Identical Twins Reared Apart"

(2) Repeating words, phrases, structures, or ideas to link a sentence to those that precede it

In paragraph 28, the repetition of the shortened forms of *No Child Left Behind* links sentences to preceding sentences, as does the repeated use of the pronoun *they.*

28   I recently encountered a mother who told me that her school "had some of those **Nickleby** kids" . . . in reference to **No Child Left Behind** kids. **NCLB**. It was said in a derogatory way, like the school was being dragged down because of these children. So who are these "**Nickleby**" kids? The voiceless ones who slipped through the system because **they** were someone else's problem. **They** were in someone else's school. But you know what? **They** weren't. And aren't. **They** are in almost every school. Your child's school. My daughters' schools. And **they** are gifted young people with much to offer our communities, our country and our world.

—MARGARET SPELLINGS, "Spellings Addresses PTA Convention"

Secretary of Education Spellings also uses parallelism (another kind of repetition) in the sentences beginning with *they.* Parallelism is a key tool for writing coherent sentences and paragraphs (Chapter **30**).

(3) Using conjunctions and other transitional words or phrases to indicate how ideas are related

Conjunctions and other transitional words or phrases indicate the logical relationship between ideas. In the following sentences, in which two clauses are linked by different conjunctions, notice the subtle changes in the relationship between the two ideas:

The toddler cried, **and** he listened helplessly.

The toddler cried **while** he introduced her to the babysitter.

The toddler cried **because** he was putting on his coat.

The toddler cried, **so** he gave her a cookie.

The toddler cried; **later** he was glad he had been patient.

The following list of frequently used transitional connections, arranged according to the kinds of relationships they establish, can help you with your reading as well as your writing.

TYPES OF TRANSITIONAL CONNECTIONS

Addition	and, and then, further, furthermore, also, too, again, in addition, besides
Alternative	or, nor, either, neither, on the other hand, conversely, otherwise
Comparison	similarly, likewise, in like manner
Concession	although this may be true, even so, still, nevertheless, at the same time, notwithstanding, nonetheless, in any event, that said
Contrast	but, yet, or, and yet, however, on the contrary, in contrast
Exemplification	for example, for instance, in the case of
Intensification	in fact, indeed, moreover, even more important, to be sure
Place	here, beyond, nearby, opposite to, adjacent to, on the opposite side
Purpose	to this end, for this purpose, with this objective, in order to, so that
Repetition	as I have said, in other words, that is, as has been noted, as previously stated
Result or cause	so, for, therefore, accordingly, consequently, thus, thereby, as a result, then, because, hence
Sequence	next, first, second, third, in the first place, in the second place, finally, last, then, afterward, later
Summary	to sum up, in brief, on the whole, in sum, in short
Time	meanwhile, soon, after a few days, in the meantime, now, in the past, while, during, since

---

When revising an essay, you must consider the effectiveness of the individual paragraphs at the same time as you consider how well those paragraphs work together to achieve the overall purpose, which your thesis statement declares. Some writers like to revise at the paragraph level before addressing larger concerns; other writers cannot work on individual paragraphs until they have grappled with larger issues related to the rhetorical situation (the rhetorical opportunity, overall purpose, audience, and context; **1b–e**) or have finalized their thesis statement (**2c**).

The following checklist can guide you in revising your paragraphs.

✔ **CHECKLIST** *for Revising Paragraphs*

- Does the paragraph have a clear (or clearly implied) topic sentence (**3c(1)**)?

- Do all the ideas in the paragraph relate to the topic sentence (**3c(2)**)? Does each sentence link to previous and later ones? Are the sentences arranged in chronological, spatial, emphatic, or logical order, or are they arranged in some other pattern (**3c(3)**)?

- Are sentences connected to each other with effective transitions (**3d**)?

- What rhetorical method or methods have been used to develop the paragraph (**2g**)?

- What evidence do you have that the paragraph is adequately developed (**2f**)? What idea or detail might be missing (**3a(2)**)?

- How does the paragraph itself link to the preceding and following ones (**3d**)?

Since there is no predetermined order to the writing process, you can do whatever works best for you each time you revise. Be guided by the principles and strategies discussed in this chapter but trust also in your own good sense.

3e   PEER REVIEW

Because writing is a medium of communication, good writers check to see whether they have successfully conveyed their ideas to their readers. Instructors are one set of readers you need to think about. But often they are the last people to see your finished writing. Before you submit your work to an instructor, take advantage of other opportunities for getting responses to it. Consult with readers—at the writing center, in your classes, or in online writing groups—asking them for honest responses to your concerns about your writing.

(1) Establishing specific evaluation standards

Although you will always write within a rhetorical situation (1a), you will often do so in the context of a class assignment that is explicit about rhetorical opportunity, audience, purpose, and format. If you are fortunate, you will be responding to a clearly stated assignment and working with specific evaluation standards (addressing everything from thesis statement and topic sentences to correctness and format) that your instructor has provided in class, on assignment sheets, or on separate handouts. Such standards serve as a starting point when discussing your draft with your writing group, a classmate, or a writing center tutor. For example, if your instructor has told you that your essay will be evaluated primarily in terms of whether you have a clear thesis statement (2c) and adequate support for it (2f and 2g), then those features should be your primary focus. Your secondary concerns may be the overall effectiveness of the introduction (3b(1)), sentence length and variety (Chapter 32), or mechanical correctness (Chapters 41–44).

Although evaluation standards cannot guarantee useful feedback, they can help you describe the type of feedback you want in a writer's memo (3e(2)). They can also help your reviewers focus on specific kinds of advice to give as they respond to your draft.

A reviewer's comments should be based on the evaluation standards, pointing out what the writer has done well and suggesting how to improve particular passages. A reviewer may frame a recommendation in terms of personal engagement with the text: "This is an interesting point! However, it's not clear if this is your thesis." A reviewer can be honest and helpful simultaneously. If a reviewer sees a problem that the writer did not identify, the reviewer should ask the writer if she or he wants to discuss it and should abide by the writer's decision. Ultimately, the success of the essay is the responsibility of the writer, who weighs the reviewer's advice, rejecting comments that might take the essay in a different direction and applying any suggestions that help fulfill the rhetorical purpose (1c).

If you are developing your own criteria for evaluation, the following checklist can help you get started. Based on the elements of the rhetorical situation, this checklist can be easily adjusted so that it meets your specific needs for a particular assignment.

✔ CHECKLIST for Evaluating a Draft of an Essay

- Does the essay fulfill all the requirements of the assignment?
- What rhetorical opportunity does the essay address (1a)?
- What is the specific audience for the essay (1d)? Is that audience appropriate for the assignment?
- What is the tone of the essay (3a(3))? How does the tone align with the overall purpose, the intended audience, and the context for the essay (1c–e)?
- Is the larger subject focused into a topic (2b)? What is the thesis statement (2c)?
- What assertions support the thesis statement? What specific evidence (examples or details) support these assertions?
- What pattern of organization is used to arrange the paragraphs (3c(3))? What makes this pattern effective for the essay? What other pattern(s) might prove to be more effective?
- How is each paragraph developed (2f and 2g)?
- What specifically makes the introduction effective (3b(1))? How does it address the rhetorical opportunity and engage the reader?
- How is the conclusion appropriate for the essay's purpose (3b(2))? How exactly does it draw the essay together?

(2) Informing reviewers about your purpose and your concerns

When submitting a draft for review, you can increase your chances of getting the kind of help you want by introducing your work and indicating what your concerns are. You can provide such an orientation orally to a writing group, tutor, or peer reviewer in just a few minutes. Or, when doing so is not possible, perhaps because you are submitting a draft online, you can attach to your draft a cover letter consisting of a paragraph or two—sometimes called a **writer's memo**. In either case, adopting the following model can help ensure that reviewers will give you useful responses.

SUBMITTING A DRAFT FOR REVIEW

Topic and Purpose

State your topic and the rhetorical opportunity for your writing (**1b**). Identify your thesis statement (**2c**), purpose (**1c**), and intended audience (**1d**). Such information gives reviewers useful direction.

Strengths

Mark the passages of your draft you are confident about. Doing so directs attention away from areas you do not want to discuss and saves time for all concerned.

Concerns

Put question marks by the passages you find troublesome and ask for specific advice wherever possible. For example, if you are worried about your conclusion, say so. Or if you suspect that one of your paragraphs may not fit the overall purpose, direct attention to that paragraph. You are most likely to get the kind of help you want and need when you ask for it specifically.

Mary LeNoir's writer's memo follows.

Topic, Rhetorical Opportunity, Audience, and Purpose: I'm focusing on the way student-athletes actually choose a college. Because I've gone through the decision-making process, I know that many people—adults and students alike—think we student-athletes make our choice on the basis of "how good a deal" we're getting from our chosen school, a deal in terms of scholarship money and playing time. I want to address this opportunity to change their thinking. Yes, many high school student-athletes hope or secretly hope that they will go to college, play well, get noticed, and turn pro—no matter what kind of school they attend. But most of us know that we're playing college sports because we love to play, not because of the money we're offered or even the dream of going pro. I want to inform people of how we student-athletes actually make our college choice, a decision not always based on what the most logical reason (a monetary one) might be.

Concerns: I'm concerned about being able to spell out the three kinds of thinking that go into our decision making. I'm also concerned about how to provide support for those three kinds of thinking. Even though I've interviewed some of my friends at other schools, I'm not sure the interviews work well. I'm also not confident about my current conclusion, if it actually shows the importance of my topic and my thinking.

Mary submitted the draft on pages 69–72 for peer review in a first-year writing course. She worked with two classmates, giving them a set of criteria she had prepared. Because the reviewers were learning how to conduct peer evaluations, their comments are representative of responses you might receive in a similar situation. As members of writing groups gain experience and learn to employ the strategies outlined in this section, their advice usually becomes more helpful.

◉ TECH SAVVY

Some instructors require students to do peer reviewing online, rather than during class time, and usually provide specific peer-review guidelines and procedures for doing so. What follows are some general suggestions for online reviewing.

- If you are responding to a classmate's draft via e-mail, reread your comments before sending them to be sure that your tone is appropriate and that you have avoided the kinds of misunderstandings that can occur with e-mail messages (**5b** and **5c**).
- Always save a copy of your comments in case your e-mail message is lost or inadvertently deleted.
- If you are responding to a classmate's draft using an online course-management program, such as WebCT, ANGEL, or Blackboard, remember that your comments may be read by other classmates, too.
- Follow the advice in **3e(1)**, just as you would if you were commenting on a paper copy of your classmate's draft.

As you read the following assignment and then Mary's draft, remember that a first draft will not be a model of perfect writing—and also that this is the first time peer reviewers Ernie Lujan and Andrew Chama responded to it. Mary sent Ernie and Andrew her essay electronically, and they both used Track Changes to add their comments.

The assignment: Draft a three- to four-page, double-spaced essay in which you analyze the causes or consequences of a choice you have had to make in the last year or two. Whatever choice you analyze, make sure that it concerns a topic you can develop with confidence and without violating your sense of privacy. Also, consider the expectations of your audience and whether the topic you have chosen will allow you to communicate something meaningful to readers. As you draft, establish an audience for your essay, a group that might benefit from or be interested in any recommendation or new knowledge that grows out of your analysis.

1

First Draft

The Search: Student-Athletes' Choice of College

Mary LeNoir

There are over 380,000 NCAA student-athletes, and most of us will go pro in something other than sports. However, an academically weighted decision holds a higher probability for future success than one biased towards athletics. Many high school student athletes strive to play their sport at the collegiate level; they're tempted by the idea of turning an average volleyball team into champs or of reviving the football glory of the school.

It all begins in the hearts of little leaguers and peewee soccer players. Though we begin our athletic careers hitting off a tee or paddling in the pool on a kickboard, many of us grow to hone our athletic abilities and practice our skills to be the best and play against the best. We play sports year round; for our schools, club teams, all-star teams, AAU teams. We attend camps, separate workouts, and practices. Our love of picking grass during peewee soccer games evolves into the love of the competition and triumph over our opponents. Aspirations of great collegiate careers and even dreams of playing professional athletics consume our minds' thoughts, driving the discipline behind our work ethic. College prospects come knocking on our doors, prepared to enable our dreams and paint before us the golden vision of our future athletic careers wearing blue and white or orange and maroon. Tempting is the sound of turning an average volleyball team into champs or reviving the football glory of the school. Yes, we see our futures, we've prepared for our futures, and our futures will last us maybe four to five years if we are so lucky; perhaps seven to

2

ten years for those more fortunate. And those favorites of the heavens, they will make lasting careers. Our young hearts are ignorant of the cruel reality of this "love of the game," for who would ever think it could end?

These dreams become reality for about 16 percent of collegiate athletes; a percent that feeds all professional men's sports (basketball, baseball, football, ice hockey, and soccer) and one professional women's sport being basketball. In addition, if one is able to make the pros, a professional athletic career, on average, lasts around five years. This 16 percent fails to include the many other sports offered at competitive college levels. Most collegiate athletes do not even have the option of professional careers, for the extent of their sport lies in playing at the collegiate level, coaching after college or the Olympics. Furthermore, injuries keep numbers of great athletes from reaching their athletic peak; either cutting their college career short or ruining any professional chances.

High school athletes recruited for highly competitive collegiate athletics approach their decision with a heavy emphasis on both athletics and academics. Though the recruiting process for the athlete's sport may appear to cloud the academic reputation of the school, the athlete is first and foremost enrolling for the academics offered. A thorough examination of the college as a whole may afford the athlete the best of both worlds.

Having spoken to numbers of collegiate student athletes, three major factors played a huge role in their decision and none of them had to do with athletics or academics: tuition, location, and atmosphere of the school. Could they see themselves happy further from home or closer to

3

home? Would they prefer an urban or rural location, the size of a huge state school or the more intimate setting of a small liberal arts college?

Finally, is the school affordable? Then, the next step included the academics and athletics. How important was the athletic and academic reputation for their decision? Future playing time may affect the decision—would the athletes have a chance to play or would they ride the bench for four years? With that said, could the students handle both the academics and athletics of the school? Most of these collegiate athletes admitted to not examining these questions to their full extent. Many relied on the first three factors with some emphasis on academics and the majority on their future athletic careers.

However, three athletes stood out as examples of performing thorough college searches and finally deciding on three schools that fit their academic, athletic, and personal needs: Johns Hopkins University, Penn State University and The University of Richmond. The athlete who chose Johns Hopkins grew up about a half hour from the university. She desired to play lacrosse at an institution that offered stellar academics and a solid lacrosse program and, preferably, one closer to home. Johns Hopkins was of particular interest for her due to the nursing program. She was prepared for the rigorous academics along with the commitment to a division one lacrosse program and, therefore, was not caught off guard by neither demand.

The second athlete, also a lacrosse player, chose Penn State University. She is from Ohio and desired a school a bit further from home. She wanted a big school with a great academic reputation that offered a

4

variety of majors from which to choose. A contrast to the first athlete, she was not set on a particular profession such as nursing, rather, she wanted the flexibility to explore her academic endeavors as an underclassman. Penn State's academic appeal was the school's broad range of academics offered and the academic support extending to career services. The second athlete, too, desired a competitive lacrosse program; however, she also aimed to play and contribute, whereas the first was content with being a member of the team, focusing more on her nursing major. Penn State's lacrosse program had been building and gaining a considerable reputation. This second athlete desired to help take the team to a higher level and help grow Penn State's lacrosse reputation.

The third athlete was a baseball player for the University of Richmond. He desired good academics, however, his main focus was baseball and he wanted a potential professional career in baseball. Tuition did play a major role in that he needed to earn a scholarship if he were to attend a college out of state, which he did. Location and size also became relevant factors after he examined the school's baseball program. A baseball scholarship offer and good academics paved the way for him to visit the school and then decide if he loved it or if the baseball scholarship was enough for him to accept the other aspects of the school. Unlike the first two athletes, he chose primarily based on his sport and his potential chance of a professional baseball career.

5

Dear Mary,

Until I read your draft, I hadn't thought at all about how student-athletes make their college choice. I guess I just thought that they went wherever they got the most money. Or, if they weren't all that good, they attended a school where they'd get some playing time. So I think you have a rhetorical opportunity to address. Lots of your readers won't have a clue.

What I'm unsure about is your organization. I'm torn between thinking you should organize according to student-athlete or by the reason for choosing a college. Mostly, I think that the second organizational pattern would be more effective, because you'd have a basis for arranging the material. You could move from least to most important reason, whatever that is.

So I think that your thesis, purpose, and audience are primary concerns in this draft. And the surface errors, lack of citations, and need for quotations (from the interviews) are secondary concerns. I also think that you need to strengthen the list of criteria or reasons student-athletes choose their college. Maybe you can talk to these people again and see if you can come up with some reasons they all share.

Great first draft! Thanks for letting me read it and respond.

Ernie

6

Dear Mary,

This is an interesting topic—one that I think you have strong feelings about, judging from your very descriptive second paragraph. It seems that you have a lot you want to say about student-athletes and the college search, and I think with more drafting you'll be better able to pinpoint your exact purpose for writing.

I love your idea of doing research by talking to actual students about their enrollment decisions. What a great idea! Because you are interviewing several students, your essay has the potential to contrast the experiences of the students, which might be instructive to some readers. On one hand, the essay might work as a how-to guide for athletes who have a college decision ahead of them. On the other hand, the essay might counter some misinformation held by college students who don't play sports.

As a next step, I'd try to identify the specific audience you want to address and clarify what you want that audience to know. If you compare and/or contrast what you hear from the athletes you interview, you might want points of similarity and difference to serve as your main points. Maybe the three factors you mention in the essay could be these points.

I'd love to read another draft of this essay. Great work so far!

Andrew

Before revising, Mary considered the comments she received from Ernie and Andrew. Since she had asked them to respond to her introduction, conclusion, and organization, she had to weigh all of their comments—relevant and irrelevant—and use the ones that seemed to be most useful as she prepared her next draft.

Exercise 4

Reread Mary's first draft and the peer reviewers' responses. Identify the comments you think are the most useful, and explain why. Which comments seem to be less useful? Explain why. What additional comments would you make if Mary had asked you to review her draft?

After Mary had time to reconsider her first draft and to think about the responses she received from Ernie and Andrew, she made a number of large-scale changes, especially with regard to organization. She also strengthened her thesis statement and cleaned up the surface errors. After these and other revisions, more peer review, and some careful editing and proofreading, Mary was ready to submit her essay to her instructor. Her final draft is on pages 79–88.

3f   EDITING FOR CLARITY

If you are satisfied with the revised structure of your essay and the content of your paragraphs, you can begin editing individual sentences for clarity, effectiveness, and variety (Chapters **27–32**). The following checklist for editing contains cross-references to chapters or sections where you can find more specific information.

✔ CHECKLIST *for Editing*

1 Sentences

- What is the unifying idea of each sentence (**27**)?

- How have you varied the lengths of your sentences? How many words are in your longest and shortest sentences?

- How have you varied the structure of your sentences? How many are simple? How many use subordination or coordination? If you overuse any one sentence structure, revise for variation (**32**).

- Does each verb agree with its subject (**24e**)? Does every pronoun agree with its antecedent (**25c**)?

- Which sentences have or should have parallel structure (**30**)?

- Do any sentences contain misplaced or dangling modifiers (**26d** and **26e**)?

- Do any of your sentences shift in verb tense or tone (**24b**)? Is the shift intentional?

2 Diction

- Have you repeated any words (**31**)? Is your repetition intentional?

- Are your word choices exact, or are some words vague or too general (**34**)?

- Have you used any language that is too informal (**33b**)?

- Is the vocabulary you have chosen appropriate for your audience, purpose, and context (**1c–e** and **33**)?

- Have you defined any technical or unfamiliar words for your audience (**33b(4)**)?

3g   PROOFREADING FOR AN ERROR-FREE ESSAY

Once you have revised and edited your essay, it is your responsibility to format it properly and proofread it. Proofreading means making a special search to ensure that the final product you submit is free from error, or nearly so. An error-free essay allows your reader to read for meaning, without encountering incorrect spelling or punctuation that can interfere with meaning. As you proofread, you may discover problems that call for further revision or editing, but proofreading is usually the last step in the writing process.

Because the eye tends to see what it expects to see, many writers miss errors—especially minor ones, such as a missing comma or apostrophe—even when they think they have proofread carefully. To proofread well, then, you need to read your work more than once and read it aloud. Some people find it useful to read through a paper several times, checking for a different set of items on each pass. Other writers rely on peer editors to provide help with proofreading.

The proofreading checklist that follows refers to chapters and sections in this handbook where you will find detailed information to help you. Also, keep your dictionary (**33d**) at hand to look up any words whose meaning or spelling you are unsure about.

3h   THE FINAL PROCESS-ANALYSIS ESSAY

After her intensive revision, Mary edited and proofread her essay. The version that she ultimately submitted to her instructor follows.

✓ *CHECKLIST* for Proofreading

1 Spelling (41)

- Have you double-checked the words you frequently misspell and any the spell checker may have missed (for example, misspellings that still form words, such as *form* for *from*)?

- If you used a spell checker, did it overlook homophones (such as *there/their, who's/whose,* and *it's/its*) (41c)?

- Have you double-checked the spelling of all foreign words and all proper names?

2 Punctuation (36–40) and Capitalization (42)

- Does each sentence have appropriate closing punctuation, and have you used only one space after each end punctuation mark (40)?

- Is all punctuation within sentences—commas (36), semicolons (37a), apostrophes (38), dashes (40d), and hyphens (41f)—used appropriately and placed correctly?

- Are direct quotations carefully and correctly punctuated (39a)? Where have you placed end punctuation with a quotation (39d)? Are quotations capitalized properly (39a and 42c(1))?

- Are all proper names, people's titles, and titles of published works correctly capitalized (42a and 42b)?

- Are titles of works identified with quotation marks (39b) or italics (43a)?

Mary LeNoir

Professor Glenn

English 15

1 November 2010

How Student-Athletes Really Choose a College

It all begins in the hearts of little leaguers, peewee soccer players, and little swimmers with their kickboards—that yearning to play and win. Student-athletes may start small, but they grow and hone their athletic abilities in order to be the best and play against the best. They play sports year round—for their schools, club teams, all-star teams, Amateur Athletic Union (AAU) teams, and for themselves. They attend camps, workouts, and practices, lots of practices. Aspirations of great collegiate careers and even dreams of playing professional athletics begin to consume their dreams, driving their self-discipline and work ethic. Eventually, college prospects come knocking on their doors, the recruiters wearing blue and white or orange and maroon and talking to these young athletes of dreams that might come true. In those recruiters, student-athletes see their future. The smart ones know that their future as a competitive athlete might last through the college years, if they're lucky. They realize that only a very select few ever reach professional status.

So with the odds of becoming a professional against them, why do student-athletes agree to such a heavy commitment as playing college sports, knowing that the experience will take them only so far? Most people think student-athletes base their choice of college on financial gain and promised playing time. To find out how student-athletes actually made their choice

> The urge to win is a familiar feeling; mentioning it in the first sentence is a good way to hook readers.

> To answer this question, the author interviewed student-athletes and thereby built her thesis statement.

of college, I decided to interview five college student-athletes who played various sports at five different kinds of schools. My goal was to uncover the personal reasons or criteria student-athletes used as they made their choices.

The author explains how she went about answering the question posed in the previous paragraph.

To answer my question, I selected both male and female student-athletes who play either a highly publicized or lesser-known sport. In addition, I chose athletes who attended big state universities, system schools, and smaller liberal arts colleges. Paige Wright represents lacrosse at Johns Hopkins University; Nick Huang, football at Capitol University; Bobby Dorsey, baseball at the University of Richmond; Marye Taranto, lacrosse at the University of Virginia; and Theresa Morales, lacrosse at Penn State University. I asked about their college search process (including why they wanted to play college athletics) and soon discovered that, despite their diverse goals and circumstances, the student-athletes all worked with three criteria when choosing their college: (1) the potential playing time at the school or how this school might help further the athlete's career as either a player or a coach, (2) the material conditions associated with attending the school (mainly financial aid and geographic location), and (3) whatever emotional connection the athlete had (for whatever reasons) with the school. In this essay, I demonstrate how the five student-athletes dealt with these three criteria.

A strong topic sentence begins this paragraph.

College coaches recruit high school athletes because they believe those athletes will contribute to their athletic programs. The coach or recruiter cannot make promises about the student's collegiate athletic career: the coach cannot promise an athlete that he or she will start, play all four years, or play a specific number of games each year.

LeNoir 3

However, the coach can offer the athlete tentative ideas of how the coach believes the athlete will contribute to the team and when the coach anticipates the student-athlete will be able to play in competitive games. These ideas help a student-athlete visualize himself or herself at that school on that team.

Knowing that his chances were good but not guaranteed, Bobby still wanted to pursue a professional baseball career after playing in college; therefore, the rising success of the Richmond baseball program had a major influence on Bobby's choice. "In high school, I was not set on playing professional baseball, but I knew it could potentially be what I wanted. That meant I needed to be seen playing" (personal interview). He went on to explain that professional baseball teams do not recruit players based on the college they attend. He continued:

> Well, yes, obviously if you play at a big-time baseball program your odds are pretty great of getting drafted. But what's more important than winning college championships is building your reputation as a player, and that means you need to play. You're more likely to get talked about [having] played and done well at a less well-known school than if you sat on the bench for four years at some top-ten program. Richmond needed my position [shortstop] and made me feel like I had a good chance of playing, if not my freshman year, most definitely my sophomore year. (Dorsey)

Nick described similar circumstances. In his interview, he said that he wanted an intimate campus and small student body, but the

An effective topic sentence moves the essay forward.

Interview material is used effectively here.

LeNoir 4

opportunity to be noticed by a pro football team was just as important to him. Fortunately for Nick, football is akin to baseball in that, if the player is good enough, professional recruiters will find him, even at a Division III program like Capitol University. For Nick, Capitol offered the small-school atmosphere he desired along with a competitive football program that made a professional career a real possibility. Bobby and Nick both wanted a chance to play professionally, and their two sports happen to be two of the most popular professional sports.

This paragraph opens with a question that the writer goes on to answer.

That said, what were student-athletes thinking when they signed on to play a college sport with no professional opportunity? Theresa admitted her athletic career would be over after four years of college:

> Even though there is no professional lacrosse league, I could always coach or help start a program at a school. But I wanted to do something else—that's one of the reasons Penn State appealed to me. The school offered so many majors and amazing academic support. I felt I needed that freedom to explore and figure out what I wanted to do with my life. (Morales)

Theresa went on to explain that her professional goals in no way diminished her competitive nature or desire to excel on the lacrosse field:

> Sports have been so much a part of my life that I could not imagine not playing in college. And because I'm competitive, there was no way I was going to commit to some school that was not serious about winning, that did not have a real chance, or where I would not have a chance to play. Besides, college athletics is a good way to prepare for any profession: I am competitive.

LeNoir 5

I love to win, and in order to win I train, work hard, practice
discipline, and budget my time—all qualities vital to success in
life. Job recruiters are well aware of an athlete's commitments,
and it looks great on a résumé to have played a varsity sport in
college while having kept up a good GPA. (Morales)

Marye and Paige, who also play lacrosse, also mentioned their
competitiveness and the importance of getting to play. They, too, felt
that being able to add varsity athletics to their résumés was important.
However, Marye and Paige went on to present criteria other than "playing
time" that had a strong influence on their final decision about a college.

The second cluster of criteria that student-athletes use when making
their decision includes the material conditions associated with a college,
things that are the same for students and student-athletes alike. Costs and
the geographical location of the school—these are logistics that do not
disappear just because you are an athlete. Being recruited does not imply
the athlete has only to say yes to the school and all these factors will fall
into place. In Marye's case, her athletic scholarship was the key to attending
her dream school, the University of Virginia (UVA). Marye loved UVA
and its team and had been accepted academically, but she had received no
academic scholarship. She would have had to pay the full tuition, which she
and her parents simply could not afford. Fortunately, Marye was a highly
recruited lacrosse player, one UVA became very interested in after she had
been admitted on academic grounds. The athletic scholarship offered to
Marye made UVA affordable for her, giving her the opportunity to receive
an education from one of the best academic institutions in the country and

Use of
supporting
details and
explanation
strengthens
this paragraph.

LeNoir 6

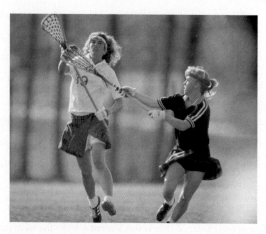

Fig. 1. Playing lacrosse for a top college team is a dream of many high school players. Photograph © Paul A. Souders/Corbis.

to live her dream of playing college lacrosse, neither of which would have been possible without her athletic scholarship. (See Fig. 1.)

This is a strong paragraph, with good transitions.

Paige's situation presented an insurmountable obstacle: geographic location. Because her parents could not afford traveling expenses (neither for themselves nor for her), Paige simply had to attend a school close to home. Thus, Paige could not consider, let alone commit to, a school across the country. Johns Hopkins was particularly appealing because it was about a forty-minute car ride from her home. Bobby spoke about circumstances that combined Marye's and Paige's. Bobby did not want to go to school in state. He wanted to move away from home and experience another region of the country. However, he could not afford out-of-state tuition in addition to the traveling expenses. Bobby's parents told him that he would either have to attend a school in the

LeNoir 7

state of Delaware or earn some kind of scholarship in order to go out of state. His baseball scholarship not only afforded him an opportunity to play ball and be drafted, but also fulfilled his desire to attend college away from home.

All five athletes emphasized the importance of the "right" atmosphere in their college search, which actually meant an atmosphere that they connected with on an emotional level. When I asked each athlete to explain what she or he meant by "atmosphere," why it ranked higher than the other factors, and what exactly was the "right atmosphere" for each of them, they responded fully to all three aspects of the question.

This transitional paragraph leads into the following ones.

For all of them, the school's atmosphere included athletic, academic, and social factors, the physical look and geographic location of the school, and the way all these features came together to enhance the student-athlete's emotional connection with the school.

Paige emphasized the size and social reputation of the school, the weather, and the look and layout of the campus. She claimed that visiting the school was crucial to her decision because the atmosphere is "felt," not described or quantified in statistics:

> A good couple days was what I needed to really test the feel [of the school]. What I had heard about the athletics and academics was the thing that kind of attracted me to look at the school and prompted me to visit in the first place. But, how I felt walking on campus, observing the students . . . this would be my home for the next four years! I wanted to fall in love. (Wright)

Nick and Theresa offered similar comments about the size and social aspects of their schools. Theresa knew she wanted a college town with a large student body. She wanted social options and a general camaraderie of school spirit among the faculty and students. In contrast, Nick desired a more intimate setting with a less intense social scene.

Having an idea of what "atmosphere" meant, I then asked them to touch on the academic and athletic aspects, explaining how those contributed to the emotional connection. Bobby wanted a smaller school with a solid academic reputation and the chance to play baseball. For him, it was important to play baseball at a school with a competitive reputation in the sport. Academically, Bobby had no specific career goal in mind. However, he did not totally disregard the academics; a university with a good academic reputation but a manageable coursework load was what he wanted. Paige, however, did have a specific career as a nurse in mind. This factor attracted her to Johns Hopkins, which is known for its medical program. Unlike Bobby, Paige emphasized the academic aspect of her college experience and desired a top-notch nursing program; thus, she knew she would be embarking on a rigorous academic schedule and was fully prepared for that commitment.

Marye offered me a slightly different definition of "atmosphere." Still including what the others mentioned, Marye simply named the atmosphere she already had in mind: her dream school, the University of Virginia. She had grown up loving UVA; she had a long history of an emotional connection. Playing lacrosse as a young girl, Marye imagined wearing the UVA uniform, which she thought "was the coolest-looking uniform ever," and winning national championships in the blue and orange. She had visited the school numerous times in high school to see games and visit her sister. For Marye, "atmosphere" meant attending

LeNoir 9

her dream school and playing lacrosse there. The reputation of UVA lacrosse ranks among the highest in the country; UVA teams are always in the top ten of polls and compete for ACC (Atlantic Coast Conference) championships. As for academics, Marye said,

> Yes, my love of the school was primarily based on this childhood dream of playing lacrosse there. UVA happens to have a stellar academic reputation too, which is a bonus for me. Not to say I would have thrown away my academics and gone to any old school if it had great lacrosse. It's just, to be honest, I saw my future through this kind of tunnel-vision dream . . . I didn't think about what I wanted to do after college. Now, having graduated, I feel a bit ashamed about my ignorance of UVA's academics. [We are] among the best in the country! I don't know how many kids dreamt of a UVA education, which I now can't describe how much I appreciate. But back in high school, I wanted to go to UVA to play lacrosse. (Taranto)

All these student-athletes described complex reasons for choosing a college, just as mine were. My love for lacrosse propelled my decision to take my sport into college, where I would pursue my professional goals, which would not include lacrosse. All my decisions were based on my wanting to achieve my goals of playing my sport in college and pursuing my career after college. And just like all of these other student-athletes, I thought about other factors than the sport I would play. In some ways, whether we hope to play sports after college or not, we all made an emotional connection with the college of our choice.

The essay ends with a reasonable and thoughtful conclusion

LeNoir 10

Works Cited

Dorsey, Robert. Personal interview. 20 Oct. 2010.

Huang, Nick. Personal interview. 14 Oct. 2010.

Morales, Theresa. Personal interview. 22 Oct. 2010.

Taranto, Marye. Personal interview. 18 Oct. 2010.

Wright, Paige. Personal interview. 26 Oct. 2010.

Exercise 5

Compare the two versions of "How Student-Athletes Really Choose a College" that appear in this chapter and write a two-paragraph summary describing how Mary revised and edited her work. If she had shown her final draft to you, asking for your advice before submitting it for a grade, what would you have advised? Write a one-paragraph response to her draft.

4 | MANAGING ACADEMIC WRITING

As you realize by now, the writing you do in college differs from the writing you did in high school or any you have done on the job in terms of schedule, genre, intellectual challenge, and evaluation. In college, you have to produce much of your writing within tight time frames. Current events sometimes prompt unscheduled writing assignments that must take the form of specific genres (reports, proposals, or analyses). Furthermore, your writing is often evaluated cumulatively, rather than one assignment at a time. In addition, rather than asking you to demonstrate what you know or comprehend, many of your college writing assignments require you to synthesize information, make decisions, support views, and solve problems.

Since you entered high school, the expectations for you as a writer have been expanding in exciting (and challenging) ways. By now, you are not only writing more papers more quickly than ever before, but also learning to write in various genres, across the curriculum. By the end of your first year of college, you will focus on rhetorical opportunity, purpose, and audience, regardless of your format or genre. And you will likely be able to write in different genres (report, proposal, research essay, evaluation, argument, literary analysis, and so on) in ways that meet the expectations of readers across academic fields. These expectations concern such elements as formatting, documentation, and specialized vocabulary. As your writing becomes more complex, your critical thinking will become more sophisticated.

Thus, college writing brings with it new challenges to your creativity, speed, and adaptability. Planning, drafting, revising, getting feedback on, and editing a piece of writing over a stretch of days or weeks may often be a luxury, one available only if you prepare a portfolio of your best writing. This chapter will help you

- manage deadlines (**4a**),
- abbreviate the writing process (**4b**),
- plan for essay examinations (**4c**), and
- prepare a portfolio of your writing (**4d**).

4a | MANAGING DEADLINES

While you are expanding your writing abilities, you will need to learn how to manage ever-increasing writing assignments. You will almost always be working under deadlines—whether for academic essays, job application packages, grant proposals, or other time-sensitive documents. Preparing ahead of time always helps, and there are a number of ways you can do that. For instance, in-class essay exams are often scheduled around midterm, and you can start preparing for such an exam on the first day of class. As you read your assignments, listen to lectures, and participate in class discussions, make an effort to determine what your instructor considers most important about the material you are learning. If you are paying careful attention but cannot tell exactly what the instructor deems most important, ask. And whenever an instructor gives you instructions on a writing assignment, ask questions until you know exactly what is expected of you.

The best way to approach a writing assignment with a longer deadline, such as a research paper, is to start early. If you are choosing your own topic, begin as soon as you can to record your ideas on paper or an electronic notepad and then narrow these down (**2b**). The sooner you identify a subject, the sooner you can discuss it with your instructor. You can make a deadline work for you by establishing your own timeline, working from the due date backward. The timeline should include intermediate deadlines for writing an introduction with a thesis statement, composing a first draft, meeting with a classmate for review, revising your draft, and editing. Do your best to stick to your timeline.

FOR BETTER OR FOR WORSE © 2000 Lynn Johnston Productions. Dist. by Universal Uclick. Reprinted with permission. All rights reserved.

4b | ABBREVIATING THE WRITING PROCESS

Students and employees, who are often expected to write well with little notice, can successfully abbreviate the writing process by following the process experienced writers use. When faced with a short deadline, you can try to narrow down the topic as quickly as possible, and connect the assignment to your knowledge. A topic with a sharp focus can be handled more thoughtfully and thoroughly in a short time than a broad topic. Once you have a focused topic, quickly organize your ideas, using a rough outline or the clustering technique.

The following tips will help you abbreviate the writing process.

TIPS FOR ABBREVIATING THE WRITING PROCESS

- Generate ideas about the assignment or topic with a friend or colleague who is facing or has faced the same kind of deadline. That person can help you clarify your line of reasoning and develop counterarguments. Take notes.

- Draft an introductory paragraph that frames your position or approach and includes a clear thesis statement. E-mail your paragraph to your instructor, a classmate, or a colleague to get assurance that you are on the right track.

- If your thesis statement and basic approach are on track, write down your main points. Then, flesh out those points with examples and supporting text until you have a first draft.

- Read your draft aloud, slowly. Make sure that your topic sentences are clear. Reading aloud will help you locate passages that need transitional words or phrases to help your reader along.

- Write a conclusion that reiterates your main points and suggests their implications.

- Read over your text to make sure that it fulfills the assignment. Reread your introduction and conclusion to see whether they frame your piece. Examine your topic sentences and supporting details to make sure that they help you fulfill your purpose and are appropriate for your audience.

- Proofread one last time. Submit your work on time.

⬛ *TECH SAVVY*

You can use your computer to help you manage writing tasks efficiently.

- If you do not have much time for revising and editing, you can use the grammar checker and spell checker of your word-processing program to help you proofread, even while you are drafting.
- Many on-campus writing centers can receive drafts of student writing via e-mail or through a website; tutors at these centers can usually schedule appointments electronically. Writing tutors will often respond to a draft or an appointment request within twenty-four hours. If the writing center on your campus offers these services, you can use the center as a source of helpful advice on short notice when you have a tight deadline.

4C | TAKING ESSAY EXAMINATIONS

If your instructor has posed a clear question, one that includes an operative term to initiate your thinking (see the list of terms on pages 93–94), and has provided explicit instructions, you are (almost) home free if you have studied well and planned for the essay exam all semester. Write out your answer, framing it with a thesis statement and developing your main points in line with the meaning of the operative term. As you develop those points, weave in supporting arguments, details, and examples. If a question does not clearly convey what is expected of you, ask your instructor for clarification. The steps described in the following sections will help you improve your ability to take essay examinations and write effectively while under pressure.

(1) Allocating time

If the exam has more than one question, determine how much time to allot to each one. If you are faced with two questions that are worth the same number of points, give half the time to one and half to the other. When certain questions are weighted more heavily than others, however, you need to divide your time accordingly. However you allocate your time, allow ten minutes for final revising and proofreading.

Stick to the time allotment for each question. If you do not finish, leave room to complete your answer later and move on to the next question. Partial answers to *all* questions usually gain you more points than complete answers to only *some* questions. Besides, you can use the ten minutes you saved to add to any incomplete answers, even if you have to draw arrows to the margins or to the back of the page or supply rough notes (**4c(3)**). Your instructor will probably appreciate the extra effort.

(2) Reading instructions and questions carefully

Students who take time to read instructions and questions carefully do better than those who do not. So invest a few minutes in studying each question, identifying its operative terms, putting the question in your own words, and then jotting down a few notes in the margin next to it. If you have been given a choice of questions to answer, choose those that best suit your knowledge yet do not overlap.

Most exam questions contain specific instructions about how, as well as what, to answer. Be alert for operative terms such as those in the list below, which identify the writing task and provide specific cues for organizing your response. When you are given more general directions, look for such words as *similar* or *different, identify*, and *why*. You will also need to determine whether you are being asked to call up course-related knowledge from memory or to respond more creatively with your own interpretations, hypotheses, or solutions. Words such as *think, defend*, and *argue* signal that you are to frame a thesis and support it.

Most essay exam questions begin with or contain one of the operative terms in the following list and end with a reference to the information you are to work with. Understanding these terms and framing your answers in response to them will help you focus on what is being asked.

TERMS USED IN ESSAY EXAM QUESTIONS

Compare	Examine the points of similarity (compare) or difference (contrast) between two ideas or things (**2g(5)**) drawing upon your clear understanding of information.
Define	State the class to which the item to be defined belongs, and clarify what distinguishes it from the others of that class (**2g(6)**), tapping into your remembered knowledge.

(continued on page 94)

(continued from page 93)

Describe	Use details in a clearly defined order to give the reader a clear mental picture of what you are being asked to describe (**2g(2)**), again calling on information that you remember and understand.
Discuss	Examine, analyze, evaluate, apply information, or state pros and cons. This term gives you wide latitude in addressing the topic and thus can be more difficult to work with than some of the others in this list, since you must decide on a focus. *Discuss* can be interpreted in various ways and is, unfortunately, the term that appears most frequently on exam questions.
Evaluate	Appraise the advantages and disadvantages of the idea or thing specified. This term draws on your comprehension as well as on your ability to analyze—to take something apart, to examine it, and perhaps categorize it. Often an evaluation question requires you to recommend a course of action.
Explain	Clarify and interpret (**2g(3)**), reconcile differences, or state causes (**2g(4)**). When you *explain*, you draw upon your remembered knowledge as well as your ability to analyze and apply information.
Illustrate	Offer concrete examples, or, if possible, create figures, charts, or tables that provide information about the topic, summoning up the concrete knowledge that you can apply as support for your assertions.
Summarize	State the main points in a condensed form, omitting details and curtailing examples. Fully comprehended knowledge must be boiled down into easy-to-understand terms.
Trace	Narrate a sequence of events that show progress toward a goal or comprise a process (**2g(1)** and **2g(3)**). Both creativity and analysis are in play in a narration of this sort.

(3) Organizing your answer

Even under time constraints, you should be able to draft a rough outline or jot down a few phrases for an informal list (**2d**) within the time allotted for each question. Focus your thesis immediately. Then list the most important points you plan to cover. You might decide to rearrange ideas later, but the first step is to get some down on paper. Before you begin to compose your answer, quickly review your list, deleting any irrelevant or unimportant points and adding any better ones that come to mind. Number the points in a logical sequence determined by chronology (reporting events in the order in which they occurred), by causation (showing how one event led to another), or by order of importance (given the possibility that you might run out of time, move from the most important to the least important point). As an example, consider the thesis statement and list of supporting points that biology major Trish Parsons quickly composed and edited during the first few minutes of an essay exam. Trish was responding to the following question: "Discuss whether the term 'junk DNA' is an appropriate name for the nucleic DNA that does not code for proteins."

THESIS: The term "junk" applied to DNA with no apparent purpose is a misnomer; there are many possible purposes, both past and present, for the allegedly "junk" DNA.

1a.

1b. Though junk DNA sequences do not code for specific proteins, they may play an important role in DNA regulation. ⟶ go to point #5

2. Microbiology technology has had many amazing advances since the discovery of DNA. ~~Indeed,~~ DNA itself was not immediately recognized as the "plan for life." Further technological advances that are sure to come may find a definite purpose for "junk" DNA.

3. Junk DNA may have coded for proteins in our evolutionary past and a mechanism for disposing of it ~~never has~~ yet to evolve ∧ evolved.

4. During DNA replication, the possibilities for mistakes are endless. The junk (filler) DNA decreases the chances of the more important, protein-coding DNA being mutated during this process.

5. Junk DNA may yet play an important role in the new field of eugenics, where it has been found that certain traits are heritable, but not directly coded for (possible relation to DNA regulation role in point #1)

1a Many terms have been applied in genetics that end up creating confusion because scientists came to conclusions too quickly — e.g., dominant and recessive alleles are too simplistic. b/c genetics is a relatively new field we have only recently begun to understand. (BEGIN WITH THIS ONE)

© 2013 Cengage Learning

Sometimes, the language of the question will tell you how you should organize your answer. Consider this example:

Discuss how the two-party political system of the United States influenced the outcome of the last presidential election.

At first glance, this exam question might seem to state the topic without indicating how to organize a discussion of it. *To influence*, however, is to be responsible for certain consequences. In this case, the two-party political system is being viewed as a cause, and you are being asked to identify its effects (**2g(4)**). Once you have recognized the meaning of *influence*, you might decide to discuss the effects you identify in different paragraphs.

Here is another example:

> Consider Picasso's treatment of the human body early and late in his career. How did his concept of bodily form persist throughout his career? How did it change?

The reference to two different points in the artist's career, along with the words *persist* and *change*, indicates that your task is to compare and contrast. You could organize your response to this question by discussing Picasso's concept of the body's form when his paintings were realistic and when they were cubist—preferably covering the same points in the same order in each part of the response. Or you could begin by establishing similarities and then move on to discuss differences. There is almost always more than one way to organize a thoughtful response. Devoting at least a few minutes to organizing your answer can help you better demonstrate what you know.

(4) Stating the main points clearly

If you state your main points clearly, your instructor will see how well you have understood the course material. Make your main points stand out from the rest of the answer to an exam question by making them the first sentence of each paragraph; by using transitional words such as *first, second,* and *third*; or by creating headings to separate your points. Once you have outlined your essay exam answer, you will know which points you want to emphasize, even if they change slightly as you write. Use your conclusion to summarize your main points. Just in case you develop points that differ from those you had in mind when you started, leave space for an introduction at the beginning of the answer and then write it after you have written the rest.

(5) Sticking to the question

Always answer each essay exam question as precisely and directly as you can, perhaps using some of the instructor's language in your thesis statement. If your thesis statement implies an organizational plan, follow that plan as closely as possible. If you move away from your original thesis because better ideas occur to you as you write, simply go back and revise your thesis statement (2c). If you find yourself drifting into irrelevance, stop and draw a line through that material.

If you face a vague or truly confusing question and your instructor does not clarify it, go ahead and construct a clear(er) question and then answer it. Rewriting the instructor's question can seem like a risky thing to do, but figuring out a reasonable question that is related to what the instructor has written is actually a responsible move, if you can answer the question you have posed.

(6) Revising and proofreading each answer

Save a few minutes to reread each answer, making whatever deletions and corrections you think are necessary. If time allows, ask yourself if there is anything you have left out that you can still manage to include (even if you have to write in the margins or on the back of the page). Unless you are certain that your instructor values neatness more than knowledge, do not hesitate to make additions and corrections. Simply draw a caret (∧), marking the exact place in the text where you want an addition or correction to be placed. Making corrections will allow you to focus on improving what you have already written, whereas recopying your answer just to make it look neat is an inefficient use of time (and you may have recopied only half your essay when the time is up). Finally, check spelling, punctuation, and sentence structure.

4d   PREPARING A WRITING PORTFOLIO

College writing brings with it new demands: unfamiliar genres and purposes, time-management issues, and more writing overall. Though challenging, these demands are often balanced by opportunities for you to submit your best writing for final evaluation. You probably already know that artists, architects, designers, photographers, musicians, and even teachers often assemble a representative selection of their work for the consideration of gallery owners, schools, potential employers, or potential clients. Just as those professionals revise and reflect on the work they submit, so will you, as you go through the process of preparing a writing portfolio for your instructor's evaluation.

The purpose of a writing portfolio is to display your accomplishments—their range, depth, and quality—for another person, usually your instructor but sometimes a potential employer. Sometimes, you will be given free rein to decide what to include, but most often, your instructor will specify how many pieces and kinds of writing should make up the portfolio. For instance, if your semester-long writing course includes six writing assignments, you might be asked to submit your four best pieces, each representing a different genre, purpose, or stage of revision. Or your instructor might indicate that you can include five pieces of writing, as long as one of them is based on library research and contains correctly formatted citations and documentation of sources. In addition to the finished pieces of writing, you might also be expected to include organizing tools (such as notes or outlines), a rationale for your choices, and a letter of reflection on your progress. Some writing portfolios also include examples of group work, peer reviews, or disks or portable hard drives that showcase work delivered electronically. Whatever you ultimately decide to include in your portfolio, it should be writing that you feel good about. Keep in mind that your grade will be based on a summative evaluation of the portfolio, not on the individual examples.

As you select, revise, and assemble pieces of writing for your portfolio, then, you are evaluating your writing, just as your instructor will do as he or she deliberates on the writing portfolio as a whole. Given the evaluative nature of portfolios, you will want to present the most persuasive and informative selection of your writing that you can. To that end, consider including the following elements in your portfolio:

- **Cover sheet.** Includes your name, your instructor's name, the course title and number, and the date.
- **Table of contents.** Directs the reader to the types, lengths, and titles of the various pieces; compels you to label and consciously sequence your writing.
- **Page numbers.** Make locating pieces easier.
- **Reflective essay.** Usually the opening essay, describing the contents of the portfolio, providing a rationale for the selections, and reflecting on your strengths and weaknesses as a college writer, summarizing where you are and where you want to be.

After assembling a portfolio, many college writers request a peer review, taking full advantage of their writing group's expertise and help to evaluate the portfolio's effectiveness. Peer evaluation can alert you to strengths and weaknesses in everything pertaining to your portfolio, from arguments in your reflective essay and surface errors to issues of sequencing and selection.

5 ‖ ONLINE WRITING

If you regularly use word-processing software, you already know how it facilitates your writing. The software helps you capture and arrange ideas, as well as plan, compose, revise, edit, proofread, and format professional-looking documents. In addition to word-processing capabilities, computers also offer you the opportunity to communicate with a wider, often global, audience when you compose for websites and other online forums, such as blogs, listservs, and social networking sites.

Online writing is often **interactive** (that is, a writer is linked to other writers, and a document is linked to other documents), dramatically expanding a work's audience and context. Because composing in this medium differs somewhat from writing essays or research papers delivered in hard copy, online writing calls for different skills—many of which you already have. This chapter will help you

- assess the rhetorical situation for online writing (**5a**),
- participate in online discussions (**5b**),
- understand conventions for online communication (**5c**),
- compose effective documents in an online environment (**5d**), and
- manage the visual elements of a website (**5e**).

5a ‖ ASSESSING THE ONLINE RHETORICAL SITUATION

Whenever you compose an e-mail message, create a web page, engage in an online discussion, or post a note on Facebook or an update on a blog, you are using rhetoric, or purposeful language, to influence the outcome of an interaction (**1a**). Some online communication is so quick and casual you may forget that you are responding to a rhetorical situation, one in which your message can carry an impact just as powerful (negative or positive) as any created by a static, print document. For that reason, online communication, like print and oral communication, merits attention to audience, purpose, context, and tone.

The key difference between online communication and other kinds of communication is the former's instant access to many different audiences. You may have already learned the hard way how easily your so-called private e-mail can be forwarded to, accidentally copied to, or printed out for an unintended audience. Thus, online communication offers enormous challenges in terms of audience, which are evident whether you are composing within an online learning platform (or course management program) like Blackboard, ANGEL, or WebCT; contributing to a campus club's listserv or website; or updating your status on Facebook or Twitter. For example, if your instructor asks you to contribute regularly to a class-related blog, the instructor and your classmates comprise your primary audience. But as soon as you post an entry on the blog, your work is available to a variety of secondary audiences (**1d(3)**) via the Internet. Therefore, as you compose online, you will want to consider the responses of all possible readers.

Online audiences are just as varied as those for print and oral communication; they can be primary or secondary, as well as specialized, diverse, or multiple (**1d**). When writing an e-mail to an individual recipient, for instance, you are addressing a small primary audience and will adjust your tone depending on that recipient's identity. When you are posting a message on an online course management system, in contrast, you are addressing a broader, more specialized primary audience. In this case, your tone will be appropriate for contributions to a class discussion, and your message will fit into the context established by previous posts.

If you decide to create a web page about a current issue or controversy, such as the airport screening protocols of the Transportation Security Administration (TSA) or the debate over genetically modified food, you will be composing for a diverse audience, whose members have varying levels of knowledge, understanding of specialized terms, and interest in your subject matter. Therefore, factual accuracy and appropriate tone should be major concerns.

Purpose is another important feature of any online rhetorical opportunity, whether you are responding to an e-mail or creating a website. You will always want to identify your purpose, connecting it with your audience, just as you do in print. Whether you wish to express your point of view, create a mood, or amuse or motivate your audience, you need to make your purpose clear. In an e-mail message, you can often state a purpose in the subject line. In a course-related blog, you can

Figure 5.1. This home page of a website for a technical writing course states the purpose of the site.

Michael Faris

announce the subject, so that your audience has a sense of your purpose and of how your comments connect to it. You might state the purpose of a web page as a mission statement. For instance, the website for English 202C, Technical Writing (Figure 5.1), a course designed for students in the sciences, states that one of the site's primary purposes is to "serve as a respository for the syllabus, assignment sheets, and resources for the course." However readers encounter your online composition (by receiving an e-mail message, by finding your web page through a search engine, or by participating in a class's online course management system), they want to be able to identify your purpose without effort. Therefore, you need to take extra care to clarify your purpose and make it readily apparent to any audience.

In addition to attention to purpose and audience, online composing requires a sensitivity to rhetorical context that sometimes exceeds that demanded by conventional academic writing projects (1e). In an online context, the boundary between writer and audience can often become blurred, as writer and audience are both participants in the rhetorical situation, responding to one another nearly simultaneously. In addition, the accessibility of online discussion communities (5b) encourages many people to add to or comment on what has already been written and posted. This flow of new material contributes to an always evolving rhetorical context, requiring you to be familiar with the preceding discussion and to understand the conventions of the forum in order to communicate effectively.

Timeliness is another important feature of an online rhetorical situation. Internet users expect online compositions to be up-to-date, given the ease of altering an electronic document (as opposed to a print publication). Just think of the constant updates you receive via Twitter and Facebook. Web pages, too, must be constantly updated in order to be useful. As you know, it is frustrating to access a web page only to discover that it is months or even years out of date. For example, a web page about TSA screening procedures that came online in November 2010 should differ markedly from one produced before that date. In order for such a document to be current, it would have to include continuous updates on various new passenger-screening procedures, imaging technologies for screening, and the TSA's 3-1-1 policy for liquids, gels, and aerosols. Whether you are reading or composing online material, you want the information to be current, detailed, and correct.

5b PARTICIPATING IN ONLINE DISCUSSION COMMUNITIES

Participating in an online discussion community is a good way to learn more about a topic that interests you or to network with friends, classmates, and online acquaintances while developing your writing skills. However, just as you evaluate information in print sources (Chapter 9), you need to evaluate the information and advice you receive from this kind of online source.

The two main types of online discussion groups are asynchronous forums and synchronous forums. **Asynchronous forums**, such as blogs, listservs, and various discussion forums, allow easy access, regardless of time and place, because participants do not need to be online at the same time. The delay between the posting and viewing of messages can lead to thoughtful discussions because it emphasizes the importance of *responding* to the existing rhetorical situation. On the other hand, **synchronous forums**, provided by electronic meeting software and instant-messaging (IM) programs (such as iChat, Skype, and Gchat), allow users to view text (and any multimedia elements) in real time—that is, as it is being posted—and to respond immediately. Such discussions resemble face-to-face interactions. Both asynchronous and synchronous forums are used by a variety of groups—social groups, students, scholarly or special-interest groups, and business groups—as a convenient way to communicate across geographic distances. Whenever you are involved in an online forum, you need to pay attention to your rhetorical situation, taking care to post and respond respectfully (see Figure 5.2).

Whenever—and however—you participate in an online forum, take care to present yourself as a trustworthy, credible writer and person. To do so, start by reading what has already been said about the topic

Heather Brook Adams | January 18, 2011 8:12 PM | Reply

Your points are well taken. I am most interested in your feeling like there is a level of political engagement you "should" embrace. Where does that sense of responsibility and obligation come from? Do you really feel that you "should" follow politics and current events? Or do you think that these are the sorts of things that we are supposed to feel? After all, you articulate some level of hopelessness in light of an "underlying power struggle."

Do public speakers hold themselves to a higher standard of this obligation? If so, where and when does that obligation break down?

These are just questions for thinking. Of course, anyone is welcome to respond!

JOSEPHINE SEUNGAH LEE | January 19, 2011 9:41 AM | Reply

Well, being a college student who is thinking about making some kind of difference in this world or in someone's life, I know that there really is not much I can do to help anyone as I would like to if I don't know what their problems are. I am a sociology major, and we learn that people are influenced not only by one another directly but also by larger groups or powers indirectly. Even if I want to help people on a more personal level, often times, the source of their problems stem from what is happening around them, and this includes political issues. Part of me wants to just keep my head in the sand, but I feel as though I am missing out on something big if I continue to do that.

Perhaps I do see politics as an endless power struggle, but as I said, I do not really know much about it. Debate is just so complex to me. It is an exchange that does not work if someone does not listen. Without listening, it is just an exchanging of words. I am more concerned about action to back up words. Without a following action, I don't know what the purpose of debate was.

I think everyone is equal in their obligation to speak. Some people actually speak in public, others speak out visually or in other ways. Some people can not speak, but they are there crying out silently. It all depends on who listens and responds with actions.

Figure 5.2. A thread from a course blog, *Rhetoric and Civic Life*, featuring messages between an instructor (Adams) and her student (Lee).

before adding your comments to an existing thread or starting a new one. Keep in mind both the specific information and the overall tone of the messages posted by others, and monitor your own messages for tone and clarity. For instance, in the exchange in Figure 5.2, the instructor draws inferences from the student's previous post and poses several pointed questions to spark further reflection by the student.

Because tone is difficult to convey in online postings, take care when responding to others, making sure to stay on topic or to announce when you are changing the topic. Avoid jokes, criticism, or any other kinds of comments that might be misinterpreted as rude or mean-spirited. (Your purpose is to enrich the conversation, not to criticize the posts of others.) If you have a question about a previous post, raise it respectfully. If you detect a factual error, diplomatically present what you believe to be the correct information. And if someone criticizes you online (an attack referred to as **flaming**), try to remember how difficult tone is to convey and give that person the benefit of the doubt. Except in the most informal of e-mail correspondence, stay alert to all the conventions of correct English. If you use all lowercase letters, misspell words, or make usage errors, readers of your online writing may come away with a negative impression of you, especially if the writing is business, academic, or professional correspondence. Finally, given that friends, teachers, and professional colleagues can easily access your online writing, take care to establish a professional relationship with the multiple audiences in your online groups and always monitor your privacy settings.

Exercise 1

Locate a blog devoted to a subject you are interested in or conduct a Twitter search for terms related to that subject. Read through the recent and archived posts, clarifying the rhetorical situation for yourself before introducing yourself to others in the group. Then, ask a question or post a comment related to the subject under discussion. After reading responses to your posting, write a paragraph describing the experience.

5C   NETIQUETTE AND ONLINE WRITING

Netiquette (from the phrase *Internet etiquette*) is a set of social practices developed by Internet users in order to regulate online interactions so that they are always conducted respectfully.

TIPS FOR USING NETIQUETTE IN ONLINE INTERACTIONS

Audience

- Keep in mind the potential audience(s) for your message: those for whom it is intended and others who may read it. If privacy is important, do not use online communication.

- Make the subject line of your message as descriptive as possible so that your reader(s) will immediately recognize the topic.

- Keep your message focused and limit it to one screen, if possible. If you want to attach a text or graphic file, keep its size under 1 MB. Readers' time or bandwidth may be limited, or their mobile device may be subject to an expensive usage plan.

- Before uploading a large file, consider reducing the resolution (and file size) of an image, which rarely affects quality.

- Avoid using fancy fonts and multiple colors unless you are certain that they will appear on your audience's screen.

- Give people adequate time to respond, remembering that they may be away from their computers or may be contemplating what to say.

- Consider the content of your message, making sure that it pertains to the interests and needs of your audience.

- Respect copyright. Never post something written by someone else or pass it off as your own.

Style and Presentation

- Maintain a respectful tone, whether your message is formal or informal.

- Be sure of your facts, especially when you are offering a clarification or a correction.

- Present ideas clearly and logically, using bullets or numbers if doing so will help.

(continued on page 106)

(continued from page 105)

- Pay attention to spelling and grammar. If your message is a formal one, you will certainly want to proofread it (perhaps even in hard copy) and make corrections before sending it out.

- Use emoticons (such as ☺) and abbreviations (such as IMHO for "in my humble opinion" or LOL for "laughing out loud") only when you are sure your audience will understand them and find them appropriate.

- Use all capital letters only when you want to be perceived as SHOUTING.

- Use boldface only if you wish the reader to be able to quickly locate a key item in your message, such as the due date for a report or the name of someone to contact.

- Abusive, critical, or profane language is never appropriate.

Context

- Observe what others say and how they say it before you engage in an online discussion; note what kind of information participants find appropriate to exchange.

- If someone is abusive, ignore that person or change the subject. Do not respond to flaming.

- Tone is difficult to convey online, and thus gentle sarcasm and irony may inadvertently come across as personal attacks.

- Do not use your school's or employer's network for personal business.

Credibility

- Use either your real name or an appropriate online pseudonym to identify yourself to readers. Avoid suggestive or inflammatory pseudonyms.

- Be respectful of others even when you disagree, and be welcoming to new members of an online community.

5d   COMPOSING IN AN ONLINE ENVIRONMENT

The Internet offers you the chance to communicate with many different audiences for a variety of purposes. More than an electronic library for information and research, it is also a kind of global marketplace, allowing people all over the world to exchange ideas as well as goods.

As you know, websites are sets of electronic pages, anchored to a home page. Instead of the linear arrangement of print texts (in which

Figure 5.3. The Memphis Zoo's website illustrates successful integration of text and graphics and features easy-to-use hyperlinks for navigation.

arguments, passages, and paragraphs unfold sequentially, from start to finish), websites rely on **hypertext** (electronic text that includes **hyperlinks**, or **links**, to other online text, graphics, and animations) to emphasize arrangement and showcase content. That is, websites are created and delivered with text, graphics, and animations integrated into their content. You are probably accustomed to navigating websites by clicking on hyperlinks. The Memphis Zoo's home page (Figure 5.3) illustrates both the integration of text and graphics on a web page and the use of hyperlinks for navigation within a website.

Another important online tool is the navigation bar that stretches across the top of a web page. The home page of the White House's website (Figure 5.4) features a well-organized navigation bar that includes tabs for current issues on its left side and tabs for more stable information about the administration, the White House and its staff, and the U.S. government on the right side. Each of these tabs redirects users to other web pages with more information. The **arrangement** (the pattern of organization of the ideas, text, and visual elements in a composition) of the site is clear because information is grouped meaningfully. The site is thus easy to use: at the top of each page, below a purpose statement, is a list of main topics, each of which links to more detailed information. Arrangement also involves the balance of visual elements and text. The White House's home page is unified by the use of several shades of blue for accent boxes, links, and headings, and the

Navigation bar — White House seal

Courtesy of The White House

Figure 5.4. The navigation bar on the home page of the White House's website provides coherence.

entire website is given coherence by the navigation bar, which appears on every page. Finally, the White House seal, prominent in the middle of the navigation bar, and the American flag, at the left corner of the navigation bar, are visual cues that remind users of the official nature of this site. Visual links—such as the current images that are presented as a slide show on the home page and that link to in-depth blog posts and videos—combine arrangement and **delivery** (the presentation and interaction of visual elements with content).

Your web documents will likely be less elaborate than the White House site. Nevertheless, remember that websites (and other online compositions) are available to diverse audiences, and so their context, purpose, tone, and message should be given as much forethought as possible (1a). Because of the flexible nature of electronic composition, you can be creative when planning, drafting, and revising web documents.

(1) Planning a website

As you develop any web document, including a website, you need to keep all the elements of the rhetorical situation in mind: audience, message, context, and purpose. Considering your audience and purpose, you must decide which ideas or information to emphasize and then work out how best to arrange your web document to achieve that emphasis. And you also need to consider the overall impression you want the document to make. Do you want it to be motivational, informative, entertaining, or analytical? Do you want it to look snazzy, soothing, fun, or serious?

While you are generating the content (with your overall purpose in mind), you need to consider the supplementary links that will help you achieve your overall purpose. But you do not have to do everything at once; fine-tuning the visual design can wait until the content is in place.

When you are planning a website, you may find it helpful to create a storyboard or other visual representation of the site's organization. You can sketch a plan on paper or in a word-processing file if your site is fairly simple, or you can use index cards tacked to a bulletin board if it is more complex. If you have some time to devote to the planning process, you may want to learn how to use a program such as Web Studio or Dreamweaver to help you map out your site (such website design software is often available on computers in school labs).

The possibilities for organizing a website are endless. As starting points, you can consider three basic arrangement patterns—linear, hierarchical, and radial. A linear site (Figure 5.5) is easy to set up, as it is presented with a narrative structure, running from beginning to end. Hierarchical arrangements and radial arrangements are more complex to develop and may be better suited to group projects. The hierarchical arrangement (Figure 5.6) branches out at each level, and the radial arrangement (Figure 5.7) features individual pages that can be linked and viewed in a variety of sequences. Whatever arrangement you choose, keep in mind how your arrangement will affect a user's experience in navigating the website. However you decide to organize your site, be sure to represent each main element in your plan. A good plan will be invaluable to you as you draft text, incorporate visual and multimedia elements, and refine your arrangement.

Figure 5.5. Linear pattern for organizing a website. (© 2013 Cengage Learning)

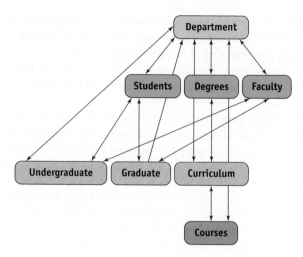

Figure 5.6. Hierarchical pattern for organizing a website.
(© 2013 Cengage Learning)

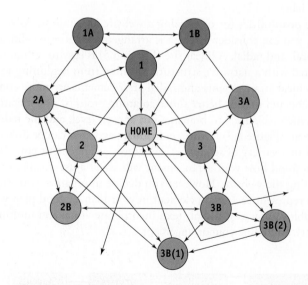

Figure 5.7. Radial pattern for organizing a website.
(© 2013 Cengage Learning)

(2) Creating effective online documents

When you plan and compose a web page or website, you will rely on hypertext. You will also rely on design or visual elements (such as background and color) and links (to the home page as well as to all other pages of the website) to establish consistency and orienting guideposts for your readers. Those design and visual elements and links create important associations among the concepts and ideas in your web document and serve as valuable tools for its development. Your inclusion of links allows the website user (your audience) to read the information in whatever sequence is most productive for that user. Thus, a hypertext document (one created with online capabilities in mind) offers unlimited options for ordering the content, as users click on the various links in any order they choose. Clearly, the individual interests and personalities of those who read your web document will lead them to navigate it in different ways. Therefore, you will want to consider how users' different approaches may affect the intended purpose of your document and try to arrange your document accordingly.

Some basic principles can help you use hyperlinks effectively in your web documents.

(a) Enhancing coherence with hyperlinks

The choice and placement of hyperlinks should be a vital part of your organizational plan. A site map, located on the home page, is essential for a large site and helpful for a compact one, as it provides a snapshot of the site's content and arrangement as well as direct access to its various pages. Hyperlinks to the individual pages of a website not only indicate logical divisions of the document but also provide transitions based on key words or ideas. As navigational signposts, hyperlinks serve as powerful rhetorical tools that provide coherence and reflect an effective arrangement.

(b) Taking advantage of the flexibility of hyperlinks

You can use individual words, phrases, or even sentences as textual hyperlinks. Hyperlinks can also be icons or other graphical elements, such as pictures or logos that reflect the information contained in each link (see Figure 5.8). If you do use graphical links, be sure that their appearance is appropriate for the transitions you are indicating. In addition, you must get permission to use text, graphics, or multimedia elements

Figure 5.8. The hyperlinks on this charity's "About Us" web page parallel the labels on the navigation bar and are accompanied by icons that reflect the information accessed through the links.

taken from other sources. Even though such material is often free, its source must be acknowledged (**10g**).

Internal hyperlinks are those that take the user between pages or sections of the website in which they appear. When creating links to content *external* to your website (such as a hyperlink in a web page about hurricanes that links to a meteorologist's website), be sure to select sites containing relevant, accurate, and well-presented information. You should use any contact information provided on a site to request permission to link to it, and you should check your links periodically to be sure that they are still active.

(c) Evaluating the rhetorical impact of hyperlinks

Textual and graphical links establish persuasive rhetorical associations for users. Compare the rhetorical impact of linking an image of the World Trade Center towers to a page about public memorials with that of linking the same image to a page about global terrorism. Because hyperlinks serve various rhetorical purposes, be sure to evaluate the impact of any you include on your web document as you plan, compose, and revise it. You will also want to evaluate the rhetorical impact of the hyperlinks on web documents you are reading or using.

> ### ◉ *TECH SAVVY*
>
> To create a web page, you do not have to understand the computer code (HTML) that allows a browser to display text. Programs such as Moveable Type (a blogging platform) and iWeb, referred to generally as WYSIWYG (What You See Is What You Get) HTML editors, will do such coding for you automatically. But some writers find that knowledge of the basic HTML commands can be useful for troubleshooting and editing a web page. A number of tutorials on the use of HTML are available on the Internet.

(3) Drafting web documents

When drafting a web document, you will undoubtedly consider various ways to organize your material. You may draft text for a linear arrangement and then later break the text into separate sections for different pages, which you link in sequence. At times, however, the arrangement and means of delivery required for an online document will force you to draft in unfamiliar ways. For example, you may find that you need to write the text for a website in chunks, drafting the text for a single page, including hyperlinks, and then moving on to the next page. Or you might wait until you revise your site to add hyperlinks or to replace some of your initial text links with graphical ones.

Once you have drafted and revised your site, get feedback from your classmates or colleagues, just as you would for an essay or a report. Since a website can include many pages with multiple links and images, you may want to ask for feedback not only about the content of your site but also about layout, graphics, and navigation (5e).

Professional web developers often put a site that is still in a draft stage on the Internet and solicit reactions from users, a process called **usability testing**. The developers then refine the site based on those reactions. Because websites are more interactive than printed texts, it is a good idea to seek input from users during site development. To solicit feedback, specify on your home page how users can contact you, taking care to consider your online security. To that end, you may want to open a free e-mail account through Gmail, Hotmail, or Yahoo! Mail to which users can send their comments, rather than making your personal e-mail address available. Usability testing is particularly important given the wide variety of potential audiences for online documents. Be sure to make your web document accessible to users who do not have a fast Internet connection or who have physical limitations affecting seeing, hearing, or keyboarding. Consider simplifying the design by using a restricted number of graphical elements, facilitating the downloading of materials by using low-resolution images (which have smaller file sizes), and avoiding animated graphics. To accommodate users with physical disabilities or different means of accessing web documents (for example, visually impaired users who employ talking computer programs that read web pages), incorporate basic accessibility features such as **alt tags** (descriptive lines of text for each visual image that can be read by screen-reading software). Such accommodations will make your online writing accessible to the greatest number of users.

The following checklist will help you plan a website and develop ideas for each page.

✅ CHECKLIST for Planning and Developing a Website

- What information, ideas, or perspective should a user take away from your site?
- How does the arrangement of your site reflect your overall purpose? How does it assist your intended users in understanding your purpose?
- Ideally, how would a user navigate your website? What are the other options for navigating within your site?
- Should you devote each page to a single main idea or combine several ideas on one page?
- How will you help users return to the home page and find key information quickly?
- What key connections between ideas or pieces of information might be emphasized through the use of hyperlinks?
- Will a user who follows external links be able to get back to your site?
- To ensure that your website has more impact than a paper document, have you used web-specific resources—such as

hyperlinks, sound and video clips, and animations—in creating it? How do those multimedia elements help you achieve your purpose?

- Do you need graphics—charts, photos, cartoons, clip art, logos, and so on—to enhance the site so that it will accomplish your purpose? Where should key visual elements be placed to be most effective?
- How often will you update your site?
- How will you solicit feedback for revisions to your site?
- Will your site be accessible to users with slow Internet access and those with physical limitations?

Exercise 2

Plan and compile information for a web page that supports a paper you are writing for one of your classes. If you have access to software that converts documents to web pages, start by converting your document. Make adjustments to it based on the criteria in the preceding checklist. Finally, critique your web page.

5e   VISUAL ELEMENTS AND RHETORICAL PURPOSE

Visual design sends messages to users: an effective design not only invites them to explore a website but also conveys the designer's rhetorical purpose (Chapter 6). All the design elements of an online document, like the tone and style of a printed one, are rhetorical tools that help you achieve your purpose and reach your intended audience. For instance, if a user has a negative reaction to a photograph of dead seals on a website devoted to protecting wildlife, that reaction is likely to affect the user's view of the site in general. When you choose visual elements such as photographs, try to anticipate how your audience may react.

(1) Basic design principles for easy navigation

A number of basic principles apply to the visual design of web documents.

- **Balance** involves the way in which the design elements used in a document are related to one another spatially. Web pages with a symmetrical arrangement of elements convey a formal, static impression, whereas asymmetrical arrangements are informal and dynamic.
- **Proportion** has to do with the relative sizes of design elements. Large elements attract more attention than small ones and will be perceived as more important.
- **Movement** concerns the way in which our eyes scan a page for information. Most of us look at the upper-left corner of a page first and the lower-right corner last. Therefore, the most important information on a web page should appear in those locations. Vertical or horizontal arrangement of elements on a page implies stability; diagonal and zigzagging arrangements suggest movement.
- **Contrast** between elements can be achieved by varying their focus or size. For instance, a web page about the Siberian Husky might show a photo of one of these dogs in sharp focus against a blurred background; the image of the dog might also be large relative to other elements on the page to enhance contrast. In text, you can emphasize an idea by presenting it in a contrasting font—for example, a playful display font such as **Marker Felt Thin** or an elegant script font such as *Edwardian Script*. An easy-to-read (sans serif) font such as Arial or Helvetica, however, should be used for most of the text on a web page.
- **Unity** refers to the way all the elements (and pages) of a site combine to give the impression that they are parts of a complete whole. For instance, choose a few colors and fonts to reflect the tone you want to convey, and use them consistently throughout your site. Creating a new design for each page of a website makes the site seem chaotic and thus is ineffective.

(2) Using color and background in online composition

Like the other elements of a web document, color and background are rhetorical tools that can be used to achieve various visual effects (Figure 5.9). Current web standards allow the display of a wide array

Courtesy of the International Federation of Organic Agriculture Movements (IFOAM)

Figure 5.9. The use of a consistent color palette on this web page enhances the purpose of the website. The Organic World Foundation promotes organic farming; the visual composition suggests simplicity and purity.

of colors for backgrounds, text, and frames. You can find thousands of background graphics on the Internet or create them with software.

Designers recommend using no more than three main colors for a document, although you may use varying intensities, or shades, of a color (for example, light blue, dark blue, and medium blue) to connect related materials. Using more than three colors may create confusion on your web pages. Besides helping to organize your site, color can have other specific effects. Bright colors, such as red and yellow, are more noticeable and can be used on a web page to emphasize a point or idea. In addition, some colors have associations you may wish to consider. For instance, reds can indicate danger or an emergency, whereas brown shades such as beige and tan suggest a formal atmosphere. Textual hyperlinks usually appear in a color different from that of the surrounding text on a web page so that they are more visible to users. Also, such links generally appear in one color before they are clicked and change to a different color when a user clicks on them. Select colors for textual hyperlinks that fit in with the overall color scheme of your document and help readers navigate between pages on your site.

Background, too, contributes to a successful website. Although a dark background can create a dramatic appearance, it often makes text difficult to read and hyperlinks difficult to see. A dark background can also cause a printout of a web page to be blank or unreadable. If you do use a dark background, be sure that the color of the text is bright enough to be readable on screen and that you provide a version that will print clearly. Similarly, a background with a pattern can be dramatic but can obscure the content of a web page or other online document. If you want to use a pattern for your background, check the readability of the text. You may need to change the color of the text or adjust the background to make the page easier to read.

Use different background colors or patterns for different pages of your online document only if you have a good rhetorical reason for doing so (as you might, for instance, if you were using a different color for each of several related categories of information). When you do this, adhere closely to the other design principles in **5e(1)** so that your site appears coherent to your audience.

✔ *CHECKLIST for Designing an Online Document*

- Have you chosen background and text colors that allow users to print readable copies of your pages if they wish?
- Have you used no more than three colors, perhaps varying the intensity of one or more of them?
- Does a background pattern on your page make the text difficult or easy to read?
- Have you chosen a single, easy-to-read font such as Arial or Helvetica for most of your text? Are the type styles (bold, italic, and so on) used consistently throughout the document?
- Have you used visual elements sparingly? Are any image files larger than 4 or 5 MB, making it likely that they will take a long time to transfer? If so, can you reduce their size using a lower resolution or by cropping?
- Have you indicated important points graphically by using bullets or numbers or visually by dividing the text into short blocks?
- Is any page or section crowded? Can users scan the information on a single screen quickly?
- Does each page include adequate white space for easy reading?
- Have you made sure that all links work?
- Have you identified yourself as the author and noted when the site was created or last revised?
- Have you run a spell checker and proofread the site yourself?

6 ‖ COMPOSING WITH VISUALS

All of us use visual elements to interpret messages every day—even if we are not consciously aware of how we "read" these photos, graphics, and design features. Just as important as understanding how we make sense of visuals is understanding how to compose print and electronic documents that use visuals in combination with words to communicate information to an intended audience.

In this chapter, you will learn the rhetorical principles of combining visual elements with text, the genres of visual documents, and the conventions of layout—all of which will help you achieve your rhetorical purpose. More specifically, this chapter will help you

- understand visual documents in terms of the rhetorical situation (**6a**),
- employ the design principles of visual rhetoric (**6b**),
- combine visual and verbal elements effectively (**6c**), and
- identify the common genres and effective design features of visual documents (**6d**).

6a ‖ VISUAL DOCUMENTS AND THE RHETORICAL SITUATION

Opportunity, audience, purpose, message, and context—the rhetorical elements underlying the interpretation and composition of verbal texts—apply to visual documents as well. Like a verbal text, a **visual document**, which combines visual elements (images or graphics) with verbal text, can respond to a rhetorical opportunity, express meaning, and deliver a message to an intended audience. In addition to images and **graphics** (such as diagrams and tables), visual elements include the design features and the layout of a document. Whether their purpose is expressive, expository, or argumentative (**1c**), visual documents—ranging from magazine advertisements to posters, billboards, brochures, newsletters, and websites—must always take into account the relationship between purpose and audience.

Consider the brochure in Figure 6.1, which features "WINNING SOLUTIONS" to the problem of global warming. This brochure serves a distinct purpose and employs rhetorical strategies that appeal to a specific audience: readers with a vested interest in the topic who are already predisposed to the message. This audience likely sought out the brochure and shares at least some of its creator's views and opinions about the importance of reversing global warming. Therefore, the brochure need only respond to (rather than elicit) the audience's interest. With no need to argue the importance of paying attention to global warming, the brochure's creator could concentrate instead on outlining various strategies for slowing the progress of the problem. In other words, the purpose of the brochure is not to argue a point but to deliver new information to a specific audience. Thus, the intended audience and the rhetorical purpose of the brochure are linked by the seven winning solutions.

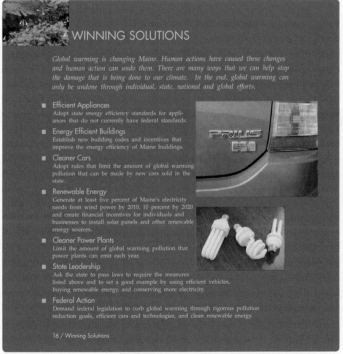

WINNING SOLUTIONS

Global warming is changing Maine. Human actions have caused these changes and human action can undo them. There are many ways that we can help stop the damage that is being done to our climate. In the end, global warming can only be undone through individual, state, national and global efforts.

■ Efficient Appliances
Adopt state energy efficiency standards for appliances that do not currently have federal standards.

■ Energy Efficient Buildings
Establish new building codes and incentives that improve the energy efficiency of Maine buildings.

■ Cleaner Cars
Adopt rules that limit the amount of global warming pollution that can be made by new cars sold in the state.

■ Renewable Energy
Generate at least five percent of Maine's electricity needs from wind power by 2010, 10 percent by 2020 and create financial incentives for individuals and businesses to install solar panels and other renewable energy sources.

■ Cleaner Power Plants
Limit the amount of global warming pollution that power plants can emit each year.

■ State Leadership
Ask the state to pass laws to require the measures listed above and to set a good example by using efficient vehicles, buying renewable energy, and conserving more electricity.

■ Federal Action
Demand federal legislation to curb global warming through rigorous pollution reduction goals, efficient cars and technologies, and clean renewable energy.

16 / Winning Solutions

Courtesy of Natural Resources Council of Maine

Figure 6.1. An effective brochure that is aimed at a specific audience.

The rhetorical situation also influences the genre of visual document that is chosen to deliver a message. Most posters, billboards, and advertisements contain a small amount of text, allowing the audience to absorb the message visually, with only a brief glance. The ease of access helps these predominantly visual documents reach a large, diverse audience. By contrast, the creator of the global warming brochure has assumed that those in the intended audience will take the time to read the more extensive text. The volume of information in a brochure, as well as the specialized focus, makes this genre particularly appropriate for an educated, already interested audience.

Exercise 1

Select a visual document that has caught your attention. Write for five to ten minutes in response to that document. Then, working with one or two classmates, analyze the document in terms of the rhetorical opportunity it addresses, the components of the rhetorical situation, and the relationship between words and images.
Be prepared to share your document and analysis with the rest of the class.

6b   THE DESIGN PRINCIPLES OF VISUAL RHETORIC

After considering the context of a visual document as a whole, you can analyze how the various elements work together to create a coherent message. Just as writers organize words into sentences and paragraphs, designers structure the visual elements of their documents in order to achieve coherence, develop ideas, and make a point. Experienced designers know to stand back several feet from a document in order to see which elements draw their attention. If the visual elements compete, no part of the document gets sufficient attention. Thus, presenting complicated material in visual form requires a set of strategies different from those used in writing academic papers. Rather than relying on paragraph breaks and topic sentences, designers of visual documents call on four important principles to organize, condense, and develop ideas: alignment, proximity, contrast, and repetition. These four design principles will help you organize complex information, making it visually appealing and easily accessible to your audience.

(1) The principle of alignment

The principle of alignment involves the use of an invisible grid system, running vertically and horizontally, to place and connect elements on a page. The fewer the invisible lines, the stronger the document design. For instance, the poster in Figure 6.2 has two

Digital Image © The Museum of Modern Art/Licensed by SCALA/Art Resource, NY.
Art © Lester Beall, Jr. Trust/Licensed by VAGA, New York, NY.

Figure 6.2. This Rural Electrification Administration poster by Lester Beall (1934) was purposefully designed to herald progress.

obvious sets of primary lines: one set that moves from left to right over the top half of the poster and a strong line down the center of the bottom half. These lines organize and unify the poster and give it a sharp, clean look, directing the viewer's eye to the smiling young people leaning on the fence. The words along the bottom of the poster, "RURAL ELECTRIFICATION ADMINISTRATION," reveal that the happy expressions are related to the expectation of electrification. The broad red-and-white and blue-and-white stripes affirm the patriotism of the federal program for rural electrification. Overall, the poster communicates that rural Americans can look forward to a better future because of electricity.

(2) The principle of proximity

The principle of **proximity** requires the grouping of related textual or visual elements, such as the vertical stripes and the fence rails in the poster in Figure 6.2. Dissimilar elements are separated by **white space** (blank areas around blocks of text or around graphics or images). The audience perceives each grouping (or chunk) of elements in a well-designed visual document as a single unit and interprets it as a whole before moving on to the next group. In other words, the chunks serve a function similar to sections in a written document, organizing the page and reducing clutter. In the poster in Figure 6.2, the proximity of the text to the image of the young people links the textual and visual elements and allows them to be interpreted together.

(3) The principle of contrast

The principle of **contrast** establishes a visual hierarchy, providing clear clues as to which elements are most important and which are less so. The most salient textual or visual elements (such as the red, white, and blue stripes in the poster in Figure 6.2) stand out from the rest of the document, while other elements (the line of text, for instance) are not as noticeable. The most significant elements of a document are generally contrasted with other elements by differences in size, color, or typeface. Academic and professional documents, for example, usually have their headings in bold or italic type or capital letters to distinguish them from the rest of the text. The brochure in Figure 6.1 (on page 121) features a large title in capital letters, "WINNING SOLUTIONS," which dominates the page; the identical size and typeface of all the headings indicate that they are of equal importance but subordinate to the title. Just a brief glance at this brochure allows the viewer to determine the hierarchy of information and the basic structure.

(4) The principle of repetition

The principle of **repetition** has to do with the replication throughout a document of specific textual or visual elements, such as the headings in the brochure in Figure 6.1 and the stripes in the poster in Figure 6.2. For example, nearly all academic and professional papers use a consistent typeface for large blocks of text, which creates a unified look throughout these documents. Visual documents follow a similar strategy, purposefully limiting the number of typefaces, colors, and graphics in order to enhance coherence with repetition. The repeated bullets and the repeated typefaces in the headings and text of the brochure on global warming as well as the stripes in the poster for rural electrification structure these visual documents and reinforce their unity.

6c	COMBINING VISUAL AND VERBAL ELEMENTS

Although words or images alone can have a tremendous impact on an audience, the combination of the two is often necessary, especially when neither verbal nor visual elements alone can successfully respond to a rhetorical opportunity, reach an intended audience, or fulfill the rhetorical purpose. As you know, newspaper and magazine articles often include powerful images to heighten the emotional impact of the text. Diagrams that accompany a set of product-assembly instructions reinforce the process analysis and make assembly easier for the reader. Tag clouds—visual depictions of textual content on blogs and websites—indicate the frequency with which words are used in that content: the bigger the word, the more frequently it is used. With just a glance at the tag cloud on the blog *UVM Career Services Blog* (Figure 6.3), students at the University of Vermont can identify the key concepts and issues related to their career concerns. Thus, when used together, words and images can reinforce each other to deliver a message—or even deliberately contradict each other to establish an ironic tone.

TAG CLOUD

advice alumni alumni
profile boston burlington Career
career connection career
path Catamount Job Link
choosing a major Doing Good
Doing Well Employers
etiquette events
Experience federal
government google how to
inspiration internship hop
Internships internship
search Interviewing Job Fair
Jobs job search majors
mission-driven work
Networking new york
non-profit On Campus
Recruiting online identity
photos Prezi quotes resume
search socially responsible
social media tips

Courtesy UVM Career Services

Figure 6.3. Informative tag cloud on
UVM Career Services Blog.

(1) Advertisements

The words and image in the advertisement in Figure 6.4 work together to argue that the viewer should consider buying a particular car. The image depicts a row of vehicles, two of which have been crushed by a falling tree. Considering the image alone, a viewer can see that the small vehicle is the focal point: prominently placed at the center of the frame, its unscathed body provides a strong contrast to the badly damaged vehicles on either side. The setting also contributes to the analysis, as the tall trees (one of which has fallen on the bigger, more rugged vehicles) convey an outdoorsy, back-to-nature mood. Ironically, the large vehicles are destroyed; the smaller vehicle remains intact. Along with the compelling image, the advertisement has three verbal elements.

The first, printed on the license plate of the small car, is "ELECTRIC," a word that alerts the reader to the car's energy efficiency. Second, the sentence "HELLO, PARKING KARMA" appears below that car, the only ecologically sensitive vehicle in the image. Finally, the small type at the bottom of the image reads, "With the right car, everything's better. Introducing the electric ZAP Worldcar L.U.V.," followed by the company's contact information and logo.

Without the accompanying text, the image in Figure 6.4 might convey the message that the central car was lucky to have been parked between two bigger vehicles. But combined with the three verbal elements, the image's message is clarified: the electric vehicle is environment-friendly, whereas the larger vehicles are gas hogs that burn fossil fuel and pollute the environment. The sentence about parking karma strongly suggests that the tree's falling was not accidental but was, in

Figure 6.4. Both words and image are necessary to communicate the message of this ad.

fact, an ethical consequence; that is, nature is punishing the gas hogs and sparing the electric vehicle. The argument of this advertisement is clear: pick the "right car," one that is compact and environmentally sound, and you will be rewarded.

(2) Graphics

Many academic and professional documents that are primarily composed of text also include visual displays, or **graphics**, to clarify written material. Graphics can be used to illustrate a concept, present data, provide visual relief, or simply attract readers' attention. Different types of graphics—tables, charts or graphs, and pictures—serve different purposes, and some may serve multiple purposes in a given document. Any of these types of graphics can enable readers to absorb a message more quickly than they would by reading long sections of text. However, if there is any chance that readers might not receive the intended message, it is a good idea to supplement graphics with textual discussion.

(a) Tables

Tables use a row-and-column arrangement to organize data (numbers or words) spatially; they are especially useful for presenting great amounts of numerical information in a small space, enabling the reader to draw direct comparisons among pieces of data or even to locate specific items. When you design a table, be sure to label all of the columns and rows accurately and to provide both a title and a number for the table. In Table 6.1, you can see that the columns, labeled "Season," "Season Total," and "Biggest One-Day Snowfall for the Season and the Amount," contain important information for people interested in Great Lakes snow-belt weather conditions. The table number and title traditionally appear above the table body, as Table 6.1 demonstrates, and any notes or source information are placed below it.

Most word-processing programs have settings that let you insert a table wherever you need one. You can determine how many rows and columns the table will have, and you can also size each row and each column appropriately for the information it will hold.

(b) Charts and graphs

Like tables, charts and graphs also display relationships among statistical data in visual form; unlike tables, they do so using lines, bars, or other visual elements rather than just letters and numbers. Data can be displayed in several different graphic forms: pie charts, line graphs, and bar charts are the most common examples.

Pie charts are especially useful for showing the relationship of parts to a whole (see Figure 6.5), but these graphics can only be used to display sets of data that add up to 100 percent. (In the chart in Figure 6.5, twenty-four hours represents 100 percent of a day.)

Line graphs show the change in the relationship between one variable (indicated as a value on the vertical axis, or y axis) and another variable (indicated as a value on the horizontal axis, or x axis). The most common x-axis variable is time. Line graphs are very good at showing how a variable changes over time. A line graph might be used, for example, to illustrate the progression of sleep stages during one night, increases or decreases in student achievement from semester to semester, or trends in financial markets over a number of years.

Bar charts show correlations between two variables that do not involve smooth changes over time. For instance, a bar chart might illustrate gross national product for several nations, the relative speeds of various computer processors, or statistics about the composition of the U.S. workforce (see Figure 6.6).

Table 6.1 Snowfall in Cleveland, Ohio, by Season (in inches)

Season	Season Total	Biggest One-Day Snowfall for the Season and the Amount	
2010–2011	69.5	February, 25, 2011	8.9
2009–2010	59.8	January 4, 2010	4.5
2008–2009	80.0	February 4, 2009	10.9
2007–2008	77.2	March 8, 2008	10.8
2006–2007	76.5	February 13, 2007	10.4
2005–2006	50.6	February 8, 2006	6.9
2004–2005	117.9	December 22, 2004	9.4
2003–2004	91.2	March 16, 2004	7.1
2002–2003	94.9	December 25, 2002	10.2
2001–2002	45.8	March 25, 2002	6.9
2000–2001	74.3	March 25, 2001	7.7
1999–2000	59.2	January 26, 2000	6.5
1998–1999	61.6	February 13, 1999	6.5
1997–1998	33.7	December 6, 1997	5.6
1996–1997	55.4	November 11, 1996	7.2
1995–1996	101.1	December 19, 1995	12.0
1994–1995	43.6	January 7, 1995	7.2
1993–1994	72.5	January 4, 1994	5.5
1992–1993	88.5	February 23, 1993	13.6
1991–1992	65.7	January 14, 1992	6.2
1990–1991	47.1	February 15, 1991	6.6

Source: http//:blog.cleveland.com/datacentral/index.ssf/2010/07/annual_cleveland_snowfall
_total.html

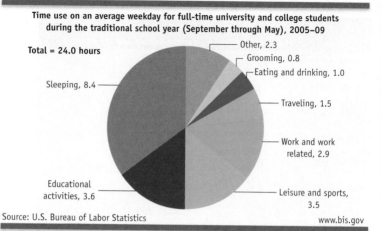

Figure 6.5. This easy-to-read pie chart shows how the average full-time university or college student spends time on an average weekday.

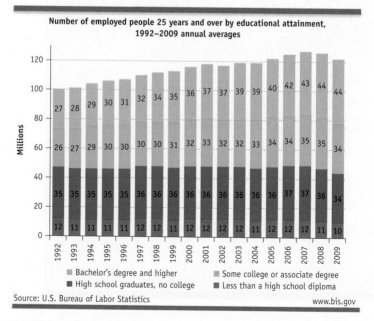

Figure 6.6. This bar chart illustrates the composition of the US workforce with respect to level of education.

Figure 6.7. A photo and a drawing of the same printer.

(c) Pictures

Pictures include photos, sketches, technical illustrations, paintings, icons, and other visual representations. Photographs are often used to reinforce textual descriptions or to show a reader exactly what something looks like. Readers of a used-car ad, for instance, will want to see exactly what the car looks like, not an artistic interpretation of its appearance. Likewise, a travel brochure about Costa Rica needs to contain lots of full-color photos of dazzling beaches, verdant forests, and azure water.

But photographs are not always the most informative type of picture. Compare the two images in Figure 6.7. Although the photograph is a more realistic image of the actual printer, the illustration more clearly shows the printer's important features: buttons, panels, and so forth. With its simple lines and clear labels, the illustration suits its purpose: to help the viewer set up and use the printer. Line drawings enable the designer of a document such as a user manual to highlight specific elements of an object while deemphasizing or eliminating unnecessary information. The addition of arrows, pointers, and labels adds useful detail to such an illustration.

(3) Effective integration of visual and verbal elements

To integrate visual elements into written text, you want to position them purposefully, whether you place images close together in a document or you put an image at the beginning or end of a document so as not to disrupt the text.

(a) Considering proximity

Proximity—placing an image as close as possible to the text that refers to it—is one way of establishing a connection between the verbal and visual elements. Think of how helpful it can be to have images accompanying printed instructions for assembling a piece of furniture, setting up a new computer, or following a complicated recipe. When an image aligns with verbal instructions, the document is effective and instructive. Wrapping the text around an image also serves to integrate visual and verbal elements; wrapping places an image and its corresponding text in very close proximity. In addition, cropping unnecessary elements from an image strengthens connections between it and the textual components of a document, highlighting what is most important while preserving what is authentic. When a visual element (a graph or table) is too large to fit on the same page as the related text, it is placed on a separate page or moved to an appendix. Thus, proximity must occasionally be forfeited for the sake of in-depth explanation or detailed support.

(b) Including captions and labels

Captions and labels are also crucial to the integration of visual and verbal components of a document. In academic texts, figures and tables are labeled by being numbered consecutively and separately. Moreover, the body of an academic text includes **anchors**, specific references to each image or graphic used, such as "see Figure 5" and "as shown in Table 2" (see the research paper in **17d**). In popular magazines and newspapers, on the other hand, images and graphics are rarely labeled and anchored in this way. More often, these text-enhancing visuals are integrated into the text through the use of captions and layout. Although the conventions of academic and professional documents vary, no figure or table should be inserted into a text document without either a caption or a label (or both) to explain its relevance in the larger context of the work.

6d   COMMON GENRES AND EFFECTIVE FEATURES OF VISUAL DOCUMENTS

Although all visual documents adhere to the same rhetorical principles, each of the common genres is distinguished by its effective features. Posters, flyers, brochures, and newsletters are among the most common genres of visual documents. Publishing software, such as PagePlus or Microsoft Publisher, offer standard templates for designing these documents.

(1) Posters and flyers

Posters and **flyers**, colorful sheets that paper walls, utility poles, and bulletin boards around most college and university campuses, are used to advertise organizations, events, issues, and services. Although posters and flyers often fulfill the same purpose, they are not always aimed at the same audiences. Therefore, their effectiveness depends on how and where they appear. Posters, for instance, usually appear on large walls and are seen from afar. For those reasons, a poster usually employs much more visual than verbal (or textual) information so that its audience can absorb the message at a glance. By contrast, the smaller, usually more text-heavy, single-sheet flyer is intended for mass distribution and is often handed out to passersby. Yet, despite these differences, both posters and flyers are meant to be seen by as many people as possible—with text and images that readily appeal to a target group (the intended audience).

Because the purpose of posters and flyers is to reach as many people as possible—and quickly—it is vitally important that the audience be able to locate the important information immediately. Both posters and flyers need a focal point that captures attention and highlights the basic information. Thus, artfully minimalistic posters and flyers are more effective than those that overwhelm viewers with too many images or fancy typefaces.

The poster in Figure 6.8 relies heavily on color, repetition, and contrast to convey its message: "Live Heart Smart." Sponsored by the Centers for Disease Control and Prevention and circulated just before and during February (American Heart Month), the poster shows an ageless and generic woman wearing Valentine's Day red, with hearts forming her hair and serving as her words. Red and hearts are repeated throughout the poster, both in images and in words. The text of the poster is aligned in two blocks at the top and bottom, and the lines of text within each block are in close proximity. The white space works to focus the viewer's attention on the figure of the woman. Her graceful hands encircling her heart further emphasize the poster's serious message.

Centers For Disease Control and Prevention

Figure 6.8. This poster combines text and image effectively. It was designed to be scanned by viewers in the backward S pattern, as shown on the right.

Most people "read" posters and flyers by scanning them in a backward S pattern, beginning at the top left and ending at the bottom right. The poster in Figure 6.8 was designed to take advantage of that scanning strategy. The large lines of type at the top, centering on the red boldfaced word "Heart," provide a natural starting point. The eye is drawn downward over the curve of the hearts in the woman's hair, then across her hands and heart as a turning point, and, finally, to the words "WEAR RED" in all capital letters just below the waist of her red dress.

The flyer in Figure 6.9, by contrast, uses two major lines of text, one vertical and the other horizontal, to deliver its message about the health risks of tanning beds. Additional information about the dangers of UVA radiation appears in a separate chunk in the lower portion of the flyer. The image at the upper left not only breaks up the text but is positioned where the eye goes first. Though the flyer is somewhat text-heavy,

Want to look and feel your best?

Then rethink that trip to the tanning bed.

Using tanning beds increases your exposure to UVA radiation.

What can UVA do?

- Prematurely age your skin
- Increase your risk of developing melanoma by 74%
- Weaken your immune system
- Lead to cataracts and other eye damage

Think tanning is healthy?
Think again.

Figure 6.9. This student-produced flyer draws attention to the dangers of tanning, using the design principles of alignment, proximity, contrast, and repetition.

its layout and the chunking of its text make it easy to read. In addition to using both text and image, the student designer used a sans serif typeface in two colors. With its visual impact and its unwavering focus on the message, this flyer is effective.

TIPS FOR DESIGNING EFFECTIVE POSTERS AND FLYERS

- Identify your intended audience.
- Determine your purpose.
- Consider where your poster will appear or how your flyer will be distributed.
- Provide a clear focal point.
- Aim for visual simplicity.
- Strive for coherence.
- Chunk information.
- Remember the backward S scanning pattern.

(2) Brochures

Like posters and flyers, **brochures** rely on engaging text, visual elements, and effective design to appeal to their target audience. The audience has usually already indicated an interest in the topic by requesting the brochure or by picking it out of a holder or rack. It is up to the designer of the brochure to maintain that interest by effectively integrating visual and textual material. To that end, brochures often include striking photographs and bold colors that contrast with the text color. Like all successful communicators, designers of brochures are guided by several basic rhetorical principles.

Because many readers have voluntarily become part of the audience, designers of brochures can assume that these documents will be read, but not necessarily word for word. Therefore, they choose a layout that allows for easy scanning. They know their readers want to locate relevant information quickly and easily. For these reasons, a brochure incorporates certain characteristics or design features that serve as signposts for readers, helping them navigate the document. Headings and subheadings allow a reader to gain an overview of the document's contents and pinpoint specific information. Bullets are often used to organize information and make it quickly accessible. The principle of repetition is applied to the document's overall structure: Each page may have the same basic layout, with variations in content and color, or a simple image or symbol may appear throughout the document to unify it. In the brochure for cancer patients in Figure 6.10, each left-hand page contains an image of a survivor; the facing page has the same layout throughout the document, with variations in the content. The statement "I LIVE STRONG" is repeated beneath each picture.

Brochures break text into blocks or chunks. In a typical brochure, the folds differentiate the blocks of text. In addition, the brochure in Figure 6.10 uses a box with a background color to distinguish the checklist from the introductory paragraph at the top of the page.

TIPS FOR DESIGNING EFFECTIVE BROCHURES

- Identify your intended audience.
- Design each page of the brochure for ease of scanning (remember the Z pattern).
- Provide verbal and visual signposts for your readers: headings, subheadings, shading, and bullets.
- Chunk the text to emphasize main points.
- Employ striking photographs and bold colors to contrast with black type.

I AM JASON
I LIVE STRONG
CANCER SURVIVOR

Physical Concerns
Pain, Body, Lifestyle

Now that you have finished treatment, you may have special needs in caring for your body. Ask your doctor about these changes or what you can expect.

Do you have concerns about changes in your body?
Make a check next to the things you would like help with or write down your own concerns.

Pain or Swelling
☐ I have pain that does not go away.
☐ I have swelling in parts of my body.

Body Changes
☐ I am not sure how the surgery, treatment or medicines I have taken or am taking will affect my body.
☐ My feelings about my body have changed.
☐ I feel tired often.
☐ I have trouble remembering things and my mind works more slowly than before.

Lifestyle
☐ I want to know how much I should exercise.
☐ I want to know what type of diet I should follow.
☐ I am having changes in my intimate life.

Other Concerns:

The Road to Survivorship 3

LIVESTRONG ™ is a trademark of the Lance Armstrong Foundation

Figure 6.10. This brochure's repeated design features provide the reader with signposts.

Exercise 2

Choose a document containing one or more images that you composed for another class or for an extracurricular activity. Bring the document (or a color photocopy of it) to class. Have your classmates look at the document from several feet away and ask them to report what their eyes are drawn to. As you lead a discussion about the document, be prepared to explain how you created it and chose the image(s). Be receptive to suggestions from your classmates for improving your document—they can tell you if the elements are competing for or directing their attention.

7 WRITING ARGUMENTS

You write arguments on a regular basis, usually to address an issue or resolve a problem. When you send a memo reminding your colleague that a client needs to sign a contract, when you e-mail your parents to ask them for a loan, when you petition your academic advisor for a late drop, or when you demand a refund from a mail-order company, you are writing an argument in response to a rhetorical opportunity. You are expressing a point of view and using logical reasoning as you invite a specific audience to adopt that point of view or engage in a particular course of action.

Argument and *persuasion* are often used interchangeably, but they differ in two basic ways. **Persuasion** has traditionally referred to winning or conquering with the use of emotional reasoning, whereas **argument** has been reserved for the use of logical reasoning to convince listeners or readers that a particular course of action is the best one. But because writing often involves some measure of "winning" (even if that means just gaining the ear of a particular audience) and uses both emotion and reason to affect an audience, this book uses *argument* to cover the meanings of both terms.

© Bruno Joachim/Index Stock/Photolibrary

Argumentation is used to determine the best course of action.

When writing arguments, you follow the same process as for all your writing: once you decide to respond to a rhetorical opportunity, you begin planning, drafting, and revising, as well as considering the intended audience, purpose, and context (**1d** and **1e**). A respectful acknowledgment of the beliefs, values, and expertise of a targeted audience is crucial for achieving the rhetorical purpose of an argument, which always goes beyond mere victory over an opponent. After all, argument is an important way to invite exchange, understanding, cooperation, consideration, joint decision making, agreement, or negotiation of differences. Thus, argument serves three basic and sometimes overlapping purposes: to analyze a complicated issue or question an established belief, to express or defend a point of view, and to invite or convince an audience to change a position or adopt a course of action (in order to address or resolve a problem).

This chapter will help you

- determine the purpose of an argument (**7a**),
- consider different viewpoints (**7b**),
- distinguish fact from opinion (**7c**),
- take a position or make a claim (**7d**),
- provide evidence to support a claim (**7e**),
- use the rhetorical appeals to ground an argument (**7f**),
- select an appropriate type of argument (**7g**),
- reason effectively and ethically (**7h**),
- avoid rhetorical fallacies (**7i**), and
- analyze an argument (**7j**).

As you proceed, you will understand the importance of determining your purpose, identifying your audience, marshaling your arguments, arguing ethically, and treating your audience with respect.

7a   DETERMINING THE PURPOSE OF AN ARGUMENT

What opportunity for change calls to you? Why have you decided to respond to that opportunity? What topic is under discussion? What is at stake? What is likely to happen as a result of making this argument? How important are those consequences? Who is in a position to act or react in response to your argument?

When writing an argument, take care to establish the relationships among your topic, purpose, and audience. The relationship between audience and purpose is particularly significant because the audience often shapes the purpose.

- If there is little likelihood that you can convince members of your audience to change a strongly held opinion, you might achieve a great deal by inviting them to understand your position and offering to understand theirs.
- If the members of your audience are not firmly committed to a position, you might be able to convince them to agree with the opinion you are expressing or defending or at least to consider it.
- If the members of your audience agree with you in principle, you might invite them to undertake a specific action—such as voting for a proposed school tax or supporting a particular candidate.

No matter how you imagine those in your audience responding to your argument, you must establish **common ground** with them, stating a goal toward which you both want to work (our neighborhood streets should be safe and clean) or identifying a belief, assumption, or value that you both share (all our nation's children deserve a good education). In other words, common ground is a necessary starting point, regardless of your ultimate purpose.

7b CONSIDERING DIFFERING VIEWPOINTS

Because people invariably hold different points of view, a good deal of the writing you will do in school or at work will require you to take an arguable position on a topic. The first step toward finding a topic for argumentation is to consider issues that inspire different opinions and offer opportunity for change.

Behind any effective argument is a question that can generate more than one reasonable answer that goes beyond "yes" or "no." If you ask "Are America's schools in trouble?" almost everyone will say "yes." But if you ask "In what ways can America's schools be improved?" or "How can colleges better prepare teachers?" you will hear different answers. Answers differ because people approach questions with various backgrounds, experiences, and assumptions. As a consequence, they are often tempted to use reasoning that supports what they already believe. As a writer, you, too, will be tempted to employ such reasoning, but as you shape your argument, you need to demonstrate that you are well informed about your topic as well as aware and considerate of other views about it.

You write an argument in order to solve a problem, answer a question, or determine a course of action—with or for an audience. When you choose a topic for argumentation, you take a stance that allows you to question, while providing you an opportunity (or reason) for writing. You first focus on a topic, on the part of some general subject that you will address (**2b**), and then pose a question about it. As you formulate your question, consider (1) your values and beliefs with respect to the topic, (2) how your assumptions might differ from those of your intended audience, (3) what your ultimate purpose is for writing to this audience, and (4) how you might establish common ground with them, while respecting any differences between your opinion and theirs. The question you raise will evolve into an arguable statement, your thesis.

The most important criterion for choosing an arguable statement for an essay is knowledge of the topic, so that you will be an informed writer, responsive to the expectations of your audience and faithful to your purpose. While in the process of identifying your topic, stay alert for issues about which you have strong opinions or ideas that circulate in classes, on television, on the Internet, in your reading, and in conversations.

To determine whether a topic might be suitable, make a statement about the topic ("I believe strongly that . . . " or "My view is that . . . ") and then check to see if that statement can be argued. If you can answer all the questions in the following box to your satisfaction, you should feel confident about your topic.

TIPS FOR ASSESSING AN ARGUABLE STATEMENT ABOUT A TOPIC

- What reasons can you state that support your belief (or point of view) about the topic? List those reasons. What else do you need to know?

- Who or what groups might disagree with your statement? Why? List those groups.

- What are other viewpoints on the topic and reasons supporting those viewpoints? List them. What else do you need to know?

- What is your purpose in writing about this topic?

- How does your purpose connect with your intended audience? Describe that audience.

- What do you want your audience to do in response to your argument? In other words, what do you expect from your audience? Write out your expectation.

As you move further into the writing process, researching and exploring your topic at home, in the library, and online (Chapter 8), you will clarify your purpose and refine your thesis statement.

7C	DISTINGUISHING BETWEEN FACT AND OPINION

As you develop your thesis statement into an argument, you use both facts and opinions. You must distinguish between these two kinds of information so that you can use both to your advantage as you establish your credibility (7f(1)), an essential feature of successful argumentation. **Facts** are reliable pieces of information that can be verified through independent sources or procedures. **Opinions**, on the other hand, are assertions or inferences that may or may not be based on facts. Opinions that are widely accepted, however, may seem to be factual when they are not. And just because facts are reliable does not mean that they speak for themselves. Facts must be used responsibly in support of an argument; otherwise, a thoughtful and well-informed opinion might have more impact. So, neither facts nor opinions are preferable. Their power depends on how you employ them.

To determine whether a statement you have read is fact or opinion, ask yourself questions like these: Can it be proved? Can it be challenged? How often is the same result achieved? If a statement can consistently be proved true, then it is a fact. If it can be disputed, then it is an opinion, no matter how significant or reasonable it may seem.

Fact	Milk contains calcium.
Opinion	Americans should drink more milk.

To say that milk contains calcium is to state a well-established fact: it can be verified by consulting published studies or by conducting laboratory tests. Whether or not this fact is significant depends on how a writer chooses to use it. To say that Americans need to drink more milk is to express an opinion that may or may not be supported by facts. When considering the statement "Americans should drink more milk," a thoughtful reader might ask, "How much calcium does a human need? Why do humans need calcium? Is cow's milk good for humans? Might leafy green vegetables provide a richer source of calcium?" Anticipating questions such as these can help you develop an argument as well as help you recognize the evidence that will best support that argument, where you can obtain such evidence, and what to do if you discover conflicting evidence.

Because the line between fact and opinion is not always clear, writers and readers of arguments must be prepared to assess the reliability of the information before them. They need to evaluate the beliefs supporting the argument's stance, the kinds of sources used, and the objections that could be made to the argument.

Exercise 1

Determine which of the following statements are facts and which are opinions. In each case, what kind of verification would you require in order to accept the statement as reliable?

1. China's Liu Xiaobo won the 2010 Nobel Peace Prize.
2. A college degree guarantees a higher income over the course of a lifetime.
3. Women who are overweight or who have a family history of diabetes have a higher risk of gestational diabetes.
4. The Phantom of the Opera is the longest running show on Broadway.
5. Every American student can and should learn to write well in college.
6. Santa Fe's Chapel of San Miguel is the oldest church in the United States.
7. Aerobic exercise is good for your health.
8. The United States entered World War II because of the bombing of Pearl Harbor.
9. When combined, ammonia and chlorine bleach produce a poisonous gas.
10. New Orleans will never fully recover from Hurricane Katrina.

7d   TAKING A POSITION OR MAKING A CLAIM

When making an argument, a writer takes a position on a particular topic. Whether the argument analyzes, questions, expresses, defends, invites, or convinces, the writer's position needs to be clear. That position, which is called the **claim**, or **proposition**, clearly states what the writer wants the audience to do with the information being provided. The claim is the thesis of the argument and usually appears in the introduction and sometimes again in the conclusion.

(1) Extent of a claim

Claims vary in extent; they can be absolute or moderate, large or limited. Absolute claims assert that something is always true or false, completely good or bad; moderate claims make less sweeping assertions.

Absolute claim	Any great college athlete can go pro.
Moderate claim	Most pro athletes went to college.
Absolute claim	Harry Truman was the best president the United States has ever had.
Moderate claim	Truman's domestic policies helped advance civil rights.

Moderate claims are not necessarily superior to absolute claims. After all, writers frequently need to take a strong position for or against something. But the stronger the claim, the stronger the evidence needed to support it. Be sure to consider the quality and the significance of the evidence you use—not just its quantity.

(2) Types of claims

(a) Substantiation claims
Without making a value judgment, a **substantiation claim** asserts that something exists or is evident. This kind of point can be supported by evidence.

The job market for those with a liberal arts degree is limited.

The post office is raising rates and losing money again.

(b) Evaluation claims

According to an **evaluation claim**, something has a specific quality: it is good or bad, effective or ineffective, successful or unsuccessful.

> The high graduation rate for athletes at Penn State is a direct result of the school's supportive academic environment.

> The public transportation system in Washington DC is reliable and safe.

Sometimes, writers use an evaluation claim as a way to invite their audience to consider an issue.

> It is important for us to consider the graduation rate of all Big Ten athletes, regardless of the sport they play.

(c) Policy claims

When making **policy claims**, writers call for specific action.

> We must establish the funding necessary to hire the best qualified high school teachers.

> We need to build a light-rail system linking downtown with the western suburbs.

Photo by The Conservative Party Archive/Getty Images

Much writing involves sub-stantiation, evaluation, and policy claims. When writing about the job market for engineers with recent degrees, you might tap your ability to substantiate a claim; when writing about literature (Chapter 11), you might need to evaluate a character. Policy claims are commonly found in arguments about social or political issues such as health care, social security, affirmative action, or defense spending. These claims often grow out of substantiation or evaluation

Policy claims, such as the one made by this 1961 British political poster, call for specific action. In this case, the requested action is to vote for Conservative candidates.

claims: first, you demonstrate that a problem exists; then, you establish the best solution for that problem.

TIPS FOR MAKING A CLAIM ARGUABLE

- Write down your opinion.
- Describe the situation and experiences that produced your opinion.
- Decide who constitutes the audience for your opinion and what you want that audience to do about your opinion.
- Write down the verifiable and reliable facts that support your opinion.
- Transform your initial opinion into a thoughtful claim that reflects those facts and considers at least two sides of the issue.
- Ask yourself, "So what?" If the answer to this question shows that your claim leads nowhere, start over, beginning with the first tip.

Exercise 2

The following argument is an excerpt from a book analyzing racial strife in the United States and written by Cornel West, a scholar specializing in race relations. Evaluate the claims it presents. Are they absolute or moderate? Can you identify a substantiation or evaluation claim? What policy claim is implicit in this passage? (The sentences are numbered for ease of reference.)

[1]To engage in a serious discussion of race in America, we must begin not with the problems of black people but with the flaws of American society—flaws rooted in historic inequalities and longstanding cultural stereotypes. [2]How we set up the terms for discussing racial issues shapes our perception and response to these issues. [3]As long as black people are viewed as a "them," the burden falls on blacks to do all the "cultural" and "moral" work necessary for healthy race relations. [4]The implication is that only certain Americans can define what it means to be American—and the rest must simply "fit in."   —CORNEL WEST, *Race Matters*

7e   PROVIDING EVIDENCE FOR AN EFFECTIVE ARGUMENT

Effective arguments are well developed and supported. You should explore your topic in enough depth that you have the evidence to support your position intelligently and ethically, whether that evidence is based on personal experience or on research (Chapters **2** and **8**). You want to consider the reasons others might have to disagree with you and be prepared to respond to those reasons.

(1) Establishing the claim

If you want readers to take your ideas seriously, you must establish the reasons that have led to your claim and the opinions, values, and assumptions that underlie your thinking. So as you explore your topic, make a list of the reasons that have led to your belief (**2d** and **2f**). When Anna Seitz was working on her argumentative essay (at the end of this chapter; see pages 171–76), she listed the following reasons for her belief that universities should not allow individuals or corporations to buy naming rights to campus buildings:

1. By purchasing naming rights, donors gain influence over educational policy decisions, even though they are not qualified to make such decisions.
2. Significant donations can adversely affect overall university finances by replacing existing funding sources.
3. Donors who purchase naming rights are associated with the university, in spite of the fact that they or their corporations may subscribe to a different set of values.

Although it is possible to base an argument on one good reason (such as "The selling of naming rights distracts from the educational purposes of universities"), doing so can be risky. If your audience does not find this reason convincing, you have no other support for your position. When you show that you have more than one reason for believing as you do, you increase the likelihood that your audience will find merit in your argument. Sometimes, however, one reason is stronger—and more appropriate for your audience—than several others you could advance. To develop an argument for which you have only one good reason, explore the opinions, values, and assumptions that led you to take such a stand. By revealing the thinking behind the single reason on which you are building your case, you can create a well-developed argument.

Whether you have one reason or several, be sure to provide sufficient evidence from credible sources to support your claim:

- facts,
- statistics,
- examples, and
- testimony (based on personal experience or professional expertise).

This evidence must be accurate, representative, and sufficient. Accurate information should be verifiable by others (7c). Recognize, however, that even if the information a writer provides is accurate, it may not be representative or sufficient if it was drawn from an exceptional case, a biased sample, or a one-time occurrence. If, for example, you are writing an argument about the advantages of using Standardized English but you draw all of your supporting evidence from a proponent of the English-Only movement, your evidence represents only the views of that movement. Such evidence is neither representative of all the support for the use of Standardized English nor sufficient to support a thoughtful argument. In order to better represent your viewpoint, you should gather supporting evidence from sociolinguists, speakers of other dialects and languages, education specialists, professors, and other experts. In other words, consult more than a single source (Chapter 8).

When gathering evidence, be sure to think critically about the information you find. If you are using the results of polls or other statistics or statements by authorities, determine how recent and representative the information is and how it was gathered. Consider, too, whether the authority you plan to quote is qualified to address the topic under consideration and is likely to be respected by your readers.

Whatever form of evidence you use—facts, statistics, examples, or testimony—you need to make clear to your audience exactly *why* and *how* the evidence supports your claim. After all, even accurate information has to be interpreted by the writer and the reader. As soon as the relationship between your claim and your evidence is clear to you, make that connection explicit to your readers, helping them understand your thinking.

(2) Responding to diverse views

Issues are controversial because good arguments can be made on all sides. Therefore, effective arguments consider and respond to other points of view. Fairness, respect, and acknowledgment of other points of view are crucial for connecting with your audience. When you introduce diverse views and then respectfully demonstrate why you disagree with each of them, you are using **refutation**, the most common strategy for addressing opposing points of view. As you consider opposing points of view, you are likely to discover some you cannot refute, perhaps because they are based in a belief system markedly different from your own. You are also likely to discover that some of those other views have real merit. If you understand the reasons behind opposing viewpoints but remain unconvinced, you will need to demonstrate why.

When you find yourself agreeing with a point that supports another side of an issue, you can benefit from offering a **concession**. By openly admitting that you agree with opponents on one or more specific points, you demonstrate that you are fair-minded and credible (7f(1)). Your concessions also increase the likelihood that your opponents will find merit in parts of your argument.

Whether you agree or disagree with other positions, you must recognize and assess them. It is hard to persuade people to agree with you if you insist that they are entirely wrong. If you admit that they are partially right, they are more likely to admit that you could be partially right as well. In this sense, then, argument involves working with an audience as much as getting them to work with you.

Exercise 3

The following paragraph is the conclusion of an argument written by Tucson writer Debra Hughes shortly after the January 2011 shooting of Representative Gabrielle Giffords and eighteen other people at a local political rally. Hughes's piece connects inflammatory rhetoric with such acts of violence. Write a short analysis of this paragraph in which you note (a) an opposing viewpoint to which she is responding, (b) a refutation she offers to this viewpoint, (c) a concession she makes, and (d) any questions this excerpt raises for you.

[1]Habits are hard to break. [2]Only days after the shooting, Arizona passed laws prohibiting picketing within three hundred feet of any home, cemetery, funeral home, or house of worship before, during, or after a ceremony or burial. [3]As the shooting victims were being laid to rest, a group called Angel Action donned white wings and stood with hundreds of others dressed in white, to shield mourners from potential protests by fanatics, such as the Westboro Baptist Church congregants, who have been disrupting services for US soldiers slain in Iraq and Afghanistan. [4]The Westboro group is emblematic of the flashpoints of opinion and controversy across the land. [5]In the weeks and months ahead, only determined national leadership and conscientious, principled activity and restraint on the part of major media, and on the part of each citizen, can restore humanity and civility to American discourse.

—**DEBRA HUGHES, "The Tucson Shootings: Words and Deeds"**
© 2011. Reprinted by permission.

7f USING THE RHETORICAL APPEALS TO GROUND AN ARGUMENT

Human beings do not form their beliefs or act on the basis of facts or logic alone; if we did, we would all agree and would act accordingly. Scientific findings would stop us from indulging in unhealthy eating, drinking, and smoking; we would never speed or use a cell phone while driving. Our actions and attitudes would change as soon as we learned the facts. But logical reasoning alone is never enough to get anybody to change. If you want your argument to be heard, understood, and even acted on, you need to follow the necessary steps for gaining a fair hearing.

You can shape effective arguments through a combination of persuasive strategies, which include the **rhetorical appeals** of ethos, logos, and pathos. **Ethos** (an ethical appeal) establishes the speaker's or writer's credibility and trustworthiness. An ethical appeal demonstrates goodwill toward the audience, good sense or knowledge of the subject at hand, and good character. Establishing common ground with the audience is another feature of ethos. However, ethos can rarely carry an argument by itself; therefore, you also need to use **logos** (a logical appeal). Logos demonstrates an effective use of reason and judicious use of evidence, whether that evidence consists of facts, statistics, comparisons, anecdotes, expert opinions, or observations. You employ logos when you are supporting claims, drawing reasonable conclusions, and avoiding rhetorical fallacies (7i). But logic may not be sufficient to persuade an audience, unless the audience feels emotionally stirred by the topic under discussion. Therefore, **pathos** (an emotional appeal) involves using language that will connect with the beliefs and feelings of the audience. If you misuse pathos in an attempt to manipulate your audience (as sentimental movies and manipulative speakers often do), your attempt can easily backfire. Still, pathos can be used successfully when it establishes empathy, authentic understanding, and a human connection with the audience. The most effective arguments are those that combine these three persuasive appeals—ethos, logos, and pathos—responsibly and knowledgeably.

In the next three subsections, additional passages from Debra Hughes's "Tucson Shootings: Words and Deeds" illustrate how a writer can use all three of the classical rhetorical appeals.

(1) Ethical appeals

The ethical appeal, ethos, establishes a writer's credibility, moral character, and goodwill. In her introductory paragraphs, Debra Hughes captures the atmosphere of downtown Tucson on the evening of the shootings and demonstrates her knowledge of the day's events, her credibility as a local Tucsonan, and her goodwill toward her readers, who have "their own heavy feelings." She also establishes her thesis.

> The night of the mass shootings in Tucson, a downtown art gallery hosted an already scheduled [exhibition of images] from François Robert's photography series *Stop the Violence* . . . of human bones arranged in the shapes of a handgun, grenade, knife, Kalashnikov, fighter jet, and other symbols of violence, all starkly set on black backgrounds. Those images confronted viewers with their own heavy feelings. That morning six people had been killed and thirteen wounded in the shooting rampage at Gabrielle Giffords's political rally at a local Safeway. Jared Lee Loughner had tried to assassinate the Arizona congresswoman, using a Glock 19 semiautomatic pistol and firing thirty-one rounds into the crowd in about fifteen seconds.
>
> The shooting took place at a small shopping center in my neighborhood. . . . Our bank is there, along with the stores where we mail our packages, buy pastries, toothpaste, and paper towels, and where we regularly

run errands. That morning people had gathered to hear what their state representative had to say. She called the event "Congress at Your Corner."

In the afternoon, . . . Pima County Sheriff Clarence Dupnik, a seventy-five-year-old with the sagging cheeks and drooping eyes of a bulldog, spoke his mind. "People tend to pooh-pooh this business about all the vitriol that we hear inflaming the American public . . . ." He was alluding to talk-show hosts and politicians who use inflammatory rhetoric, and he added that the effect of their words should not be discounted. "That may be free speech, but it's not without consequences." Almost immediately a heated public debate began over whether or not political rhetoric had spurred Jared Lee Loughner to kill.

(2) Logical appeals

Logos, the logical appeal, is considered to be especially trustworthy, as it is rooted in a writer's reliance on reason and supporting evidence (facts, statistics, observations, interviews with authorities, survey results, and so on) to build an argument. Logical appeals, however, need to be examined closely to determine whether facts are accurate, testimony has been considered within its context, and sources are reliable. To help her audience appreciate the connection she's trying to make, Debra Hughes builds on the sheriff's testimony, building her logos with facts, expert opinions, observations, and vivid examples, while recognizing all sides of the controversy. She ends the following excerpt by quoting an obvious (and ironic) logical fallacy:

> Tucson forensic psychologist Dr. Gary Perrin, a professional familiar with violent crime, was asked if a mentally disturbed person might distort strong messages into a belief that violent acts are noble. Perrin replied, "In . . . the past few years, rhetoric has increased. Words are powerful, and certainly words can make a [mentally unstable] person act in a certain way." But he emphasized that violent acts are "situational, and many things contribute. Words can be one of the factors."
>
> . . . Within a week of the shooting a Google search produced 55 million results about the event, including myriad bloggers arguing over free speech. Steven Colbert, on his Comedy Central TV show, aired a segment entitled "The Word: Life, Liberty, and the Pursuit of Angriness," in which he deadpanned, "If incendiary rhetoric isn't connected to the Arizona tragedy, it logically follows that it must be good."

(3) Emotional appeals

Emotional appeals, pathos, stir feelings and help a writer connect with the audience. Although emotional appeals can be manipulative (like unethical appeals to faulty logic or to false authority), they can be used ethically and logically to move the audience to a new way of thinking or acting.

In the following passage, which moves toward her conclusion (see page 151), Debra Hughes continues to use logos while alluding to moderation and personal responsibility, thus evoking feelings that people on all sides of the issue can share.

> The night before Gabrielle Giffords was shot, she sent an email offering congratulations to Kentucky Secretary of State Trey Grayson, . . . [newly] named director of Harvard University's Institute of Politics. . . . "After you get settled, I would love to talk about what we can do to promote centrism and moderation. I am one of twelve Democrats in a GOP district (the only woman) and we need to figure out how to tone our rhetoric and partisanship down." . . .
>
> The Tucson shooting and its aftermath are being followed around the world, especially in places where violence is a problem. Venezuelan magazine editor Sergio Dahbar wrote, "The Giffords shooting is being followed very closely in Latin America because we also have this illness. We have the illness of intolerance." A well-known maxim from Victor Hugo commenting on unrest in France in the 1830s runs, "The guilty one is not he who commits the sin, but the one who causes the darkness."
>
> —DEBRA HUGHES, "The Tucson Shootings: Words and Deeds"

Although ethos is often developed in the introduction to an argument, logos in the body, and pathos in the conclusion, these classical rhetorical appeals can overlap and appear throughout an argument.

7g   TYPES OF ARGUMENTS

All arguments are not alike. Arguments differ in the use of rhetorical appeals, the arrangement of the components, and the reliance on various kinds of reasoning. The most noticeable difference among the different types of argument is the arrangement of their components.

Unless your instructor asks you to demonstrate a particular type of argument, the decisions you make about developing your argument should be based on your topic, your audience, and your purpose. You can develop a good plan by simply listing the major points you want to make (2d), deciding what order to put them in, and then determining where to include refutation or concession (7e(2)). You must also decide whether to place your thesis statement (or claim) at the beginning or the end of your argument. Once you sort out the reasons supporting your claim, you need to develop each reason with a separate paragraph (unless, of course, you are summarizing the reasons in the conclusion).

No matter which type of argument you use, your conclusion should move beyond a mere summary of what has already been stated and instead emphasize your connection with your audience, a connection that reinforces your rhetorical purpose: getting readers to take a particular course of action, to further their understanding, or to accept the implications of your claim (7d). The student paper by Anna Seitz (pages 171–76) ends with a conclusion that not only reinforces her purpose but also links it with the mission of universities.

(1) Classical argument

If your audience has not yet taken a position on your issue, you may want to use a classical argument, which assumes that an audience is prepared to follow a well-reasoned argument. A classical argument takes advantage of the power of the rhetorical appeals in its opening, or introduction, by establishing the writer's ethos; at the same time, it establishes common ground with the audience and introduces the issue. The body of the classical argument relies on the power of logos: it provides background information, introduces the claim (proposition), offers reasons supporting the claim (proof or confirmation), and presents refutation and concession. Where refutation is best located depends largely on the audience. If the audience is familiar with classical arrangement, refutation appears after the proof or confirmation. If not, it is better to first establish common ground and then acknowledge and respond to opposing viewpoints. Finally, classical argument typically closes with a strong appeal to pathos, making an emotional connection with the audience.

FEATURES OF THE CLASSICAL ARRANGEMENT

- **Introduction.** Introduce the issue and capture the attention of the audience. Try using a short narrative or a strong example (2f(2) and 2g). Begin establishing your credibility (using the rhetorical appeal of ethos) and common ground with the audience.

- **Background information.** Provide your audience with a history of the situation and state how things currently stand. Define any key terms. Draw the

(continued on page 156)

(continued from page 155)

attention of your audience to those points that are especially important and explain why they are meaningful.

- **Proposition.** Introduce the position you are taking and outline the basic reasons that support it. Frame your position as a thesis statement or a claim (**2c** and **7d**).

- **Proof or confirmation.** Discuss the reasons that have led you to take your position. Each reason must be clear, relevant, and representative. Provide facts, expert testimony, and any other evidence that supports your claim and demonstrates logos.

- **Refutation.** Recognize and disprove the arguments of people who hold a different position and with whom you continue to disagree.

- **Concession.** Concede any point with which you agree or that has merit; show why this concession does not damage your case.

- **Conclusion.** Summarize your most important points and appeal to your audience's feelings, making a personal connection. Describe the consequences of your argument in a final attempt to connect with your audience (using the emotional appeal of pathos) and encourage your audience to consider (if not commit to) a particular course of action.

(2) Rogerian argument

When you are addressing an audience strongly opposed to your position, you can show that you understand that opposing point of view by using a Rogerian argument. This type of argument derives from the work of psychologist Carl R. Rogers, who believed that many problems are the result of a breakdown in communication. Rogers claimed that people often fail to understand each other because of their natural tendency to judge and evaluate, agree or disagree, before they listen to, let alone understand, what is being said. Thus, Rogers's model for an argument calls for the suspension of judgment (positive or negative) until you are able to restate fairly and accurately what others believe—thereby demonstrating that you understand them. When each person in a conflict demonstrates this ability, the likelihood of misunderstanding is significantly reduced, and that of moving forward together is significantly increased.

Skills such as paraphrasing (**10d(3)**) and summarizing (**10d(4)**) are essential to a Rogerian argument. Although this model can be used to achieve a number of goals, it is especially useful for building consensus.

To demonstrate that you have given fair consideration to the views of others, you begin a Rogerian argument not by refuting those views but by paraphrasing them, demonstrating that you understand the thinking behind them and recognize the value they have. Only then do you introduce your own position, weaving in as much agreed-on information as possible, and explaining why you believe your position has merit. Because the Rogerian model relies on consensus, you conclude your argument by describing how everyone concerned about the issue could benefit from adopting your position. This emphasis on being fair-minded, nonconfrontational, and inclusive gives ethos (**7f(1)**) an essential place in a Rogerian argument.

However, some readers may react negatively to an argument that responds to opposing views before providing any reasons in support of its claim. These readers want to know from the start where an argument is headed. For this reason, writers often alter the Rogerian model by stating their position at the beginning of an argument and offer at least one strong reason to support it before turning to opposing views. They sometimes keep at least one other reason in reserve (often one responsibly appealing to emotion, or pathos), so that they can present it after responding to opposing views, thereby ending with an emphasis on their proof or confirmation.

The summary of benefits with which a Rogerian argument concludes gives you the opportunity to draw together the threads of your argument and appeal to the audience to accept your position. In the following conclusion to an argument for using writing to change the world, notice how the author cites benefits for the natural world and for all people, including terrorists:

> As writers, we can extend the circle of caring to plants and animals, to rivers and oceans and coral reefs. And we can form a caring circle of human beings that includes young and old, rich and poor, gay and straight, the immigrant, the homeless, the emotionally sturdy and the mentally ill, and those in prison, no matter what their religion. I would even include "terrorists" in the circle. They too are human, and can only be properly dealt with if we see them as people with needs, desires, and ideals like ourselves. Ultimately, placing them outside the circle will only hurt all of us. When any humans are dehumanized, we all lose some of our humanity.
>
> —**MARY PIPHER**, *Writing to Change the World*

To write an argument based on the Rogerian models, use the following plan as your guide.

FEATURES OF THE ROGERIAN ARRANGEMENT

- **Introduction.** Establish that you have paid attention to views different from your own, which helps you establish your ethos. Build trust by stating these views clearly and fairly.
- **Concessions.** Reassure the people you hope will adopt your position by showing that you agree with them to some extent, can employ some of their ideas, and thus do not think that they are completely wrong.
- **Thesis.** Having earned the confidence of your audience, state your claim, or proposition.
- **Support.** Explain why you have taken this position and provide support for it, employing logos, the appeal to logic and reason.
- **Conclusion.** Conclude by describing how you, your audience, and other people can benefit from adopting your position; employ pathos to make an emotional connection with the audience. Indicate the extent to which adopting this position will resolve the problem you are addressing. If you are offering a partial solution to a complex problem, concede that further work may be necessary.

(3) Toulmin argument

The Toulmin model, devised by philosopher Stephen Toulmin, defines an *argument* as a logical progression from the **data** (accepted evidence or reasons that support a claim) to the **claim** (a debatable or controversial statement), based on the **warrant** (the underlying assumption, like the major premise). If the warrant is controversial, it requires **backing** (independent support or justification). Writers who draw evidence from what they view as reliable authorities (scientists, researchers, government agencies, and so on) should be able to cite the credentials of those authorities. Writers who base an argument on the law or another written code that has been widely accepted (a university's mission statement, for instance) should be able to cite the exact statute, code, precedent, or regulation in question or even quote it verbatim.

Thus, a Toulmin argument establishes a reasonable relationship among data, the claim, and the warrant, which links the other two components (see Figure 7.1). The following argument demonstrates such a relationship:

Universities should not sell naming rights to buildings because education, not pleasing corporate sponsors, should be the universities' primary goal.

Data	Selling naming rights to buildings makes pleasing the sponsors a top priority.
Claim	Universities should not sell naming rights to buildings.
Warrant	Education is the first priority of universities.

Of course, few arguments are as simple as this example. For instance, universities may view education as their first priority but see the sale of naming rights as a means of supporting that goal. Thus, writers often need to make allowances for exceptions. Qualifiers such as *usually, probably, should,* and *possibly* show the degree of certainty of the conclusion, and rebuttal terms such as *unless* indicate exceptions.

> Because universities seek to promote education rather than business, they **should** avoid selling naming rights to buildings **unless** doing so supports their primary goal of educating students.

When using the Toulmin model to shape your arguments, you may be able to identify the claim, the data, and the qualifiers more easily than the warrant. Like an unstated premise in a syllogism (7h(2)), the warrant is often an assumption whose backing is not presented explicitly. In the example above, the backing is the definition of a university—an institution established to provide higher education. To determine the backing for a warrant in an argument you are writing, trace your thinking back to the assumptions with which you began. As you do so, remember that backing can take different forms—it may be a law or regulation, a belief

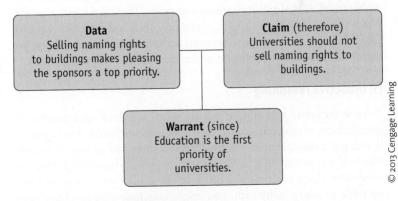

Figure 7.1. A warrant linking data and a claim.

that the data came from a reliable source or that what is true of a sample is true of a larger group, or a widely accepted value.

Exercise 4

Read the editorial pages of several consecutive issues of your school newspaper. Look for editorials that analyze or question an established belief, express or defend an opinion, invite consideration, or try to convince. Choose an editorial that strikes you as well argued, well developed, and well organized—even if it does not change your belief or your action (but perhaps your understanding). Bring several copies of the editorial to class, and be prepared to discuss its purpose, audience, use of rhetorical appeals, and conclusion.

7h REASONING EFFECTIVELY AND ETHICALLY

Although many people believe that successful arguments are always purely logical, such arguments in fact rely on a considered combination of ethical, emotional, and logical components. However, logos (logical reasoning) underpins all ethical and compelling arguments. Logic is a means through which you can develop your ideas, realize new ones, and determine whether your thinking is clear enough to persuade readers to agree with you. Thus, the quality of the logic either enhances or detracts from your overall argument.

(1) Inductive reasoning

You use inductive reasoning every day when you draw on a number of specific facts or observations to reach a logical conclusion. For example, if you get a stomachache within fifteen minutes of eating ice cream, you might conclude that there is a connection. Perhaps you are lactose intolerant. If you clear out the brush by the side of your house and end up with an angry, itchy rash, you might conclude that you have been exposed to poison ivy. This use of evidence to form a generalization is called an **inductive leap**, and the extent of such a leap should be in proportion to the amount of evidence gathered.

Inductive reasoning involves moving (or leaping) from discovering evidence to interpreting it, and it can help you arrive at probable, believable conclusions (but not absolute, enduring truth). Making a small leap from evidence (a stomachache or a rash) to a probable conclusion (lactose intolerance or exposure to poison ivy) is more effective and ethical than using the same evidence to make a sweeping claim that could easily be challenged (ice cream is bad for everyone or no one should clear brush) (**7d(1)**). Generally, the greater the weight of the evidence, the more reliable the conclusion.

When used in argument, inductive reasoning often employs facts (**7c**) and examples (**2f(2)**). When writers cannot cite all the information that supports their conclusions, they choose the evidence that is most reliable and most closely related to the point they are making.

(2) Deductive reasoning

You also use deductive reasoning daily, whenever you apply a generalization (or generalized belief) to series of specific cases. For instance, if you believe that you are lactose intolerant, you will decline offers of milk, ice cream, cheese, and any other food that contains lactose. At the heart

11-5 ©2003 WM. HOEST ENTERPRISES, INC. Distributed by King Features Syndicate.

"IF IGNORANCE IS BLISS, LEROY, WHY AREN'T YOU HAPPIER?"

LOCKHORNS © 2003 WM HOEST ENTERPRISES, INC. KING FEATURES SYNDICATE

wmhoest@aol.com

Mrs. Lockhorn has worked out a deductive argument relating her husband's alleged ignorance to his not-yet-realized state of bliss, but her reasoning is flawed.

of a deductive argument is a **major premise** (a generalized belief that is assumed to be true), which the writer applies to a specific case (the **minor premise**), thereby yielding a conclusion, or claim. For example, if you know that all doctors must complete a residency and that Imogen is in medical school, then you can conclude that Imogen must complete a residency. This argument can be expressed in a three-part structure called a **syllogism.**

Major premise	All doctors must complete a residency. [generalized belief]
Minor premise	Imogen is studying to become a doctor. [specific case]
Conclusion	Imogen must complete a residency. [claim]

Sometimes the premise is not stated, for the simple reason that the writer assumes that an audience shares the belief.

> Imogen has graduated from medical school, so she must complete a residency.

In this sentence, the unstated premise is that all doctors must complete a residency. A syllogism with an unstated premise—or even an unstated conclusion—is called an **enthymeme**. Frequently found in written arguments, enthymemes can be very effective because they presume shared beliefs or knowledge. For example, the argument "The college needs to build a new dormitory because the present overcrowded dorms are unsafe" contains the unstated premise that the college has a responsibility to reduce unsafe conditions.

7i AVOIDING RHETORICAL FALLACIES

Logical reasoning fortifies the overall effectiveness of an argument as well as builds the ethos of the speaker or writer. Constructing an argument effectively means avoiding errors in logic known as **rhetorical fallacies**, which weaken an argument as well as the writer's ethos. These fallacies signal to your audience that your thinking is not entirely trustworthy and that your argument is not well reasoned or researched.

Therefore, you need to recognize and avoid several kinds of rhetorical fallacies. As you read the arguments of others (9a) and revise the arguments you draft (Chapter 3), keep the following common fallacies in mind.

(1) Non sequitur

A *non sequitur,* the basis for most of the other rhetorical fallacies, attempts to make a connection where none actually exists (the phrase is Latin for "it does not follow"). Just because the first part of a statement is true does not mean that the second part is true, will become true, or will necessarily happen.

> **Faulty**   Heather is married and will start a family soon.

This assertion is based on the faulty premise that *all* women have children soon after marrying (7h(2)).

(2) Ad hominem

The *ad hominem* fallacy refers to a personal attack that draws attention away from the issue under consideration (the Latin phrase translates to "toward the man himself").

> **Faulty**   With his penchant for expensive haircuts, that candidate cannot relate to the common people.

The fact that a candidate pays a lot for a haircut may say something about his vanity but says nothing about his political appeal. When private or personal information about political candidates is used in criticizing them, the focus is on the person, not the political issues in play.

(3) Appeal to tradition

The appeal to tradition argues that because things have always been done a certain way, they should continue that way. Assuming a mother will stay home and take care of children or that a father will be the sole breadwinner is an appeal to tradition.

> **Faulty**   Because they are a memorable part of the pledge process, fraternity hazings should not be banned.

Times change; what was considered good practice in the past is not necessarily considered acceptable now.

Maiming and pillaging have a long history, but that does not mean they should continue.

(4) Bandwagon

The bandwagon fallacy argues that everyone is doing, saying, or thinking something, so you should, too. It makes an irrelevant and disguised appeal to the human desire to be part of a group.

Faulty   Everyone uses cell phones while driving, so why won't you answer my calls?

Even if the majority of people talk on the phone while driving, doing so has proven to be dangerous. The majority is not automatically right.

(5) Begging the question

The begging-the-question fallacy presents the conclusion as though it were a major premise. What is assumed to be fact actually needs to be proved.

Faulty   If we get rid of the current school board, we will see an end to all the school district's problems.

Any connection between the current school board and the school district's problems has not been established.

(6) Equivocation

The rhetorical fallacy of equivocation falsely relies on the use of one word or concept in two different ways.

Faulty   Today's students are illiterate; they do not know the characters in Shakespeare's plays.

The major premise about penguins is true, but it does not relate to the minor premise about old television shows, let alone lead to the conclusion.

Traditionally, *literacy* has meant knowing how to read and write, how to function in a print-based culture. Knowing about Shakespeare's characters is not the equivalent of literacy; someone lacking this special kind of knowledge might be characterized as uneducated or uninformed but not as illiterate.

(7) False analogy

A false analogy assumes that because two things are alike in some ways, they are alike in others as well.

> **Faulty**   The United States lost credibility with other nations during the war in Vietnam, so we should not get involved in the Middle East, or we will lose credibility again.

The differences between the war in Southeast Asia in the 1960s and 1970s and the current conflict in the Middle East may well be greater than their similarities.

(8) False authority (or appeal to authority)

The fallacy of false authority assumes that an expert in one field is credible in another. Every time you see a movie star selling cosmetics, a sports figure selling shirts, or a talk-show host selling financial advice, you are the target of an appeal to authority.

Faulty   We must stop sending military troops into Iran, as Zack de la Rocha has argued.

De la Rocha's membership in the politically engaged band Rage Against the Machine does not qualify him as an expert in foreign policy.

(9) False cause

Sometimes called *post hoc, ergo propter hoc* (meaning "after this, so because of this"), the fallacy of false cause is the assumption that because one event follows another, the first is the cause of the second.

Faulty   If police officers did not have to carry carry guns and batons as part of their job, there would be no incidents of violence by off-duty officers.

The assumption is that because police officers carry weapons, they use those weapons indiscriminately. Making such a connection is like announcing that you are not going to wash your car any more because every time you do, it rains (as though a clean car causes rain).

(10) False dilemma

Sometimes called the *either/or fallacy*, a false dilemma is a statement that only two alternatives exist, when in fact there are more than two.

Faulty   We must either build more nuclear power plants or be completely dependent on foreign oil.

Other possibilities for generating energy without using foreign oil exist.

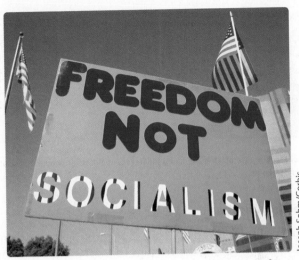

This sign exemplifies a false dilemma, as though only two alternatives exist when, in reality, there are more than two.

(11) Guilt by association

An unfair attempt to besmirch a person's credibility by linking that person with untrustworthy people or suspicious actions is the fallacy of guilt by association.

Faulty   You should not vote for her for class treasurer because her mother was arrested for shoplifting last year.

The mother's behavior should not be held against the daughter.

(12) Hasty generalization

A hasty generalization is a conclusion based on too little evidence or on exceptional or biased evidence.

Faulty   Ellen is a poor student because she failed her first history test.

Ellen's performance may improve in the weeks ahead. Furthermore, she may be doing well in her other subjects.

Without careful thinking, we often make hasty judgments about other people, especially about those who are not like us.

(13) Oversimplification

A statement or argument that implies a single cause or solution for a complex problem, leaving out relevant considerations and complications, relies on the oversimplification fallacy.

Faulty   We can eliminate unwanted pregnancies by teaching birth control and abstinence.

Teaching people about birth control and abstinence does not guarantee the elimination of unwanted pregnancies.

(14) Red herring

Sometimes called *ignoring the question*, the red herring fallacy dodges the real issue by drawing attention to a seemingly related but irrelevant one.

Faulty   Why worry about violence in schools when we ought to be worrying about international terrorism?

International terrorism has no direct relationship with school violence.

(15) Slippery slope

The slippery slope fallacy assumes that one thing will inevitably lead to another—that if one thing is allowed, it will be the first step in a downward spiral.

Faulty   Handgun control will lead to a police state.

Handgun control has not led to a police state in England.

"It started out with lactose, but now he's intolerant of everything."

Applying a slippery slope argument, this cartoon suggests that lactose intolerance leads to general intolerance.

Be alert for rhetorical fallacies in your writing. When you find such a fallacy, be sure to moderate your claim, clarify your thinking, or, if necessary, eliminate the fallacious statement. Even if your argument as a whole is convincing, rhetorical fallacies can damage your credibility (**9a**).

Exercise 5

For each of the following statements, write one or two sentences in which you identify and explain the faulty reasoning. Next, rewrite each statement so that it avoids rhetorical fallacies.

1. The university must either build more classrooms or admit fewer new students.

2. If we censor neo-Nazi demonstrations, we will ultimately lose freedom of speech.

3. If more women had advanced degrees, they would break through the glass ceiling.

4. If the government cuts social services, people on welfare will try harder to get jobs.

5. Our nation's children would not be fighting obesity if they watched less television.

7j   SAMPLE ARGUMENT

The following argumentative essay was Anna Seitz's response to an assignment asking her to identify a specific problem in her living quarters, on her campus, in her town, or in the world at large and then recommend a solution for that problem. As you read Anna's essay (which she formatted according to MLA guidelines; see Chapter **12**), consider how she argued her case and whether she argued effectively. Note her use of the rhetorical appeals (ethos, logos, and pathos) and classical arrangement and her inductive reasoning. Also, identify the kinds of evidence she uses (facts, examples, testimony, and authority).

Seitz 1

Anna Seitz

Professor Byerly

Library Science 313

30 November 2007

Naming Opportunities: Opportunities for Whom?

All over the nation, football stadiums, business schools, law schools, dining halls, and even coaching positions have become naming opportunities (also known as "naming rights" and "legacy opportunities"). Since 1979, when Syracuse University signed a deal with the Carrier Corporation for lifetime naming rights to its sports stadium—the Carrier Dome—naming has become a common practice with an alleged twofold payoff: universities raise money and donors get their names writ large. Universities use the money obtained from naming opportunities to hire more faculty, raise salaries, and support faculty research. Reser Stadium (Oregon State), The Donald Bren School of Law (University of California–Irvine), or the Malloy Paterno Head Football Coach Endowment (Penn State University)—all these naming opportunities seem like a good solution for raising money, especially at a time when state legislatures have cut back on university funding and when wealthy alumni are being besieged for donations from every college they have ever attended. Naming opportunities seem like a good solution for donors, too, because their donations will be broadly recognized. While naming opportunities may seem like a perfect solution for improving colleges and universities and simplifying funding, in reality they are not. In this paper, I argue against naming opportunities on college and

The writer's last name and the page number appear as the running head on each page of the paper.

In her introduction (the first paragraph), the writer uses concrete examples to catch her readers' attention and set up her argument.

The last sentence in the first paragraph is the thesis statement.

Seitz 2

university campuses because they create more problems than they solve.

The naming of sports stadiums is a familiar occurrence. But naming opportunities in other spheres of academic life are unfamiliar to most people, even though such naming is an established practice. A quick search of the Web pages of university libraries reveals that many of them, especially those in the midst of major development campaigns, have created a price list just for naming opportunities. Entire buildings are available, of course. For example, a $5 million donation earns the right to name the music library at Northwestern University (Northwestern). But parts of buildings are also available these days. North Carolina State University will name an atlas stand according to the donor's wishes for only $7,500 or put a specific name on a lectern for $3,500 (North Carolina).

Naming opportunities can clearly bring in a good deal of money. It has become commonplace for schools to offer naming opportunities on planned construction in exchange for 51 percent of the cost of the building! That's a big head start to a building project, and naming opportunities may be what allow some schools to provide their students with better facilities than their counterparts that do not offer naming opportunities. In fact, donors are often recruited for the opportunity to pay for named faculty chairs, reading rooms, or major library or art collections—all of which enhance student life.

Clearly the more opportunities and resources any university can offer current and potential students and even alumni, the more that university enhances its own growth and that of its faculty. Library donors and recipients say that if it is possible for a library to pay for a new computer lab just by

The writer provides background information in the second, third, and fourth paragraphs.

The writer's use of specific information helps establish her ethos as knowledgeable and trustworthy.

The writer's use of the phrase *enhance student life* at the end of third paragraph demonstrates an effort to establish common ground with her readers.

Seitz 3

adding a sign with someone's name over the door, the advantages often seem to outweigh the disadvantages. Proponents of naming opportunities point out that small donors are often hailed as library supporters, even when big donors are maligned as corporate flag-wavers.

Few would argue that these donations necessarily detract from the educational mission of the institution. However, selling off parts of a university library, for example, does not always please people, especially those whose responsibility includes managing that donation. The curator of rare books and manuscripts at a prominent state university told me that one of the most frustrating parts of her job is dealing with "strings-attached" gifts, which is what too many library donations turn out to be. Some major donors like to make surprise visits, during which they monitor the prominence of their "legacy opportunity." Others like to create rules which limit the use of their funds to the purchase of certain collections or subjects; still others just need constant personal maintenance, including lunches, coffees, and regular invitations to events. But this meddling after the fact is just a minor inconvenience compared to some donors' actions.

Donors who fund an ongoing educational program and who give money on a regular basis often expect to have regular input. Because major donors want major prestige, they try to align themselves with successful programs. Doing that can result in damage to university budgets. First of all, high-profile programs can become increasingly well funded, while less prominent, less glamorous ones are continually ignored. Second, when corporate or private funds are regularly available, existing funding sources can erode. Simply put, if a budgeted program

The writer lays out specific opposing arguments without losing her focus on her own argument or alienating her readers. She is maintaining her ethos while using logos.

The writer's refutation of opposing arguments is fair-minded.

This paragraph and the next introduce the proposition.

The writer uses cause-and-consequence analysis in these paragraphs to support her thesis.

Seitz 4

becomes funded by donation, the next time the program needs funding, the department or unit will likely be told that finding a donor is its only option. Essentially, once donor-funded, always donor-funded.

Additionally, many academics believe that selling off naming rights can create an image problem for a university. While buildings, schools, endowed chairs, even football stadiums were once named for past professors, university presidents, or others with strong ties to the university, those same facilities are now named for virtually anyone who can afford to donate, especially corporations. Regular input from a corporation creates the appearance of a conflict of interest in a university, which is exactly the reason such arrangements are so often vehemently opposed by the university community. Boise State University in Idaho received such negative press for negotiating a deal with labor-unfriendly Taco Bell that it was finally pressured to terminate the $4 million contract (Langrill 1).

This paragraph provides the proof, or confirmation. Here the writer describes a reasonable middle ground, a way to encourage endowments, enhance student life, and protect the integrity of the university.

Given these drawbacks, many universities are establishing guidelines for the selection of appropriate donors for named gifts. To that end, fundraising professional and managing director of Changing Our World, Inc. Robert Hoak suggests that naming opportunities should be mutually beneficial for the donor (whether a corporation or an individual) and the university and that these opportunities should be viewed as the start of a long-term relationship between the two. Additionally, he cautions that even if the donor seems the right fit for the organization, it is in the best interest of both parties to add an escape clause to the contract in order to protect either side from potential embarrassment or scandal.

Seitz 5

He provides the example of Seton Hall University, which regrettably had both an academic building and the library rotunda named for Tyco CEO Dennis Kozlowski. When Kozlowski was convicted of grand larceny, the university pulled the names (Hoak).

Although many people prefer that naming be an honor given to recognize an accomplished faculty member or administrator, most realize that recruiting major donors is good business. Whether it is "good education" is another question. Naming university property for major donors is not a recent phenomenon. New College in Cambridge, Massachusetts was just that—until local clergyman John Harvard died and left half his estate and his entire library to what would soon become Harvard College. Modern naming opportunities, however, do not necessarily recognize and remember individuals who had significant influence on university life; rather, they create obligations for the university to operate in such a way as to please living donors or their descendants. Pleasing wealthy donors should not replace educating students as a university's primary goal.

Although the writer uses the final paragraph for a refutation of opposing arguments, she also emphasizes her common ground with her readers.

The conclusion repeats the writer's main point.

Seitz 6

Works Cited

Hoak, Robert. "Making the Most of Naming Opportunities." *onPhilanthropy*.

   Changing Our World, 28 Mar. 2003. Web. 5 Nov. 2007.

Langrill, Chereen. "BSU Faculty Says 'No Quiero' to Taco Bell." *Idaho

   Statesman* [Boise] 27 Oct. 2004: 1+. Print.

North Carolina State University Libraries. "NCSU Libraries East Wing

   Renovation: Naming Opportunities." *NCSU Libraries*. North Carolina

   State U, n.d. Web. 5 Nov. 2007. <http://www.lib.ncsu.edu/renovation/

   namingOp/>.

Northwestern University Library. "Making a Gift: Naming Opportunities."

   Naming Opportunities: Library Development Office. Northwestern U,

   2007. Web. 20 Nov. 2007.

Exercise 6

Reread Anna Seitz's essay and identify what you consider to be her values. Which ones does she reveal as she argues against naming opportunities? What personal experiences might have shaped those values?

RESEARCH

inhauscreative/Stockphoto.com

8 | FINDING SOURCES ONLINE, IN PRINT, AND IN THE FIELD

When research is part of a writing assignment, students sometimes ask, "Why do we have to do research? Why can't we just use our own opinions?" A personal opinion is a good starting point, but research can help you broaden and even challenge your initial perspective. For example, you might believe that students should not use credit cards because they may spend more money than they can afford. When doing research on student credit-card use, you could be tempted to use only those sources that support your belief and perhaps reveal other disadvantages of credit-card use. However, if you keep an open mind, you might find out how some students manage to use credit cards wisely. Doing research is a way of joining a larger conversation on a topic—a conversation that often holds surprises.

This chapter will help you

- use the rhetorical situation to frame your research (**8a**),
- find online sources (**8b**),
- find books (**8c**),
- find articles (**8d**), and
- conduct field research (**8e**).

8a | RESEARCH AND THE RHETORICAL SITUATION

To make the most of the time you spend doing research, think carefully about your rhetorical situation early in the research process. Identifying your research question and understanding your rhetorical opportunity, audience, and purpose will allow you to gather relevant sources efficiently.

(1) Identifying a research question

The starting point for any writing project is the rhetorical opportunity—the issue or problem that has prompted you to write. For research assignments, it is helpful to turn the issue or problem into a question that can guide your research. This question will help you choose relevant articles, books, and other materials. Research questions often arise when you try to relate what you are studying for a course to your own experience. For instance, you may start wondering about voting regulations while reading about past elections for a history class and, at the same time, noticing news stories about the role technology plays in current elections or the unfair practices reported in some states. Each of these observations, however, may give rise to a different question. Focusing on the influence of technology may prompt you to ask, "What are the possible consequences of having only electronic ballots?" However, if you focus on unfair voting practices, you may ask, "How do voting procedures differ from state to state?" Because you can ask a variety of research questions about any topic, choose the one that interests you the most and also allows you to fulfill the assignment.

To generate research questions, you may find it helpful to ask yourself about causes, consequences, processes, definitions, or values, as in the following examples:

Questions about causes

What are the causes of low achievement in our schools?

What causes power outages in large areas of the country?

Questions about consequences

What are the consequences of taking antidepressants for a long time?

How might stronger gun control laws affect the frequency of public shootings?

Questions about processes

How can music lovers prevent corporations from controlling the development of new music?

How are presidential campaigns funded?

Questions about definitions

How do you know if you are addicted to something?

What is the opportunity gap in the American educational system?

Questions about values

Should the result of a parental DNA test be the deciding factor in a custody case?

Would the construction of wind farms be detrimental to the environment?

If you have trouble coming up with a research question, you may need a jump start. The following tips can help you.

TIPS FOR FINDING A RESEARCH QUESTION

- What rhetorical opportunity (problem or issue) presented in one of your classes would you like to address?
- What have you observed recently (on television, in the newspaper, on campus, or online) that piqued your curiosity?
- What widely discussed local or national problem would you like to help solve?
- Is there anything that you find unusual or intriguing and would like to explore? Consider lifestyles, fashion trends, political views, and current news stories.

Research and writing require a commitment of time and effort. You will find these tasks more pleasant, even easier, if you first share your ideas with others. To start a conversation about your research ideas, have a friend or classmate ask you the following questions. If no one is available, sharpen your ideas by *writing* answers to these questions.

- Why is it important for you to answer this research question?
- Why is it important for your audience to know the answer to the question?
- Why does the answer to your question require research?
- What types of research might help you answer your question?
- Will you be able to carry out the necessary research in the amount of time allowed?

Exercise 1

Each of the following subjects would need to be narrowed down for a research paper. To experiment with framing a research question, compose two questions about each subject that could be answered in a ten-page paper (refer to the list on pages 180–81 for examples of questions).

1. college education
2. water supply
3. environment
4. extreme sports
5. body image
6. social networking

(2) Conducting research with your audience and purpose in mind

Your audience and your purpose are interconnected. In general terms, your purpose is to have an impact on your audience; in more specific terms, your purpose may be to entertain your readers, to inform them, to explain something to them, or to persuade them to do something. Research can help you achieve any of these goals.

A research paper often has one of the following rhetorical purposes.

- *To inform an audience.* The researcher reports current thinking on a specific topic, including opposing views, without analyzing them or siding with a particular position.

  Example   To inform an audience about current nutritional guidelines for children

- *To analyze and synthesize information and then offer possible solutions.* The researcher analyzes a topic and synthesizes the available information about it, looking for points of agreement and disagreement as well as gaps in coverage. Thus, part of the research consists of finding out what other researchers have written about the topic. After presenting the analysis and synthesis, the researcher sometimes offers possible ways to address any problems found.

  Example   To analyze and synthesize various proposals for alternative energy sources

- *To convince or issue an invitation to an audience.* The researcher states a position and supports it with data, statistics, examples, testimony, or relevant experience. The researcher's purpose is to persuade or invite readers to take the same position.

  Example   To persuade people to support a political candidate

A researcher presenting results from an original experiment or study must often achieve all of these purposes. In the introduction of a lab report, for example, the researcher analyzes and synthesizes previous work done on the same topic and locates a research niche—an area needing further study. The researcher then attempts to convince the readers that his or her current study will help address the need for more research. The body of the report is informative: it describes the materials used, explains the procedures followed, and presents the results. In the conclusion, the researcher may try, based on the results of the experiment or study, to persuade the audience to take some action (for example, give up smoking, eat fewer carbohydrates, or fund future research).

(3) Preparing a working thesis

At some point during the research process, you may find it beneficial to state a **working thesis**—essentially, an answer to your question, which you will test against the research you do. Because you form a working thesis during the early stages of writing, you will need to revise it during later stages. Note how the following research question, working thesis, and final thesis statement differ:

  Research question: What is happiness?

  Working thesis: Being happy is more than feeling cheerful.

  Final thesis statement: Although most people think of cheerfulness when they hear the word *happiness*, they should not exclude contentment and confidence.

Clearly, each successive version becomes more specific.

(4) Using primary and secondary sources

As you proceed with research, be aware of whether your sources are primary or secondary. **Primary sources** for researching topics in the humanities are generally documents such as archived letters, records, and papers, as well as literary, autobiographical, and philosophical texts. In the social sciences, primary sources may be field observations, case histories, or survey data. In the natural sciences, primary sources may be field observations, measurements, discoveries, or experimental results. **Secondary sources** are commentaries on primary sources. For example, a review of a new novel is a secondary source, as is a discussion of adolescence based on survey data. Experienced researchers usually consult both primary and secondary sources.

Compare the following excerpts. The first is from a primary source, a book published in 1789. The second, which comments on that book, is from a secondary source, a book published in 2010. (The superscript numbers in the second excerpt direct readers to bibliographic information at the end of the book.)

Primary source

Now private ethics has happiness for its end: and legislation can have no other. Private ethics concerns every member, that is, the happiness and the actions of every member, of any community that can be proposed; and legislation can concern no more.

—JEREMY BENTHAM, *The Principles of Morals and Legislation*

Secondary source

One writer, Jeremy Bentham, gained enduring fame through his pronouncement that the overriding aim of government should be to secure the greatest happiness of the greatest number of people by maximizing pleasures and minimizing pain.[10] In his more optimistic passages, he wrote about a science of happiness, a "felicific calculus" by which governments could measure the expected pleasures and pains resulting from policy proposals and choose the one that would produce the greatest net happiness.[11]   —DEREK BOK, *The Politics of Happiness*

If you were writing about Bentham and decided to quote him, using a quotation you found in Bok's book, you would have to cite Bok's book as an indirect source (see the style guidelines for citing and documenting indirect sources on pages 261 [Modern Language Association], 343 [American Psychological Association], and 409 [the *Chicago Manual of Style*]).

8b | FINDING ONLINE SOURCES

You are probably well acquainted with search engines such as Google and Bing. Unlike these search engines, **subject directories** are collections of Internet sources arranged topically. They include categories such as "Arts," "Health," and "Education." Researchers often find subject directories easier to use than search engines because most of the irrelevant Internet sites have been weeded out. Some useful subject directories for academic and professional research are Academic Info, Internet Public Library, and WWW Virtual Library.

Although searching the Internet is a popular research technique, it is not the only technique you should use. Search engines cover only the portion of the Internet that allows free access. You will not find library books or database materials through an Internet search because library and database services are available only to paid subscribers (students fall into this category).

> ### ❶ CAUTION
>
> AllTheWeb, AltaVista, Ask, Bing, Google, Yahoo!, and other search engines list both reliable and unreliable sources. Choose only sources that have been written and reviewed by experts (see Chapter 9). Entries in *Wikipedia* include links to useful information, but avoid using *Wikipedia* itself, or any other wiki, as a research source. Because nonexperts can write or alter entries, the information on a wiki is not considered reliable.

(1) Keeping track of online sources

As you click from link to link, you can keep track of your location by looking at the **URL (uniform resource locator)** at the top of the screen. These addresses generally include the server name, domain name, directory (and perhaps subdirectory) name, file name, and file type.

When you click on a link, you sometimes end up on a totally different website, so be sure to check the server and domain names when you are unsure of your location. If you find that a URL of a site you are looking for has changed (which is likely if a site is regularly updated), you may still be able to find the site by dropping the last part of the address and trying again. You may need to do this several times. If this strategy does not work, you can also run a search or look at the links on related websites.

A convenient way to keep track of any useful website you find is to create a **bookmark**—a record of a URL that allows you to go to the website with one click. The bookmarking function of a browser can usually be opened by selecting Bookmarks or Favorites on the brower's main menu bar.

Because sites change and even disappear, scholarly organizations such as the Modern Language Association (Chapter 12) require that bibliographic entries for websites include both the **access date** (the date on which the site was visited) and the **publication date** (the date when the site was published or last modified). When you print out material from the Internet, the access date usually appears at the top or bottom of the printout. The publication date generally appears on the site itself. Keeping a separate record of this information can help you when you need to verify information on a site or list it in a bibliography. If a site does not have a publication date, note that it is undated; doing so will establish that you did not accidentally omit a piece of information.

(2) Finding US government documents

If you need information on particular federal laws, court cases, or population statistics, US government documents may be your best sources. You can find these documents by using online databases such as Congressional Universe, MARCIVE, LexisNexis Academic, and STAT-USA. In addition, the following websites may be helpful:

FedStats	www.fedstats.gov
FirstGov	www.firstgov.gov
US Government Printing Office	www.gpoaccess.gov
US Courts	www.uscourts.gov
FedWorld	www.fedworld.gov

(3) Finding images

If your rhetorical situation calls for the use of images, the Internet offers you billions from which to choose. However, if an image you choose is copyrighted, you need to contact the author, artist, or designer for permission to use it. Figure 8.1 is an example of an image with a caption and a credit line, which signifies that the image is used with permission. You do not need to obtain permission to use

Figure 8.1. Genetically modified foods look like naturally produced foods. (Photo © Tom Grill/ Getty Images)

images that are in the public domain (meaning that they are not copyrighted) or those that are cleared for reuse.

Many search engines allow you to search for images. Collections of specific types of images are also available at the following Internet sites:

Advertisements

Ad*Access   scriptorium.lib.duke.edu/adaccess

Adflip   www.adflip.com

Art

Artchive   www.artchive.com

The Web Gallery of Art   www.wga.hu

Clip art

Microsoft Office   microsoft.office.com

Clipart.com   www.clipart.com

Photography

National Geographic   photography.nationalgeographic.com

Smithsonian Images   smithsonianimages.com

8c | FINDING BOOKS

Three types of books are commonly used in the research process. **Scholarly books** are written by experts to advance knowledge of a certain subject. Most include original research. Before being published, these books are reviewed by scholars in the same field as the author(s). **Trade books** are also written by experts or scholars and often by journalists or freelance writers as well. Authors of trade books write to inform a general audience of research that has been done by others. **Reference books** such as encyclopedias and dictionaries provide factual information in short articles or entries written and reviewed by experts in the field. The audience for these books includes both veteran scholars and those new to a field of study.

(1) Locating sources through an online catalog

The easiest way to find books related to your research question is to consult your library's online catalog, doing either a keyword search or a subject search. To perform a **keyword search**, choose a word or phrase that you think might be found in the title of a book or in notes in the catalog's records. Some online catalogs allow users to be quite specific. Figure 8.2 shows the keyword search page Marianna Suslin used to begin researching her paper on genetically modified foods (12c). Notice that it allows a user to list a number of related items and to specify a library (Penn State has more than one), a language, the type of material desired (periodicals, books, or archival materials, for example), publication date(s), and the way the results should be organized.

By inserting into the keyword search box a word or part of a word followed by asterisks, you can find all sources that include that root, even when suffixes have been added. For example, if you entered *environment***, your search would yield not only sources with *environment* in the title, subject headings, and content notes but also sources with *environments, environmental,* or *environmentalist* in those locations. This search technique is called **truncation**.

Figure 8.2. Keyword search page from a university library's website.

The keyword search page at most libraries also allows the user to select a **logical** (or **Boolean**) **operator**—*and, or,* or *not.* These words narrow or broaden an electronic search.

LOGICAL OPERATORS

The words *and, or,* and *not* are the most common logical operators. However, online catalogs and periodical databases have various instructions for using them. If you have trouble following the guidelines presented here, check the instructions for the particular search box you are using.

and   narrows a search (Entering "genetically modified **and** food" returns only those records that contain both keywords.)

or   broadens a search (Entering "genetically modified **or** food" finds all records that contain information about either keyword.)

not   excludes specific items (Entering "genetically modified **and** food **not** humans" excludes any records that mention genetic modification of human beings.)

Although you will probably begin your research by using keyword searches, you may employ **subject searches** as well. To perform a successful subject search, you need to enter words that correspond to the subject categories established by the Library of Congress. You can try entering words familiar to you; if the search does not yield any results, ask a reference librarian for a subject-heading guide. Author searches and title searches can also be useful, though only when you already have a particular author or title in mind.

Once you find the online catalog record for a book you would like to use, write down its **call number**. This number appears on the book itself and indicates where the book is shelved. The online record will reveal the status of the book, letting you know whether it is currently checked out or has been moved to a special collection. To find the book, consult the key to your library's shelving system, usually posted throughout the library. Library staff can also help you find books.

(2) Locating specialized reference books

A specialized encyclopedia or dictionary can often provide background information about people, events, and concepts related to the topic you are researching. To find such sources using a library's search page, enter the type of reference book and one or two keywords identifying your topic. For example, entering "encyclopedia of alcoholism" resulted in the following list of titles:

Encyclopedia of Drugs, Alcohol, and Addictive Behavior

Encyclopedia of Drugs and Alcohol

The Encyclopedia of Alcoholism

USEFUL REFERENCE BOOKS

For a detailed list of reference books and a short description of each, consult *Guide to Reference Books* and *American Reference Books Annual* (*ARBA*). A few widely used reference books are listed here.

Specialized Dictionaries and Encyclopedias

Dictionary of American History

Dictionary of Art

Encyclopedia of Bioethics

Encyclopedia of Higher Education

Encyclopedia of Psychology

Collections of Biographies

American National Biography
Dictionary of Literary Biography
Dictionary of Scientific Biography
Notable American Women
Who's Who in America

(3) Consulting books not listed in a library's online catalog

If you cannot find a particular book in your school's library, you have several options. Frequently, library websites have links to the catalogs of other libraries. By using such links, you can determine whether another library has the book you want and order it directly from that library or through the interlibrary loan service. In addition, your library may offer access to the database WorldCat, which locates books as well as images, sound recordings, and other materials.

Exercise 2

Choose a research question, perhaps one you composed in Exercise 1. Find the titles of a scholarly book, a trade book, and a reference book related to your choice.

8d   FINDING ARTICLES

Because articles offer information that is often more recent than that found in books, they can be crucial to your research. Articles can be found in various **periodicals** (publications that appear at regular intervals). **Scholarly journals** contain reports of original research written by experts for an academic audience. **Professional** (or **trade**) **magazines** feature articles written by staff writers or industry specialists who address on-the-job concerns. **Popular magazines** and **newspapers**, generally written by staff writers, carry a combination of news stories that attempt to be objective and essays that reflect the opinions of editors or guest contributors. The following are examples of the various types of periodicals:

Scholarly journals: *The Journal of Developmental Psychology, The Journal of Business Communication*

Trade magazines: *Farm Journal, Automotive Weekly*

Magazines (news): *Time, Newsweek*

Magazines (public affairs): *The New Yorker, National Review*

Magazines (special interest): *National Geographic, Discover*

Newspapers: *The New York Times, The Washington Post*

A library's online catalog lists the titles of periodicals; however, it does not provide the titles of individual articles within these periodicals. The best strategy for finding print articles is to use an **electronic database**, which is a collection of articles compiled by a company that indexes them according to author, title, date, subject, keywords, and other features. The electronic databases available in libraries are sometimes called **database subscription services**, **licensed databases**, or **aggregated databases.**

A database search will generally yield an **abstract**, a short summary of an article. By scanning the abstract, you can determine whether to locate the complete text of the article, which can often be downloaded and printed. You can access your library's databases by using its computers or, if you have a password, by linking from a remote computer. College libraries subscribe to a wide variety of database services, but the following carry articles on the widest range of topics: EBSCO Academic Search Complete, LexisNexis Academic, JSTOR, and CQ Researcher. You may also be able to search databases that focus on a single field, for example, ERIC for education and PsycINFO for psychology.

Your school's library is likely to provide access to a number of databases. To find those related to your research, go to the library's database search page and enter a word or a part of a word that might be in the titles of relevant databases. You may also find relevant databases by entering a description, category, type, or database vendor. During her research on genetically modified foods, Marianna Suslin inserted "food" in the title box and selected "Agriculture + Biology" as a category (see the boxes at the left of the screen in Figure 8.3).

Figure 8.3. A database search page from a university's website.

Most database search pages also allow you to view an alphabetical listing of the various databases available. If you were using such a list of databases to research the status of genetically modified foods in the United States, as Marianna did for her paper (12c), you could select Agropedia (agriculture encyclopedias), Consumer Health, or Engineered Materials. To research tattooing trends, as Rachel L. Pinter and Sarah M. Cronin did for their paper (14c), you could select PsycARTICLES or Social Sciences Citation Index.

TIPS FOR CONDUCTING A DATABASE SEARCH

■ Identify keywords that clearly represent the topic.

■ Determine the databases you want to search.

■ Perform your search, using logical operators (8c(1)).

(continued on page 194)

(continued from page 193)

- Refine your search strategy if the first search returns too many or too few citations or (worse) irrelevant ones.
- Download and print the relevant articles or save them to a folder you have created for your research project.
- Be sure that the name of the database is on the printout or electronic copy. If it is not, jot down the name so that you will have it when you prepare your bibliography.

Exercise 3

Choose a research question, perhaps one from Exercise 1. Find the titles of a scholarly article, a magazine article, and a newspaper article related to your choice.

Exercise 4

Perform a database search and an Internet search, using the same keywords for each. Print the first screen of the hits (results) you get for each type of search. Compare the two printouts, describing how the results of the two searches differ.

8e   FIELD RESEARCH

Although much of your research will be done in a library or online, you may also find it helpful to conduct **field research**—to gather information in a natural setting. Interviews, questionnaires, and observations are the most common methods for such research.

(1) Interviewing an expert

After you have consulted articles, books, or other sources on your topic, you may find that you still have questions that might best be answered by someone who has firsthand experience in the area you are researching—a teacher, government official, business owner, or other person who may be able to provide the information you are seeking. If your assignment calls for an expert, be sure the person you contact has educational or professional credentials in the relevant area.

To arrange an interview, introduce yourself, briefly describe your project, and then explain your reasons for requesting the interview. Most people are busy, so try to accommodate the person you hope to interview by asking him or her to suggest an interview date. If you intend to record your interview, ask for permission ahead of time.

Start preparing your list of questions before the day of the interview. Effective interviews usually contain a blend of open (or broad) questions and focused (or narrow) questions. Here are a few examples:

Open questions

What do you think about _____?

What are your views on _____?

Why do you believe _____?

Focused questions

How long have you worked as a/an _____?

When did you start _____?

What does _____ mean?

If you ask a question that elicits just "yes" or "no," reformulate the question so that it begins with *why, when, what, who, where,* or *how.* By doing so, you give your interviewee a chance to elaborate. If you know that the person you are interviewing has published articles or a book on your topic, ask questions that will advance your knowledge, rather than questions that the author has already answered in print.

Preparing a list of questions before an interview is essential, but do not just recite your questions during the meeting. An interview is a special kind of conversation. Although you will be guiding it, the person you are speaking with is likely to say something you did not expect but would like to know more about. Do not be afraid to ask questions that are not on your list but come to mind during the interview. Along with your list of questions, be sure to bring pen and paper so that you can take notes and a voice recorder if you will be recording the interview.

After the interview, take some time to review your notes. It will be hard to take down everything that is said during the interview, so expand on the notes you do have. If you recorded the interview, transcribe the relevant parts of the recording. The next step is to write extensively about the interview. Ask yourself what you found most important, most surprising, and most puzzling. You will find this writing especially worthwhile when you are able to use portions of it in your final paper.

(2) Using a questionnaire

Whereas an interview elicits information from one person whose name you know, a questionnaire provides information from a number of anonymous people. To be effective, a questionnaire should be short and focused. If the list of questions is too long, people may not be willing to take the time to answer them all. If the questions are not focused on your research topic, you will find it difficult to integrate the results into your paper.

The types of questions you decide to ask will depend on the purpose of your survey. The first four types of questions in the following box are the easiest for respondents to answer. Open questions, which require much more time to answer, should be asked only when the other types of questions cannot elicit the information you want.

EXAMPLES OF TYPES OF SURVEY QUESTIONS

Questions that require a simple yes-or-no answer:
Do you commute to work in a car? (Circle one.)
Yes   No

Multiple-choice questions:
How many people do you commute with? (Circle one.)
0   1   2   3   4

Questions with answers on a checklist:
How long does it take you to commute to work? (Check one.)
___ 0–30 minutes   ___ 30–60 minutes
___ 60–90 minutes   ___ 90–120 minutes

Questions with a ranking scale:
If the car you drive or ride in is not working, which of the following types of transportation do you rely on? (Rank the choices from 1 for most frequently used to 4 for least frequently used.)
___ bus ___ shuttle van ___ subway ___ taxi

Open questions:
What feature of commuting do you find most irritating?

Begin your questionnaire with an introduction stating what the purpose of the questionnaire is, how the results will be used, and how many questions it contains or approximately how long it should take to complete. In the introduction, you should also assure participants that their answers will remain confidential. To protect survey participants' privacy, colleges and universities have **institutional review boards (IRBs)** set up to review questionnaires. Before you distribute your questionnaire, check with the institutional review board on your campus to make certain that you have followed its guidelines.

If you decide to mail a questionnaire, provide a self-addressed envelope and directions for returning it. It is a good idea to send out twice as many questionnaires as you would like returned because the proportion of responses is generally low. Questionnaires can sometimes be distributed in college dormitories or in classes, but this procedure must be approved by school officials. Listservs (5b(1)) can also be used to conduct surveys. Just remember that a survey limited to people who have a strong interest in a topic will not yield results representative of other groups, such as the students at your school or the citizens of your state.

Once the questionnaires have been completed and returned, tally the results for all but the open questions on an unused copy. To find patterns in the responses to the open questions, first read through them all; you might find that you can create categories for the responses. For example, the open question "What feature of commuting do you find most irritating?" might elicit answers that fall into such categories as "length of time," "amount of traffic," or "bad weather conditions." By first creating categories, you will find it easier to tally the answers to the open questions.

✓ CHECKLIST *for Creating a Questionnaire*

- Does each question relate directly to the purpose of the survey?
- Are the questions easy to understand?
- Are they designed to elicit short, specific responses?
- Are they designed to collect concrete data that can be analyzed easily?
- Have respondents been given enough space to write their answers to open questions?
- Do you have access to the group you want to survey?
- Have you asked a few classmates to "test-drive" your questionnaire?

9 ‖ EVALUATING PRINT AND ONLINE SOURCES

As you find sources that seem to address your research question, you have to evaluate them to determine how, or even whether, you can use them in your paper. In short, you need to establish whether the information they contain is credible, relevant, and timely. This chapter will help you

- assess an author's credibility (9a),
- evaluate a publisher's credibility (9b),
- evaluate online sources (9c), and
- determine the relevance and timeliness of a source (9d).

9a ‖ CREDIBILITY OF AUTHORS

To be considered credible, authors must be trustworthy: they must present facts accurately, support their opinions with evidence, connect their ideas reasonably, and demonstrate respect for any opposing views. Evaluating the credibility of authors involves determining what their credentials are, what beliefs and values they hold, and how other readers respond to their work.

(1) Evaluating an author's credentials

When evaluating sources, consider whether the authors have credentials that are relevant to the topics they address. Although many works have only one author, some are composed collaboratively, so be sure to take into account the credentials of all the authors responsible for the material in the sources you use.

Credentials take various forms, including academic or professional training, publications, and experience. A college biology professor who specializes in genetics is likely to be credible when writing about genes, for example, and a civil engineer who specializes in bridges should have credibility when writing about the risk of bridge collapse. However, given their areas of specialization, the biologist would not necessarily be considered a credible source of information on the foraging habits of black bears, and the engineer would not have credibility concerning the design of hydroelectric power plants.

To find information about the credentials of an author whose work you want to use, look

- on the jacket of a book,
- on a separate page near the front or back of the book,
- in the preface of the book,
- in a note at the bottom of the first or last page of an article in print, or
- on a separate page of a periodical or a web page devoted to providing background on contributors.

As you read about an author, ask yourself the following questions.

✔ CHECKLIST for Assessing an Author's Credentials

- Does the author's education or profession relate to the subject of the work?
- With what institutions, organizations, or companies does the author affiliate?
- What awards has the author won?
- What other works has the author produced?
- Do other experts speak of the author as an authority?

---

(2) Examining an author's values and beliefs

An author's values and beliefs underpin his or her research and publications. To determine what these values and beliefs are, consider the author's purpose and intended audience. For example, a lawyer may write an article about malpractice suits to convince patients to sue health providers, a doctor may write a presentation for a medical convention to highlight the frivolous nature of malpractice claims, and a linguist might prepare a conference paper proposing that miscommunication is at the core of malpractice suits.

As you read and use sources, keep in mind that they reflect the views of the authors and often of the audience for whom they were written. By identifying the underlying values and beliefs, you can responsibly report the information you retrieve from various sources. When you find source material that suggests economic, political, religious, or social biases, you should point out such flaws, as Natalie Angier does when she questions the views of certain evolutionary psychologists.

> Now, it makes sense to be curious about the evolutionary roots of human behavior. It's reasonable to attempt to understand our impulses and actions by applying Darwinian logic to the problem. We're animals. We're not above the rude little prods and jests of natural selection. But evolutionary psychology as it has been disseminated across mainstream consciousness is a cranky and despotic Cyclops, its single eye glaring through an overwhelmingly masculinist lens. I say masculinist rather than male because the view of male behavior promulgated by hardcore evolutionary psychologists is as narrow and inflexible as their view of womanhood is.   —NATALIE ANGIER, *Woman: An Intimate Geography*

The following questions may help you determine the beliefs and values of an author whose work you hope to use.

✓ CHECKLIST for Determining an Author's Beliefs and Values

- What is the author's educational and professional background?
- What are the author's and publisher's affiliations; that is, with what types of organizations do they align themselves?
- What is the editorial slant of the organization publishing the author's work? Where does it lie on the political spectrum from conservative to liberal?
- Can you detect any signs of bias on the part of the author or the publisher?
- Is the information purported to be factual and objective? Or is it subjective?
- Who advertises in the source?
- To what types of websites do any links lead?
- How can you use the source—as fact, opinion, support, authoritative testimony, or material to be refuted?

9b   CREDIBILITY OF PUBLISHERS

When doing research, you need to consider not only the credibility of authors but also the credibility of the media through which their work is made available to you. Some publishers hold authors accountable to higher standards than others do. When evaluating books, you can usually assume that publishers associated with universities demand a high standard of scholarship—because the books they publish are reviewed by experts before publication. Books published by commercial (or trade) presses, in contrast, typically do not undergo the same scrutiny. To determine how a trade book has been received by others writing in the same area, you may have to rely on book reviews available through your library's databases (**8d**).

Similarly, journals that carry scholarly articles are considered more credible than magazines that publish articles for a general audience. Authors of journal articles must include both in-text citations and bibliographies so that expert reviewers and other researchers can consult the sources used (Chapters **12**, **14**, **16**, and **18**). Articles that appear in magazines and newspapers may also be reliable, but keep in mind that they are usually written by someone on the periodical's staff—not by an expert in the field. Because magazines and newspapers often discuss research initially published elsewhere, try to find the original source to ensure the accuracy of their reports. Because in-text citations and bibliographies are rarely provided in these periodicals, your best bet for finding the original source is to search databases (**8d**) or the Internet (**8b**).

The following excerpt from an article about overconfidence in business professionals, published in *The New Yorker,* includes direct quotations and identifies the author of those statements but provides no article title, publication date, or page numbers:

> "In conflicts involving mutual assessment, an exaggerated assessment of the probability of winning increases the probability of winning," Richard Wrangham, a biological anthropologist at Harvard, writes. "Selection therefore favors this form of overconfidence." Winners know how to bluff. And who bluffs the best? The person who, instead of pretending to be stronger than he is, actually believes himself to be stronger than he is. According to Wrangham, self-deception reduces the chances of "behavioral leakage"; that is, of "inadvertently revealing the truth through an inappropriate behavior."
>
> —MALCOLM GLADWELL, "Cocksure"

If readers want to know more about Wrangham's thoughts on overconfidence, they will have to do extra work, because the writer includes no bibliographic information.

Compare the excerpt from Gladwell's magazine article to the following excerpt from Richard Wrangham's journal article, published in *Evolution and Human Behavior*:

> According to Hinde (1993: 33), for example, in-group bias is associated with increased cohesiveness and cooperation and, thus, more effective social action. Among individuals in competition, self-deception may enhance performance by deflecting attention from anxiety, pain, and fatigue (Starek and Keating 1991).
>
> —RICHARD WRANGHAM, "Is Military Incompetence Adaptive?"

In this article on overconfidence, Wrangham also refers to the work of others, but because he is writing for an academic audience, he is expected to include dates with the names of those whose work he mentions and corresponding bibliographic entries at the end of the article, as well as page numbers for any direct quotations. Readers are thus able to consult the original sources mentioned. By checking the references that the author of a source uses, you can find out how reliable and valid the author's claims are.

9C | EVALUATION OF ONLINE SOURCES

If you are evaluating a source from a periodical that you obtained online, you can follow the guidelines for print-based sources (9a and 9b). But if you are evaluating a website, also consider the nature of the site and its sponsor. Although many sites are created by individuals working on their own, many others are sponsored by colleges or universities, professional or nonprofit organizations, and commercial enterprises. The type of sponsor is typically indicated in the site's address, or URL, by a suffix that represents the domain. Colleges and universities are indicated by the suffix **.edu**, government departments and agencies by **.gov**, professional and nonprofit organizations by **.org**, network sites by **.net**, and businesses by **.com**. Depending on the nature of your research paper, you can access any or all of the various types of sites. As you evaluate the content of websites, remember that every site has been created to achieve a specific purpose and to address a target audience.

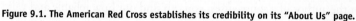

Figure 9.1. The American Red Cross establishes its credibility on its "About Us" page.

Suppose, for example, you wanted to write a paper about financial reform. An organization site could alert you to relevant news and current debates; a government site could contain data compiled by the Federal Trade Commission (FTC); a business site could convey information from one of the companies that will be affected by the reform. Each of these sites would offer different content, which would be shaped by the rhetorical situation as envisioned by each site's sponsor.

You can find out more about the sponsor of a website by clicking on a navigational link such as About Us or Our Vision. Figure 9.1 shows a page from the website of the American Red Cross, reached by clicking on About Us on the site's home page. In the text on the page, the Red Cross establishes its credibility by explaining its history, its mission, and the scope of its services. It also discloses information about the donations it receives.

For criteria you can use to evaluate both online and print sources, see pages 206–7.

Exercise 1

Find three websites that have different kinds of sponsors but contain material about a specific subject, such as global warming, saving energy, or disaster relief efforts. Explain the differences and similarities among the three sites you choose.

9d | RELEVANCE AND TIMELINESS OF SOURCES

A source is useful only when it is relevant to your research question. Given the ever-growing amount of information available on most topics, you should be prepared to put aside a source that will not help you answer your research question or achieve your rhetorical purpose. Some writers get off track when they cannot bring themselves to abandon a source they like, even if it is no longer relevant—as often happens when their focus has changed during the process of conducting research, drafting the paper, and revising it. It is better to abandon an irrelevant source than to write a poorly focused paper.

Seldom will an entire book, article, or website be useful for a specific research paper. A book's table of contents can lead you to relevant chapters or sections, and its index can lead you to relevant pages. Websites have links that you can click on to locate relevant information. Once you find potentially useful material, read it with your research question and rhetorical purpose in mind.

Useful sources are also up to date. A common research error is to do a simple search on the Internet or in a library database and use the first sources listed. These sources, however, may not be the most recent. An advanced search, which is an option offered by search engines and database search pages, allows you to select the dates of articles you would like to review. If you are writing about a specific era in the past, you should also consult **contemporary sources**—sources written during that period.

CRITERIA FOR EVALUATING SOURCES

TYPE OF SOURCE	PURPOSE	AUTHORS/PUBLISH.
Scholarly books	To advance knowledge among experts	Experts/University presses
Trade (or commercial) books	To provide information of interest to the general public	Experts, journalists, professional writers, Commercial presses
Reference books	To provide factual information	Experts/Commercial and university presses
Articles from scholarly journals	To advance knowledge among experts	Experts/Publishers associated with professions or universities
Articles from magazines or newspapers	To report current events or provide general information about current research	Journalists and professional writers (sometimes experts) Commercial presses
Editorials from newspapers	To state a position on an issue	Journalists/Commer. presses
Sponsored websites	To report information	Often a group autho.
Interviews with experts	To report views of an expert	Professional or stude. writer reporting view. of expert

SOURCES DOCUMENTED?	PRIMARY AUDIENCE	CHIEF ADVANTAGE
Yes	Other experts	Reliable because they are written and reviewed by experts
Sometimes	Educated public	Accessible because the language is not overly technical
Yes	Other experts and educated public	Reliable because the entries are written by experts
Yes	Other experts	Reliable because the entries are written and reviewed by experts
No	General public	Accessible because the language is not overly technical
No	General public	Current because they are published daily
No	General public	Accessible by computer
No	General public	Reliable because the interviewee is an expert

To determine when a source was published, look for the date of publication. In books, it appears with other copyright information on the page following the title page. (See the example on page 279.) Dates of periodicals appear on their covers and frequently at the top or bottom of pages throughout each issue (see page 274). The publication date on a website (the date when the site was published or last modified) frequently appears at the bottom of each screen on the site.

✓ CHECKLIST *for Establishing Relevance and Timeliness*

- Does the table of contents, index, or directory of the work include key words related to your research question?
- Does the abstract of a journal article contain information on your topic?
- If an abstract is not available, are any of the article's topic sentences relevant to your research question?
- Do the section heads of the source include words connected to your topic?
- On an Internet site, are there links that lead to relevant information?
- Is the work recent enough to provide useful information?
- If you need a source from another time period, is the work from the right period?

Exercise 2

Using the questions in the preceding checklist, evaluate the relevance and timeliness of the sources you found for Exercise 1.

10 | INTEGRATING SOURCES AND AVOIDING PLAGIARISM

To use sources effectively, you need to think and write about them critically. Instead of just reporting information, you need to comment on the strengths or shortcomings of each source, note any questions it raises, and relate the information to your own experience or to other research you have done. Essentially, you will add your voice to an ongoing conversation about a topic or issue. To use sources responsibly, you must acknowledge the ideas and words of other writers as you incorporate them into your paper. This chapter will help you

- consider the rhetorical situation for a research paper (**10a**);
- take notes and organize them effectively (**10b**);
- compile a working bibliography or an annotated bibliography (**10c**);
- quote, paraphrase, and summarize sources (**10d**);
- analyze and respond to sources (**10e**);
- synthesize sources (**10f**); and
- avoid plagiarism (**10g**).

10a | THE RHETORICAL SITUATION AND THE RESEARCH PAPER

Although you might think that a research paper is simply a paper that reports research on a topic, it is much more than that. A research paper not only describes what others have discovered but also points out the connections between those discoveries and explains the writer's response to them.

The following introduction to a research article from the *Journal of Film and Video* reveals how the author, Marsha Orgeron, has addressed her rhetorical situation. In the first paragraph, she mentions a problem: a gap in the historical research on the effects of movie magazines on their readers. To help fill this gap is Orgeron's purpose. In the last line of the excerpt, she states that her intention is to determine a specific effect that movie magazines published between 1910 and 1950 had on their readers. Orgeron shows her understanding of the journal's academic audience and context by discussing the work of others, by indicating endnotes with superscript numbers, and by appropriately identifying the work of another researcher she has quoted.

There exists a significant critical literature about motion picture marketing and advertisement, especially concerning the related subject of American movie fan magazines. Much of this scholarship revolves around the gendering of discourse aimed at the fan magazine reader, especially over the course of the 1910s and 20s, and the degree to which these magazines increasingly spoke to women who were confronted with a range of entertainment options and related forms of consumerism.[2] However, there have been few attempts by scholars to account for the ways that the readers of movie magazines both were encouraged to behave and, indeed, responded to this institutionalizing of fan culture. Jane Gaines makes a point akin to this in her 1985 essay "War, Women, and Lipstick": "Our most sophisticated tools of structural analysis can't tell us who read fan magazines, in what spirit or mood, or in what social context. Were they read on magazine stands next to bus stops, in waiting rooms, or under the dryers at beauty parlors? Or maybe they were never read at all, but purchased only for images, to cut up, tack on walls, or paste into scrapbooks" (46).

Where Gaines abandons this quest, casting it aside as an ancillary and perhaps even futile pursuit, I want to investigate one relatively unexplored avenue for understanding how fans both read and responded to movie magazines and the culture they created. Although this article begins somewhat conventionally with a discussion of how fan magazines from Hollywood's heyday (the 1910s through the 40s) were encoded, its ultimate aim is to assess how the magazines shaped their readers' understanding of their own relation to star culture.

—MARSHA ORGERON, "'You Are Invited to Participate':
Interactive Fandom in the Age of the Movie Magazine"

By conducting research and acknowledging sources, you demonstrate that you have

- educated yourself about your topic,
- drawn accurately on the work of others (including diverse points of view),
- understood what you have discovered,
- integrated published research into a paper that is clearly your own, and
- provided all the information readers need to consult the sources you have used.

The rest of this chapter and Chapters 11–18 will help you fulfill these responsibilities.

10b TAKING AND ORGANIZING NOTES

Taking accurate notes and organizing those notes are both critical when you are preparing to write a research paper in which you attribute specific words and ideas to others while adding your own ideas. Some researchers are most comfortable taking notes in notebooks. Others write notes on index cards (three-by-five cards) or type them into computer files—two methods that allow notes to be rearranged easily. Still others like to write notes directly on pages they have photocopied or printed out from an online source. Many researchers rely on web-based research tools, such as Zotero, which allow them not only to collect and organize materials but also to take notes and keep track of bibliographic information. Choose the method that best meets the requirements of your research project and fits your working style. However, your notes will be most useful for drafting a paper if you include the elements identified in the following box.

TIPS ON TAKING NOTES AND ORGANIZING THEM

- **Subject heading.** Use a short descriptive phrase to summarize the content of the note. This phrase will help you retrieve the information later.

- **Type of note.** Indicate whether the note is a quotation (10d(2)), a paraphrase (10d(3)), a summary (10d(4)), or your own thoughts. Place quotations between quotation marks (39a). Indicate any changes you made to the quoted material with square brackets (40f) or ellipsis points (40g). If you are using a computer to take notes, you can use a different font color to indicate your own thoughts (see Figure 10.1).

- **Bibliographic information.** Jot down the author's name and/or the title of the source. If the source has page numbers, indicate which pages your notes refer to. You can provide complete bibliographic information in a working bibliography (10c).

- **Computer folders.** If you are using a computer, create a master folder (or directory) for the paper. Within that folder, create separate folders for your notes, drafts, and bibliography. In your notes folder, create files or documents to correspond to each source you use.

Figure 10.1 shows one of the notes Marianna Suslin took before drafting her paper on genetically modified foods (12c).

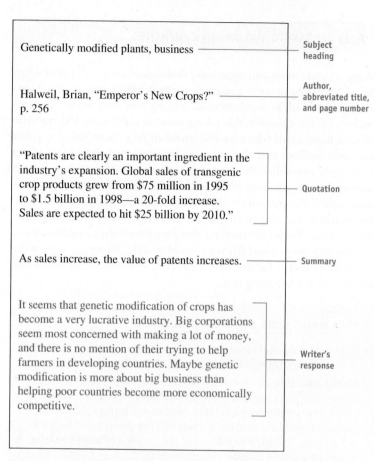

Genetically modified plants, business —————— Subject heading

Halweil, Brian, "Emperor's New Crops?" —————— Author, abbreviated title, and page number
p. 256

"Patents are clearly an important ingredient in the industry's expansion. Global sales of transgenic crop products grew from $75 million in 1995 to $1.5 billion in 1998—a 20-fold increase. Sales are expected to hit $25 billion by 2010." —— Quotation

As sales increase, the value of patents increases. —————— Summary

It seems that genetic modification of crops has become a very lucrative industry. Big corporations seem most concerned with making a lot of money, and there is no mention of their trying to help farmers in developing countries. Maybe genetic modification is more about big business than helping poor countries become more economically competitive. —— Writer's response

Figure 10.1. Contents of a useful note.

Another way to take notes is to use photocopies of articles and excerpts from books or printouts of sources from the Internet. On a printout or a photocopy, you can highlight quotable material and jot down your own ideas in the margins. The example in Figure 10.2 also comes from the work Marianna Suslin did for her research paper (**12c**). Make sure to record the bibliographic information if it is not shown on the photocopy or printout. If you have downloaded an article from a database (**8d**) as a PDF file, consider using the commenting feature of Adobe Acrobat or Adobe Reader to make notes.

Genetic tinkering is the process of adding a gene or genes (the transgene) to plant or animal DNA (the recipient genome) to confer a desirable trait, for example, inserting the genes of an arctic flounder into a tomato to give antifreeze properties, or inserting human genes into fish to increase growth rates.

But, as we are about to discover, this is a technology that no one wants, that no one asked for, and that no one but the biotech companies will benefit from. This is why the biotech lobby has such a vast, ruthless, and well-funded propaganda machine. If they can reinvent our food and slap a patent on it all, they have just created an unimaginably vast new market for themselves.

And to try to convince a suspicious public, they have given us dozens of laudable reasons why the world will benefit from this tinkering. The companies who so enthusiastically produce millions of tons of pesticides every year are now telling us that GMOs will help reduce pesticide use. The companies who have so expertly polluted the world with millions of tons of toxic chemicals are now telling us that GM will help the environment. The companies who have so nonchalantly used child labor in developing countries, and exported dangerous pesticides that are banned in the developed countries to the developing countries, are now telling us that they really do care about people and that we must have GM to feed the world.

Rees, Andy. *Genetically Modified Food: A Short Guide for the Confused.* Ann Arbor: Pluto, 2006. 8.

Author defines "genetic engineering"; his use of the word "tinkering" reveals how he feels about the technology.

examples of genetic modification

Author believes no one but big corporations will benefit from this technology.

Author seeks to discredit biotech companies.

Figure 10.2. Photocopied source with notes.

10C	WORKING BIBLIOGRAPHY AND ANNOTATED BIBLIOGRAPHY

A **working bibliography**, or preliminary bibliography, contains information about the materials you think you might use for your research paper. Creating a working bibliography can help you evaluate the quality of your research. If you find that your most recent source is five years old, for example, or that you have relied exclusively on information from magazines or websites, you may need to find some other sources.

Some researchers find it convenient to compile a working bibliography using a web-based research tool or a word processor, which can sort and alphabetize automatically, making it easier to move material directly to the final draft. Others prefer to put each bibliographic entry on a separate index card.

It is a good idea to use the bibliographical format your instructor prefers when compiling your working bibliography. This book covers the most common formats:

Modern Language Association (MLA), Chapter **12**

American Psychological Association (APA), Chapter **14**

The Chicago Manual of Style (CMS), Chapter **16**

The Council of Science Editors (CSE), Chapter **18**

The examples given in the rest of this chapter follow the MLA's bibliographical and citation style.

If you are asked to prepare an **annotated bibliography** (also called an **annotated list of works cited**), you should list all your sources alphabetically according to the last name of the author. Then, at the end of each entry, summarize the content of the source in one or two sentences.

Zimmer, Carl. *Soul Made Flesh: The Discovery of the Brain—and How It Changed the World.* New York: Free, 2004. Print. This book is a historical account of how knowledge of the brain developed and influenced ideas about the soul. It covers a span of time and place, beginning four thousand years ago in ancient Egypt and ending in Oxford, England, in the seventeenth century.

If you prepare an annotated bibliography as a preliminary assignment, ask your instructor whether you should include the annotations in your final bibliography or works-cited list.

| **10d** | QUOTING, PARAPHRASING, AND SUMMARIZING SOURCES |

You can integrate sources into your writing in a number of ways: quoting exact words, paraphrasing sentences, and summarizing longer sections of text or even entire texts. Whenever you borrow others' ideas in these ways, be careful to integrate the material—properly cited—into your own sentences and paragraphs. Once you have represented source material accurately and responsibly, you will be ready to respond to it.

(1) Introducing sources

When you borrow textual material, introduce it to readers by establishing the source, usually by providing the name(s) of the author(s). You may also need to include additional information about an author, especially if he or she is unfamiliar to your audience. For example, in a paper on the origins of literacy, the following statement becomes more credible if it includes the added information about Oliver Sacks's background:

professor of neurology and psychiatry at Columbia University,
According to Oliver Sacks, "[t]he origin of writing and reading cannot be understood as a direct evolutionary adaptation" (27).

Phrases such as *According to Oliver Sacks* and *from the author's perspective* are called **signal phrases** (or *attributive tags*) because they indicate the source from which information was taken. Most signal phrases in academic writing consist of the name of an author (or a related noun or pronoun) and a verb to report what that author has said or written. The following box suggests phrases to use when you quote, paraphrase, or summarize information, as well as verbs to use in variations of some of the phrases.

SIGNAL PHRASES FOR QUOTING, PARAPHRASING, AND SUMMARIZING

- According to __author's name__ ,....
- In __author's name__ 's view,....
- In __title of article or book__ , __author's name__ states that ....
- The author points out that .... She [or he] also stresses that ....

(continued on page 216)

(continued from page 215)

You can vary the last two of the preceding signal phrases by using one of the following verbs instead of *state, point out,* or *stress.* For a list of the types of complements that follow such verbs, see **27d(5)**.

admit	conclude	find	propose
advise	deny	imply	reject
argue	disagree	indicate	reply
believe	discuss	insist	report
claim	emphasize	note	suggest
concede	explain	observe	think

Signal phrases often begin a sentence, but they can also appear in the middle or at the end:

According to Jim Cullen, "The American Dream would have no drama or mystique if it were a self-evident falsehood or a scientifically demonstrable principle" (7).

"The American Dream," **claims Jim Cullen,** "would have no drama or mystique if it were a self-evident falsehood or a scientifically demonstrable principle" (7).

"The American Dream would have no drama or mystique if it were a self-evident falsehood or a scientifically demonstrable principle," **asserts Jim Cullen in his book** *The American Dream: A Short History of an Idea That Shaped a Nation* (7).

When you integrate sources, be sure to find out whether it is appropriate to add evaluative remarks. If your assignment requires that you be objective, refrain from injecting your own opinions when introducing the ideas of another writer. You can convey your opinion of the material when responding to it (**10e**). If, on the other hand, your assignment allows you to voice your opinion when presenting ideas, you can easily add an adverb to the verb in a signal phrase to indicate your attitude toward the material: the authors *persuasively* argue, *strongly* oppose, or *inaccurately* represent.

If you decide to integrate visual elements such as photos or graphs as source material, you must label them as figures and assign them arabic numerals. You can then refer to them within the text of your paper, as in this example: "The markings on the sixspine butterfly fish (*Parachaetodon ocellatus*) resemble those on the wings of some butterflies (see fig. 10.3)." Under the visual element, include both the figure number and a title or caption.

Offscreen/Shutterstock.com

Figure 10.3. Sixspine butterfly fish.

(2) Using direct quotations

Direct quotations draw attention to key passages. Include a direct quotation in a paper only if

- you want to retain the beauty or clarity of someone's words,
- you need to reveal how the reasoning in a specific passage is flawed or insightful, or
- you plan to discuss the implications of the quoted material.

Keep quotations as short as possible and make them an integral part of your text.

Any quotation of another person's words should be placed in quotation marks or, if longer than four lines, set off as an indented block

(12a(2)). If you need to clarify a quotation by changing it in any way, place square brackets around the added or changed words.

"In this role, he [Robin Williams] successfully conveys a diverse range of emotion."

If you want to omit part of a quotation, replace the deleted words with ellipsis points (40g).

"Overseas markets ... are critical to the financial success of Hollywood films."

When modifying a quotation, be sure not to alter its essential meaning.

Each quotation you use should be accompanied by a signal phrase to help readers understand why the quotation is important. A sentence that consists of only a quotation is called a **dropped quotation**. Notice how the signal phrase improves the following passage:

Joel Achenbach recognizes that compromises
Compromises must be made to promote safer sources of energy: "To accommodate green energy, the grid needs not only more storage but more high-voltage power lines" (Achenbach 137).

Readers will also want to know how a quotation is related to the point you are making. When the connection is not readily apparent, provide an explanation in a sentence or two following the quotation.

Joel Achenbach recognizes that compromises must be made to promote safer sources of energy: "To accommodate green energy, the grid needs not only more storage but more high-voltage power lines" (137). If we are going to use green energy to avoid dependence on types of energy that cause air pollution, we may have to tolerate visual pollution in the form of power lines strung between huge towers.

✔ **CHECKLIST** *for Using Direct Quotations*

- Have you copied all the words and punctuation accurately?
- Have you attributed the quotation to a specific source?
- Have you used square brackets around anything you added to or changed in a direct quotation (**40f**)?
- Have you used ellipsis points to indicate anything you omitted (**40g**)?
- Have you included a signal phrase with the quotation?
- Have you included a sentence or two after a quotation to indicate its relevance?
- Have you used quotations sparingly? Rather than using too many quotations, consider paraphrasing or summarizing the information instead.

(3) Paraphrasing another person's ideas

A **paraphrase** is a restatement of someone else's ideas in approximately the same number of words. Paraphrasing allows you to demonstrate that you have understood what you have read; it also enables you to help your audience understand it. Paraphrase when you want to

- clarify difficult material by using simpler language,
- use someone else's idea but not his or her exact words,
- create a consistent tone (**3a(3)**) for your paper as a whole, or
- interact with a point that a source has made.

Your paraphrase should be almost entirely in your own words and should accurately convey the content of the original passage.

(a) Using your own words and sentence structure

As you compare the source below with the paraphrases that follow, note the similarities and differences in both sentence structure and word choice.

Source

Zimmer, Carl. *Soul Made Flesh: The Discovery of the Brain—and How It Changed the World.* New York: Free, 2004. Print.

> The maps that neuroscientists make today are like the early charts of the New World with grotesque coastlines and blank interiors. And what little we do know about how the brain works raises disturbing questions about the nature of our selves. (page 7)

Inadequate paraphrase

The maps used by neuroscientists today resemble the rough maps of the New World. Because we know so little about how the brain works, we must ask questions about the nature of our selves (Zimmer 7).

If you simply change a few words in a passage, you have not adequately restated it. You may be committing plagiarism (**10g**) if the wording of your version follows the original too closely, even if you provide a page reference for the source.

Adequate paraphrase

Carl Zimmer compares today's maps of the brain to the crude maps made of the New World. He believes that the lack of knowledge about the workings of the brain makes us ask serious questions about human nature (7).

In the second paraphrase, both vocabulary and sentence structure differ from those in the original. This paraphrase also includes a signal phrase ("Carl Zimmer compares").

(b) Maintaining accuracy

Any paraphrase must accurately maintain the sense of the original. If you unintentionally misrepresent the original because you did not understand it, you are being *inaccurate.* If you deliberately change the gist of what a source says, you are being *unethical.* Compare the original statement below with the paraphrases.

Source

Hanlon, Michael. "Climate Apocalypse When?" *New Scientist* (17 Nov. 2007): 20.

> Disastrous images of climate change are everywhere. An alarming graphic recently appeared in the UK media showing the British Isles reduced to a scattered archipelago by a 60-metre rise in sea level. Evocative scenes of

melting glaciers, all-at-sea polar bears and forest fires are routinely attributed to global warming. And of course Al Gore has just won a Nobel prize for his doomsday flick *An Inconvenient Truth,* starring hurricane Katrina.

… There is a big problem here, though it isn't with the science. The evidence that human activities are dramatically modifying the planet's climate is now overwhelming—even to a former paid-up sceptic like me. The consensus is established, the fear real and justified. The problem is that the effects of climate change mostly haven't happened yet, and for journalists and their editors that presents a dilemma. Talking about what the weather may be like in the 2100s, never mind the 3100s, doesn't sell.

Inaccurate or unethical paraphrase

Evocative scenes of melting glaciers, landless polar bears, and forest fires are attributed to global warming in Al Gore's *An Inconvenient Truth.* The trouble is that Gore cannot predict what will happen (Hanlon 20).

Accurate paraphrase

According to Michael Hanlon, the disastrous images of climate change that permeate the media are distorting our understanding of what is actually happening globally and what might happen in the future (20).

Although both paraphrases include a reference to an author and a page number, the first focuses misleadingly on Al Gore, whereas the second paraphrase notes the much broader problem, which can be blamed on the media's focus on selling a story.

(4) Summarizing an idea

When you summarize, you condense the main point(s) of your source. Although a summary omits much of the detail used by the writer of the original source, it accurately reflects the essence of that work. In most cases, then, a **summary** reports a writer's main idea (2c) and the most important support given for it.

Whereas the length of a paraphrase (10d(3)) is usually close to that of the original material, a summary is shorter than the material it reports. When you paraphrase, you restate an author's ideas in order to present or examine them in detail. When you summarize, you present just the gist of the author's ideas, without including background information and details. Summaries can include short quotations of key words or phrases, but you must always enclose another writer's exact words in quotation marks when you blend them with your own.

Source

Marshall, Joseph M., III. "Tasunke Witko (His Crazy Horse)." *Native Peoples* (Jan./Feb. 2007): 76-79. Print.

The world knows him as Crazy Horse, which is not a precise translation of his name from Lakota to English. *Tasunke Witko* means "his crazy horse," or "his horse is crazy." This slight mistranslation of his name seems to reflect the fact that Crazy Horse the man is obscured by Crazy Horse the legendary warrior. He was both, but the fascination with the legendary warrior hides the reality of the man. And it was as the man, shaped by his family, community and culture—as well as the events in his life—that he became legend.

Summary

The Lakota warrior English speakers refer to as "Crazy Horse" was actually called "his crazy horse." That mistranslation may distort impressions of what Crazy Horse was like as a man.

This example reduces five sentences to two, retaining the key idea but eliminating the source author's analysis and speculation. A writer who believes that the audience needs to read such an analysis might decide to paraphrase the passage instead.

Exercise 1

Find a well-developed paragraph in one of your recent reading assignments. Rewrite it in your own words, varying the sentence structure of the original. Make your paraphrase approximately the same length as the original. Next, write a one-sentence summary of the same paragraph.

10e **ANALYZING AND RESPONDING TO SOURCES**

Though quotations, paraphrases, and summaries are key to academic writing, thinking critically involves more than referring to someone else's work. Quotations, paraphrases, and summaries call for responses.

Readers of your papers will want to know what you think about an article, a book, or another source. They will expect you to indicate its strengths and weaknesses and to mention the impact it has had on your own ideas.

Your response to a source will be based on your analysis of it. You can analyze a source in terms of its rhetorical situation (**1a**), its use of rhetorical appeals (**7f**), or its reasoning (**7h** and **7i**). You can also evaluate a source by using some common criteria: currency, coverage, and reliability.

(1) Considering the currency of sources

Depending on the nature of your research, the currency of sources may be an important consideration. Using up-to-date sources is crucial when researching most topics. (Historical research may call for sources from a specific period in the past.) When you consider the currency of a source, start by looking for the date of its publication. Then, examine any data reported. Even a source published in the same year that you are doing research may include data that are several years old and thus possibly irrelevant. In the following example, the writer questions the usefulness of an out-of-date statistic mentioned in a source:

According to Jenkins, only 50% of all public schools have web pages (23). However, this statistic is taken from a report published in 1997; a more recent count would likely yield a much higher percentage.

(2) Noting the thoroughness of research

Coverage refers to the comprehensiveness of research. The more comprehensive a study is, the more convincing are its findings. Similarly, the more examples an author provides, the more compelling are his or her conclusions. Claims or opinions that are based on only one instance are often criticized for being merely anecdotal or otherwise unsubstantiated. The writer of the following response suggests that the author of the source in question may have based his conclusion on too little information:

Johnson concludes that middle-school students are expected to complete an inordinate amount of homework given their age, but he bases his conclusion on research conducted in only three schools (90). To be more convincing, Johnson needs to conduct research in more schools, preferably located in different parts of the country.

(3) Checking the reliability of findings

Research, especially when derived from experiments or surveys, must be reliable. Experimental results are considered **reliable** if they can be reproduced by researchers using a similar methodology. Results that cannot be replicated in this way are not reliable because they are supported by only one experiment.

Reliability is also a requirement for reported data. Researchers are expected to report their findings accurately and honestly, not distorting them to support their own beliefs or claiming others' ideas as their own. To ensure the reliability of their work, researchers must also report all relevant information, not intentionally excluding any that weakens their conclusions. When studies of the same phenomenon give rise to disputes, researchers should discuss conflicting results or interpretations. The writer of the following response focuses on the problematic nature of her source's methodology:

Jamieson concludes from her experiment that a low-carbohydrate diet can be dangerous for athletes (73), but her methodology suffers from lack of detail. No one would be able to confirm her experimental findings without knowing exactly what and how much the athletes consumed.

Researchers often use certain phrases when responding to sources. The following list presents a few examples.

COMMON PHRASES FOR RESPONDING TO SOURCES

Agreeing with a source

- Recent research confirms that ___author's name___ is correct in asserting that....

- ___Author's name___ aptly notes that....

- I agree with ___author's name___ that....

Disagreeing with a source

- Several of the statements made by ___author's name___ are contradictory. She [or he] asserts that ..., but she [or he] also states that....

- In stating that ..., ___author's name___ fails to account for....

- I disagree with ___author's name___ on this point. I believe that....

Expressing both agreement and disagreement with a source

- Although I agree with ___author's name___ that ..., I disagree with his [or her] conclusion that....

- In a way, ___author's name___ is correct:.... However, from a different perspective, one can say that....

- Even though ___author's name___ may be right that..., I must point out that....

10f   SYNTHESIZING SOURCES

The word *synthesis* may remind you of another word—*thesis*. The two words are, of course, related. A *thesis* is typically defined as a claim, a proposition, an informed opinion, or a point of view; a *synthesis* refers to a combination of claims, propositions, opinions, or points of view. When you synthesize sources, you combine them, looking for similarities, differences, strengths, weaknesses, and so on. Like summarizing and responding, synthesizing is not only a writing skill but also a critical-thinking skill.

In the following excerpt, a writer reports two similar views on the topic of ecotourism.

> The claim that ecotourism can benefit local economies is supported by the observations of Ellen Bradley, tour leader in Cancun, Mexico, and Rachel Collins, county commissioner in Shasta County, California. Bradley insists that ecotourism is responsible for creating jobs and improved standards of living in Mexico (10). Similarly, Collins believes that ecotourism has provided work for people in her county who had formerly been employed by the timber industry (83).

Notice that the writer uses the transitional word *similarly* (**3d(3)**) to indicate a comparison. In the next excerpt on the topic of voting fraud, a writer contrasts two different views, using the transitional word *although*.

> Although Ted Kruger believes voting fraud is not systematic (45), that does not mean there is no fraud at all. Kendra Berg points out that voter rolls are not updated often enough (18), which leaves the door open for cheaters.

In both of the previous examples, the writers not only summarize and respond to sources but synthesize them as well. The box below suggests phrases you can use when synthesizing sources.

COMMON PHRASES FOR SYNTHESIZING SOURCES

- The claim that...is supported by the observations of ___author 1's name___ and ___author 2's name___. ___Author 1's name___ insists that.... Similarly, ___author 2's name___ believes that....

- ___Author 1's name___ asserts that.... ___Author 2's name___ supports this position by arguing that....

- Although ___author 1's name___ believes that..., this interpretation is not accepted universally. For example, ___author 2's name___ notes that....

- ___Author 1's name___ asserts that...; however, he [or she] fails to explain why [or how].... ___Author 2's name___ points out that....

10g   AVOIDING PLAGIARISM

To use the work of other writers responsibly, you need to give credit for all information you gather through research. Your audience must be able to distinguish between the ideas of other writers and your own contributions. It is not necessary, however, to credit information that is **common knowledge**, which includes well-known facts such as the following: "The *Titanic* hit an iceberg and sank on its maiden voyage." This event has been the subject of many books and movies, so some information about it has become common knowledge.

If, however, you are writing a research paper about the *Titanic* and wish to include the ship's specifications, such as its overall length and gross tonnage, you will be providing *un*common knowledge, which must be documented. After you have read about a given subject in a number of sources, you will be able to distinguish between common knowledge and the distinctive ideas or interpretations of specific writers. If you have been scrupulous about identifying your own thoughts while taking notes, you should have little difficulty distinguishing between what you knew to begin with and what you learned through your research.

Taking even part of someone else's work and presenting it as your own leaves you open to criminal charges. In the film, video, music, and software businesses, this sort of theft is called **piracy**. In publishing and education, it is called **plagiarism**. Whatever it is called, it is illegal, and penalties range from failing a paper or course to being expelled from school. Never compromise your integrity or risk your future by submitting someone else's work as your own.

> ❶ **CAUTION**
>
> Although it is fairly easy to copy material from a website or even to purchase a paper on the web, it is just as easy for a teacher or employer to locate that same material and determine that it has been plagiarized. Many teachers routinely use Internet search tools such as Google or special services such as Turnitin if they suspect that a student has submitted a paper that was plagiarized.

To review how to draw responsibly on the words and ideas of others, consider the following examples:

Source

McConnell, Patricia B. *The Other End of the Leash.* New York: Ballantine, 2002. 142. Print.

Status in male chimpanzees is particularly interesting because it is based on the formation of coalitions, in which no single male can achieve and maintain power without a cadre of supporting males.

Paraphrase with documentation

Patricia B. McConnell, an authority on animal training, notes that by forming alliances with other male chimpanzees, a specific male can enjoy status and power (142).

This example includes not only the author's name but also a parenthetical citation, which marks the end of the paraphrase and provides the page number where the original material can be found.

Quotation with documentation

Patricia B. McConnell, an authority on animal training, argues that male chimpanzees achieve status "based on the formation of coalitions, in which no single male can achieve and maintain power without a cadre of supporting males" (142).

Quotation marks show where the copied words begin and end; the number in parentheses indicates the exact page in McConnell's book on which those words appear. Again, the author is identified at the beginning of the sentence. However, the quoted material can instead be completely documented in a parenthetical reference at the end of the sentence:

Male chimpanzees achieve status "based on the formation of coalitions, in which no single male can achieve and maintain power without a cadre of supporting males" (McConnell 142).

If, after referring to the following checklist, you cannot decide whether you need to cite a source, the safest policy is to cite it.

✔ CHECKLIST of Sources That Should Be Cited

- Writings, both published and unpublished
- Opinions and judgments that are not your own
- Statistics and other facts that are not widely known
- Images and graphics, such as works of art, drawings, charts, graphs, tables, photographs, maps, and advertisements
- Personal communications, such as interviews, letters, and e-mail messages
- Public electronic communications, including television and radio broadcasts, motion pictures and videos, sound recordings, websites, and posts to online discussion groups or blogs

Exercise 2

After reading the source material, decide which of the quotations and paraphrases that follow it are written correctly and which would be considered problematic. Be prepared to explain your answers.

Source

Despommier, Dickson D. "A Farm on Every Floor." *New York Times.* New York Times, 23 Aug. 2009. Web. 19 July 2010.

If climate change and population growth progress at their current pace, in roughly 50 years farming as we know it will no longer exist. This means that the majority of people could soon be without enough food or water. But there is a solution that is surprisingly within reach: Move most farming into cities, and grow crops in tall, specially constructed buildings. It's called vertical farming.

1. Vertical farming is a way to provide food in the future.
2. Dickson D. Despommier believes that vertical farming may be the solution to the growing demand for food and water.
3. According to Dickson D. Despommier, in fifty years "farming...will no longer exist."
4. Dickson D. Despommier claims that the farming we are accustomed to will no longer be in existence in fifty years.
5. Vertical farming is the use of specially designed city buildings to grow crops (Despommier).
6. "If climate change and population growth progress at their current pace, in roughly 50 years farming as we know it will no longer exist" (Despommier).

DISCIPLINES and DOCUMENTATION STYLES

Martin Child/Getty Images

11 WRITING ABOUT LITERATURE

You have been interpreting and writing about literature—talking about plot, characters, and setting—ever since you wrote your first book report. When you write about literature in college—whether the work is fiction, drama, poetry, an essay, or a memoir—you will still discuss plot, characters, and setting. But you will also apply many of the same strategies you use when writing about other topics: you will establish a rhetorical opportunity for writing, explore and focus your subject, formulate a purposeful thesis statement that is supported by reference to the literary work itself, address an audience, and arrange your thoughts in the most effective way. In short, when you write about literature, you respond to the rhetorical situation. This chapter will help you

- recognize the various genres of literature (**11a**),
- realize the value of careful reading (**11b**),
- use the specialized vocabulary for discussing literature (**11c**),
- employ various critical approaches for interpreting literature (**11d**), and
- apply the conventions for writing about literature (**11e** and **11f**).

11a LITERATURE AND ITS GENRES

Works of literature can be divided into categories, which are referred to as **genres**. A genre can be identified by its particular features and conventions. Some genres are timeless and universal (drama and poetry, for instance); others are context-specific and develop within particular cultures (the graphic novel, for instance, is a fairly recent cultural phenomenon).

Just as you can recognize film genres—action, suspense, horror, comedy, animation, Western, and science fiction—you can identify various literary genres: from poetry and drama to essays and narratives. And just as film genres sometimes overlap (for example, when an action film, such as *Beowulf,* is also animated), so do literary genres: some poems are referred to as prose poems, whereas some plays (Shakespeare's plays, for example) are written in verse. But even when genres overlap, the identifiable features of each genre are still evident.

Some of the most widely studied literary genres are fiction, drama, and poetry, though many forms of nonfiction (including personal essays and memoirs, literacy narratives, and manifestos) are being studied in college courses on literature. All imaginative literature can be characterized as fictional, but the term **fiction** is applied specifically to novels and short stories.

Drama differs from all other imaginative literature in one specific way: it is meant to be performed—whether on stage, on film, or on television—with the director and actors imprinting the lines with their own interpretations. In fact, the method of presentation distinguishes drama from fiction, even though the two genres share many of the same elements (setting, character, plot, and dialogue). For instance, novels usually include extensive descriptions of characters and setting as well as passages revealing what characters are thinking. In drama, however, characters reveal what they are thinking through either spoken dialogue with other characters or a **dramatic soliloquy** (a speech delivered to the audience by an actor alone on the stage). Drama can also be read rather than watched, in which case, you bring your interpretive abilities to the printed page rather than to the performance.

Poetry shares the components of both fiction and drama. Dramatic monologues and narrative poems sometimes feature a narrator with a point of view, a plot, a setting, and characters. But poetry distinguishes itself from the other literary genres with its extensive use of connotative language, imagery, allusions, figures of speech, symbols, sound, meter, and rhythm.

11b	RHETORICAL READING AND LITERARY INTERPRETATION

The most successful writing about literature starts with rhetorical (or active) reading. Both understanding and interpretation of a literary work are fostered by such reading. Therefore, as you read, examine your own reactions. Were you amused, moved, or confused? Which characters interested you? Were you able to follow the plot? Did the work remind you of any experience of your own or other works you have read? Did it introduce you to a different historical or geographical setting, or did you encounter a familiar setting and cast of characters? These first impressions can provide the seeds from which strong essays will grow, especially when they are later modified as you consider the work further.

(1) Your personal response to reading literature

When reflecting on your response to some element in a work of literature, consider how your reading might be shaped by the factors that define who you are. After all, what you bring to the page is important. If you feel yourself responding positively or negatively to a character, a plot twist, or the setting in a novel or play, you might ask yourself whether this response has anything to do with your psychological makeup, political beliefs, gender or sexual orientation, cultural or ethnic group, social class, religion, or geographic location.

Thinking about what your individual reading contributes to a work of literature helps you focus on a rhetorical opportunity for writing and may suggest a theoretical approach to use as a basis for your interpretation (11d). Keep in mind, though, that just as your life experiences and values can enhance your understanding of a literary work, they can also limit that understanding—yet another way your identity can shape your response.

(2) Developing your topic using evidence in the text

If you are choosing your own topic, your first step is to reflect on your personal response as you formulate a tentative thesis statement. Next, consider what specific evidence from the text will best explain and support your interpretation and thesis statement.

Most readers (including your instructor) will be interested in what *you* think, so you need to discover a way to demonstrate your originality by focusing on a topic you can develop adequately and then applying one or more rhetorical methods (2g). You might explain why you consider a character heroic, classify a play as a comedy of manners, or describe a setting that anchors a literary work's meaning. Perhaps you can compare and contrast two poems on a similar subject or explore cause-and-consequence relationships in a novel. What circumstances, for instance, lead to an otherwise intelligent character's monumentally bad decision? You might point out how features of a family's house in a novel illustrate the values or underlying conflicts of that family. Or you might trace the repeated appearance of an object (hands, dark skies, or a cat, for example) throughout a story and explain how that repetition serves to remind the reader of some particular idea or theme.

(3) Researching what other readers have said about a literary work

You will undoubtedly anchor your essay in your own interpretation, but you enrich that interpretation with the sometimes conflicting responses of others, from literary experts to classmates. Every time you read works of literary criticism, visit online discussion groups (5b), participate in class discussions, or take part in a book club or reading group, you are engaging in literary-based dialogue with others. Although it is tempting to lean heavily on the interpretations of scholarly experts, you should use them in the same way you use other outsides sources: to enrich your own interpretation and support your own points. No matter what outside sources you tap, be sure to give credit to them by citing them.

To locate scholarly material on a specific writer, work, or literary theory, you can start by consulting your library's resources. Your library's catalog (8b and 8c) and certain reference books are the best starting points. For instance, *The MLA International Bibliography*, an index of books and articles about literature, is an essential resource for literary studies and is available in print and online. Works such as *Contemporary Authors, The Oxford Companion to English Literature,* and *The New Princeton Handbook of Poetic Terms* can be useful when you are beginning your research or when you have encountered terms you need to clarify.

(4) Types of literary interpretation

Writing about a literary work requires you to focus on the work itself and to demonstrate that you have read it carefully—a process known as **close reading**. (Compare close reading with reading rhetorically, discussed in Chapter 1 and in 11b.) Close reading allows you to offer an **interpretation**, an explanation of what you see in a work. When your interpretation explains the contribution of one feature of a literary work (such as the setting or main character) to the work's overall meaning, it is called an **analysis**. A common form of analysis is **character analysis**, in which a writer interprets the significance of one or more features of a single character. An analysis can also focus on a single scene, symbol, or theme.

Explication, usually used only with poetry, is an interpretation that attempts to explain every element in a literary work. When explicating William Wordsworth's "A Slumber Did My Spirit Seal," a writer might note that the *s* sound reinforces the hushed feeling of sleep and death in the poem. But it would also be necessary to consider the meanings of *slumber, spirit,* and *seal.*

An **evaluation** of a literary work gauges how successfully the author communicates meaning to readers or how successfully one part of the work contributes to the meaning conveyed by the other parts. The most common types of evaluation are book, theater, and film reviews. Like any other interpretation, an evaluation is a type of argument in which a writer cites both positive and negative textual evidence to persuade readers to accept a clearly formulated thesis. (See Chapters 2 and 7.)

Summarizing a literary work can be a useful way to make sure that you understand it, that you have read it closely. But do not confuse a summary with an analysis, an explication, or an evaluation. Those who have read the work do not need to read a summary of it; there is no need to provide a summary unless your instructor has specifically asked for one.

11C	VOCABULARY FOR DISCUSSING LITERATURE

Like all specialized fields, literature has its own vocabulary, which describes the various features of literary texts and the concepts of literary analysis. As you learn this vocabulary, you will learn more than just a list of terms: you will learn how to understand, interpret, and write about literature.

(1) Characters

The **characters** are the humans or humanlike personalities (aliens, robots, animals, and other creatures) who carry the plot forward; they usually include a main character, called a **protagonist**, who is in external conflict with another character or an institution or in internal conflict with

Understanding how a particular character moves the plot forward will help you interpret a work as a whole.

himself or herself. This conflict usually reveals the **theme**, or the central idea of the work (**11c(7)**).

Because writing about literature often requires character analysis, you need to understand the characters in any work you read. You can do so by paying close attention to their appearance, their language, and their actions. You also need to pay attention to what the narrator or other characters say about them and how the other characters treat and react to them. Whether you are writing about characters in a novel, a play, or a poem, you will want to concentrate on what those characters do and say—and why.

(2) Imagery

The imagery in a piece of literature is conveyed by **descriptive language**, or words that describe a sensory experience. Notice the images in the following excerpt from a prose poem by Pinkie Gordon Lane that focuses on the death—and life—of a mother.

> My mother died walking along a dusty road on a Sunday morning in New Jersey. The road came up to meet her sinking body in one quick embrace. She spread out like an umbrella and dropped into oblivion before she hit the ground. In that one swift moment all light went out at the age of forty-nine. Her legacy: the blackened knees of the scrub-woman who ransomed her soul so that I might live, who bled like a tomato whenever she fought to survive, who laughed fully when amused—her laughter rising in one huge crescendo—and whose wings soared in dark despair . . . .
>
> —**PINKIE GORDON LANE**, "Prose Poem: Portrait"
>
> © 1991. Reprinted by permission.

The dusty road, the sinking body, the quick embrace—these images convey the loneliness and swiftness of death. The blackened knees, tomato-like bleeding, and rising laughter are, in contrast, images of a life's work, struggle, and joy.

© Reuters/Michael Daniel/Landov

(3) Narrator

The **narrator** of a literary work tells the story. The voice doing the telling can seem to be that of the author himself or herself (but such a voice is that of the author's **persona**, which is a fictional construction and not actually the author). The voice might instead be that of a specific character (or one of several characters who are taking turns telling the story). Or the voice can be that of an all-knowing presence (referred to as an **omniscient narrator**) that transcends characters and author alike. Whatever the voice, the narrator's tone reveals his or her attitude toward events and characters and even, in some circumstances, toward readers. By determining the tone and the impact it has on you as a reader, you can gain insight into the author's purpose (**3a(3)**).

(4) Plot

The plot is what happens in the story, the sequence of events (the narrative)—and more. The plot establishes how events are patterned or related in terms of conflict and resolution. Narrative answers "What comes next?" and plot answers "Why?" Consider this example:

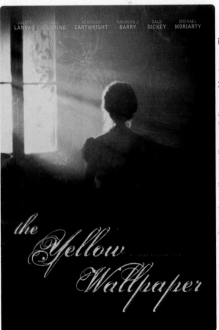

Image from the feature film "The Yellow Wallpaper," directed by Logan Thomas, starring Juliet Landau, Aric Cushing, Veronica Cartwright, Dale Dickey, Raymond J. Barry, and Michael Moriarty

Narrative

A woman is confined to a room with yellow wallpaper.

Plot

The physician husband of a highly imaginative woman moves her into a room with yellow wallpaper, where she is restricted to silence and idleness.

In "The Yellow Wallpaper," a doctor confines his wife to an upstairs bedroom in an attempt to restore her mental health by means of a rest cure.

A plot usually begins with a conflict, an unstable situation that sets events in motion (for instance, the state of tension or animosity between the powerful, patronizing husband and his confined wife). In what is called the **exposition**, the author introduces the characters, setting, and background—the elements that not only constitute the unstable situation but also relate to the events that follow. The subsequent series of events leads to the **climax**, the most intense event in the narrative. The climax is also referred to as the **turning point** because what follows is **falling action** (or **dénouement**) that leads to a resolution of the conflict and a more stable situation, though not necessarily a happy ending.

(5) Setting

Setting involves place—not just the physical setting, but also the social setting (the morals, manners, and customs of the characters). Setting also involves time—not only historical time, but also the length of time covered by the narrative. Setting includes **atmosphere**, or the emotional response to the situation, often shared by the reader with the characters. For example, San Francisco in the nineteenth century is a markedly different setting from the same city in the twenty-first century. Not only has the physical appearance of the city changed, but so has the social setting and the atmosphere. Being aware of the features of the setting will help you better understand a story, whether it is written as fiction, drama, or poetry.

© Photo collection Alexander Allard, Sr/Corbis

This nineteenth-century scene, illustrating a time when both people and vehicles moved more slowly, suggests the atmosphere of early San Francisco.

(6) Symbols

Frequently used by writers of literature, a **symbol** is usually a physical object that stands for something else, usually something abstract.

For example, at the beginning of *A Streetcar Named Desire,* a play by
Tennessee Williams, one of the main characters buys a paper lantern
to cover a naked lightbulb. During the scenes that follow, she frequently talks about light, emphasizing her preference for soft lighting. At the end of the play, another character tears off the lantern,
and a third character tries to return the ruined lantern to the main
character as she is being taken away to a mental hospital. Anyone
seeing this play performed or reading it carefully would note that the
paper lantern is a symbol. It is an object that is part of the setting and
the plot, but it also stands for something more—a character's avoid-
ance of harsh truths.

When you write about a particular symbol, first note where it appears in the literary work. To determine what the symbol might mean,
consider why it appears in those places and to what effect. Once you
have an idea about the meaning, trace the incidents in the literary work
that reinforce that interpretation.

(7) Theme

The main idea of a literary work is its **theme**. Depending on how they
interpret a work, different readers may identify different themes. To test
whether an idea is central to the work in question, check to see if the
idea is supported by the setting, plot, characters, and symbols. If you
can relate these components to the idea you are considering, then it can
be considered the work's theme. The most prominent literary themes
arise out of external or internal conflict: character versus character,
character versus herself or himself, character versus nature, or character
versus society.

When you believe you have identified the theme of a literary work,
state it as a sentence—and be precise. A theme conveys a specific idea;
it should not be confused with a topic.

Topic	a physician's care of his ill wife
Vague theme	the subordination of nineteenth-century married women
Specific theme	"The Yellow Wallpaper" deals with a conflict between an imaginative woman and a society that insists that she abandon her artistic endeavors.

> ✔ **CHECKLIST** *for Interpreting a Literary Work*
>
> - From whose point of view is the story told?
> - Who is the protagonist? How is his or her character developed?
> - With whom or what is the protagonist in conflict?
> - How are the other characters depicted and distinguished through dialogue?
> - What symbols, imagery, or figures of speech (**33a(3)**) does the author use? To what effect?
> - What is the theme of the work? How does the author use setting, plot, characters, and symbols to establish that theme?

11d   APPROACHES TO INTERPRETING LITERATURE

An interpretation of a literary work can be shaped by your personal response to what you have read, by the views of other readers whom you wish to support or challenge, or by a specific type of literary theory.

Literary theory, the scholarly discussion of how the nature and function of literature can be determined, ranges from approaches that focus almost exclusively on the text itself (its language and structure) to approaches that show how the text relates to author, reader, language, society, culture, economics, or history. Familiarity with literary theory enriches your reading of literature as well as your understanding of the books and essays about literature that you will discover when you do research (Chapter **8**). Literary theory can also help you decide how you want to focus your writing about literature.

Although the most popular theoretical approaches to literature overlap somewhat, each has a different primary focus: the reader, some feature of the social or cultural context, the text itself, or the author or characters. Interpreting literature involves a responsible reliance on one or more of these approaches—*for whatever your interpretation, the text should support it.*

(1) Reader-response theory

According to **reader-response theory**, readers construct meaning as they read and interact with the elements within a text, with each reader bringing something different (intellectual values and life experiences) to the text with every reading. Thus, meaning is not fixed *on* the page but rather depends on what each reader brings *to* the page. Furthermore, the same reader can have different responses to the same literary work when rereading it later: a father of teenagers, for example, might find Gwendolyn Brooks's "we real cool" more disturbing now than when he first read it in high school. Although a reader-response approach to literature encourages diverse interpretations, you cannot simply say, "Well, that's what this work means to me," or "That's my interpretation." You must demonstrate to your audience how the elements of the work support your interpretation.

(2) Feminist and gender-based literary theories

The significance of sex, gender, or sexual orientation within a particular social context is the interpretive focus of **feminist** and **gender-based literary theories**. These theories enable a reader to analyze the ways in which a work (through its characters, theme, or plot) promotes or challenges the prevailing intellectual or cultural assumptions of its day regarding issues related to gender and sexuality, such as patriarchy and compulsory heterosexuality. For instance, Edith Wharton's *The Age of Innocence* compares two upper-class nineteenth-century women with respect to the specific social pressures that shaped and constricted their lives and loves. A feminist critic might emphasize the oppression of these women and the repression of their sexuality. Using a gender-based approach, another critic might read Henry James's *The Bostonians* and focus on the positive features of the domestic relationship between the financially independent Olive Chancellor and Verena Tarrant, the feminist activist she supports. That same critic might also try to explain why Jake Barnes in Ernest Hemingway's *The Sun Also Rises* bonds with some men and is contemptuous of others.

(3) Race-based literary theory

A useful form of race-based literary criticism, **critical race theory**, focuses on the significance of race relations within a specific historical and social setting in order to explain the experience and literary production

Harper Perennial Modern Classics

In *Their Eyes Were Watching God*, a mature and complex black woman recounts her life in three "acts," based on her relationships with three very different men.

of any people whose history is characterized by political, social, or psychological oppression. Not only does this theoretical approach seek out previously neglected literary works, but it also illuminates the ways in which race, ethnicity, and the imbalance of power inform many works. Previously neglected works such as Zora Neale Hurston's *Their Eyes Were Watching God,* Rudolfo Anáya's *Bless Me, Ultima,* and Frederick Douglass's *Narrative,* which demonstrate how racism affects the characters' lives, have taken on considerable cultural value in the last twenty years. **African American literary criticism**, for example, has been particularly successful in invigorating the study of great African American writers, whose works can be more fully appreciated when readers consider how literary elements of the works have been informed by the social forces that helped produce them. Closely associated with critical race theory is **postcolonial theory**, which takes into account the relationship of the colonized with the colonizer and the challenge a text can direct at the dominant powers at a particular time and place, asserting a drive toward the liberation of oppressed social groups. Joseph Conrad's *Heart of Darkness,* Jean Rhys's *Wide Sargasso Sea,* Daniel Defoe's *Robinson Crusoe,* and E. M. Forster's *A Passage to India* can all be read productively through the lens of postcolonial theory.

(4) Class-based literary theory

To explain the conflict between literary characters or between a character and a community or institution, **class-based literary theory** draws on the work of Karl Marx, Terry Eagleton, and others who have addressed the implications of social hierarchies and the accompanying economic tensions. These theorists argue that differences in socioeconomic class—in the material conditions of daily life—divide people in profoundly significant ways, more so than differences in race, ethnicity, culture, and gender. Thus, a class-based approach can be used to explain why Emma Bovary is unhappy, despite her "good" (that is, financially advantageous) marriage, in Gustave Flaubert's *Madame Bovary,* why Bigger Thomas gets thrown into such a confused mental state in Richard Wright's *Native Son,* or why a family loses its land in John Steinbeck's *The Grapes of Wrath.*

(5) Text-based literary theory

Text-based literary theory demands concentration on the piece of literature itself; that is, it calls for a close reading. With this approach, only the use of concrete, specific examples from the text validates an interpretation. The reader must pay careful attention to the elements within the literary work—plot, characters, setting, tone, dialogue, imagery, and so on—to evaluate their interaction, overall effect, and meaning. According to this theory, nothing more than what is contained within the text itself—not information about the author's life, culture, or society—is needed to understand and appreciate the text's unchanging meaning. Readers may change, but the meaning of the text does not. A close reading of the work is essential, then, in order to account for all of its particularities, including the ways in which the language and the structure fit within a specific literary genre.

(6) Context-based literary theory

Context-based literary theory considers the historical period during which a work was written and the cultural and economic patterns that prevailed during that period. For example, recognizing that Willa Cather published *My Ántonia* during World War I can help account for the darker side of that novel about European immigrants' harsh life in the American West; similarly, understanding that Arthur Miller wrote *The Crucible* in response to the accusations of the House Un-American Activities Committee in the 1950s helps explain why that play generated so much excitement when it was first produced. Critics who use a context-based and class-based approach known as **cultural studies**

consider how a literary work interacts with economic conditions, socio-economic classes, and other cultural artifacts (such as songs or fashion) of the period in which it was written.

(7) Psychoanalytic theories

Psychoanalytic theories seek to explain human experience and behavior in terms of sexual impulses and unconscious motivations (drives, desires, fears, needs, and conflicts). When applied to literature, these theories (based on the work of Nancy Chodorow, Hélène Cixous, Sigmund Freud, Melanie Klein, and Jacques Lacan, among others) focus on the psychological states of the author and the characters as well as the reader. The theories help readers discern the motivations of characters, envision the psychological state of the author as implied by the text, and evaluate the psychological reasons for their own interpretations. Readers may apply a psychoanalytic approach to explain why Hamlet is deeply disturbed by his mother's remarriage, why Holden Caulfield rebels at school (in J. D. Salinger's *The Catcher in the Rye*), or why Rochester is blinded (in Charlotte Brontë's *Jane Eyre*).

Theorists who use the work of psychiatrist Carl Jung to explore **archetypes** (meaningful images that arise from the human unconscious and that appear as recurring figures or patterns in literature) are also using a psychoanalytic approach to interpret literature, whether the literary form is a fairy tale, fable, epic poem, Greek drama, postmodern novel, or movie script. Archetypal figures include the hero, the earth mother, the warrior, the outcast, and the cruel stepmother. Archetypal patterns include the quest, the initiation, the test, and the return.

Exercise 1

Attend a film, a play, or a poetry reading at your school or in your community. Write a two- to three-page essay evaluating the work, using one of the theoretical approaches discussed in this section.

11e CONVENTIONS FOR WRITING ABOUT LITERATURE

Writing about literature involves adhering to several conventions.

(1) Using first person

When writing an analysis of a piece of literature, you may use the first-person singular pronoun, *I*.

Although some critics believe Rudolfo Anáya's novel to be about witchcraft, I think it is about the power of belief.

By using *I*, you indicate that you are presenting your opinion about a work. When you propose or argue for a particular belief or interpretation or offer an opinion, you must support it with specific evidence from the text itself.

(2) Using present tense

Use the present tense when discussing a literary work, since the author of the work is communicating to the reader at the present time (**24b(1)**).

In "A Good Man Is Hard to Find," the grandmother reaches out to touch her killer just before he pulls the trigger.

Similarly, use the present tense when reporting how other writers have interpreted the work you are discussing.

As Toni Morrison demonstrates in her analysis of the American literary tradition, black Americans continue to play a vital role.

(3) Documenting sources

When writing about a work assigned by your instructor, you may not need to give the source and publication information. However, if you are using an edition or translation that may be different from the one your reader(s) will use, you should indicate this. You can document the version of the work you are discussing by using the MLA format for listing works cited (**12b**), although your bibliography in this case will consist of only a single entry.

An alternative way of providing documentation for a single source is by acknowledging the first quotation from or reference to the work using a superscript number and then providing an explanatory note on a separate page at the end of your paper.

In-text citation

… as Toni Morrison states (127).[1]

OR

… tendency to misread texts by African American writers (Morrison 127).[1]

Note

1. Toni Morrison, *Playing in the Dark: Whiteness and the Literary Imagination* (New York: Vintage, 1992). All subsequent references to this work will be identified with page numbers in parentheses within the text.

If you use this note form, you do not need to repeat the bibliographical information in a separate entry or include the author's name in subsequent parenthetical references to page numbers. Check with your instructor about the format he or she prefers.

When you use a bibliography to provide publication data, you must indicate specific references whenever you quote a line or passage. According to MLA style, such bibliographic information should be placed in the text in parentheses directly after the quotation. A period, a semicolon, or a comma should follow the parentheses (**12a(1)** and **39d(1)**). Quotations from short stories and novels are identified by the author's name and page number:

"A man planning to spend money on me was an experience rare enough to feel odd" (Gordon 19).

Quotations from poems are referred to by line number:

"O Rose, thou are sick!" (Blake 1).

Quotations from Shakespeare's plays are identified using abbreviations of the titles; the following line is from act I, scene I, line 28 of Shakespeare's play *Much Ado about Nothing*:

"How much better it is to weep at joy than to joy at weeping" (*Ado* 1.1.28).

(4) Quoting poetry

When quoting from poems and verse plays, type quotations involving three or fewer lines in the text and insert a slash (see **40h**) with a space on each side to separate the lines.

"Does the road wind uphill all the way? / Yes, to the very end" (Rossetti 1-2). Christina Rossetti opens her poem "Uphill" with this two-line question and answer.

Quotations of more than three lines should be indented one inch from the left-hand margin and double-spaced. Do not use slashes at the ends of lines, and make sure to follow the original text for line breaks, special indenting, or spacing. For this type of block quotation, place your citation after the final punctuation mark.

(5) Referring to authors' names

Use the full name of the author of a work in your first reference and only the last name in all subsequent references. For instance, write "Charles Dickens" or "Willa Cather" the first time and use "Dickens" or "Cather" after that. Never refer to a female author differently than you do a male author. For example, use "Robert Browning and Elizabeth Barrett Browning" or "Browning and Barrett Browning" (not "Browning and Mrs. Browning" or "Browning and Elizabeth").

11f	LITERARY INTERPRETATION OF A SHORT STORY

In the following literary interpretation, English major Kristin Ford focuses on (**2b**) the political and personal implications of a woman's mental illness as portrayed in Charlotte Perkins Gilman's short story "The Yellow Wallpaper."

Ford 1

Kristin Ford

Professor Glenn

English 232

19 November 2010

The Role of Storytelling in Fighting Nineteenth-Century Chauvinism

Widely considered to be one of the most influential pieces of

early feminist literature, "The Yellow Wallpaper," published in 1892 by

Charlotte Perkins Gilman, illustrates nineteenth-century men's patronizing

treatment of and abusive power over women, exploring the smudged line

between sanity and insanity, men's alleged ability to distinguish between

the two, and women's inability to pull themselves out of depression or

any form of mental illness without seeming to further demonstrate their

insanity. The protagonist of Gilman's story descends into madness, a

mental state unnecessarily exacerbated, if not caused, by her husband's

prescribed "rest cure," which entailed total inactivity and isolation. Such

was her double bind: the stronger the constraints of the cure, the worse

her mental illness. She had no way to resolve her problem.

During Gilman's time, women were understood largely in relation

to the "Cult of True Womanhood," which prescribed women's "proper"

place in society, especially within the middle and upper classes. Piety,

purity, submissiveness, and domesticity were not merely encouraged but

demanded in order for a woman to avoid breaking this strict social code

(Lavender). Such virtues meant that a "true woman" of that time was

a wife, housewife, and mother—always yielding to the demands of her

husband and her family. Any woman who went against these norms risked

The writer provides a critical overview of the story, demonstrating her understanding of it.

The writer defines *double bind,* which is the operative term for her thesis.

The writer includes historical background for the story. She uses past tense to refer to these actions and beliefs.

Ford 2

being cast out or labeled insane (Mellor 156). Men dominated medicine, and mental illness remained largely unexplored and thus misunderstood. Many doctors still feared it and thus ignorantly tried to pass off serious psychological disorders as cases of "nervousness" or "hysteria" or "fragile constitutions" (Tierny 1456). One of the most influential doctors at that time, Silas Weir Mitchell, made popular his "rest cure," which was thought to be especially effective for such disorders.

These societal views are reflected in "The Yellow Wallpaper." The physician husband of the main character imposes the "rest cure" on her. She is forced to obey her husband and has no choice in her treatment. Furthermore, her husband does not listen when she tries to tell him more about her condition, her fears, and her aspirations. This feature of the story—men not listening to their wives—accurately reflects the social climate of the late nineteenth century, when husbands could impose their rules on their wives, with little (if any) thought given to what the women knew, felt, or wanted.

The writer uses the literary present tense to describe the action in the story itself.

Such a male-centered ideology fostered the development of the "rest cure," initiated by Weir Mitchell in the late 1880s. He describes his "Rest Treatment for Nervous Disorders" (Tierny 1456) as well as the temperament of women in his book *Fat and Blood: and How to Make Them*:

> The American woman is, to speak plainly, too often physically unfit for her duties as woman, and is perhaps of all civilized females the least qualified to undertake those weightier tasks which tax so heavily the nervous system of man. She is not fairly

The writer uses information from a physician's writings to support her interpretation and bolster her historical connection.

Ford 3

up to what nature asks from her as wife and mother. How
will she sustain herself under the pressure of those yet more
exacting duties which nowadays she is eager to share with the
man? (13)

Because of this general belief about American women's fragility (or
weakness), Weir Mitchell often diagnosed patients as having neurasthenia,
a catch-all term for any nervous disorder that affected mainly women.
Many cases, like the one depicted in "The Yellow Wallpaper," were
what would now be considered postpartum depression, a legitimate
psychological disorder requiring medication and therapy.

Conversely, Weir Mitchell's theory was that neurasthenia was all in
a woman's head. His rest treatment, prescribed only for women, involved
complete rest, little mental stimulation, and overfeeding. A woman was
not allowed to leave her bed for months at a time, and she was certainly
never allowed to read or write (Weir Mitchell 39). This tendency to
diagnose women as "hysterical," coupled with the era's chauvinism, made
it easy for doctors like Weir Mitchell to simply, almost flippantly, dismiss
the protesting pleas of mentally ill women.

The writer
presents relevant
biographical
information
about the author
of the story.

Gilman herself was prescribed this treatment. In "Why I Wrote 'The
Yellow Wallpaper,'" Gilman describes how she tried the "rest cure" for
three months and "came so near the border of mental ruin that I could see
over" (820). In the end, in order to save herself from insanity, Gilman had
to ignore what society told her. She could not lead a domestic, sedentary life
without falling into insanity. However, according to Weir Mitchell, such a life
was considered sane for a woman, a prime indicator of her mental stability.

Ford 4

The resulting conflict between Gilman's personal experience and Weir Mitchell's impersonal theory begs the question "What is true sanity?" For Gilman, the only way to cure herself of her madness was the very thing she was told she could not do: write and engage in mental stimulation. This is the double bind that women of the day faced. What Gilman was prescribed to do caused her to fall further into mental illness, but doing what she needed to do to get over the illness was considered a symptom of insanity. This is the same double bind trapping Gilman's protagonist throughout the story.

The rest cure is a tool to suppress all mental activity in women (Tierny 1457). At the beginning of the story, the struggle is among competing factors: what the protagonist is told, what she knows is right, and what she feels she should do. She wants to listen to her husband, but she senses that her illness will not be cured by his proposed remedy. All the while her husband assures her that she only needs the "rest cure" and she will be the wife and mother she should be. Throughout "The Yellow Wallpaper," the wife repeatedly says that although she may be getting physically better, mentally she is not. Her husband repeatedly replies, "Never for one instant let that idea enter your mind! There is nothing so dangerous, so fascinating to a temperament like yours" (Gilman, "Yellow Wallpaper" 814). In addition, he often admonishes her to get well. Gilman juxtaposes what men believed at this time with the actual implications of this cure for the female mind. Although her husband remarks that she seems to be getting better and better, the woman slowly descends further into her madness, showing just how oblivious men, even renowned physicians, were to the struggles of women.

Gilman's goal in this story is to expose this "rest cure" for what it truly is and make clear the struggle women have in a society in which they are expected to be entirely domestic and submissive to men. Gilman makes a particular yet subtle argument when she demonstrates the "domesticated" woman's double bind: If she uses her imagination in an "unsuitable" way, she is exhibiting mental illness. The cure for that illness is constraint, a prohibition on imagination and activity, which only worsens her mental condition. Gilman experienced another double bind as a female author functioning within a realm of male control and expectations. Any woman who published, particularly if her stories dealt with mentally ill women, was revealing her own mental instability. Of course, if an author was not able to write and publish, she would feel even worse.

Gilman portrays the feminist challenge to society's standards through character development and the interactions between the physician husband and his wife. When developing the character of the husband, Gilman illustrates his dominance over his wife through much of their dialogue. The physician speaks to his wife much like an adult speaking to a child. Gilman juxtaposes the husband's view of the woman's improving health against what the reader actually sees happening: the woman creeps around the room becoming completely involved in the pattern of the wallpaper, clearly a sign that she is becoming increasingly ill. This disconnect between what the husband wants to believe and the reality of his wife's condition exemplifies the disconnect in their marital life. It demonstrates the lack of understanding

Ford 6

men had toward women and the lack of concern with which they reacted
to women's problems.

In "The Yellow Wallpaper," Gilman produced an insightful work
using the symbolism of a room turned jail cell to express her views on
the way women were treated in her society. Gilman masterfully crafted a
story that describes a woman's descent into madness, using that descent
as an allegory for the oppression of women of the late nineteenth century.
Beyond its importance as a powerful piece of feminist literature, "The
Yellow Wallpaper" made a profound impact on its society. After the
publication of "Why I Wrote 'The Yellow Wallpaper,' " Weir Mitchell
quietly changed his "rest cure." For a respected physician in the late
nineteenth century to change his practice based on the literary work of a
woman is powerful testimony to the impact of "The Yellow Wallpaper."

Ford 7

Works Cited

Gilman, Charlotte P. "Why I Wrote 'The Yellow Wallpaper.'" *The Norton*
  Anthology of American Literature. 7th ed. Vol. C. New York:
  Norton, 2007. Print.

---. "The Yellow Wallpaper." *The Norton Anthology of American*
  Literature. 7th ed. Vol. C. New York: Norton, 2007. Print.

Lavender, Catherine. "The Cult of Domesticity & True Womanhood."
  Women in New York City, 1890–1940. The College of Staten Island of
  CUNY, Fall 1998. Web. 21 Nov. 2008. <http://www.csi.cuny.edu/dept/
  history/lavender/386/truewoman.html>.

Mellor, Ann K. *Romanticism and Feminism*. Bloomington: Indiana UP,
  1988. Print.

Tierny, Helen. *Women's Studies Encyclopedia*. Westport: Greenwood,
  1997. Print.

Weir Mitchell, Silas. *Fat and Blood: and How to Make Them*. Philadelphia:
  Lippincott, 1882. Print.

Exercise 2

Based on your reading of Kristin Ford's essay on "The Yellow
Wallpaper," what personal or political values do you think she
brought to her interpretation of that text? Which of the theoretical
approaches to literature did she use as the basis for her interpretation (**11d**)? Write a one- or two-page paper analyzing her interpretation of the story.

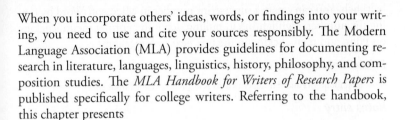

12 ‖ MLA DOCUMENTATION

When you incorporate others' ideas, words, or findings into your writing, you need to use and cite your sources responsibly. The Modern Language Association (MLA) provides guidelines for documenting research in literature, languages, linguistics, history, philosophy, and composition studies. The *MLA Handbook for Writers of Research Papers* is published specifically for college writers. Referring to the handbook, this chapter presents

- guidelines for citing sources within the text of a paper (**12a**),
- guidelines for documenting sources in a works-cited list (**12b**), and
- a sample student paper (**12c**).

12a ‖ MLA-STYLE IN-TEXT CITATIONS

(1) Citing material from other sources

The citations you use within the text of a research paper refer your readers to the list of works cited at the end of the paper, tell them where to find the borrowed material in the original source, and indicate the boundaries between your ideas and those you have borrowed. In the following example, the parenthetical citation guides the reader to page 88 of the book by Pollan in the works-cited list:

In-text citation

Since the 1980s virtually all the sodas and most of the fruit drinks sold in supermarkets have been sweetened with high-fructose corn syrup (HFCS)—after water, corn sweetener is their principal ingredient (Pollan 88).

Works-cited entry

Pollan, Michael. *The Omnivore's Dilemma: A Natural History of Four Meals*. New York: Penguin, 2006. Print.

The MLA suggests reserving numbered notes for supplementary comments—for example, when you wish to explain a point further but the subject matter is tangential to your topic. When numbered notes are used, superscript numbers are inserted in the appropriate places in the text, and the notes are gathered at the end of the paper on a separate page with the heading *Notes* (not italicized). The first line of each note is indented one-half inch. You can create a superscript number in Microsoft Word by typing the number, highlighting it, pulling down the Format menu, clicking on Font, and then clicking in the box next to Superscript.

In-text note number

Most food found in American supermarkets is ultimately derived from corn.[1]

Notes entry

1. Nearly all farm animals—from cows and chickens to various kinds of farmed fish—are fed a diet of corn.

An in-text citation usually provides two pieces of information about borrowed material: (1) information that directs the reader to the relevant source on the works-cited list and (2) information that directs the reader to a specific page or section within that source. An author's last name and a page number generally suffice. To create an in-text citation, either place both the author's last name and the page number in parentheses or introduce the author's name in the sentence and supply just the page number in parentheses.

A "remarkably narrow biological foundation" supports the variety of America's supermarkets (Pollan 18).

Pollan explains the way corn products "feed" the familiar meats, beverages, and dairy products that we find on our supermarket shelves (18).

When referring to information from a range of pages, separate the first and last pages with a hyphen: (34-42). If the page numbers have the same hundreds or thousands digit, do not repeat it when listing the final page in the range: (234-42) or (1350-55) but (290-301) or (1395-1402). If you refer to an entire work or a work with only one page, no page numbers are necessary.

The following examples are representative of the types of in-text citations you might be expected to use. For more details on the placement and punctuation of citations, including those following long quotations, see pages 263–65.

1. Work by one author

Set on the frontier and focused on characters who use language sparingly, Westerns often reveal a "pattern of linguistic regression" (Rosowski 170).

OR

Susan J. Rosowski argues that Westerns often reveal a "pattern of linguistic regression" (170).

2. More than one work by the same author(s)

When your works-cited list includes more than one work by the same author(s), provide a shortened title in your in-text citation that identifies the relevant work. Use a comma to separate the name (or names) from the shortened title when both are in parentheses. For example, if you listed two books by Antonio Damasio, *Looking for Spinoza* and *The Feeling of What Happens*, on your works-cited page, then you would cite one of them within your text as follows:

According to one neurological hypothesis, "feelings are the expression of human flourishing or human distress" (Damasio, *Looking* 6).

OR

Antonio Damasio believes that "feelings are the expression of human flourishing or human distress" (*Looking* 6).

3. Work by two or three authors

Some environmentalists seek to protect wilderness areas from further development so that they can both preserve the past and learn from it (Katcher and Wilkins 174).

Use commas to separate the names of three authors: (Bellamy, O'Brien, and Nichols 59).

4. Work by more than three authors

Use either the first author's last name followed by the abbreviation *et al.* (from the Latin *et alii,* meaning "and others") or all the last names. (Do not italicize the abbreviated Latin phrase, which ends with a period.)

In one important study, women graduates complained more frequently about "excessive control than about lack of structure" (Belenky et al. 205).

OR

In one important study, women graduates complained more frequently about "excessive control than about lack of structure" (Belenky, Clinchy, Goldberger, and Tarule 205).

5. Works by different authors with the same last name

When your works-cited list includes works by different authors with the same last name, provide a first initial, along with the last name, in parenthetical citations, or use the author's first and last name in the text. For example, if your works-cited list included entries for works by both Richard Enos and Theresa Enos, you would cite the work of Theresa Enos as follows.

Pre-Aristotelian rhetoric still has an impact today (T. Enos 331-43).

OR

Theresa Enos mentions the considerable contemporary reliance on pre-Aristotelian rhetoric (331-43).

If two authors have the same last name and first initial, spell out each author's first name in a parenthetical citation.

6. Work by a corporate author

A work has a corporate author when individual members of the group that created it are not identified. If the corporate author's name is long, you may use common abbreviations for parts of it—for example, *Assn.* for "Association" and *Natl.* for "National." Do not italicize the abbreviations.

Strawbale constructions are now popular across the nation (Natl. Ecobuilders Group 2).

7. Two or more works in the same citation

When two sources provide similar information or when you combine information from two sources in the same sentence, cite both sources, listing them in alphabetical order by the first author of each one and separating them with a semicolon.

Agricultural scientists believe that crop productivity will be adversely affected by solar dimming (Beck and Watts 90; Harris-Green 153-54).

8. Multivolume work

When you cite material from more than one volume of a multivolume work, include the volume number (followed by a colon and a space) before the page number.

Katherine Raine claims that "true poetry begins where human personality ends" (2: 247).

You do not need to include the volume number in a parenthetical citation if your list of works cited includes only one volume of a multivolume work.

9. Anonymous work

The Tehuelche people left their handprints on the walls of a cave, now called Cave of the Hands ("Hands of Time" 124).

Use the title of an anonymous work in place of an author's name. If the title is long, provide a shortened version, beginning with the word by which it is alphabetized in the list of works cited. For example, the shortened title for "Chasing Down the Phrasal Verb in the Discourse of Adolescents" is "Chasing Down."

10. Indirect source

If you need to include material that one of your sources quoted from another work because you cannot obtain the original source, use the following format (*qtd.* is the abbreviation for "quoted"):

The critic Susan Hardy Aikens has argued on behalf of what she calls "canonical multiplicity" (qtd. in Mayers 677).

A reader turning to the list of works cited should find a bibliographic entry for Mayers, the source consulted, but not for Aikens.

11. Poetry, drama, and sacred texts

When you refer to poetry, drama, or sacred texts, you should give the numbers of lines, acts and scenes, or chapters and verses, rather than page numbers. This practice enables readers to consult an edition other than the one you have used. Act, scene, and line numbers (all arabic numerals) are separated by periods with no space before or after them. The MLA suggests that biblical chapters and verses be treated similarly, although some writers prefer to use colons instead of periods in such citations. In all cases, the progression is from larger to smaller units.

The following citation refers to lines of a poem:

Emily Dickinson alludes to her dislike of public appearance in "I'm Nobody! Who Are You?" (5-8).

The following citation shows that the famous "To be, or not to be" soliloquy from *Hamlet* appears in act 3, scene 1, lines 56-89:

In *Hamlet*, Shakespeare presents the most famous soliloquy in the history of the English theater: "To be, or not to be . . ." (3.1.56-89).

Citations of biblical material identify the book of the Bible, the chapter, and the pertinent verses. In the following example, the writer refers to the creation story in Genesis, which begins in chapter 1 with verse 1 and ends in chapter 2 with verse 22:

The Old Testament creation story, told with remarkable economy, culminates in the arrival of Eve (*New American Standard Bible*, Gen. 1.1-2.22).

Mention in your first citation which version of the Bible you are using; list only book, chapter, and verse in subsequent citations. Note that the names of biblical books are neither italicized nor enclosed in quotation marks.

The *MLA Handbook* provides standard abbreviations for the parts of the Bible, as well as for the works of Shakespeare and Chaucer and certain other literary works.

12. Constitution

When referring to the US Constitution, use the full title in the list of works cited. For in-text citations, use the following common abbreviations:

United States Constitution	US Const.
article	art.
section	sec.

The testimony of two witnesses is needed to convict someone of treason (US Const., art. 3, sec. 3).

13. Online sources

If paragraphs or sections in an online source are numbered, cite the number(s) of the paragraph(s) or section(s) after the abbreviation *par.* (or *pars.* for more than one paragraph) or *sec.* (or *secs.* for more than one section).

Alston describes three types of rubrics for evaluating customer service (pars. 2-15).

Hilton and Merrill provide examples of effective hyperlinks (sec. 1).

PDFs (stable files that can be viewed on and downloaded from the Internet) usually have numbered pages, which you should cite.

If an online source includes no numbers that distinguish one part from another, either indicate an approximate location of the cited passage within the sentence that introduces the material or treat the source as unpaginated in the parenthetical citation.

Raymond Lucero's *Shopping Online* offers useful advice for consumers who are concerned about transmitting credit-card information over the Internet.

Shopping Online offers useful advice for consumers who are concerned about transmitting credit-card information over the Internet (Lucero).

If an electronic source is only one page long, you may omit the page number in your citation. However, including a page number demonstrates to your readers that you did not unintentionally omit it and gives the citation the proper form.

(2) Guidelines for in-text citations and quotations

(a) Placement of in-text citations

When you acknowledge your use of a source by placing the author's name and a relevant page number in parentheses, insert this parenthetical citation directly after the information you used, generally at the end of a sentence but *before* the final punctuation mark (a period, question mark, or exclamation point).

Oceans store almost half the carbon dioxide released by humans into the atmosphere (Wall 28).

However, you may need to place a parenthetical citation earlier in a sentence to indicate that only the first part of the sentence contains borrowed material. Place the citation after the clause containing the material but before a punctuation mark (a comma, semicolon, or colon).

Oceans store almost half the carbon dioxide released by humans into the atmosphere (Wall 28), a fact that provides hope for scientists studying global warming but alarms scientists studying organisms living in the oceans.

If you cite the same source more than once in a paragraph, with no intervening citations of another source, you can place one parenthetical citation at the end of the last sentence in which the source is used: (Wall 28, 32).

(b) Lengthy quotations

When a quotation is more than four lines long, set it off from the surrounding text by indenting all lines one inch from the left margin. Such quotations (sometimes referred to as **block quotations**) are usually introduced by a colon, but other punctuation marks or none at all may be more appropriate. The first line should not be indented more than the others. The right margin should remain the same as it is for the surrounding text. Double-space the entire quotation and do not enclose it in quotation marks.

In *Nickel and Dimed*, Barbara Ehrenreich describes the dire living conditions of the working poor:

> The lunch that consists of Doritos or hot dog rolls, leading to faintness before the end of the shift. The "home" that is also a car or a van. The illness or injury that must be "worked through," with gritted teeth, because there's no sick pay or health insurance and the loss of one day's pay will mean no groceries for the next. These experiences are not part of a sustainable lifestyle, even a lifestyle of chronic deprivation and relentless low-level punishment. They are, by almost any standard of subsistence, emergency situations. And that is how we should see the poverty of millions of low-wage Americans—as a state of emergency. (214)

A problem of this magnitude cannot be fixed simply by raising the minimum wage.

Note that the period precedes the parenthetical citation at the end of an indented (block) quotation. Note, too, how the writer introduces and then comments on the quotation from Ehrenreich.

Rarely will you need to quote more than a paragraph, but if you do, indent the first line of each paragraph an extra quarter of an inch.

(c) Punctuation within citations and quotations

Punctuation marks clarify meaning in quotations and citations. The following list summarizes their common uses:

- A colon separates volume numbers from page numbers in a parenthetical citation.

  (Raine 2: 247)

- A comma separates the author's name from the title when it is necessary to list both in a parenthetical citation.

  (Kingsolver, *Animal Dreams*)

  A comma also indicates that page or line numbers are not sequential.

  (44, 47)

- Ellipsis points indicate an omission within a quotation.

  "They lived in an age of increasing complexity and great hope; we in an age of . . . growing despair" (Krutch 2).

  When an ellipsis indicates that the end of a sentence has been omitted, the final punctuation follows the in-text citation.

  "They lived in an age of increasing complexity and great hope . . ." (Krutch 2).

- A hyphen indicates a continuous sequence of pages or lines.

  (44-47)

- A period separates acts, scenes, and lines of dramatic works.

  (3.1.56)

  A period also distinguishes chapters from verses in biblical citations.

  (Gen. 1.1)

- A question mark placed inside the final quotation marks indicates that the quotation itself is a question. Notice that the period after the parenthetical citation marks the end of the sentence.

  Peter Elbow asks, "What could be more wonderful than the pleasure of creating or appreciating forms that are different, amazing, outlandish, useless—the opposite of ordinary, everyday, pragmatic?" (542).

  When placed outside the final quotation marks, a question mark indicates that the quotation has been incorporated into a question posed by the writer of the paper.

  What does Kabat-Zinn mean when he advises people to practice mindfulness "as if their lives depended on it" (305)?

- Square brackets enclose words that have been added to the quotation as clarification and are not part of the original material.

  "The publication of this novel [*Beloved*] establishes Morrison as one of the most important writers of our time" (Boyle 17).

12b MLA LIST OF WORKS CITED

All of the works you cite should be listed at the end of your paper, beginning on a separate page that has the heading *Works Cited*. Use the following tips as you prepare your list.

TIPS FOR PREPARING A LIST OF WORKS CITED

- Center the heading *Works Cited* (not italicized) one inch from the top of the page.
- Arrange the list of works alphabetically by the authors' last names.
- If a source has more than one author, alphabetize the entry according to the last name of the first author.
- If you use more than one work by the same author, alphabetize the works by the first major word in each title. For the first entry, provide the author's complete name (last name given first), but substitute three hyphens (---) for the author's name in subsequent entries. If the author is also the first of two or more authors of another work in the list, do not use three hyphens for the author's name but instead write it out in full. A multiple-author entry follows all entries for the first author's works.
- For a work without an author or editor, alphabetize the entry according to the first important word in the title.
- Type the first line of each entry flush with the left margin and indent subsequent lines one-half inch (a hanging indent).
- Double-space equally throughout—between lines of an entry and between entries as well as between the heading *Works Cited* and the first entry.

---

❶ CAUTION

Automatic bibliography composers found online and included in some software packages often make mistakes. They may fail to include all elements of a bibliographic entry or may order the elements incorrectly. If you decide to use an automatic composer, be sure to check the results against the model entries provided in this chapter.

Directory of MLA-Style Entries for a Works-Cited List

When writing down source information for your bibliography, be sure to copy the information directly from the source (e.g., the table of contents of a journal or the title page of a book). (See Figure 12.1 on page 274 for an example of a journal's table of contents and Figure 12.2 on page 278 for an example of a book's title page.)

GENERAL DOCUMENTATION GUIDELINES FOR PRINT-BASED SOURCES

Author or Editor

One author. Place the last name before the first, separating them with a comma. Add any middle name or initial after the first name. Use another comma before any abbreviation or number that follows the first name. Titles, affiliations, and degrees should be omitted. Indicate the end of this unit of the entry with a period.	Halberstam, David. Johnston, Mary K. King, Martin Luther, Jr.
Two or three authors. List names in the same order used in the original source. The first person's name is inverted (that is, the last name appears first); the others are not. Separate all names with commas, placing the word *and* before the final name.	West, Nigel, and Oleg Tsarev. Green, Bill, Maria Lopez, and Jenny T. Graf.
Four or more authors. List the names of all the authors or provide just the first person's name (inverted) and the abbreviation *et al.* (for *et alii,* meaning "and others").	Quirk, Randolph, Sidney Greenbaum, Geoffrey Leech, and Jan Svartvik. or Quirk, Randolph, et al.
Corporate or group author. Omit any initial article (*a, an,* or *the*) from the name.	Institute of Medicine. Department of Natural Resources.
Editor. If an editor or editors are listed instead of an author or authors, include the abbreviation *ed.* for "editor" or *eds.* for "editors."	Espinoza, Toni, ed. Gibb, Susan, and Karen Enochs, eds.

Title

Italicized titles. Italicize the titles of books, magazines, journals, newspapers, films, plays, and screenplays. Capitalize all major words (nouns, pronouns, verbs, adjectives, adverbs, and subordinating conjunctions). Do not use a period after the title of a periodical.	*Hamlet.* *Weird English.* *The Aviator.* *Newsweek*
Titles in quotation marks. Use quotation marks to enclose the titles of short works such as journal or magazine articles, short stories, poems, and songs (**39b**).	"Three Days to See." "Selling the Super Bowl." "Generations."
Subtitles. Always include a subtitle if the work has one. Use a colon to separate a main title and a subtitle. However, if the main title ends in a question or exclamation mark, no colon is used.	*Lost in Translation: Life in a New Language.* "Silence: Learning to Listen."
Titles within titles. When an italicized title includes the title of another work normally italicized, do not italicize the embedded title.	*Essays on* Death of a Salesman. but *Death of a Salesman.*
If the embedded title normally requires quotation marks, it should be italicized as well as enclosed in quotation marks.	*Understanding "The Philosophy of Composition" and the Aesthetic of Edgar Allan Poe.* but "The Philosophy of Composition."
When a title in quotation marks includes the title of another work normally italicized, retain the italics.	"A Salesman's Reading of *Death of a Salesman.*"

(continued on page 272)

Title *(continued from page 271)*

If the embedded title is normally enclosed in quotation marks, use single quotation marks.	"The European Roots of 'The Philosophy of Composition.'"

Publication Data

City of publication. If more than one city is listed on the title page, mention only the first. Place a colon after the name of the city.	Boston: New York:
Publisher's name. Provide a shortened form of the publisher's name, and place a comma after it. To shorten the name of the publisher, use the principal name. For books published by university presses, abbreviate *University* and *Press* without periods or italics.	Knopf (for Alfred A. Knopf) Random (for Random House) Harvard UP (for Harvard University Press)
If two publishers are listed, provide the city of publication and the name of the publisher for each. Use a semicolon to separate the two.	Manchester: Manchester UP; New York: St. Martin's
Publisher's imprint. You will sometimes need identify both a publisher and an imprint. The imprint is usually listed above the publisher's name on the title page. In a works-cited entry, the imprint is listed first with a hyphen to separate the two names.	Quill-Harper Vintage-Random
Copyright date. Although the copyright date may be found on the title page, it is usually found on the next page—the copyright page (see Figure 12.3 on page 279). Place a period after the date.	

Medium of publication. Entries for all print publications—books, newspapers, magazines, journals, maps, articles, reviews, editorials, letters to the editor, pamphlets, published dissertations, and so on—must include the medium of publication: *Print.* Do not italicize the medium of publication; follow it with a period.

PRINT PUBLICATIONS

Print Articles

A **journal** is a publication written for a specific discipline or profession. **Magazines** and **newspapers** are written for the general public. You can find most of the information required for a works-cited entry for a journal article in the table of contents for the issue (Figure 12.1) or at the bottom of the first page of the article.

Title of article and name of periodical

Put the article title in quotation marks with a period inside the closing quotation marks. Italicize the name of the periodical, but do not add any punctuation following the name. Capitalize all major words (nouns, pronouns, verbs, adjectives, adverbs, and subordinating conjunctions). Omit the word *A, An,* or *The* from the beginning of the name of a periodical.

"Activities to Create Yearlong Momentum." *English Journal*

Volume and issue numbers

In an entry for an article from a journal, provide the volume number. If the issue number is available, put a period after the volume number and add the issue number.

Contemporary Review 194   *Studies in the Literary Imagination* 26.3

Date

For journals, place the year of publication in parentheses after the volume or issue number. For magazines and newspapers, provide the date of issue

ENGLISH JOURNAL — Name of journal

Vol. 98 No. 1 September 2008

Date of publication

Volume number Issue number

Name of author

Title of article

continued

THE JOURNAL OF THE SECONDARY SECTION OF THE NATIONAL COUNCIL OF TEACHERS OF ENGLISH. PUBLISHED SINCE 1912.
Printed on recycled paper.

Figure 12.1. Table of contents of a journal.

after the name of the periodical. Note the day first (if provided), followed by the month (abbreviated except for May, June, and July) and year.

Journal	*American Literary History* 20.1-2 (2008)
Magazine	*Economist* 13 Aug. 2005
Newspaper	*Chicago Tribune* 24 July 2002

Page numbers
Use a colon to separate the date from the page number(s). Note all the pages on which the article appears, separating the first and last page with a hyphen: 21-39. If the page numbers have the same hundreds or thousands digit, do not repeat it when listing the final page in the range: 131-42 or 1680-99. Magazine and newspaper articles are often interrupted by advertisements or other articles. If the first part of an article appears on pages 45 through 47 and the rest on pages 92 through 94, give only the first page number followed by a plus sign: 45+.

Medium of publication
Identify the medium of publication, *Print* (not italicized), at the end of the entry.

1. Article in a journal

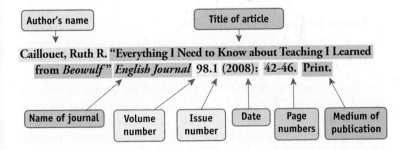

Author's name

Title of article

Caillouet, Ruth R. "Everything I Need to Know about Teaching I Learned from *Beowulf*" *English Journal* 98.1 (2008): 42-46. Print.

Name of journal

Volume number

Issue number

Date

Page numbers

Medium of publication

2. Article in a monthly magazine

Keizer, Garret. "How the Devil Falls in Love." *Harper's* Aug. 2002: 43–51. Print.

3. Article in a weekly magazine or newspaper

Chown, Marcus. "Into the Void." *New Scientist* 24 Nov. 2007: 34-37. Print.

4. Article in a daily newspaper

Moberg, David. "The Accidental Environmentalist." *Chicago Tribune* 24 Sept. 2002, final
ed., sec. 2: 1+. Print.

When the name of the city is not part of a locally published newspaper's name, it should be given in brackets after the name of the paper: *Star Telegram* [Fort Worth]. If an edition is specified on the newspaper's masthead, include this information (using *ed.* for "edition") after the date. If a specific edition is not identified, put a colon after the date and then provide the page number(s). Specify a section by using the number and/or letter that appears in the newspaper (7, A, A7, or 7A, for example).

5. Unsigned article or wire service article

"View from the Top." *National Geographic* July 2001: 140. Print.

6. Editorial in a newspaper or magazine

Beefs, Anne. "Ending Bias in the Human Rights System." Editorial. *New York Times* 22 May
2002, natl. ed.: A27. Print.

7. Book or film review in a magazine

Denby, David. "Horse Power." Rev. of *Seabiscuit*, dir. Gary Ross. *New Yorker* 4 Aug. 2003:
84–85. Print.

Include the name of the reviewer, the title of the review (if any), the phrase *Rev. of* (for "Review of"), the title of the work being reviewed, and the name of the editor (preceded by the abbreviation *ed.*, not italicized), the author (preceded by the word *by*), or the director (preceded by the abbreviation *dir.*).

8. Book or film review in a journal

Graham, Catherine. Rev. of *Questionable Activities: The Best*, ed. Judith Rudakoff. *Canadian
Theatre Review* 113 (2003): 74–76. Print.

Print Books

9. Book by one author

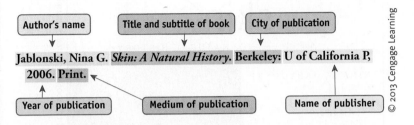

Author's name

Title and subtitle of book

City of publication

Jablonski, Nina G. *Skin: A Natural History*. Berkeley: U of California P,

2006. Print.

Year of publication

Medium of publication

Name of publisher

© 2013 Cengage Learning

The title page and copyright page of a book (see Figures 12.2 and 12.3) provide the information needed to create a bibliographic entry. Be sure to include the medium of publication at the end of the entry.

10. Book by two authors

West, Nigel, and Oleg Tsarev. *The Crown Jewels: The British Secrets at the Heart of the KGB Archives*. New Haven: Yale UP, 1999. Print.

11. Book by three authors

Spinosa, Charles, Ferdinand Flores, and Hubert L. Dreyfus. *Disclosing New Worlds: Entrepreneurship, Democratic Action, and the Cultivation of Solidarity*. Cambridge: MIT P, 1997. Print.

12. Book by more than three authors

Bullock, Jane A., George D. Haddow, Damon Cappola, Erdem Ergin, Lissa Westerman, and Sarp Yeletaysi. *Introduction to Homeland Security*. Boston: Elsevier, 2005. Print.

OR

Bullock, Jane A., et al. *Introduction to Homeland Security*. Boston: Elsevier, 2005. Print.

13. Book by a corporate author

Institute of Medicine. *Blood Banking and Regulation: Procedures, Problems, and Alternatives*. Washington: Natl. Acad., 1996. Print.

14. Book by an anonymous author

Primary Colors: A Novel of Politics. New York: Warner, 1996. Print.

Begin the entry with the title. Do not use *Anonymous* or *Anon*.

Figure 12.2. A title page includes most, if not all, of the information needed for a bibliographic entry. In this case, the title page omits the publication date.

15. Book with an author and an editor

Stoker, Bram. *Dracula*. 1897. Ed. Glennis Byron. Peterborough: Broadview, 1998. Print.

Include both the name of the author and the name of the editor (preceded by *Ed.*). The original publication date, followed by a period, can be included after the title.

16. Book with an editor instead of an author

Kachuba, John B., ed. *How to Write Funny*. Cincinnati: Writer's Digest, 2000. Print.

University of California Press, one of the most distinguished
university presses in the United States, enriches lives around the
world by advancing scholarship in the humanities, social sciences,
and natural sciences. Its activities are supported by the UC Press
Foundation and by philanthropic contributions from individuals
and institutions. For more information, visit www.ucpress.edu.

University of California Press
Berkeley and Los Angeles, California

University of California Press, Ltd.
London, England

Copyright year

©2006 by Nina G. Jablonski

Figure 12.3. If the title page does not give the book's date of publication, turn to the copyright page, which is usually the page following the title page.

17. Edition after the first

Murray, Donald. *The Craft of Revision*. 4th ed. Boston: Heinle, 2001. Print.

18. Introduction, preface, foreword, or afterword to a book

Olmos, Edward James. Foreword. *Vietnam Veteranos: Chicanos Recall the War*. By Lea Ybarra.

Austin: U of Texas P, 2004. ix-x. Print.

The name that begins the entry is that of the author of the section of the book, not the author of the entire book. The section author's name is followed by the title of the section (Introduction, Preface, Foreword, or Afterword).

19. Anthology (a collection of works by different authors)

Buranen, Lisa, and Alice M. Roy, eds. *Perspectives on Plagiarism and Intellectual Property in a*

Postmodern World. Albany: State U of New York P, 1999. Print.

Include the name(s) of the editor(s), followed by the abbreviation *ed.* (or *eds.*). (For documenting individual works within an anthology, see items 20–22.)

20. A work originally published in an anthology

Rowe, David. "No Gain, No Game? Media and Sport." *Mass Media and Society*. Ed. James
Curran and Michael Gurevitch. 3rd ed. New York: Oxford UP, 2000. 346-61. Print.

Use this form for an article, essay, story, poem, or play that was published for the first time in the anthology. Place the title of the anthology
after the title of the individual work. Provide the name(s) of the editor(s)
after the abbreviation *Ed.* for "edited by," and note the edition if it is not
the first. List the publication data for the anthology and the range of
pages on which the work appears. (See pages 258 and 275 for information on inclusive page numbers.)

If you cite more than one work from an anthology, provide only the
name(s) of the author(s), the title of the work, the name(s) of the editor(s),
and the inclusive page numbers in an entry for each work. Also provide
an entry for the entire anthology, in which you include the relevant publication data (see the sample entry for an anthology in item 19).

Clark, Irene L. "Writing Centers and Plagiarism." Buranen and Roy 155-67.

Howard, Rebecca Moore. "The New Abolitionism Comes to Plagiarism." Buranen and
Roy 87-95.

21. A work from a journal reprinted in a textbook or an anthology

Selfe, Cynthia L. "Technology and Literacy: A Story about the Perils of Not Paying
Attention." *College Composition and Communication* 50.3 (1999): 411-37. Rpt. in *Views
from the Center: The CCCC Chairs' Addresses 1977-2005*. Ed. Duane Roen. Boston:
Bedford; Urbana: NCTE, 2006. 323-51. Print.

Use the abbreviation *Rpt.* (not italicized) for "Reprinted." Two cities
and publishers are listed in the sample entry because the collection was
copublished.

22. A work from an edited collection reprinted in a textbook or an anthology

Brownmiller, Susan. "Let's Put Pornography Back in the Closet." *Take Back the Night: Women on
Pornography*. Ed. Laura Lederer. New York: Morrow, 1980. 252-55. Rpt. in *Conversations:
Readings for Writing*. By Jack Selzer. 4th ed. New York: Allyn, 2000. 578-81. Print.

See item 20 for information on citing more than one work from the
same anthology.

23. Translated book

Garrigues, Eduardo. *West of Babylon*. Trans. Nasario Garcia. Albuquerque: U of New

Mexico P, 2002. Print.

Place the abbreviation *Trans.* (not italicized) for "Translated by" before the translator's name.

24. Republished book

Alcott, Louisa May. *Work: A Story of Experience*. 1873. Harmondsworth: Penguin, 1995. Print.

After the title of the book, provide the original publication date, followed by a period.

25. Multivolume work

Young, Ralph F., ed. *Dissent in America*. 2 vols. New York: Longman-Pearson, 2005. Print.

Cite the total number of volumes in a work when you have used material from more than one volume. If all the volumes were not published in the same year, provide inclusive dates: 1997–99 or 1998–2004. If publication of the work is still in progress, include the words *to date* (not italicized) after the number of volumes. If you have used material from only one volume of a multivolume work, include that volume's number (preceded by the abbreviation *Vol.*) in place of the total number of volumes.

Young, Ralph F., ed. *Dissent in America*. Vol. 1. New York: Longman-Pearson, 2005. Print.

Note that the publisher's name in this entry is hyphenated: the first name is the imprint, and the second is the publisher.

26. Article in a multivolume work

To indicate a specific article in a multivolume work, provide the author's name and the title of the article in quotation marks. Provide the page numbers for the article after the date of publication.

Baxby, Derrick. "Jenner, Edward." *Oxford Dictionary of National Biography*. Ed. H. C. G.

Matthew and Brian Harrison. Vol. 30. Oxford: Oxford UP, 2004. 4-8. Print.

If required by your instructor, include the number of volumes and the inclusive publication dates after the medium of publication: 382-89. Print. 23 vols. 1962-97.

27. Book in a series

Sumner, Colin, ed. *Blackwell Companion to Criminology*. Malden: Blackwell, 2004. Print.

Blackwell Companions to Sociology 8.

When citing a book that is part of a series, add the name of the series after the medium of publication. If one is listed, include the number designating the work's place in the series. The series name is not italicized. Abbreviate words in the series name according to the MLA guidelines; for example, the word *Series* is abbreviated *Ser.*

Other Print Texts

28. Encyclopedia entry

Robertson, James I., Jr. "Jackson, Thomas Jonathan." *Encyclopedia of the American Civil War: A Political, Social, and Military History*. Ed. David S. Heidler and Jeanne T. Heidler.

Santa Barbara: ABC-CLIO, 2000. 1058-66. Print.

When the author of an encyclopedia article is indicated by initials only, check the table of contents for a list of contributors. If an article is anonymous, begin the entry with the article title.

Page numbers and full publication information are not necessary in an entry for an article from a well-known reference work that is organized alphabetically. After the author's name, the title of the article, and the name of the encyclopedia, provide the edition and/or year of publication, for example, *5th ed. 2004.* or *2002 ed.* (not italicized). Conclude with the medium of publication.

Petersen, William J. "Riverboats and Rivermen." *The Encyclopedia Americana*. 1999 ed. Print.

29. Dictionary entry

When citing a specific dictionary definition for a word, use the abbreviation *Def.* (for "Definition"), and indicate which definition you used if the entry has two or more.

"Reactive." Def. 2a. *Merriam-Webster's Collegiate Dictionary*. 10th ed. 2001. Print.

30. Sacred text

Begin your works-cited entry for a sacred text with the title of the work, rather than information about editors or translators, and, if appropriate, end the entry with the name of the version of that work.

The Bible. Anaheim: Foundation, 1997. Print. New American Standard Bible.

The Qur'an. Trans. Muhammad A. S. Abdel Haleem. Oxford: Oxford UP, 2004. Print.

31. Government publication

United States. Office of Management and Budget. *A Citizen's Guide to the Federal Budget.*
  Washington: GPO, 1999. Print.

When citing a government publication, list the name of the government (e.g., United States or Minnesota) and the agency that issued the work. Italicize the title of a book or pamphlet. Indicate the city of publication. Federal publications are usually printed by the Government Printing Office (GPO) in Washington, DC, but be alert for exceptions.

When the name of an author, editor, or compiler appears on a government publication, you can begin the entry with that name, followed by the abbreviation *ed.* or *comp.* if the person is not the author. Alternatively, insert that name after the publication's title and introduce it with the word *By* or the abbreviation *Ed.* or *Comp.* to indicate the person's contribution.

32. Law case

Chavez v. Martinez. 538 US 760. Supreme Court of the US. 2003. *United States Reports.*
  Washington: GPO, 2004. Print.

Include the last name of the first plaintiff, the abbreviation *v.* for "versus," the last name of the first defendant, data on the law report (volume, abbreviated name, and page or reference number), the name of the deciding court, the year of the decision, and appropriate publication information for the medium consulted. Although names of law cases are italicized in the text of a paper, they are *not* italicized in works-cited entries.

33. Public law

No Child Left Behind Act of 2001. Pub. L. 107-10. 115 Stat. 1425-2094. 8 Jan. 2002. Print.

Include the name of the act, its Public Law number (preceded by the abbreviation *Pub. L.*), its Statutes at Large volume number and page numbers (separated by the abbreviation *Stat.*), the date it was enacted, and the medium of publication.

Although no works-cited entry is needed for familiar sources such as the US Constitution, an in-text citation should still be included (see page 262).

34. Pamphlet or bulletin

Stucco in Residential Construction. St. Paul: Lath & Plaster Bureau, 2000. Print.

If the pamphlet has an author, begin with the author's name, as you would in an entry for a book.

35. Published dissertation

Fukuda, Kay Louise. *Differing Perceptions and Constructions of the Meaning of Assessment in*

Education. Diss. Ohio State U, 2001. Ann Arbor: UMI, 2002. Print.

After the title of the dissertation, include the abbreviation *Diss.*, the name of the university granting the degree, the date of completion, and the publication information. In the example, *UMI* stands for "University Microfilms International," which publishes many dissertations. If a dissertation was published by its author, use *privately published* (not italicized) instead of a publisher's name.

36. Published letter

In general, treat a published letter like a work in an anthology, adding the date of the letter and the number (if the editor assigned one).

Jackson, Helen Hunt. "To Thomas Bailey Aldrich." 4 May 1883. *The Indian Reform*

Letters of Helen Hunt Jackson, 1879-1885. Ed. Valerie Sherer Mathes. Norman: U of

Oklahoma P, 1998. 258-59. Print.

Print Cartoons, Maps, and Other Visuals

37. Cartoon or comic strip

Cheney, Tom. Cartoon. *New Yorker* 9 June 2003: 93. Print.

Trudeau, Garry. "Doonesbury." Comic strip. *Daily Record* [Ellensburg] 21 Apr. 2005:

A4. Print.

After the creator's name, place the title of the work (if given) in quotation marks and include the descriptor *Cartoon* or *Comic strip.*

38. Map or chart

Cincinnati and Vicinity. Map. Chicago: Rand, 2008. Print.

Include the title and the appropriate descriptor, *Map* or *Chart.*

39. Advertisement

Nu by Yves Saint Laurent. Advertisement. *Allure* June 2003: 40. Print.

The name of the product and/or that of the company being advertised is followed by the designation *Advertisement.*

ONLINE PUBLICATIONS

Many of the MLA guidelines for documenting online sources are similar to those for print sources. For sources you find online, provide electronic publication information and access information. (However, if you conduct all your research online, you may want to consult *The Columbia Guide to Online Style*, which offers formatting guidelines, sample in-text citations, and sample bibliographic entries.)

Electronic publication information
Indicate the author's name, the title of the work, the title of the website (and version or edition used), the site's sponsoring organization (usually found at the bottom of the site's home page; see Figure 12.4), the date of publication, and the medium of publication (*Web*). All of this information precedes the access information.

Access information
When you document an online source, you must include the date of access: the day, month, and year on which you consulted the source. Either keep track of the date of access or print out the source so that you have a record (see Figure 12.5).

You are not required to include the URL if your readers can easily locate the online source by searching for the author's name and

Centers for Disease Control and Prevention

Figure 12.4. A page on the website of the Centers for Disease Control and Prevention indicates the name of the sponsoring organization and the date of publication (most recent update).

the title of the work. For cases in which your readers cannot easily locate a source, you should provide the complete URL (between angle brackets), including the protocol (*http, ftp, telnet,* or *news*). When a URL does not fit on a single line, break it only after a slash or a double slash. Make sure that the URL is accurate. Take care to distinguish between uppercase and lowercase letters and to include hyphens and underscores. The URL follows the date of access, appearing after a period and a space. The closing angle bracket should also be followed by a period.

Figure 12.5. When you print a page from a website, the URL and the date of access usually appear at the top or bottom of the page.

Online Articles

The following formats apply to articles available only online. For articles available through online databases, see pages 288–91. If you need to include a URL, follow the instructions on page 286.

40. Scholarly journal article

Harnack, Andrea, and Gene Kleppinger. "Beyond the *MLA Handbook*: Documenting

　　Sources on the Internet." *Kairos* 1.2 (1996): n. pag. Web. 14 Aug. 1997.

If no page numbers are provided for an online journal, write *n. pag.* (for "no pagination"). If page numbers are provided, place them after the publication date and a colon. The entry ends with the date of access.

41. Popular magazine article

Plotz, David. "The Cure for Sinophobia." *Slate.com*. Newsweek Interactive, 4 June 1999.

　　Web. 15 June 1999.

42. Newspaper article

"Tornadoes Touch Down in S. Illinois." *New York Times*. New York Times, 16 Apr. 1998.

　　Web. 20 May 1998.

When no author is identified, begin with the title of the article. If the article is an editorial, include *Editorial* (not italicized) after the title: "America's Promises." Editorial. (In the sample entry, the first mention of *New York Times* is the title of the website, and the second, which is not italicized, is the name of the site's sponsor.)

Online Books

43. Book available only online

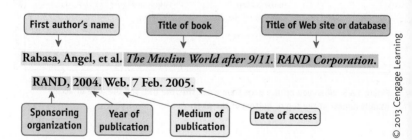

Because there are more than three authors, the abbreviation *et al.* has been used in the example entry, but listing all names is also acceptable: Rabasa,

Angel, Cheryl Benard, Peter Chalk, C. Christine Fair, Theodore W. Karasik, Rollie Lal, Ian O. Lesser, and David E. Thaler.

44. Book available online and in print

Rohrbough, Malcolm J. *Days of Gold: The California Gold Rush and the American Nation.* Berkeley: U of California P, 1997. *History E-book Project.* Web. 17 Feb. 2005.

Begin the citation with print citation information: the author's name, the title of the work, city of publication, publisher, and date. Follow this information with the title of the database or website (italicized) where the book was accessed, the medium of publication (*Web*), and the date of access.

45. Part of an online book

Strunk, William, Jr. "Elementary Rules of Usage." *The Elements of Style.* Ithaca: Humphrey, 1918. n. pag. *Bartleby.com.* Web. 6 June 2003.

Online Databases

Many print materials are available online through databases such as JSTOR, Project MUSE, ERIC, PsycINFO, Academic Search Premier, LexisNexis, ProQuest, InfoTrac, and Silver Platter. To cite material from an online database, begin with the author, the title of the article (in quotation marks), the title of the publication (in italics), the volume and issue numbers, the year of publication, and the page numbers (or the abbreviation *n. pag.*). Then add the name of the database (in italics), the medium of publication (*Web*), and the date of access. You can find most of the information you need for a works-cited entry for an article on the abstract page from the database (see Figure 12.6).

46. ERIC

Taylor, Steven J. "Caught in the Continuum: A Critical Analysis of the Principle of the Least Restrictive Environment." *Research and Practice for Persons with Severe Disabilities* 29.4 (2004): 218-30. *ERIC.* Web. 3 Mar. 2009.

Name of database —

Title of article —

Author —

Name of journal —

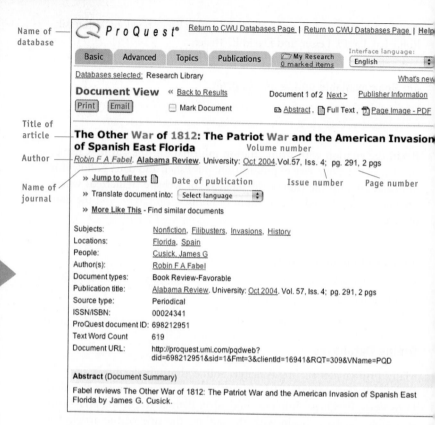

Figure 12.6. Abstract page from an online subscription database.

47. Academic Search Premier

Folks, Jeffrey J. "Crowd and Self: William Faulkner's Sources of Agency in *The Sound and the Fury*." *Southern Literary Journal* 34.2 (2002): 30+. *Academic Search Premier*. Web. 6 June 2003.

For sources that list only the page number on which a work begins, include that number and a plus sign.

48. LexisNexis

Suggs, Welch. "A Hard Year in College Sports." *Chronicle of Higher Education* 19 Dec. 2003: 37. *LexisNexis*. Web. 17 July 2004.

49. ProQuest

Fabel, Robin F. A. "The Other War of 1812: The Patriot War and the American Invasion of
Spanish East Florida." *Alabama Review* 57.4 (2004): 291-92. *ProQuest.* Web. 8 Mar. 2005.

50. InfoTrac

Priest, Ann-Marie. "Between Being and Nothingness: The 'Astonishing Precipice' of Virginia
Woolf's *Night and Day*." *Journal of Modern Literature* 26.2 (2002-03): 66-80. *InfoTrac.*
Web. 12 Jan. 2004.

51. JSTOR

Blum, Susan D. "Five Approaches to Explaining 'Truth' and 'Deception' in Human
Communication." *Journal of Anthropological Research* 61.3 (2005): 289-315. *JSTOR.*
Web. 3 Mar. 2009.

52. Project MUSE

Muñoz, Alejandro Anaya. "Transnational and Domestic Processes in the Definition of
Human Rights Policies in Mexico." *Human Rights Quarterly* 31.1 (2009): 35-58. *Project
MUSE.* Web. 3 Mar. 2009.

53. Encyclopedia entry from a subscription database

Turk, Austin T. "Terrorism." *Encyclopedia of Crime and Justice.* Ed. Joshua Dressler. 2nd ed.
Vol. 4. New York: Macmillan Reference USA, 2002. *Gale Virtual Reference Library.* Web. 7
Feb. 2005.

54. Abstract from a subscription database

Landers, Susan J. "FDA Panel Findings Intensify Struggles with Prescribing of Antidepressants."
American Medical News 47.37 (2004): 1-2. *ProQuest Direct.* Web. 7 Feb. 2005.

Online Communications and Web Sites

55. Web site

McGann, Jerome, ed. *The Complete Writings and Pictures of Dante Gabriel Rossetti.* Inst. for
Advanced Technology in the Humanities, U of Virginia, n.d. Web. 16 Mar. 2009.

Include the name of the author, editor, or compiler, followed by the title
of the site (italicized), the version or edition (if given), the publisher
or sponsor (if not available, use *N.p.*), the date of publication (if not

available, use *n.d.*), the medium of publication (*Web*), and the date of access.

56. Web site with incomplete information

Breastcancer.org. N.p., 2 Feb. 2008. Web. 5 Feb. 2008.

If a site does not provide all the information usually included in a works-cited entry, list as much as is available.

57. Section of a Web site

Altman, Andrew. "Civil Rights." *Stanford Encyclopedia of Philosophy.* Ed. Edward N. Zalta. Center for the Study of Lang. and Information, Stanford U, 3 Feb. 2003. Web. 12 June 2003.

Mozart, Wolfgang Amadeus. "Concerto No. 3 for Horn, K. 447." *Essentials of Music.* Sony Music Entertainment, 2001. Web. 3 Mar. 2009.

58. Personal home page

Gladwell, Malcolm. Home page. N.p., 8 Mar. 2005. Web. 2 Mar. 2009.

After the name of the site's creator, provide the title or include the words *Home page* (not italicized).

59. E-mail

Peters, Barbara. "Scholarships for Women." Message to Rita Martinez. 10 Mar. 2003. E-mail.

The entry begins with the name of the person who created the e-mail. Put the subject line of the e-mail message in quotation marks. The recipient of the message is identified after the words *Message to*. If the message was sent to you, use *the author* rather than your name. The date of the message and the medium complete the citation.

60. Discussion group or forum

Schipper, William. "Re: Quirk and Wrenn Grammar." *Ansaxnet.* N.p., 5 Jan. 1995. Web. 12 Sept. 1996.

Provide the name of the forum (in this case, *Ansaxnet*) between the title of the work and the sponsor (use *N.p.* if no sponsor is identified). If the posting is untitled, note the genre (for example, *Online posting*) in place of the title.

61. Newsgroup

May, Michaela. "Questions about RYAs." *Generation X.* N.p., 19 June 1996. Web.

29 June 1996.

The name of the newsgroup (for example, *Generation X*) takes the place of the title of the website.

62. Blog

Cuthbertson, Peter. "Are Left and Right Still Alright?" *Conservative Commentary.* N.p., 7 Feb.

2005. Web. 18 Feb. 2005.

Other Online Documents

63. Online encyclopedia entry

"Iran." *Encyclopaedia Britannica Online.* Encyclopaedia Britannica, 2002. Web. 6 Mar. 2004.

64. Online congressional document

United States. Cong. Senate. Special Committee on Aging. *Global Aging: Opportunity or*

Threat for the U.S. Economy? 108th Cong., 1st sess. S. Hrg. 108-30. Washington: GPO,

2003. *GPO Access.* Web. 7 Jan. 2005.

Provide the number and session of Congress and the type and number of publication. (*S* stands for "Senate"; *H* or *HR* stands for "House of Representatives.")

Bills	S 41, HR 82
Reports	S. Rept. 14, H. Rept. 18
Hearings	S. Hrg. 23, H. Hrg. 25
Resolutions	S. Res. 32, H. Res. 52
Documents	S. Doc. 213, H. Doc. 123

65. Online document from a government office

United States. Dept. of State. Bureau of Democracy, Human Rights, and Labor. *Guatemala*

Country Report on Human Rights Practices for 1998. Feb. 1999. Web. 1 May 1999.

Begin with the name of the country, state, or city whose government is responsible for the document and the name of the department or agency that issued it. If a subdivision of the larger organization is responsible, also name the subdivision. If an author is identified, provide his or her name, preceded by the word *By*, between the title and the date of issue of the document.

66. Online law case

Tennessee v. Lane. 541 US 509. Supreme Court of the US. 2004. *Supreme Court Collection.*

  Legal Information Inst., Cornell U Law School, n.d. Web. 28 Jan. 2005.

67. Online public law

Individuals with Disabilities Education Act. Pub. L. 105-17. 104 Stat. 587-698. *Thomas.*

  Lib. of Cong., 4 June 1997. Web. 29 Jan. 2005.

Thomas is an online government resource that makes federal legislative information available to the public.

68. Online sacred text

Sama Veda. Trans. Ralph T. H. Griffith. 1895. *Sacred-Texts.com.* Ed. John B. Hare. N.p.,

  2008. Web. 6 Mar. 2008.

Online Recordings and Images

69. Online music

Moran, Jason. "Jump Up." *Same Mother.* Blue Note, 2005. *Blue Note.* Blue Note Records.

  Web. 7 Mar. 2005.

In this entry, the first mention of "Blue Note" identifies the manufacturer of the CD, *Blue Note* is the title of the website where the song was accessed, and "Blue Note Records" identifies the sponsor of that site.

70. Online speech

Malcolm X. "The Ballot or the Bullet." Detroit. 12 Apr. 1964. *American Rhetoric: Top One*

  Hundred Speeches. Ed. Michael E. Eidenmuller. N.p., 2005. Web. 14 Jan. 2005.

In this entry, "12 Apr. 1964" identifies the date the speech was originally delivered, "2005" specifies the year of the speech's electronic publication, and "14 Jan. 2005" gives the date of access.

71. Online video

Riefenstahl, Leni, dir. *Triumph of the Will.* Reichsparteitag-Film, 1935. *Movieflix.com.*

  MovieFlix, 2005. Web. 17 Feb. 2005.

In this entry, "1935" specifies the year in which the movie was originally released, "2005" identifies the year in which it was made available online, and "17 Feb. 2005" gives the date of access. An entry like this one can begin with either the name of the director or the title of the work, depending on the emphasis of the discussion of the work.

72. Online television or radio program

"Religion and the American Election." Narr. Tony Hassan. *The Religion Report*. ABC Radio
    National, 3 Nov. 2004. Web. 18 Feb. 2005.

73. Online interview

McLaughlin, John. Interview by Wolf Blitzer. *CNN.com*. Cable News Network, 14 July
    2004. Web. 21 Dec. 2004.

74. Online work of art

Vermeer, Johannes. *Young Woman with a Water Pitcher*. c. 1660. Metropolitan Museum of
    Art, New York. *The Metropolitan Museum of Art*. Web. 2 Oct. 2002.

75. Online photograph

Marmon, Lee. *Engine Rock*. 1985. *Lee Marmon Gallery*. Web. 9 Feb. 2009.

76. Online map or chart

"Virginia 1624." Map. *Map Collections 1544-1996*. Lib. of Cong. Web. 26 Apr. 1999.

United States. Dept. of Health and Human Services. Centers for Disease Control and
    Prevention. "Daily Cigarette Smoking among High School Seniors." Chart. 27 Jan. 2005.
    National Center for Health Statistics. Web. 25 Feb. 2005.

77. Online advertisement

Adflip LLC. "Got Milk?" Advertisement. *Adflip.com*. May 2001. Web. 16 Feb. 2005.

78. Online cartoon or comic strip

Cagle, Daryl. "Social Security Pays 3 to 2." Cartoon. *Slate.com*. Newsweek Interactive,
    4 Feb. 2005. Web. 5 Feb. 2005.

OTHER COMMON SOURCES
Live and Recorded Performances
79. Play performance

Proof. By David Auburn. Dir. Daniel Sullivan. Walter Kerr Theater, New York. 8 Oct. 2002.
Performance.

Cite the date of the performance you attended.

80. Lecture or presentation

Guinier, Lani. Barbara Jordan Lecture Ser. Schwab Auditorium, Pennsylvania State U,
University Park. 4 Oct. 2004. Address.

Scharnhorst, Gary. English 296.003. Dane Smith Hall, U of New Mexico, Albuquerque. 30
Apr. 2008. Class lecture.

Identify the site and the date of the lecture or presentation. Use the title
if available; otherwise, provide a descriptive label.

81. Interview

Furstenheim, Ursula. Personal interview. 16 Jan. 2003.

Sugo, Misuzu. Telephone interview. 20 Feb. 2003.

For an interview you conducted, give only the name of the person you
interviewed, the type of interview, and the date of the interview. If the
interview was conducted by someone else, add the name of the inter-
viewer, a title or a descriptive label, and the name of the source.

Harryhausen, Ray. Interview by Terry Gross. *Fresh Air*. Natl. Public Radio. WHYY,
Philadelphia. 6 Jan. 2003. Radio.

82. Film

My Big Fat Greek Wedding. Dir. Joel Zwick. IFC, 2002. Film.

The name of the company that produced or distributed the film (IFC, in
this case) appears before the year of release. It is not necessary to cite the
city in which the production or distribution company is based.

When you want to highlight the contribution of a specific person,
list the contributor's name first. Other supplementary information may
be included after the title.

Gomez, Ian, perf. *My Big Fat Greek Wedding.* Screenplay by Nia Vardalos. Dir. Joel Zwick.

IFC, 2002. Film.

83. Radio or television program
When referring to a specific episode, place quotation marks around its title. Italicize the title of the program.

"'Barbarian' Forces." *Ancient Warriors.* Narr. Colgate Salsbury. Dir. Phil Grabsky. Learning

Channel. 1 Jan. 1996. Television.

To highlight a specific contributor or contributors, begin the entry with the name or names and note the nature of the contribution.

Abumrad, Jad, and Robert Krulwich, narrs. "Choice." *Radiolab.* New York Public Radio.

WNYC, New York, 14 Nov. 2008. Radio.

Works of Visual Art

84. Painting
Gauguin, Paul. *Ancestors of Tehamana.* 1893. Oil on canvas. Art Inst. of Chicago, Chicago.

Identify the artist's name, the title of the work (italicized), the date of composition (if known; otherwise, write *N.d.*), the medium of composition, the organization or individual holding the work, and the city in which the work is located. For a photograph or reproduction of a work of art, provide the preceding information followed by complete publication information for the source, including medium of publication.

85. Photograph
Marmon, Lee. *White Man's Moccasins.* 1954. Photograph. Native American Cultural Center,

Albuquerque.

An entry for a photograph parallels one for a painting; see item 84.

Digital Sources

86. CD-ROM
"About *Richard III.*" *Cinemania 96.* Redmond: Microsoft, 1996. CD-ROM.

Indicate which part of the CD-ROM you are using, and then provide the title of the CD-ROM. Begin the entry with the name of the author if one has been provided.

Jordan, June. "Moving towards Home." *Database of Twentieth-Century African American Poetry on CD-ROM*. Alexandria: Chadwyck-Healey, 1999. CD-ROM.

87. Work from a periodically published database on CD-ROM

Parachini, John V. *Combating Terrorism: The 9/11 Commission Recommendations and the National Strategies*. CD-ROM. *RAND Electronically Distributed Documents*. RAND. 2004. Disc 8.

If the work was issued in print at the same time, the print publication information appears before the CD-ROM information.

88. DVD

A River Runs through It. Screenplay by Richard Friedenberg. Dir. Robert Redford. 1992. Columbia, 1999. DVD.

Cite relevant information about the title and director as you would for a film. Provide both the original release date of the film and the release date for the DVD. If the company that originally produced the film did not release the DVD, list the company that released the DVD instead.

89. Sound recording on CD

Franklin, Aretha. *Amazing Grace: The Complete Recordings*. Atlantic, 1999. CD.

For a sound recording on another medium, identify the type (*Audiocassette* or *LP*).

Raitt, Bonnie. *Nick of Time*. Capitol, 1989. Audiocassette.

When citing a recording of a specific song, begin with the name of the performer or composer (depending on your emphasis) and place the song title in quotation marks. Identify the composer(s) or performer after the song title. If the performance is a reissue from an earlier recording, provide the original date of recording (preceded by *Rec.* for "Recorded").

Horne, Lena. "The Man I Love." By George Gershwin and Ira Gershwin. Rec. 15 Dec. 1941. *Stormy Weather*. BMG, 1990. CD.

(1) Title page

The MLA recommends omitting a title page and instead providing the title of the paper and your name and other pertinent information on the first page of the paper (see page 301). If your instructor requires a title page but does not supply specific instructions for one, include the title of the paper, your name, the instructor's name, the course title with its section number, and the date—all centered on the page. A sample title page is shown in Figure 12.7. (If your instructor requires a title page, omit the heading on the first page of your paper.) Some instructors require a final outline with a paper, which serves as a table of contents. If you are asked to include an outline, prepare a title page as well.

(2) Sample paper

Interested in the controversy surrounding genetically modified foods, Marianna Suslin explores both sides of the debate as she comes to her conclusion. As you study her paper, notice how she develops her thesis statement, considers more than one point of view, and observes the conventions for an MLA-style paper.

TIPS FOR PREPARING AN MLA-STYLE PAPER

- Number all pages (including the first one) with an arabic numeral in the upper-right corner, one-half inch from the top. Put your last name before the page number.
- On the left side of the first page, one inch from the top, type a heading that includes your name, the name of your professor, the course number, and the date of submission.
- Double-space between the heading and the title of your paper, which should be centered on the page. If your title consists of two or more lines, double-space them and center each line.
- Double-space between your title and the first line of text.
- Indent the first paragraph, and every subsequent paragraph, one-half inch.
- Double-space throughout.

Genetically Modified Foods and Developing Countries

Marianna Suslin

Professor Squier
Sociology 299, Section 1
27 November 2007

Figure 12.7. Sample title page for an MLA-style paper.

One-half inch

One inch

The writer's last name and the page number appear as the running head on each page.

Marianna Suslin

Professor Squier

Sociology 299, Section 1

27 November 2007

A header consisting of writer's name, instructor's name, course title, and date is aligned at the left side.

Genetically Modified Foods and Developing Countries

Center the title.

Genetic engineering first appeared in the 1960s. Since then, thousands of genetically modified plants, also referred to as "genetically modified organisms" (GMOs) and "transgenic crops," have been introduced to global markets. Those who argue for continued support of genetic modification claim that the crops have higher yield, grow in harsher conditions, and benefit the ecology. Some experts even argue that genetic engineering has the potential to benefit poor farmers in developing countries, given that genetically modified plants increase the production of food, thereby alleviating world hunger. Despite these claims, the practice of genetic engineering—of inserting genetic material into the DNA of a plant—continues to be controversial, with no clear answers as to whether genetically engineered foods can be the answer for developing countries, as proponents insist.

Double-space throughout.

Use one-inch margins on all sides of the page.

The last sentence in the first paragraph is the thesis statement.

One of the most important potential benefits of the technology to both proponents and opponents of genetic engineering is its potential to improve the economies of developing countries. According to Sakiko Fukuda-Parr, "Investing in agricultural technology increasingly turns up these days on the lists of the top ten practical actions the rich world could take to contribute to reducing global poverty" (3). Agriculture is the source of income for the world's poorest—70 percent of those living on less than

The second paragraph provides background information.

Direct quotations are used as evidence.

One-inch bottom margin

Suslin 2

a dollar a day support themselves through agriculture. These farmers could benefit greatly from higher yielding crops that could grow in nutrient-poor soil. Genetic modification "has shown how high-yielding varieties developed at international centers can be adapted to local conditions, dramatically increasing yields and farm incomes" (Fukuda-Parr 3).

Indent each paragraph one-half inch.

Theoretically, genetic engineering can bring about an increase in farm productivity that would give people in developing countries the chance to enter the global market on better terms. Developing countries are often resource poor and thus have little more than labor to contribute to the world economy. Farming tends to be subsistence level as farmers can grow only enough on the land—which tends to be nutrient poor—to feed themselves. But the higher yield of genetically modified crops along with the resistance to pests and ability to thrive in nutrient-poor soil can enable the farmers to produce more crops, improve the economy, and give their countries something more to contribute globally by exporting extra crops not needed for subsistence (Fukuda-Parr 1). Genetic modification can also help poor farmers by delaying the ripening process. If fruits and vegetables don't ripen as quickly, the farmer is able to store the crops longer and thus have more time in which to sell the crops without fear of spoilage. Small-scale farmers often "suffer heavy losses because of uncontrolled ripening and spoiling of fruits and vegetables" (Royal Society et al. 238).

The writer describes some advantages of growing genetically modified crops.

A work by an organization is cited.

Today, eighteen percent of people living in developing countries do not have enough food to meet their needs (Royal Society et al. 235). "Malnutrition plays a significant role in half of the nearly 12 million deaths each year of children under five in developing countries"

Suslin 3

(UNICEF, qtd. in Royal Society et al. 235). Genetically modified foods that produce large yields even in nutrient-poor soils could potentially help to feed the world's increasing population. Moreover, scientists are working on ways to make the genetically modified foods more nutritious than unmodified crops, which would feed larger numbers of people with less food while, at the same time, combating malnutrition. The modification of the composition of food crops has already been achieved in some species to increase the amount of protein, starch, fats, or vitamins. For example, a genetically modified rice has already been created, one that "exhibits an increased production of beta-carotene," which is a precursor to vitamin A (Royal Society et al. 240). Because vitamin A deficiencies are common in developing countries and contribute to half a million children becoming partially or totally blind each year, advances in genetic engineering offer hope for millions of people who live with nutrient deficiencies (Royal Society et al. 239).

Proponents of genetic engineering have also argued that genetically modified crops have the potential to decrease the amount of damage modern farming technologies inflict on ecology, thereby improving the economy of developing countries without the ecological damage many developed countries have suffered. For example, genetically modified plants with resistance to certain insects would decrease the amount of pesticides that farmers have to use. Genes for insect resistance have already been introduced into cotton, making possible a huge decrease in insecticide use (Royal Society et al. 238). A decrease in the amount of pesticides used is good from an ecological perspective.[1] Not only can pesticides be washed into streams and be harmful to wildlife, but they

A superscript number indicates an endnote.

Suslin 4

have also been known to appear in groundwater, thus potentially causing harm to humans.

Scientists have argued that genetic engineering is only the latest step in the human involvement in plant modification that has been going on for thousands of years.[2] Since the dawn of the agricultural revolution, people have been breeding plants for desirable traits and thus altering the genetic makeup of plant populations. The key advantage of genetic engineering over traditional plant breeding is that genetic engineering produces plants with the desirable trait much faster (Fukuda-Parr 5).

The writer describes the disadvantages of eating genetically modified foods.

While there are many potential benefits that can come from genetic engineering for farmers in developing countries and even in the United States, many people remain skeptical about this new technology. Research shows that many Americans are uneasy about consuming foods that have been genetically enhanced. That same research points out potential risks of consuming GMOs, which some believe outweigh the benefits of this new technology (Brossard, Shanahan, and Nesbitt 10). Considering the risks of genetically modified foods, people in developing countries are likely to feel the same way: that the risks outweigh the benefits. No matter how many potential benefits genetically modified crops may bring, if they are not safe for consumption, they will hurt the economies of developing countries.

In "Genetically Modified Food Threatens Human Health," Jeffrey Smith argues that inserting foreign genetic material into food is extremely dangerous because it may create unknown toxins or allergens. Smith argues that soy allergies increased significantly after genetically modified

Suslin 5

soybean plants were introduced in the United Kingdom (103). Smith also points to the fact that gene insertion could damage a plant's DNA in unpredictable ways. For example, when scientists were working with the soybean plant, the process of inserting the foreign gene damaged a section of the plant's own DNA, "scrambling its genetic code" (105). The sequence of the gene that was inserted had inexplicably rearranged itself over time. The protein the gene creates as a result of this rearrangement is likely to be different, and since this new protein has not been evaluated for safety, it could be harmful or toxic (105).

A direct quotation of a phrase from a cited work is integrated into the text.

In *Genetically Modified Food: A Short Guide for the Confused*, Andy Rees argues a similar point: genetically modified foods carry unpredictable health risks. As an example, he cites the 1989 incident in which bacteria genetically modified to produce large amounts of the food supplement L-tryptophan "yielded impressively toxic contaminants that killed 37 people, partially paralyzed 1,500 and temporarily disabled 5,000 in the US" (75). Rees also argues that genetically modified foods can have possible carcinogenic effects. He states that "given the huge complexity of genetic coding, even in very simple organisms such as bacteria, no one can possibly predict the overall, long-term effects of GM [genetically modified] foods on the health of those who eat them" (78). Rees cites a 1999 study on male rats fed genetically modified potatoes to illustrate the possible carcinogenic effect. The study found that the genetically modified potatoes had "a powerful effect on the lining of the gut (stomach, small bowel, and colon)" leading to a proliferation of cells. According to histopathologist Stanley Ewen,

Suslin 6

this proliferation of cells caused by genetically modified foods is

Three ellipsis points mark an omission in quoted material.

then likely to "act on any polyp present in the colon ... and drastically accelerate the development of cancer in susceptible persons" (qtd. in Rees 78).

In addition to the health risks involved in consuming genetically modified foods, some experts also argue that such foods will not benefit farmers in developing countries but will aid big corporations here in the United States. Brian Halweil, author of "The Emperor's New Crops," brings up the fact that global sales for genetically modified crops grew

The writer cites statistical evidence.

from seventy-five million dollars in 1995 to one and a half billion dollars in 1998, which is a twenty-fold increase. Genetically modified crops are obviously lucrative for large companies. In addition, of the fifty-six transgenic products approved for commercial planting in 1998, thirty-three belong to just four corporations (Halweil 256).

The writer focuses on social issues related to genetically modified crops.

The spread of genetic engineering can change power relations between nations (Cook 3). The big American corporations that sell genetically modified seeds can hold power over the governments of developing countries, hindering their further economic development. For example, all transgenic seeds are patented. Because the seeds are patented, it is illegal for farmers to practice "seed saving"—reserving a certain amount of seeds from the harvest to plant in the next growing season. Farmers thus have to depend entirely on the big corporations for their seeds. Since these corporations have a monopoly on genetically modified seeds, the prices for these seeds are likely to remain high, and poor farmers are unlikely to be able to afford them. Genetically altered seeds can then

Suslin 7

become just one more way that rich countries and their corporations exploit the people of developing countries. Genetic engineering could then become one more way of hindering the development of poor countries, and not the opportunity for economic improvement and increased social equality that its proponents claim it is. Thus, unscrupulous companies could use the economic vulnerability of developing countries to develop and test genetically modified products that have been rejected in the United States or Europe (Newell 68). People in developing countries would be the ones to suffer if the genetically modified products turned out to be hazardous.

With many concerned about the health risks associated with GMOs, there has been a push to institute the practice of labeling genetically modified foods. International organizations such as Greenpeace and Friends of the Earth have advocated food labeling for GMOs because they believe that consumers should have the right to choose whether or not to buy genetically modified foods and expose themselves to the risks associated with consuming GMOs (Huffman 3). The FDA, however, contends that scientific studies "detect no substantial difference between food from traditional crops and GM crops" (*Federal Register*) and regards genetic modification as not altering the product enough to require labeling. Interestingly, one of the reasons for not labeling genetically modified food is the concern that consumers will shun the products with the GMO label, and thus the industry producing genetic modifications will suffer (Weirich 17). The interests of corporate giants, therefore, appear to be able to influence decision making in the United States, where the

The writer continues to explore both sides of the controversy.

government and economy are comparatively strong. The impact of corporations on the governments of poorer countries, then, is likely to be much more pronounced, and poorer countries are likely to be victimized by big corporations.

Moreover, there is some evidence that genetically modified foods do not live up to their promise and, therefore, lack the benefits that could help farmers in poor countries. For example, Rees argues against the assertion that genetically modified crops will be able to ameliorate world hunger. Rather, he believes that more than enough food is produced to feed everyone in the world without these crops and that people go hungry because they cannot afford to buy from the plenty around them for socioeconomic reasons (49). Rees also argues that genetically modified crops have not increased farmers' incomes, regardless of what proponents of genetic engineering may claim. He points to a 2003 study by Professor Caroline Saunders at Lincoln University, New Zealand, which found that "GM food releases have not benefited producers anywhere in the world" and that "the soil association's 2002 'Seeds of Doubt' report, created with feedback from farmers and data from six years of commercial farming in North America, shows that GM soy and maize crops deliver less income to farmers (on average) than non-GM crops" (50-51). The potential benefit of genetically modified crops thus remains uncertain.

While proponents of genetic engineering insist that genetically modified crops can increase yield and help feed the hungry, opponents point to health risks and challenge the research that appears to prove

Suslin 9

that genetically modified foods are beneficial. However, even if these

foods do prove to be as beneficial as proponents claim, there is nothing

to ensure that this technology will benefit poor farmers in developing

countries. Since large corporations hold patents on all genetically

modified seeds, poor farmers may not have access to these seeds.

Developing countries continue to be at a disadvantage despite the

creation and wide distribution of genetically modified crops. Therefore,

it is far from certain whether this new technology will benefit developing

nations in the dramatic way its proponents assert.

The writer's conclusion is based on her own insights as well as on research reported on the previous pages.

One inch

Suslin 10

Notes

1. There is some concern, however, about the long-term effects of

crops genetically engineered for pest resistance. Since these plants are

engineered to continually produce the pesticide, insects are constantly

exposed to the chemical. Such exposure increases the likelihood that the

insects will develop a tolerance for the pesticide.

2. The main difference between genetic engineering and the breeding

of plants for desired traits that people have practiced for thousands of

years is that genetic engineering alters the DNA of a particular plant.

Traditional breeding cannot do this but instead increases the number of

plants that have a naturally occurring trait.

Center the heading.

The numbers on the notes match the superscript numbers in the body of the paper.

One inch

Suslin 11

Center the
heading.

Works Cited

Alphabetize
the entries
according to
the authors'
last names.

Indent the
second and
subsequent
lines of each
entry one-half
inch.

Brossard, Dominique, James Shanahan, and T. Clint Nesbitt, eds. *The Public, the Media, and Agricultural Biotechnology.* Cambridge: CABI, 2007. Print.

Cook, Guy. *Genetically Modified Language: The Discourse of Arguments for GM Crops and Food.* New York: Routledge, 2005. Print.

Easton, Thomas A., ed. *Taking Sides: Clashing Views on Controversial Environmental Issues.* 11th ed. Dubuque: McGraw, 2005. Print.

Federal Register 54.104 (1992): 22991. Print.

Fukuda-Parr, Sakiko, ed. *The Gene Revolution: GM Crops and Unequal Development.* London, England: Earthscan, 2007. Print.

Halweil, Brian. "The Emperor's New Crops." Easton 249-59.

Huffman, W. E. "Production, Identity Preservation, and Labeling in a Marketplace with Genetically Modified and Non-Genetically Modified Foods." *Plant Physiology* 134 (2004): 3-10. Web. 5 Nov. 2007.

Newell, Peter. "Corporate Power and 'Bounded Autonomy' in the Global Politics of Biotechnology." *The International Politics of Genetically Modified Food: Diplomacy, Trade, and Law.* Ed. Robert Falkner. Hampshire: Palgrave, 2007. 67-84. Print.

Rees, Andy. *Genetically Modified Food: A Short Guide for the Confused.* Ann Arbor: Pluto, 2006. Print.

Royal Society et al. "Transgenic Plants and World Agriculture." Easton 234-45.

Smith, Jeffrey M. "Genetically Modified Food Threatens Human Health."

Humanity's Future. Ed. Louise I. Gerdes. Detroit: Gale, 2006. 103-08. Print.

Weirich, Paul, ed. *Labeling Genetically Modified Food: The Philosophical and Legal Debate.* New York: Oxford UP, 2007. Print.

13 ‖ WRITING IN THE SOCIAL SCIENCES

The **social sciences** include such disciplines as psychology, anthropology, sociology, political science, and economics. Researchers in these disciplines study how humans behave as members of groups—families, peer groups, ethnic communities, political parties, and many others. The goal of research in the social sciences is to examine and explain behavior occurring under a particular set of circumstances. For example, Danielle Dezell, the student whose report is featured later in this chapter (**13e**), investigated whether students depend on gender stereotypes to assign status to certain occupations. Typical assignments in the social sciences are library research papers, case studies, and laboratory or field reports.

This chapter will help you

- determine the audience, purpose, and research question for a paper in the social sciences (**13a**);
- decide which types of evidence, sources, and reasoning to use in such a paper (**13b**);
- use appropriate language, style, and formatting when writing the paper (**13c**);
- understand the types of writing assignments you might receive in social sciences courses (**13d**); and
- learn the conventions for writing a laboratory report (**13e**).

13a ‖ AUDIENCE, PURPOSE, AND THE RESEARCH QUESTION

The first step toward completing a writing assignment for a course in the social sciences is to determine your audience and purpose. Your audience will always include your instructor, but it could include students in your class and sometimes people outside your class. For example, you may have the opportunity to present your work at a student research conference. Identifying your audience will help you decide how much background information to present, how much technical language to include, and what types of reasoning and sources to use.

Most researchers in the social sciences write either to inform or to persuade. If they are simply reporting the results of a study, their purpose is informative. However, if they urge their audience to take some action, their purpose is persuasive. Once you know what your purpose is and to whom you are writing, you can craft a research question that will help you find sources, evaluate them, and use them responsibly (Chapters 8–10). Here are some examples of types of research questions that could be posed about the topic of community service performed by students:

Questions about causes or purposes

Why do students perform community service?

Questions about consequences

What do students believe they have learned through their community service?

Questions about process

How do college instructors help students get involved in community service?

Questions about definitions or categories

What does community service entail?

Questions about values

What values do instructors hope to cultivate by encouraging students to perform community service?

All of the writers of the student papers in this book started with a research question. For example, Rachel Pinter and Sarah Cronin, whose paper appears at the end of Chapter 14 (see pages 367–76), asked a question about process:

How have trends in tattooing changed over the years?

13b EVIDENCE, SOURCES, AND REASONING

Researchers in the social sciences study the behavior of humans and other animals. To make accurate observations of their subjects' activities, these researchers either design controlled laboratory experiments or conduct field research. Interviews and surveys are the two most common techniques for gathering data in the field, although observations are also widely used. Both laboratory experiments and field research yield data that social-science researchers can use as evidence to make statements (or claims) about the behavior of humans and other animals.

Researchers in the social sciences distinguish between quantitative studies and qualitative studies. **Quantitative studies**, such as laboratory experiments and surveys, yield data that can be presented in numerical form, as statistics. Using statistical data and formulas, researchers show how likely it is for a behavior to occur or to have certain consequences. If you decide to undertake a quantitative study, you should turn your research question into a **hypothesis**, a prediction of what the results of your experiment or survey will be. The study you design will be based on this hypothesis, which should be as objective as possible. Obviously, you cannot entirely eliminate the influence of your own preconceptions, but you can strive to be impartial by avoiding value judgments. The results of your study will either prove or disprove your hypothesis. Be prepared to provide possible explanations for either result.

Hypotheses are best formed after a sustained period of observation and preliminary research. When presenting her hypothesis about gender stereotypes and occupational status, Danielle Dezell states her prediction in the context of existing research.

Although studies have not correlated participant gender and occupational status (Parker et al., 1989), Teig and Susskind (2008) found that occupational gender did correlate with occupational status. The current study expects to find that people's ranking of occupational status correlates with the stereotyped gender of the occupation.

Researchers who perform **qualitative studies**, such as observations and interviews, are interested in interpreting behavior by first watching, listening to, or interacting with individuals or a group. If you decide to conduct a qualitative study, you will not reason *from* a hypothesis but will reason *to* a hypothesis. You will observe a phenomenon and note what you see or hear. Then, instead of reporting numbers as evidence, you will provide detailed descriptions and discuss their significance. Although you may not be able to demonstrate the degree of impartiality prescribed for quantitative research, you should be as objective as possible.

Social scientists often study gender stereotyping. For example, a social-science researcher might conduct an experiment to investigate participants' reactions to photographs such as these—of a female CEO and a male nurse.

Researchers in the social sciences recognize that some studies have both quantitative and qualitative features. They also expect to use both primary and secondary sources (see **8a(4)**) in many of their research projects. Primary sources consist of data derived from experiments, observations, surveys, or interviews. Secondary sources are articles or case studies written about a research topic. Be sure to cite any sources you use and to provide a corresponding bibliographic entry on the reference list at the end of your paper.

13C ‖ CONVENTIONS OF LANGUAGE AND ORGANIZATION

(1) Style guidelines

The words and grammatical structures you use in a paper in the social sciences will depend on the style manual prescribed by the discipline in which you are writing. Most of the social sciences follow the guidelines presented in the *Publication Manual of the American Psychological Association* (see Chapter **14**). This manual stresses the importance of writing

---

TIPS FOR PREPARING A PAPER IN THE SOCIAL SCIENCES

- Use the active voice as often as possible, although the passive voice may be acceptable for describing methodology. (See page 24c(2).)

- Choose verb tenses carefully. Use the present tense to discuss results and report conclusions (as in "The findings suggest . . ."). Reserve the past tense for referring to specific events in the past and for describing your procedures (as in "Each participant signed a consent form . . .").

- Use a first-person pronoun rather than referring to yourself or to any coauthor(s) and yourself in the third person.

    ∧I ~~The experimenter~~ described the procedure to each participant.

    ∧We ~~The experimenters~~ retested each participant after a rest period.

- Clarify noun strings by placing the main noun first.
  the method for testing literacy NOT the literacy testing method

---

prose that is clear, concise, unbiased, and well organized. The following specific tips can help you write in the style recommended by the manual.

(2) Organization

Assignments in the social sciences will generally require you to (1) state a research question, thesis, or hypothesis; (2) discuss research that has already been published about your topic; (3) describe your methodology; and (4) present your conclusions or results. Specific types of assignments are discussed in 13d.

To organize the information they are presenting, writers in the social sciences use tables and graphs as well as headings, which are designed to signal levels of importance (14a(3)). Danielle Dezell includes a table to display her results (see page 327). If you decide to use a table in your paper, be sure to refer to the table by number (for example, Table 1) and explain the significance of the information it provides. Without a brief discussion of the table, your readers may have difficulty understanding why you included it.

Graphs provide a visual representation of data. Danielle uses line graphs to highlight her comparison of gender stereotypes and perceptions of occupational status (see page 328). Graphs are labeled as numbered figures. Like tables, they should be discussed in the text.

⬛ *TECH SAVVY*

Table
To insert a table into a document, choose Table on the main menu bar of your word processor and click on Insert and then on Table in the pulldown menu. You will see a dialogue box that allows you to choose the number of rows and columns for your table.

Graph
To insert a graph into a document, choose Insert on the main menu bar and select Object from the pulldown menu. Then choose Create New. From the list of object types, choose Microsoft Graph Chart. You can then enter your data into the spreadsheet provided.

(3) Reference list

At the end of any paper you write for a course in the social sciences, you should include a list of all the sources you used. By doing so, you provide your readers with the details they need to consult these sources on their own. You can find guidelines for creating a reference list in **14b** and sample lists of references on pages 331–32 and 375–76.

13d EXAMPLES OF WRITING IN THE SOCIAL SCIENCES

(1) Library research report

Library research reports are written by both students and professionals. The purpose of such reports is to bring together several related sources on a specific topic in order to examine that topic closely. Writing such a report will require you to read a number of sources and then summarize, critique, and synthesize those sources (see Chapter **10**). Library research reports generally include the following elements:

- Statement of the research question or thesis
- Presentation of background information, using sources
- Discussion of major findings presented in the sources
- Application of those findings to the specific research question

- Conclusions
- References

An excerpt from a library research report is shown in Figure 13.1. In the report's introduction, authors Matthew Gervais and David Sloan Wilson present background information for their study. Notice that the authors maintain a neutral stance that conveys an impression of impartiality, although they clearly and strongly state their point of view.

The first paragraph presents past studies on the topic.

INTRODUCTION

LAUGHTER AND HUMOR were accorded high evolutionary significance by Darwin (1872) and have received increasing attention from biologists and psychologists during the last 30 years. This attention has resulted in myriad empirical advances and has left laughter and humor well characterized on multiple proximate levels (see Provine 2000; Vaid 2002; Bachorowski and Owren 2003; van Hooff and Preuschoft 2003; Wild, Rodden et al. 2003). Laudably, this research has spawned a number of hypotheses attempting to explain the ultimate evolutionary origins of laughter and humor (e.g., Eibl-Eibesfeldt 1989; Weisfeld 1994; Pinker 1997; Ramachandran 1998; Harris 1999; Miller 2000; Provine 2000; Owren and Bachorowski 2001; Caron 2002; Howe 2002; Jung 2003; Storey 2003). Nevertheless, the scientific study of laughter and humor is still in its infancy relative to other comparable subjects in emotions and communication research.

Many empirical questions about laughter and humor remain unanswered or neglected. For example, most researchers (e.g., Provine 2000; Owren

and Bachorowski 2003; Vettin and Todt 2004) have failed to make the important distinction between Duchenne (stimulus-driven and emotionally valenced) and non-Duchenne (self-generated and emotionless) laughter (Keltner and Bonanno 1997; see also Wild, Rodden et al. 2003). While laughter has recently been found to occur most frequently during casual conversation and not following deliberate humor (Provine 1993; LaGreca et al. 1996; Vettin and Todt 2004), researchers have yet to question whether such conversational laughter is different in kind from that following humor. This oversight might well be the root cause of the widespread confusion concerning the diversity of forms and functions that characterizes laughter today (Keltner and Bonanno 1997).

As regards theory, the results of empirical findings of laughter and humor research remain disjointed and only partially accounted for by any one framework. In most cases, such hypotheses are not mutually exclusive but potentially complementary, yet a synthesis remains unrealized. As a result, theoretical limitations abound.

The next two paragraphs discuss gaps in the research.

Figure 13.1. An excerpt from the introduction of a library research report.

Another example of a library research report is Rachel Pinter and Sarah Cronin's paper on tattooing (see **14c**).

(2) Case study

A case study is a qualitative project that requires a researcher to describe a particular participant or group of participants. The researcher refrains from making generalizations about the participant(s) in the study and instead focuses on the behavior of the participant(s). After describing the behavior, the researcher usually suggests a solution to the problem faced by the participant(s). Most case studies include the following information:

- An introduction to the participant(s)
- A description of the problem
- Observations
- A presentation of strategies to solve the problem

Figure 13.2 is an excerpt from a case study, one of many that can be found on the website *Improving Provision for Disabled Psychology Students.*

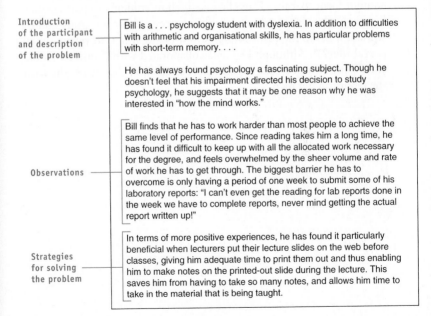

Figure 13.2. An excerpt from a case study posted online.

(3) Laboratory or field (observation) report

Social science students and professionals often conduct research in a laboratory or in the field (that is, in a natural setting). Reports based on this type of research contain standard sections: introduction, method, results, and discussion. An example of a laboratory report is Danielle Dezell's paper on gender stereotypes and occupations (13e).

13e	LABORATORY REPORT ON A GENDER-STEREOTYPING EXPERIMENT

Written according to the style guidelines of the American Psychological Association (APA), which are discussed in Chapter 14, the following laboratory report by Danielle Dezell includes the standard sections mentioned in 13d(3). Danielle's report also includes several appendices: a copy of the prompt she used, a script for the study, and a participant consent form. Because Danielle asked fellow students to participate in her study, she was required to submit a proposal for her study and the consent form to the institutional review board at her university for approval (8e(2)). Although Danielle collaborated with Cameron Dooley and Elaine Acosta on the experiment described in the report, she wrote the report on her own.

Gender Stereotypes and Perceptions of Occupational Status

Among University Students

Danielle Dezell

Central Washington University

Abstract

This study investigated whether the gender of participants affected their view of certain occupations and whether the gender typically associated with an occupation affected participants' ranking of the status of that occupation. Participants were asked (1) to write a response to a prompt designed to elicit gender-specific pronouns and (2) to rate the status of one of three occupations typically associated with a gender. The results were compared to see whether the interaction between participant gender and stereotypical occupational gender influenced the perception of the status of the occupation and to discover whether participant gender influenced the perception of occupational gender.

The writer introduces the purpose of the study.

GENDER STEREOTYPES AND PERCEPTIONS   3

Gender Stereotypes and Perceptions of Occupational Status

Among University Students

The writer establishes the importance of her report.

Occupational gender stereotypes are important to examine for their possible influence not only on a person's occupational choice but also on perceptions of status associated with occupations. When university-age students consider possible careers, they often choose one based on their own gender and on the stereotypical gender assigned to an occupation (Evans & Diekman, 2009). They may also choose an occupation according to the status they believe it to have. An investigation into gender stereotypes about occupations is a first step in limiting their influence on students' career choices.

By discussing the work of other researchers, the writer not only provides readers with necessary information but also demonstrates her credibility.

Gender stereotypes begin in early childhood, when children see how society views certain professions. These societal influences can have long-term effects on how children may stereotype various occupations (Firestone, Harris, & Lambert, 1999). Several studies using school-age children as participants have examined the strength of these early stereotypes. Miller and Hayward (2006) showed that participants often preferred occupations that were stereotyped to their own gender (i.e., boys preferred stereotypically male jobs, and girls preferred stereotypically female jobs). Another study conducted by Teig and Susskind (2008) looked at both status and stereotypes. When participants were asked to rate the status of jobs, the researchers found that out of the 18 highest ranked jobs, only 3 were classified as feminine. Of all the occupations, 27.8% of masculine occupations had a high status ranking, while 15.4% of female occupations had a high status ranking. Participants in this study

GENDER STEREOTYPES AND PERCEPTIONS   4

classified both *librarian* and *elementary school teacher* as stereotypically
feminine occupations. The researchers found that there was a significant
correlation between the gender of the participant and how he or she ranked
the status of an occupation. However, the researchers pointed out that as
girls grew older, their tendency to stereotype lessened. Boys, though,
continued to carry gender stereotypes into adulthood. Miller and Hayward
(2006) noted that men generally prefer occupations traditionally performed
by men.

In a study whose participants were college-age students, Shinar (1975)
looked at how the participants rated the masculinity and femininity of various
occupations on a 1-to-7 Likert scale (1 being *masculine* and 7 being *feminine*).
The study showed that both men and women held gender stereotypes about
certain occupations. The participants rated *miner* as a fully masculine job
(mean rating of 1.000) and *manicurist* as a mostly feminine job (mean rating
of 6.667). Shinar also reported that *head librarian* had a mean rating of 5.583,
high school teacher a mean rating of 4.000, and *carpenter* a mean rating of
1.667. What is interesting is that Shinar showed that both women and men
demonstrated gender stereotyping, whereas, over 30 years later, Seguino (2007)
and Miller and Hayward (2006) found that men had much stronger stereotypes
than women. Miller and Hayward also suggested that women grow out of a
stereotyping mindset by age 18.

The writer refers to previous studies and synthesizes their findings.

Although certain occupations clearly seem to be gender stereotyped,
occupational status is not always related to gender. Parker, Chan, and Saper
(1989) found that there was no significant correlation between participant
gender and occupational status ratings. It might be tempting to believe

GENDER STEREOTYPES AND PERCEPTIONS   5

that jobs associated with masculinity would be ranked as having higher social status, but these researchers showed that the status of many traditionally masculine jobs (e.g., *heavy equipment operator*) was considered low. This finding is especially interesting because it suggests that when people choose an occupation, they might rely more on the perception of the gender associated with an occupation than on the perception of status.

> The writer adds her own voice to the discussion of gender stereotypes.

One way to test how people stereotype a job according to gender is to ask them to assign a pronoun to a certain occupation. This simple test provides insight into how gender stereotypes of occupations work and whether males or females are more likely to hold such stereotypes. A study looking at the gender people attributed to different gender-neutral characters introduced in a dialogue script found that both men and women were more likely to assume that a character was male. The same study also found that men and women had equal biases toward gender assumptions (Merritt & Kok, 1995). In a similar study, participants were asked to attribute a gender to various stuffed animals. Both children and adults used the male pronoun to describe stuffed animals that were gender-neutral (Lambdin, Greer, Jibotian, Wood, & Hamilton, 2003).

> After reporting the work of other researchers in previous paragraphs, the writer now introduces her hypothesis.

This study aims to discover both whether participants stereotype certain occupations as being either male or female and whether participants rate the status of an occupation based on whether the occupation has historically been a masculine, feminine, or gender-neutral occupation. The findings of previous studies suggest that both males and females do stereotype certain occupations. Although studies have not correlated participant gender and occupational

GENDER STEREOTYPES AND PERCEPTIONS   6

status (Parker et al., 1989), Teig and Susskind (2008) found that occupational

gender did correlate with occupational status. The current study expects to find

that people's ranking of occupational status correlates with the stereotyped

gender of the occupation.

Method

Participants

A total of eight groups participated in the study. Numbers of

participants in each group varied. Overall, there were 40 participants,

11 males and 29 females. All participants were students at Central

Washington University and were 19 years old or older. The participants

were all volunteers and were randomly assigned to one of three

experimental conditions.

Materials

The materials for each experimental condition were a sheet of paper

that presented one of three different writing prompts and asked for four

pieces of demographic information (Appendix A). A script from which

the researcher read (Appendix B) was also used. Each writing prompt was

a scenario about an employee of a school who had a problem; however,

the employee's occupation in each prompt differed. The occupations and

their associated gender stereotypes were as follows: *librarian* (female),

woodshop teacher (male), and *high school teacher* (gender neutral). The

occupations were chosen based on the percentage of females employed in

each occupation, according to statistics from the Bureau of Labor Statistics

(Bureau of Labor Statistics, 2010). The statistics showed that *high school

teacher* was the most gender-neutral occupation (54.9% female).

Information on
methodology
helps readers
decide whether
the researcher's
findings are
reliable and
valid.

GENDER STEREOTYPES AND PERCEPTIONS   7

The occupation *librarian* was found to be gender segregated toward females (81.8% female). There were no statistics for *woodshop teacher*, though there were statistics for *carpenter* (1.6% female). Because most carpenters are male, it is quite likely that most people would stereotype the occupation of woodshop teacher as male. A focus on jobs that were all in a school environment prevented the creation of confounds based on the status of a work environment.

The writing prompts excluded any language that might allow the participant to infer the gender of the person in the prompt (e.g., no pronouns were used). A five-point Likert scale was used to measure how participants rated the status of an occupation. Each of the three prompt sheets used identical wording in the directions, prompts, Likert scale, and demographic items (i.e., gender, age, class standing, and major); the only difference among the prompts was the occupation used.

Procedure

Each group of participants had two administrators. The study took approximately 15 minutes. One administrator passed out consent forms (Appendix C), collected them, and then distributed the prompts, while the other administrator read the appropriate directions from the script (Appendix B). Once the participants had the prompt, they were given 10 minutes to complete the story. After the administrators collected the stories, participants were debriefed and provided with the opportunity to ask questions.

Results

Statistics are used to report results.

The descriptive statistics can be found in Table 1. A two-way between-subjects ANOVA with $\alpha = .05$ showed that the interaction

GENDER STEREOTYPES AND PERCEPTIONS 8

Table 1
Descriptive Statistics

Gender of Participant	Occupation in Prompt	Mean	Std. Deviation	N
F	High School Librarian	2.75	.452	12
	High School Teacher	2.75	.463	8
	High School Woodshop Teacher	2.56	.527	9
	Total	2.69	.471	29
M	High School Librarian	5.00	.545	1
	High School Teacher	3.20	1.304	5
	High School Woodshop Teacher	3.20	.837	5
	Total	3.36	1.120	11
Total	High School Librarian	2.92	.760	13
	High School Teacher	2.92	.862	13
	High School Woodshop Teacher	2.79	.699	14
	Total	2.88	.757	40

between participant gender and occupation in the prompts was not significant, $F(2, 34) = .88$, $p > .05$. Of the two main effects, only gender was significant, $F(1, 34) = .001$, $p < .05$. However, occupation had a nonsignificant main effect, $F(2, 34) = .052$, $p > .05$. The averages of means are graphed in Figure 1. The homogeneity of variance test was significant, $F(5, 34) = .003$, $p < .05$. The first chi-square test, which was run on the interaction between participant gender and type of pronoun used by the participant in responding to the prompt, had a Pearson's correlation of .267, which is not significant. The second chi-square test between occupation in the prompt and pronoun type had a highly significant Pearson's correlation of .000.

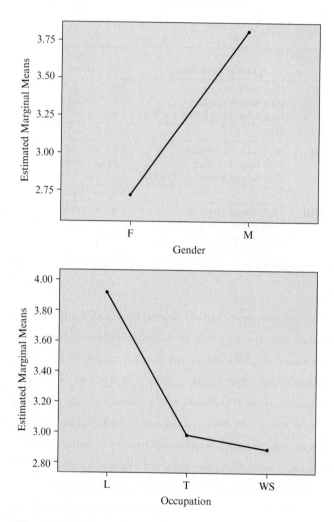

Figure 1. Means for main effects.

Discussion

The results of the study showed that there was no interaction between the status ranking of an occupation and the gender stereotyping of that occupation. This is contrary to the findings of Teig and Susskind (2008), who found that the gender stereotype of an occupation affects the rating of its status. However, it is similar to the findings of Parker et al. (1989), who showed that the gender of a participant had no bearing on occupational status. All three occupations were ranked on average as having medium status (mean of 2.875). *Librarian* had a mean status of 2.92; *high school teacher*, a mean status of 2.92; and *woodshop teacher*, a mean status of 2.79. While there may not be a significant difference, the mean status ranking is lowest for *woodshop teacher*, which agrees with the finding of Parker et al. (2008) that manual labor jobs were rated as having a lower status. Neither part of this study's hypothesis was supported by the results. Levene's test of homogeneity of variance had a significant outcome, indicating that the groups were unequal and the result is not due to random sampling.

The results from the gender-stereotyping tests were more intriguing. There was a significant correlation between the occupation mentioned in the prompt and the type of pronoun chosen by the participant to respond to the prompt (feminine, masculine, or neutral). Participants did stereotype the occupations, but what is interesting is that females used gender-specific pronouns much more than males did. When writing their stories about the various occupations, male participants used gender-neutral pronouns 72% of the time, whereas female participants used

The statistics reported in the previous section are explained in this section.

GENDER STEREOTYPES AND PERCEPTIONS   11

The writer compares her results with those of other researchers.

gender-neutral pronouns only 41% of the time. These findings are contrary to those of Merritt and Kok (1995), who found that when participants are presented with unspecified characters, they generally designate the gender as male. The findings of this study also contradict the occupational-stereotype findings of Shinar (1975), who stated that men use stereotypes more than women, and of Miller and Hayward (2006), who reported that females tend to use fewer stereotypes once they are enrolled in college.

The writer acknowledges some limitations of the study.

    One of the biggest limitations of the study was that there were so few participants, especially men. Data elicited from a larger number of male participants would have provided a more accurate picture of how men view occupational stereotypes. The prompts could also have been worded better. Because of the awkward wording of the prompts, participants had a good idea of what the study was looking for and so may have adjusted their responses. Another limitation is that there were only three occupations. Including a greater number of occupations would have made it possible to state conclusions about gender stereotypes more firmly. Future studies should include not only more occupations but also occupations that obviously have different statuses. This study chose occupations that were all in the same environment in order to avoid confounds; however, if there were many different types of occupations from a variety of environments, participants might not be able to determine as easily the researcher's intent. Despite these limitations, this study suggests that people are starting to have fewer assumptions about the relation between gender and occupation.

GENDER STEREOTYPES AND PERCEPTIONS   12

References

Bureau of Labor Statistics. (2010). *Household data: Annual averages* [Data file]. Retrieved from http://www.bls.gov/cps/cpsaat11

Evans, C., & Diekman, A. (2009). On motivated role selection: Gender beliefs, distant goals, and career interest. *Psychology of Women Quarterly, 33*(2), 235–249. doi:10.1111/j.1471-6402.2009.01493.x

Firestone, J., Harris, R., & Lambert, L. (1999). Gender role ideology and the gender based differences in earnings. *Journal of Family and Economic Issues, 20*(2), 191–215. doi:10.1023/A:1022158811154

Lambdin, J. R., Greer, K. M., Jibotian, K. S., Wood, K. R., & Hamilton, M. C. (2003). The animal = male hypothesis: Children's and adult's beliefs about the sex of non-sex-specific stuffed animals. *Sex Roles, 48*(11/12), 471–482. doi:10.1023/A:1023567010708

Merritt, R. D., & Kok, C. J. (1995). Attribution of gender to a gender-unspecified individual: An evaluation of the people = male hypothesis. *Sex Roles, 33*(3/4), 145–157. doi:10.1007/BF01544608

Miller, L., & Hayward, R. (2006). New jobs, old occupational stereotypes: Gender and jobs in the new economy. *Journal of Education & Work, 19*(1), 67–93. doi:10.1080/13639080500523000

Parker, H., Chan, F., & Saper, B. (1989). Occupational representativeness and prestige rating: Some observations. *Journal of Employment Counseling, 26*(3), 117–131. Retrieved from http://www.employmentcounseling.org

Seguino, S. (2007). Plus ça change? Evidence on global trends in gender norms and stereotypes. *Feminist Economics, 13*(2), 1–28. doi:10.1080/13545700601184880

Shinar, E. (1975). Sexual stereotypes of occupations. *Journal of Vocational Behavior, 7*(1), 99–111. Retrieved from http://www.sciencedirect.com /science/journal/00018791

Teig, S., & Susskind, J. (2008). Truck driver or nurse? The impact of gender roles and occupational status on children's occupational preferences. *Sex Roles, 58*(11/12), 848–863. doi:10.1007/s11199-008-9410-x

GENDER STEREOTYPES AND PERCEPTIONS   14

Appendix A
Sample Prompts

DO NOT WRITE YOUR NAME ANYWHERE ON THIS PAGE.
THANK YOU.

Instructions: Please read the following scenario; then write one or two
paragraphs describing what the person would do in response to this
situation. If you run out of room, you may use the back of the page. Then
go to the bottom of the page to rate the occupational status of the
profession and fill out the demographic information.

*The high school woodshop teacher arrives late to school. Upon arriving at
the classroom with no keys, the woodshop teacher realizes the door is locked.
There is a group of students waiting to go to class. What does the woodshop
teacher do?*

*The high school librarian arrives late to school. Upon arriving at the library
with no keys, the librarian realizes the door is locked. There is a group of
students waiting to go in. What does the librarian do?*

*The high school teacher arrives late to school. Upon arriving at the
classroom with no keys, the teacher realizes the door is locked. There is a
group of students waiting to go to class. What does the teacher do?*

On a scale of 1 to 5, where 1 is a low-status occupation and 5 is a high-
status occupation, how would you rate the occupation of the person in the
story? Please circle your choice.

Lowest Status   1   2   3   4   5   Highest Status

Your gender: _____ Age: _____ Class standing: _____ Major: _____

GENDER STEREOTYPES AND PERCEPTIONS   15

Appendix B
Script for the Study

(As participants enter room, Administrator 2 gives each a consent
form and a pencil and asks each one to take a seat anywhere. When all are
seated, Administrator 1 says the following:)

*Thank you for volunteering to participate in this study. You have been
given a consent form. When you have read and signed the consent form, we
will collect them and begin. I'm going to highlight some main points while
you are reading through it. The total testing time is 15 minutes. You do not
have to participate in the study; refusal to participate will not affect your
grade in any class or any of your privileges at CWU. You can agree to this
study now and then leave at any time if you change your mind. If you wish
to stop at any time, please tell us right away. The data collected from you in
this study are completely anonymous.*

(Administrator 2 collects consent forms. Administrator 1 says the
following:)

*You will now be given a pencil and the writing prompt. When you
receive the paper, please leave it face down until instructed. Once you have
turned over the story, you will have 10 minutes to read the prompt and write
a response. When you have completed writing, please remain seated and
quiet until the 10 minutes have passed. The administrator will then collect
your papers. Please ask any questions you have now. You will be able to ask
more questions once the stories have been collected.*

*Please turn over your paper and read the instructions. Please do not
write your name on the paper.*

GENDER STEREOTYPES AND PERCEPTIONS   16

(After 10 minutes have gone by, Administrator 1 continues:)

Please stop writing. Be sure you have filled in the bottom of the page.

Debrief: *This study was designed to discover whether students associate the type and status of an occupation with a particular gender. Your prompt did not give any indication of the gender of the occupation. We will analyze your pronoun choice to see what gender you assumed the occupation to be.*

Are there any questions? Thank you for your participation. You are free to leave. This is a week-long study, so please do not discuss it.

Appendix C

Consent Form

CENTRAL WASHINGTON UNIVERSITY

RESEARCH PARTICIPANT CONSENT FORM

Study Title:	Gender Stereotypes and Occupational Status
Principal Investigator(s):	Danielle Dezell, Cameron Dooley, and Elaine Acosta. Dept. of Psychology, Central Washington University. (509) 555-1234, student321@university.edu
Faculty Sponsor:	Dr. Sally Lifland. Dept. of Psychology, Central Washington University. (509) 555-4321, ProfessorSL@university.edu

1. **What you should know about this study:**
   - You are being asked to take part in a research study.
   - This consent form explains the research study and your part in the study.
   - Please read it carefully and take as much time as you need.
   - Ask questions about anything you do not understand, now or later.
   - You are a volunteer. If you change your mind about participating, you may quit at any time without fear of penalty.
   - While you are in this study, the study team will keep you informed of any new information that could affect whether you want to stay in the study.

2. **Why is this research being done?**
   This research is to show how college students perceive occupational status in order to better understand occupational stereotypes.

3. **Who can take part in this study?**
   Any CWU student over the age of 18 is able to participate in this study.

4. **What will happen if you join this study?**
   If you agree to be in this study, you will be asked to write a short response to a prompt. The prompt consists of three sentences. It

GENDER STEREOTYPES AND PERCEPTIONS   18

describes a situation in which the subject is a professional. Your
response will consist of one or two paragraphs describing what the
subject should do in this situation.

[Some of the consent form items have been omitted.]

13. What does your signature on this consent form mean?
By signing this consent form, you are not giving up any legal rights.
Your signature means that you understand the study plan, have been
able to ask questions about the information given to you in this form,
and agree to take part in the study.

Participant's Name (print): _____

Participant's Signature: _____ Date: _____

Phone Number: _____ E-mail: _____

Signature of Investigator: _____ Date: _____

Appendix D
Raw Data

Subject	Gender	Occupation	Pronoun	Status
1	F	L	F	3
2	F	L	F	3
3	F	L	N	3
4	F	L	F	3
5	F	L	F	3
6	F	L	F	3
7	F	L	F	2
8	F	L	N	3
9	F	L	F	3
10	F	L	F	2
11	F	L	N	2
12	F	L	F	3
13	F	WS	M	3
14	F	WS	M	3
15	F	WS	M	3
16	F	WS	M	2
17	F	WS	M	2
18	F	WS	N	2
19	F	WS	N	3
20	F	WS	M	2

(continued)

GENDER STEREOTYPES AND PERCEPTIONS 20

Subject	Gender	Occupation	Pronoun	Status
21	F	WS	M	3
22	F	T	N	3
23	F	T	N	3
24	F	T	N	3
25	F	T	M	2
26	F	T	N	3
27	F	T	N	2
28	F	T	N	3
29	F	T	N	3
30	M	L	N	5
31	M	WS	M	4
32	M	WS	N	3
33	M	WS	N	3
34	M	WS	M	2
35	M	WS	N	4
36	M	T	N	5
37	M	T	F	4
38	M	T	N	2
39	M	T	N	3
40	M	T	N	2

14 | APA DOCUMENTATION

The American Psychological Association (APA) publishes a style guide entitled *Publication Manual of the American Psychological Association.* Its documentation system (called an *author-date system*) is used for work in psychology and many other disciplines, including education, economics, sociology, and business management. Updates to the style guide are provided at www.apastyle.org. This chapter presents

- guidelines for citing sources within the text of a paper (**14a**),
- guidelines for documenting sources in a reference list (**14b**), and
- a sample student paper (**14c**).

14a | APA-STYLE IN-TEXT CITATIONS

(1) Citing material from other sources

APA-style in-text citations usually include just the last name(s) of the author(s) of the work and the year of publication. However, be sure to specify the page number(s) for any quotations you use in your paper. The abbreviation *p.* (for "page") or *pp.* (for "pages") precedes the number(s). If you do not know the author's name, use a shortened version of the source's title instead. If your readers want to find more information about a source, they will look for the author's name or, in its absence, the title of the work in the bibliography at the end of your paper.

You will likely consult a variety of sources for a research paper. The following examples are representative of the types of in-text citations you can expect to use.

Directory of APA-Style Parenthetical Citations

1. Work by one author

Yang (2006) admits that speech, when examined closely, is a "remarkably messy means of communication" (p. 13).

OR

When examined closely, speech is "a remarkably messy means of communication" (Yang, 2006, p. 13).

Use commas within a parenthetical citation to separate the author's name from the date and the date from the page number(s). Include a page number or numbers only when you are quoting directly from the source.

2. Work by two authors

Waldron and Dieser conclude from their interview data that the media are responsible for shaping student perceptions of health and fitness (2010).

OR

The media are greatly responsible for shaping student perceptions of health and fitness (Waldron & Dieser, 2010).

When the authors' names are in parentheses, use an ampersand (&) to separate them.

3. Work by more than two authors

Students have reported the benefits of talking with a teacher about their academic progress (Komarraju, Musulkin, & Bhattacharya, 2010).

For works with three, four, or five authors, cite all the authors the first time the work is referred to, but in subsequent references give only the last name of the first author followed by *et al.* (which means "and others" and is not italicized).

According to Komarraju et al. (2010), when students find a teacher accessible, they "are more likely to report being confident of their academic skills and being motivated, both intrinsically and extrinsically" (p. 339).

For works with six or more authors, provide only the last name of the first author followed by *et al.* in the first and subsequent citations.

4. Anonymous work

Use a shortened version of the title to identify an anonymous work.

Chronic insomnia often requires medical intervention ("Sleep," 2009).

This citation refers to an article listed in the bibliography as "Sleep disorders: Standard methods of treatment."

If the word *Anonymous* is used in the source itself to designate the author, it appears in place of an author's name.

The documents could damage the governor's reputation (Anonymous, 2009).

5. Two or more works by different authors in the same parenthetical citation

Smokers frequently underestimate the long-term effects of smoking (O'Conner, 2005; Polson & Truss, 2007).

Arrange the citations in alphabetical order, using a semicolon to separate them.

6. Two or more works by the same author in the same parenthetical citation

The amygdala is active when a person experiences fear or anger (Carey, 2001, 2002).

Jameson (2007a, 2007b) has proposed an anxiety index for use by counselors.

Order the publication dates of works by the same author from earliest to most recent; however, if two or more works have the same publication date, distinguish the dates with lowercase letters (*a, b, c,* and so on) assigned according to the order in which the entries for the works are listed in your bibliography (see page 346).

7. Personal communication

State educational outcomes are often interpreted differently by teachers in the same school
(J. K. Jurgensen, personal communication, May 4, 2009).

Personal communications include letters, memos, e-mail messages, interviews, and telephone conversations. These sources are cited in the text only; they do not appear in the reference list.

8. Indirect source

Korovessis (2002, p. 63) points out Toqueville's description of the "strange melancholy" exhibited by citizens living amid abundance.

Toqueville (as cited in Korovessis, 2002, p. 63) observed the "strange melancholy" exhibited by citizens living amid abundance.

In the reference list, include a bibliographic entry for the source you read, not for the original source. (Use an indirect source only when you are unable to obtain the original.)

9. Electronic source

Cite an electronic source such as an online newspaper or a website according to the guidelines already mentioned. If there is no date, use the abbreviation *n.d.* If no page numbers are provided in a source, give the number of the paragraph containing the words you are quoting, preceded by the abbreviation *para.*

Researchers believe that athletes should warm up before exercising, but according to Kolata (2010), "what's missing is evidence showing actual effects on performance" (para. 18).

If the source is divided into sections, use the section heading and the number of the paragraph following that heading: (Methods, para. 2).

(2) Guidelines for in-text citations and quotations

(a) Placement of in-text citations

According to APA guidelines, there are two ways to cite a source: one focuses on the researcher and the other on the researcher's findings. If you focus on the researcher, use that person's name in the sentence and place the publication date of the source in parentheses directly after the name.

Diaz (2011) reported that all-night cram sessions do not improve performance.

When making subsequent references to a researcher within the same paragraph, you do not need to repeat the date.

If you decide to focus on the researcher's findings, place the researcher's name and the date (separated by a comma) in parentheses at the end of the sentence.

All-night cram sessions do not improve performance (Diaz, 2011).

Parenthetical citations that include a researcher's name must also include a publication date.

(b) Punctuation for citations and quotations

Quotations should be incorporated into the text when they include fewer than forty words. Use double quotation marks to enclose the quotation. Then cite the source and page number in parentheses. Use *p.* for "page" and *pp.* for "pages." Place a period after the last parenthesis.

According to recent research on the effects of birth order, "laterborns are 1.5 times more likely than first-borns to engage in such activities, including football, soccer, rugby, bobsledding, and skydiving" (Sulloway & Zweigenhaft, 2010, p. 412).

OR

Sulloway and Zweigenhaft (2010) report that "laterborns are 1.5 times more likely than first-borns to engage in such activities, including football, soccer, rugby, bobsledding, and skydiving" (p. 412).

If a quotation has forty or more words, format it as a block quotation. Because a block quotation is set off from the rest of the text, quotation marks are not used. Notice that the parenthetical citation is placed at the end of the paragraph *after* the end punctuation (in this case, a period).

Sulloway and Zweigenhaft (2010) report the effect of birth order on individuals' decisions to take more risks in sports:

> Data on 700 brothers whose major league careers ended by 2008, and who collectively played in more than 300,000 baseball games, reveal significantly heterogeneous results for birth order and its relationship to specific abilities in baseball, including skill, power, self-restraint, and risk taking. As predicted, younger brothers were more likely to engage in the risky business of stealing bases; they attempted more steals per game, and they were more likely to succeed in doing so. (p. 412)

(3) Headings

In research reports, headings set off sections and subsections. The APA specifies five levels of headings:

- Level 1 headings are centered and boldfaced, with each major word capitalized:

Method

- Level 2 headings are flush with the left margin and boldfaced, with each major word capitalized:

Materials and Procedure

- Level 3 headings are boldfaced, begin on a paragraph indent, have only the first word capitalized, and end with a period:

    Sampling procedures.

- Level 4 headings are boldfaced and italicized, begin on a paragraph indent, have only the first word capitalized, and end with a period:

    Use of a random generator.

- Level 5 headings are italicized, begin on a paragraph indent, have only the first word capitalized, and end with a period:

    Problems with generated data points.

Most papers that students write have two or three levels of headings. For a paper with two levels, use levels 1 and 2; for a paper with three levels, use levels 1, 2, and 3. For examples of headings, see Danielle Dezell's paper (13e).

14b APA-STYLE REFERENCE LIST

All of the works you cite should be listed at the end of your paper, beginning on a separate page with the heading *References* (not italicized). The following tips will help you prepare your list.

TIPS FOR PREPARING A REFERENCE LIST

- Center the heading *References* one inch from the top of the page.

- Include in your reference list only the sources you explicitly cite in your paper. Do not, however, include entries for personal communications or for original works cited in indirect sources.

- Arrange the list of works alphabetically by the author's last name. If a source has more than one author, alphabetize by the last name of the first author.

- If you use more than one work by the same author(s), arrange the entries according to the date of publication, placing the entry with the earliest date first. If two or more works by the same author(s) have the same publication date, the entries are arranged so that the titles of the works are in alphabetical order, according to the first important word in each title; lowercase letters are then added to the date (for example, 2008a and 2008b) to distinguish the works.

- When an author's name appears both in a single-author entry and as the first name in a multiple-author entry, place the single-author entry first.

- For a work without an author, alphabetize the entry according to the first important word in the title.

- Type the first line of each entry flush with the left margin and indent subsequent lines one-half inch or five spaces (a hanging indent).

- Double-space throughout—between lines in each entry and between entries.

Whether you are submitting an APA-style paper in a college course or preparing a manuscript for publication, you can be guided by the format of the following sample entries.

❶ *CAUTION*

Automatic bibliography composers found online and included in some software packages often make mistakes. They may fail to include all elements of a bibliographic entry or may order elements incorrectly. If you decide to use an automatic composer, be sure to check the results against the model entries provided in this chapter.

Directory of APA-Style Entries for a Reference List

The following guidelines are for books, articles, and most electronic sources. For additional guidelines for documenting electronic sources, see pages 358–64.

When preparing entries for your reference list, be sure to copy the bibliographic information directly from each source (for example, the title page of a book). (See Figure 14.1, on page 353.)

GENERAL DOCUMENTATION GUIDELINES FOR PRINT-BASED SOURCES

Author or Editor

One author. Use the author's first initial and middle initial (if given) and his or her last name. Invert the initials and the last name; place a comma after the last name. Include a space between the first and middle initials. Any abbreviation or number that is part of a name, such as *Jr.* or *II,* is placed after a comma following the initials. Indicate the end of this information unit with a single period.	Walters, D. M. Thayer-Smith, M. S. Villa, R. P., Jr.

Two to seven authors. Invert the last names and initials of all authors. Use commas to separate last names from initials. Use an ampersand (&) (in addition to the comma) before the last name of the last author.	Vifian, I. R., & Kikuchi, K. Kempf, A. R., Cusack, R., & Evans, T. G.
Eight or more authors. List the first six names, add three ellipsis points, and include the last author's name.	Bauer, S. E., Berry, L., Hacket, N. P., Bach, R., Price, T., Brown, J. B., … Green, J.
Corporate or group author. Provide the author's full name.	Hutton Arts Foundation. Center for Neuroscience.
Editor. If a work has an editor or editors instead of an author or authors, include the abbreviation *Ed.* for "editor" or *Eds.* for "editors" in parentheses after the name(s).	Harris, B. E. (Ed.). Stroud, D. F., & Holst, L. F. (Eds.).

Publication Date

Books and journals. Provide the year of publication in parentheses, placing a period after the closing parenthesis. For books, this date can be found on the copyright page, which is the page following the title page (see Figure 14.2, on page 354). The publication date of a journal article can be found at the bottom of the first page of the article (see Figure 14.3, on page 357). For a work that has been accepted for publication but has not yet been published, place *in press* in parentheses. For a work without a date of publication, use *n.d.* in parentheses.	(2008). (in press). (n.d.).

(continued on page 350)

Publication Date *(continued from page 349)*

Magazines and newspapers. For monthly publications, provide both the year and the month, separated by a comma. For daily publications, provide the year, month, and day. Use a comma between the year and the month.	(2007, January). (2008, June 22).
Conferences and meetings. If a paper presented at a conference, symposium, or professional meeting is published, the publication date is given as the year only, in parentheses. For unpublished papers, provide the year and the month in which the gathering occurred, separated by a comma.	(2008) (2009, September).

Title

Books. Capitalize only the first word and any proper nouns in a book title. Italicize the entire title and place a period at the end of this information unit.	*An introduction to Vygotsky.* *Avoiding work-related stress.*
Journals, magazines, or newspapers. In the name of a journal, magazine, or newspaper, capitalize all major words, as well as any other words consisting of four or more letters. Italicize the entire name and place a comma after it.	*Journal of Child Psychology,* *Psychology Today,* *Los Angeles Times,*
Articles and chapters. Do not italicize the titles of short works such as journal articles or book chapters. The title of an article or chapter appears before the book title or the name of the journal, magazine, or newspaper. Capitalize only the first word of the title and any proper nouns.	Treating posttraumatic stress disorder.

Subtitles. Always include any subtitle provided for a source. Use a colon to separate a main title and a subtitle. Capitalize only the first word of the subtitle and any proper nouns.

Reading images: The grammar of visual design.

Living in Baghdad: Realities and restrictions.

Volume, Issue, Chapter, and Page Numbers

Journal volume and issue numbers. A journal paginated *continuously* designates only the first page of the first issue in a volume as page 1. The first page of a subsequent issue in the same volume is given the page number that follows the last page number of the previous issue. In contrast, each issue of a journal paginated *separately* begins with page 1. When you use an article from a journal paginated continuously, provide only the volume number (italicized). When you use an article from a journal paginated separately, provide the issue number (placed in parentheses) directly after the volume number. Do not insert a space between the volume and issue numbers. Italicize only the volume number. Place a comma after this unit of information.

Journal of Applied Social Psychology, 32,

Behavior Therapy, 33(2),

Book chapters. Provide the numbers of the first and last pages of the relevant chapter preceded by the abbreviation *pp.* (for "pages"). Place this information in parentheses. Use an en dash (a short dash; see **40d** and **44g(2)**) between the page numbers.

New communitarian thinking (pp. 126–140).

Articles. List the page numbers after the comma that follows the volume or issue number.

TESOL Quarterly, 34(2), 213–238.

(continued on page 352)

Publication Data

City and state. Identify the city in which the publisher of the work is located, including the two-letter U.S. Postal Service abbreviation for the state. If two or more cities are given on the title page, use the first one listed. If the publisher is a university press whose name mentions a state, do not include the state abbreviation. When a work has been published in a city outside the United States, include the name of the country.

Boston, MA:

Lancaster, PA:

University Park: Pennsylvania State University Press.

Oxford, England:

Publisher's name. Provide only enough of the publisher's name so that it can be identified clearly. Omit words such as *Publishers* and abbreviations such as *Inc.* However, include *Books* and *Press* when they are part of the publisher's name. The publisher's name follows the city and state or country, after a colon. A period ends this unit of information.

New Haven, CT: Yale University Press.

New York, NY: Harcourt.

Cambridge, England: Cambridge University Press.

BOOKS

1. Book by one author

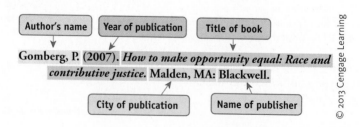

Author's name   Year of publication   Title of book

Gomberg, P. (2007). *How to make opportunity equal: Race and contributive justice.* Malden, MA: Blackwell.

City of publication   Name of publisher

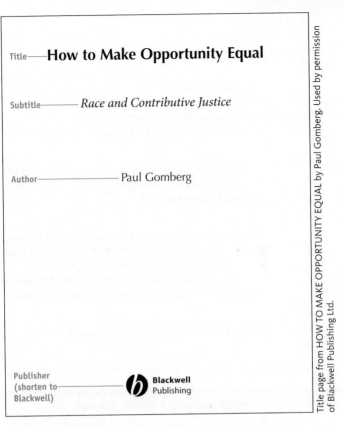

Figure 14.1. The title page of a book provides most of the information necessary for creating a bibliographic entry for a research paper.

2. Book by two or more authors

Edwards, M., & Titman, P. (2010). *Promoting psychological well-being in children with acute and chronic illness.* London, England: Jessica Kingsley.

If there are eight or more authors, list the first six names followed by three ellipsis points and the last author's name.

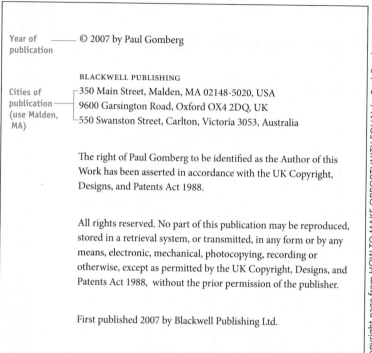

Year of publication — © 2007 by Paul Gomberg

BLACKWELL PUBLISHING

Cities of publication (use Malden, MA) — 350 Main Street, Malden, MA 02148-5020, USA
9600 Garsington Road, Oxford OX4 2DQ, UK
550 Swanston Street, Carlton, Victoria 3053, Australia

The right of Paul Gomberg to be identified as the Author of this Work has been asserted in accordance with the UK Copyright, Designs, and Patents Act 1988.

All rights reserved. No part of this publication may be reproduced, stored in a retrieval system, or transmitted, in any form or by any means, electronic, mechanical, photocopying, recording or otherwise, except as permitted by the UK Copyright, Designs, and Patents Act 1988, without the prior permission of the publisher.

First published 2007 by Blackwell Publishing Ltd.

Figure 14.2. The year in which a book was published and the city where it was published can be found on the copyright page, which follows the title page.

3. Book with editor(s)

Wolfe, D. A., & Mash, E. J. (Eds.). (2005). *Behavioral and emotional disorders in adolescents: Nature, assessment, and treatment.* New York, NY: Guilford Press.

4. Book with a corporate or group author

U.S. War Department. (2003). *Official military atlas of the Civil War.* New York, NY: Barnes & Noble.

5. Edition after the first

Lycan, W., & Prinz, J. (Eds.). (2008). *Mind and cognition* (3rd ed.). Malden, MA: Blackwell.

Identify the edition in parentheses immediately after the title. Use abbreviations: *2nd, 3rd,* and so on for the edition number and *ed.* for "edition."

6. Translation

Rank, O. (2002). *Psychology and the soul: A study of the origin, conceptual evolution, and nature of the soul* (G. C. Richter & E. J. Lieberman, Trans.). Baltimore, MD: Johns Hopkins University Press. (Original work published 1930)

A period follows the name of the publisher but not the parenthetical note about the original publication date.

7. Republished book

Petersen, J. (2009). *Our street.* (B. Rensen, Trans.) London, England: Faber. (Original work published 1938)

8. Multivolume work

Fitzduff, M., & Stout, C. (Eds.). (2006). *The psychology of resolving global conflicts: From war to peace* (Vols. 1–3). Westport, CT: Praeger.

9. Government report

Executive Office of the President. (2003). *Economic report of the President, 2003* (GPO Publication No. 040-000-0760-1). Washington, DC: U.S. Government Printing Office.

10. Selection from an edited book

Empson, R. (2007). Enlivened memories: Recalling absence and loss in Mongolia. In J. Carsten (Ed.), *Ghosts of memory: Essays on remembrance and relatedness* (pp. 58–82). Malden, MA: Blackwell.

Italicize the book title but not the title of the selection.

11. Selection from a reference book

Wickens, D. (2001). Classical conditioning. In *The Corsini encyclopedia of psychology and behavioral science* (Vol. 1, pp. 293–298). New York, NY: John Wiley.

ARTICLES IN PRINT

12. Article with one author in a journal with continuous pagination

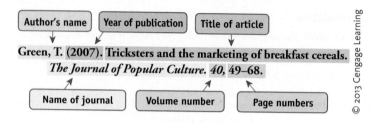

Figure 14.3 shows where the information for this type of entry is found on the first page of an article.

13. Article with two authors in a journal with each issue paginated separately

Rudisill, J. R., & Edwards, J. M. (2002). Coping with job transitions. *Consulting Psychology Journal, 54*(1), 55–62.

14. Article with three to seven authors

Frost, R. O., Steketee, G., & Williams, L. (2002). Compulsive buying, compulsive hoarding, and obsessive-compulsive disorder. *Behavior Therapy, 33*(2), 201–213.

15. Article with eight or more authors

Lockenhoff, C. E., De Fruyt, F., Terracciano, A., McCrae, R. R., De Bolle, M., Costa, P. T., Jr., …Yik, M. (2009). Perceptions of aging across 26 cultures and their culture-level associates. *Psychology and Aging, 24*, 941–954.

16. Article in a monthly, biweekly, or weekly magazine

Winson, J. (2002, June). The meaning of dreams. *Scientific American, 12*, 54–61.

For magazines published weekly or biweekly, add the day of the issue: (2003, May 8).

17. Article in a newspaper

Simon, S. (2007, October 14). Winning hearts, minds, homes. *Los Angeles Times,* p. A1.

Include the letter indicating the section with the page number.

Title —— Tricksters and the Marketing of
Breakfast Cereals

Author —— THOMAS GREEN

CULTURE, Vol. 40, No. 1, 2007. Reprinted by permission of Blackwell Publishing Ltd.

REAKFAST CEREALS ARE SOLD BY TRICKSTERS. FROM LUCKY THE
Leprechaun to the Cookie Crook to the mischievous live-action
squirrels who vend General Mills Honey Nut Clusters, an astounding number of Saturday morning television commercials feature 30-second
dramatizations of trickster tales that are designed to promote breakfast
cereals. True, breakfast cereals are not the only products sold by tricksters,
and not all cereals are sold by tricksters—especially in the last decade. But
the association is common enough to persist as an unexamined assumption
that seems obvious to most Americans once it is pointed out. Naturally,
breakfast cereals are often sold by animated tricksterish mascot characters,
and naturally such commercials feature motifs and narrative patterns that
are common in trickster tales. But the perception of an inherent internal
logic in this scheme overlooks a couple of key questions. Why, for example,
are tricksters considered a particularly appropriate or effective means of
marketing breakfast cereals? And why breakfast cereals in particular (and a
few other breakfast products), almost to the exclusion of tricksters in other
types of marketing campaigns? The answers to these questions, it turns out,
may lie back in the semi-mystical, pseudoreligious origins of prepared
breakfast foods and the mating of the mythology of those foods with the
imperatives of the competitive, prepared-foods marketplace.

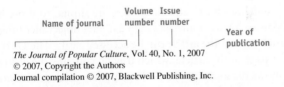

Name of journal | Volume number | Issue number | Year of publication

The Journal of Popular Culture, Vol. 40, No. 1, 2007
© 2007, Copyright the Authors
Journal compilation © 2007, Blackwell Publishing, Inc.

Figure 14.3. The first page of a journal article provides the information needed to
complete a bibliographic entry for that source.

18. Letter to the editor

Budington, N. (2010, July 20). Social class and college admissions [Letter to the editor]. *The
New York Times,* p. A26.

After the title, indicate within brackets that the work is a letter to the editor.

19. Book review
If the review lacks its own title, use a descriptive phrase (like that shown below) in brackets.

Orford, J. (2007, November). [Review of the book *Drug addiction and families,* by M. Barnard]. *Addiction, 102,* 1841–1842.

If the review has a title, include that title before the bracketed information.

Herman, O. (2011, April 10). A little help from your friends: How evolution explains altruism. [Review of the book *Supercooperators,* by M. A. Nowak with R. Highfield]. *The New York Times Book Review,* p. 18.

20. Conference paper
Dodgen, L. (2010, May). *Perceptions of coercion.* Paper presented at the Symposium on University Research and Creative Expression, Central Washington University, Ellensburg, WA.

SOURCES PRODUCED FOR ACCESS BY COMPUTER

The APA guidelines for electronic sources are similar to those for print sources. Many scholarly journals assign a digital object identifier (DOI) to each article so that the article can be accessed easily. The DOI is listed on the first page of the article, which usually contains the abstract. Figure 14.4 shows the location of a DOI and other pertinent bibliographic information on the first page of an online journal. Whenever possible, end a reference list entry for a journal article with the DOI (without a period following it). In an entry for an article without a DOI, use the URL for the periodical's home page. If the URL has to continue on a new line, break it before a punctuation mark or other special character. Do not include a period at the end of the URL.

Name of journal — Page numbers

Journal of Personality and Social Psychology
2011, Vol. 100, No. 2, 365–385
— Volume and issue numbers

© 2010 American Psychological Association
0022-3514/10/$12.00 DOI: 10.1037/a0021341 — DOI

— Year of publication

Implicit Self-Esteem: Nature, Measurement, and a New Way Forward

Title of article

Michael D. Buhrmester
University of Texas at Austin

Hart Blanton
University of Connecticut

Authors' names

William B. Swann, Jr.
University of Texas at Austin

Gaining insight into the nature and consequences of people's global self-evaluations (i.e., their self-esteem) has been fraught with difficulty. Nearly 2 decades ago, researchers suggested that such difficulties might be addressed by the development of a new class of measures designed to uncover implicit self-esteem. In this article, we evaluate the construct validity of the 2 most common measures of implicit self-esteem, the Implicit Association Test (IAT) and Name–Letter Test (NLT). Our review indicates that the research literature has not provided strong or consistent support for the validity of either measure. We conclude that both tests are impoverished measures of self-esteem that are better understood as measures of either generalized implicit affect (IAT) or implicit egotism (NLT). However, we suggest that there surely are aspects of self-esteem that people are unwilling or unable to report and suggest a general approach that may allow researchers to tap these unspoken aspects of self-esteem.

Keywords: self-esteem, implicit measures, Implicit Association Test, name–letter effect, implicit egotism

Proper self-esteem [is] a state of mind that ought to be. Those, moreover, who estimate their own worth correctly, do so on the basis of their past deeds, and so, what they have done, they dare to try again. Those who estimate their worth too highly, or who pretend to be what they are not, or who believe flatterers, become disheartened when dangers actually confront them.

—Thomas Hobbes, *De Homine*

As Hobbes's remarks testify, the construct of self-esteem has a long history in Western culture. But his remarks also acknowledge the difficulty of accurately assessing and reporting one's value. And so, although self-esteem has soared in popularity among both laypersons (e.g., Branden, 1994) and academics (e.g., Bosson & Swann, 2009), some have registered gnawing doubts regarding the capacity of people to report faithfully their true self-evaluations. These concerns have recently dovetailed with growing interest in implicit, nonconscious processes to produce an exciting new construct: Implicit self-esteem. Here, we focus on the nature and measurement of this new construct, what is known about its relation to theoretical correlates of self-esteem, and how researchers might approach this new construct in the future. To place our analysis in context, we begin with a brief discussion of challenges associated with measuring self-esteem using traditional, explicit methods.

Measuring Self-Esteem

Throughout most of the 6 decades since the introduction of the first measure of self-esteem (Raimy, 1948), theorists agreed that explicit self-esteem refers to feelings of self-worth or the global evaluation of the self (Bosson & Swann, 2009; Rosenberg, 1965; Shavelson, Hubner, & Stanton, 1976). But, if there is consensus regarding the nature of self-esteem, there is less agreement regarding the most appropriate means of assessing it. To date, the most widespread approach has been to explicitly ask people a series of questions regarding their global self-evaluation. Critics have faulted such measures on at least three counts. First, the verbal questionnaires designed to assess explicit self-esteem may fail to capture self-views of which people are unaware (e.g., Greenwald & Farnham, 2000). Second, even if people are aware of a given self-view, they might fail to express it due to self-presentational pressures that tempt them to inflate their self-evaluations (e.g., Paulhus, 1991, 2002). Third, perhaps due to the foregoing limitations, researchers have failed to uncover strong and consistent support for the predictive validity of measures of explicit self-esteem (see Baumeister, Campbell, Krueger, & Vohs, 2003).

Although some have countered the foregoing critiques (e.g., Marsh & Craven, 2006; Swann, Chang-Schneider, & McClarty, 2007), it is certainly possible that measures of explicit self-esteem may fail to capture important aspects of self-knowledge. With this possibility in mind, researchers developed several measures of implicit self-esteem (see Bosson, Swann & Pennebaker, 2000). By far the most popular of these measures have been a pair dubbed the Implicit Association Test (IAT) and the Name–Letter Test (NLT). Both measures are based on the assumption that implicit self-esteem is a valenced association that a person has toward himself or herself. Although researchers differ in how they characterize this association, some consensus has emerged regarding its nature

This article was published Online First November 1, 2010.

Michael D. Buhrmester and William B. Swann, Jr., Department of Psychology, University of Texas at Austin; Hart Blanton, Department of Psychology, University of Connecticut.

Correspondence concerning this article should be addressed to William B. Swann, Jr., Department of Psychology, University of Texas at Austin, 1 University Station, Austin, TX 78712. E-mail: swann@mail.utexas.edu

Figure 14.4. First page of an online journal article.

21. Online journal article with a digital object identifier (DOI)

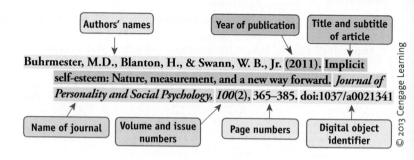

Authors' names → Buhrmester, M.D., Blanton, H., & Swann, W. B., Jr.

Year of publication → (2011).

Title and subtitle of article → Implicit self-esteem: Nature, measurement, and a new way forward.

Name of journal → *Journal of Personality and Social Psychology,*

Volume and issue numbers → *100*(2),

Page numbers → 365–385.

Digital object identifier → doi:1037/a0021341

© 2013 Cengage Learning

22. Online journal article without a DOI

Tuladhar-Douglas, W. (2007). Leaf blowers and antibiotics: A Buddhist stance for science and technology. *Journal of Buddhist Ethics, 14,* 200–238. Retrieved from http://blogs .dickinson.edu/buddhistethics/

Instead of a DOI, the URL for the journal's home page, preceded by the phrase *Retrieved from*, appears at the end of the entry.

23. Online magazine article based on a print source

Acocella, J. (2008, May 26). A few too many. *The New Yorker, 84*(15), 32–37. Retrieved from http://www.newyorker.com

24. Online magazine article not found in print

Saletan, W. (2008, August 27). Unfinished race: Race, genes, and the future of medicine. *Slate.* Retrieved from http://www.slate.com

25. Article in an online newspaper

Redden, J. (2011, April 18). Portland, Lake Oswego councils endorse streetcar proposal. *Portland Tribune.* Retrieved from http://www.portlandtribune.com

In Figure 14.5, you can see where to find the author's name, the date, the title of the article, and the name of the newspaper. Be sure to use the URL for the newspaper's home page (for example, http://www .portlandtribune.com), not the URL for the page on which you found the article.

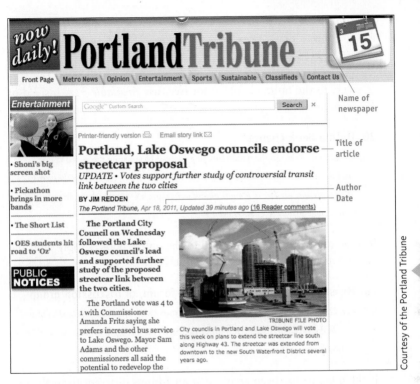

Figure 14.5. Article from an online newspaper.

26. Article from a database

Include the article's DOI if it has one; if it does not have a DOI, list the URL of the journal's home page (see items 21 and 22). Note that the name of the database is not included.

Hill, E. J., Erickson, J. J., Holmes, E. K., & Ferris, M. (2010). Workplace flexibility, work

    hours, and work-life conflict: Finding an extra day or two. *Journal of Family Psychology,*

    24(3), 349–358. doi:10.1037/a0019282

Shellenbarger, S. (2010, July 21). Kids quit the team for more family time. *The Wall Street*

    Journal. Retrieved from http://online.wsj.com/home-page

27. Online book

Pine, R. C. (2004). *Science and the human prospect.* Retrieved from http://home.honolulu
.hawaii.edu/~pine/book1-2.html

If access to the online book is not free, use *Available from* instead of
Retrieved from.

28. Online book chapter

Brady, V. (2006). A flaw in the nation-building process: Negotiating the sacred in our
multicultural society. In E. B. Coleman & K. White (Eds.), *Negotiating the sacred:
Blasphemy and sacrilege in a multicultural society* (pp. 43–49). Retrieved from http://
epress.anu.edu.au/nts_citation.html

If page numbers are not provided in the online book, simply omit the
parenthetical identification of such numbers.

29. Message posted to a newsgroup, forum, or discussion group

Vellenzer, G. (2004, January 24). Synonyms of entreaty [Msg 2]. Message posted to http://
groups.google.com/groups?selm=MPG.1a7cacccd54e9c27989b95%40news.CIS.DFN
.DE&output=gplain

If the message has been archived at an address different from the one
it was posted to, a comma should be placed after the first URL, followed by *archived at* (not italicized) and the URL for the archived
version.

30. Blog posting

Chatham, C. (2008, August 29). Action without intention: Parietal damage alters attention
awareness. Message posted to http://scienceblogs.com/developingintelligence/2008/08
/action_without_intention_parie.php

31. Lecture notes posted online

Wolfe, J. (2004). *Lecture 18: Freud and fairy tales.* Retrieved from Massachusetts Institute of
Technology OpenCourseWare website: http://ocw.mit.edu/OcwWeb/Brain-and
-Cognitive-Sciences/9-00Fall-2004/LectureNotes/index.htm

32. Authored document from a website

Ennis, R. H. (2002, July 20). *An outline of goals for a critical thinking curriculum and its assessment.*
Retrieved from http://faculty.ed.uiuc.edu/rhennis/outlinegoalsctcurassess3.html

33. Online document with no identified author

American School Counselor Association. (2006). *Position statement: Equity for all students.*
Retrieved from http://asca2.timberlakepublishing.com/content.asp?contentid=503

Use the name of the organization sponsoring the website as the author
of the document.

34. Personal communication

Entries for personal communications such as e-mail messages, letters,
interviews, and telephone conversations are not included in the reference list. Such sources should be cited in the text as follows: (S. L.
Johnson, personal communication, September 3, 2003).

35. Online encyclopedia

Dowe, P. (2007). Causal processes. In E. N. Zalta (Ed.), *The Stanford encyclopedia of philosophy.*
Retrieved from http://plato.stanford.edu/archives/sum2007/entries/cognitive-science/

36. Online dictionary

Paranormal. (2000). In *The American Heritage dictionary of the English language* (4th ed.).
Retrieved from http://www.bartleby.com/61/35/P0063500.html

37. Online consumer brochure

American Psychological Association. (2008). *Elder abuse and neglect: In search of solutions*
[Brochure]. Retrieved from http://www.apa.org/pi/aging/eldabuse.html

38. Online government document

Pashler, H., Bain, P., Bottge, B., Graesser, A., Koedinger, K., McDaniel, M., & Metcalfe, J.
(2007, September). *Organizing instruction and study to improve student learning: IES
practice guide* (NCER 2007-2004). Washington, DC: National Center for Education
Research, Institute of Education Sciences, U.S. Department of Education. Retrieved
from http://ies.ed.gov/pubsearch/pubsinfo.asp?pubid=NCER20072004

If no authors are identified, an entry for an online government document is formatted as follows:

U.S. Department of Health and Human Services, National Institutes of Health,

National Institute on Alcohol Abuse and Alcoholism. (2010). Beyond hangovers:

Understanding alcohol's impact on your health (NIH Publication No. 10-7604).

Retrieved from http://www.niaaa.nih.gov/Publications/PamphletsBrochuresPosters

/English/Pages/default.aspx

39. Online audio or video file

Begin the entry with the name of the contributor whose role is most relevant to the topic of your paper. Identify the contributor's role (for example, *Producer, Director, Writer, Host,* or *Presenter*) in parentheses. The medium (for example, *Audio file, Video file, Audio podcast,* or *Video webcast*) is placed in square brackets after the title of the work.

Davies, D. (Host). (2010, July 13). A psychiatrist's prescription for his profession

[Audio file]. In T. Gross & D. Miller (Executive producers), *Fresh air.*

Retrieved from http://www.npr.org/templates/rundowns/rundown.php

?prgrid=13&prgDate=7-13-2010

Gopnik, A. (Presenter). (2009, July 28). Moments of absolute absorption [Video file]. In

D. McGee & P. W. Kunhardt (Executive producers), *This emotional life: The meaning*

of happiness (Chapter 6). Retrieved from http://www.pbs.org/thisemotionallife

/perspective/meaning-happiness

OTHER SOURCES

40. Motion picture

Gaviria, M. (Producer/Director), & Smith, M. (Producer/Writer). (2001). *Medicating kids*

[Motion picture]. United States: Public Broadcasting Service.

Begin with the relevant contributor(s), identifying the nature of the contribution in parentheses following each name. Then provide the release date and the title, followed by a descriptive label in square brackets. The entry ends with the name of the country where the film was produced and the name of the studio or organization.

41. Television program

Holt, S. (Producer). (2002, October 1). *The mysterious lives of caves* [Television program].

Alexandria, VA: Public Broadcasting Service.

Give the title of the program in italics. If citing an entire series (for example, *Nova* or *The West Wing*), use the name of the producer of the series as a whole and the descriptive label *Television series* in the square brackets. If the program is a single episode of a series, its title is not italicized, and the descriptive label in the brackets is *Television series episode*.

42. Advertisement

Rosetta Stone [Advertisement]. (2010, July). *National Geographic, 218*(1), 27.

14C | APA-STYLE RESEARCH PAPER

The APA recognizes that a paper may have to be modified so that it adheres to an instructor's requirements. The following boxes offer tips for preparing a title page, an abstract page, and the body of a typical student paper. For tips on preparing a reference list, see **14b**.

TIPS FOR PREPARING THE TITLE PAGE OF AN APA-STYLE PAPER

- The title page includes both the full title of the paper and a shortened version of it. The shortened version appears in the header. On the left side of the header, place the words *Running head:* (not italicized, followed by a colon) and the shortened version of your title. The shortened version should consist of no more than fifty characters (including punctuation and spaces), and all letters should be capitals. On the right side of the header, insert the page number. The title page is page 1 of your paper.

- Place the full title in the upper half of the page, with your name and your institutional affiliation below it. You may include the course name and number instead of the affiliation if your instructor requests it. Double-space and center these lines.

TIPS FOR PREPARING THE ABSTRACT AND THE BODY OF AN APA-STYLE PAPER

- The header for the abstract page and each page in the body of the paper consists of the shortened title on the left and the page number on the right. The abstract is on page 2; the body of the paper begins on page 3.

- Center the word *Abstract* (not italicized or boldfaced) one inch from the top of the paper.

- Be sure that the abstract is no more than 250 words. For advice on summarizing, see 10d(4).

- Double-space throughout the body of the abstract. Do not indent the first line of the abstract.

- Center the title of the paper one inch from the top of the page on page 3.

- Use one-inch margins on both the left and right sides of all pages.

- Double-space throughout the body of the paper, indenting each paragraph one-half inch, or five to seven spaces.

- If there are headings within the body of the paper, format them according to their levels (14a(3)).

↕ 1/2 inch

The shortened title
in the page header
should consist of
no more than 50
characters.

Place the
page number
in the top
right corner.

Use 1-inch
margins on
both sides of
the page.

The Social Status of an Art: Historical and Current Trends in Tattooing

Rachel L. Pinter and Sarah M. Cronin

Central Washington University

If required by the
instructor, the
course name and
number replace
the institutional
affiliation.

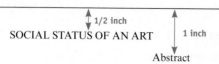

↕ 1/2 inch

SOCIAL STATUS OF AN ART | 1 inch | 2

Center the heading.

Abstract

The maximum length for an abstract is 250 words.

Current research demonstrates that the social practice of tattooing has changed greatly over the years. Not only have the images chosen for tattoos and the demographic of people getting tattoos changed, but the ideology behind tattooing itself has evolved. This paper first briefly describes the cross-cultural history of the practice. It then examines current social trends in the United States and related ideological issues.

The Social Status of an Art: Historical and Current Trends in Tattooing

Tattoos, defined as marks made by inserting pigment into the skin, have existed throughout history in countless cultures. Currently, tattoos are considered popular art forms. They can be seen on men and women from all walks of life in the United States, ranging from a trainer at the local gym to a character on a television show or even a sociology professor. Due to an increase in the popularity of tattooing, studies of tattooing behavior have proliferated as researchers attempt to identify trends. This paper seeks to explore both the history of tattooing and its current practice in the United States.

Tattooing has a long history in most of the world, though its origin is currently unknown. Krcmarik (2003) provides a helpful geographical overview. In Asia, tattooing has existed for thousands of years in Chinese, Japanese, Middle Eastern, and Indian cultures. Evidence of its existence can be seen on artifacts such as 7,000-year-old engravings. In Europe, tattooing flourished during the 19th century, most notably in England. Many of the sailors traveling with Captain James Cook returned with tales of exotic tattooing practices and sometimes with tattoos themselves. The Samoans in the South Pacific are famous for their centuries-old tattooing practice, known as *tatau*—the word from which *tattoo* is said to have originated. The Maori of New Zealand are also well known for their hand-carved facial tattoos, known as *Moko* (see Figure 1).

In Africa, tattoos can be found on Egyptian and Nubian mummies, which date back to approximately 2000 BCE. Tattooing is noted in the written accounts of Spanish explorers' encounters with tattooed Mayans

Center the title.

Use 1-inch margins on both sides of the page.

The writers' thesis statement forecasts the content of the essay.

The writers provide historical and cultural information about tattooing.

SOCIAL STATUS OF AN ART   4

Figure 1. A Maori man with a facial tattoo. *Note.* Photo © Tim Graham/Getty Images.

The writers discuss changing perspectives on the appropriateness of tattoos.

in Central America. Finally, in North America, tattooing became popular in the early part of the 20th century and has experienced advances and retreats in social acceptance since then. Starting in the 1960s, its popularity rose dramatically.

Clearly, the history of tattooing spans generations and cultures. The practice has gained and lost popularity, often as a result of rather extreme changes in the ideologies supporting or discouraging it. This roller-coaster pattern of acceptance is well demonstrated in the United States. Since the 19th century, the wearing of tattoos has allowed for subculture identification among such persons as sailors, bikers, circus "freak" performers, and prison inmates (DeMello, 1995). As a collective group behavior indicating deviant subculture membership, tattooing flourished during the 20th century but remained plagued by negative stereotypes and associations. In the last 10 years, however, the practice has represented a more individualistic yet mainstream means of body adornment. As Figure 2 illustrates, it is not unusual to see a white-collar worker sporting a tattoo.

Tattooing is now common among both teenagers and older adults, men and women, urbanites and suburbanites, the college-educated and the uneducated, and the rich as well as the poor (Kosut, 2006). Table 1 indicates the wide range of Americans wearing tattoos in 2003 and 2008.

SOCIAL STATUS OF AN ART 5

Figure 2. Tattoos are becoming more common among middle-class professionals. *Note.* Photo © Eric Anthony Johnson/Photolibrary.com

> The writers include a photograph to support a point.

The trend toward acceptance of tattoos may be a result of how American society views the people who wear them. Earlier, tattoos were depicted in mainstream print and visual media as worn by people with low socioeconomic or marginal status; now, they are considered to be a means of self-expression among celebrities as well as educated middle- and upper-class individuals (Kosut, 2006). This shift in the symbolic status of tattoos—to a form of self-expression among the social elite rather than a deviant expression among the lower classes—has allowed tattoos to be obtained in greater numbers, owing in great part to the importance placed on self-expression in the United States. Even in the workplace, where employees had often been forbidden to display tattoos, employers now "take advantage of the open-mindedness and innovation that younger [tattooed] employees bring into the workplace" (Org, 2003, p. D1).

> Citation of a work by one author

> To clarify a direct quotation from a source, the writers insert a word in square brackets.

As the popularity and acceptability of tattoos have increased, tattooing has become part of the greater consumer culture and has thus

SOCIAL STATUS OF AN ART   6

Table 1

Percentages of American Adults with One or More Tattoos

	Year	
Category	2003	2008
All adults	16	14
Region		
East	14	12
Midwest	14	10
South	15	13
West	20	20
Age range		
18–24	13	9
25–29	36	32
30–39	28	25
40–49	14	12
50–64	10	8
65+	7	9
Sex		
Male	16	15
Female	15	13

Note. Adapted from "Three in Ten Americans with a Tattoo Say Having One Makes Them Feel Sexier," by R. A. Corso, 2008, *Harris Interactive.* Copyright 2008 by Harris Interactive.

undergone the process of commercialization that frequently occurs in the United States. Tattoos are now acquired as status symbols, and their prevalence helps to sell tattoo maintenance products, clothing, and skateboards (Kosut, 2006). This introduction into the consumer culture allows tattoos to gain even more popularity; they are now intertwined with mainstream culture.

SOCIAL STATUS OF AN ART   7

Researchers have been tracking the popularity of tattoos, though no one seems able to agree on exact numbers (Libbon, 2000). In 2000, MSNBC aired an investigative piece called *Tattoos—Skin Deep*, which cited the tattooing rate at 20% of the U.S. population (Rosenbaum, 2000). In 2003, citing a lower number, Harris Interactive reported that 16% of all adults in the United States have at least one tattoo (Sever, 2003). The actual number of individuals with tattoos is unknown, but most researchers believe the trend has been consistently gaining ground since the 1960s. Statistics on the frequency of tattooing among specific age groups generally show increases (Armstrong, Owen, Roberts, & Koch, 2002; Mayers, Judelson, Moriarty, & Rundell, 2002) although one study (Corso, 2008) showed a slight decrease. However, because of the limitations of the various research designs, more research on a national level is needed to obtain truly representative figures.

Significantly, the increase in acceptance of tattoos has resulted in trends concerning the images and locations of tattoos, which appear to be divided along lines of gender. Many of the tattoo images commonly found on men include, but are not limited to, death themes, various wildlife, military insignia, tribal armbands, and family crests or last names. During the 1980s, cartoon images such as Bugs Bunny and the Tasmanian Devil were also popular for males. Males choose various locations for tattoos, but the most popular sites are the upper back, back of the calves, and the upper arm, according to tattoo artist Ben Reames (personal communication, July 12, 2007). Conversely, females often obtain tattoos that symbolize traditional femininity, such as flowers, stars, hearts, and butterflies. A noticeable trend

The writers list statistics to support a claim.

Two citations of articles, both written by four authors, are separated by a semicolon.

Citation of an interview with a tattoo artist

SOCIAL STATUS OF AN ART   8

for females in the 1980s was the rose tattoo, which was often located on the breast or ankle. Stars and butterflies now rival the rose in popularity. The ankle continues to be a popular location for females today. Other popular spots for tattoos include the hip, the foot, and the lower back. In fact, the lower back experienced a huge surge in popularity during the 1990s (B. Reames, personal communication, July 12, 2007).

The last paragraph is the conclusion.

     The art of tattooing has existed in many culturally determined forms throughout human history, and its current manifestations are as varied as the cultures themselves. However, based on the current literature, the social behavior of tattooing is still quite common in the United States. In fact, Kosut (2006) argues, "New generations of American children are growing up in a cultural landscape that is more tattoo-friendly and tattoo-flooded than any other time in history" (p. 1037). Because today's children see tattoos and tattoo-related products everywhere, usually in neutral or positive situations, they will likely be more accepting of tattoos than earlier generations were. Certainly, the tattooing trend shows no signs of decreasing significantly.

References

Center the
heading.

Armstrong, M. L., Owen, D. C., Roberts, A. E., & Koch, J. R. (2002).

College students and tattoos: Influence of image, identity, family,

and friends. *Journal of Psychosocial Nursing, 40*(10), 20–29.

Corso, R. A. (2008, February 12). *Three in ten Americans with a tattoo

say having one makes them feel sexier.* Retrieved from http://www

.harrisinteractive.com/harris_poll/index.asp?PID=868

DeMello, M. (1995). Not just for bikers anymore: Popular representations

of American tattooing. *Journal of Popular Culture, 29*(3), 37–53.

Retrieved from http://www.wiley.com/bw/journal.asp?ref=0022-3840

Kosut, M. (2006). An ironic fad: The commodification and consumption

of tattoos. *Journal of Popular Culture, 39*(6), 1035–1049. Retrieved

from http://www.wiley.com/bw/journal.asp?ref=0022-3840

Krcmarik, K. L. (2003). *History of tattooing.* Retrieved from Michigan

State University website: http://www.msu.edu/~krcmari1/individual

/history.html

Libbon, R. P. (2000). Dear data dog: Why do so many kids sport tattoos?

American Demographics, 22(9), 26. Retrieved from http://amiga

.adage.com/de

Mayers, L. B., Judelson, D. A., Moriarty, B. W., & Rundell, K. W. (2002).

Prevalence of body art (body piercing and tattooing) in university

undergraduates and incidence of medical complications. *Mayo Clinic

Proceedings, 77,* 29–34.

Org, M. (2003, August 28). The tattooed executive. *The Wall Street

Journal.* Retrieved from http://online.wsj.com/public/us

Alphabetize
the entries
according to the
author's (or the
first author's)
last name.

Indent second
and subsequent
lines of each
entry one-half
inch or five
spaces.

SOCIAL STATUS OF AN ART   10

Rosenbaum, S. (Executive Producer). (2000, August 20). *MSNBC*

investigates: Tattoos—skin deep [Television program]. New York and

Englewood Cliffs, NJ: MSNBC.

Sever, J. (2003, October 8). *A third of Americans with tattoos say*

they make them feel more sexy. Retrieved from http://www

.harrisinteractive.com/Insights/HarrisVault.aspx

Identification
of the type
of medium is
placed in square
brackets.

No period follows
a URL at the end
of an entry.

15 | WRITING IN THE HUMANITIES

The humanities include disciplines such as philosophy, art history, history, foreign languages, religion, comparative literature, cultural studies, women's and gender studies, and English. (For information on writing about literature, see Chapter 11.) Scholars in the humanities study the artifacts of human culture (works of art, novels, plays, architecture, musical compositions and forms, philosophical treatises, and handicrafts, as well as popular media). The humanities differ from the creative arts (such as painting, music, and drama) in their focus on *analyzing* cultural artifacts rather than *creating* them. Many students as well as professional researchers study cultural artifacts in order to better understand the wide variety of human experience, both past and present, and to help explain why people think and feel as they do. Common writing assignments in the humanities include informal reflection papers (also called response papers), historical research papers, position papers, critical reviews, and critical analyses.

In courses in the humanities, you will write in a variety of ways and for various purposes; it is therefore important to analyze your rhetorical situation and identify a rhetorical opportunity before you begin drafting. This chapter will help you

- determine the audience, purpose, and research question for a paper in the humanities (**15a**);
- decide which types of evidence, sources, and reasoning to use in such a paper (**15b**);
- follow appropriate style, formatting, and documentation conventions when writing the paper (**15c**);
- understand the types of writing assignments you are likely to receive in humanities courses (**15d**); and
- analyze a sample critical review (**15e**) and a sample critical analysis (**15f**).

15a   AUDIENCE, PURPOSE, AND THE RESEARCH QUESTION

Before writing a paper for a humanities course, you need to determine your rhetorical opportunity (**1b**), your intended audience (**1d**), and your purpose (**1c**). Thinking about your rhetorical opportunity (what you are writing in response to, and why) will not only help you shape your research question; it will also help you narrow your purpose and identify your audience. Of course, your audience will include your instructor, but it may also include other readers, such as your classmates, other students on campus, and even alumni. If you are writing a review for the school paper of a play staged by the drama department, your audience might include all those types of readers. Knowing who comprises your audience helps you determine how much background information on your topic to provide, how technical your language should be, and what kinds of evidence will be most persuasive.

© Geraint Lewis/Alamy

A review of a contemporary production of a Shakespearean play could be assigned in a humanities course.

Most researchers in the humanities write to convey a particular interpretation of a cultural artifact to a specific audience or to inform readers about the history of a particular event, individual, artifact, or social movement. Writers in the humanities may also write to evaluate a work of art or a performance. Once you have determined your purpose for writing, you can develop a research question that will help you find and evaluate sources and use those sources responsibly (see Chapters 8–10). Research papers in the humanities often focus on texts or cultural products that help the researcher answer a specific question. The following are some research questions that scholars in the humanities might pose about the experience of African Americans during the civil rights movement:

Questions about causes or purposes

What events stimulated the Montgomery bus boycott during the civil rights movement?

Questions about consequences

How did jazz musician John Coltrane contribute to the success of the civil rights movement?

Questions about process

What did civil rights workers do to gain national attention for their cause?

Questions about definitions or categories

What kinds of protest tactics did different African American leaders, such as Martin Luther King and Malcolm X, advocate during the civil rights movement?

Questions about values

What does the struggle for equal rights for African Americans reveal about the values of white Americans during the 1960s?

15b EVIDENCE, SOURCES, AND REASONING

The aim of writers in the humanities is to understand human experience by observing and interpreting cultural artifacts; therefore, most claims in the humanities are not put forth as statements of absolute fact. Instead, researchers in the humanities often seek to demonstrate the validity of their interpretations through detailed analyses of texts or other works. Scholars in the humanities rely on textual evidence, logical reasoning, and the work of other scholars in a particular field to present a compelling argument for an interpretation. After considering the available evidence, researchers in the humanities advance a claim, or **thesis**, that expresses their interpretation of a work of art, a performance, or some other object or event (**2c**).

(1) Using primary sources

Most researchers in the humanities begin their studies by working directly with a **primary source**, which can be a person, an object, or a text. For art historians, this primary source might be a drawing, a painting, or a sculpture. Art historians evaluate their primary sources by paying attention to the formal qualities of the work (line, color, shape, texture, composition, and so forth) and to images or themes that might have symbolic importance; they then write an explanation of how these features work together to create meaning in the work. For instance, in a classic analysis of Jan van Eyck's *Arnolfini Portrait* in his book *Early Netherlandish Painting*, art historian Erwin Panofsky argues that the elaborate details of the scene, such as the dog (representing fidelity), the two additional figures reflected in a mirror on the wall who may have served as

© SuperStock/SuperStock

Jan van Eyck's *Arnolfini Portrait*, from the fifteenth century, has been the subject of many analyses by art historians.

witnesses, and van Eyck's signature on the wall indicate that the scene documents a wedding. More recently, art historians have challenged this interpretation: in her article "In the Name of God and Profit: Jan van Eyck's *Arnolfini Portrait*," Margaret Carroll argues that the painting does not portray a wedding but is an important document that gives the wife power of attorney; in "The Arnolfini Double Portrait: A Simple Solution," Margaret Koster suggests instead that the painting is a memorial for Arnolfini's wife, painted after her death. Each of these different interpretations draws on formal and stylistic evidence from the painting itself as well as on expert knowledge of the cultural context in which it was created.

For historians, primary sources include letters, government documents, newspapers, pamphlets, and other materials produced during a particular time period about some person, group, or event. For example, when writing her biography of nineteenth-century Paiute activist Sarah Winnemucca, Sally Zanjani used letters written by Winnemucca, transcriptions of her public speeches, newspaper accounts of her activities, photographs, diaries, and other first-hand accounts to reconstruct Winnemucca's personal life and motivations. Like other historians, Zanjani analyzed these sources by comparing what they say, evaluating the reliability of their creators, and then generating her own interpretation of the information they present.

(2) Using secondary sources

Researchers in the humanities also use **secondary sources**, or works written by other scholars on their topic, to understand what these scholars think about the topic and to help establish the social and historical context for the topic. For instance, Zanjani referred to earlier biographies of Winnemucca and then demonstrated how her work offers new evidence about Winnemucca's life. Zanjani also relied on other historians for historical context that was not explicitly discussed in her primary sources, such as information about nineteenth-century American Indian reservations, government military policies regarding Indians, and so forth.

(3) Using logic and observation

In addition to using primary and secondary sources, some researchers in the humanities, such as philosophers and other theorists, rely on evidence that is grounded in the rules of formal logic and individual observation. A theory or interpretation is considered valid if it adequately explains a particular phenomenon of human experience and if the reasons used to support the conclusion are logically sound (**7h**). Consider, for example, the following passage:

> Free will in the sense that matters, in the sense that makes you responsible for your actions and that gives meaning to both your strivings and your regrets, is determined by *how* your brain deals with the reasons it finds for acting. Philosophers have established that you can still have free will and moral responsibility when the decisions your brain arrives at are *your* decisions, based on your very own reasoning and experience, not on any brainwashing or manipulation by others. If your brain is normal, it enables you to consider and reconsider your options and values indefinitely, and to reflect on what kind of a person you want to be, and since these reflections can lead to decisions and the decisions can lead to actions, you can be the author of your deeds and hence have free will in a very important sense.
>
> —**DANIEL C. DENNETT, "Some Observations on the Psychology of Thinking about Free Will"**

Here, Dennett concludes that humans with normally functioning brains have free will, based on the following logical premises:

The ability to act consciously constitutes free will. [major premise]

A normally functioning brain allows humans to act consciously. [minor premise]

Humans with normally functioning brains have free will. [conclusion]

15C | CONVENTIONS OF LANGUAGE AND ORGANIZATION

(1) Following conventions of style

When writing a paper for a course in the humanities, you will use language and apply formatting as prescribed by the style manual of the particular discipline. Some writers in the humanities, particularly those writing about languages and literature, use MLA style (Chapter **12**). Other writers in the humanities, including historians and art historians, follow the conventions outlined in *The Chicago Manual of Style* (CMS) or in Kate Turabian's *A Manual for Writers of*

Term Papers, Theses, and Dissertations, which is based on CMS style (Chapter **16**).

Unlike writers in the sciences, who strive for objectivity in their writing, most writers in the humanities recognize that an interpretation is colored by the perspective of the person expressing it. Thus, writers in the humanities often acknowledge their own position on a topic, especially if it has a clear effect on their interpretation. In particular, many writers in the humanities use the first-person pronoun *I* when describing the results of their research. Writers in the humanities also use the active voice, which focuses readers' attention on the agent performing the action (**24c**).

(2) Organizing information in particular ways

Papers in the humanities often have a less formal structure than those in the sciences, but nearly all humanities papers include a thesis statement that indicates the author's position on the topic (**2c**), evidence that supports the thesis statement, and a conclusion that restates the major claim and explains why the topic is important. (Specific formats for organizing papers in the humanities are discussed in **15d**.)

Headings can help you organize your writing. Most short humanities papers do not require headings, but for longer papers, Turabian's style manual suggests the following levels of headings:

- First-level headings are centered and boldfaced (or italicized), with major words capitalized.

A First-Level Heading

- Second-level headings are centered and not boldfaced (or italicized), with major words capitalized.

A Second-Level Heading

- Third-level headings are flush with the left margin and boldfaced (or italicized), with major words capitalized.

A Third-Level Heading

(3) Including a bibliography

Include any sources you have used in your paper in a bibliography at the end of the paper. A bibliography not only demonstrates that you have done sufficient research but also allows your readers to obtain any of the sources they are interested in. You can find information on putting together a bibliography according to CMS style in **16a** and a sample bibliography in **16b**.

15d   EXAMPLES OF WRITING IN THE HUMANITIES

(1) Reflection paper

Your humanities instructors may require you to write **reflection papers** (also known as *response papers*): short, informal pieces that express your thoughts on a reading, a performance, or a work of art studied in a course. Often, your instructor will want to know how well you understood the text, performance, or artwork and what you thought of the ideas it presented. Sometimes, your instructor might ask you to reflect on how a book, an art exhibit, or a performance related to the course content, what you thought about it before you encountered it, and how your experience of it affected your thinking. An informal reflection paper may also be assigned to encourage you to start thinking about a topic for a research paper and to help you identify a rhetorical opportunity for that paper.

To write a reflection paper, start by summarizing your understanding of the event or work. Even if your instructor (and others in the class) have seen the same exhibit or performance or have read the same text, they may have understood it differently. Next, go on to explain what you think about the event or work. Consider also how the event or work relates to other material you have read or discussed in class; instructors often want evidence that you are making connections among various topics covered in a course. As you write, make sure that you refer to specific elements of the event or work to support your interpretation. Finally, if your instructor has given you specific instructions for your reflection paper (for example, posing one or more questions to be answered or requiring a specific pattern of organization), strive to meet those requirements.

In the following excerpt from a reflection paper, student Matthew Marusak makes a connection between his response to a film about sexual harassment and an article on the role of silence in sexual harassment that was a class assignment. He begins by summarizing his understanding of the reading and the film and then offers his own interpretation of their message.

In "Witnessing Silence," Cheryl Glenn discusses the critical role silence plays in cases of sexual harassment, specifically in Anita Hill's famous testimony against Clarence Thomas. Glenn places particular emphasis on the double bind in which Hill found herself: she could continue to remain silent about the incident, or she could speak up and face public humiliation, with the added risk that no one would take her seriously. I would like to discuss the elements of Hill's initial decision to remain silent in connection with the 2005 film *North Country*, a fictionalized account of the first landmark sexual harassment class action lawsuit. The film stars Charlize Theron as Josey Aimes, a single mother who takes a job in an iron mine in Minnesota, despite protests from her father, who insists the mine is no place for a woman. Unfortunately, Josey's male coworkers feel the same, and she and her few female coworkers are harassed daily. Josey, however, is the only one to speak out; the other women, fearing for their jobs, remain silent and turn on Josey, demanding that she keep silent. Ultimately, Josey quits and brings a lawsuit against the company. Like Anita Hill, the character of Josey Aimes is treated with scorn and experiences public humiliation for speaking out against male tyranny. She feels the same emotions as Hill did, including disbelief and a loss of self-worth. Where Hill and Aimes differ is in their class positions; yet Glenn suggests that both working-class and professional women often put up with sexual harassment for the same reason: they need their job.

I can imagine I would go through a similar response to sexual harassment: trying to cope with the loss of my own sense of worth as a respectable human being, while deciding if I was willing to put my job on the line. It's a difficult call in any case, though I think it's not always as easy to spot sexual harassment as it was in these cases. Sexual harassment can be someone purposefully making you uncomfortable solely on the basis of your sex; the harassment need not be lewd remarks made to or about you. The decision to remain silent can be devastating, but I think I would have greater trouble living with never saying anything at all than facing what might come from speaking up. Both the Anita Hill case and *North Country* have the same message: you must stand up for your rights, even if you stand alone.

(2) Historical research paper

Another kind of assignment you may be given in a humanities course is a historical research paper, which is written to reconstruct a past event or era or to profile an individual. Most historians use a combination of primary sources (newspapers, diaries, cookbooks, medical guides, and so forth, published at the time of the event or during the lifetime of the person being profiled) and secondary sources (writings by later historians about the event or person or about the primary sources) to explain or interpret some feature of the past. When your instructor assigns a historical research paper, he or she wants to see that you understand how to compare different primary sources to reconstruct what might have happened during a particular time or to a specific person. A historical research paper also allows you to place your interpretation in the context of others that have been offered, using some sources to support your interpretation and other sources to refute the alternative interpretations.

The introduction to a historical research paper explains the importance of the topic and provides the thesis. Following the introduction and thesis, the body of the paper provides evidence from both primary and secondary sources to support the thesis. Finally, the conclusion of a historical research paper should reconsider the major claim of the paper in terms of its overall significance and implications (for research, teaching, practice, and so forth). See **16b** for an example of this kind of humanities paper.

(3) Position paper

Some humanities courses, particularly those in philosophy, may require you to write a position paper. The purpose of a position paper is to present critical and careful thinking about a specific topic, such as the nature of reality, ethical practices in science and medicine, the existence of free will, or the purpose of human life. In a position paper, you state what you believe about the topic and provide reasons to support your claim. You may be asked to take a side in an existing philosophical debate or to express your own thoughts on the topic. In either case, you need to consider both what you agree with and what you disagree with.

A position paper is likely to be organized using a variation of the classical arrangement (**7g(1)**). The paper begins with a brief introduction to the topic and its importance and includes a statement of the **claim**. For instance, if you are asked to write about the existence of free will, you might claim that people have some agency to choose their actions but that most actions are based on what society expects, rather than on independent judgments. Following the statement of the claim, you provide an **explication**, which explains the basis for your belief.

In this section, you define any terms that are important to your topic (*free will*, for instance) and provide any necessary background information. The next section in a position paper discusses any possible **counterarguments** to your position. Here, you summarize some of the most prominent scholarly positions on the topic, particularly those that are opposed to yours. This section is likely to require some research. Because you are trying to demonstrate your ability to think critically and rationally, you want to present the counterarguments in as fair and unbiased a manner as possible. Following the discussion of counterarguments, you need to provide a **resolution**. After restating your own position, explain why the counterarguments are convincing or flawed. You concede or refute each counterargument based on its logic or its supporting information. Next, you provide reasons that support your argument. In the conclusion, briefly restate the purpose of your paper, your major claim, and the primary reasons supporting your claim.

As you write your position paper, focus on what you want to prove. Choose a feature of the topic that you can reasonably defend in three to five pages. Your instructor will be more impressed with a concise, well-reasoned paper on a narrow topic than a longer paper that offers only shallow proof for its points. As you frame your argument, be sure to avoid any logical fallacies that could weaken it (7i).

The following excerpt from student Kaycee Hulet's position paper on the existence of numbers illustrates an introduction and a claim:

> The metaphysical question of whether or not numbers exist is one that has been debated for hundreds of years. There are two basic positions that have historically been held on the matter: that numbers do exist and are therefore not invented but discovered, and, conversely, that numbers are a human invention that do not exist but yet have a usefulness in describing objects or explaining the relationship of objects in the natural world. I posit that numbers do not exist in the real world but have a value entirely dependent on their relation to objects in the real world. Brief consideration is given to the existence of numbers in the currently dominant schools of thought regarding mathematics: formalism, neo-platonism, and constructivism.

Following her claim that numbers are a human invention, Kaycee gives a definition of *numbers* (her explication) and describes formalist, neo-platonist, and constructivist positions regarding the existence of numbers (potential counterarguments). She then provides a resolution by suggesting that there is no evidence that numbers exist, but that this fact does not diminish their usefulness as symbols.

(4) Critical review

Students in humanities courses, as well as professional writers, are often asked to write reviews of various creative works, including films, literary works, exhibits of artwork, musical performances, theatrical performances, and dance performances. The purpose of a critical review is to evaluate the quality of the work for an interested audience. The audience for a review wants to know what the work is about as well as whether it would be worthwhile to experience it themselves. Accordingly, when you write a critical review, begin with some basic information about the work (the title and the artist, composer, or director and perhaps the location where the work can be seen or heard) and some kind of evaluative statement, or thesis, that gives readers your general opinion of the work. Following this introduction, you may provide a brief description of the work that helps readers unfamiliar with it to understand the review. As you evaluate the strengths and weaknesses of the work, be sure to provide examples from it to support your evaluation. Finally, most reviews conclude with a summary statement that drives home the final evaluation of the work. (See Matthew Marusak's critical review in **15e**.)

(5) Critical analysis

Many researchers in the humanities write critical analyses—of visual arts, musical and theatrical performances, literary works, and other works—in which they argue for a specific interpretation of the work in question and aim at deepening an audience's understanding of and appreciation for that work. If your assignment is to write a critical analysis, your instructor is likely interested in assessing both your understanding of the work and your ability to think critically about it. Critical analyses usually focus on formal, stylistic, and/or symbolic features of a work and explain how these elements work together to create meaning. (See **15b** for more information on evidence in critical analyses.) Such analyses sometimes explore the ways in which class, gender, or racial relationships are expressed in a work (**11c**).

Most critical analyses include the following sections:

- **Introduction.** The introduction provides a brief historical context for the work. It may also explain why the work ought to be reexamined—perhaps scholars have overlooked the work's significance or have not considered other possible meanings of the work. At the end of the introduction, the **thesis**, a clearly focused claim, states the writer's interpretation of the work.
- **Body.** The body of the paper provides the evidence—the formal, stylistic, symbolic, or contextual details that support the writer's interpretation. Many analyses also address differing interpretations of the work, explaining why the writer's interpretation is more convincing. This section can be organized in a number of ways—for example, through comparison and contrast of data or artifacts or with chronological, thematic, or emphatic (from less to more familiar or from less to more contestable) arrangement.
- **Conclusion.** The conclusion should review the thesis as well as the most important evidence supporting the writer's interpretation. Frequently, the conclusion also addresses implications—in other words, the writer explains to readers why his or her interpretation is so important, what effect the work may have had on other works or the cultural context, and/or what the writer's interpretation may mean to readers today.

Carla Spohn's critical analysis of two paintings appears in **15f**.

15e   CRITICAL REVIEW OF A THEATER PRODUCTION

In the following critical review, student Matthew Marusak makes an argument for his negative response to a production of Tennessee Williams's play *Suddenly Last Summer*.

1

Not So *Suddenly Last Summer*

Matthew Marusak

Theatre 464

March 15, 2008

The writer introduces the performance and gives a brief evaluation of the production.

I began to nod off halfway through Carla Gugino's ardent, over-the-top, twenty-minute monologue at the end of Tennessee Williams's *Suddenly Last Summer* (Roundabout at Laura Pels Theatre, Harold and Miriam Steinberg Center for Theatre; November 4, 2007). It's not that there is anything inherently wrong with the material: Williams's stark, deeply ambiguous play about the dangers of sexual repression, denial, and deception remains as potent as ever. Rather, Roundabout's production turns an urgent and emotionally explosive work into an uncomfortably dull, embarrassingly archaic exercise in trying an audience's patience.

This paragraph describes the basic plot of the play for readers.

In theory, any revival of this play should be utterly and wholly riveting. In its production at the Laura Pels theatre, however, something has gone inexplicably awry. Violet Venable (an imposing Blythe Danner) is a wealthy widow—mannered and shrouded in a contradictory haze of unrelenting misery and dreamy-eyed idealism—suffering from the great loss of her son, Sebastian (discussed but never seen), who perished under a veil of mystery the previous summer. As her story unfolds, Mrs. Venable does her best to cloud Sebastian's implicit homosexuality and the events surrounding his death by praising him as a great artist—the way she

2

Gale Harold and Carla Gugino perform
in Tennessee Williams's play *Suddenly
Last Summer.* (Photo © Joan Marcus.)

wants him to be remembered. Mrs. Venable sends the sophisticated
yet suspicious Dr. Cukrowicz (a debonair Gale Harold) to evaluate her
niece, Catharine Holly (a woefully miscast Carla Gugino), who, having
allegedly witnessed Sebastian's death, was sent away to a psychiatric
hospital after her experience. The decision is made to perform a
lobotomy on the young woman, against her will and at the wishes of
her clandestinely cruel, manipulative aunt. Only under the influence
of a powerful truth serum does Catharine finally reveal the shocking
circumstances of her cousin's death.

    Suddenly Last Summer is a staggering achievement of drama;
but this revival, directed with a heavy hand by Mark Brokaw, has no
life. Noteworthy, though, is Santo Loquasto's dazzling set design.
Sebastian's magical greenhouse garden is wonderfully staged, and scenes
in the interior of the house are simple yet elegant. Loquasto's costume

The writer cites
both positive
and negative
features of the
production as
he continues his
evaluation.

3

design is also impressive, while Peter Golub's original score is by turns lovely and haunting. A baffling technical aspect, however, is David Weiner's lighting design, which seems both inappropriate from scene to scene and peculiarly inconsistent.

Unfortunately, there are problems with the cast as well. Blythe Danner, while giving a respectable performance, is nowhere near as good as she could have been. She speaks in a distracting, maddeningly uneven dialect and gives the character far more nervous tics than are necessary. Lost is the nuance of the character, as is her caustic wit (as seen in Katharine Hepburn's superior portrayal in the 1959 film version). Danner's polished poise works for the character in many ways, but too often she seems overly rehearsed. Moreover, Carla Gugino should never have been cast as Catharine. She has neither the presence nor the charm to pull off the role convincingly, and Catharine's fiery passion is lost in what seems to be little more than a bid for a Tony nomination in the monologue. Rounding out the leads is Gale Harold, who does his best with the play's most underwritten role, making Dr. Cukrowicz at once both charismatic and calculating.

The conclusion summarizes the major strengths and weaknesses of the production and indicates why the weaknesses outweigh the strengths.

Roundabout's revival of *Suddenly Last Summer,* while technically robust, leaves its audience exhausted and bored. Everyone involved tries too hard to make an impression, instead of allowing genuine talent and Williams's wonderful material to speak for themselves. I cannot rightfully recommend this production, though it might be worth seeing for Gale Harold alone. He's an underrated, underused actor, and watching him is an unmitigated pleasure.

15f   CRITICAL ANALYSIS OF TWO PAINTINGS

In the following critical analysis, student Carla Spohn analyzes two early Italian Renaissance paintings by comparing and contrasting stylistic elements of the two works.

1

Two Annunciations

Carla Spohn

Art History 341

April 15, 2009

The introduction provides a brief historical context for the paper and concludes with the thesis.

The Annunciation of Christ's birth to the Virgin Mary by the Angel Gabriel is a sacred scene that is revered and that was portrayed by many artists throughout the Middle Ages and the Renaissance. Fra Angelico and Leonardo da Vinci, both transitional artists, painted two different Annunciation paintings that reflect the changing artistic styles and techniques of the fifteenth century. However, while Fra Angelico's *Altarpiece of the Annunciation* is still in some ways reminiscent of medieval conventions, Leonardo's *The Annunciation* depicts a complete embracing of Renaissance ideals.

This section provides evidence for the different styles of Fra Angelico and Leonardo da Vinci that supports the writer's thesis statement.

The most obvious difference between the two Annunciations can be seen in their use of color. The medieval influence in Fra Angelico's painting is shown by the bright blue, which contrasts with the lighter primary colors. While this contrast creates bold visual interest, it emphasizes the unreality of the image. Leonardo, however, uses shading to blend the colors, creating subtle hues which provide variation and a much more naturalistic effect than the stark use of dark and light by Fra Angelico. The color used is also affected by the artists' depiction of light. While Fra Angelico's scene is one of bright sunlight that bathes the figures in vibrant luminosity, the solid beam of light upon the Virgin again

2

Fra Angelico's *Altarpiece of the Annunciation*
(c. 1430–1432; tempera and gold on panel). (Source: Prado,
Madrid, Spain, Giraudon/The Bridgeman Art Library.)

Leonardo da Vinci's *The Annunciation* (c. 1472–1475; oil on panel).
(Source: Galleria degli Uffizi, Florence, Italy/The Bridgeman Art Library.)

creates a sense of unreality, with little depth. In contrast, Leonardo creates reality through his use of natural light and atmospheric effects, which allow for greater solidity and substance than in Fra Angelico's depiction.

The setting in which the two scenes are placed also contributes to the paintings' differences. While both use the Annunciation convention of enclosing the figures, Fra Angelico's is much more apparent with a Roman-style portico; Leonardo's is simply implied by the stone wall whose cornerstones frame Mary. Both paintings also convey Renaissance characteristics through classical details, such as the Corinthian columns and round arches in Fra Angelico's and the stone table carved with Roman-like designs in Leonardo's. In contrast to these Renaissance attributes, Fra Angelico exercises the medieval tradition of depicting more than one story in a single scene, which in this instance are separated by the Roman architecture; the figures of Adam and Eve being expelled from the Garden combined with the Annunciation of Christ's birth link salvation to the Fall.

The last feature reflecting the artists' use of or departure from Renaissance conventions is their portrayal of the figures. Both Fra Angelico and Leonardo portray naturalistic figures that demonstrate a sculptural quality in themselves and their draperies. Fra Angelico depicts the angel and Mary as devout figures in profile. Their serene religious attitude is conveyed by the soft curve in their bow of reverence toward each other. While the emotions evoked are those of ethereal spirituality and piety, their faces and gestures capture humanity. Mary is depicted as humble and

4

human, and yet still celestial as she receives a vision from a ray of light.

Leonardo's figure suggests a slightly more regal Mary; while the angel bows and greets her, Mary remains upright and only raises her left hand in greeting. The Virgin is also turned more, for a frontal view rather than a profile view. This view somewhat recalls the Byzantine and medieval depiction of Mary enthroned as the central figure, so as to completely convey her majesty to the viewer. Leonardo's Mary is the Queen of Heaven, but depicted as beautifully human and realistic, embodying the Renaissance humanistic belief that humanity is God's greatest creation.

Both Fra Angelico's and Leonardo's Annunciations capture the reverential nature of the subject, despite their many differences. Fra Angelico's painting is truly a transitional piece, combining medieval and Renaissance artistic elements. Leonardo, however, demonstrates that he is a true Renaissance man with his skillful mastery of the newly emerging techniques. Their diverse treatments of the Annunciation reveal two separate ideals concerning religious depictions of Mary: Fra Angelico's Mary reflects her ethereal piety and the medieval notion of humanity's ultimate submission to God; whereas Leonardo's Mary exemplifies naturalistic regality and the Renaissance belief in human greatness.

> The conclusion reasserts the main argument for the artists' stylistic differences and explains the implications of this argument.

16 | CMS DOCUMENTATION

The Chicago Manual of Style (CMS), published by the University of Chicago Press, provides guidelines for writers in history and other subject areas in the humanities. The manual recommends documenting sources by using either footnotes or endnotes and, for most assignments, a bibliography. (Updates to the latest edition of the manual can be found at http://www.press.uchicago.edu.) College-level writers often turn to Kate L. Turabian's *A Manual for Writers of Research Papers, Theses, and Dissertations,* which bases its formatting and style guidelines on CMS.

This chapter includes

- guidelines for citing sources within a CMS-style research paper and documenting the sources in a bibliography (**16a**) and
- a sample CMS-style research paper (**16b**).

16a | CMS NOTE AND BIBLIOGRAPHIC FORMS

The documentation system that CMS recommends for papers in the humanities calls for in-text citations in the form of sequential numbers that refer to **footnotes** (notes at the bottom of each page) or **endnotes** (notes at the end of the paper). For either footnotes or endnotes, a superscript number is placed in the text wherever documentation of a source is necessary. The number should be as close as possible to the information requiring documentation, generally at the end of a sentence or a clause or following the punctuation that appears at the end of a direct quotation or paraphrase. If a bibliography lists all the sources used in the paper, the information in footnotes or endnotes is condensed to the point that it includes only the author's last name, the title (shortened if longer than four words), and the relevant page number(s): Eggers, *Court Reporters,* 312–15. When no bibliography is provided for a paper, the full note form is used.

TIPS FOR PREPARING FOOTNOTES

- Each footnote begins with a full-size number followed by a period and a space.
- Indent the first line of a footnote five spaces.
- Single-space lines within a footnote.
- Double-space between footnotes when more than one appears on a page.
- Use the abbreviation *Ibid.* (not italicized) to indicate that the source documented by a footnote is identical to the one in the preceding entry (*Ibid.* is short for *ibidem*, Latin for "in the same place.") If the page number(s) for a source differ from those appearing in the preceding note, include the number(s) after a comma: Ibid., 331–32.
- A bibliography is not necessary when the footnotes provide complete bibliographic information for all sources.

⊙ *TECH SAVVY*

Most word-processing programs will footnote your paper automatically. In Microsoft Word, position the cursor where you want a superscript number to appear, pull down the Insert menu, and choose Footnote. A superscript number (with no period) will appear in the cursor's position. A box will also appear at the bottom of the page, in which you can insert the content of the footnote.

TIPS FOR PREPARING ENDNOTES

- Place endnotes on a separate page, following the last page of the body of the paper and preceding the bibliography (if one is included).
- Center the word *Notes* (not italicized) at the top of the page.
- Use the abbreviation *Ibid.* (not italicized) to indicate that the source documented in an endnote is identical to the one in the preceding note. If the page number(s) for a source differ from those appearing in the preceding note, include the number(s) after a comma: Ibid., 331–32.

(continued on page 400)

(continued from page 399)

- Indent the first line of a note five spaces.

- Single-space between lines in each endnote and double-space between endnotes.

- A bibliography is not necessary when the endnotes provide complete bibliographic information for all sources used in the paper.

TIPS FOR PREPARING A BIBLIOGRAPHY

- Start the bibliography on a separate page, following the last page of the body of the paper if footnotes are used or following the last page of endnotes.

- Center the word *Bibliography* (not italicized) at the top of your paper. (Some instructors may prefer that you title this section *Works Cited*.)

- Alphabetize entries in the bibliography according to the authors' last names.

- If a source has more than one author, alphabetize by the last name of the first author.

- For a work without an author, alphabetize the entry according to the first important word in the title.

- To indicate that a source has the same author(s) as in the preceding entry, begin an entry with a three-em dash (——) instead of the name(s) of the author(s). (If you do not know how to create this dash, open the Help function of your word processor and type *em dash* in the Search box.)

- Indent the second and subsequent lines of an entry five spaces.

- Single-space between lines in each entry and double-space between entries.

❶ *CAUTION*

Automatic bibliography composers found online and included in some software packages often make mistakes. They may fail to include all elements of a bibliographic entry or may order elements incorrectly. If you decide to use an automatic composer, be sure to check the results against the model entries provided in this chapter.

Directory of CMS Note and Bibliographic Forms

The following guidelines are for books and articles. Both full note forms and bibliographic forms are provided. Remember that a condensed or short note form consists of just the author's last name, the title (shortened if longer than four words), and relevant page numbers.

GENERAL DOCUMENTATION GUIDELINES FOR PRINT-BASED SOURCES

Author or Editor

One author—note form. Provide the author's full name, beginning with the first name and following the last name with a comma. For the short note form, use only the last name of the author.	***Full note form*** 1. Jamie Barlowe,
One author—bibliographic form. Invert the author's name so that the last name appears first. Place a period after the first name.	***Bibliographic form*** Barlowe, Jamie.
Two authors—note form. Use the word *and* between the names.	***Full note form*** 2. Pauline Diaz and Edward Allan,
Two authors—bibliographic form. Invert the first author's name only. Place a comma and the word *and* after the first author's name. A period follows the second author's name.	***Bibliographic form*** Diaz, Pauline, and Edward Allan.
Three authors—note form. Use commas after the names of the first and subsequent authors. Include *and* before the final author's name.	***Full note form*** 3. Joyce Freeland, John Bach, and Derik Flynn,
Three authors—bibliographic form. Invert the order of the first author's name only. Place a comma after this name and after the second author's name. Use *and* before the final author's name.	***Bibliographic form*** Freeland, Joyce, John Bach, and Derik Flynn.

Author or Editor

Corporate or group author—note and bibliographic forms. Provide the full name of the group in all forms— full note, short note, and bibliographic entry.

Note form
4. Smithsonian Institution,

Bibliographic form
Smithsonian Institution.

Editor—note and bibliographic forms. Place the abbreviation *ed.* or *eds.* after the name(s) of the editor(s).

Full note form
5. Peggy Irmen, ed.,
6. Cheryl Glenn, Margaret Lyday, and Wendy Sharer, eds.,

Bibliographic form
Irmen, Peggy, ed.
Glenn, Cheryl, Margaret Lyday, and Wendy Sharer, eds.

Titles

Italicized titles. Italicize the titles of books, magazines, journals, newspapers, and films. Capitalize all major words (nouns, pronouns, verbs, adjectives, adverbs, and conjunctions except for *and, but, for, or,* and *nor*). A book title is followed by the publication data enclosed in parentheses in the full note form, by a comma and a page number in the short note form, and by a period in the bibliographic form. In the short note form, a title longer than four words is shortened by omitting any article at its beginning and using only important words from the rest of the title.

Full note form
The Great Design of Henry IV from the Memoirs of the Duke of Sully

Short note form
Great Design of Henry IV,

Bibliographic form
The Great Design of Henry IV from the Memoirs of the Duke of Sully.

(continued on page 404)

Titles *(continued from page 403)*

Titles in quotation marks. Use quotation marks to enclose the titles of journal or magazine articles, selections from anthologies, and other short works (39b). In the note form, a title of a short work is followed by a comma. In the bibliographic form, it is followed by a period.

Note form
"The Humor of New England,"

Bibliographic form
"The Humor of New England."

Subtitles. Include a subtitle of a book or article (which appears after a colon) in the full note and bibliographic forms but not in the short note form.

Full note form
Appreciations: Painting, Poetry, and Prose
"Cooperation and Trust: Some Theoretical Notes,"

Short note form
Appreciations,
"Cooperation and Trust,"

Bibliographic form
Appreciations: Painting, Poetry, and Prose.
"Cooperation and Trust: Some Theoretical Notes."

Publication Data

For a book, list the city of publication, the publisher's name, and the date of publication. A colon follows the city of publication, and a comma follows the publisher's name. In the full note form, this information should be placed within parentheses. No parentheses are needed for the bibliographic form. The short note form does not include publication data.

Full note form
(New York: Alfred A. Knopf, 2005),

Bibliographic form
New York: Alfred A. Knopf, 2005.

Whenever possible, include both the volume number and the issue number for any journal article you use. The volume number should appear after the title, and the issue number should appear after the volume number (preceded by the abbreviation *no.*). Use a comma to separate the two numbers. Place the year of publication in parentheses after the volume or issue number. For a magazine, provide the full date of publication.

International Social Work 47 (2004)

Journal of Democracy 14, no. 1 (2003)

Time, January 24, 2005

City and state. Identify the city in which the main office of the publisher of a book is located. If the city is not widely known, add the appropriate two-letter state abbreviation (or, for a city outside the United States, the abbreviation for the country). If the city of publication is Washington, include the abbreviation for the District of Columbia, *DC* (not italicized). When two or more cities are listed on a book's title page, use only the first in the bibliographic entry. A colon follows the city name or the state or country abbreviation.

Baltimore:

Carbondale, IL:

Waterloo, ON:

Harmondsworth, UK:

Publisher's name. Provide either the full name of a book's publisher, as given on the title page, or an abbreviated version. The style chosen must be consistent throughout the notes and bibliography. Even when the full name is provided, some words may be omitted: an initial *The,* words such as *Company* and *Corporation,* or abbreviations such as *Co.* and *Inc.* The word *University* may be abbreviated to *Univ.* (not italicized).

Univ. of Chicago Press

Penguin Books

HarperCollins

(continued on page 406)

Page Numbers

If you are citing information from a specific page or pages of a book or article, place the page number(s) at the end of the footnote or endnote. If you are citing more than one page, separate the first and last page with an en dash (a short dash, typically created by pressing the Option and hyphen keys simultaneously): 35–38. If the page numbers have the same hundreds or thousands digit, do not repeat it when listing the final page in the range: 123–48. Page numbers are not included in a bibliographic entry for an entire book; however, a bibliographic entry for an article ends with the range of pages on which the article appears.

The following list presents examples of the full note form and the bibliographic form. The short note form is illustrated in the first entry. For more examples of notes in short form, see the endnotes of the sample student paper (page 423).

BOOKS

1. Book with one author

Full note form

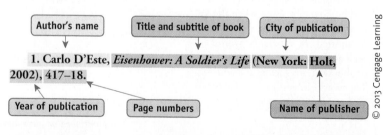

Author's name → Title and subtitle of book → City of publication →

1. Carlo D'Este, *Eisenhower: A Soldier's Life* (New York: Holt, 2002), 417–18.

Year of publication ← Page numbers ← Name of publisher

© 2013 Cengage Learning

Short note form

1. D'Este, *Eisenhower*, 417–18.

Bibliographic form

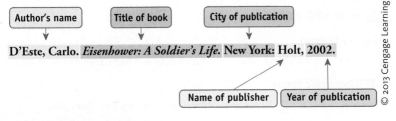

D'Este, Carlo. *Eisenhower: A Soldier's Life.* New York: Holt, 2002.

© 2013 Cengage Learning

2. Book with two authors

Full note form

2. Cathy Scott-Clark and Adrian Levy, *The Stone of Heaven* (Boston: Little, Brown, 2001), 28.

Bibliographic form

Scott-Clark, Cathy, and Adrian Levy. *The Stone of Heaven.* Boston: Little, Brown, 2001.

3. Book with three authors

Full note form

3. Karen A. Foss, Sonja K. Foss, and Cindy L. Griffin, *Feminist Rhetorical Theories* (Thousand Oaks, CA: Sage, 1999).

Bibliographic form

Foss, Karen A., Sonja K. Foss, and Cindy L. Griffin. *Feminist Rhetorical Theories.* Thousand Oaks, CA: Sage, 1999.

4. Book with more than three authors

In the note form, just the first author's name is used, followed by the phrase *et al.* (not italicized). The bibliographic form includes all the authors' names.

Full note form

4. Mike Palmquist et al., *Transitions: Teaching Writing in Computer-Supported and Traditional Classrooms* (Greenwich, CT: Ablex, 1998), 153.

Bibliographic form

Palmquist, Mike, Kate Kiefer, James Hartvigsen, and Barbara Goodlew. *Transitions: Teaching Writing in Computer-Supported and Traditional Classrooms.* Greenwich, CT: Ablex, 1998.

5. Book with an editor

Full note form

5. Hanna Schissler, ed., *The Miracle Years* (Princeton, NJ: Princeton Univ. Press, 2001).

Bibliographic form

Schissler, Hanna, ed. *The Miracle Years.* Princeton, NJ: Princeton Univ. Press, 2001.

6. Book with an author and an editor

Full note form

6. Ayn Rand, *The Art of Fiction,* ed. Tore Boeckmann (New York: Plume, 2000).

Use the abbreviation *ed.* for "edited by."

Bibliographic form

Rand, Ayn. *The Art of Fiction.* Edited by Tore Boeckmann. New York: Plume, 2000.

Write out the words *Edited by* (not in italics).

7. Translated book

Full note form

7. Murasaki Shikibu, *The Tale of Genji,* trans. Royall Tyler (New York: Viking, 2001).

Use the abbreviation *trans.* for "translated by."

Bibliographic form

Shikibu, Murasaki. *The Tale of Genji.* Translated by Royall Tyler. New York: Viking, 2001.

Write out the words *Translated by* (not in italics).

8. Edition after the first

Full note form

8. Edward O. Wilson, *On Human Nature,* 14th ed. (Cambridge: Harvard Univ. Press, 2001).

Bibliographic form

Wilson, Edward O. *On Human Nature.* 14th ed. Cambridge: Harvard Univ. Press, 2001.

9. One volume in a multivolume work

Full note form

9. Thomas Cleary, *Classics of Buddhism and Zen: The Collected Translations of Thomas Cleary* (Boston: Shambhala Publications, 2001), 3:116.

Bibliographic form

Cleary, Thomas. *Classics of Buddhism and Zen: The Collected Translations of Thomas Cleary.* Vol. 3. Boston: Shambhala Publications, 2001.

10. Government document

Documents issued by departments and agencies of the US government are usually published by the Government Printing Office in Washington, DC.

Full note form

10. U.S. Bureau of the Census, *Statistical Abstract of the United States,* 120th ed. (Washington, DC: Government Printing Office, 2001), 16.

Bibliographic form

U.S. Bureau of the Census. *Statistical Abstract of the United States.* 120th ed. Washington, DC: Government Printing Office, 2001.

11. Selection from an anthology

When only one selection from an anthology is used, inclusive page numbers end the footnote or endnote and precede the publication data in the bibliographic entry.

Full note form

11. Elizabeth Spencer, "The Everlasting Light," in *The Cry of an Occasion,* ed. Richard Bausch (Baton Rouge: Louisiana State Univ. Press, 2001), 171–82.

Bibliographic form

Spencer, Elizabeth. "The Everlasting Light." In *The Cry of an Occasion,* edited by Richard Bausch, 171–82. Baton Rouge: Louisiana State Univ. Press, 2001.

12. Published letter

Full note form

12. Lincoln to George McClellan, Washington, DC, 13 October 1862, in *This Fiery Trial: The Speeches and Writings of Abraham Lincoln,* ed. William E. Gienapp (New York: Oxford Univ. Press, 2002), 178.

Bibliographic form

Lincoln, Abraham. Abraham Lincoln to George McClellan, Washington DC, 13 October 1862. In *This Fiery Trial: The Speeches and Writings of Abraham Lincoln,* edited by William E. Gienapp, 178. New York: Oxford Univ. Press, 2002.

13. Indirect source

Cite both the original work and the secondary source in which you found it quoted. Begin with the name of the author you have quoted, and provide information about the work (which should be available in the notes or bibliography of the indirect source you used). Then provide information about the secondary source.

Full note form

13. Toni Morrison, *Playing in the Dark* (New York: Vintage, 1992), 26, quoted in Jonathan Goldberg, *Willa Cather and Others* (Durham, NC: Duke Univ. Press, 2001), 37.

Bibliographic form

Morrison, Toni. *Playing in the Dark.* New York: Vintage, 1992, 26. Quoted in Jonathan Goldberg, *Willa Cather and Others,* 37. Durham, NC: Duke Univ. Press, 2001.

ARTICLES

14. Article in a journal

Full note form

14. A. Schedler, "The Menu of Manipulation," *Journal of Democracy* 13, no. 2 (2002): 48.

Use an initial for an author's first name only when the name appears that way in the original publication.

Bibliographic form

Schedler, A. "The Menu of Manipulation." *Journal of Democracy* 13, no. 2 (2002): 36–50.

15. Article in a popular (general-circulation) magazine

Full note form

> 15. John O'Sullivan, "The Overskeptics," *National Review,* June 17, 2002, 23.

Bibliographic form

O'Sullivan, John. "The Overskeptics." *National Review,* June 17, 2002, 22–26.

For a magazine published monthly, include only the month and the year, with no comma inserted between them.

16. Article from an online journal

In documentation of electronic sources, CMS recommends that either a URL (uniform resource locator) or a DOI (digital object identifier) conclude the note or bibliographic entry. (A DOI is preferable because it is a unique and permanent label that is assigned to a source and leads to all versions of it in any medium.)

Full note form

> 16. Lars Wik et al., "Quality of Cardiopulmonary Resuscitation during Out-of-Hospital Cardiac Arrest," *Journal of the American Medical Association* 293, no. 3 (2005): 300, doi:10.1001/jama.293.3.299.

Bibliographic form

Wik, Lars, Jo Kramer-Johansen, Helge Myklebust, Hallstein Sorebo, Leif Svensson, Bob Fellows, and Petter Andreas Steen. "Quality of Cardiopulmonary Resuscitation during Out-of-Hospital Cardiac Arrest." *Journal of the American Medical Association* 293, no. 3 (January 19, 2005): 299–304. doi:10.1001/jama.293.3.299.

If your instructor requires you to provide the date on which you accessed an electronic source, the word *accessed* and the date should immediately precede the DOI (or the URL). In a note, the word is lowercased and the word and date are set off by commas; in a bibliographic entry, the word is capitalized and the word and date are set off by periods.

17. Article from a journal database

Full note form

> 17. Samuel Guy Inman, "The Monroe Doctrine and Hispanic America," *Hispanic America Historical Review* 4, no. 4 (1921): 635, http://links.jstor.org/sici?sici=0018-2168(192111)4%3A4%3C635%3ATMDAHA%3E2.0.CO%3B2-8.

Include a stable URL (or any identification number provided for the source in the database). A URL that runs onto a second line may be broken *after* a colon or a double slash (//) or *before* a single slash (/), a comma, a period, a hyphen, a question mark, a percent symbol, a number sign (#), a tilde (~), or an underscore (_). It can be broken either before or after an ampersand (&) or an equals sign. Include the access date in parentheses after the URL and before the final period if it is required by your instructor.

Bibliographic form

Inman, Samuel Guy. "The Monroe Doctrine and Hispanic America." *Hispanic America*

Historical Review 4, no. 4 (1921): 635–76. http://links.jstor.org/sici?sici=

0018-2168(192111)4%3A4%3C635%3ATMDAHA%3E2.0.CO%3B2-8.

18. Article from an online magazine

Full note form

18. Mark Frank, "Judge for Themselves: Why a Supreme Court Ruling on Sentencing Guidelines Puts More Power Back on the Bench," *Time*, January 24, 2005, http://www.time .com/time/magazine/printout/0,8816,1018063,00.html.

Bibliographic form

Frank, Mark. "Judge for Themselves: Why a Supreme Court Ruling on Sentencing

Guidelines Puts More Power Back on the Bench." *Time*, January 24, 2005.

http://www.time.com/time/magazine/printout/0,8816,1018063,00.html.

19. Newspaper article

Full note form

19. Rick Bragg, "An Oyster and a Way of Life, Both at Risk," *New York Times*, June 15, 2002, national edition, sec. A.

Bibliographic form

Bragg, Rick. "An Oyster and a Way of Life, Both at Risk." *New York Times*. June 15, 2002,

national edition, sec. A.

If the city of publication is not part of the newspaper's name, it should be added at the beginning and italicized as if part of the name: *St. Paul Pioneer Press*. If the city is not well known or could be confused with another city with the same name, add the state name or abbreviation within parentheses after the city's name. If the paper is a well-known national one, such as the *Wall Street Journal,* it is not necessary to add the city of publication.

If the name of the newspaper and the date of publication are mentioned in the text of the paper, no bibliographic entry is needed.

OTHER SOURCES

20. Interview

Unpublished interviews are usually cited in the text or in notes. Published or broadcast interviews are documented in a note or a bibliographic entry. The entry includes the name of the person who was interviewed, the title of the interview (if any), the name of the person who conducted it, and the publication data.

Full note form

20. Yoko Ono, "Multimedia Player: An Interview with Yoko Ono," by Carolyn Burriss-Krimsky, *Ruminator Review,* no. 10 (Summer 2002): 28.

Bibliographic form

Ono, Yoko. "Multimedia Player: An Interview with Yoko Ono." By Carolyn Burriss-Krimsky. *Ruminator Review,* no. 10 (Summer 2002): 26–29.

21. Videocassette or DVD

Full note form

21. *Araby,* produced and directed by Dennis J. Courtney (Los Angeles: American Street Productions, 1999), videocassette (VHS).

Bibliographic form

Araby. Produced and directed by Dennis J. Courtney. Los Angeles: American Street Productions, 1999. Videocassette (VHS).

Place *Videocassette* (not capitalized in the full note form and followed by the format, if known, in parentheses in both forms) or *DVD* at the end of the entry.

22. E-book

Most e-books have a print counterpart, but the two versions may differ. Therefore, the e-book's format or brand (such as, Kindle edition, PDF e-book, Microsoft Reader e-book, or Palm e-book) is identified at the end of the entry.

Full note form

22. Stieg Larsson, *The Girl with the Dragon Tattoo* (New York: Vintage, 2008), Kindle edition.

Bibliographic form

Larsson, Stieg. *The Girl with the Dragon Tattoo.* New York: Vintage, 2008. Kindle edition.

23. Website content

When possible, include a title, the author's name, the name of the site owner or sponsor, a publication or revision date (or an access date if neither of those is available), and the URL, followed by a period.

Full note form

23. "De Klerk Apologises Again for Apartheid," South African Press Assoc., last modified May 14, 1997, http://www/doj.gov.za.trc/media/1997/9705/s970514a.htm.

Bibliographic form

South African Press Association. "De Klerk Apologises Again for Apartheid." Last modified May 14, 1997. http://www/doj.gov.za.trc/media/1997/9705/s970514a.htm.

16b CMS-STYLE RESEARCH PAPER

The following student essay, a historical research paper, addresses an ongoing struggle in South Africa related to electricity usage. Because this essay includes a full bibliography, the endnotes are written in short form (see page 398). CMS does not provide specific guidelines for a title page for a student paper, but you can refer to the sample in Figure 16.1 if your instructor requires a title page. Your instructor may prefer that you format the first page of your paper so that it includes the information that would appear on a title page (see page 390 for this format).

Local Politics and National Policy in a Globalized World:
South Africa's Ongoing Electricity Dilemma

Cristian Nuñez
Political Science 87
December 15, 2010

Figure 16.1. Sample title page for a CMS-style paper.

1

Since the end of the apartheid system in South Africa in 1994, the government has struggled to alleviate national poverty without alienating the global financial community. Even though the government has adopted a business-friendly stance, intended to reduce poverty, it continues to provide too little support to the nation's poor—and is thus harshly criticized by citizen-advocate groups. One such group is the Soweto Electricity Crisis Committee (SECC), a civic organization advocating free basic utilities for all South Africans. The SECC charges that the government is not living up to the human-rights core of its constitution, which guarantees all South Africans access to basic resources.[1] The SECC addresses human rights through its controversial—and illegal—practice of delivering free electricity to South Africa's poorest people.

The Electricity Crisis

Following the end of apartheid in 1993, the majority (African National Congress [ANC]) government swept into power with a mandate to reverse the injustices prevalent in South Africa. Millions of poor nonwhites hoped that affordable housing, modern education, and basic utilities would become available in their long-neglected neighborhoods (see fig. 1). However, carrying out these goals would prove to be extremely difficult for the new ANC president Nelson Mandela, who inherited a huge financial crisis from the old National Party regime. In order to avert a spending crisis (which would devalue South African currency both locally and globally), the ANC government implemented broad economic

2

Figure 1. This settlement in Soweto typifies the
poverty and lack of access to public services
that many South African citizens must endure.
(Photograph courtesy of Jon Hrusa/Corbis.)

reforms to attract the foreign investment and capital inflows necessary for
strengthening the South African economy.[2]

One of the economic reforms included privatizing the nation's many
parastatals (state-owned enterprises). To prepare for privatization, each
parastatal enacted cost-recovery pricing to make itself more competitive
and more attractive to foreign investors. Unfortunately, such cost-recovery
measures eliminated both subsidized utilities and rents in nonwhite
neighborhoods like those of Soweto, a part of Johannesburg that had
long been a hotbed of revolutionary actions and ideas. In response, a
number of civics (community action groups) protested the government's
economic reforms. The most brash of these civics was the SECC.

By 2001, in an effort to remain financially solvent, South Africa's
public utility company, the Electricity Supply Commission (Eskom),

The writer
outlines steps
Mandela and
the new
government
took in order
to address
the financial
problems they
had inherited.

3

was disconnecting 20,000 households a month for not paying their bills.
The SECC illegally reconnected more than 3,000 Soweto households in
a program called "Reconnect the Power."[3] No workable solutions to
this problem were discovered, so the reconnections remained in place.
In fact, in 2009, SECC's electricians reconnected nearly forty houses
per week, until an estimated 60 percent of Soweto residents were
receiving electricity without charge. Many of the SECC electricians
view having electric power as a constitutional right, not a luxury. One
of them argues that he and the other electricians "are giving back what
belongs to the people," thereby justifying SECC's ongoing activism.[4]

The Legacy of Apartheid and Perceptions of Eskom

The rest of the paper describes the ways in which the SECC has intervened in order to provide electricity to poor, nonwhite South Africans.

Although the SECC was established in 2000, the practice of
nonpayment for basic needs has a much longer history in South Africa.
During apartheid, the ANC urged residents of Soweto and other black
townships to stop paying their rent and their electricity and water bills
(which were often higher than those of households in upper-class white
neighborhoods). The boycott the ANC organized was a powerful weapon
against apartheid, eventually bankrupting local authorities. Many people
retained this stance of resistance following the end of apartheid. "We did
not expect this," said Chris Ngcobo, an organizer of the Soweto boycott
under apartheid, who now helps oversee an ANC/Eskom project to
reverse the culture of nonpayment. "We expected that after the elections
people would just pay. But it will not be so easy."[5]

4

For many residents, nonpayment as protest continued as an intentional act during the Mandela years. During these early post-apartheid years, bill payment was presented as a patriotic gesture in support of the Mandela government.[6] The residents, however, wanted to see improvements first before resuming payment. Without revenues, the government did not have the necessary resources to make substantial investments in improving essential national infrastructure.

Still, Eskom did not take a completely hands-off approach; it invested $1.2 billion in electrification in rural and nonwhite urban areas, estimating that if each household consumed 300 kilowatt-hours of electricity per month, the project would be profitable.[7] Instead, the average monthly consumption per household has hovered around 80 kilowatt-hours, far below the expected levels.[8] By 2000, Eskom decided that it was not profitable to continue providing service for nonpaying customers whose monthly energy consumption was only 80 kilowatt-hours.[9] Energy consumption was not high enough to justify creating the infrastructure to make power available to poor areas. Furthermore, transience, poor mail delivery, and substandard banking institutions in poor districts rendered the use of charge accounts impossible. Thus, today's poor customers—whose payments for electricity may be as much as twenty years in arrears—find it easier to perpetuate the culture of nonpayment than to pay Eskom's cost-recovery prices.[10]

Many poor South Africans believe that the ANC government, which ended apartheid, could provide free or low-cost utilities to them as citizens. Therefore, the fact that the ANC asks them to pay for

> Throughout this research paper, the evidence comes from both primary sources such as newspaper interviews with political activists and secondary sources such as relevant historical scholarship and annual business reports.

5

utilities represents to many, especially Soweto residents, an extension of apartheid's exclusionary practices. According to the SECC, Soweto is discriminated against by the government because its residents are poor, a message that harks back to the apartheid era when race was the central concern.

Ironically, just as SECC has worked to link the ANC with the apartheid government, the ANC has worked to distance itself from apartheid in an effort to negotiate with the poor.[11] In fact, riots broke out in 1997 within mixed-race communities around Johannesburg because of residents' claims that poor black communities, which maintained a culture of nonpayment, were being favored by the government.[12] Clearly, many long-standing traditions and perceptions—not merely the lack of money—have complicated the provision of electricity in South Africa.

Eskom's Moral and Financial Dilemma

Eskom's 1999 annual report included a message from then-chairman Reuel J. Khoza emphasizing the organization's commitment to providing electricity to the poor as a vehicle for economic progress.[13] That commitment on paper, though, has not become a reality, as a result of Eskom's financial situation. Without government support, Eskom cannot remain solvent.

The South African government and Eskom are faced with a moral dilemma that extends beyond the streets of Soweto. Should government

6

policies be pro-business or pro–social welfare? An internal study commissioned by the new government in 1994 (the Regional Development Plan, or RDP) investigated how to increase the gross domestic product (GDP) and lower the unemployment rate. The study concluded that South Africa's economy would have to grow by 6 percent annually, a doubling of the 1994 GDP growth rate, to bring unemployment down to a desirable level.[14] In pursuit of this ambitious growth goal, the South African government enacted stringent government spending controls.

Critics of Eskom's cost-recovery pricing argue that if Eskom would increase the rates it charges businesses and wealthy clients, the additional income could be used to subsidize electricity for the poor. Yet, the government fears that doing so will discourage foreign business investment and thereby hinder long-term economic growth.

Turning a Blind Eye

Although the SECC accuses the ANC of abandoning people in its pursuit of conservative economic policies, the ANC believes that a business-friendly economic climate will promote the growth necessary to increase the standard of living for all citizens, regardless of race or socioeconomic class. The even larger problem for the ANC is that foreign investors can disinvest at short notice, limiting the government's options. Michael Sachs, head of policy and research for the ANC, notes that when South Africa eliminated apartheid in 1994, it "immediately had to confront the issue of globalization" and that in the global climate, "you've got to play the

7

game."[15] The power and influence of the South African government on the global financial stage are extremely limited—much less extensive than the people of Soweto think they are.

Despite these economic challenges, the ANC appears somewhat sympathetic to the needs of poor South Africans and the goals of the SECC. The SECC's electricians have reconnected power for local police officers, who have reduced their arrests and charges.[16] There is no evidence that the ANC directly supports such local-level decisions, but the fact that the electricians can do this illegal activity openly suggests that the government is taking a purposefully relaxed stance.

As the writer brings his paper to a conclusion, he reminds his readers why emerging democracies merit the kind of global economic support that will ensure their stability.

The SECC believes that the ANC, via Eskom, has the agency to provide free or heavily subsidized energy to the poor. The ANC, however, pressured by the need to improve the economy quickly and to compete within the world economy, wants to run the government like a business, with its effectiveness measured by a balance sheet for the world's economic powers to read. The world has entered an era in which the lack of efficiency in government operations translates into stagnation and increased poverty. Thus, numerous other sub-Saharan African countries are facing a similar power crunch.[17] The conflict between Eskom (as a state-run enterprise) and the SECC illustrates an ongoing dilemma for developing countries around the world: how can the government do just enough to support the poor without alienating the business community that has the power to provide the poor with jobs? South Africa's inability to balance the needs of its citizens and its investors, even after twenty years of negotiation, suggests that no clear answer is in sight.

8

Notes

1. *Countries of the World.*

2. McNeil, "Shedding State Companies."

3. Bond, *Against Global Apartheid*, 170.

4. Fisher, "South Africa Crisis."

5. Daley, "In South Africa."

6. Ibid.

7. Bond, *Against Global Apartheid*, 162.

8. Ibid.

9. Ibid.

10. Fisher, "South Africa Crisis."

11. Eskom, *Annual Report 1999.*

12. Daley, "Seeing Bias."

13. Ibid.

14. Chang, *Privatisation and Development*, 100.

15. Kingsnorth, *One No, Many Yeses*, 1.

16. Fisher, "South Africa Crisis."

17. Wines, "Toiling in the Dark."

9

Bibliography

Bond, Patrick. *Against Global Apartheid: South Africa Meets the World Bank, IMF and International Finance*. Cape Town: Univ. of Cape Town Press, 2003.

Chang, Claude V. *Privatisation and Development: Theory, Policy and Evidence*. Hampshire, UK: Ashgate, 2006.

Countries of the World and Their Leaders Yearbook 2011. 2 vols. Detroit: Gale, 2010. Accessed November 30, 2010. http://go.galegroup.com.

Daley, Suzanne. "In South Africa, a Culture of Resistance Dies Hard." *New York Times*, July 19, 1995. Accessed December 1, 2010. http://www.nytimes.com/1995/07/19/world/in-south-africa-a -culture-of-resistance-dies-hard.html.

———. "Seeing Bias in Their Utility Rates, Mixed-Race South Africans Riot." *New York Times,* February 7, 1997. Accessed November 30, 2010. http://www.nytimes.com/1997/02/07/world/seeing-bias-in -their-utility-rates-mixed-race-south-africans-riot.html.

Eskom. *Annual Report 1999*. Accessed December 7, 2010. http://www .eskom.co.za/annreport/main.htm.

Fisher, Jonah. "South Africa Crisis Creates Crusading Electricians." *BBC News*, November 24, 2009. Accessed December 2, 2010. http://news .bbc.co.uk/2/hi/8376400.stm.

Kingsnorth, Paul. *One No, Many Yeses*. Sydney: Simon and Schuster, 2003.

McNeil, Donald G., Jr. "Shedding State Companies, If Sometimes Reluctantly." *New York Times,* February 27, 1997. Accessed November 25, 2010. http://select.nytimes.com/gst/abstract.html? res=F60917F63F550C748EDDAB0894DF494D81&scp=6&sq= eskom+privitize&st=cse&pagewanted=print.

Wines, Michael. "Toiling in the Dark: Africa's Power Crisis." *New York Times*, July 29, 2007. Accessed November 30, 2010. http://www .nytimes.com/2007/07/29/world/africa/29power.html?pagewanted= 1&_r=1.

17 | WRITING IN THE NATURAL SCIENCES

The **natural sciences** include mathematics, the biological sciences (biology, botany, and zoology), the physical sciences (chemistry and physics), and the earth sciences (geology and astronomy). They also include **applied sciences** such as medicine and allied health studies, engineering, and computer science. The natural sciences are problem-solving disciplines that report or analyze results derived from meticulous observation and experimentation. For example, Heather Jensen, whose paper appears at the end of this chapter, examined onion root tip cells during five stages of mitosis (cell division). On the basis of her results, she was able to describe how this cell division occurs.

Writing assignments you can expect to receive in natural science courses include literature reviews, field reports, and laboratory reports. To allow you to complete such assignments, this chapter will help you

- determine the audience, purpose, and research question for a paper in the natural sciences (**17a**);
- decide which types of evidence, sources, and reasoning to use in such a paper (**17b**);
- use appropriate language, style, and formatting when writing the paper (**17c**);
- understand typical assignments in the natural sciences (**17d**); and
- learn the conventions for writing a field report (**17e**) and a laboratory report (**17f**).

17a | AUDIENCE, PURPOSE, AND THE RESEARCH QUESTION

Before you start working on a writing assignment for a course in the natural sciences, be sure to consult with your instructor as you determine your audience and your purpose. Your instructor will always be one of your readers, but he or she may ask you to share your work with other readers as well. If you are enrolled in an advanced class, you may be expected to present your work at a local, regional, or national conference. By knowing who constitutes your audience(s), you will be able to gauge how much background information is adequate, how much technical language is appropriate, and what types of evidence and reasoning are necessary.

Researchers in the sciences generally write to inform their readers, either by discussing studies pertaining to a specific topic or by reporting their observations of some phenomenon or the results of an experiment. However, these researchers' purpose may be evaluative if they are critiquing a journal article or argumentative if they are encouraging readers to take a specific action. After you have determined your purpose and audience, formulate a research question that will guide you to sources and help you to use them responsibly (Chapters **8–10**). The following example research questions focus on global warming:

Questions about cause

What causes global warming?

Questions about consequences

What are the effects of global warming?

Questions about process

How can global warming be stopped?

Questions about definitions or categories

What types of greenhouse gases are responsible for global warming?

Questions about values

What are a scientist's responsibilities concerning the public in the face of global warming?

Research questions in the sciences are often narrowed to enable precise measurements:

Questions about length, distance, frequency, and so on

How far has Mendenhall Glacier receded each year for the past decade, and do the values show any trend?

Questions about comparisons and correlations

How are emission intensities related to the total amount of emissions?

The question Heather Jensen responds to in her laboratory report (**17f**) focuses on a process:

> What happens to onion root tip cells during mitosis?

Kayla Berg, whose paper appears in **18c**, asks a question about cause:

> What factors account for the varying types of damage done in Thailand by the 2004 tsunami?

17b ‖ EVIDENCE, SOURCES, AND REASONING

Researchers in the natural sciences attempt to quantify phenomena in the world around them. They look for **empirical evidence**—facts that can be measured or tested—to support their claims. Most of their investigations, then, are set up as experiments. If you conduct an experiment for a course in the natural sciences, you will be expected to start with a **hypothesis**, a prediction that serves as a basis for experimentation. To test the hypothesis, you will follow a procedure—one designed by yourself, established in another study, or specified by your instructor. The results of your experiment will either validate your hypothesis or show it to be in error. This systematic way of proceeding from a hypothesis to verifiable results is called the **scientific method**. Consisting of six steps, this method helps ensure the objectivity and accuracy of experimental findings.

THE SCIENTIFIC METHOD

1. *State a problem.* When you recognize and then state a problem, you establish your rhetorical opportunity (the reason for your writing).

2. *Collect evidence.* Close observation is the key technique for collecting evidence. Be sure to record all details as accurately as you can. Alternatively, you may read the reports of other researchers who have addressed a problem similar to yours. If you draw on observations or experiments, you are using primary sources; if you use scientific articles and statistical charts, you are using secondary sources.

(continued on page 428)

(continued from page 427)

3. *Form a hypothesis*. A hypothesis is a tentative claim, or prediction, about the phenomenon you are studying.

4. *Test the hypothesis*. Although you will have conducted some research before formulating the hypothesis, you continue that research through additional observation or experimentation.

5. *Analyze the results*. Look at your results in light of your hypothesis. Attempt to find patterns, categories, or other relationships.

6. *State the conclusion*. If you have validated your hypothesis, explain why it accounts for *all* of your data. If your hypothesis is disproved, suggest revisions to it or offer a new one.

Reports based on the six steps of the scientific method are **quantitative studies**, because their results are presented as numerical data. Heather Jensen's lab report on cell division is a quantitative study. Another type of study performed by scientists, especially those working in the field, is a **qualitative study**. The data in qualitative studies are produced through observation and analysis of natural phenomena. It is not uncommon, however, for studies to have both quantitative and qualitative features.

Regardless of the type of study they perform, scientists depend on previous research to place their work in context. They draw from both primary sources (experiments, observations, surveys, and so on) and secondary sources (books and articles already published on a topic). All sources used in a report or paper in the natural sciences are cited in the body of the text and documented on a reference list. (See Chapter **18**.)

17C   CONVENTIONS OF LANGUAGE AND ORGANIZATION

(1) Style guidelines

The conventions that most writers in the sciences follow are presented in a manual titled *Scientific Style and Format,* compiled by the Council of Science Editors (CSE). However, you may sometimes be asked to use one of the following manuals:

American Chemical Society. *The ACS Style Guide: Effective Communication of Scientific Information.* 3rd ed. Washington, DC: American Chemical Society, 2006.

American Institute of Physics. *AIP Style Manual.* 4th ed. New York: American Institute of Physics, 1990. (This manual is no longer in print but is available as a free PDF file at http://www.aip.org /pubservs/style/4thed/toc.html.)

American Mathematical Society. *A Manual for Authors of Mathematical Papers.* 8th ed. Providence, RI: American Mathematical Society, 1990.

American Medical Association. *AMA Manual of Style: A Guide for Authors and Editors.* 10th ed. New York: Oxford Univ. Press, 2007.

United States Geological Society. *Suggestions to Authors of the Reports of the United States Geological Survey.* 7th ed. Washington, DC: Government Printing Office, 1991.

Before starting any writing project, check with your instructor to see which style manual you should use.

The CSE manual says that effective scientific prose has the qualities of accuracy, clarity, conciseness, and fluency. The following tips can help you write in the style recommended by the manual.

TIPS FOR PREPARING A PAPER IN THE NATURAL SCIENCES

- Select words that convey meaning precisely (34a).

- Avoid gender bias (33c).

- If two different wordings are possible, choose the more succinct alternative (35a).

- Clarify noun strings by placing modifiers after the main noun.

    the system for measuring frequency NOT the frequency measuring system

- When using an introductory participial phrase, be sure that it modifies the subject of the sentence (26e). Participial phrases that begin with *based on* are particulary troublesome, so double-check to make sure that such a phrase modifies the subject.

    Based on the promising results, the decision to approve the new medication seemed reasonable.

    NOT Based on the promising results, the new medication was approved.

(2) Organization

The most frequent writing assignments in the natural sciences are various types of reports—literature reviews, field reports, and laboratory reports. The specific formats for these reports are presented in **17d–f.**

All scientific reports include headings and often subheadings to help readers find and understand information. Heather Jensen uses three levels in her lab report (**17f**). Writers in the natural sciences also use tables and figures (such as graphs, drawings, and maps) to organize information. Essential for presenting numerical data, tables should be numbered and titled. Each table should be introduced in the text so that readers will understand its purpose. Heather includes two tables in her lab report: one to show the number of cells in each phase of mitosis and one to show the percentage of cells in each phase. She introduces her first table this way: "Table 1 shows the number of cells found in each phase of mitosis." Heather also uses six figures in her report. The first five are drawings that illustrate the five phases of cell division. The sixth is a graph that indicates how much time the onion root tip cells she examined spent in each phase. Like tables, figures should be numbered, titled, and introduced in the text. For instructions on how to create tables and bar graphs with a word processor, see **6c(2)**. For an example of a map used as a figure, see Kayla Berg's paper on the tsunami that hit Thailand in 2004 (**18c**).

(3) Reference lists

CSE provides three options for citing sources and listing them at the end of a paper: the citation-sequence system, the citation-name system, and the name-year system. You can find specific guidelines for creating a reference list in Chapter **18**.

17d | **EXAMPLES OF WRITING IN THE NATURAL SCIENCES**

(1) Literature review

A **literature review** is essentially an evaluative overview of research directly related to a specific topic. It focuses on both strengths and weaknesses of previous research—in methodology or interpretation—with the goal of establishing what steps need to be taken to advance research on the topic. A literature review may be assigned as part of a longer paper, in which case the information it contains appears in the introductory section of the paper. In a paper on agate formation, student Michelle Tebbe included the following paragraphs, which provide, respectively, a historical account of research on her topic and a review of relevant current studies:

> Scientific interest in agate dates back at least to the 18th century when Collini (1776) contemplated the source of silica for agate formation and suggested a mechanism for producing repetitive banding. In the mid-19th century, Noeggerath (1849) hypothesized that the repetitive banding of agate is indicative of natural, external (to the agate-bearing cavity), rhythmic processes such as bedrock leaching of silica by a fluid that enters into cavities via infiltration canals, forming agate after many separate infiltrations. Other processes such as variation in water-table height (Bauer 1904) and alternating wet-dry seasons (Linck and Heinz 1930) have been credited as responsible for rhythmic infilling of cavities by silica-rich solutions.
>
> These now traditional ideas on agate formation imply fluid-rock interaction at low temperatures (<250 °C). Empirical support for low formation temperatures comes from several published studies. Based on hydrogen and oxygen isotope data, Fallick et al. (1985) estimated the temperature of formation of Devonian and Tertiary basalt-hosted Scottish agate to be approximately 50 °C. Using the same methods, Harris (1989) inferred the temperature of formation for basalt-hosted agate from Namibia to be approximately 120 °C. Lueth and Goodell (2005) performed fluid-inclusion analyses for agate from the Paraná Basalts, Rio do Sul, Brazil, and inferred the temperature of formation to be <50 °C for darker-colored samples and 140–180 °C for lighter-colored samples.

(2) Field report

Field work is research done in a natural environment rather than in a laboratory. Examples of field work range from recording beach erosion to studying avalanche patterns. To record their observations and analyses, researchers working in the field write **field reports**. These reports consist mainly of description and analysis, which may be presented together or in separate sections. A field report sometimes includes a reference list of sources mentioned in the text. (See **17e** for a sample field report.)

(3) Laboratory report

The most common writing assignment in the natural sciences is a **laboratory report**. The purpose of a lab report is to describe an experiment, including the results obtained, so that other researchers understand the procedure used and the conclusions drawn. When writing a lab report, you should explain the purpose of your research, recount the procedure you followed, and discuss your results. The format of this type of report follows the steps of the scientific method by starting with a problem and a hypothesis and concluding with a statement proving, modifying, or disproving the hypothesis.

- The **abstract** states the problem and summarizes the results. (You may not have to include an abstract if your report is short or if your instructor does not require it.)
- The **introduction** states the research question or hypothesis clearly and concisely, explains the scientific basis for the study, and provides brief background material on the subject of the study and the techniques to be used. The introduction usually includes citations referring to relevant sources.
- The **methods and materials** section is a narrative that describes how the experiment was conducted. It lists the materials that were used, identifies where the experiment was conducted, and describes the procedures that were followed. (Your lab notes should help you remember what you did.) Anyone who wants to repeat your work should be able to do so by following the steps described in this section.
- **Results** are reported by describing (but not interpreting) major findings and supporting them with properly labeled tables or graphs showing the empirical data.
- The **discussion** section includes an analysis of the results and an explanation of their relevance to the goals of the study. This section also reports any problems encountered and offers suggestions for further testing of the results.
- **References** are listed at the end of the paper. The list includes only works that are referred to in the report. The comprehensiveness and the accuracy of this list allow readers to evaluate the quality of the report and put it into a relevant context.

These sections appear in the sample laboratory report in **17f**.

Alyssa Jergens wrote the following field report for a biology course. Her assignment was to form and test a hypothesis on the density and positioning of lichen growth on tree trunks. She worked as a member of a research group, but all the members wrote their own reports. Following the guidelines she was given by her instructor, Alyssa describes the observational study in the Methods section and analyzes the findings in the Results section.

1

Lichen Distribution on Tree Trunks

Alyssa Jergens

General Biology I

October 1, 2009

Method

Our group formulated the hypothesis that lichens grow more densely on higher parts of tree trunks than on lower parts of tree trunks. Our null hypothesis was as follows: there will be no difference in lichen density at various heights on tree trunks. Our hypothesis on lichen density led us to predict that the largest clusters of lichens would be found predominately on higher portions of tree trunks.

The writer describes the observational research.

We conducted our study by sampling 20 trees in a designated area of the Central Washington University campus. Each tree trunk was divided into three sections based on height: from ground level to 0.5 m above the ground; from 0.5 m to 1.0 m above the ground; and from 1.0 m to 1.5 m above the ground. Data were recorded on a diagram (Figure 1). To the right in the diagram

A diagram used for data collection is presented in the Method section.

Figure 1   Method for recording lichen density

2

are the height ranges of the sections of tree trunks. The tick marks indicate how many trees had most of their lichens in that section of trunk.

Results

    Our observations of lichen growth revealed that lichens are more commonly found on the lower parts of tree trunks. Data from our observational study can be found in Table 1 and Figure 2. Note that 15 of 20 trees had the densest lichen growth on the lowest section of the trunk (ground level to 0.5 m above the ground).

The Results section presents the findings.

Table 1   Summary of data

Section of tree trunk	0.0–0.5 m	0.5–1.0 m	1.0–1.5 m
Number of trees with highest lichen density in given trunk section	15	3	2

A bar graph provides a visual representation of the data.

Figure 2   Association of trunk height with lichen distribution

    To ensure that the pattern of lichen growth we found was not random, we performed a chi-square test. The observed number, f_o, was determined by counting the total number of trees having the most lichens in each height division. The expected number, f_e, was calculated

The writer explains the statistical test that was used to ensure that the results were not random.

3

by taking the total number of trees observed (20) and dividing it by the total number of height divisions (3), to arrive at an expected value of 6.67. The chi-square test results are summarized in Table 2; the calculated value is 15.69.

Table 2   Results of chi-square test

	Observed number (f_o)	Expected number (f_e)	$f_o - f_e$	$(f_o - f_e)^2$	$\dfrac{(f_o - f_e)^2}{f_e}$
0.0–0.5 m	15	6.67	8.33	69.39	10.40
0.5–1.0 m	3	6.67	−3.67	13.47	2.02
1.0–1.5 m	2	6.67	−4.67	21.81	3.27
Total	20	20			15.69

The concluding paragraph acknowledges that the findings did not support the original hypothesis.

The critical value for the chi-square test given to us in class was 5.99. Our calculated chi-square value, 15.69, is greater than the critical value. Therefore, because the data from this observational study do not exhibit a random pattern, it can be concluded that a real nonrandom pattern is present. The results of the chi-square test show that our null hypothesis can be refuted. Although a pattern does exist in the sample of trees we observed, it was not the result we hypothesized. Our hypothesis stated that lichens would grow more densely on the upper portions of tree trunks rather than on the lower portions. Contrary to our expectations, our data and the results of the chi-square test indicate that lichens grow more densely on the lower portions of tree trunks than on the upper portions.

17f | LABORATORY REPORT ON A CELL-DIVISION EXPERIMENT

Heather Jensen's paper is representative of a report based on an experiment outlined in a lab manual for a first-year biology course. It includes section headings and graphics—drawings of the various stages of mitosis and a graph showing the results. The report ends with a reference list formatted according to CSE's citation-sequence system.

1

Observations and Calculations of Onion Root Tip Cells

Heather Jensen

Biology 101

January 9, 2011

Abstract

The first paragraph provides a summary of the experiment.

This laboratory experiment examined *Allium* (onion) root tip cells in the five stages of mitosis. The five stages of mitotic division were identified and recorded, and a 50-cell sample was chosen for closer examination. Of those 50 cells, 64% were found to be in interphase, 20% in prophase, 6% in metaphase, 6% in anaphase, and only 4% in telophase. The results showed that onion root tip cells spend the majority of their life cycle in a rest period (interphase). Prophase was calculated to be the longest phase of active division, while telophase was the shortest. These results were consistent with the experiments completed by other students and scientists.

Introduction

The Introduction section describes the purpose of the experiment.

This lab report outlines a laboratory experiment on mitosis, the division of the nucleus of a cell to form two new cells with the same number of chromosomes as the parent cell. Mitotic cell division consists of five visually identifiable stages: interphase, prophase, metaphase, anaphase, and telophase. The purpose of this experiment was to identify and observe cells in each phase of mitosis, as well as to calculate an estimate of the time involved in each stage of mitosis in an onion root tip cell. The onion root tip was chosen for this experiment because of easy

2

availability and rapid growth. Rapid root growth made it easy to observe multiple cells in the phases of mitosis in a small sample, on one or two slides. Onion root cells complete the entire cycle of division in 80 minutes,[1] and it was expected that larger numbers of cells would be found in interphase, because the majority of a life cycle is spent performing normal cell functions.

A superscript number refers to the first source on the References list.

Materials and Methods

The materials required for this experiment include a compound microscope and prepared slides of a longitudinal section of *Allium* (onion) root tip. First, the slides were placed on a compound microscope under low power, a 40× magnification level. The end of the root tip was located; then the cells immediately behind the root cap were examined. These cells appeared as a darker area under low power. This area of cells was identified as the apical meristem,[1] an area of rapid growth and division in the onion root tip. This area of cells was examined, while keeping the microscope on low power, to find and identify cells in interphase, prophase, metaphase, anaphase, and telophase. Then high power, a 400× magnification, was used to further examine and record the appearance of these cells.

The first paragraph in the Materials and Methods section lists the materials used and describes the methodology of the experiment.

After the multiple phases of mitosis were observed, a large area of 50 cells in mitosis was selected for further examination. This area was observed under low power in order to assess rows of cells in an easily countable space. Then the number of cells in each stage of mitosis was counted. These numbers were divided by the total number of cells examined, 50 cells, and multiplied by 100 in order to calculate the percentage of cells in each phase of mitosis. For example, if 10 cells were observed in interphase, then $10/50 = 0.20$ and $0.20 \cdot 100 = 20\%$ of cells

The writer describes the calculations performed on the data.

3

were in interphase. The actual time of each phase of mitosis in this sample of cells was calculated by multiplying the percentage by the total time of the division cycle, 80 minutes for the onion root tip cell.[1] For example, if 20% (20/100 = 0.20) of the cells were observed in interphase, then 0.20 • 80 minutes = 16 minutes total time were spent in interphase.

The Results section describes the phases of cell division, with labeled drawings as support.

Results

Drawings and Observations

INTERPHASE

This phase lasts from the completion of a division cycle to the beginning of the next cycle. All regular cell functions occur in this phase (except reproduction). It is not part of mitosis.[2]

The superscript number refers to the second source.

Figure 1   Two cells observed in interphase

PROPHASE

Technically the first phase of mitosis, this stage is marked by the thickening and shortening of chromosomes, which makes them visible under a compound microscope. The nucleus appears grainy at first and then the chromosomes appear more clearly defined as prophase progresses.

Figure 2   Two cells observed in prophase

4

METAPHASE

This phase is identified by the lining up of double chromosomes along the center line, the equator, of the cell.

Figure 3   Two cells observed in metaphase

ANAPHASE

This phase is classified by the separation of the double chromosomes. They begin to pull apart to opposite poles of the cell.

Figure 4   Two cells observed in anaphase

TELOPHASE

In telophase, the chromosomes have reached the opposite poles of the cell, and the connection between the chromosomes begins to break down as the nuclear membrane begins to form around each chromosomal clump. At the end of telophase, cytokinesis, or the division of the cytoplasm, takes place. In plant cells, a cell plate begins to form in the center of the cell and then grows outward to form a new cell wall,

5

completely dividing the old cell into two new cells, both with a complete

set of chromosomes.

Figure 5   Two cells observed in telophase

Table 1 shows the number of cells found in each phase of mitosis.

Tables summarize findings.

Table 1   Number of cells in each phase

Interphase	Prophase	Metaphase	Anaphase	Telophase
32 cells	10 cells	3 cells	3 cells	2 cells

Table 2 shows the calculated percentage of cells in each phase of mitosis.

Table 2   Percentage of cells in each phase

Interphase	Prophase	Metaphase	Anaphase	Telophase
64%	20%	6%	6%	4%

Figure 6 shows the actual time cells spent in each phase of mitosis.

The writer includes a graph that presents key results clearly.

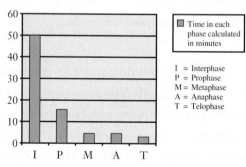

Figure 6   Time spent in each phase of mitosis

6

Discussion

This laboratory experiment provided firsthand experience with the phases of cell division. The five phases became more easily recognizable as each cell was examined and classified. Cells often looked like they could be classified in interphase or prophase or like they were between phases. Observation led to the confirmation that mitosis is a fluid process and not just a series of distinct phases. During the experiment, difficulties with overdyed and gray areas caused uncertainty because visual indications of phase were impossible to detect. This problem was lessened through the careful selection of clear patches of cells for observation. The expectation that a large number of cells would be found in interphase was confirmed by the numbers of cells counted in the cell sample of the onion root tip. Online comparison of the results of this experiment to those of other similar experiments confirmed the results found here as typical of an onion (*Allium*) root tip.[3] This indicated that the careful selection of clear patches of cells for sampling proved an effective method for eliminating error that might have been caused by the incorrect labeling of cells or the poor visibility of cells in overdyed or gray areas. Further studies might include larger samples of cells. Experiments with larger numbers of cells would offer additional evidence to confirm the results found in this experiment.

The writer explains how the results of the experiment fulfilled its purpose.

The writer describes a problem that was encountered.

The superscript number refers to the third source.

7

References

1. Schraer WD, Stoltze H. Biology: the study of life. 7th ed. Needham (MA): Prentice Hall; 1999. Mitosis and asexual reproduction; pp. 398–403.

2. The biology project [Internet]. Tucson (AZ): Department of Biochemistry and Molecular Biophysics, University of Arizona; 1997 [modified 2004; cited 2011 Jan 9]. Available from: http://www.biology.arizona.edu/cell_bio/tutorials/cell_cycle/cells3.html

3. Yesnik A, Jaster K. The bio 1 super virtual lab book [Internet]. Washington (DC): Sidwell Friends School; 1998 [modified 2002; cited 2011 Jan 9]. Mitosis lab. Available from: http://classic.sidwell.edu/us/science/vlb/mitosis/

The list of references is formatted according to the citation-sequence system.

18 | CSE DOCUMENTATION

The Council of Science Editors (CSE) has established guidelines for writers in the life and physical sciences. *Scientific Style and Format: The CSE Manual for Authors, Editors, and Publishers* covers general style conventions for spelling, punctuation, capitalization, and so forth, as well as specific scientific conventions for such items as chemical names and formulas. In addition, the manual presents three systems for citing and documenting research sources: the citation-sequence system, the name-year system, and the citation-name system. This chapter includes

- guidelines for citing sources and organizing material within a CSE-style research paper (**18a**),
- guidelines for documenting sources in a reference list (**18b**), and
- a sample CSE-style research paper (**18c**).

18a | CSE CITATION-SEQUENCE, NAME-YEAR, AND CITATION-NAME SYSTEMS

(1) Citing material from other sources

As you prepare to write your paper, find out which system your instructor prefers—the citation-sequence system, the name-year system, or the citation-name system. Because these systems differ significantly, it is important to know before you get started which one you will be expected to use. Once you know your instructor's preference, use the guidelines in one of the following boxes for formatting your in-text references.

TIPS FOR FORMATTING CITATION-SEQUENCE IN-TEXT REFERENCES

- Place a superscript number after each use of information from a source. This number corresponds to the number assigned to the bibliographic entry for the source in the list at the end of your paper.

- Insert the superscript number after the information taken from the source or after the word or phrase indicating the source; a single space precedes the number:

  Herbert's original method [1] was used.

- Insert the same number each time you use information from the source.

- Order the numbers according to the sequence in which you introduce the sources:

  Both Li [1] and Holst [2] have shown . . .

- When referring to more than one source in the same in-text reference, use commas to separate the superscript numbers corresponding to the sources; notice that there is no space after each comma. Use an en dash between two numbers to indicate a sequence of sources:

  The early studies [1,2,4–7] found . . .

TIPS FOR FORMATTING NAME-YEAR IN-TEXT REFERENCES

- Place the author's last name and the year of publication in parentheses after mentioning the source or information from it:

  In a more recent study (Karr 2011), these findings were not replicated.

  Using the author's last name, the reader will be able to find the corresponding entry in the reference list, which is arranged alphabetically.

- Omit the author's name from the in-text reference if the name appears in the text preceding it:

  In Karr's study (2011), these findings were not replicated.

- If the source has two authors, use both of their last names:

  (Phill and Richardson 2011)

  If there are three or more authors, use the first author's last name and the abbreviation *et al.*:

  (Drake et al. 2010)

- Use semicolons to separate multiple in-text references within a single set of parentheses. Order references chronologically when the years differ but alphabetically when the years are the same:

  (Li 2010; Holst 2011)   BUT   (Lamont 2010; Li 2010)

TIPS FOR FORMATTING CITATION-NAME IN-TEXT REFERENCES

- Arrange your bibliographic list of references alphabetically. Then assign each reference a number. Use the superscript form of this number in the text immediately after the information taken from the source or after the word or phrase indicating the source:

   Stress-related illnesses are common among college students. [1]

   According to Li's study [6] of such illnesses . . .

- Use the same number each time you use material from or refer to the source.

- When referring to more than one source in the same in-text reference, use commas to separate the superscript numbers corresponding to the sources; note that there is no space after each comma. Use an en dash between two numbers to indicate a sequence of sources:

   Recent studies of posttraumatic stress disorder [1,2,4–7] show . . .

---

(2) Guidelines for quotations and headings

(a) Direct quotations

If a quotation is brief, incorporate it into a sentence. A comma or period at the end of a quotation is placed inside the quotation marks. A lengthy quotation should be set off as a block quotation (see **12a(2)**).

(b) Headings

Headings and subheadings indicate how the various sections of a research paper or report are related. The CSE manual recommends that levels of headings be readily distinguishable and presents the following style as an illustration:

First level	**Boldfaced Uppercase and Lowercase Letters**
Second level	Uppercase and Lowercase Letters
Third level	*ITALICIZED SMALL UPPERCASE LETTERS*
Fourth level	*Italicized Uppercase and Lowercase Letters*

Two or three levels of subheadings are usually sufficient for most college-level assignments.

18b | CSE-STYLE REFERENCE LIST

All of the works you cite should be listed at the end of your paper, beginning on a separate page with the heading *End References, References,* or *Reference List.* The following tips will help you prepare such a list.

TIPS FOR PREPARING A REFERENCE LIST

- Place the heading (*End References, References* or *Reference List,* not italicized) at the upper left of the page.

- If you are using the citation-sequence system, list the entries for your sources in the order in which they were introduced in the text. If your paper employs the citation-name system, your list of bibliographic entries should be ordered alphabetically according to the first author's last name and then numbered. If your paper employs the name-year system, your list should be ordered alphabetically. See page 466 for an example of a reference list in alphabetical order.

- CSE-style reference lists differ in overall organization: With the citation-sequence system, the entries in the reference list follow the order in which the sources were introduced in the text. With the citation-name or the name-year system, entries are listed alphabetically by the first author's last name.

- The name-year system differs from both the citation-sequence and the citation-name systems in the placement of the date of publication within entries: the name-year system calls for the date to be placed after the author's name; the citation-sequence and the citation-name systems call for the date to be placed after the publisher's name in entries for books and after the name of the periodical in entries for articles.

---

❶ *CAUTION*

Automatic bibliography composers found online and included in some software packages often make mistakes. They may fail to include all elements of a bibliographic entry or may order elements incorrectly. If you decide to use an automatic composer, be sure to check the results against the model entries provided in this chapter.

The following directory guides you to sample bibliographic entries for the citation-sequence system or the citation-name system.

Directory of CSE-Style Reference-List Entries (Citation-Sequence or Citation-Name System)

The following guidelines are for the citation-sequence or the citation-name system. For examples of reference-list entries for the name-year system, see pages 456 and 466.

GENERAL DOCUMENTATION GUIDELINES FOR PRINT AND ONLINE SOURCES

Author or Editor

One author. Begin the bibliographic entry with the author's last name followed by the initials for the first name and the middle name (if one is given). Notice that there is no	Klemin TK. Laigo MS.

(continued on page 450)

Author or Editor *(continued from page 449)*

comma after the last name and no period or space between initials.

Two or more authors. Invert the names and initials of all authors, using commas to separate the authors' names.

Stearns BL, Sowards JP.

Collum AS, Dahl PJ, Steele TP.

Organization as author. Whenever possible, use an abbreviation or acronym for the name of an organization in the text of the paper. The bibliographic entry begins with the abbreviation or acronym in square brackets, followed by the full name.

[AMA] American Medical Association.

[UNICEF] United Nations Children's Fund.

Editor. Add the word *editor* or *editors* after the last name.

Walter PA, editor.

Mednick VB, Henry JP, editors.

Titles

Books. Use the title given on the book's title page. Titles are neither underlined nor italicized. Capitalize only the first word of the title and any proper nouns or adjectives. A subtitle does not begin with a capital letter unless its first word is a proper noun or adjective. If the book is a second or subsequent edition, follow the title with a period and then the number of the edition.

The magpies: the ecology and behaviour of black-billed and yellow-billed magpies.

Genetics. 5th ed.

Journals, magazines, and newspapers. For the names of journals and magazines that are longer than one word, use standard abbreviations (for example, *Sci Am* for *Scientific American*). Rules for abbreviating journal

J Mamm. (for *Journal of Mammology*)

New York Times.

names are given in Appendix 29.1 of the CSE manual and can also be found using a search engine (enter "CSE journal abbreviations"). Use full names of newspapers, but omit any initial *The*.

Publication Data

Books. Include the place of publication, the publisher's name, and the year of publication. The place of publication can usually be found on the title page. If more than one city is mentioned, use the first one listed. If the city is not well known, clarify its location by including an abbreviation for the state, province, or country in parentheses after the name of the city. The publisher's name is separated from the place of publication by a colon and one space. (Standard abbreviations for publishers' names may be used.) List the source's year of publication after the publisher's name, following a semicolon and one space.

London: Chatto & Windus; 2010.

Orlando (FL): Harcourt; 2011.

Journals and magazines. Use one space after the name of the journal or magazine; then provide the year of publication, the volume number, and the issue number. Place a semicolon between the year of publication and the volume number. Put the issue number in parentheses. Notice that there are no spaces separating the year, the volume number, and the issue number.

Nature. 2009;420(6911)

Natl Geogr Mag. 2009;211(3)

(continued on page 452)

Publication Data *(continued from page 451)*

Newspapers. Place the year, month, and day of publication (if any) after the name of the newspaper.	New York Times. 2011 Aug 1

Page Numbers

Books. Page numbers are not always required, so ask your instructor for guidance. If page numbers are required, that information is provided at the end of an entry. When you are citing an entire book, list the total number of pages, excluding preliminary pages with roman numerals. If you have used only part of a book, list just the pages you used. Use the abbreviation *p* for *pages* after the total number of pages but before a range of pages.	University of Chicago Press. 315 p. OR Taylor and Francis. p. 136–164.
Journals and magazines. Page numbers should be expressed as a range at the end of an entry.	Natl Geogr Mag. 2011;219(4):82–89.
Newspapers. At the end of the entry, include the section letter, the page number, and the column number.	Houston Chronicle. 2001 Apr 19; Sect. A:2 (col. 1).

Electronic Sources

Entries for electronic sources are similar to those for print sources; however, they include three additional pieces of information:

1. The word *Internet* is placed in square brackets after the title of the book or the name of the journal to indicate that the work is an online source. If you are not using an

Internet-based source, indicate the medium of the electronic source: [CD-ROM] or [disk].

2. The date of access, preceded by the word *cited*, is given in square brackets after the date of publication.

3. The Internet address (URL) is included at the end of the entry, preceded by the phrase *Available from:* (notice the colon). If the Internet address is excessively long, provide the URL for a home page or a main page, such as a table of contents, and instruct the reader to click on a link.

Duru M, Ansquer P, Jouany C, Theau JP, Cruz P. Comparison of methods for assessing the impact of different disturbances and nutrient conditions upon functional characteristics of grassland communities. Ann Bot [Internet]. 2010 [cited 2010 Nov 13]; 106(5):833–842. Available from: http://aob.oxfordjournals.org/content/current after clicking on the article link.

See pages 454 and 455 for other examples.

BOOKS

1. Book with one author

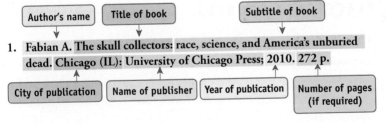

1. Fabian A. The skull collectors: race, science, and America's unburied dead. Chicago (IL): University of Chicago Press; 2010. 272 p.

© 2013 Cengage Learning

2. Book with two or more authors

2. Easley D, Kleinberg J. Networks, crowds, and markets: reasoning about a highly connected world. Cambridge (GB): Cambridge University Press; 2010.

3. Book with an organization (or organizations) listed as author

3. Seattle Times. Natural wonders: the flora, fauna & formations of Washington. Seattle (WA): Seattle Times; 2003.

4. Book with editor(s)

4. Lund B, Hunter P, editors. The microbiological safety of food in healthcare settings. Malden (MA): Blackwell; 2007.

5. Chapter or part of an edited book

5. Martin DJ. Social data. In: Wilson J, Fotheringham AS, editors. The handbook of geographic information science. Malden (MA): Blackwell; 2008. p. 35–48.

ARTICLES

6. Article in a scholarly journal

6. Hilli S, Stark S, Derome J. Litter decomposition rates in relation to litter stocks in boreal coniferous forests along climatic and soil fertility gradients. Appl Soil Ecol. 2010;46(2):200–208.

7. Article in a popular (general-circulation) magazine

7. McKibben B. Carbon's new math. Natl Geogr Mag. 2007;212(4):33–37.

8. Article in a newspaper

8. O'Connor A. Heart attack risk linked to time spent in traffic. New York Times. 2004 Oct 26;Sect. F:9 (col. 4).

ELECTRONIC SOURCES

9. Online book

9. Committee on Planetary and Lunar Exploration. National Research Council. The quarantine and certification of Martian samples [Internet]. Washington (DC): National Academy Press; 2002 [cited 2007 Oct 31]. Available from: http://www.nap.edu/openbook.php?isbn=0309075718

10. Article in an online journal

10. Thom DH, Wong ST, Guzman D, Wu A, Penko J, Miaskowski C. Physician trust in the patient: development and validation of a new measure. Ann Fam Med [Internet]. 2011 [cited 2011 Apr 20]; 9(2):142–147. Available from: http://www.annfammed.org/cgi/content/full/9/2/142

11. Article in an online magazine

11. Shermer M. Weirdonomics and quirkology: how the curious science of the oddities of everyday life yields new insights. Sci Am [Internet]. 2007 [cited 2007 Nov 1]; 1297(5):45. Available from: http://www.sciam.com/issue.cfm after clicking on the article link.

12. Article in an online newspaper

12. Singer N. Making ads that whisper to the brain. New York Times [Internet]. 2010 Nov 13 [cited 2010 Nov 29]; [1 p.]. Available from: http://www.nytimes.com/2010/11/14/business/14stream.html?ref=health

13. Website content

13. Corvus corax [Internet]. Bay Shore (NY): Long Island Ravens MC; c2000–2002 [updated 2001 Dec 3; cited 2003 Jan 3]. Available from: http://www.liravensmc.org/About/about_ravens.htm

14. Database

14. Honey Bee Genome Project [Internet]. Houston (TX): Baylor College of Medicine. [date unknown] -   [updated 2005 Jan 27; cited 2007 Nov 1]. Available from: http://www.hgsc.bcm.tmc.edu/projects/honeybee/

If you do not know the date of publication, place the words *date unknown* (not italicized) in square brackets; then add a space, a hyphen, and three more spaces.

Name-year system

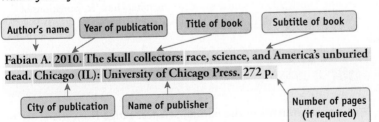

The following sample entries for a reference list in the name-year format correspond to those listed as items 1 through 8 for the citation-sequence or citation-name system. (Because the CSE manual provides only one format for online sources, the entries for those sources are not repeated in this list.) The individual entries for books and articles differ from those in the citation-sequence and citation-name formats only in the placement of the date. In the name-year system, the date follows the author's name. For more examples of entries in name-year format, see page 466.

References

Easley D, Kleinberg J. 2010. Networks, crowds, and markets: reasoning about a highly connected world. Cambridge (GB): Cambridge University Press.

Fabian A. 2010. The skull collectors: race, science, and America's unburied dead. Chicago (IL): University of Chicago Press.

Hilli S, Stark S, Derome J. 2010. Litter decomposition rates in relation to litter stocks in boreal coniferous forests along climatic and soil fertility gradients. Appl Soil Ecol. 46(2):200–208.

Lund B, Hunter P, editors. 2007. The microbiological safety of food in healthcare settings. Malden (MA): Blackwell.

Martin DJ. 2008. Social data. In: Wilson J, Fotheringham AS, editors. The handbook of geographic information science. Malden (MA): Blackwell. p. 35–48.

McKibben B. 2007. Carbon's new math. Natl Geogr Mag. 212(4):33–37.

O'Connor A. 2004 Oct 26. Heart attack risk linked to time spent in traffic. New York Times. Sect. F:9 (col. 4).

Seattle Times. 2003. Natural wonders: the flora, fauna & formations of Washington. Seattle (WA): Seattle Times.

18c   CSE-STYLE RESEARCH PAPER

Writing assignments in the natural sciences range from literature reviews to laboratory reports (17d). Kayla Berg, whose paper follows, was asked to review the causes and impacts of a natural disaster for a geology course. Kayla applied the guidelines in the CSE manual in formatting her paper. However, those guidelines do not cover all features of under-graduate papers, and Kayla's title page was formatted according to her instructor's directions. Kayla used the CSE name-year system to cite and document her sources.

Thailand Tsunami

Kayla Berg

Geology 380: Environmental Geology

November 5, 2009

1

Abstract

In 2004, an earthquake off the coast of Sumatra caused a tsunami that struck the coasts of several countries, causing not only a great deal of human suffering but also much environmental damage. This paper reports on various types of damage caused by the tsunami and the safety precautions that have been put into place to avoid similar destruction in the future.

2

Introduction

In December 2004, an earthquake with a magnitude of 9.0 occurred about 250 km off the west coast of Sumatra (in Indonesia) (Figure 1). The epicenter of the earthquake was located in the Indian Ocean at 3.3°N and 95.9°E. (Lukkunprasit and Ruangrassamee 2008). This earthquake caused a series of tsunami waves that struck the coasts of Thailand, Indonesia, Sri Lanka, India, Somalia, Madagascar, Kenya, Tanzania, Malaysia, Myanmar, and Bangladesh (At-a-glance 2005). These waves had a negative impact on these areas. They caused damage to groundwater, wells, ecosystems, mangrove trees, coral reefs,

Figure 1   Epicenter of the earthquake and the areas affected by the tsunami (© GraphicMaps.com)

3

and buildings (Szczucinski et al. 2006). This paper investigates the damage caused by this tsunami, commonly known as the Thailand Tsunami.

The thesis states the purpose of the paper.

Causes and Consequences of the Tsunami

Plate Tectonics

Tsunamis are commonly generated by earthquakes that arise in subduction zones. These earthquakes are created when one plate subducts beneath (descends under) another plate and becomes stuck as a result of friction. The motion of the subducting plate causes distortion of the overriding plate, which results in an accumulation of energy. At some point, the energy built up in the overriding plate is released, causing the plates to unlock. When the plates unlock, the bottom plate continues to move downward while the top plate snaps upward. The amount the seafloor moves as a result of movement of the upper plate determines the size of the tsunami that will be created (Geist et al. 2006).

The writer explains how tsunamis are created.

Cause of the 2004 Tsunami

Off the coast of Sumatra in the Indian Ocean, the India Plate and the Eurasia Plate meet to form a subduction zone (Geist et al. 2006). In this zone, the India Plate, because it is denser, subducts beneath the Eurasia Plate. It is believed that on the day of the tsunami, the Eurasia Plate moved upward a small amount at first and then jumped violently. When this occurred, a magnitude 9.0 earthquake occurred and caused the seafloor to rise 8 m in some areas and a tsunami to form. When the earthquake happened, waves formed on the surface of the water. These

Section headings indicate the hierarchy of information.

4

waves were seen by satellite and looked no bigger than 1 m high.
However, when the waves reached the coast of Sumatra about 2 hours
later, they were about 30 m in height (Geist et al. 2006).

Loss of Life and Property

In this section and the following sections, the writer discusses the types of harm caused by the tsunami.

More than 1 million people were displaced because of the tsunami's
environmental impact, and more than 285,000 people were killed. The
greatest loss of human life occurred along the coast of Sumatra. In addition,
the tsunami caused over $10 billion worth of damage to houses, buildings,
and farms (Szczucinski et al. 2006). Buildings have been reconstructed and
improved since the disaster. To help protect houses from future tsunamis,
openings have been built to create a path for the water to flow through. Low
sea walls have also been created. These will reduce the force of the waves
before they hit the shoreline (Lukkunprasit and Ruangrassamee 2008).

Environmental Impacts

Erosion

In the countries affected by the tsunami, major coastal erosion
occurred. The two main causes of the erosion were wave scour and
subsidence. Wave scour is caused when waves hit the coast with enough force
to carry sediment displaced by the wave back out to sea. Subsidence is a
decrease in elevation of the land, generally caused by the depletion of water
that underlies the area that subsided. In some areas along the coast, human
activity such as cast mining had already caused the ground to subside.
Therefore, when the waves hit the coast, the depressions were filled with salty
water. This water sat in the depressions and contaminated the groundwater.
In areas with flat beaches, there was a large amount of wave scour and

5

Figure 2   Points along the coast affected by the tsunami. Graphs A through G show inundation and run-up amounts. The vertical axis shows the height in meters the water attained above the average sea level. The horizontal axis shows the distance in meters the water traveled inland from the shoreline (Szczucinski et al. 2006).

Captions help readers understand graphs.

erosion. The areas with flatter coastal regions also experienced inundation by seawater that extended between 340 m and 560 m inland. Along coasts with steep rocky cliff faces, the water was not able to travel inland more than 100 m (Figure 2). Reefs and dunes also prevented run-up in some areas. If coral reefs or dunes are present, less run-up occurs because the reefs or dunes reduce the force of the waves (Szczucinski et al. 2006).

Following CSE style, the writer uses abbreviations for units of measurement.

6

Tsunami Deposits

Most erosion occurred within 50 m of the shoreline. Within this high erosion area, no tsunami deposits could be found. However, beyond 50 m inland, tsunami deposits have been found. These deposits were composed of sand and marine sediments consisting of shells, corals, and microorganisms (Szczucinski et al. 2006). The thickness of these deposits varied based on the amount of run-up, the vegetation, the topography, and other obstructions. The average thickness of the tsunami deposits was 8 cm. However, in some places, the deposits were 52 cm thick and completely covered some of the vegetation. Figure 3 shows a typical

Figure 3   Cross section of a typical tsunami deposit (Szczucinski et al. 2006)

tsunami deposit that occurred in an inundation zone. The bottom layer is the original layer of soil; on top of this layer is the tsunami deposit with layers of coarse sand and fine sand (Szczucinski et al. 2006). Large amounts of salt and heavy metals were found in the tsunami deposits. Of great concern were the deposits that included potassium, sodium, copper, lead, and zinc, substances that could reach toxic levels in crops (Szczucinski et al. 2006). In addition, small amounts of mercury sulfide were discovered in the seawater in the depressions that were due to cast mining in the area. Because it is highly toxic, mercury sulfide can pose a threat to humans and other living organisms. It can also leak into the groundwater system and pollute drinking water (Boszke and Astel 2007).

Salinity

The high salinity of the ocean water in the tsunami and of the tsunami deposits greatly affected groundwater and inland surfaces. Over time, the salt in tsunami deposits seeped into the soil and eventually into the groundwater, thus polluting it. The amount of pollution depended on the extent of inundation in an area. Groundwater and wells were also polluted by fecal bacteria that leaked into the soil when septic systems were damaged by the tsunami (Szczucinski et al. 2006).

Ecosystems

Ecosystems were greatly affected by the tsunami. Coral reefs were destroyed, damaged, or moved. The closer the reefs were to the shoreline, the more they were affected by wave impact and backwash. Another part of the ecosystem that was destroyed was the sea grass beds, which are important sources of income for local fisherman and fishing companies.

8

The beds were buried under sand from inland erosion and backwash (Szczucinski et al. 2006).

Vegetation

Mangrove trees located close to the shoreline were completely destroyed, while mangrove trees further inland experienced little to no damage. When the high-energy wave hit the mangroves close to the shoreline, it had a devastating effect because they have not evolved to withstand such conditions. Even though mangrove trees near the coast were destroyed, they helped protect vast areas of land from great damage. In areas where these trees were abundant, the amount of damage done by the water was greatly reduced (Yanagisawa et al. 2009). Many trees that were not as protective as the mangroves were completely destroyed. Some were pulled out of the ground by the force of the wave (Szczucinski et al. 2006).

Other vegetation was affected by the salinity of the ocean water in the wave and the large amounts of tsunami deposits. Plants either withered from the intake of the salty water or died because they were buried under the tsunami deposits.

Conclusion

The amount of damage that different areas received was determined by multiple factors. For example, the bathymetry (the depth of water along the shoreline) and the morphology of the shoreline affected the amount of force the tsunami had when it hit the coast. If an area had offshore coral reefs or coastal mangroves, the amount of erosion and damage inland was often reduced. However, within 50 days

9

of the tsunami, ecosystems in areas like Thailand were already beginning to heal and to rebuild themselves, and about 4 months after the event, water, animals, and sea grass, which had been depleted, were beginning to return to their original quantities (Szczucinski et al. 2006). Scientists have been able to study damage in different areas and determine factors that increase or decrease it.

By studying this tsunami, scientists have become able to predict which areas are prone to tsunami effects. They have also gained information that helps them predict the orientation of tsunami waves, where they will go and how far they will travel inland (Geist et al. 2006). Early prediction, along with the construction of seawalls and the improvement of houses, should lessen the impact of any future tsunami in the area devastated by the Thailand Tsunami.

The writer describes what was learned from studying the effects of the tsunami.

10

References

At-a-glance: countries hit. 2005 Dec 22. BBC News [Internet]. [cited 2011 Jan 9]; [1 p.] Available from: http://news.bbc.co.uk/2/hi/4126019.stm

Boszke, L, Astel A. 2007. Fractionation of mercury in sediments from coastal zone inundated by tsunami and in freshwater sediments from the rivers. J Environ Sci Health, Pt A: Toxic/Hazard Subst Environ Eng. (42)7:847–858.

Geist, EL, Titov, VV, Synolakis, CE. 2006. Tsunami: wave of change. Sci Am. (294)1:56–63.

Lukkunprasit P, Ruangrassamee, A. 2008. Building damage in Thailand in the 2004 Indian Ocean tsunami and clues for tsunami-resistant design. IES J Part A: Civ & Struct Eng. 1(1):17–30.

Szczucinski W, Chaimanee N, Niedzielski G, Rachlewicz G, Saisuttichai D, Tepsuwan T, Lorenc S, Siepak J. 2006. Environmental and geological impacts of the 26 December 2004 tsunami in coastal zone of Thailand—overview of short- and long-term effects. Polish J of Environ Stud. 15(5):793–810.

Yanagisawa H, Koshimura S, Goto K, Miyagi T, Imamura F, Ruangrassamee A, Tanavud C. 2009. Damage to mangrove forest by 2004 tsunami at Pakarang Cape and Namkem, Thailand. Polish J of Environ Stud. 18(1):35–42.

19 | WRITING IN BUSINESS

Writing in business, like writing in any other environment, requires close attention to the rhetorical situation: opportunity, audience, purpose, message, and context. It differs from other writing, however, in the nature of authorship: as a business writer, you need to present yourself and your employer as credible and reliable—whether you are writing to explain, solve a problem, gather information, analyze, or argue a point. One way to project that positive image is to follow the conventions and formats expected by the business community.

On the job or in business courses, you will receive a variety of writing assignments: letters, memos and e-mails, PowerPoint presentations, oral reports, and business reports. This chapter will help you

- recognize the stylistic conventions of standard business writing (**19a**),
- draft a business letter (**19b**),
- produce business memos and e-mails (**19c**),
- compose a résumé (**19d**) and a letter of application (**19e**),
- prepare an oral report including a PowerPoint presentation (**19f**), and
- research and write a formal business report (**19g**).

19a | CONVENTIONS OF LANGUAGE AND ORGANIZATION

Whether you are using a word processor or writing on paper, preparing a memo or a business plan, you will face both anticipated and unexpected deadlines for business documents. The following strategies for effective business communication will help you produce comprehensive, concise, and well-organized documents on time.

STRATEGIES FOR EFFECTIVE BUSINESS COMMUNICATION

Be direct.

- Know who your audience members are and consider their needs.
- State the purpose of your document in your opening sentence or paragraph.
- Write straightforward sentences, beginning with a subject and including an active verb (24c(2)).
- Use technical language sparingly, unless the document is intended for a specialized audience (33b(4)).

Be concise.

- Compose direct, uncomplicated sentences.
- Include only necessary details.
- Use numbers, bullets, or descriptive headings that guide readers to information.
- Use graphs, tables, and other visual elements that convey information succinctly.

Use conventional formatting.

- Follow the standard formats that have been established within a business or industry or use the formats outlined in this chapter (19b–f).
- Avoid informal language unless you know that a casual tone is acceptable.
- Edit and proofread your documents carefully. Typos, grammatical mistakes, sentence fragments, and missing words detract significantly from your ethos.

19b BUSINESS LETTERS

Business letters serve a variety of purposes—to inquire, to inform, to complain, or to respond, for example. (For letters of application, see 19e.) Regardless of its purpose, a business letter is usually single-spaced and fits on one sheet of paper. It also follows a standard block format: each element is aligned flush with the left margin, with double spacing between paragraphs.

ELEMENTS OF A STANDARD BUSINESS LETTER

- **Return address.** Your employer may require you to use stationery with a letterhead. If not, type your mailing address one inch from the top of the paper, flush left on a one-inch margin, and single-spaced.

- **Date.** Type the date beneath your return address. If you are using letterhead stationery, type the date one or two lines below the letterhead's last line.

- **Recipient's name and address.** Provide the full name and address of the recipient. Single-space these lines, and allow an extra line space above them. If you do not know the person's name, try to find it by checking the company's website or phoning the company. If you cannot find the recipient's name, use an appropriate title such as *Personnel Director* or *Customer Service Manager* (not italicized).

- **Greeting.** Type your greeting two lines below the last line of the recipient's address. The conventional greeting is *Dear* (not italicized) followed by the recipient's name and a colon. If you and the recipient use first names to address each other, use the person's first name. Otherwise, use *Mr.*, *Ms.*, *Mrs.*, or *Miss* and the last name. (Choose *Ms.* when you do not know a woman's preference.) Avoid the sexist *Dear Sir*, *Gentlemen*, or *Dear Madam* and the stilted *To Whom It May Concern* or *Dear Sir or Madam*.

- **Body of the letter.** Begin the first paragraph two lines below the greeting. Single-space lines within a paragraph; double-space between paragraphs. If your letter must continue on a second page, include the recipient's last name, the date, and the page number in three single-spaced lines at the top left on the second page.

- **Closing.** Close your letter two lines after the end of the body with an expression such as *Sincerely* or *Cordially* (not italicized) followed by a comma.

- **Signature.** Type your full name four lines below the closing. Then, in the space above your typed name, sign your full name, using blue or black ink. If you have addressed the recipient by his or her first name, sign just your first name.

- **Additional information.** If you are enclosing extra material such as a résumé, type the word *Enclosure* or the abbreviation *Encl.* (not italicized) two lines below your name. You may also note the number of enclosures or the identity of the document(s): for example, *Enclosures (3)* or *Encl.: 2002 Annual Year-End Report*. If you would like the recipient to know the names of people receiving copies of the letter, use the abbreviation *cc* (for "carbon copy") and a colon followed by the other recipients' names. Place this element on the line directly below the enclosure line or, if there is no enclosure, two lines below your name.

The sample **letter of inquiry** (a letter intended to elicit information) in Figure 19.1 illustrates the parts of a typical business letter.

Return address and date	550 First Avenue Ellensburg, WA 98926 February 4, 2009
Name and address of recipient	Mr. Mark Russell Bilingual Publications 5400 Sage Avenue Yakima, WA 98907
Greeting	Dear Mr. Russell:
Body of letter	I am a junior in the Bilingual Education Program at Central Washington University. For my coursework, I am investigating positions in publishing that include the use of two languages. Your name and address were given to me by my instructor, Marta Cole, who worked for you from 2003 through 2007. I have learned something about your publications on your website. I am most interested in dual documents—those in both English and Spanish. Could you please send me samples of such documents so that I can have a better idea of the types of publications you produce? I am also interested in finding out what qualifications I would need to work for a business like yours. I am fluent in both Spanish and English and have taken a course in translation. If possible, I would like to ask you a few questions about your training and experience. Would you have time for an interview some day next week?
Closing	Sincerely,
Signature	*Chris Humphrey* Chris Humphrey

Figure 19.1. A sample letter of inquiry. (© 2013 Cengage Learning)

19C   BUSINESS MEMOS AND E-MAILS

A **memo** (short for *memorandum*) is a brief document, usually focusing on one topic, sent within a business to announce a meeting, explain an event or situation, set a schedule, or request information or action (see Figure 19.2). Like memos, e-mail messages are used for internal communication, but they are also used for external communication, for initiating and maintaining relationships with clients, prospective employees, or people at other companies. The basic guidelines for writing memos also apply to e-mail messages.

Because it is circulated internally, a memo or e-mail is usually less formal than a letter. Nonetheless, it should still be direct and concise: a memo should be no longer than a page, and an e-mail no longer than a screen. The following guidelines for formatting these kinds of documents are fairly standard, but a particular company or organization may establish its own format.

To:	Intellectual Properties Committee	Heading
From:	Leo Renfrow, Chair of Intellectual Properties Committee	
Date:	March 15, 2010	
Subject:	Review of Policy Statement	

At the end of our last meeting, we decided to have our policy statement reviewed by someone outside our university. Clark Beech, chair of the Intellectual Properties Committee at Lincoln College, agreed to help us. Overall, as his review shows, the format of our policy statement is sound. Dr. Beech believes that some of the content should be further developed, however. It appears that we have used some ambiguous terms and included some conditions that would not hold up in court.   *Body of memo*

Early next week, my assistant will deliver a copy of Dr. Beech's review to each of you. Please look it over before our next meeting, on March 29. If you have any questions or comments before then, please call me at ext. 1540. I look forward to seeing all of you at the meeting.

Figure 19.2. A sample business memo. (© 2013 Cengage Learning)

ELEMENTS OF A STANDARD BUSINESS MEMO OR E-MAIL

- **Heading.** On four consecutive lines, type *To* (not italicized) followed by a colon and the name(s) of the recipient(s), *From* followed by a colon and your name and title (if appropriate), *Date* followed by a colon and the date, and *Subject* followed by a colon and a few words identifying the memo's subject. (The abbreviation *Re*, for "regarding," is sometimes used instead of *Subject.*) This information should be single-spaced. If you are sending copies to individuals whose names are not included in the *To* line, place those names on a new line beginning with *cc* ("carbon copy") and a colon. Most e-mail software supplies these header lines on any new message.

- **Body.** Use the block format (**19b**), single-spacing lines within each paragraph and double-spacing between paragraphs. Double-space between the heading and the body of the memo. Open your memo with the most important information and establish how it affects your audience. Use your conclusion to establish goodwill.

The effectiveness of memos and e-mails depends on several essential features: tone, length, and directness. As you know, different audiences appreciate different tones, so adjust your style and tone accordingly. A conversational tone is acceptable for an internal message to a coworker, but a more formal tone is required for a memo or an e-mail to a supervisor or a larger group of associates. One way to enhance the professional tone of your e-mails is to use an e-mail signature: a set of information that identifies you and your institution and is appended to the end of all your outgoing messages. In addition to the level of formality, tone also includes the content of a message, so take care not to mention, let alone forward, any information that you or other correspondents might prefer to keep private. When in doubt, seek the other person's permission before making information public. Also keep in mind that anything you send in an e-mail can easily be forwarded by others. (For information on writing to multiple audiences, see **1d**.)

Although speed and ease are hallmarks of e-mailing, these advantages can lead to an inappropriate tone, allowing senders to hit the Send or Forward button without giving the message enough thought. Other obvious results of the speed and ease of e-mailing are misspellings, poor grammar, violations of privacy, and junk mail. Since no one appreciates any of these results, consider carefully every e-mail message you send.

Excessive length also detracts from the effectiveness of your memos and e-mails. People tend to read only one rhetorical unit, so keep your messages to just that: one page for a memo, one screen (or twenty lines) for an e-mail. Your memo or e-mail should fit on a single page or screen but retain enough white space to allow for easy reading.

Regular e-mail users receive a large volume of messages every day. For that reason, most of them are in the habit of scanning messages, deleting many without reading them, and responding quickly (sometimes too quickly) to the rest. To ensure that an e-mail receives the attention it merits, you should announce your topic in the subject line and then arrange and present your message in concise, readable chunks (perhaps bulleted or numbered lists) that incorporate white space and guide recipients to important information. Short paragraphs also allow for white space, which helps readers to maintain their attention and absorb the key points.

TIPS FOR SENDING ATTACHMENTS WITH E-MAIL MESSAGES

- Before you send any attachment, consider the size of the file—many in-boxes have limited space and cannot accept large files or multiple files (totalling over 1000 KB) or files that contain streaming video, photographs, or sound clips. If there is a chance that a large file might crash a recipient's e-mail program, call or e-mail the recipient to ask permission before sending it.

- When you do not know the type of operating system or software installed on a recipient's computer, send text-only documents in rich text format (indicated by the file suffix **.rtf**), which preserves most formatting and is recognized by many word-processing programs.

- Attachments are notorious for transmitting computer viruses; therefore, never open an attachment sent by someone you do not know or any attachment if your computer does not have active antivirus software. You can get virus-related updates and alerts on the website for your computer's operating system or from suppliers such as McAfee and Symantec.

❶ CAUTION

E-mail messages that you send from or receive at your workplace are not necessarily private or secure. For this reason, avoid using your work e-mail for personal communications, whether you are forwarding someone else's private message to you or sending jokes, chain letters, or petitions for good causes. Employers have been vindicated in cases in which they were charged with privacy violations for reading employees' e-mail. Most companies and organizations have an e-mail policy specifying employees' responsibilities and appropriate employer responses to violations of the policy. Be sure you know what the policy of your employer is.

19d   RÉSUMÉS

A **résumé** is essentially an argument (Chapter 7) designed to emphasize a person's job qualifications by highlighting his or her experience and abilities. Along with its accompanying letter of application (19e), a résumé should command attention and establish a positive first impression—immediately. Most interviewers say they spend less than a minute scanning each résumé as they search for what exactly the applicant can contribute to the organization. Thus, your résumé should be easy to read, with clear headings, adequate white space, and traditional format. It should also highlight the parts of your education and experience and the particular skills that best suit the specific position you are applying for.

Writing an impressive résumé requires smart choices about what to include, exclude, and emphasize. Start by placing all your contact information at the top center of the page, including your name, address, phone number(s), and e-mail address. Then, briefly state your career objective, including short-term as well as long-term goals, if appropriate. In the next section, establish a strong link between you and the organization to which you are applying, leading with your work or educational experience, whichever one is more suitable. (No matter what you decide to present first, you need to include information about both kinds of experience.) Many college students showcase their educational background, including their degrees or diplomas, special honors, participation in advanced programs, grade point average (either in general or in their major), and relevant courses. List your extra-curricular activities if they relate directly to the position for which you are applying or demonstrate distinctive leadership, athletic, or artistic abilities. When describing your work experience, include all your jobs (paying, volunteer, and internships, as well as military service). Include dates, places of employment, and job titles, describing your duties with active verbs (**24c(2)**) that emphasize your initiative and your sense of responsibility.

Once you have listed all of your potentially relevant work and educational information, decide what to exclude, include, and emphasize by reviewing what the specific job advertisement says about desired experience and traits. To familiarize yourself with a company's goals and philosophy, check its website. If you create and save your résumé as a word-processing file, you can easily tailor it to various positions during your job search.

The next step is to decide how to organize your résumé. A **chronological résumé** lists positions and activities in *reverse* chronological order; that is, your most recent experience comes first. This format works well if you have a steady job history and want to emphasize your most recent experience because it is closely related to the position for which you are applying. An alternative way to organize a résumé is to list experience in terms of job skills rather than jobs held. This format, called a **functional résumé**, is especially useful when you have the required skills, but your work history in the particular field is modest or you are just starting your career.

Regardless of the format you choose, remember that your résumé is, in effect, going to someone's office for a job interview. Make sure that it is dressed for success. Effective résumés are brief, so try to design your résumé to fit on a single page. Use good-quality paper (preferably white or off-white) and a laser printer. Choose a standard format and a traditional typeface, applying them consistently throughout. Use boldface or italic type only for headings. Remember that your choices regarding indentations, spacing, white space, typeface, and margins contribute to the overall readability and effectiveness of your résumé. Resist the impulse to make the design unnecessarily complicated: when in doubt, opt for simplicity.

🖥 *TECH SAVVY*

When you are ready to create your résumé, you may find it helpful to use a software program (such as Résumé Wizard from Microsoft) that allows you to select the kind of résumé you need and then prompts you to complete the various sections. Such software also allows you to view your completed document in its entirety and redesign any or all of it. Some job applicants create an **online résumé**, a web-based version that may include links to documents representative of the applicant's work. In addition, these applicants create a non-web version to be downloaded and printed out and possibly scanned into a résumé database. If a job advertisement instructs you to e-mail your résumé, you should send both a web-based and a non-web version (in case the recipient wants to print it out for any reason).

Joe Delaney's résumé (Figure 19.3) incorporates features of both the chronological and the functional formats. He starts with his education, then proceeds to a description of his computer skills, clubs, and activities because those skills and experiences relate directly to the position he is applying for; his library job, which he lists later, is less relevant.

Joseph F. Delaney III
138 Main Street, Apt. 10D
Cityville, PA 16800
(555) 544-9988
JoeDel4@psu.edu

OBJECTIVE   To obtain a position specializing in project and risk management

EDUCATION
Pennsylvania State University, University Park, PA, 2003–2007
Majors: IST BS (Information Context Option), Psychology BS
Dean's List: Summer 2006, Fall 2006, and Spring 2007
Cumulative GPA: 3.60
Relevant Classes:
- Project Management in Technology—dealt with the application of basic concepts and tools of project management to the information sciences
- Database Management—managed a project team that applied MySql, PHP, and HTML in completing Rabble Mosaic Creator, described at www.schoolproject.psu.edu/~100

COMPUTER AND TECHNICAL SKILLS
- MySql, PHP, GD Library, C++ (2 years experience), Java (1 year experience)
- TCP/IP, network security, LANs and WANs
- HTML, XML, and project and risk management

CLUBS/ACTIVITIES
IST Student Government:
- Regular participation in the student government's Academic Committee
- Student resource for the IST Student Executive Board
IST Academic Committee:
- Participated in regularly scheduled meetings with the dean, Henry C. Foley, and the professor in charge, John Yen
- Worked with the administration to address students' problems

WORK EXPERIENCE
Penn State Pollock Library, University Park, PA, May–July 2006
- Assisted patrons of the library in using computers, printers, and the Internet via a wireless network using VPN
- Coordinated computers in my designated area and assisted with defragmenting, rebooting, reformatting, charging, and normal maintenance of laptops

HONORS
- 2005 scholarship student in the College of IST; recipient of the Cingular Wireless Trustee Scholarship
- Pollock Library 2006 student employee of the year

Figure 19.3. Sample résumé.

TIPS FOR RÉSUMÉ WRITING

- Include your name, address, telephone number, e-mail address, and a fax number, if available.

- Identify your career or job objective, but only if you have a compelling one. A résumé can be effective without a career objective. You can provide details about your future plans when you are asked about them during an interview.

- Whenever possible, establish a clear relationship between jobs you have had and the job you are seeking, connecting tasks and responsibilities that most closely correspond with the position you seek.

- List your college or university degree and any pertinent areas in which you have had special training, highlighting educational details that best demonstrate your qualifications for the job at hand. Consider including your GPA (your overall GPA or your GPA in your major, whichever is more impressive), particular coursework (list specific classes or note areas of specialization, such as twenty hours of coursework in accounting), and relevant class projects.

- Do not include personal data such as age, marital status, race, religion, or ethnicity.

- Even if an advertisement or posting asks you to state a salary requirement, avoid any mention of salary in your résumé. That topic is usually deferred until an interview or a job offer.

- The names and addresses of **references** (people who have agreed to speak or write on your behalf) are not usually listed on a résumé, though you may want to mention that references are available on request. Instead, job candidates are advised to take a list of references to interviews. Make sure that the individuals on your list understand the nature of the position you are seeking. The list should include their names and addresses as well as their telephone numbers and/or e-mail addresses.

- To show that you are well organized and thoughtful, use a clean, clear format (see page 477).

- Meticulously proofread your résumé before sending it, and have others read it carefully as well. Errors in business writing always detract from your credibility, but errors in a résumé or letter of application (19e) can destroy your chances of getting an interview.

19e LETTERS OF APPLICATION

Writing a letter of application, or cover letter, is an essential step in applying for a job. Because this letter usually accompanies a résumé (**19d**), it is crucial that it guide the reader to the relevant high points of the résumé, rather than repeating that information. Your letter of application provides you with the chance to sound articulate, interesting, and professional, and to put a personal face on the factual content of the résumé—in other words, to make a good first impression. (See Figure 19.4 for a sample letter of application.)

In your opening paragraph, identify the position you are applying for, explain how you learned about it, and—in a single sentence—state why you believe you are qualified to fill it. This statement serves as the thesis for the rest of the letter. In the paragraphs that follow, describe the specific ways your education, experience, and abilities qualify you for the position. Remember, your reader wants to find out quickly what exactly you can contribute to his or her organization. Generally, two body paragraphs follow the introductory paragraph: one describing relevant education, the other relevant work experience. (Many applicants find that their education and their work experience are not equally pertinent to the job at hand. In that case, you might use these two paragraphs to describe two particular course projects or two particular jobs.) In your closing paragraph, offer any additional useful information and make a direct request for an interview.

Letters of application follow the general format of all business letters (**19b**).

Joseph F. Delaney III
138 Main Street, Apt 10D
Cityville, PA 16800
June 4, 2007

Mr. Jim Konigs, Human Resource Director
E. G. Hickey Technical Enterprise
333 Cumberville State Road, Suite 110
West Cumberville, PA 19428-2949

Dear Mr. Konigs:

I am applying for the position of project manager advertised on Monster.
com. I graduated on May 15 with a B.S. degree in information sciences
and technology from Pennsylvania State University. I believe that my
in-depth research and education in information technology make me an
ideal candidate for this position.

I have completed the required coursework and an internship in
information technology, consulting, and security, working under such
distinguished professors as James Wendle and David Markison. I am
currently a teaching instructor with Dr. Markison, responsible for
student evaluation and advising. I have served as a project team leader in
database management; my team created Rabble Mosaic Creator, a Web
site that allows users to create mosaics out of images.

In addition to my studies, I have applicable experience as a member of
the student government's Academic Committee, which analyzes students'
problems in light of policy before presenting the issues to the dean and
professor in charge. I have also worked in the Penn State libraries.

I would appreciate the opportunity to talk with you about the position and
my interest in risk and project management. I am available for an interview
and can be reached at the phone number or e-mail address at the top of my
résumé.

Sincerely,

Joseph F. Delaney

Joseph F. Delaney III

Encl.: résumé

Figure 19.4. Model letter of application. (© 2013 Cengage Learning)

TIPS FOR WRITING LETTERS OF APPLICATION

- Address your letter to a specific person. If you are responding to an ad that mentions a department without giving a name, call the company and find out who will be doing the screening. If you cannot obtain a specific name, use an appropriate title such as *Human Resources Director* (not italicized).

- Be brief. You can assume that the recipient will be screening many applications, so keep your letter to one easy-to-read page.

- Mention that you are enclosing a résumé or refer to it, but do not summarize it. Your goal is to attract the attention of a busy person (who will not want to read the same information in both your letter and your résumé).

- Indicate why you are interested in working for the company or organization to which you are applying. Demonstrating that you already know something about the company and the position, that you can contribute to it, indicates your seriousness and motivation. If you want more information about the company, locate an annual report and other information by searching the web (8d).

- In your closing, be sure to specify how and where you can be reached and emphasize your availability for an interview.

19f ‖ ORAL PRESENTATIONS WITH POWERPOINT

Oral reports accompanied by PowerPoint presentations are commonplace in business. Such reports can be either internal (for supervisors and colleagues) or external (for clients or investors). They may take the form of project status reports, demonstrations of new equipment or software, research reports, or recommendations.

Keep in mind the following guidelines as you compose an oral report and create PowerPoint slides to accompany it.

ELEMENTS OF A STANDARD ORAL PRESENTATION

- **Introduction.** Taking no more than one-tenth of your overall presentation time (for example, one minute of a ten-minute presentation), your introduction should indicate who you are, your qualifications, your topic, and the relevance of that topic to your audience. The introduction provides an outline of your main points so that listeners can easily follow your presentation.

- **Body.** Make sure the organization of your presentation is clear through your use of transitions. You can number each point (*first, second, third,* and so on) and use cause-and-consequence transitions (*therefore, since, due to*) and chronological transitions (*before, following, next, then*). Provide internal summaries to remind your listeners where you have been and where you are going and offer comments to help your audience sense the weight of various points (for example, "Not many people realize that ..." or "The most important thing I have to share is ...").

- **Conclusion.** Anyone can simply restate the main ideas in the conclusion to an oral presentation; you will want to consider ways to make your conclusion memorable. To do so, you may want to end with a proposal for action, a final statistic, recommendations, or a description of the benefits of a certain course of action. In general, conclusions should be even shorter than introductions.

TIPS FOR INCORPORATING POWERPOINT INTO AN ORAL PRESENTATION

- Design your slides for your audience, not for yourself. If you need speaking notes for your talk, write them on note cards or type them into the notes section provided below each slide in the PowerPoint program.

- Use text and visuals on the PowerPoint slides that complement the oral part of your presentation and do not repeat what you have said. If everything you are saying is on the slides, your audience will skim each slide and then become bored listening to you catch up.

- Be aware of the limitations of PowerPoint. For example, PowerPoint slides do not accommodate large amounts of text. In general, use no more than five lines of text per slide. Because PowerPoint tends to encourage oversimplification of information, be sure to tell your audience whenever you had to simplify the information presented on a slide (for example, in order to fit time constraints) and let them know where they can find more details.

- In general, keep text and visuals separate. Alternating predominantly visual slides with slides of text will keep your audience's attention. Let visuals (charts, pictures, or graphs) stand alone with just a heading or a title. Use text slides to define terms, to present block quotes that might be difficult to follow orally, and to list the main points you will be making.

- Time your speaking with your presentation of the slides so that the two components are synchronized. Make sure to give your audience enough time to absorb complex visuals.

Student Emily Cohen and fellow group members created Power-Point slides to accompany an oral presentation in a business class in which they were writing a business plan. The group created a draft set of slides, then realized that the slides did not follow basic guidelines for effective PowerPoint presentations. Figure 19.5 shows two slides from the first draft of the presentation. Figure 19.6 shows the same slides, revised so that they better serve as visuals accompanying an oral presentation. Emily's group revised the slides in several ways:

- Using a solid background color and a contrasting typeface to make reading easier
- Limiting the slides to one sans-serif typeface
- Writing more concise bulleted points to cover main ideas
- Removing subpoints that were discussed in the presentation
- Making all bulleted items parallel in structure (by starting each point with an active verb)
- Incorporating simple graphics created with PowerPoint software

Figure 19.5. These PowerPoint slides incorporate too much text, and the blue-on-blue design makes the text hard to read. Unnecessary repetition of the subpoints in the lower slide adds clutter and distracts listeners from what the presenter is saying.

Figure 19.6. A more precise title and concise bulleted points will help audience members skim, not read, the upper slide, letting them focus more on what the presenter is saying. Reducing the amount of text and using contrasting colors make slides easier to read.

19g | BUSINESS REPORTS

Business reports take many forms, including periodic reports, sales reports, progress reports, incident reports, and longer reports that assess relocation plans, new lines of equipment or products, marketing schemes, and so on. The following box describes elements of such reports.

ELEMENTS OF A STANDARD BUSINESS REPORT

- **Front matter.** Depending on the audience, purpose, and length of a given report, the front matter materials may include a letter of transmittal (explaining the relevance of the report), a title page, a table of contents, a list of illustrations, and/or an abstract.

- **Introduction.** This section should identify the problem addressed by the report (the rhetorical opportunity), present background information about it, and include a purpose statement and a description of the scope of the report (a list of the limits that framed the investigation). In a long report, each of these elements may be several paragraphs long, and some may have their own subheadings. An introduction should not take up more than ten to fifteen percent of the length of a report.

- **Body or discussion.** This, the longest section of the report, presents the research findings. It often incorporates charts and graphs to help make the data easy to understand. This section should be subdivided into clear subsections by subheadings or, for a shorter report, paragraph breaks.

- **Conclusion(s).** This section summarizes any conclusions and generalizations deduced from the data presented in the body of the report.

- **Recommendation(s).** Although not always necessary, a section that outlines what should be done with or about the findings is included in many business reports.

- **Back matter.** Like the front matter, the back matter of a report depends on the audience, purpose, and length of the report. Back matter may include a glossary, a list of the references cited, and/or one or more appendixes.

In the following sample business report, a student makes recommendations for changes in a business communication curriculum based on research into day-to-day business practices.

Changing Forms of Business Communication:
Implications for Business Communication Curricula

Joseph F. Delaney III

Penn State University

June 11, 2007

2

Table of Contents

3

Abstract

American businesses gain a competitive advantage in today's global economy by properly and effectively using various means of business communication. The use of different communication strategies in the workplace is essential to the success of businesses ranging from large corporations to on-campus student technology centers. Thus, any successful business education program must also prepare students to use and choose between the diverse media available for business communication today. This report discusses the strengths and weaknesses of different communication modes such as telephone, e-mail, and face-to-face communication, relying largely on an in-depth study of the Computer Store at Penn State University. Based on research and observations of staff, managers, and executives of the organization, the research team developed some strategies for successful business communication, in particular a critique of the overuse of e-mail in business settings. Finally, this report proposes changes to the business communication curriculum at Penn State University, in light of the team's research into real-world business communication practices.

Introduction

Background

Business communication is constantly evolving as technology provides new methods of communication. In the past two decades, e-mail, instant messaging, video conferencing, and cell phone technology have allowed colleagues to cooperate with unparalleled efficiency. The number of e-mails sent daily in 2006 was estimated at around 62 billion. The

4

International Data Corporation has also reported 600 billion minutes of usage per year by mobile phone users (Berkeley School of Information Management and Systems, 2003, p. 10). However, these new methods have not replaced more traditional forms of communication. The average office worker uses about 12,000 sheets of paper per year. With so many options available, it is sometimes difficult to choose the best one for a given situation. Furthermore, the range of options for communication necessitates changes to business communication curricula.

Problem

In the world of modern business, it can be difficult to choose between memos, telephone calls, voice mails, e-mails, meetings, and other modes of communication. All too often employees choose a form of communication that may not be properly suited to their purpose. More specifically, e-mail is easy to use, but at the same time it leads to impersonal interactions between the sender and the receiver. Many employees use e-mail when contacting individuals they are not closely acquainted with, such as new clients. The problem with this strategy is that, in business, building relationships and networking are valuable activities and can increase productivity and quality throughout an organization.

Jeremy Burton, Vice-President of VERITAS Software Corporation in Silicon Valley, like many other executives, has taken this issue to heart. Burton banned e-mails on Fridays, imposing a small fine for each e-mail sent. Though his 240 employees initially resisted the change, they began to think more critically about their communication with others, and productivity increased (Walker, 2004). The real problem, however, is that this kind of critical thinking should be encouraged before employees reach the workforce. Business communication skills like those that innovative employers like Burton are teaching their employees should be addressed in college coursework, not just on the job. The research team believes that the Penn State College of Business is not currently addressing this need.

Purpose

The object of this report is to encourage the College of Business at Penn State to consider changes to the business communication curriculum. Specifically, this report examines a few major forms of communication, evaluates their strengths and weaknesses, and gives suggestions for when and how to use them effectively. This analysis shows that such topics need to be more thoroughly addressed in business classes at Penn State. The analysis is followed by a set of recommendations for the college.

Scope

This report includes a general analysis of various types of communication and their uses. A case study of communication practices at Penn State's Computer Store examines, in particular, e-mail overuse and some factors that may contribute to it. The report shows the value of employees who can properly identify appropriate communication strategies and media. The recommendations suggest the relevance and consequences of the findings for the business curriculum at Penn State.

Discussion

Successful Business Communication

Like those at many other contemporary businesses, the employees of the Computer Store at Penn State University use many forms of

6

communication. As Robin Becker, the Director of Sales and Marketing, said, "There is no one ideal form of communication" (personal communication, June 5, 2007). Besides e-mail, the Computer Store uses three effective forms of communication for communicating with clients. During in-house technical consulting, employees assist students and parents in person as they purchase and learn to use a laptop. Second, consultants use the telephone to advise individuals about purchasing laptops and accessories. The last medium, which has taken off recently, is the store's website. The Computer Store website has become a very useful tool for assisting people in their decision making and preparing them for computer ownership, and it complements the first two methods for communicating with clients. The site helps the meeting with a consultant run more smoothly, whether it takes place face to face or over the phone.

As for communication between workers at the Computer Store, no one form is ideal. Table 1 shows the different modes of communication and ranks their appropriateness for different purposes. Generally, e-mail is used for follow-ups or quick notes. For other tasks, such as negotiating with a corporation to make its software available to all Penn State students, a face-to-face conference or a conference call is preferred. For passing quick notes and bits of information within the Computer Store, Becker explains, e-mail or instant messaging works best (personal communication, June 5, 2007). James Murphy, team leader for the consultants, advised, "Use a mix [of communication], try not to limit yourself to one style, and try to cater to other people. If I need to get a lot of information across, I'll write a memo and send it via e-mail, but if I

7

Table 1

Business Communication Methods

How Well Method Is Suited To:	Hard Copy	Phone Call	Voice Mail	E-mail	Meeting	Web-site
Assessing commitment	3	2	3	3	1	3
Building consensus	3	2	3	3	1	3
Mediating a conflict	3	2	3	3	1	3
Resolving a misunderstanding	3	1	3	3	2	3
Addressing negative behavior	3	2	3	2	1	3
Expressing support/ appreciation	1	2	2	1	2	3
Encouraging creative thinking	2	3	3	1	3	3
Making an ironic statement	3	2	2	3	1	3
Conveying a reference document	1	3	3	3	3	2
Reinforcing one's authority	1	2	3	3	1	1
Providing a permanent record	1	3	3	1	3	3
Maintaining confidentiality	2	1	2	3	1	3
Conveying simple information	3	1	1	1	2	3
Asking an informational question	3	1	1	1	3	3
Making a simple request	3	1	1	1	3	3
Giving complex instructions	3	3	2	2	1	2
Addressing many people	2	2	2	2	3	1

Key: 1 = Excellent   2 = Adequate   3 = Inappropriate
Note. From *Email Composition and Communication (EMC2)* by T. Galati.
Practical Communications, Inc. (www.praccom.com), 2001.

just need to get across one thing to one person, I will walk over there and tell that person face to face" (personal communication, June 5, 2007).

Research into business communication confirms the necessity of the Computer Store's reliance on modes of communication other than e-mail. When working with a large number of people, businesses need to be able to get a message across accurately and promptly. If a message is misinterpreted by just one individual, a large-scale problem might result. When an e-mail message requires immediate attention, some businesses, like the Computer Store, address the problem of delayed response by using instant messaging.

Though instant messaging may alleviate in-house communication lapses, other media, like websites, are more suited to reaching foreign audiences. Foreign investment by U.S. companies was approximately $9 trillion in 1966 but had grown to $300 trillion in 2002 (Blalock, 2005). This rising foreign investment by U.S. companies has increased the need for better global communication media. Though the Penn State Computer Store is, for the most part, not communicating on a global scale, its practices demonstrate the same need for a variety of communication media, without an uncritical overreliance on e-mail.

E-mail Overuse

Many factors go into choosing the proper medium for a given situation, such as privacy concerns, size of the group, type of information, and desired level of immediacy. People tend to overuse e-mail because it is an easy, inexpensive way to send information to several people. When asked why sending an e-mail to a large group is not as effective as sending one to a small group, CIO Carol Hildenbrand, answered:

9

As a group increases in size, you have a whole slew of management challenges. Communicating badly exponentially increases the possibility of making fatal mistakes. A large-scale project has a lot of moving parts, which makes it that much easier to break down. Communication is the oil that keeps everything working properly. It's much easier to address an atmosphere of distrust among a group of five team members than it is with a team of 500 members. (Schwalbe, 2006, p. 399)

Information distribution, therefore, involves more than creating and sending status reports, and different media are suited to different contexts, purposes, and audiences. Table 1 shows some findings about the suitability of forms of communication to particular business goals, but each situation should be assessed individually.

Implementation of Communication Strategies

One of the most important functions of business communication is to transfer information from one level in a hierarchy to another: from employee to manager, for example, or vice versa. After examining the functioning of the Penn State Computer Store, the research team found that it had a very effective communication structure. Employees shared their insights as to how different kinds of information are conveyed through different media. Ideas, proposals, and other important information are generally communicated in person or over the phone. E-mail is relied on for notifications and follow-ups, but not for complex tasks where interactivity and collaboration are desired.

10

Personal Relationships

It is vital for a business to build successful relationships that might prove beneficial in the future. Yet in today's workplace, it is becoming harder to develop a network of relationships because of the overuse of e-mail. The Penn State Computer Store avoids this problem by having employees within the office interact face to face. The store also maintains good relationships with customers at other campuses by sending out consultants to meet with them. Face-to-face communication creates perceived added value for the store's services and products. When a consumer buys a product or a warranty from the Computer Store, he or she reaps the benefits of the store's strong network of coworkers who have good communication skills.

Conclusion

Over the past few decades, modes of communication have changed rapidly. When we have something to say, we have the option of sending an instant message or an e-mail, making a phone call, sending a text message, posting information on a web site or a blog, or even creating a podcast. The rise of these new means of communication has posed some problems for businesses that are not operating with a high level of efficiency. Without employees who can both use the technologies and, more importantly, choose the most fitting technology for a given situation, businesses will not be able to communicate efficiently either internally or externally, with clients and other businesses.

Research at the Penn State Computer Store showed that each form of communication has its own benefits and drawbacks. If an important

11

message needs to be conveyed, a face-to-face meeting is recommended.
If an employee wants to check with a supervisor before leaving the office
for an hour, an instant message is sufficient. However, there is an
overuse of e-mail, which has become a mode used between people who
are unfamiliar with each other and are likely, if using this medium, to
remain that way. This impersonality may hurt businesses because
networking and building relationships are crucial to business success.

Recommendation

Overview of the Problem

Business curricula are not devoting enough time to teaching
potential new employees strategies and procedures for communicating
properly through different media. This issue needs to be addressed
immediately by the College of Business at Penn State.

Possible Solutions

The way to correct this problem is to increase the amount of business
communication courses offered in the College of Business. The
inclusion of more communication-oriented material will increase
graduates' abilities to begin and maintain careers in the business world.
The curriculum should cover topics such as the use and misuse of
e-mail and the advantages and disadvantages thereof. Courses should
cover networking within businesses and explore how this networking
can create successful relationships among employees. The curriculum
should also present students with multiple opportunities to work in
groups using various media as well as the opportunity to develop their
communication skills before entering the business community.

12

Benefits

Implementation of this new curriculum will put Penn State business students in an enviable position for future employment with successful companies. Businesses need employees well versed in communication techniques crucial to a global market. Penn State students will be well placed with these revisions to the business communication curriculum. Ultimately, as Penn State students achieve more success in business, the prestige and reputation of the College of Business will continue to grow.

13

References

Berkeley School of Information Management and Systems. (2003). *Executive summary: How much information?* Retrieved from http://www2.sims .berkeley.edu/research/projects/how-much-info-2003/execsum.htm

Blalock, M. (2005, December 23). *Why good communication is good business.* Retrieved from http://www.bus.wisc.edu/update/winter05 /business_communication.asp

Schwalbe, K. (2006). *Information technology project management* (4th ed.). Waterloo, Ontario, Canada: Thomson Course Technology.

Walker, M. (2004, August 26). The day the e-mail dies. *The Wall Street Journal Online.* Retrieved from http://www.lucid-minds.com/public /p66.htm

G

GRAMMAR

yo-ichi/Veer

◉ *TECH SAVVY*

Using a Grammar Checker

Most word-processing programs have a grammar checker, which can help you identify grammar errors as well as problems with usage and style; however, any grammar checker has significant limitations. A grammar checker will usually identify

- fused sentences, sometimes called run-on sentences (Chapter 23),
- some misused prepositions (34c),
- wordy or overly long sentences (32a and 35a), and
- missing apostrophes in contractions (38b).

However, a grammar checker can easily miss

- sentence fragments (Chapter 22),
- problems with adverbs or adjectives (26a),
- misplaced or dangling modifiers (26d and 26e),
- problems with pronoun-antecedent agreement (25c),
- errors in subject-verb agreement (24e), and
- misused or missing commas (Chapter 36).

Because these errors can weaken your credibility as a writer, you should never rely solely on a grammar checker to find them. Furthermore, grammar checkers can mark as wrong words or phrases that are actually correct. Some of these "errors" may be choices you have made deliberately to suit your rhetorical situation (Chapter 1).

Used carefully, a grammar checker can be a helpful tool, but keep the following advice in mind:

- Use a grammar checker only in addition to your own editing and proofreading. When in doubt, consult the appropriate chapters in this handbook.
- Always evaluate any sentences flagged by a grammar checker to determine whether there is, in fact, a problem.
- Adjust the settings on your grammar checker to look for specific types of errors. If you are using Microsoft Word, select Tools; then select either Spelling and Grammar or Options to customize your settings.
- Carefully review the revisions proposed by a grammar checker before accepting them. Sometimes the proposed revisions create new errors.

20 | SENTENCE ESSENTIALS

When you think of the word *grammar*, you might also think of the word *rule*—a regulation that you must obey. But *rule* has another meaning: "a description of what is true in most cases." A grammar rule, then, describes how language is commonly or conventionally used. However, what is appropriate in one rhetorical situation (Chapter 1) may not be appropriate in another. To know which rules to follow, you must first determine your intended audience, overall purpose, and specific context. Once you establish your rhetorical situation, you will be ready to select from the array of words and word arrangements the English language offers. By also learning basic grammar terms and concepts, you will better understand how to choose among the options available to you.

This chapter will help you

- identify the parts of speech (**20a**),
- recognize the essential parts of a sentence (**20b**),
- identify complements (**20c**), and
- recognize basic sentence patterns (**20d**).

20a | PARTS OF SPEECH

When you look up a word in the dictionary, you will often find it followed by one or more of these labels: *adj., adv., conj., interj., n., prep., pron.,* and *v* (or *vb.*). These are the abbreviations for the traditional eight parts of speech: *adjective, adverb, conjunction, interjection, noun, preposition, pronoun,* and *verb*.

(1) Verbs

Verbs that indicate action (*walk, drive, study*) are called **action verbs**. Verbs that express being or experiencing are called **linking verbs**; they include *be, seem,* and *become* and the sensory verbs *look, taste, smell,* *feel,* and *sound.* Both action verbs and linking verbs are frequently accompanied by **auxiliary** or **helping verbs** that add shades of meaning, such as information about time (*will* study this afternoon), ability (*can* study), or obligation (*must* study). See Chapter **24** for more details about verbs.

The dictionary (base) form of most action verbs fits into this frame sentence:

We should _____ (it). [With some verbs, it is not used.]

The dictionary (base) form of most linking verbs fits into this frame sentence:

It can _____ good (terrible, fine).

❓ *THINKING RHETORICALLY*

VERBS

Decide which of the following sentences evokes a clearer image.

The team captain **was** absolutely ecstatic.

Grinning broadly, the team captain **shot** both her arms into the air.

You probably chose the sentence with the action verb *shot* rather than the sentence with *was.* Most writers avoid using the verb *be* in any of its forms (*am, is, are, was, were,* or *been*) when their rhetorical situation calls for vibrant imagery. Instead, they use vivid action verbs.

(2) Nouns

Nouns usually name people, places, things, or ideas. **Proper nouns** are specific names. You can identify them easily because they are capitalized: *Bill Gates, Redmond, Microsoft Corporation.* **Common nouns** refer to any member of a class or category: *person, city, company.* There are three types of common nouns.

- **Count nouns** refer to people, places, things, and ideas that can be counted. They have singular and plural forms: *boy, boys; park, parks; car, cars; concept, concepts.*

- **Noncount nouns** refer to things or ideas that cannot be counted: *furniture, information.*
- **Collective nouns** are nouns that can be either singular or plural, depending on the context: *The **committee** published its report* [singular]. *The **committee** disagree about their duties* [plural]. (See **24e(7)**.)

Most nouns fit into this frame sentence:

(The) _____ is (are) important (unimportant, interesting, uninteresting).

❓ *THINKING RHETORICALLY*

NOUNS

Nouns like *entertainment* and *nutrition* refer to concepts. They are called **abstract nouns**. In contrast, nouns like *guitar* and *apple* refer to things perceivable by the senses. They are called **concrete nouns**. When your rhetorical situation calls for the use of abstractions, balance them with tangible details conveyed through concrete nouns. For example, if you use the abstract nouns *impressionism* and *cubism* in an art history paper, also include concrete nouns that will enable readers to visualize the colors, shapes, and brushstrokes of the paintings you are discussing.

(3) Pronouns

Pronouns function as nouns, and most pronouns (*it, he, she, they,* and many others) refer to nouns that have already been mentioned. These nouns are called **antecedents** (**25c**).

My parents bought the cheap, decrepit house because **they** thought **it** had charm.

A pronoun and its antecedent may be found either in the same sentence or in separate, though usually adjacent, sentences.

The <u>students</u> collaborated on a research project last year. **They** even presented their findings at a national conference.

The pronouns in the preceding examples are called **personal pronouns**. There are also several other types of pronouns: indefinite, possessive, relative, interrogative, and reflexive/intensive. For a detailed discussion of pronouns, see Chapter **25**.

(4) Adjectives

Adjectives most commonly modify nouns: *spicy* food, *cold* day, *special* price. Sometimes they modify pronouns: *blue* ones, any-one *thin*. Adjectives usually answer one of these questions: Which one? What kind of . . . ? How many? What color (or size or shape, and so on)? Although adjectives usually precede the nouns they modify, they occasionally follow them: *enough* time, time *enough*. Adjectives may also follow linking verbs such as *be, seem,* and *become*:

The <u>moon</u> is **full** tonight.   <u>He</u> seems **shy.**

When an adjective follows a linking verb, it modifies the subject of the sentence (**20b**).

Most adjectives fit into one of these frame sentences:

He told us about a/an _____ idea (person, place).

The idea (person, place) is very _____.

Articles are a subclass of adjectives because, like adjectives, they are used before nouns. There are three articles: *a, an,* and *the.* The article *a* is used before a consonant sound (**a** yard, **a** university, **a** VIP); *an* is used before a vowel sound (**an** apple, **an** hour, **an** NFL team).

For a detailed discussion of adjectives, see **26a**.

ñ *MULTILINGUAL WRITERS*

ARTICLE USAGE

English has two types of articles: indefinite and definite. The **indefinite articles** *a* and *an* indicate that a singular noun is used in a general way, as when you introduce the noun for the first time or when you define a word:

> Pluto is **a** dwarf <u>planet</u>.

> There has been **a** <u>controversy</u> over the classification of Pluto.

> **A** <u>planet</u> is a celestial body orbiting a star such as our sun.

The **definite article**, *the,* is used before a noun that has already been introduced or when a reference is obvious. *The* is also used before a noun that is related in form or meaning to a word mentioned previously.

> Scientists distinguish between planets and <u>dwarf planets</u>. Three of **the** <u>dwarf planets</u> in our solar system are Ceres, Pluto, and Eris.

> Scientists were not sure how to <u>classify</u> some celestial bodies. **The** <u>classification</u> of Pluto proved to be particularly controversial.

The definite article also appears before a noun considered unique, such as *moon, universe, solar system, sun, earth,* or *sky.*

> **The** <u>moon</u> is full tonight.

For more information on articles, see Chapter 45.

(5) Adverbs

Adverbs most frequently modify verbs. They provide information about time, manner, place, and frequency, thus answering one of these questions: When? How? Where? How often?

The conference <u>starts</u> **tomorrow.** [time]

I **rapidly** <u>calculated</u> the cost. [manner]

We <u>met</u> **here.** [place]

They **often** <u>work</u> late on Thursdays. [frequency]

Adverbs that modify verbs can often move from one position in a sentence to another.

He **carefully** removed the radio collar.

He removed the radio collar **carefully.**

> Most adverbs that modify verbs fit into this frame sentence:
>
> They _____ moved (danced, walked) across the room.

Adverbs also modify adjectives and other adverbs by intensifying or otherwise qualifying the meanings of those words.

I was **extremely** <u>curious</u>. [modifying an adjective]

The team played **surprisingly** <u>well</u>. [modifying an adverb]

For more information on adverbs, see **26a**.

❓ *THINKING RHETORICALLY*

ADVERBS

What do the adverbs add to the following sentences?

The scientist **delicately** places the slide under the microscope.

"You're late," he whispered **vehemently.**

She is **wistfully** hopeful.

Adverbs can help you portray an action, indicate how someone is speaking, and add detail to a description.

(6) Prepositions

A **preposition** is a word that combines with a noun and any of its modifiers to establish a relationship between the words or to provide additional detail—often by answering one of these questions: Where? When?

In the early afternoon, we walked **through** our old neighborhood. [answer the questions *When?* and *Where?*]

A preposition may also combine with a pronoun.

We walked **through** it.

SOME COMMON PREPOSITIONS				
about	behind	except	of	through
above	beside	for	on	to
after	between	from	out	toward
around	by	in	over	under
as	despite	into	past	until
at	down	like	regarding	up
before	during	near	since	with

Phrasal prepositions consist of more than one word.

Except for the last day, it was a wonderful trip.

The postponement was **due to** inclement weather.

PHRASAL PREPOSITIONS		
according to	except for	in spite of
as for	in addition to	instead of
because of	in case of	with regard to
due to	in front of	with respect to

ñ **MULTILINGUAL WRITERS**

PREPOSITIONS IN IDIOMATIC COMBINATIONS

Some verbs, adjectives, and nouns combine with prepositions to form idiomatic combinations.

Verb + Preposition	Adjective + Preposition	Noun + Preposition
apply to	fond of	interest in
rely on	similar to	dependence on
trust in	different from	fondness for

(7) Conjunctions

Conjunctions are connectors; they fall into four categories: coordinating, correlative, subordinating, and adverbial.

A **coordinating conjunction** connects similar words or groups of words; that is, it generally links a word to a word, a phrase to a phrase (**21a**), or a clause to a clause (**21b**).

English **and** Spanish [*And* joins two words and signals addition.]

in school **or** at home [*Or* joins two phrases and marks them as alternatives.]

We did not share a language, **but** somehow we communicated. [*But* joins two independent clauses and signals contrast.]

There are seven coordinating conjunctions. Use the made-up word *fanboys* to help you remember them.

F	A	N	B	O	Y	S
for	and	nor	but	or	yet	so

A coordinating conjunction such as *but* may also link independent clauses (**21b(1)**) that stand alone as sentences.

The momentum in the direction of globalization seems too powerful to buck, the economic logic unmatchable. **But** in a region where jobs are draining away, and where an ethic of self-reliance remains a dim, vestigial, but honored memory, it seems at least an outside possibility.

—BILL McKIBBEN, "Small World"

A **correlative conjunction** (or **correlative**) consists of two parts. The most common correlatives are *both . . . and, either . . . or, neither . . . nor,* and *not only . . . but also.*

> **either** Pedro **or** Sue [*Either . . . or* joins two words and marks them as alternatives.]

> **neither** on the running track **nor** in the pool [*Neither . . . nor* joins two phrases and marks them both as false or impossible.]

> **Not only** did they run ten miles, **but** they **also** swam twenty laps. [*Not only . . . but also* joins two independent clauses and signals addition.]

As the preceding examples show, correlative conjunctions join words, phrases, or clauses, but they do not join sentences. Generally, a correlative conjunction links similar structures. The following sentence needed to be revised because the correlative conjunction was linking a phrase to a clause:

> Not only~~saving~~ the lives of the accident victims, **but** he **also** prevented
> many spinal injuries.
>
> *(inserted above: did he save)*

A **subordinating conjunction** introduces a dependent clause (**21b(2)**). It also carries a specific meaning; for example, it may indicate cause, concession, condition, purpose, or time. A dependent clause that begins a sentence is followed by a comma.

> **Unless** the project receives more funding, the research will stop. [*Unless* signals a condition.]

> The project continued **because** it received additional funding. [*Because* signals a cause.]

SUBORDINATING CONJUNCTIONS

after	how	than
although	if	though
as if	in case	unless
as though	in that	until
because	insofar as	when, whenever
before	once	where, wherever
even if	since	whether
even though	so that	while

The word *that* can be omitted from the subordinating conjunction *so that* if the meaning remains clear.

> I left ten minutes early **so** I would not be late. [*That* has been omitted.]

However, when *that* is omitted, the remaining *so* can be easily confused with the coordinating conjunction *so*.

> I had some extra time, **so** I went to the music store.

Because sentences with subordinating conjunctions are punctuated differently from sentences with coordinating conjunctions, be careful to distinguish between them. If *so* stands for "so that," it is a subordinating conjunction. If *so* means "thus," it is a coordinating conjunction.

Adverbial conjunctions—such as *however, nevertheless, then,* and *therefore*—link independent clauses (**21b(1)**). These conjunctions, also called **conjunctive adverbs,** signal relationships such as cause, condition, and contrast. Adverbial conjunctions are set off by commas. An independent clause preceding an adverbial conjunction may end in a semicolon instead of a period.

> The senator thought the plan was reasonable**; however,** the voters did not.
>
> . **However,** the voters did not.
>
> . The voters, **however,** did not.
>
> . The voters did not, **however.**

ADVERBIAL CONJUNCTIONS			
also	however	moreover	still
consequently	instead	nevertheless	then
finally	likewise	nonetheless	therefore
furthermore	meanwhile	otherwise	thus

(8) Interjections

Interjections most commonly express a simple exclamation or an emotion such as surprise, dread, or resignation. Interjections that come before a sentence end in a period or an exclamation point.

Oh. Now I understand.

Wow! Your design is astounding.

Interjections that begin or interrupt a sentence are set off by commas.

Hey, what are you doing?

The solution, **alas,** was not as simple as I had hoped it would be.

Exercise 1

Identify the part of speech for each word in the sentences below.

1. Hey, are you a fan of both anime and manga?
2. If you are, you should join the university's Anime and Manga Club.
3. Every Tuesday at noon, we watch current anime or swap favorite manga.
4. Membership is free; however, donations are always welcome.
5. Whenever you have time, you can simply look for us in the Student Union.

20b ‖ SUBJECTS AND PREDICATES

A sentence consists of two parts:

> SUBJECT + PREDICATE

The **subject** is generally someone or something that either performs an action or is described. The **predicate** expresses the action initiated by the subject or gives information about the subject.

The <u>landlord</u> + <u>had</u> <u>renovated</u> the apartment.
[The subject performs an action; the predicate expresses the action.]

<u>The rent</u> + <u>seemed</u> reasonable.
[The subject is described; the predicate gives information about the subject.]

The central components of the subject and the predicate are often called the **simple subject** (the main noun or pronoun) and the **simple predicate** (the main verb and any auxiliary verbs). They are underlined in the examples above.

Compound subjects and **compound predicates** include a connecting word (conjunction) such as *and, or,* or *but.*

<u>The Republicans</u> **and** <u>the Democrats</u> are debating this issue.
[compound subject]

The candidate <u>stated his views on abortion</u> **but** <u>did not discuss stem-cell research</u>. [compound predicate]

To identify the subject of a sentence, find the verb and then use it in a question beginning with *who* or *what*, as shown in the following examples.

Jennifer works at a clinic.	Meat contains cholesterol.
Verb: **works**	Verb: **contains**
Who works? **Jennifer**	*What* contains? **Meat**
(not the clinic) **works.**	(not cholesterol) **contains.**
Subject: **Jennifer**	Subject: **Meat**

Some sentences begin with an **expletive**—*there* or *it.* Such a word occurs in the subject position, forcing the true subject to follow the verb.

    exp   v   s
There were **no exercise machines.**

A subject following the expletive *it* is often an entire clause. You will learn more about clauses in Chapter **21**.

  exp v   s
It is essential **that children learn about nutrition at an early age.**

ñ *MULTILINGUAL WRITERS*

BEGINNING A SENTENCE WITH *THERE*

In sentences beginning with the expletive *there,* the verb comes before the subject. The verb *are* is often hard to hear, so be careful to include it when you write a sentence like the following:

     are
  There_∧ many good books on nutrition.

❓ *THINKING RHETORICALLY*

SUBJECT AND PREDICATES

Generally, sentences have the pattern subject + predicate. However, writers often vary this pattern to provide cohesion, emphasis, or both.

He + elbowed his way into the lobby and paused.
[subject + predicate]

From a far corner came + shrieks of laughter.
[predicate + subject]

These two sentences are cohesive because the information in the predicate that begins the second sentence is linked to information in the first sentence. The reversed pattern in the second sentence (predicate + subject) also places emphasis on the subject: *shrieks of laughter.*

| 20C | COMPLEMENTS |

Complements are parts of the predicate required by the verb to make a sentence complete. For example, the sentence *The chair of the committee presented* is incomplete without the complement *his plans*. A complement is generally a pronoun, a noun, or a noun with modifiers.

The chair of the committee introduced
- **her.** [pronoun]
- **Sylvia Holbrook.** [noun]
- **the new member.** [noun with modifiers]

There are four different types of complements: direct objects, indirect objects, subject complements, and object complements.

(1) Direct object

A **direct object** follows an action verb and either receives the action of the verb or identifies the result of the action.

Steve McQueen invented **the bucket seat** in 1960.
I. M. Pei designed **the East Building of the National Gallery.**

Compound direct objects include a connecting word, usually *and.*

Thomas Edison patented **the phonograph <u>and</u> the microphone.**

To identify a direct object, first find the subject and the verb; then use them in a question ending with *what* or *whom.*

Marie Curie discovered radium.	They hired a new engineer.
Subject and verb:	Subject and verb:
Marie Curie discovered	**They hired**
Marie Curie discovered *what*?	They hired *whom*?
radium	**a new engineer**
Direct object: **radium**	Direct object: **a new engineer**

A direct object may be a clause (**21b**).

Researchers found **that patients benefited from the new drug.**

(2) Indirect object

Indirect objects typically name the person(s) receiving or benefiting from the action indicated by the verb. Verbs that often take indirect objects include *bring, buy, give, lend, offer, sell, send,* and *write.*

The supervisor gave **the new employees** computers.
[*To whom* were the computers given?]

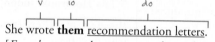

She wrote **them** recommendation letters.
[*For whom* were the recommendation letters written?]

Like subjects and direct objects, indirect objects can be compound.

She offered **Elena and Octavio** a generous benefits package.

(3) Subject complement

A **subject complement** follows a linking verb (**20a(1)**) and renames, classifies, or describes the subject. The most common linking verb is *be* (*am, is, are, was, were, been*). Other linking verbs are *become, seem,* and *appear* and the sensory verbs *feel, look, smell, sound,* and *taste.* A subject complement can be a pronoun, a noun, or a noun with modifiers. It can also be an adjective (**20a(4)**).

The winner was —
- **you.** [pronoun]
- **Harry Solano.** [noun]
- **the person with the highest score.** [noun with modifiers]
- **ecstatic.** [adjective]

(4) Object complement

An **object complement** renames, classifies, or describes a direct object and helps complete the meaning of a verb such as *call, elect, make, name,* or *paint*. The object complement can be either a noun or an adjective, along with any modifiers.

do   oc

Reporters called the rookie **the best player.** [noun with modifiers]

do   oc

His recent performance left the fans **somewhat disappointed.**
[adjective with modifier]

Exercise 2

Identify the subject and the predicate in each sentence. Then, looking just at the predicate, identify the underlined complements.

1. A naturalist gave us a short lecture on the Cascade Mountains.
2. He showed slides of mountain lakes and heather meadows.
3. Douglas fir predominates in the Cascade forests.
4. Mountaineers and artists consider the North Cascades the most dramatic mountains in the range.
5. Timberlines are low because of the short growing season.
6. Many volcanoes are in the Cascades.
7. Mt. Rainier is the highest volcano in the range.
8. Many visitors to this area hike the Pacific Crest Trail.
9. My friend lent me his map of the trail.
10. The trail begins in southern California, passes through Oregon and Washington, and ends in British Columbia.

20d   BASIC SENTENCE PATTERNS

The six basic sentence patterns presented in the following box are based on three verb types: intransitive, transitive, and linking. Notice that *trans* in the words *transitive* and *intransitive* means "over or across."

Thus, the action of a **transitive verb** carries across to an object, but the action of an **intransitive verb** does not. An intransitive verb has no complement, although it is often followed by an adverb (pattern 1). A transitive verb is followed by a direct object (pattern 2), by both a direct object and an indirect object (pattern 3), or by a direct object and an object complement (pattern 4). A linking verb (such as *be, seem, sound,* or *taste*) is followed by a subject complement (pattern 5) or by a phrase that includes a preposition (pattern 6).

BASIC SENTENCE PATTERNS

Pattern 1 SUBJECT + INTRANSITIVE VERB

Prices dropped.

Prices dropped precipitously.

Pattern 2 SUBJECT + TRANSITIVE VERB + DIRECT OBJECT

He writes detective stories.

Pattern 3 SUBJECT + TRANSITIVE VERB + INDIRECT OBJECT + DIRECT OBJECT

My father sent me a care package.

Pattern 4 SUBJECT + TRANSITIVE VERB + DIRECT OBJECT + OBJECT COMPLEMENT

The new leaders declared the country a separate nation.

Pattern 5 SUBJECT + LINKING VERB + SUBJECT COMPLEMENT

Dr. Vargas is the discussion leader.

Pattern 6 SUBJECT + LINKING VERB + PREPOSITIONAL PHRASE

They are in the library.

ⓝ MULTILINGUAL WRITERS

WORD ORDER

Some languages, such as French and Cantonese, have sentence patterns similar to English sentence patterns. These languages are called **SVO (subject-verb-object) languages**, even though not all sentences have objects. Sentence patterns differ from those of English in **SOV (subject-object-verb) languages** (such as Japanese) and **VSO (verb-subject-object) languages** (such as Arabic). Keep the SVO pattern in mind to help you write English sentences. For more on word order in English, see Chapter 47.

When declarative sentences, or statements, are turned into questions, the subject and the auxiliary verb are usually inverted; that is, the auxiliary verb is moved to the beginning of the sentence, before the subject.

Statement: A Chinese skater (has) won a gold medal.

Question: Has a Chinese skater won a gold medal?

Often, a question word such as *what* or *why* opens a question. As long as the question word is *not* the subject of the sentence, the auxiliary verb precedes the subject.

Question: What has a Chinese skater won? [*What* is the object of *has won*.]

COMPARE: Who has won a gold medal? [*Who* is the subject of the sentence.]

If a statement does not include an auxiliary verb or a form of the linking verb *be,* a form of *do* is added to produce the corresponding question. Again, the auxiliary verb is placed in front of the subject.

Statement: A Chinese skater won a gold medal.

Question: Did a Chinese skater win a gold medal?

As you study sentences more closely, you will find patterns other than the six presented in this section. For example, another pattern requires mention of a destination or location. The sentence *I put the documents* is incomplete without a phrase such as *on your desk.* Other sentences have phrases that are not essential but do add pertinent information. These phrases can sometimes be moved. For example, the phrase *on Friday* can be placed either at the beginning or at the end of the following sentence.

I finished my assignment **on Friday.**
On Friday, I finished my assignment.

To learn how to write effective sentences by varying their structure, see Chapter **32**.

ñ MULTILINGUAL WRITERS

INVERTING THE SUBJECT AND THE VERB IN QUESTIONS

English is one of a few languages in which the subject and the verb are inverted in questions. Most languages rely on intonation, rather than a change in word order, to indicate that a question is being asked. (English speakers do occasionally use uninverted questions to ask for clarification or to indicate surprise.) In languages other than English, a frequently occurring option for making a statement into a question is to add a particle (see **24a(3)**), such as the Japanese *ka.*

Exercise 3

1. Identify the basic pattern of each sentence in Exercise 2.
2. Write a question corresponding to each of the sentences. Put a check mark next to those questions in which the subject and the verb are inverted.

❓ *THINKING RHETORICALLY*

SENTENCE PATTERNS

If you want to emphasize a contrast or intensify a feeling, alter the sentence pattern by placing the direct object at the beginning of the sentence.

I acquired English at home. I learned **French** on the street.

I acquired English at home. **French** I learned on the street.

A comma is sometimes used after the direct object in such sentences.

They loved the queen. They despised **the king**.

They loved the queen. **The king**, they despised.

Exercise 4

Shift the emphasis in the underlined sentences by moving the direct objects to the beginning of the sentence.

1. Leah considers her medical studies her priority. <u>She calls her rock band a hobby</u>.

2. He learned to play the clarinet when he was eight. <u>He mastered the saxophone later on</u>.

3. They renovated the state house. <u>They condemned the old hotel</u>.

4. We played volleyball in the fall. <u>We played basketball in the winter</u>.

5. They named their first child Lewis. <u>They named their second child Clark</u>.

21 | PHRASES, CLAUSES, AND SENTENCES

Within a sentence, groups of words form phrases and clauses. Like single words, these larger units function as specific parts of speech. By understanding how word groups can serve as nouns, verbs, adjectives, or adverbs, you will be able to make your sentences clear, concise, and complete. This chapter will help you

- recognize phrases (**21a**),
- recognize clauses (**21b**), and
- identify sentence forms and functions (**21c** and **21d**).

21a | PHRASES

A **phrase** is a sequence of grammatically related words without a subject, a predicate, or both. A phrase is categorized according to its most important word. This section introduces noun phrases, verb phrases, verbal phrases, prepositional phrases, appositives, and absolute phrases.

(1) Noun phrases

A noun phrase consists of a main noun and its modifiers. It can serve as a subject (**20b**) or as a complement (**20c**). It can also be the object of a preposition such as *in, of, on, at,* and *to.* (See **20a(6)** for a longer list of prepositions.)

The heavy frost killed **many fruit trees.** [subject and direct object]

My cousin is **an organic farmer.** [subject and subject complement]

His farm is in **eastern Oregon.** [subject and object of the preposition *in*]

❓ *THINKING RHETORICALLY*

NOUN PHRASES

In the preceding example sentences, the adjectives *heavy, organic,* and *eastern* add specificity. For example, the noun phrase *an organic farmer* tells the reader more than *farmer* alone would. By composing noun phrases carefully, you will make your sentences more precise.

Much of Greenland lies within the Arctic Circle. ~~The area~~ This large island is owned by Denmark. Its name is Kaballit Nunaat. ^native

[*The area* could refer to either Greenland or the area within the Arctic Circle. *This large island* clearly refers to Greenland. *Its native name* is more precise than just *Its name*.]

ñ *MULTILINGUAL WRITERS*

NUMBER AGREEMENT IN NOUN PHRASES

Some words must agree in number with the nouns they precede. The words *a, an, this,* and *that* are used before singular nouns; *some, few, these, those,* and *many* are used before plural nouns:

an/that opportunity [singular noun]

some/few/those opportunities [plural noun]

The words *less* and *much* precede nouns representing abstract concepts or masses that cannot be counted (noncount nouns; 20a(2)):

less freedom, **much** water

For more information, see Chapter 45.

(2) Verb phrases

A verb is essential to the predicate of a sentence (**20b**). It generally expresses action or a state of being. Besides a main verb, a verb phrase includes one or more **auxiliary verbs**, sometimes called *helping verbs,* such as *be, have, do, will,* and *should.*

> The passengers **have deplaned.** [auxiliary verb + main verb]
>
> The flight **will be departing** at 7:00 p.m.
> [two auxiliary verbs + main verb]

For a comprehensive discussion of verbs, see Chapter **24**.

(3) Verbal phrases (gerund, participial, and infinitive phrases)

A **verbal phrase** differs from a verb phrase (**21a(2)**) in that the verb form in a verbal phrase serves as a noun or a modifier rather than as a verb.

> He <u>was</u> **reading** the story aloud. [*Reading* is part of the verb phrase *was reading.*]
>
> **Reading** is fundamental to academic success. [*Reading* serves as a noun. COMPARE: **It** is fundamental to academic success.]
>
> The student **reading** aloud is an education major. [*Reading aloud* modifies *the student.*]

Because of their origin as verbs, verbals in phrases often have their own complements (**20c**) and modifiers (Chapter **26**).

> He decided **to read the story aloud.** [The object of the verbal *to read* is *the story. Aloud* is a modifier.]

Verbal phrases are divided into three types: gerund phrases, participial phrases, and infinitive phrases.

Gerund phrases include a verb form ending in *-ing* (see **24a(1)**). A gerund phrase serves as a noun, usually functioning as the subject (**20b**) or the object (**20c**) in a sentence.

> **Writing a bestseller** was her only goal. [subject]
>
> My neighbor enjoys **writing about distant places.** [object]

Because gerund phrases act as nouns, pronouns can replace them.

That was her only goal.

My neighbor enjoys **it.**

❓ *THINKING RHETORICALLY*

GERUNDS

What is the difference between the following sentences?

They bundle products together, which often results in higher consumer costs.

Bundling products together often results in higher consumer costs.

In the first sentence, the actor, *they,* is the focus. In the second sentence, the action of the gerund phrase, *bundling products together,* is the focus. As you draft or revise, ask yourself whether you want to emphasize actors or actions.

Participial phrases include either a present participle (a verb form ending in *-ing*) or a past participle (a verb form ending in *-ed* for regular verbs or another form for irregular verbs). (See **24a** for more information on verb forms.)

<u>**Planning**</u> **her questions carefully,** she was able to hold fast-paced and engaging interviews. [present participle]

<u>**Known**</u> **for her interviewing skills,** she was asked to host her own radio program. [past participle]

Participial phrases function as modifiers (**26a(2)**). They may appear at the beginning, in the middle, or at the end of a sentence. In the following sentences, the participial phrases modify *farmers.*

<u>**Fearing**</u> **a drought,** the farmers used less irrigation water.

The farmers, <u>**fearing**</u> **a drought,** used less irrigation water.

Farmers conserved water, <u>**fearing**</u> **a drought.**

Remember that gerund phrases and participial phrases have different functions. A gerund phrase functions as a noun; a participial phrase functions as a modifier.

Working together can spur creativity. [gerund phrase]

Working together, the students designed their own software.
[participial phrase]

For advice on using punctuation with participial phrases, see **36d**.

---

❷ *THINKING RHETORICALLY*

PARTICIPIAL PHRASES

If some of your sentences sound monotonous or choppy, try combining them by using participial phrases.

Fans crowded along the city streets. They were celebrating their team's first state championship.

REVISED

Crowded along the city streets, fans celebrated their team's first state championship.

OR

Celebrating their team's first state championship, fans crowded along the city streets.

Infinitive phrases serve as nouns (**20a(2)**) or as modifiers (Chapter **26**). The form of an infinitive is distinct—the infinitive marker *to* is followed by the base form of the verb.

The company intends **to hire twenty new employees.** [noun]

We discussed his plan **to use a new packing process.** [modifier of the noun *plan*]

To attract customers, the company changed its advertising strategy. [modifier of the verb *changed*]

Some instructors advise against putting words between the infinitive marker *to* and the base form of the verb.

Under the circumstances, the
∧The jury was unable to~~, under the circumstances,~~ convict the defendant.

This is good advice to remember if the intervening words create a cumbersome sentence. However, most writers today recognize that a single word splitting an infinitive can provide emphasis.

He did not expect **to** actually **publish** his work.

ñ MULTILINGUAL WRITERS

VERBS FOLLOWED BY GERUNDS AND/OR INFINITIVES

Some verbs in English can be followed by a gerund, some can be followed by an infinitive, and some can be followed by either.

Verbs Followed by a Gerund

admit   avoid   consider   deny   dislike   enjoy   finish   suggest

Example: She **enjoys playing** the piano.

Verbs Followed by an Infinitive

agree   decide   deserve   hope   need   plan   promise   seem

Example: She **promised to play** the piano for us.

Verbs Followed by Either a Gerund or an Infinitive

begin   continue   like   prefer   remember   stop   try

Examples: She **likes to play** the piano. She **likes playing** the piano.

For more information on verbs and verb forms, see Chapters **24** and **46**.

(4) Prepositional phrases

Prepositional phrases are modifiers. They provide information about time, place, cause, manner, and so on. They can also answer one of these questions: Which one? What kind of . . . ?

> **With great feeling,** Martin Luther King expressed his dream **of freedom.**
> [*With great feeling* describes the way the speech was delivered, and *of freedom* specifies the kind of dream.]

> King delivered his most famous speech **at a demonstration in Washington, DC.**
> [Both *at a demonstration* and *in Washington, DC* provide information about place.]

A **prepositional phrase** consists of a **preposition** (a word such as *at, of,* or *in*) and a pronoun, noun, or noun phrase (called the **object of the preposition**). A prepositional phrase modifies another element in the sentence.

> Everyone **in class** went to the play. [modifier of the pronoun *everyone*]

> Some students met the professor **after the play.** [modifier of the verb *met*]

A prepositional phrase sometimes consists of a preposition and an entire clause (**21b**).

> They will give the award **to whoever produces the best set design.**

A grammar rule that has been controversial advises against ending a sentence with a preposition. Most professional writers now follow this rule only when they adopt a formal tone. If their rhetorical situation calls for an informal tone, they will not hesitate to place a preposition at the end of a sentence.

> He found friends **on** whom he could depend. [formal]

> He found friends he could depend **on.** [informal]

(5) Appositives

An **appositive** is most often a noun or a noun phrase that refers to the same person, place, thing, or idea as a preceding noun or noun phrase but in different words. The alternative wording either clarifies the reference or provides extra details. When the appositive simply specifies the referent, no commas are used.

> Cormac McCarthy's novel ***The Road*** won a Pulitzer Prize.
> [The appositive specifies which of McCarthy's novels won the award.]

When the appositive provides extra details, commas set it off.

> *The Road*, **a novel by Cormac McCarthy,** won a Pulitzer Prize.
> [The appositive provides extra details about the book.]

For more information on punctuating nonessential appositives, see **36d(2)**.

(6) Absolute phrases

An **absolute phrase** is usually a noun phrase modified by a prepositional phrase or a participial phrase (**21a(3)**). It provides descriptive details or expresses a cause or condition.

> <u>Her guitar</u> **in the front seat,** she pulled away from the curb.

> She left town at dawn, <u>**all her belongings**</u> **packed into a Volkswagen Beetle.**

The preceding absolute phrases provide details; the following absolute phrase expresses cause.

> **Her friend's directions lacking clarity,** she frequently checked her map.

Be sure to use commas to set off absolute phrases.

Exercise 1

Label the underlined phrases in the following sentences as noun phrases, verb phrases, prepositional phrases, or verbal phrases. For verbal phrases, specify the type: gerund, participial, or infinitive. When a long phrase includes a short phrase, identify just the long phrase. Finally, identify any appositive phrases or absolute phrases in the sentences.

1. <u>After the Second World War</u>, <u>fifty-one countries</u> formed <u>the United Nations</u>, <u>an international organization dedicated to peace, tolerance, and cooperation</u>.

2. <u>The Charter of the United Nations</u> <u>was written</u> <u>in 1945</u>.

3. <u>According to this charter</u>, the United Nations <u>may address</u> a wide range <u>of issues</u>.

4. <u>The United Nations</u> devotes most of its energies to <u>protecting human rights</u>, <u>maintaining peace</u>, and <u>encouraging social development</u>.

5. <u>To reach its goals</u>, the United Nations depends on funding <u>from its member states</u>.

6. <u>Its blue flag easily recognized everywhere</u>, the United Nations now includes <u>192 countries</u>.

7. <u>Symbolizing peace</u>, the emblem <u>on the flag</u> is a map <u>enclosed by olive branches</u>.

21b CLAUSES

(1) Independent clauses

A **clause** is a group of related words that contains a subject and a predicate. An **independent clause**, sometimes called a *main clause,* has the same grammatical structure as a simple sentence: both contain a subject and a predicate (see **20b**).

The students earned high grades.

An independent clause can stand alone as a complete sentence. Other clauses can be added to an independent clause to form a longer, more detailed sentence.

(2) Dependent clauses

A **dependent clause** also has a subject and a predicate (**20b**). However, it cannot stand alone as a complete sentence because of the word introducing it—usually a relative pronoun or a subordinating conjunction.

The athlete **who placed first** grew up in Argentina. [relative pronoun]

She received the gold medal **because she performed flawlessly.**
[subordinating conjunction]

If it is not connected to an independent clause, a dependent clause is considered a sentence fragment (**22c**).

(a) Noun clauses

Dependent clauses that serve as subjects (**20b**) or objects (**20c**) are called **noun clauses** (or **nominal clauses**). They are introduced by *if, that,* or a *wh-* word such as *what* or *why.* Notice the similarity in usage between noun phrases and noun clauses.

Noun phrases	Noun clauses
The testimony may not be true. [subject]	**What the witness said** may not be true. [subject]
We do not understand **their motives.** [direct object]	We do not understand **why they did it.** [direct object]

When no misunderstanding would result, the word *that* can be omitted from the beginning of a noun clause.

The scientist said **she was moving to Australia.** [*that* omitted]

However, *that* should always be retained when there are two noun clauses.

> The scientist said **that she was moving to Australia** and **that her research team was planning to accompany her.** [*that* retained in both noun clauses]

(b) Adjectival (relative) clauses

An **adjectival clause**, or **relative clause**, follows a pronoun, noun, or noun phrase and answers one of these questions: Which one? What kind of . . . ? Such a clause usually begins with a **relative pronoun** (*who, whom, that, which,* or *whose*). Notice the similarity in usage between adjectives and adjectival clauses.

Adjectives	Adjectival clauses
Effective supervisors give clear directions. [answers the question *Which supervisors?*]	Supervisors **who give clear directions** earn the respect of their employees. [answers the question *Which supervisors?*]
Long, complicated directions confuse employees. [answers the question *What kind of directions?*]	Directions **that are long and complicated** confuse employees. [answers the question *What kind of directions?*]

An **essential (restrictive) adjectival clause** contains information that is necessary to identify the main noun that precedes the clause. Such a clause is *not* set off by commas. The essential adjectival clause in the following sentence is needed for the reader to know which state carries a great deal of influence in a presidential election.

> The state **that casts the most electoral votes** greatly influences the outcome of a presidential election.

A **nonessential (nonrestrictive) adjectival clause** provides extra details that, even though they may be interesting, are not needed for identifying the preceding noun. An adjectival clause following a proper noun (**20a(2)**) is almost always nonessential. A nonessential adjectival clause should be set off by commas.

California**, which has fifty-five electoral votes,** greatly influences the outcome of any presidential election.

Many writers use *that* to begin essential clauses and *which* to begin nonessential clauses. Follow this convention if you are required to use APA, CMS, or MLA guidelines (although the MLA accepts *which* instead of *that* in essential clauses). For more information on the use of *which* and *that*, see **25a(3)**.

A relative pronoun can be omitted from an adjectival clause as long as the meaning of the sentence is still clear.

Mother Teresa was someone **the whole world admired.**
[*Whom,* the direct object of the clause, has been omitted: the whole world admired *whom.*]

She was someone **who cared more about serving than being served.**
[*Who* cannot be omitted because it is the subject of the clause.]

The relative pronoun is not omitted when the adjectival clause is set off by commas (that is, when it is a nonessential clause).

Mother Teresa**, whom the whole world admired,** cared more about serving than being served.

❓ THINKING RHETORICALLY

ADJECTIVAL CLAUSES

If you find that your sentences tend to be short, try using adjectival clauses to combine them into longer sentences.

Dub is a car magazine. It appeals to drivers with hip-hop attitudes.

Dub is a car magazine **that appeals to drivers with hip-hop attitudes.**

A Hovercraft can go where many vehicles cannot. It is practically amphibious.

A Hovercraft**, which can go where many vehicles cannot,** is practically amphibious.

(c) Adverbial clauses

An **adverbial clause** usually answers one of the following questions: Where? When? How? Why? How often? In what manner? Adverbial clauses are introduced by subordinating conjunctions such as *because, although,* and *when.* (For a list of subordinating conjunctions, see **20a(7)**.) Notice the similarity in usage between adverbs and adverbial clauses.

Adverbs	Adverbial clauses
Occasionally, the company hires new writers. [answers the question *How often does the company hire new writers?*]	**When the need arises,** the company hires new writers. [answers the question *How often does the company hire new writers?*]
She acted **selfishly.** [answers the question *How did she act?*]	She acted **as though she cared only about herself.** [answers the question *How did she act?*]

Adverbial clauses can appear at various points in a sentence. Use commas to set off an adverbial clause placed at the beginning or in the middle of a sentence.

Because they disagreed, the researchers made little progress.

The researchers, **because they disagreed,** made little progress.

An adverbial clause at the end of a sentence is rarely preceded by a comma.

The researchers made little progress **because they disagreed.**

However, if a final adverbial clause in a sentence contains an extra detail—information you want the reader to pause before—use a comma to set it off.

I slept soundly that night, **even though a storm raged outside.**

❷ *THINKING RHETORICALLY*

ADVERBIAL CLAUSES

In an adverbial clause that refers to time or establishes a fact, both the subject and any form of the verb *be* can be omitted. Using such **elliptical clauses** will make your writing more concise.

While fishing, he saw a rare owl.
[COMPARE: **While he was fishing,** he saw a rare owl.]

Though tired, they continued to study for the exam.
[COMPARE: **Though they were tired,** they continued to study for the exam.]

Be sure that the omitted subject of an elliptical clause is the same as the subject of the independent clause. Otherwise, revise either the adverbial clause or the main clause.

While∧reviewing your report, a few questions occurred to me.
      I was

OR

While reviewing your report,∧a few questions occurred to me.
                          I thought of   ~~occurred to me~~.

For more information on the use of elliptical constructions, see **35b**.

Exercise 2

Identify the dependent clauses in the following paragraph.

[1]If you live by the sword, you might die by the sword. [2]However, if you make your living by swallowing swords, you will not necessarily die by swallowing swords. [3]At least, this is the conclusion Brian Witcombe and Dan Meyer reached after they surveyed forty-six professional sword swallowers. [4](Brian Witcombe is a radiologist, and Dan Meyer is a famous sword swallower.) [5]Some of those surveyed mentioned that they had experienced either "sword throats" or chest pains, and others who let their swords drop to their stomachs described perforation of their innards, but the researchers could find no listing of a sword-swallowing mortality in the medical studies they reviewed. [6]The researchers did not inquire into the reasons for swallowing swords in the first place.

| **21C** | SENTENCE FORMS |

You can identify the form of a sentence by noting the number of clauses it contains and the type of each clause. There are four sentence forms: simple, compound, complex, and compound-complex.

(1) Simple sentences

> ONE INDEPENDENT CLAUSE

A **simple sentence** is equivalent to one independent clause; thus, it must have a subject and a predicate.

The lawyer presented her final argument.

However, you can expand a simple sentence by adding one or more verbal phrases (**21a(3)**) or prepositional phrases (**21a(4)**).

> **Encouraged by the apparent sympathy of the jury,** the lawyer presented her final argument. [The verbal phrase adds detail.]

> The lawyer presented her final argument **in less than an hour.** [The prepositional phrase adds information about time.]

(2) Compound sentences

> INDEPENDENT CLAUSE + INDEPENDENT CLAUSE

A compound sentence consists of at least two independent clauses but no dependent clauses. The independent clauses of a compound sentence are most commonly linked by a coordinating conjunction. However, punctuation may sometimes serve the same purpose (**37a**).

> The Democrats proposed a new budget, **but** the Republicans opposed it. [The coordinating conjunction *but* links two independent clauses and signals contrast.]

The Democrats proposed a new budget; the Republicans opposed it.
[The semicolon serves the same purpose as the coordinating
conjunction.]

(3) Complex sentences

> INDEPENDENT CLAUSE $+$ DEPENDENT CLAUSE

A complex sentence consists of one independent clause and at least
one dependent clause. A dependent clause in a complex sentence
can be a noun clause, an adjectival clause, or an adverbial clause
(**21b(2)**).

> **Because he was known for architectural ornamentation,** no one
> predicted **that the house <u>he designed for himself</u> would be so plain.**
> [This sentence has three dependent clauses. *Because he was known for
> architectural ornamentation* is an adverbial clause. *That the house he
> designed for himself would be so plain* is a noun clause, and *he designed
> for himself* is an adjectival clause within the noun clause. The relative
> pronoun *that* has been omitted from the beginning of the embedded
> adjectival clause.]

(4) Compound-complex sentences

> INDEPENDENT CLAUSE $+$ INDEPENDENT CLAUSE $+$
> DEPENDENT CLAUSE

The combination of a compound sentence and a complex sentence
is called a **compound-complex sentence**. A compound-complex
sentence consists of at least two independent clauses and at least one
dependent clause.

> Conflict is essential to good storytelling, **so** fiction writers often create
> a character **who faces a major challenge.**
> [The coordinating conjunction *so* joins the two independent clauses;
> the relative pronoun *who* introduces the dependent clause.]

❓ *THINKING RHETORICALLY*

SENTENCE FORMS

If one of your paragraphs has as many simple sentences as the one below, try combining some of your ideas into compound, complex, or compound-complex sentences. As you do, you might need to add extra detail as well.

> I rode the school bus every day. I didn't like to, though. The bus smelled bad. And it was always packed. The worst part was the bumpy ride. Riding the bus was like riding in a worn-out sneaker.

REVISED

> As a kid, I rode the school bus every day, but I didn't like to. I hated the smell, the crowd, and the bumpy ride itself. Every seat was filled, and many of the kids took their shoes off for the long ride home on roads so bumpy you couldn't even read a comic book. Riding that bus was like riding inside a worn-out sneaker.

Exercise 3

Identify each sentence in the paragraph in Exercise 2 as simple, compound, complex, or compound-complex.

Exercise 4

Vary the sentence forms in the following paragraph. Add details as needed.

Most people write on a computer. Many still keep a pencil nearby. They most likely use it to jot notes. They rarely think about its role in history. This common writing instrument was invented during the sixteenth century. It was used by George Washington while surveying the Ohio Territory. It was used by Meriwether Lewis and William Clark during their expedition to the Northwest. And Ulysses S. Grant used a pencil to make battle plans. The authors Henry David Thoreau, John Steinbeck, and Ernest Hemingway were other well-known pencil users. The graphite pencil began as an alternative to a stylus made of lead. In fact, we still speak of a pencil lead because the stylus contained this compound. However, the marks a pencil makes are nothing more than flecks of graphite.

21d   SENTENCE FUNCTIONS

Sentences serve a number of functions. Writers commonly state facts or report information with **declarative sentences**. They give instructions with **imperative sentences (commands)**. They use questions, or **interrogative sentences**, to elicit information or to introduce topics. And they express emotion with **exclamatory sentences (exclamations)**.

Declarative	The runners from Kenya won the race.
Imperative	Compare their times with the record.
Interrogative	What were their times?
Exclamatory	The runners from Kenya won the race! Check their times! What an incredible race that was!

Although most of the sentences you are likely to write will be declarative, an occasional command, question, or exclamation will add variety (32c).

Taking note of end punctuation can help you identify the function of a sentence. Generally, a period indicates the end of a declarative

Expect great things.

Now more daily nonstops to China from the U.S. than any other airline.

■ UNITED
It's time to fly.

Advertisers often use imperatives to attract the reader's attention.

sentence or an imperative sentence, and a question mark ends an interrogative sentence. An exclamation point indicates that a sentence is exclamatory. To distinguish between an imperative sentence and a declarative sentence, look for a subject (**20b**). If you cannot find one, the sentence is imperative. Because an imperative is directed to another person or persons, the subject *you* is implied:

Look over there.
[COMPARE: You look over there.]

ñ **MULTILINGUAL WRITERS**

SENTENCE FUNCTIONS

Declarative, imperative, interrogative, and exclamatory sentences can be used for a variety of purposes. For example, imperative sentences are used not only to give directions but also to make suggestions (*Try using a different screwdriver*), to issue invitations (*Come in*), to extend wishes (*Have a good time*), and to warn others (*Stop there*). Furthermore, a particular purpose, such as getting someone to do something, can be accomplished in more than one way.

Imperative   Close the window, please.
Declarative   You should close the window.
Interrogative Would you please close the window?

❓ THINKING RHETORICALLY

QUESTIONS

One type of interrogative sentence, the **rhetorical question**, is not a true question, because an answer is not expected. Instead, like a declarative sentence, it is used to state an opinion. However, a positive rhetorical question can correspond to a negative assertion, and vice versa.

Rhetorical questions	Equivalent statements
Should we allow our rights to be taken away?	We should not allow our rights to be taken away.
Isn't it time to make a difference?	It's time to make a difference.

Because they are more emphatic than declarative sentences, rhetorical questions focus the reader's attention on major points.

Exercise 5

Identify each sentence type in the passage below. What type is used most often? Why?

¹Think of the thousand cartoons you have seen—in the *New Yorker* or a multitude of other places—of the marooned human or pair of humans (in whatever combination of sexes) on some microscopic tropical atoll, a little sand, one palm tree, one rock, the vastness of the sea. ²Humor and pathos live together in these scenes. ³Here at last, we think, life is cut down to the bone so that we can see what stuff it is made of. ⁴If two men, they are The Odd Couple; if man and woman, they will find the roots of the old sex wars and quarrel, as they might on a street in New York; if only one [person], there is a message in a bottle, generally with cheerless news. ⁵Do we love this cartoon scene because we imagine we can discover the bedrock of human nature inside it?

—**BILL HOLM**, *Eccentric Islands: Travels Real and Imaginary*

22 | SENTENCE FRAGMENTS

As its name suggests, a **sentence fragment** is only a piece of a sentence; it is not complete. This chapter can help you

- recognize sentence fragments (**22a**) and
- revise fragments resulting from incorrectly punctuated phrases and dependent clauses (**22b** and **22c**).

22a   RECOGNIZING SENTENCE FRAGMENTS

A sentence is considered a fragment when it is incomplete in any of the following ways:

- It is missing a subject or a verb.

    Derived from a word meaning "nervous sleep." Hypnotism actually refers to a type of focused attention. [no subject]

    Alternative medical treatment may include hypnosis. **The placement of a patient into a relaxed state.** [no verb]

- It is missing both a subject and a verb.

    The hypnotic state differs from sleep. **Contrary to popular belief.**

- It is a dependent clause.

    Most people can be hypnotized easily. **Although the depth of the trance for each person varies.**

Note that imperative sentences (**21d**) are not considered fragments. In these sentences, the subject, *you,* is not stated explicitly. Rather, it is implied.

Find out as much as you can about alternative treatments.
[COMPARE: You find out as much as you can about alternative treatments.]

MULTILINGUAL WRITERS

SUBJECT PRONOUNS

In some languages, subject pronouns are dropped when there is no risk of misunderstanding. In Japanese, a sentence such as *Sushi o tabemasu* ("Eat sushi") is permissible when the subject pronoun can be determined from the context. In Spanish, a verb form reveals information about the subject; unless needed for clarity or emphasis, a subject pronoun can thus be omitted, as in *Trabajo en un banco* ("I work in a bank"). In English, however, subject pronouns must be included in all except imperative sentences.

FOUR METHODS FOR IDENTIFYING FRAGMENTS

If you have trouble recognizing fragments in your own writing, try one or more of these methods:

1. Read each paragraph backwards, sentence by sentence. When you read your sentences out of order, you may more readily note the incompleteness of a fragment.

2. Locate the essential parts of each sentence. First, find the main verb and any accompanying auxiliary verbs. Remember that gerunds and participles cannot function as main verbs (**21a(3)**). After you find the main verb, identify the subject (**20b**). Finally, make sure that the sentence does not begin with a relative pronoun (**21b(2)**) or a subordinating conjunction (**20a(7)**).

Test sentence 1: The inventor of the Frisbee.

Test: Main verb? *None.*
[Because there is no verb, this test sentence is a fragment.]

Test sentence 2: Walter Frederick Morrison invented the Frisbee.

Test: Main verb? *Invented.*
Subject? *Walter Frederick Morrison.*
Relative pronoun or subordinating conjunction? *None.*
[The test sentence is complete: it contains a subject and a verb and does not begin with a relative pronoun or a subordinating conjunction.]

(continued on page 544)

(continued from page 543)

3. Put any sentence you think might be a fragment into this frame sentence:

   They do not understand the idea that _____.

   Only a full sentence will make sense in this frame sentence. If a test sentence, other than an imperative, does not fit into the frame sentence, it is a fragment.

   Test sentence 3: Because it can be played almost anywhere.

   Test: They do not understand the idea that *because it can be played almost anywhere.*
   [The frame sentence does not make sense, so the test sentence is a fragment.]

   Test sentence 4: Ultimate Frisbee is a popular sport because it can be played almost anywhere.

   Test: They do not understand the idea that *Ultimate Frisbee is a popular sport because it can be played almost anywhere.*
   [The frame sentence makes sense, so the test sentence is complete.]

4. Rewrite any sentence you think might be a fragment as a question that can be answered with *yes* or *no*. Only complete sentences can be rewritten this way.

   Test sentence 5: That combines aspects of soccer, football, and basketball.

   Test: *Is that combines aspects of soccer, football, and basketball?*
   [The question does not make sense, so the test sentence is a fragment.]

   Test sentence 6: Ultimate Frisbee is a game that combines aspects of soccer, football, and basketball.

   Test: *Is Ultimate Frisbee a game that combines aspects of soccer, football, and basketball?*
   [The question makes sense, so the test sentence is complete.]

22b   PHRASES AS SENTENCE FRAGMENTS

A phrase is a group of words without a subject and/or a predicate (**21a**). When punctuated as a sentence (that is, with a period, a question mark, or an exclamation point at the end), a phrase becomes a fragment. You can revise such a fragment by attaching it to a related sentence, usually the one preceding it.

Verbal phrase as a fragment

Early humans valued color. ~~Creating~~ , creating **permanent colors with natural pigments.**

Prepositional phrase as a fragment

For years, the Scottish have dyed sweaters with soot. ~~Originally~~ , originally **from the chimneys of peat-burning stoves.**

Compound predicate as a fragment

Arctic foxes turn white when it snows. ~~And~~ and **thus conceal themselves from prey.**

Appositive phrase as a fragment

During the Renaissance, one of the most highly valued pigments was ultramarine. ~~An~~ —an **extract from lapis lazuli.**

Appositive list as a fragment

To derive dyes, we have always experimented with what we find in nature. ~~Shells,~~ : shells, **roots, insects, flowers.**

Absolute phrase as a fragment

The deciduous trees of New England are known for their brilliant autumn color. ~~Sugar~~ , sugar **maples dazzling tourists with their orange and red leaves.**

Instead of attaching a fragment to the preceding sentence, you can recast the fragment as a complete sentence. This method of revision elevates the importance of the information conveyed in the fragment.

Fragment	Humans painted themselves for a variety of purposes. **To attract a mate, to hide themselves from game or predators, or to signal aggression.**
Revision	Humans used color for a variety of purposes. For example, they painted themselves to attract a mate, to hide themselves from game or predators, or to signal aggression.

Exercise 1

Revise each fragment by attaching it to a related sentence or by recasting it as a complete sentence.

1. A brilliant twenty-three-year-old Englishman. Isaac Newton was the first person to study color.
2. By passing a beam of sunlight through a prism. Newton showed that white light comprised all the visible colors of the spectrum.
3. White light passed through the prism. And separated into the colors of the rainbow.
4. Rainbows are arcs of color. Caused by water droplets in the air.
5. Sometimes rainbows contain all the spectrum colors. Red, orange, yellow, green, blue, indigo, and violet.
6. Particles of spray in waterfalls can act as prisms. Producing a variety of colors.
7. Our brains easily fooled. We sometimes see more colors than are actually present.

| **22C** | DEPENDENT CLAUSES AS SENTENCE FRAGMENTS |

A dependent clause is a group of words with both a subject and a predicate (**21b(2)**), but because it begins with a subordinating conjunction (**20a(7)**) or a relative pronoun (**21b(2)**), it cannot stand alone as a sentence. To revise this type of fragment, attach it to a related sentence, usually the sentence preceding it.

The iceberg was no surprise. ~~Because~~ because ~~,~~the *Titanic*'s wireless operators had received reports of ice in the area.

More than two thousand people were aboard the *Titanic*. ~~Which~~ , which ~~,~~was the largest ocean liner in 1912.

You can also recast the fragment as a complete sentence by removing the subordinating conjunction or relative pronoun and supplying any missing elements. This method of revision draws attention to the information originally conveyed in the fragment. Compare the following revisions with the ones above:

The iceberg was no surprise. The *Titanic*'s wireless operators had received reports of ice in the area.

More than two thousand people were aboard the *Titanic*. In 1912, this ocean liner was the world's largest.

You can also reduce a clause that is a fragment to a phrase (**21b**) and then attach it to a related sentence.

More than two thousand people were aboard the *Titanic*, the largest ocean liner in 1912. [fragment reduced to an appositive phrase]

If you are unsure of the punctuation to use with phrases or dependent clauses, see Chapter **36**.

❓ *THINKING RHETORICALLY*

FRAGMENTS

When used judiciously, fragments—like short sentences—emphasize ideas or add surprise. However, they are generally permitted only when the rhetorical situation allows the use of a casual tone.

May. When the earth's Northern Hemisphere awakens from winter's sleep and all of nature bristles with the energies of new life. My work has kept me indoors for months now. I'm not sure I'll ever get used to it.

—KEN CAREY, *Flat Rock Journal: A Day in the Ozark Mountains*

Exercise 2

Revise each fragment by attaching it to a related sentence or by recasting it as a full sentence.

1. The ship was christened *Titanic*. Which means "of great size."
2. The shipbuilders thought the *Titanic* was unsinkable. Because it had sixteen watertight compartments.
3. The ship sank in less than three hours. Even though the damage caused by the iceberg was not massive.
4. The extent of the damage to the ship's hull was unknown. Until researchers started examining the wreckage in the late 1990s.
5. In 1987, a controversial French expedition recovered dishes, jewelry, and other artifacts from the *Titanic*. Which were later displayed in France and Germany.

Exercise 3

Follow the guidelines in this chapter to locate and revise the fragments in the following paragraph. If you find it necessary, make other improvements as well. Be prepared to explain your revisions.

[1]One of the most popular rides at any county fair or amusement park is the Ferris wheel. [2]The original Ferris wheel, designed by George Washington Gale Ferris, Jr., for a national exposition in 1893. [3]Rose to a height of 264 feet. [4]And accommodated 2,140 passengers. [5]Ferris's goal was to build something that would surpass in effect the Eiffel Tower. [6]Which was constructed just a few years earlier. [7]Though Ferris's plans were not immediately accepted. [8]Once they were, and the wheel opened to the public, it became an immediate success. [9]At times carrying 38,000 passengers a day. [10]Since the nineteenth century. [11]Engineers have designed taller and taller Ferris wheels. [12]The 541-foot Singapore Flyer holds the record, but the Beijing Great Wheel, currently under construction. [13]Will be over 100 feet taller.

23 | COMMA SPLICES AND FUSED SENTENCES

Comma splices and fused sentences are sentence-level mistakes resulting from incorrect or missing punctuation. Both are punctuated as one sentence when they should be punctuated as two sentences (or two independent clauses). By revising comma splices and fused sentences, you indicate sentence boundaries and thus make your writing easier to read. This chapter will help you

- review the rules for punctuating independent clauses (**23a**),
- recognize comma splices and fused sentences (**23b**), and
- learn ways to revise them (**23c** and **23d**).

23a | PUNCTUATING SENTENCES WITH TWO INDEPENDENT CLAUSES

In case you are unfamiliar with or unsure about the conventions for punctuating sentences with two independent clauses, here is a short review.

A comma and a coordinating conjunction can join two independent clauses (**36a**). The coordinating conjunction indicates the relationship between the two clauses. For example, *and* signals addition, whereas *but* and *yet* signal contrast. The comma precedes the conjunction.

INDEPENDENT CLAUSE**, and** INDEPENDENT CLAUSE.

The new store opened this morning, **and** the owners greeted everyone at the door.

A semicolon can join two independent clauses that are closely related. A semicolon generally signals addition or contrast.

INDEPENDENT CLAUSE; INDEPENDENT CLAUSE.

One of the owners comes from this area; the other grew up in Cuba.

A semicolon may also precede an independent clause that begins with an adverbial conjunction (conjunctive adverb) such as *however* or *nevertheless*. Notice that a comma follows this type of connecting word.

The store will be open late on Fridays and Saturdays; **however,** it will be closed all day on Sundays.

A comma used to set off an adverbial conjunction (conjunctive adverb) is sometimes omitted when there is no risk that the sentence will be misread.

The owners remodeled the interior; **then** they put up a new sign outside. [No misreading is possible, so the comma can be omitted.]

A colon can join two independent clauses. The second clause usually explains or elaborates on the first.

INDEPENDENT CLAUSE: INDEPENDENT CLAUSE.

The owners have announced a special offer: anyone who makes a purchase during the opening will receive a 10 percent discount.

If you are following MLA guidelines, capitalize the first word of a clause following a colon when the clause expresses a rule or principle (**37b(1)**).

A period separates clauses into distinct sentences.

INDEPENDENT CLAUSE. INDEPENDENT CLAUSE.

The store is located on the corner of Pine Street and First Avenue. It was formerly an insurance office.

Occasionally, commas are used between independent clauses, but only when the clauses are short, parallel in form, and unified in meaning.

They came, they shopped, they left.

For more information on punctuating sentences, see Chapters 36, 37, and 40.

23b	RECOGNIZING COMMA SPLICES AND FUSED SENTENCES

A **comma splice**, or **comma fault**, refers to the incorrect use of a comma between two independent clauses (21b).

Most stockholders favored the merger,ᴧthe management did not.
but

A **fused sentence**, or **run-on sentence**, consists of two independent clauses run together without any punctuation at all.

The first section of the proposal was approvedᴧthe budget will have to be resubmitted.
; however,

To revise a comma splice or a fused sentence, include appropriate punctuation and any necessary connecting words.

If you have trouble recognizing comma splices or fused sentences, try one of the following methods.

TWO METHODS FOR IDENTIFYING COMMA SPLICES AND FUSED SENTENCES

1. Locate a sentence that may be problematic. Put it into this frame sentence:

   They do not understand the idea that _____.

   Only complete sentences make sense when placed in the frame sentence. If just part of a test sentence fits, you have probably located a comma splice or a fused sentence.

   Test sentence 1: Plasma is the fourth state of matter.

   Test: They do not understand the idea that *plasma is the fourth state of matter.*

   [The test sentence makes sense in the frame sentence. No revision is necessary.]

Test sentence 2: Plasma is the fourth state of matter, some scientists believe that 99 percent of the universe is made of it.

Test: They do not understand the idea that *plasma is the fourth state of matter, some scientists believe that 99 percent of the universe is made of it.*

[The frame sentence does not make sense because there are two sentences completing it, rather than one. The test sentence contains a comma splice and thus should be revised.]

Revision: Plasma is the fourth state of matter. Some scientists believe that 99 percent of the universe is made of it.

2. If you think a sentence may be incorrect, try to rewrite it as a question that can be answered with *yes* or *no*. If just part of the sentence makes sense, you have likely found a comma splice or a fused sentence.

Test sentence 3: Plasma is used for a number of purposes.

Test: *Is plasma used for a number of purposes?*
[The question makes sense. No revision is necessary.]

Test sentence 4: Plasma is used for a number of purposes it may even power rockets someday.

Test: *Is plasma used for a number of purposes it may even power rockets someday?*
[The question does not make sense because only one part of the test sentence has been made into a question. The test sentence is a fused sentence and thus should be revised.]

Revision: Plasma is used for a number of purposes. It may even power rockets someday.

You can also find comma splices and fused sentences by remembering that they commonly occur in certain contexts.

■ With transitional words and phrases such as *however, therefore,* and *for example* (see also **23c(5)**)

Comma splice: The director is unable to meet with you this week‚ however‚ next week she will have time on Tuesday.

[Notice that a semicolon replaces the comma.]

- When an explanation or an example is given in the second sentence

  Fused sentence: The cultural center has a new collection of spear

  points~~,~~ _∧ <ins>. Many</ins> ~~many~~ of them were donated by a retired anthropologist.

- When a clause that includes *not* is followed by one without this word, or vice versa

  Comma splice: A World Cup victory is not just an everyday sporting

  event~~, it~~ _∧ <ins>. It</ins> is a national celebration.

- When the subject of the second clause is a pronoun whose antecedent is in the preceding clause

  Fused sentence: Lake Baikal is located in southern Russia~~it~~ _∧ <ins>. It</ins> is 394 miles long.

23C REVISING COMMA SPLICES AND FUSED SENTENCES

If you find comma splices or fused sentences in your writing, try one of the following methods to revise them.

(1) Linking independent clauses with a comma and a coordinating conjunction

By linking clauses with a comma and a coordinating conjunction (such as *and* or *but*), you signal the relationship between the clauses (addition or contrast, for example).

Fused sentence: The diplomats will end their discussions on Friday_∧ <ins>, and</ins> they will submit their final decisions on Monday.

Comma splice: Some diplomats applauded the treaty,_∧ <ins>but</ins> others opposed it vehemently.

(2) Linking independent clauses with a semicolon or a colon or separating them with a period

When you link independent clauses with a semicolon, you signal their connection indirectly. There are no explicit conjunctions to use as cues. The semicolon usually indicates addition or contrast. When you link clauses with a colon, the second clause serves as an explanation or an elaboration of the first. A period indicates that each clause is a complete and separate sentence.

> **Comma splice:** Our division's reports are posted on our web page, hard copies are available by request.

> **Revision 1:** Our division's reports are posted on our web page; hard copies are available by request.

> **Revision 2:** Our division's reports are posted on our web page. Hard copies are available by request.

> **Fused sentence:** Our mission statement is simple‸ we aim to provide athletic gear at affordable prices.

(3) Recasting an independent clause as a dependent clause or as a phrase

A dependent clause (**21b(2)**) includes a subordinating conjunction such as *although* or *because,* which indicates how the dependent and independent clauses are related (in a cause-and-consequence relationship, for example). A prepositional phrase (**21a(4)**) includes a preposition such as *in, on,* or *because of* that may also signal a relationship directly. Verbal, appositive, and absolute phrases (**21a(3)**, **21a(5)**, and **21a(6)**) suggest relationships less directly because they do not include connecting words.

> **Comma splice:** The wind had blown down trees and power lines, the whole city was without electricity for several hours.

> **Revision 1: Because the wind had blown down power lines,** the whole city was without electricity for several hours. [dependent clause]

> **Revision 2: Because of the downed power lines,** the whole city was without electricity for several hours. [prepositional phrase]

> **Revision 3: The wind having blown down power lines,** the whole city was without electricity for several hours. [absolute phrase]

(4) Integrating one clause into the other

When you integrate clauses, you will generally retain the important details but omit or change some words.

Fused sentence: The proposal covers all but one point it does not describe how the project will be assessed.

Revision: The proposal covers all the points except assessment procedures.

(5) Using transitional words or phrases to link independent clauses

Another way to revise fused sentences and comma splices is to use transitional words and phrases such as *however, on the contrary,* and *in the meantime.* (For other examples, see the list on page 63.)

Fused sentence: Sexual harassment is not just an issue for women. After all, men can be sexually harassed too.

Comma splice: The word *status* refers to relative position within a group; however, it is often used to indicate only positions of prestige.

If you have questions about punctuating sentences that contain transitional words and phrases, see **37a**.

As you edit fused sentences and comma splices, you will refine the connections between your sentences and thereby help your readers follow your train of thought. The following checklist will help you find and fix comma splices and fused sentences.

✔ **CHECKLIST** *for Comma Splices and Fused Sentences*

1 Common Sites for Comma Splices or Fused Sentences

- With transitional words such as *however* and *therefore*
- When an explanation or an example occurs in the second clause
- When a clause that includes *not* is followed by one without this word, or vice versa
- When the subject of the second clause is a pronoun whose antecedent is in the first clause

2 **Ways to Fix Comma Splices and Fused Sentences**

- ■ Link the clauses with a comma and a coordinating conjunction.
- ■ Link the clauses, using a semicolon or a colon.
- ■ Separate the clauses by punctuating each as a sentence.
- ■ Make one clause dependent.
- ■ Reduce one clause to a phrase.
- ■ Rewrite the sentence, integrating one clause into the other.
- ■ Use a transitional word or phrase.

Exercise 1

Revise each comma splice or fused sentence by using one of the strategies mentioned in this section.

1. The average human brain weighs about three pounds, the average brain of a sperm whale weighs seventeen pounds.

2. The body of a brain cell can move but most brain cells stay put they extend their axons outward.

3. The brain needs water to function properly dehydration may cause lethargy or learning problems.

4. Researchers studying brain hemispheres have found that many professional musicians process music in their left hemisphere, the notion that musicians and artists depend on the right side of their brain is considered outmoded.

5. Discoveries in neuroscience have yielded many benefits, researchers have developed medication for schizophrenia and Tourette's syndrome.

23d | DIVIDED QUOTATIONS

When dividing quotations with signal phrases such as *he said* or *she asked,* use a period between independent clauses.

Comma splice: "Beauty brings copies of itself into being," states Elaine

Scarry, ~~it~~ "It makes us draw it, take photographs of it, or describe it to

other people."

[Both parts of the quotation are complete sentences, so the signal phrase is attached to the first, and the sentence is punctuated with a period.]

A comma separates two parts of a single quoted sentence.

"Musing takes place in a kind of meadowlands of the imagination," writes Rebecca Solnit, "a part of the imagination that has not yet been plowed, developed, or put to any immediately practical use."

[Because the quotation is a single sentence, a comma is used.]

Exercise 2

Revise each comma splice or fused sentence in the following paragraph. Some sentences may not need revision.

¹In *The Politics of Happiness,* Derek Bok, former president of Harvard University, discusses recent findings that researchers studying well-being have reported. ²He mentions, for example, research showing that measurements of happiness in the United States have not risen much in the last fifty years, people are responding to survey questions about their levels of happiness in much the same way as they did in 1960. ³Even though average incomes have grown, levels of happiness have not increased. ⁴Bok believes that people become accustomed to higher standards of living they do not realize how quickly they adapt and so do not become happier. ⁵Bok recognizes that not everyone's income has increased but notes that, strangely enough, the disparity between rich and poor has not caused increased dissatisfaction among the poor, he cites further studies showing that citizens in countries with costly welfare programs are not necessarily happier than citizens in countries with welfare programs that are not as generous. ⁶Because of these studies, Bok suggests that our government not focus on economic growth alone as an indicator of well-being and instead take into account current research on what makes people happy. ⁷This discussion "is bound to contribute to the evolution of society and the refinement of its values," he explains, "that alone will be an accomplishment of enduring importance to humankind" (212).

24 | VERBS

Choosing verbs to convey your message precisely is the first step toward writing clear sentences. The next step is to ensure that the verbs you choose conform to the conventions your audience expects you to follow. This chapter will help you

- identify conventional verb forms (**24a**),
- use verb tenses to provide information about time (**24b**),
- distinguish between the active voice and the passive voice (**24c**),
- use verbs to signal the factuality or likelihood of an action or event (**24d**), and
- ensure that subjects and verbs agree in number and person (**24e**).

24a | VERB FORMS

Most English verbs have four forms, following the model for *walk*:

walk, walks, walking, walked

However, English also includes irregular verbs, which may have as few as three forms or as many as eight:

let, lets, letting   be, am, is, are, was, were, being, been

(1) Regular verbs

Regular verbs have four forms. The **base form** is the form you can find in a dictionary. *Talk, act, change,* and *serve* are all base forms.

The second form of a regular verb is the **-s form**. To derive this form, add to the base form either *-s* (*talks, acts, changes, serves*) or, in some cases, *-es* (*marries, carries, tries*). See **41d** for information on changing *y* to *i* before adding *-es*.

The third form of a regular verb is the ***-ing* form**, also called the **present participle**. It consists of the base form and the ending *-ing* (*talking, acting*). Depending on the verb, a spelling change may be required when the suffix is added (*changing, chatting*) (**41d**).

The fourth form of a regular verb consists of the base form and the ending *-ed* (*talked, acted*). Again, spelling may vary when the suffix is added (*changed, chatted*) (**41d**). The *-ed* form has two names. When this form is used *without* a form of the auxiliary verb *have* or *be*, it is called the **past form**: We *talked* about the new plan. When the *-ed* form is used *with* one of these auxiliary verbs, it is called the **past participle**: We *have talked* about it several times. A committee *was formed* to investigate the matter.

	Verb Forms of Regular Verbs		
Base Form	**-s Form (Present Tense, Third Person, Singular)**	**-ing Form (Present Participle)**	**-ed Form (Past Form or Past Participle)**
work	works	working	worked
watch	watches	watching	watched
apply	applies	applying	applied
stop	stops	stopping	stopped

❶ CAUTION

When verbs are followed by words with similar sounds, you may find their endings (*-s* or *-ed*) difficult to hear. In addition, these verb endings may seem unfamiliar because your dialect does not have them. Nonetheless, you should use *-s* and *-ed* when you write for an audience that expects you to include these endings.

> ^{seems}
> She ~~seem~~ satisfied with the report.

> ^{supposed}
> We were ~~suppose~~ to receive the results yesterday.

(2) Irregular verbs

Most irregular verbs, such as *write,* have forms similar to some of those for regular verbs: base form (*write*), *-s* form (*writes*), and *-ing* form (*writing*). However, the past form (*wrote*) and the past participle (*written*) vary from those of the regular verbs. In fact, some irregular verbs have two acceptable past forms and/or past participles (see *awake, dive, dream,* and *get* in the following chart). Other irregular verbs have only three forms because the same form serves as the base form, the past form, and the past participle (see *set* in the chart). If you are unsure about verb forms not included in the chart, consult a dictionary.

Verb Forms of Irregular Verbs				
Base Form	-s Form (Present Tense, Third Person, Singular)	-ing Form (Present Participle)	Past Form	Past Participle
arise	arises	arising	arose	arisen
awake	awakes	awaking	awaked, awoke	awaked, awoken
begin	begins	beginning	began	begun
break	breaks	breaking	broke	broken
bring	brings	bringing	brought	brought
buy	buys	buying	bought	bought
choose	chooses	choosing	chose	chosen
come	comes	coming	came	come
dive	dives	diving	dived, dove	dived
do	does	doing	did	done
dream	dreams	dreaming	dreamed, dreamt	dreamed, dreamt
drink	drinks	drinking	drank	drunk
drive	drives	driving	drove	driven
eat	eats	eating	ate	eaten
forget	forgets	forgetting	forgot	forgotten
forgive	forgives	forgiving	forgave	forgiven
get	gets	getting	got	gotten, got
give	gives	giving	gave	given
go	goes	going	went	gone
hang (suspend)	hangs	hanging	hung	hung

Base Form	-s Form (Present Tense, Third Person, Singular)	-ing Form (Present Participle)	Past Form	Past Participle
hang (execute)	hangs	hanging	hanged	hanged
keep	keeps	keeping	kept	kept
know	knows	knowing	knew	known
lay (see the Glossary of Usage)	lays	laying	laid	laid
lead	leads	leading	led	led
lie (see the Glossary of Usage)	lies	lying	lay	lain
lose	loses	losing	lost	lost
pay	pays	paying	paid	paid
rise (see the Glossary of Usage)	rises	rising	rose	risen
say	says	saying	said	said
see	sees	seeing	saw	seen
set (see the Glossary of Usage)	sets	setting	set	set
sink	sinks	sinking	sank	sunk
sit (see the Glossary of Usage)	sits	sitting	sat	sat
speak	speaks	speaking	spoke	spoken
stand	stands	standing	stood	stood
steal	steals	stealing	stole	stolen
swim	swims	swimming	swam	swum

(continued on page 564)

(continued from page 563)

Base Form	-s Form (Present Tense, Third Person, Singular)	-ing Form (Present Participle)	Past Form	Past Participle
take	takes	taking	took	taken
tell	tells	telling	told	told
throw	throws	throwing	threw	thrown
wear	wears	wearing	wore	worn
write	writes	writing	wrote	written

The verb *be* has eight forms:

be   **Be** on time!

am   I **am** going to arrive early tomorrow.

is   Time **is** of the essence.

are   They **are** always punctual.

was   The meeting **was** scheduled for 10 a.m.

were   We **were** only five minutes late.

being   He is **being** delayed by traffic.

been   How long have we **been** here?

ñ MULTILINGUAL WRITERS

OMISSION OF FORMS OF *BE* IN OTHER LANGUAGES

Forms of the verb *be* can be omitted in some languages. In English, however, they are necessary.

Sentence without an auxiliary verb: The population $\overset{is}{\wedge}$ growing.

Sentence without a linking verb: It $\overset{is}{\wedge}$ quite large.

(3) Prepositional verbs and phrasal verbs

A **prepositional verb** is a frequently occurring combination of a verb and a preposition. *Rely on, think about, look like,* and *ask for* are all prepositional verbs. A **phrasal verb** is a combination of a verb and a particle such as *up, out,* or *on.* A **particle** resembles an adverb or a preposition, but it is so closely associated with a verb that together they form a unit of meaning. *Carry out, go on, make up, take on,* and *turn out* are phrasal verbs commonly found in college-level writing. Notice that these five phrasal verbs have meanings that can be expressed in one word: *do, continue, form, accept,* and *attend.*

> **ñ MULTILINGUAL WRITERS**
>
> **PHRASAL VERBS**
>
> Definitions of phrasal verbs are often not obvious. For example, *find out* means "to discover." To learn more about phrasal verbs, see Chapter 46.

(4) Auxiliary verbs

The auxiliary verbs *be, do,* and *have* combine with main verbs, both regular and irregular.

be	am, is, are, was, were surprised am, is, are, was, were writing
do	does, do, did call doesn't, don't, didn't spend
have	has, have, had prepared has, have, had read

When you combine auxiliary verbs with main verbs, you alter the meanings of the main verbs in subtle ways. The resulting verb combinations may provide information about time, emphasis, or action in progress.

Be, do, and *have* are not just auxiliary verbs, though. They may be used as main verbs as well.

be	I **am** from Texas.
do	He **does** his homework early in the morning.
have	They **have** an apartment near a park.

A sentence may even include one of these verbs as both an auxiliary and a main verb.

They **are being** careful.

Did you **do** your taxes by yourself?

She **has** not **had** any free time this week.

Another type of auxiliary verb is called a **modal auxiliary**. There are nine modal auxiliaries: *can, could, may, might, must, shall, should, will,* and *would*. The following box provides examples of common meanings conveyed by modal auxiliaries.

SOME COMMON MEANINGS OF MODAL AUXILIARIES

Meaning	Modal Auxiliary	+	Main Verb	Example(s)
Ability	can, could		afford	They *can afford* to buy a small house.
				They *could afford* that trip to Portugal.
Certainty	will		leave	We *will leave* tomorrow.
Obligation	must		return	You *must return* your books soon.
Advice	should		talk	He *should talk* with his counselor.
Permission	may		use	You *may use* the computers in the library.

❶ *CAUTION*

When a modal auxiliary occurs with the auxiliary *have* (*must have forgotten, should have known*), *have* frequently sounds like the word *of*. When you proofread, be sure that modal auxiliaries are not followed by *of*.

They **could of taken** another route.
(have)

Writers generally do not combine modal auxiliaries unless they want to portray a regional dialect.

We **might could** plan the meeting for after the holidays.
(be able to)

> **ñ** *MULTILINGUAL WRITERS*
>
> **MODAL AUXILIARY VERBS**
> Most modal auxiliary verbs have more than one meaning. *Could*
> sometimes refers to ability (*I **could** swim a mile when I was sixteen*).
> However, *could* can also refer to possibility (*Something good **could**
> happen*). To learn more about modal auxiliary verbs and about
> phrasal modals such as *be going to* and *have to*, see Chapter **46**.

(5) Participles

Present participles (*-ing* verb forms) are used with a form of the auxiliary verb
be: We *are waiting* for the next flight. It *is arriving* sometime this afternoon.
Depending on the intended meaning, past participles can be used with either *be* or *have*: The first flight *was canceled*. We *have waited* for an hour. If a
sentence contains only a participle, it is probably a fragment (**22b**).

I sit on the same bench every day. ~~Dreaming~~ ,dreaming ∧of far-off places.

When a participle is part of a verbal phrase, it often appears without an
auxiliary verb (**21a(4)**).

Swatting at mosquitoes and **cursing** softly, we packed our gear.
[COMPARE: We **were swatting** at mosquitoes and **cursing** softly as
we packed our gear.]

Exercise 1

Revise the following sentences. Explain any changes you make.
1. Any expedition into the wilderness suffer its share of mishaps.
2. The Lewis and Clark Expedition began in May 1804 and end in
   September 1806.

(continued on page 568)

(continued from page 567)

3. Fate must of smiled on Meriwether Lewis and William Clark, for there were no fatalities under their leadership.

4. Lewis and Clark lead the expedition from St. Louis to the Pacific Ocean and back.

5. President Thomas Jefferson commission the expedition in 1803 in part because he was interest in finding the Northwest Passage—a hypothetical waterway connecting the Atlantic and Pacific Oceans.

6. By 1805, the Corps of Discovery, as the expedition was call, included thirty-three members.

7. The Corps might of lost all maps and specimens had Sacajawea, a Native American woman, not fish them from the Missouri River.

8. Sacajawea could of went off with her own people in Idaho, but she accompany Lewis and Clark to the Pacific.

9. When the Mandans had finish inspecting York, William Clark's African American servant, they assume he was the expedition's leader.

10. The success of the expedition depend on its members' willingness to help one another.

24b   VERB TENSES

Verb tenses provide information about time. For example, the tense of a verb may indicate that an action took place in the past or that an action is ongoing. Verb tenses are labeled as present, past, or future; they are also labeled as simple, progressive, perfect, or perfect progressive. The following chart shows how these labels apply to the tenses of *walk*.

Verb Tenses			
	Present	**Past**	**Future**
Simple	I/you/we/they **walk.** He/she/it **walks.**	walked	will walk
Progressive	I **am walking.** He/she/it **is walking.** You/we/they **are walking.**	I/he/she/it **was walking.** You/we/they **were walking.**	will be walking
Perfect	I/you/we/they **have walked.** He/she/it **has walked.**	had walked	will have walked
Perfect progressive	I/you/we/they **have been walking.** He/she/it **has been walking.**	had been walking	will have been walking

Some of the tenses have more than one form because they depend on the person and the number of the subject (generally, the main noun or the pronoun that precedes the verb). **Person** refers to the role of the subject. First person (expressed by the pronoun *I* or *we*) indicates that the subject of the verb is the writer or writers. Second person (*you*) indicates that the subject is the audience. Third person (*he, she, it,* or *they*) indicates that the subject is someone or something other than the writer or audience. First- and second-person references are pronouns, but third-person references can be either pronouns or nouns (such as *book* or *books*). **Number** signals whether the subject is singular (referring to just one person or thing) or plural (referring to more than one person or thing).

24C VOICE

Voice indicates the relationship between a verb and its subject. When a verb is in the **active voice**, the subject is generally a person or thing performing the action indicated by the verb. When a verb is in the **passive voice**, the subject is usually the *receiver* of the action.

Jen Wilson **wrote** the essay. [active voice]

The essay **was written** by Jen Wilson. [passive voice]

Notice that the actor, Jen Wilson, appears in a prepositional phrase beginning with *by* in the passive sentence. Some sentences, however, do not include a *by* phrase because the actor is unknown or unimportant.

Jen Wilson's essay **was published** in the student newspaper.

In the sentence above it is not important to know who accepted Jen's essay for publication, only that it was published. The best way to decide whether a sentence is in the passive voice is to examine its verb phrase.

(1) Verbs in the passive voice

The verb phrase in a sentence written in the passive voice consists of a form of the auxiliary verb *be* (*am, is, are, was, were, been*) and a past participle (**24a(1)**). Depending on the verb tense, other auxiliaries such as *have* and *will* may appear as well. The following sentences in the passive voice show which auxiliaries are used with *called*:

Simple present	The meeting *is called* to order.
Simple past	The recruits *were called* to duty.
Present progressive	The council *is being called* to act on the proposal.
Past perfect	Ms. Jones *had been called* for jury duty twice last year, but she was glad to serve again.

If a verb phrase does not include both a form of the auxiliary verb *be* and a past participle, it is in the active voice.

(2) Choosing between the active and the passive voice

Sentences in the active voice are generally clearer and more vigorous than their passive counterparts. To use the active voice for emphasizing an actor and an action, first make the actor the subject of the sentence and then choose verbs that will help your readers see what the actor is doing. Notice how the following sentences in the active voice emphasize the role of the students:

Active voice   A group of students planned the graduation ceremony. They invited a well-known columnist to give the graduation address.

Passive voice   The graduation ceremony was planned by a group of students. A well-known columnist was invited to give the graduation address.

Use the passive voice when you want to stress the recipient of the action, rather than the actor, or when the actor's identity is unimportant or unknown. For example, you may want to emphasize the topic of a discussion.

Tuition increases **were discussed** at the board meeting.

Or you may be unable to identify the actor who performed some action.

The lights **were left** on in the building last night.

Writers of scientific prose often use the passive voice to highlight the experiment rather than the experimenter. The following is an excerpt from student Heather Jensen's lab report (see **17f** for the full paper):

First, the slides **were placed** on a compound microscope under low power, a 40X magnification level. The end of the root tip **was located**; then the cells immediately behind the root cap **were examined**.

Exercise 2

Identify the voice in each sentence as active or passive. Remember: if the verb phrase includes a form of the auxiliary verb *be* (*am, is, are, was, were, been*) and a past participle (**24a(1)**), the sentence is in the passive voice.

(continued on page 572)

(continued from page 571)

1. In a *National Geographic* article, Zahi Hawass discusses recent information regarding the life and death of King Tut.
2. King Tut was enthroned at the age of nine.
3. Originally, he was called Tutankhaten.
4. Later he changed his name to Tutankhamun.
5. At nineteen years of age, King Tut died.
6. His mummy was discovered in 1922.
7. Recently, King Tut's DNA was obtained.
8. The findings of the genetic testing reveal that King Tut may have died of malaria.

Exercise 3

Rewrite the sentences in Exercise 2, making sentences in the active voice passive, and vice versa. Add or delete actors when necessary. If one version of a sentence is better than the other, explain why.

24d MOOD

The **mood** of a verb indicates the writer's attitude concerning the factuality of what is being expressed. The **indicative mood** is used for statements and questions regarding fact or opinion. The **imperative mood** is used to give commands or directions. The **subjunctive mood** is used to state requirements, make requests, and express wishes.

Indicative   I am on the board of directors.
                    Were you on the board last year?
                    The board will meet in two weeks.

| **Imperative** | Plan on attending the meeting.
Be on time! |
| **Subjunctive** | She suggests that you come early.
If you came to more meetings, you would understand the issues.
If I had attended regularly, I would have voted for the plan. |

The subjunctive mood is also used to signal hypothetical situations—situations that are not real or not currently true (for example, *If I were president, . . .*).

Verb forms in the subjunctive mood serve a variety of functions. The **present subjunctive** is the base form of the verb. It is used to express necessity.

The manager suggested that he **pay** for his own travel. [active voice]

We demanded that he **be reimbursed.** [passive voice]

The **past subjunctive** has the same form as the simple past (for example, *had, offered,* or *wrote*). However, the past subjunctive form of *be* is *were*, regardless of person or number. This form is used to present hypothetical situations.

If they **offered** me the job, I would take it. [active voice]

Even if I **were promoted,** I would not change my mind. [passive voice]

Although it is called "past," the past subjunctive refers to the present or the future.

The **perfect subjunctive** has the same form as the past perfect tense: *had* + past participle. The perfect subjunctive signals that the action did not occur.

She wishes she **had participated** in the scholarship competition.
[active voice]

If she **had been awarded** the scholarship, she would have quit her job.
[passive voice]

The following guidelines should help you avoid pitfalls when using the subjunctive.

TIPS FOR USING THE SUBJUNCTIVE

- In clauses beginning with *as if* and *as though*, use the past subjunctive or the perfect subjunctive:

  He acts as if he ˄**was** the owner.
  (were)

  She looked at me as though she ˄**heard** this story before.
  (had)

- In a dependent clause that begins with *if* and refers to a condition or action that did not occur, use the past subjunctive or the perfect subjunctive. Avoid using *would have* in such an *if* clause.

  If I ˄**was** rich, I would buy a yacht.
  (were)

  If the driver ˄**would have checked** his rearview mirror, the accident would not have happened.
  (had)

  Notice that an indicative clause beginning with *if* may describe a condition or action that can occur.

  If it is sunny tomorrow, I'm going fishing. [indicative mood]

- In dependent clauses following verbs that express wishes, requirements, or requests, use the past subjunctive or the perfect subjunctive.

  I wish I ˄**was** taller.
  (were)

  My brother wishes he ˄**studied** harder years ago.
  (had)

Some linguists believe that certain subjunctive forms are disappearing from the English language. It is not unusual to find clauses such as *I wish I was . . .* (instead of *I wish I were . . .*) in the essays of many well-known writers. Nonetheless, appropriate use of verb forms in the subjunctive mood is still expected in most academic rhetorical situations.

Exercise 4

Use subjunctive verb forms to revise the following sentences.

1. The planners of Apollo 13 acted as if the number 13 was a lucky number.
2. Superstitious people think that if NASA changed the number of the mission, the astronauts would have had a safer journey.
3. They also believe that if the lunar landing would have been scheduled for a day other than Friday the Thirteenth, the crew would not have encountered any problems.
4. The crew used the lunar module as though it was a lifeboat.
5. If NASA ever plans a space mission on Friday the Thirteenth again, the public would object.

24e   SUBJECT-VERB AGREEMENT

To say that a verb *agrees* with a subject means that the form of the verb (*-s* form or base form) is appropriate for the subject. For example, if the subject refers to one person or thing (*an athlete, a computer*), the *-s* form of the verb is appropriate (*runs*). If the subject refers to more than one person or thing (*athletes, computers*), the base form of the verb is appropriate (*run*). Notice in the following examples that the singular third-person subjects take a singular verb (*-s* form) and all the other subjects take the base form

He, she, it, Joe, a student   has, looks, writes

I, you, we, they, the Browns, the students   have, look, write

The verb *be* has three different present-tense forms and two different past-tense forms:

I	am/was
He, she, it, Joe, a student	is/was
You, we, they, the Browns, the students	are/were

ñ MULTILINGUAL WRITERS

ADDING -s TO NOUNS AND VERBS

Standardized English requires the addition of *-s* to mark most nouns as plural and most verbs as third-person singular. (Modal auxiliaries are the exception.) Be careful not to confuse the verb ending and the noun ending.

The **students** need attention. [noun + *-s*]

The student **needs** attention. [verb + *-s*]

You can refer to the following subsections for guidance on subject-verb agreement in particular situations:

- when a word or words come between the subject and the verb (**24e(1)**);
- when two or more subjects are joined by conjunctions (**24e(2)** and **24e(3)**);
- when word order is inverted (**24e(4)**);
- when the subject is a relative pronoun (**24e(5)**), an indefinite pronoun (**24e(6)**), or a collective noun or measurement word (**24e(7)**);
- when the subject is a noun that is plural in form but singular in meaning (**24e(8)**);
- when the subject and its complement differ in number (**24e(9)**); and
- when the subject is a noun clause beginning with *what* (**24e(10)**).

(1) Subject and verb separated by one or more words

When phrases such as the following occur between the subject and the verb, they do not affect the number of the subject or the form of the verb:

accompanied by	as well as	not to mention	including
along with	in addition to	no less than	together with

Her **salary**, together with tips, **is** just enough to live on.

Tips, together with her salary, **are** just enough to live on.

(2) Subjects joined by *and*

A compound subject (two nouns joined by *and*) that refers to a single person or thing takes a singular verb.

The **founder <u>and</u> president** of the art association **was** elected to the board of the museum.

Red beans <u>and</u> rice is the specialty of the house.

(3) Subjects joined by *or, either . . . or,* or *neither . . . nor*

When singular subjects are linked by *or, either . . . or,* or *neither . . . nor,* the verb is singular as well.

The **provost <u>or</u>** the **dean** usually **presides** at the meeting.

<u>Either</u> his **accountant <u>or</u>** his **lawyer has** the will.

If the subjects linked by one of these conjunctions differ in person or number, the verb agrees in number with the subject closer to the verb.

Neither the basket nor the **apples were** expensive. [plural]

Neither the apples nor the **basket was** expensive. [singular]

(4) Inverted word order

In most sentences, the subject precedes the verb.

The large **cities** [s] of the Northeast **were** [v] the hardest hit by the winter storms.

The subject and verb can sometimes be inverted for emphasis; however, they must still agree.

The hardest hit by the winter storms **were** [v] the large **cities** [s] of the Northeast.

When *there* begins a sentence, the subject and verb are always inverted (**20b**); the verb still agrees with the subject, which follows it.

There **are** [v] several **cities** [s] in need of federal aid.

(5) Clauses with relative pronouns

In an adjectival (relative) clause (**21b(2)**), the subject is generally a relative pronoun (*that, who,* or *which*). To determine whether the relative pronoun is singular or plural, you must find its antecedent (the word or words it refers to). When the antecedent is singular, the relative pronoun is singular; when the antecedent is plural, the relative pronoun is plural. In essence, the verb in the adjectival clause agrees with the antecedent.

[sing ant] [sing v]
The person who reviews applications is out of town this week.

[pl ant] [pl v]
The director met with the **students who are** studying abroad next quarter.

According to rules of traditional grammar, in sentences like the following, which contains the pattern *one + of +* plural noun + adjectival clause, the antecedent for the relative pronoun (*who,* in this case) is the plural noun (*students*). The verb in the adjectival clause is thus plural as well (*plan*).

pl ant   pl v

Julie is one of the **students who plan** to study abroad.

However, professional writers often consider *one*, instead of the plural noun, to be the antecedent of the relative pronoun and thus use the singular verb:

sing ant   sing v

Julie is **one** of the students **who plans** to study abroad.

(6) Indefinite pronouns

The indefinite pronouns *each, either, everybody, everyone,* and *anyone* are considered singular and so require singular verb forms.

Each of them **is willing** to lead the discussion.

Everybody in our class **takes** a turn giving a presentation.

Other indefinite pronouns, such as *all, any, some, none, half,* and *most,* can be either singular or plural, depending on whether they refer to a unit or quantity (singular) or to individuals (plural).

pl ant   pl v

My sister collects comic **books; some are** quite valuable.

sing ant   sing v

My sister collects antique **jewelry; some** of it **is** quite valuable.

When an indefinite pronoun is followed by a prepositional phrase beginning with the preposition *of,* the verb agrees in number with the object of the preposition.

pl obj pl v

None of **those are** spoiled.

sing obj sing v

None of the **food is** spoiled.

More than **half** of the **population** in West Texas **is** Hispanic.

sing obj — above **population**
sing v — above **is**

More than **half** of the **people** in West Texas **are** Hispanic.

pl obj — above **people**
pl v — above **are**

Some grammarians reason that *none*, like *no one*, is singular and thus should be followed by a singular verb.

None of the grant requests **has** been rejected.

Nonetheless, many reputable writers have used *none* with plural verbs, leading to the widespread acceptance of this usage.

None of the grant requests **have** been rejected.

(7) Collective nouns and measurement words

Collective nouns (**20a(2)**) and measurement words require singular verbs when they refer to groups or units. They require plural verbs when they refer to individuals or parts.

Singular (regarded as a group or unit)	Plural (regarded as individuals or parts)
The **majority rules.**	The **majority** of us **are** in favor.
Ten million gallons of oil **is** more than enough.	**Ten million gallons** of oil **were spilled.**
The **number** of errors **is** insignificant.	A **number** of workers **were** absent.

(8) Words ending in -s

Titles of works that are plural in form (for example, *Star Wars* and *Dombey and Son*) are treated as singular because they refer to a single book, movie, recording, or other work.

The Three Musketeers **is** one of the films she discussed in her paper.

A reference to a word is also considered singular.

Beans **is** slang for "the least amount": I don't know beans about football.

Some nouns ending in *-s* are actually singular: *linguistics, news,* and *Niagara Falls.*

The **news is** encouraging.

Nouns such as *athletics, politics,* and *electronics* can be either singular or plural, depending on their meanings.

Statistics is an interesting subject. [singular]

Statistics are often misleading. [plural]

(9) Subjects and subject complements

Some sentences may have a singular subject (**20b**) and a plural subject complement (**20c**), or vice versa. In either case, the verb agrees with the subject.

Her primary **concern is** rising health-care **costs.**

Rising health-care costs are her primary **concern.**

❓ *THINKING RHETORICALLY*

AGREEMENT OF RELATED SINGULAR AND PLURAL NOUNS

When a sentence has two or more nouns that are related, use either the singular form or the plural form consistently.

The **student** raised her **hand.**

The **students** raised their **hands.**

Occasionally, you may have to use a singular noun to retain an idiomatic expression or to avoid ambiguity.

They kept their **word.**

The **participants** were asked to name their favorite **movie.**

(10) Subjects beginning with *what*

In noun clauses (**21b(2)**), *what* may be understood as either "the thing that" or "the things that." If it is understood as "the thing that," the verb in the main clause is singular.

> What we need **is** a new policy.
> [*The thing that* we need is a new policy.]

If *what* is understood as plural (the things that), the verb in the main clause is plural.

> What we need **are** new guidelines.
> [*The things that* we need are new guidelines.]

Note that the main noun following the verb in these examples (*policy*, *guidelines*) also agrees with the verb: *policy* and *is* are singular; *guidelines* and *are* are plural.

According to a traditional grammar rule, a singular verb should be used in both the noun clause beginning with *what* and the main clause.

> What **is** needed **is** new guidelines.

However, many writers and editors today consider this rule outmoded.

Exercise 5

In each sentence, choose the correct form of the verb in parentheses. Make sure that the verb agrees with its subject according to the conventions for academic and professional writing.

1. There (is/are) at least two good reasons for changing motor oil: risk of contamination and danger of additive depletion.
2. Reasons for not changing the oil (include/includes) the cost to the driver and the inconvenience of the chore.

3. What I want to know (is/are) the number of miles I can drive before changing my oil.
4. Each of the car manuals I consulted (recommends/recommend) five-thousand-mile intervals.
5. Neither the automakers nor the oil station attendants (know/knows) how I drive, however.
6. My best friend and mechanic (says/say) four thousand miles.
7. But my brother says three thousand miles (is/are) not long enough.

Exercise 6

Complete the following sentences, making sure that subjects and verbs agree.

1. Applying for college and enrolling in courses . . .
2. Erik is one of the students who . . .
3. Either of them . . .
4. The list of volunteers . . .
5. Hidden beneath the stairs . . .
6. The teacher, along with her students, . . .
7. What we requested . . .

25 || PRONOUNS

When you use pronouns effectively, you add clarity and coherence to your writing. However, if you do not provide the words, phrases, or clauses that make your pronoun references clear, you might unintentionally cause confusion. This chapter will help you

- recognize various types of pronouns (**25a**),
- use appropriate pronouns (**25b**),
- make sure that pronouns agree with their antecedents (**25c**),
- provide clear pronoun references (**25d**),
- understand when to use *I, we,* and *you* (**25e**).

25a || RECOGNIZING PRONOUNS

A **pronoun** is commonly defined as a word used in place of a noun that has already been mentioned—its **antecedent**.

John said **he** would guide the trip.

A pronoun may also substitute for a group of words acting as a noun (see **21b(2)**).

The participant with the most experience said **he** would guide the trip.

Most pronouns refer to nouns, but some modify nouns.

This man is our guide.

Pronouns are categorized as personal, reflexive/intensive, relative, interrogative, demonstrative, and indefinite.

(1) Personal pronouns

To understand the uses of personal pronouns, you must first be able to recognize person, number, and case. **Person** indicates whether a pronoun refers to the writer (**first person**), to the reader (**second person**), or to another person, place, thing, or idea (**third person**). **Number** reveals whether a pronoun is singular or plural. **Case** refers to the form a pronoun takes to indicate its function in a sentence. Pronouns can be subjects, objects, or possessives. When they function as subjects (**20b(1)**), they are in the subjective case; when they function as objects (**20b(2)**), they are in the objective case; and when they indicate possession or a related meaning (**38a**), they are in the possessive case. (See **25b** for more information on case.) Possessives can be divided into two groups based on whether they are followed by nouns: *my, your, his, her, its, our,* and *their* are all followed by nouns; *mine, yours, his, hers, ours,* and *theirs* are not. (Notice that *his* is in both groups.)

> **Their** budget is higher than **ours.**
> [*Their* is followed by a noun; *ours* is not.]

CASE:	Subjective		Objective		Possessive	
NUMBER:	**Singular**	**Plural**	**Singular**	**Plural**	**Singular**	**Plural**
First person	I	we	me	us	my mine	our ours
Second person	you	you	you	you	your yours	your yours
Third person	he, she, it	they	him, her, it	them	his, her, hers, its	their theirs

(2) Reflexive/intensive pronouns

Reflexive pronouns direct the action back to the subject (*I saw myself*); **intensive pronouns** are used for emphasis (*I myself questioned the judge*). *Myself, yourself, himself, herself, itself, ourselves, yourselves,* and *themselves* are used as either reflexive pronouns or intensive pronouns. Both types of pronouns are objects and must be accompanied by subjects.

Reflexive pronoun	**He** was always talking to **himself.**
Intensive pronoun	**She herself** delivered the letter.

Avoid using a reflexive pronoun as a subject. A common error is using *myself* in a compound subject.

Ms. Palmquist and ~~myself~~ discussed our concern with the senator.

Hisself, themself, and *theirselves* are inappropriate in college or professional writing. Instead, use *himself* and *themselves.*

The interns worked by ~~theirselves~~ themselves on one of the projects.

(3) Relative pronouns

An adjectival clause (or relative clause) ordinarily begins with a relative pronoun: *who, whom, which, that,* or *whose.* To provide a link between this type of dependent clause and the main clause, the relative pronoun corresponds to its antecedent—a word or phrase in the main clause.

                                  ant   rel pro

The students talked to **a reporter who** had just returned from overseas.

Notice that if you rewrite the dependent clause as a separate independent clause, you use the antecedent in place of the relative pronoun.

    A reporter had just returned from overseas.

Who, whose, and *whom* ordinarily refer to people; *which* refers to things; *that* refers to things and, in some contexts, to people. The possessive *whose* (used in place of the awkward *of which*) usually refers to people but sometimes refers to things.

    The poem, **whose** author is unknown, has recently been set to music.

	Refers to people	Refers to things	Refers to either
Subjective	who	which	that
Objective	whom	which	that
Possessive			whose

Knowing the difference between an essential clause and a nonessential clause will help you decide whether to use *which* or *that* (see **21b(2)**). A clause that a reader needs in order to identify the antecedent correctly is an **essential clause**.

The person who presented the award was last year's winner.

If the essential clause were omitted from this sentence, the reader would not know which person was last year's winner.

A **nonessential clause** is *not* needed for correct identification of the antecedent and is thus set off by commas. A nonessential clause often follows a proper noun (a specific name).

Andrea Bowen, who presented the award, was last year's winner.

Notice that if the nonessential clause were removed from this sentence, the reader would still know the identity of last year's winner.

According to a traditional grammar rule, *that* is used in essential adjectival clauses, and *which* is used in nonessential adjectival clauses.

I need a job **that** pays well.

For years, I have had the same job, **which** pays well enough.

However, some professional writers do not follow both parts of this rule. Although they will not use *that* in nonessential clauses, they will use *which* in essential clauses. See **21b(2)** for more information on the use of *which* and *that*.

(4) Interrogative pronouns

The **interrogative pronouns** *what, which, who, whom,* and *whose* are question words. Be careful not to confuse *who* and *whom* (see **25b(5)**). *Who* functions as a subject; *whom* functions as an object.

Who won the award? [COMPARE: **He** won the award.]

Whom did you see at the ceremony? [COMPARE: I saw **him**.]

(5) Demonstrative pronouns

The **demonstrative pronouns**, *this* and *these*, indicate that someone or something is close by in time, space, or thought. *That* and *those* signal remoteness.

> **These** are important documents; **those** can be thrown away.

Demonstrative pronouns sometimes modify nouns.

> **These** documents should be filed.

---

❷ *THINKING RHETORICALLY*

PRONOUNS

Why is the following passage somewhat unclear?

> The study found that students succeed when they have clear directions, consistent and focused feedback, and access to help. This led administrators to create a tutoring center at our university.

The problem is that the pronoun *this* at the beginning of the second sentence could refer to all of the information provided by the study or just to the single finding that students need access to help. If you discover that one of your pronouns lacks a clear antecedent, replace the pronoun with more specific words.

> **The results of this study** led administrators to create a tutoring center at our university.

---

(6) Indefinite pronouns

Indefinite pronouns usually do not refer to specific persons, objects, ideas, or events.

anyone	anybody	anything
everyone	everybody	everything
someone	somebody	something
no one	nobody	nothing
each	either	neither

Indefinite pronouns do not refer to an antecedent. In fact, some indefinite pronouns *serve* as antecedents.

Someone forgot **her** purse.

25b | PRONOUN CASE

The term *case* refers to the form a pronoun takes to indicate its function in a sentence. There are three cases: subjective, objective, and possessive. The following sentence includes all three.

He [subjective] wants **his** [possessive] legislators to help **him** [objective].

(1) Pronouns in the subjective case

A pronoun that is the subject of a sentence is in the subjective case. To determine which pronoun form is correct in a compound subject (a noun and a pronoun joined by *and*), say the sentence using the pronoun alone, omitting the noun. For the following sentence, notice that "*Me* solved the problem" is not Standard English, but "*I* solved the problem" is.

~~Me and~~ Marisa ∧solved the problem.
                 and I

Place the pronoun last in the sequence. If the compound subject contains two pronouns, test each one by itself.

∧~~Him~~ and I confirmed the results.
 He

Pronouns following a *be* verb (*am, is, are, was, were, been*) should also be in the subjective case.

The first presenters were Kevin and ∧~~me~~.
                                      I

> **ñ MULTILINGUAL WRITERS**
>
> **NOUN OR PRONOUN AS SUBJECT**
> In some languages, a noun in the subject position may be followed
> by a pronoun. In Standardized English, though, such a pronoun
> should be omitted.
>
> My roommate ~~he~~ works in the library for three hours a week.

(2) Pronouns in the objective case

Whenever a pronoun follows an action verb or a preposition, it takes
the **objective case**.

Direct object	The whole staff admired **him**.
Indirect object	The staff sent **him** a card.
Object of a preposition	The staff depended on **him**.

Pronouns in compound objects are also in the objective case.

They will appoint Tom or ᴧI. [direct object]
ᴹᵉ

They sent Tom and ᴧI the appropriate forms. [indirect object]
ᴹᵉ

The manager sat between Tom and ᴧI at the meeting. [object of the
preposition]
ᴹᵉ

To determine whether to use the subjective or objective case, remember
to say the sentence with just the pronoun. Notice that "They will appoint *I*" does not sound right. Another test is to substitute *we* and *us*.
If *we* sounds fine, use the subjective case. If *us* sounds better, use the
objective case, as in "They sent *us* the appropriate forms."

(3) Possessive forms

Its, their, and *whose* are possessive forms. Be sure not to confuse them
with common contractions: *it's* (*it is* or *it has*), *they're* (*they are*), and
who's (*who is*).

(4) Appositive pronouns

Appositive pronouns are in the same case as the nouns they rename. In the following sentence, *the red team* is the subject, so the appositive pronoun should be in the subjective case.

> The red team—Rebecca, Leroy, and ₌me̶—won by only one point. [I]

In the next sentence, *the red team* is the object of the preposition *to,* so the appositive pronoun should be in the objective case.

> A trophy was presented to the red team—Rebecca, Leroy, and ₌I̶. [me]

When the order is reversed and a pronoun is followed by a noun, the pronoun must still be in the same case as the noun.

> ₌Us̶ students need this policy. [We]

(5) *Who/whoever* and *whom/whomever*

To choose between *who* and *whom* or between *whoever* and *whomever,* you must first determine whether the word is functioning as a subject (**20b**) or an object (**20c**). A pronoun functioning as the subject takes the subjective case.

> **Who** won the award? [COMPARE: **She** won the award.]
>
> The teachers know **who** won the award.
>
> The student **who** won the award was quite surprised.
>
> **Whoever** won the award deserves it.

When the pronoun is an object, use *whom* or *whomever.*

> **Whom** did they hire? [COMPARE: They hired **him.**]
>
> I do not know **whom** they hired.
>
> The student **whom** they hired graduated in May.
>
> **Whomever** they hired will have to work hard this year.

Whom may be omitted in sentences when no misunderstanding would result.

The friend he relied on moved away.

[*Whom* has been omitted after *friend*.]

Although many writers still prefer *whom* or *whomever* as object pronouns, dictionaries also allow the use of *who* or *whoever* in informal contexts.

I wonder **who** she voted for.

Give the campaign literature to **whoever** you see.

Who do you plan to vote for?

In college writing, though, it is better to use *whom* or *whomever* as the object pronoun.

Whom will they elect president?

(6) Pronouns with infinitives and gerunds

A pronoun grouped with an infinitive (*to* + the base form of a verb) takes the objective case, whether it comes before or after the infinitive.

The director wanted **me** to help **him**.

A gerund (*-ing* verb form functioning as a noun) is preceded by a possessive pronoun.

I appreciated **his** helping Denise. [COMPARE: I appreciated **Tom's** helping Denise.]

Notice that a possessive pronoun is used before a gerund but not before a present participle (*-ing* verb form functioning as an adjective).

I saw **him** helping Luke.

(7) Pronouns in elliptical constructions

The words *as* and *than* frequently introduce **elliptical constructions**— clauses in which the writer has intentionally omitted words. To check whether you have used the correct case in an elliptical construction, read the written sentence aloud, inserting any words that have been omitted from it.

> She admires Clarice as much as **I**. [subjective case]
> Read aloud: She admires Clarice as much as *I do.*
>
> She admires Clarice more than **I**. [subjective case]
> Read aloud: She admires Clarice more than *I do.*
>
> She admires Clarice more than **me**. [objective case]
> Read aloud: She admires Clarice more than *she admires me.*

Exercise 1

Revise the following paragraph, using appropriate pronouns. Some sentences may not require editing.

¹When me and my brother were in middle school, we formed a band with our friends Jason and Andrew. ²My grandmother had given Jake a guitar and I a drum kit for Christmas. ³We practiced either alone or together for the rest of the winter. ⁴Then, in the spring, we met up with Jason, who we had known for years. ⁵Him and his cousin Andrew, whom we later called Android, were excited to join me and Jake. ⁶Jason already had a guitar, and Andrew could sing. ⁷After we played together one afternoon, we decided to call ourself The Crash. ⁸Jason and Andrew came over to our house to jam whenever they're parents let them—which was most of the time. ⁹Our parents did not mind our noise at all. ¹⁰My dad said us playing reminded him of his own teenage garage band.

Exercise 2

Following the guidelines for college and professional writing, choose the pronouns that appropriately complete the following sentences.

1. Separate the white chess pieces from the black pieces and decide (who/whom) will play with the white pieces.

2. The opening move is made by (whoever/whomever) has received the white game pieces.

3. (Whoever/Whomever) the black pieces were given to makes the next move.

4. The player (who/whom) can put the other player's king in check is close to becoming the winner.

5. (Whoever/Whomever) is unable to free his or her king must concede the game.

25c   PRONOUN-ANTECEDENT AGREEMENT

A pronoun and its antecedent (the word or word group to which it refers) agree in number (both are singular or both are plural).

The **supervisor** said **he** would help.
[Both antecedent and pronoun are singular.]

My **colleagues** said **they** would help.
[Both antecedent and pronoun are plural.]

A pronoun also agrees with its antecedent in gender (masculine, feminine, or neuter).

Joseph claims **he** can meet the deadline. [masculine antecedent]

Anna claims **she** can meet the deadline. [feminine antecedent]

The **committee** claims **it** can meet the deadline. [neuter antecedent]

ⓝ MULTILINGUAL WRITERS

POSSESSIVE PRONOUNS
A possessive pronoun (*my, your, our, his, her, its,* or *their*), also
called a **possessive determiner**, agrees with its antecedent, not
with the noun it precedes.

Ken Carlson brought ^his ~~her~~ young daughter to the office today.

[The possessive pronoun *his* agrees with the antecedent, *Ken
Carlson*, not with the following noun, *daughter*.]

(1) Indefinite pronouns

Although most antecedents for pronouns are nouns, antecedents can be
indefinite pronouns (**25a(6)**). Notice that an indefinite pronoun such
as *everyone, someone,* or *anybody* takes a singular verb form.

Everyone **has** [not *have*] the right to an opinion.

Difficulties arise, however, because words like *everyone* and *everybody* seem
to refer to more than one person even though they take a singular verb.
Thus, the definition of grammatical number and our everyday notion of
number conflict. In conversation and informal writing, a plural pronoun
(*they, them,* or *their*) is often used with the singular *everyone*. Nonetheless,
when you write for an audience that expects you to follow traditional
grammar rules, make sure to use a third-person singular pronoun.

Everyone has the combination to ^his or her ~~their~~ private locker.

You can avoid the awkwardness of using *his or her* by using an article
instead, by making both the antecedent and the possessive pronoun
plural, or by rewriting the sentence using the passive voice (**24c**).

Everyone has the combination to **a** private locker. [article]

Students have combinations to **their** private lockers. [plural antecedent
and plural possessive pronoun]

The combination to a private locker **is issued** to everyone. [passive voice]

(2) Referring to both genders

When an antecedent can refer to people of either gender, rewrite the sentence to make the antecedent plural or use *he or she* or *his or her* if doing so is not too cumbersome.

Lawyers
~~A lawyer~~ represents~~,~~ ~~his~~ *their* clients. [plural pronoun and plural antecedent]

A lawyer represents the clients **he or she** has accepted.

A lawyer represents **his or her** clients.

(See **33c** for more information on using inclusive language.)

(3) Two antecedents joined by *or* or *nor*

If a singular and a plural antecedent are joined by *or* or *nor,* place the plural antecedent second and use a plural pronoun.

Either the senator **or** her <u>assistants</u> will explain how <u>they</u> devised the plan for tax reform.

Neither the president **nor** the <u>senators</u> stated that <u>they</u> would support the proposal.

(4) Collective nouns

When an antecedent is a collective noun (**20a(2)**) such as *team, faculty,* or *committee,* determine whether you intend the noun to be understood as singular or plural and then make sure that the pronoun agrees in number with the noun.

it
The choir decided that ~~they~~ would tour during the winter. [Because the choir decided as a group, *choir* should be considered singular. The singular form, *it*, replaces the plural, *they*.]

they
The committee may disagree on methods, but ~~it~~ must agree on basic aims. [Because the committee members are behaving as individuals, *committee* is regarded as plural. The plural form, *they*, replaces the singular, *it*.]

Exercise 3

Revise the following sentences so that pronouns and antecedents agree.

1. A researcher relies on a number of principles to help him make ethical decisions.

2. Everyone should have the right to participate in a study only if they feel comfortable doing so.

3. A team of researchers should provide its volunteers with consent forms, in which they describe to the volunteers the procedures and risks involved in participation.

4. Every participant should be guaranteed that the information they provide will remain confidential.

5. Institutions of higher education require that a researcher address ethical issues in their proposal.

25d CLEAR PRONOUN REFERENCE

The meaning of each pronoun in a sentence should be immediately obvious. In the following sentence, the pronouns *them* and *itself* clearly refer to their antecedents, *shells* and *carrier shell,* respectively.

The **carrier shell** gathers small empty **shells** and attaches **them** to **itself.**

A pronoun may refer to two or more antecedents.

Jack and I have collected shells since **we** were eight years old.

Sometimes an antecedent follows a pronoun.

Because of **their** beauty and rarity, **shells** attract collectors worldwide.

(1) Ambiguous or unclear pronoun references

When a pronoun can refer to either of two antecedents, the ambiguity may confuse readers. To make the antecedent clear, replace the pronoun with a noun or rewrite the sentence. The following revised sentences clarify that Mr. Eggers, not Mr. Anderson, will be in charge of the project.

Mr. Anderson told Mr. Eggers that ∧he would be in charge of the project.
Mr. Eggers

OR

Mr. Anderson put Mr. Eggers in charge of the project.

(2) Remote or awkward references

To help readers understand your meaning, place pronouns as close to their antecedents as possible. The following sentence needs to be revised so that the relative pronoun *that* is close to its antecedent, *poem*. Otherwise, the reader would wonder how a new book could be written in 1945.

The **poem** ∧has been published in a new book ~~that was originally written in 1945~~.
that was originally written in 1945

Notice, however, that a relative pronoun does not always have to follow its antecedent directly. In the following example, there is no risk of misunderstanding.

We slowly began to notice **changes** in our lives **that** we had never expected.

(3) Broad or implied references

Pronouns such as *it, this, that,* and *which* may refer to a specific word or phrase or to the sense of a whole clause, sentence, or paragraph.

The workload was manageable, once I became used to **it**. [*It* refers specifically to *workload*.]

Large corporations may seem stronger than individuals, but **that** is not true. [*That* refers to the sense of the whole first clause.]

Unless the meaning is clear, avoid reference to the general idea of a preceding clause or sentence. Instead, state clearly what *this* or *that* refers to. In the following sentence, *this* may refer to the class-attendance policy or to the students' feelings about it.

> When class attendance is compulsory, some students feel that education is being forced on them. This~~perception~~is unwarranted.

In addition, remember to express an idea explicitly rather than using a vague *it* or *they*.

> My father is a music teacher. ~~It~~Teaching music is a profession that requires much patience.

> ~~They~~Former students say my father shows a great deal of patience with everyone.

Be especially careful to provide clear antecedents when you are referring to the work or possessions of others. The following sentence requires revision because *she* can refer to someone other than Jen Norton:

> In ~~Jen Norton's~~her new book, ~~she~~Jen Norton argues for election reform.

(4) The use of *it* without an antecedent

The expletive *it* does not have a specific antecedent (see **20b**). Instead, it is used to postpone, and thus give emphasis to, the subject of a sentence. A sentence that begins with this expletive can sometimes be wordy or awkward. Revise such a sentence by replacing *it* with the postponed subject.

> ~~It~~Trying to repair the car was ~~no use trying to repair the car~~useless.

Avoid placing one *it* near another *it* with a different meaning.

> ~~It~~Staying in the old apartment would be simpler ~~to stay in the old apartment~~, but it is too far from my job. [The first *it* is an expletive; the second *it* refers to *apartment*.]

Exercise 4

Edit the following sentences to make all references clear. Some sentences may not require editing.

1. It is remarkable to read about Lance Armstrong's victories.

2. A champion cyclist, a cancer survivor, and a humanitarian, it is no wonder that Lance Armstrong is one of the most highly celebrated athletes in the world.

3. Armstrong's mother encouraged his athleticism, which led to his becoming a professional triathlete by age sixteen.

4. Though you might not believe it, Armstrong was only a senior in high school when he started training for the Olympic developmental team.

5. By the time he was twenty-five, Armstrong ranked as the top cyclist in the world.

6. Not long afterward, because of intense pain, he sought medical attention, and they told him he had testicular cancer.

7. The cancer had spread to his lungs and brain; thus, they said his chances for recovery were slim.

8. Armstrong underwent dramatic surgery and aggressive chemotherapy; this eventually helped him recover.

9. Armstrong started training five months after their diagnosis and went on to win major championships, including the Tour de France.

10. For Lance Armstrong, it hasn't been only about racing bikes; he has become a humanitarian as well, creating the Lance Armstrong Foundation to help cancer patients and to fund cancer research around the world.

25e   USE OF FIRST-PERSON AND SECOND-PERSON PRONOUNS

Using *I* is appropriate when you are writing about personal experience. In academic and professional writing, the use of the first-person singular pronoun is also a way to distinguish your own views from those of others. However, if you frequently repeat *I feel* or *I think,* your readers may suspect that you do not understand much beyond your own experience.

We, the first-person plural pronoun, is trickier to use correctly. When you use it, make sure that your audience can tell which individuals are included in this plural reference. For example, if you are writing a paper for a college course, does *we* mean you and the instructor, you and your fellow students, or some other group (such as all Americans)? Because you may inadvertently use *we* in an early draft to refer to more than one group of people, as you edit, check to see that you have used this first-person plural pronoun consistently.

If you decide to address readers directly, you will undoubtedly use the second-person pronoun *you* (as we, the authors of this handbook, have done). There is some disagreement, though, over whether to permit the use of the indefinite *you* to mean "a person" or "people in general." Check with your instructor about this usage. If you are told to avoid using the indefinite *you*, recast your sentences. For example, use *one* instead of *you*.

Even in huge, anonymous cities, ~~you find~~ ^{one finds} community spirit.

If the use of *one* is too formal, try changing the word order and/or using different words.

Community spirit arises even in huge, anonymous cities.

Exercise 5

Revise the following paragraph to eliminate the use of the first- and second-person pronouns.

[1]In my opinion, some animals should be as free as we are. [2]For example, I think orangutans, African elephants, and Atlantic bottlenose dolphins should roam freely rather than be held in captivity. [3]We should neither exhibit them in zoos nor use them for medical research. [4]If you study animals such as these you will see that, like us, they show emotions, self-awareness, and intention. [5]You might even find that some use language to communicate. [6]It is clear to me that they have the right to freedom.

26 ‖ MODIFIERS

Modifiers are words, phrases, or clauses that modify; that is, they qualify or limit the meaning of other words. For example, if you were to describe a sandwich as "humdrum," as "lacking sufficient mustard," or as something "that might have tasted good two days ago," you would be using a word, a phrase, or a clause to modify *sandwich*. When used effectively, modifiers enliven writing with details and enhance its coherence. This chapter will help you

- recognize modifiers (**26a**),
- use conventional comparative and superlative forms (**26b**),
- revise double negatives (**26c**), and
- place modifiers effectively (**26d** and **26e**).

26a ‖ RECOGNIZING MODIFIERS

The most common modifiers are adjectives and adverbs. You can distinguish an adjective from an adverb by determining what type of word is modified. **Adjectives** modify nouns and pronouns (**20a(4)**); **adverbs** modify verbs, adjectives, and other adverbs (**20a(5)**).

Adjectives	Adverbs
She looked **curious.** [modifies pronoun]	She looked at me **curiously.** [modifies verb]
productive meeting [modifies noun]	**highly** productive meeting [modifies adjective]
a **quick** lunch [modifies noun]	**very** quickly [modifies adverb]

🔴 *MULTILINGUAL WRITERS*

ADJECTIVE SUFFIXES IN OTHER LANGUAGES

In some languages, adjectives and nouns agree in number. In Spanish, for example, when a noun is plural, the adjective is plural as well: *vistas claras.* In English, however, adjectives do not have a plural form: *clear views.* For more information on adjectives, see Chapter 45.

You can also identify a modifier by considering its form. Many adjectives end with one of these suffixes: *-able, -al, -ful, -ic, -ish, -less,* or *-y.*

accept**able**   ren**tal**   event**ful**   ange**lic**   sheep**ish**   effort**less**   sleep**y**

Present and past participles (24a(5)) can also be used as adjectives.

a **determining** factor   a **determined** effort
[present participle]   [past participle]

Be sure to include the complete *-ed* ending of a past participle.

Please see the ⌃enclose̶d̶ documents for more details.
(enclosed)

❓ *THINKING RHETORICALLY*

ADJECTIVES

When your rhetorical situation calls for vivid images or emotional intensity, choose appropriate adjectives to convey these qualities. That is, instead of describing a movie you did not like with the overused adjective *boring,* you could say that it was *tedious* or *mind-numbing.* When you sense that you might be using a lackluster adjective, search for an alternative in a thesaurus. If any of the words listed there are unfamiliar, be sure to look them up in a dictionary so that you use them correctly.

WINTER'S BONE PRODUCTIONS/THE KOBAL COLLECTION

Movie posters often include descriptive adjectives.

The easiest type of adverb to identify is the adverb of manner (**20a(5)**). It is formed by adding *-ly* to an adjective.

careful**ly**   unpleasant**ly**   silent**ly**

If the adjective ends in *-y,* the *-y* is changed to *-i* before *-ly* is added.

eas**y** [adjective]   eas**ily** [adverb]

If the adjective ends in *-le,* the *-e* is dropped and just *y* is added.

simp**le** [adjective]   simp**ly** [adverb]

However, not all words ending in *-ly* are adverbs. Certain adjectives related to nouns also end in *-ly* (*friend, friendly; hour, hourly*). In addition, not all adverbs end in *-ly.* Adverbs that indicate time or place (*today, tomorrow, here, there*) do not have the *-ly* ending; neither does the negator *not.* A few words—for example, *fast* and *well*—can function as either adjectives or adverbs.

They like **fast** cars. [adjective]

They ran **fast** enough to catch the bus. [adverb]

(1) Modifiers of linking verbs and action verbs

An adjective used after a sensory linking verb (*look, smell, taste, sound,* or *feel*) modifies the subject of the sentence (**20b**). A common error is to use an adverb after this type of linking verb.

I felt~bad~badly about missing the rally. [The adjective *bad* modifies *I*.]

However, when *look, smell, taste, sound,* or *feel* is used as an action verb (**20a(1)**), it can be modified by an adverb.

She looked **angrily** at the referee. [The adverb *angrily* modifies *looked*.]
BUT She looked **angry**. [The adjective *angry* modifies *she*.]

The words *good* and *well* are easy to confuse. In academic rhetorical situations, *good* is considered an adjective and so is not used with action verbs.

The whole team played~well~good.

Another frequent error is the dropping of *-ly* endings from adverbs. Although you may not hear the ending when you speak, be sure to include it when you write.

They bought only~locally~local grown vegetables.

Exercise 1

Revise the following sentences so that all adjectives and adverbs are used in ways considered conventional in academic writing.

1. Relaxation techniques have been developed for people who feel uncomfortably in some way.

2. Meditation is one technique that is real helpful in relieving stress.

3. People searching for relief from tension have found that a breathing meditation works good.

4. They sit quiet and concentrate on both inhaling and exhaling.

5. They concentrate on breathing deep.

(2) Nouns as modifiers

Adjectives and adverbs are the most common modifiers, but nouns (**20a(2)**) can also be modifiers (***movie** critic*, ***reference** manual*). A string of noun modifiers can be cumbersome. The following example shows how a sentence with too many noun modifiers can be revised.

The ~~Friday afternoon~~ Student Affairs Committee meeting ˄has been cancelled.
  scheduled for Friday afternoon

(3) Phrases and clauses as modifiers

Participial phrases, prepositional phrases, and some infinitive phrases are modifiers (**21a(3)** and **21a(4)**).

Growing in popularity every year, mountain bikes now dominate the market. [participial phrase modifying the noun *bikes*]

Mountain bikes first became popular **in the 1980s.** [prepositional phrase modifying the verb *became*]

Some people use mountain bikes **to commute to work.** [infinitive phrase modifying the verb *use*]

Adjectival (relative) clauses and adverbial clauses are both modifiers (see **21b(2)**).

BMX bicycles have frames **that are relatively small.** [adjectival clause modifying the noun *frames*]

Although mountain bikes are designed for off-road use, many people use them on city streets. [adverbial clause modifying the verb *use*]

(4) Sentence modifers

Sentence modifiers are generally single-word adverbs that end in *ly*. A sentence modifier indicates the writer's perspective on or attitude toward the information conveyed in the sentence. When such a modifier begins a sentence, it is followed by a comma.

Clearly, some adjustments must be made to the proposal.

Fortunately, the storm veered to the east.

26b   COMPARATIVES AND SUPERLATIVES

Many adjectives and adverbs change form to show degrees of quality, quantity, time, distance, manner, and so on. The **positive form** of an adjective or adverb is the word you would look for in a dictionary: *hard, urgent, deserving*. The **comparative form**, which either ends in *-er* or is preceded by *more* or *less*, compares two elements: *I worked **harder** than I ever had before*. The **superlative form**, which either ends in *-est* or is preceded by *most* or *least*, compares three or more elements: *Jeff is the **hardest** worker I have ever met*.

Positive	Comparative	Superlative
hard	harder	hardest
urgent	more/less urgent	most/least urgent
deserving	more/less deserving	most/least deserving

(1) Complete and logical comparisons

When you use the comparative form of an adjective or an adverb, be sure to indicate what two elements you are comparing. The revision of the following sentence makes it clear that a diesel engine and a gas engine are being compared:

A diesel engine is **heavier**$_\wedge$. than a gas engine

Occasionally, the second element in a comparison is implied. The word *paper* does not have to be included after *second* in the sentence below. The reader can infer that the grade on the second paper was better than the grade on the first paper.

> She wrote **two** papers; the instructor gave her a **better** grade on the second.

A comparison should also be logical. The following example illogically compares *population* and *Wabasha*:

> The **population** of Winona is larger than **Wabasha**.

You can revise this type of faulty comparison in one of three ways:

- Repeat the word that refers to what is being compared.

  The **population** of Winona is larger than the **population** of Wabasha.

- Use a pronoun that corresponds to the first element in the comparison.

The **population** of Winona is larger than **that** of Wabasha.

- Use possessive forms.

Winona's population is larger than **Wabasha's.**

(2) Double comparatives or superlatives

Use either an ending (*-er* or *-est*) or a preceding qualifier (*more* or *most*), not both, to form a comparative or superlative.

The first bridge is **more narrower** than the second.

The **most narrowest** bridge is in the northern part of the state.

Some modifiers have *absolute meanings*. These modifiers name qualities that are either present in full or not at all:

complete eternal fatal finite identical perfect straight unique

Expressing degrees of such modifiers is illogical, so their comparative and superlative forms are rarely used in academic writing.

a ~~more~~ perfect society   the ~~most~~ unique campus

Exercise 2

Provide the correct comparative or superlative form of each modifier within parentheses.

1. Amphibians can be divided into three groups. Frogs and toads are in the (common) group.
2. Because they do not have to maintain a specific body temperature, amphibians eat (frequently) than mammals do.

3. Reptiles may look like amphibians, but their skin is (dry).

4. During the Devonian period, the (close) ancestors of amphibians were fish with fins that looked like legs.

5. In general, amphibians have (few) bones in their skeletons than other animals with backbones have.

6. Color markings on amphibians vary, though the back of an amphibian is usually (dark) than its belly.

26c DOUBLE NEGATIVES

The term **double negative** refers to the use of two negative words to express a single negation. Unless you are portraying dialogue, revise any double negatives you find in your writing.

He did**n't** keep ^any ~~**no**~~ records.

OR

He ^kept ~~did**n't** keep~~ **no** records.

Using *not* or *nothing* with *hardly, barely,* or *scarcely* creates a double negative. The following examples show how sentences containing such double negatives can be revised:

I could**n't hardly** quit in the middle of the job.

OR

I could**n't** ~~**hardly**~~ quit in the middle of the job.

The motion passed with **not scarcely** a protest.

OR

The motion passed with ^little ~~**not scarcely**~~ a protest.

ñ MULTILINGUAL WRITERS

NEGATION IN OTHER LANGUAGES

The use of two negative words in one sentence is common in languages such as Spanish:

*Yo **no** compré **nada**.* ["I didn't buy anything."]

If your native language allows this type of negation, be especially careful to check for and revise any double negatives you find in your English essays.

26d   PLACEMENT OF MODIFIERS

Effective placement of modifiers will improve the clarity and coherence of your sentences. A **misplaced modifier** obscures the meaning of a sentence.

(1) Keeping related words together

Place the modifiers *almost, even, hardly, just,* and *only* before the words or word groups they modify. Altering placement can alter meaning.

The committee can **only** nominate two members for the position. [The committee cannot *appoint* the two members to the position.]

The committee can nominate **only** two members for the position. [The committee cannot nominate more than two members.]

Only the committee can nominate two members for the position. [No person or group other than the committee can nominate members.]

(2) Placing phrases and clauses near the words they modify

Readers expect phrases and clauses to modify the nearest grammatical element. The revision of the following sentence clarifies that the prosecutor, not the witness, was skillful:

> With great skill, the
> ∧~~The~~ prosecutor cross-examined the witness ~~with great skill~~.

The following revision makes it clear that the phrase *crouched and ugly* describes the phantom, not the boy:

> The   crouched and ugly
> ∧~~Crouched and ugly, the~~ young boy gasped at the∧phantom moving
>
> across the stage.

The next sentence is fine as long as Jesse wrote the proposal, not the review. If he wrote the review, the sentence should be recast.

> I have not read the review of the proposal Jesse wrote.

> Jesse's
> I have not read∧~~the~~ review of the proposal ~~Jesse wrote~~.

(3) Revising squinting modifiers

A **squinting modifier** can be interpreted as modifying either what precedes it or what follows it. To avoid such lack of clarity, you can reposition the modifier or revise the entire sentence.

> Even though Erikson lists some advantages **overall** his vision of a successful business is faulty.

Revisions

> Even though Erikson lists some **overall** advantages, his vision of a successful business is faulty. [modifer repositioned; punctuation added]

> Erikson lists some advantages**; however, overall,** his vision of a successful business is faulty. [sentence revised]

Exercise 3

Improve the clarity of the following sentences by moving the modifiers. Not all sentences require editing.

1. Alfred Joseph Hitchcock was born the son of a poultry dealer in London.

2. Hitchcock was only identified with thrillers after making his third movie, *The Lodger*.

3. Hitchcock moved to the United States in 1939 and eventually became a naturalized citizen.

4. Hitchcock's most famous movies revolved around psychological improbabilities that are still discussed by movie critics today.

5. Although his movies are known for suspense sometimes moviegoers also remember Hitchcock's droll sense of humor.

6. Hitchcock just did not direct movie thrillers; he also produced two television series.

7. Originally a British citizen, Queen Elizabeth knighted Alfred Hitchcock in 1980.

26e   DANGLING MODIFIERS

Dangling modifiers are phrases (**21a**) or **elliptical clauses** (clauses without a subject) (**21b(2)**) that lack an appropriate word to modify. To avoid including dangling modifiers in your essays, first look carefully at any sentence that begins with a phrase or an elliptical clause. If the phrase or clause suggests an action, be sure that what follows the modifier is the actor (the subject of the sentence). If there is no actor performing the action indicated in the phrase, the modifier is dangling. To revise this type of dangling modifier, name an actor—either in the modifier or in the main clause.

Lying on the beach, time became irrelevant. [Time cannot lie on a beach.]

Revisions

While **we** were lying on the beach, time became irrelevant. [actor in the modifier]

Lying on the beach, **we** found that time became irrelevant. [actor in the main clause]

While eating lunch, waves lapped at our toes. [Waves cannot eat lunch.]

Revisions

While **we** were eating lunch, waves lapped at our toes. [actor in the modifier]

While eating lunch, **we** noticed the water lapping at our toes. [actor in the main clause]

The following sentences illustrate revisions of other common types of dangling modifiers:

To avoid getting sunburn, ⌃you should apply sunscreen ~~should be applied~~ before going outside. [Sunscreen cannot avoid getting sunburn.]

⌃Because they were in ~~In~~ a rush to get to the beach, an accident occurred. [An accident cannot be in a rush.]

Although you will most frequently find a dangling modifier at the beginning of a sentence, you may sometimes find one at the end of a sentence.

Good equipment is important ⌃for anyone ~~when~~ snorkeling. [Equipment cannot snorkel.]

Sentence modifiers and absolute phrases are *not* dangling modifiers.

The fog finally lifting, vacationers headed for the beach.

Marcus played well in the final game, **on the whole.**

Exercise 4

Revise the following sentences to eliminate misplaced and dangling modifiers. Some sentences may not require editing.

1. Climbing a mountain, fitness becomes all-important.
2. To make the climb a true adventure, climbers must doubt whether they will reach the summit.
3. Having set their goals, the mountain must challenge the climbers.
4. In determining an appropriate challenge, considering safety precautions is necessary.
5. Taking care to stay roped together, accidents are less likely to occur.
6. Even when expecting sunny weather, rain gear should be packed.
7. Knowing how to rappel, descent from a cliff is easier and safer.
8. Although adding extra weight, climbers should not leave home without a first-aid kit.
9. Climbers should not let themselves become frustrated if they are not immediately successful.
10. By taking pains at the beginning of a trip, agony can be averted at the end of a trip.

Exercise 5

Using what you have learned in this chapter, revise all modifier errors in the following sentences.

1. As a woman of both the nineteenth and twentieth centuries, the life of Gertrude Bell was unusual.

2. Young, wealthy, and intelligent, many people were impressed by the red-headed Bell.

3. Among the first women to graduate from Oxford, she couldn't hardly be satisfied with domestic life.

4. Instead, Bell traveled to what were considered the most remotest countries in the world, saw the wonders of the Ottoman Empire, and explored the desert of Iraq.

5. Several of the Arab sheiks who knew Bell thought that she acted bold.

6. The war in Iraq did not give Bell no time to pursue her research.

7. She became an Arab rebellion supporter.

8. While traveling in Iraq, meetings with important politicians took place.

9. In 1921, Winston Churchill invited Bell to a conference in the Middle East because the other Great Britain conference participants knew little about Iraq.

10. When the photo of the conference participants was taken, Bell looked elegantly in her feathered hat and silk dress among the thirty-six black-suited males.

S

EFFECTIVE SENTENCES

Dover Publications

❷ *THINKING RHETORICALLY*

SENTENCE STYLE

Most professional writers and readers use the following words to describe effective sentences.

- *Exact.* Precise words and word combinations ensure exactness and enable readers to come as close as they can to a full understanding of the writer's message.
- *Conventional.* Sentences are conventional when they conform to the usage expectations of a particular community. For most academic assignments, you will be expected to use Standardized English.
- *Consistent.* A consistent writing style is characterized by the use of the same types of words and grammatical structures throughout a piece of writing. A style that is inconsistent jars the reader's expectations.
- *Parallel.* Related to consistency, parallelism refers to the placement of similar ideas into similar grammatical structures.
- *Concise.* Concise prose is free of redundancies.
- *Coherent.* Coherence refers to clear connections between adjacent sentences and paragraphs.
- *Varied.* To write appealing paragraphs, a writer uses both short and long sentences. When sentences vary in length, they usually also vary in structure, rhythm, and emphasis.

In the following chapters, you will learn to identify the rhetorical options considered effective by most academic and professional writers. Remember, though, that appropriateness varies across rhetorical situations. You may find that it does not make sense to apply a general rule such as "Use the active voice" in all circumstances. For example, you may be expected to write a vigorous description of an event, detailing exactly what happened, but find that you need to use the passive voice when you do not know who was responsible for the event: Several of the campaign signs *were defaced*. Or, as another example, you may need to set aside the rule calling for Standardized English if you are writing dialogue in which the speakers use regional dialects. Analyzing your rhetorical situation, rather than always following general rules, will help you write clear, purposeful sentences that engage your readers.

27 | SENTENCE UNITY

Effective academic and professional writing is composed of sentences that are consistent, clear, and complete. By carefully crafting your sentences, you demonstrate concern for your audience and awareness of your rhetorical situation. Such consideration, in turn, gives you a better chance of achieving your rhetorical purpose. This chapter can help you

- choose and arrange details (**27a**),
- revise mixed metaphors and mixed constructions (**27b** and **27c**),
- relate sentence parts (**27d**),
- include necessary words (**27e**), and
- complete comparisons (**27f**) and intensifiers (**27g**).

27a | CHOOSING AND ARRANGING DETAILS

Well-chosen details add interest and credibility to your writing. As you revise, you may occasionally notice a sentence that would be clearer and more believable with the addition of a phrase or two about time, location, or cause.

Missing important detail	An astrophysicist from the Harvard-Smithsonian Center has predicted a galactic storm.
With detail added	An astrophysicist from the Harvard-Smithsonian Center has predicted **that** a galactic storm **will occur within the next 10 million years.**

Without the additional information about time, most readers would wonder when the storm was supposed to occur. The added detail makes the sentence clearer.

The details you choose will help your readers understand your message. If you provide too many within a single sentence, though, your readers may lose sight of your main point. When you revise, be sure that the details you included in your first draft are still meaningful. The writer of the following sentence deleted the mention of her uncle as she revised because this information was irrelevant to the main idea of her essay.

When I was only sixteen, I left home to attend a college in California ~~that my uncle had graduated from twenty years earlier~~.

When considering how many details to include, be sure that each one contributes to the central thought, as in the following description of brain activity:

A given mental task may involve a complicated web of circuits, which interact in varying degrees with others throughout the brain—not like the parts in a machine, but like the instruments in a symphony orchestra combining their tenor, volume, and resonance to create a particular musical effect. —JAMES SHREEVE, "Beyond the Brain"

By using parallel structures (see Chapter 30) and careful punctuation, James Shreeve created a long yet focused sentence.

Besides choosing details purposefully, you also need to indicate a clear connection between the details and the main idea of your sentence.

| **Unrelated** | Many tigers facing possible extinction live in India, **where there are many people.** |
| **Related** | Many tigers facing possible extinction live in India, **where their natural habitat is shrinking because of population pressure.** |

27b | REVISING MIXED METAPHORS

When you use language that evokes images, make sure that the images are meaningfully related. Unrelated images that appear in the same sentence are called **mixed metaphors**. The following sentence includes incompatible images.

As he climbed the corporate ladder, he ^incurred a large ~~sank into a sea of~~ debt.

The combination of two images—climbing a ladder and sinking into a sea—could create a picture in the reader's mind of a man hanging onto a ladder as it disappears into the water. The easiest way to revise such a sentence is to replace the words evoking one of the conflicting images.

27C   REVISING MIXED CONSTRUCTIONS

A sentence that begins with one kind of grammatical structure and shifts to another is a **mixed construction**. To untangle a mixed construction, make sure that the sentence includes a conventional subject—a noun, a noun phrase, a gerund phrase, an infinitive phrase, or a noun clause. Prepositional phrases and adverbial clauses are not typical subjects.

^Practicing ~~By practicing~~ a new language daily will help you become proficient.
[A gerund phrase replaces a prepositional phrase.]

^Her scholarship award ~~Although she won a scholarship~~ does not give her the right to skip classes.
[A noun phrase replaces an adverbial clause.]

If you find a sentence that has a mixed construction, you can either revise the subject, as in the previous examples, or leave the beginning of the sentence as a modifier and add a new subject after it.

By practicing a new language daily, **you** will become more proficient.

Although she won a scholarship, **it** does not give her the right to skip classes.

Exercise 1

Revise the following sentences so that details clearly support the main idea. Correct any mixed metaphors or mixed constructions.

1. In the United States, each person has one vote, but there may be problems at the polling booths.

2. Everyone's voting rights should be protected. The federal government has funded the replacement of the punch-card ballot.

3. Many states use optical scanners, which were also used on the standardized tests we took in high school. These scanners sort readable from unreadable ballots.

4. Some voters question the use of touch-screen voting systems. These systems leave no paper trail of all the ballots election officers need to swim through during a recount.

5. By providing educational materials helps citizens learn where and how to vote.

27d   RELATING SENTENCE PARTS

When drafting, writers sometimes compose sentences in which the subject is said to be something or to do something that is not logically possible. This breakdown in meaning is called **faulty predication**. Similarly, mismatches between a verb and its complement can obscure meaning.

(1) Mismatch between subject and verb

The joining of a subject and a verb must create a meaningful idea.

Mismatch   The absence of detail screams out at the reader.
[An *absence* cannot scream.]

Revision   The reader immediately notices the absence of detail.

(2) Illogical equation with *be*

When a form of the verb *be* joins two parts of a sentence (the subject and the subject complement), these two parts need to be logically related.

Free speech
 ‸~~The importance of free speech~~ is essential to a democracy.
[*Importance* cannot be essential.]

(3) Mismatches in definitions

When you write a sentence that states a formal definition, the term you are defining should be followed by a noun or a noun phrase, not an adverbial clause (**21b**). Avoid using *is when* or *is where*.

Ecology is‸ the ~~when you~~ study‸ of the relationships among living organisms and between living organisms and their environment.

Exploitative competition is‸ the contest between ~~where~~ two or more organisms‸ vying ~~vie~~ for a limited resource such as food.

(4) Mismatch of *reason* with *is because*

You can see why *reason* and *is because* are a mismatch by looking at the meaning of *because*: "for the reason that." Saying "the reason is for the reason that" is redundant. Be sure to revise any sentence containing the construction *the reason is ... because.*

The ~~reason the~~ old train station was closed ~~is~~ because it had fallen into disrepair.

(5) Mismatch between verb and complement

A verb and its complement should fit together meaningfully.

| **Mismatch** | Only a few students used the incorrect use of *there*. [To "use an incorrect use" is not logical.] |
| **Revision** | Only a few students used *there* incorrectly. |

To make sure that a relative pronoun in the object position is connected logically to a verb, replace the pronoun with its antecedent. Then check that the subject and verb have a logical connection. In the following sentence, *the inspiration* is the antecedent for *that*.

| **Mismatch** | The inspiration that the author created touched young writers. ["The author created the inspiration" does not make sense.] |
| **Revision** | The author inspired young writers. |

Verbs used to integrate information appear in *signal phrases* and are often followed by specific types of complements. Some of the verbs used in this way are listed with their typical complements. (Some verbs such as *explain* fall into more than one category.)

VERBS FOR SIGNAL PHRASES AND THEIR COMPLEMENTS

Verb + *that* noun clause

| agree | claim | explain | report | suggest |
| argue | demonstrate | maintain | state | think |

Example: The researcher <u>**reported**</u> that the weather patterns had changed.

Verb + noun phrase + *that* noun clause

| assure | convince | inform | remind | tell |

Example: He <u>**told**</u> the reporters that he was planning to resign.

Verb + *wh-* noun clause

| demonstrate | discover | explain | report | suggest |
| describe | discuss | investigate | state | wonder |

Example: She <u>**described**</u> what had happened.

Exercise 2

Revise the following sentences so that each verb is followed by a conventional complement.

1. The speaker discussed that applications had specific requirements.
2. He convinced that mass transit was affordable.
3. The two groups agreed how the problem could be solved.
4. Brown described that improvements had been made to the old house.
5. They wondered that such a catastrophe could happen.

27e   INCLUDING NECESSARY WORDS

When we speak or write quickly, we often omit small words. As you revise, be sure to include all necessary articles, prepositions, verbs, and conjunctions.

The meeting took place in∧auditorium. [missing an article]
<small>an</small>

We discussed a couple∧issues. [missing a preposition]
<small>of</small>

When a sentence has a **compound verb** (two verbs linked by a conjunction), you may need to supply a different preposition for each verb to make your meaning clear.

He neither **believes**∧nor **approves of** the plan.
<small>in</small>

All verbs, both auxiliary and main (24a(4)), should be included to make sentences complete.

She∧spoken with all the candidates.
<small>has</small>

Voter turnout has never∧and will never be 100 percent.
<small>been</small>

When a sentence consists of two short clauses and the verb in both clauses is the same, the verb in the second clause may be omitted.

The wind **was** fierce and the thunder [was] deafening.

Include the word *that* before a clause when it makes the sentence easier to read. Without the added *that* in the following sentence, a reader may stumble over *discovered the fossil* before understanding that *the fossil* is linked to *provided.*

The paleontologists discovered~that~the fossil provided a link between the dinosaur and the modern bird.

When a sentence has two *that* clauses, *that* should begin each one.

The graph indicated **that the population had increased** but **that the number of homeowners had not.**

🖥 *TECH SAVVY*

A grammar checker will sometimes alert you to a missing word, but it will just as often fail to do so. It may also tell you that a word is missing when it is not. You are better off proofreading your work yourself.

27f | COMPLETING COMPARISONS

A comparison has two parts: someone or something is compared to someone or something else. As you revise your writing, make sure that your audience knows who or what is being compared. To revise incomplete comparisons, add necessary words, phrases, or clauses.

Printers today are quite different~from those sold in the early 1990s~.

His first novel was better~than the one just published~.

After you are sure that your comparisons are complete, check to see that they are also logical.

Her test scores are higher than ^those of^ the other students.

In the original sentence, *scores* were being compared to *students.* You could also rewrite this sentence as follows:

Her test scores are higher than the other students'.

Because *test scores* have already been mentioned, it is clear that *students'* (with an apostrophe) is short for *students' test scores.*

27g COMPLETING INTENSIFIERS

In speech, the intensifiers *so, such,* and *too* are used to mean "very," "unusually," or "extremely."

That movie was **so** funny.

In academic and professional writing, however, the intensifiers *so, such,* and *too* require a completing phrase or clause.

That movie was **so** funny **that I watched it twice.**

Julian has **such** a hearty laugh **that it makes everyone else laugh with him.**

The problem is just **too** complex **to solve in one day.**

Exercise 3

Revise the following sentences to make them clear and complete.

1. The movie *Avatar* captured the imagination of new generation of moviegoers.

2. Like the *Star Wars* movies and *The Lord of the Rings* trilogy, *Avatar* introduced so many innovative special effects.

3. The 3-D techniques are different, too.

4. Reporters noted that the director, James Cameron, had such an incredible budget.

5. Some critics, however, believe that the plot in *The Lord of the Rings* movies is more interesting than *Avatar*.

28 || CONSISTENCY

A consistent writing style will make it easier for readers to understand your message and rhetorical purpose. This chapter will help you maintain consistency

- in verb tense (**28a**),
- in point of view (**28b**), and
- in tone (**28c**).

28a || VERB TENSE

By using verb tenses consistently, you help your readers understand when the actions or events you are describing took place. Verb tenses convey information about time frames and grammatical aspect. *Time frame* refers to whether the tense is present, past, or future (refer to the columns of the chart on page 569). *Aspect* refers to whether it is simple, progressive, perfect, or perfect progressive (refer to the rows in the chart on page 569). Consistency in the time frame of a verb, though not necessarily in its aspect, ensures that any sequence of reported events is clearly and accurately portrayed. In the following paragraph, notice that the time frame remains the past, but the aspect varies among simple, perfect, and progressive:

past perfect

In the summer of 1983, I **had** just **finished** my third year of architecture

simple past   *past perfect (compound predicate)*

school and **had** to find a six-month internship. I **had grown** up and **gone**

past perfect

through my entire education in the Midwest, but I **had been** to

New York City once on a class field trip and I **thought** it **seemed** like

[*simple past*] [*simple past*]

a pretty good place to live. So, armed with little more than an inflated

ego and my school portfolio, I **was** off to Manhattan, oblivious to the bad

[*simple past*]

economy and the fact that the city **was overflowing** with young architects.

[*past progressive*]

—PAUL K. HUMISTON, "Small World"

If you do need to shift to another time frame within a paragraph, you can use a time marker:

now, then, today, yesterday
in two years, during the 1920s
after you finish, before we left

For example, in the following paragraph, the time frame shifts back and forth between present and past—between today, when Edward O. Wilson is studying ants in the woods around Walden Pond, and the nineteenth century, when Thoreau lived there. The time markers are bracketed.

These woods **are** not wild; indeed, they **were** not wild [in Thoreau's day].

[*simple present*] [*simple past*]

[Today], the beach and trails of Walden Pond State Reservation **draw**

[*simple present*]

about 500,000 visitors a year. Few of them **hunt** ants, however. Underfoot

[*simple present*]

and under the leaf litter there **is** a world as wild as it **was** [before human

[*simple present*] [*simple past*]

beings **came** to this part of North America].

[*simple past*]

—JAMES GORMAN, "Finding a Wild, Fearsome World beneath Every Fallen Leaf"

On occasion, a shift in time is indicated implicitly—that is, without an explicit time marker. A writer may change tenses without using any time marker, (1) to explain or support a general statement with information about the past, (2) to compare and contrast two different time periods, or (3) to comment on a topic. Why do you think the author of the following paragraph varies verb tenses?

> Thomas Jefferson, author of the Declaration of Independence, **is** considered one of our country's most brilliant citizens. His achievements **were** many, as **were** his interests. Some historians **describe** his work as a naturalist, scientist, and inventor; others **focus** on his accomplishments as an educator and politician. Yet Jefferson **is** best known as a spokesman for democracy.

Except for the two uses of *were* in the second sentence, all verbs are in the present tense. The author uses the past tense in the second sentence to provide evidence from the past that supports the topic sentence.

Before you turn in a final draft, check the verb tenses you have used to ensure that they are logical and consistent. Revise any that are not.

The white wedding dress~~comes~~ ^{came} into fashion when Queen Victoria wore a white gown at her wedding to Prince Albert of Saxe. Soon after, brides who could afford them bought stylish white dresses for their weddings. Brides of modest means, however, ~~continue~~ ^{continued} to choose dresses they could wear more than once.

Exercise 1

Locate the shifts in tense in this passage and decide whether they are effective. Be prepared to state your reasoning.

[1]Dave Rahm lived in Bellingham, Washington, north of Seattle. [2]Bellingham, a harbor town, lies between the alpine North Cascade Mountains and the San Juan Islands in Haro Strait above Puget Sound. [3]The latitude is that of Newfoundland. [4]Dave Rahm was a stunt pilot, the air's own genius. —ANNIE DILLARD, "The Stunt Pilot"

Exercise 2

Revise the following paragraph so that there are no unnecessary shifts in verb tense.

> I **had** already **been walking** for a half hour in the semidarkness of Amsterdam's early-morning streets when I **came** to a red light. I **am** in a hurry to get to the train station and no cars **were** out yet, so I **cross** over the cobblestones, passing a man waiting for the light to change. I never **look** back when he **scolds** me for breaking the law. I **had** a train to catch. I **was** going to Widnau, in Switzerland, to see Aunt Marie. I **have** not **seen** her since I **was** in second grade.

28b	POINT OF VIEW

Whenever you write, you must establish your point of view (perspective). Your point of view will be evident in the pronouns you choose. *I* or *we* indicates a first-person point of view, which is appropriate for writing that includes personal views or experiences. If you decide to address the reader as *you*, you are adopting a second-person point of view. However, because a second-person point of view is rare in academic writing, avoid using *you* unless you need to address the reader. If you select the pronouns *he, she, it, one,* and *they,* you are writing with a third-person point of view. The third-person point of view is the most common point of view in academic writing.

Although you may find it necessary to use different points of view in a paper, especially if you are comparing or contrasting other people's views with your own, be careful not to confuse readers by shifting perspective unnecessarily. The following paragraph has been revised to ensure consistency of point of view.

To an observer, a sleeping person appears passive, unresponsive, and essentially isolated from the rest of the world and its barrage of stimuli. While it is true that ‸*someone asleep is* ~~you are~~ unaware of most surrounding noises‸*, that person's* ~~when you are asleep, our~~ brain is far from inactive. In fact, the brain can be as active during sleep as it is‸*in a waking state.* ~~when you are awake.~~ When ‸*it is* ~~our brains are~~ asleep, the rate and type of electrical activity change.

28c ‖ TONE

The tone of a piece of writing conveys a writer's attitude toward a topic (3a(3)). The words and phrases a writer chooses affect the tone he or she creates. Notice the difference in tone in the following excerpts describing the same scientific experiment. The first paragraph was written for the general public; the second was written for other researchers.

Imagine that I asked you to play a very simple gambling game. In front of you, are four decks of cards—two red and two blue. Each card in those four decks either wins you a sum of money or costs you some money, and your job is to turn over cards from any of the decks, one at a time, in such a way that maximizes your winnings. What you don't know at the beginning, however, is that the red decks are a minefield. The rewards are high, but when you lose on red, you lose *a lot*. You can really only win by taking cards from the blue decks, which offer a nice, steady diet of $50 and $100 payoffs. The question is: how long will it take you to figure this out?   —**MALCOLM GLADWELL,** *Blink*

In a gambling task that simulates real-life decision-making in the way it factors uncertainty, rewards, and penalties, the players are given four decks of cards, a loan of $2000 facsimile U.S. bills, and asked to play so that they can lose the least amount of money and win the most (1). Turning each card carries an immediate reward ($100 in decks A and B and $50 in decks C and D). Unpredictably, however, the turning of some cards also carries a penalty (which is large in decks A and B and small in decks C and D). Playing mostly from the disadvantageous decks (A and B) leads to an overall loss. Playing from the advantageous decks (C and D) leads to an overall gain. The players have no way of predicting when a penalty will arise in a given deck, no way to calculate with precision the net gain or loss from each deck, and no knowledge of how many cards they must turn to end the game (the game is stopped after 100 card selections).

—ANTOINE BECHARA, HANNA DAMASIO, DANIEL TRANEL,
AND ANTONIO R. DAMASIO, "Deciding Advantageously before
Knowing the Advantageous Strategy"

In the excerpt from *Blink*, Malcolm Gladwell addresses readers directly: "Imagine that I asked you to play a very simple gambling game." In the excerpt aimed at an audience of researchers, Antoine Bechara and his coauthors describe their experiment without directly addressing the reader. Gladwell also uses less formal language than Bechara and his colleagues do. The scientists use words such as "immediate reward" and "penalty," while Gladwell conveys the same information informally: "wins you a sum of money or costs you some money." Finally, the scientists include a reference citation in their paragraph (the number 1 in parentheses), but Gladwell does not.

Neither of these excerpts is better than the other. The tone of each is appropriate for the given rhetorical situation. However, shifts in tone can be distracting. The following paragraph was revised to ensure consistency of tone:

Scientists at the University of Oslo (Norway) ~~think they know~~ *have evidence that* ~~why~~ the common belief about the birth order of ~~kids has some truth to it.~~ *children carries some truth.* Using as data IQ tests taken from military records, the scientists found that older children ~~have~~ *score* significantly ~~more on the ball than kids in second or third place.~~ *higher than their siblings.* According to the researchers, the average variation in scores is large enough to account for differences in college admission.

Exercise 3

Revise the following paragraph so that there are no unnecessary shifts in tone.

[1]Many car owners used to grumble about deceptive fuel-economy ratings. [2]They often found, after they had already purchased a car, that their mileage was lower than that on the car's window sticker. [3]The issue remained pretty much ignored until our gas prices started to go up like crazy. [4]Because of increased pressure from consumer organizations, the Environmental Protection Agency reviewed and then changed the way it was calculating fuel-economy ratings. [5]The agency now takes into account factors such as quick acceleration, changing road grades, and the use of air conditioning, so the new ratings should reflect your real-world driving conditions. [6]Nonetheless, the ratings can never be right on target given that we all have different driving habits.

29 | SUBORDINATION AND COORDINATION

Understanding subordination and coordination can help you indicate connections between ideas as well as add variety to your sentences (Chapter **32**). This chapter will help you

- use subordination effectively (**29a**),
- use coordination effectively (**29b**), and
- avoid faulty or excessive subordination and coordination (**29c**).

29a   USING SUBORDINATION EFFECTIVELY

Subordinate means "being of lower rank." A subordinate grammatical structure cannot stand alone; it is dependent on the main (independent) clause. The most common subordinate structure is the dependent clause (**21b(2)**), which usually begins with a subordinating conjunction (**20a(7)**) or a relative pronoun (**25a(3)**).

(1) Subordinating conjunctions

A **subordinating conjunction** specifies the relationship between a dependent clause and an independent clause. For example, it might signal a causal relationship.

The painters finished early <u>**because**</u> <u>**they work well together.**</u>

Here are a few of the most frequently used subordinating conjunctions:

Cause	*because*
Concession	*although, even though*
Condition	*if, unless*
Effect	*so that*

Sequence	*before, after*
Time	*when*

By using subordinating conjunctions, you can combine short sentences and indicate how they are related.

_{After the}
_∧~~The~~ crew leader picked us up early on Friday. ~~We~~ _{, we}∧ate breakfast

together at a local diner.

If the subjects of the two clauses are the same, the dependent clause can often be shortened to a phrase.

_{eating}
After∧~~we ate~~ our breakfast, we headed back to the construction site.

(2) Relative pronouns

A **relative pronoun** (*who, whom, which, that,* or *whose*) introduces a dependent clause that, in most cases, modifies the pronoun's antecedent (**25a(3)**). By using this type of dependent clause, called an **adjectival clause**, or a **relative clause**, you can embed details into a sentence.

The temple has a <u>portico</u> **that faces west.**

An adjectival clause can be shortened as long as the meaning of the sentence remains clear.

The Parthenon is the Greek temple ~~that was~~ dedicated to the goddess Athena.

> ❶ **CAUTION**
>
> A relative clause beginning with *which* sometimes refers to an entire independent clause rather than modifying a specific word or phrase. Because this type of reference can be vague, you should avoid it if possible.
>
> _{As}   _{he should have}
> ∧~~He is~~ a graduate of a top university,∧~~which should provide him with~~ many opportunities.

29b	USING COORDINATION EFFECTIVELY

Coordinate means "being of equal rank." Coordinate grammatical elements have the same form. For example, they may be two words that are both adjectives, two phrases that are both prepositional, or two clauses that are both independent.

a **stunning** and **satisfying** conclusion [adjectives]

in the attic or **in the basement** [prepositional phrases]

The company was losing money, yet **the employees suspected nothing.**
[independent clauses]

To indicate the relationship between coordinate words, phrases, or clauses, choose an appropriate coordinating or correlative conjunction (**20a(7)**).

Addition	*and, both . . . and, not only . . . but also*
Alternative	*or, nor, either . . . or, neither . . . nor*
Cause	*for*
Contrast	*but, yet*
Result	*so*

By using coordination, you can avoid unnecessary repetition.

The hike to the top of Angels Landing has countless

switchbacks. ~~It also has~~ *and* long drop-offs.

A semicolon can also be used to link coordinate independent clauses:

Hikers follow the path; climbers scale the cliff wall.

ⓘ MULTILINGUAL WRITERS

CHOOSING CONJUNCTIONS

In English, use either a coordinating conjunction or a subordinating conjunction, but not both, to signal a connection between clauses.

Because he had a severe headache, ~~so~~ he went to the health center.

He
ʌ~~Because he~~ had a severe headache, so he went to the health center.

Exercise 1

Using subordination and coordination, revise the sentences in the following paragraph to emphasize ideas you consider important.

[1]During the summer of 1998, many booklovers, young and old alike, spent hours reading about an adolescent wizard. [2]The wizard had friends who were also wizards. [3]Little time passed before Harry Potter, Ron Weasley, and Hermione Granger became familiar names. [4]*Harry Potter and the Sorcerer's Stone* was the first of seven fantasy novels. [5]All of these novels were penned by British author J. K. Rowling. [6]Each of the novels has been a bestseller. [7]Many readers consider the introductory novel their favorite. [8]In *Sorcerer's Stone,* readers meet Harry. [9]He is an orphan with extraordinary powers. [10]Harry meets friends at a boarding school. [11]With them, he defeats the evil wizard. ([12]The wizard is so evil his name cannot be mentioned.) [13]Some fans praise Rowling's treatment of the theme of friendship. [14]They also appreciate her exploration of the theme of self-sacrifice. [15]Other fans mention her plotting, humor, and straightforward style.

29C AVOIDING FAULTY OR EXCESSIVE SUBORDINATION AND COORDINATION

(1) Choosing precise conjunctions

Effective subordination requires choosing subordinating conjunctions carefully. In the following sentence, the use of *as* is distracting because it can mean either "because" or "while."

> *Because*
> ~~As~~ time was running out, I randomly filled in the remaining circles on
>
> the exam sheet.

Your choice of coordinating conjunction should also convey your meaning precisely. For example, to indicate a cause-and-effect relationship, *so* is more precise than *and*.

> *so*
> The timer rang, ~~and~~ I turned in my exam.

(2) Avoiding excessive subordination and coordination

As you revise your writing, make sure that you have not overused subordination or coordination. In the following ineffective sentence, two dependent clauses compete for the reader's focus. The revision is clearer because it eliminates one of the dependent clauses.

Ineffective

Although researchers used to believe that ancient Egyptians were the first to domesticate cats, they now think that cats may have provided company for humans 5,000 years earlier because the intact skeleton of a cat has been discovered in a Neolithic village on Cyprus.

Revised

Although researchers used to believe that ancient Egyptians were the first to domesticate cats, they now think that cats may have provided company for humans 5,000 years earlier. They base their revised estimate on the discovery of an intact cat skeleton in a Neolithic village on Cyprus.

Overuse of coordination results in a rambling sentence in need of revision.

Ineffective

Cats hunt mice, and they also hunt other small rodents, so they are popular pets.

Revised

Because cats hunt mice and other small rodents, they are popular pets.

The following strategies should help you avoid overusing coordinating conjunctions.

(a) Using a more specific subordinating conjunction or an adverbial conjunction

I worked all summer to earn tuition money, and I didn't ~~so that I wouldn't~~ have to work during the school year.

OR

I worked all summer to earn tuition money, and ~~; thus~~ I didn't have to work during the school year.

(b) Using a relative clause to embed information

Seafood, which is nutritious and low in fat, ~~is nutritious, and it is low in fat, and it~~ has become available in greater variety.

(c) Allowing two or more verbs to share the same subject

Marie quickly grabbed a shovel, ~~and then she~~ ran to the edge of the field, and ~~then she~~ put out the fire before it could spread to the trees.

(d) Placing some information in an appositive phrase

Karl Glazebrook, *, a researcher in astronomy at Johns Hopkins University,* ~~is a researcher in astronomy at Johns Hopkins University, and he~~ has questioned the conventional theory of galaxy formations.

(e) Placing some information in a prepositional or verbal phrase

In the thick snow, ~~The snow was thick, and~~ we could not see where we were going.

After pulling ~~The plane pulled~~ away from the gate on time, *the plane* ~~and then it~~ sat on the runway for two hours.

Exercise 2

Revise the following sentences to eliminate faulty or excessive coordination and subordination. Be prepared to explain why your sentences are more effective than the originals.

1. The Duct Tape Guys usually describe humorous uses for duct tape, providing serious information about the history of duct tape on their website.

2. Duct tape was invented for the US military during World War II to keep the moisture out of ammunition cases because it was strong and waterproof.

(continued on page 646)

(continued from page 645)

3. Duct tape was originally called "duck tape" as it was waterproof and ducks are like that too and because it was made of cotton duck, which is a durable, tightly woven material.

4. Duck tape was also used to repair jeeps and to repair aircraft, its primary use being to protect ammunition cases.

5. When the war was over, house builders used duck tape to connect duct work together, and the builders started to refer to duck tape as "duct tape" and eventually the color of the tape changed from the green that was used during the war to silver, which matched the ducts.

30 | PARALLELISM

When you join two or more ideas, whether each is encapsulated in a word or expressed in an entire sentence, the linked ideas need to be parallel in form—that is, all adjectives, all prepositional phrases, all nominal clauses, and so on. **Parallelism** is the use of grammatically equivalent forms to clarify meaning and to emphasize ideas. This chapter will help you

- create parallelism by repeating words and grammatical forms (**30a**),
- link parallel forms with correlative conjunctions (**30b**), and
- use parallel forms to ensure clarity or provide emphasis (**30c**).

30a | CREATING PARALLELISM

Recognizing parallel grammatical forms is easiest when you look for the repetition of certain words. The repetition of a preposition, the infinitive marker *to,* or the introductory word of a clause is a good clue that parallel grammatical forms will follow.

Preposition	My embarrassment stemmed not **from** the money lost but **from** the notoriety gained.
Infinitive marker *to*	She wanted her audience to remember the protest song and **to** understand its origin.
Introductory word of a clause	The team members vowed **that** they would support each other, **that** they would play their best, and **that** they would win the tournament.

The infinitive marker *to* does not need to be repeated as long as the sentence remains clear.

> She wanted her audience **to remember** the protest song and **understand** its origin.

To recognize parallelism in sentences that do not include repeated words, look for a coordinating conjunction (*and, but, or, yet, so, nor,* or *for*). The parts of a sentence that such a conjunction joins are parallel if they have similar grammatical forms (all nouns, all participial phrases, and so on).

Words	The young actor was **shy** <u>yet</u> **determined.** [two adjectives joined by *yet*]
Phrases	Her goals include **publicizing student and faculty research, increasing the funding for that research,** <u>and</u> **providing adequate research facilities.** [three gerund phrases joined by *and*]
Clauses	Our instructor explained **what the project had entailed** <u>and</u> **how the researchers had used the results.** [two noun clauses joined by *and*]

As you edit a draft, look for sentences that include two or three words, phrases, or clauses joined by a conjunction and make sure the grammatical forms being linked are parallel.

People all around me are **buying, remodeling,** or ˄~~they want to sell~~ *selling* ~~their~~ houses.

Whether **mortgage rates rise** or ~~the~~ **building codes** ˄~~are changed~~ *change***,** the real estate market should remain strong this spring.

Exercise 1

Identify the parallel structures in the following sentences.

1. The conservation group's goals are to raise awareness of the natural area, to build a walking path near the creek running through it, and to construct a nature center at the east end of the parking lot.

2. She is dedicated to freedom, development, diversity, and justice.

3. Some say voting is a right, but others say it is a responsibility.

4. Because the season was over and, more important, because their team was victorious, fans flooded the streets and celebrated until midnight.

5. He said that we would conduct a similar project but that we would likely get different results.

30b LINKING PARALLEL FORMS WITH CORRELATIVE CONJUNCTIONS

Correlative conjunctions (or **correlatives**) are pairs of words that link other words, phrases, or clauses (20a(7)).

both ... and

either ... or

neither ... nor

not only ... but also

whether ... or

Notice how the words or phrases following each of the paired conjunctions are parallel.

He will major in **either** <u>biology</u> **or** <u>chemistry</u>.

Whether <u>at home</u> **or** <u>at school</u>, he is always busy.

Be especially careful when using *not only … but also*.

His team practices not only
ₐ~~Not only practicing~~ at 6 a.m. during the week, but ~~his team~~ also
~~scrimmages~~ on Sunday afternoons.

OR

    does his team practice   it
Not only ₐ~~practicing~~ at 6 a.m. during the week, but ₐ~~the team~~ also
scrimmages on Sunday afternoons.

In the first revised example, each conjunction is followed by a prepositional phrase (**21a(4)**). In the second revised example, each conjunction accompanies a clause (**21b**).

30C	**USING PARALLELISM TO PROVIDE CLARITY AND EMPHASIS**

Repeating a pattern emphasizes the relationship of ideas. The following two parallel sentences come from the conclusion of "Letter from
Birmingham Jail":

> **If I have said anything** in this letter <u>that overstates the truth and indi-
> cates an unreasonable impatience</u>, **I beg you to forgive me. If I have said
> anything** <u>that understates the truth and indicates my having a patience</u>
> that allows me to settle for anything less than brotherhood, **I beg God to
> forgive me.** —**MARTIN LUTHER KING, JR., "Letter from Birmingham Jail"**

To create this parallelism, King repeats words and uses similar grammatical forms (sentences beginning with *if* and clauses beginning
with *that*).

> ❓ *THINKING RHETORICALLY*
>
> **PARALLELISM**
>
> Parallel elements make your writing easy to read. But consider breaking from the parallel pattern on occasion to emphasize a point. For example, to describe a friend, you could start with two adjectives and then switch to a noun phrase.
>
> My friend Alison is **kind, modest,** and **the smartest mathematician in the state.**

By expressing key ideas in parallel structures, you emphasize them. However, be careful not to overuse parallel patterns, or they will lose their impact. Parallelism is especially effective in the introduction to a paragraph or an essay. The following passage from the introduction to a chapter of a book on advertising contains three examples of parallel forms:

> While **men are encouraged to fall in love with their cars, women are more often invited to have a romance,** indeed an erotic experience, with **something closer to home, something that truly does pump the valves of our hearts**—the food we eat. And the consequences become even more severe as we enter into the territory of **compulsivity** and **addiction.** —JEAN KILBOURNE, *Deadly Persuasion*

Parallel structures can also be effective in the conclusion to an essay.

> **Because these men work** with **animals,** not **machines, because they live** outside in landscapes of torrential beauty, **because they are confined** to **a place** and **a routine** embellished with awesome variables, **because calves die** in the arms that pulled others into life, **because they go to** the mountains as if on a pilgrimage to find out what makes a herd of elk tick, **their strength** is also **a softness, their toughness, a rare delicacy.**
>
> —GRETEL EHRLICH, "About Men"

Exercise 2

Make the structures in each sentence parallel. In some sentences, you may have to use different wording.

1. Helen was praised by the vice president, and her assistant admired her.

2. Colleagues found her genial and easy to schedule meetings with.

3. When she hired new employees for her department, she looked for applicants who were intelligent, able to stay focused, and able to speak clearly.

4. At meetings, she was always prepared, participating actively yet politely, and generated innovative responses to department concerns.

5. In her annual report, she wrote that her most important achievements were attracting new clients and revenues were higher.

6. When asked about her leadership style, she said that she preferred collaborating with others rather than to work alone in her office.

7. Although dedicated to her work, Helen also recognized that parenting was important and the necessity of cultivating a life outside of work.

8. She worked hard to save money for the education of her children, for her own music lessons, and investing for her retirement.

9. However, in the coming year, she hoped to reduce the number of weekends she worked in the office and spending more time at home.

10. She would like to plan a piano recital and also have the opportunity to plan a family vacation.

31 | EMPHASIS

In any rhetorical situation, some of your ideas will be more important than others. You can direct the reader's attention to these ideas by emphasizing them. This chapter will help you

- place words where they receive emphasis (**31a**),
- use cumulative and periodic sentences (**31b**),
- arrange ideas in climactic order (**31c**),
- repeat important words (**31d**),
- invert word order in sentences (**31e**), and
- use an occasional short sentence (**31f**).

You can also emphasize ideas by using subordination and coordination (Chapter **29**), parallelism (Chapter **30**), and precise word choice (Chapter **34**).

31a | PLACING WORDS FOR EMPHASIS

Words at the beginning or the end of a sentence receive emphasis. Notice how the revision of the following sentence adds emphasis to the beginning to balance the emphasis at the end:

~~In today's society, most good~~ _Good_ jobs _today_ require a college education.

You can also emphasize important words or ideas by placing them after a colon (**37b**) or a dash (**40d**).

> At a later time [rocks and clay] may again become what they once were:
> dust.   —**LESLIE MARMON SILKO, "Interior and Exterior Landscapes"**

By 1857, miners had extracted 760 tons of gold from these hills—and left behind more than ten times as much mercury, as well as devastated forests, slopes and streams.

—REBECCA SOLNIT, *Storming the Gates of Paradise: Landscapes for Politics*

Words that come before commas, especially if they are nouns, receive stress. In the following passage, the emphasis on *day, astronomy, mathematics, optics,* and *Laws* is due, in part, to comma placement.

One of the most brilliant and influential scientists of his day, [Johannes] Kepler made numerous contributions to astonomy, mathematics, and optics, including his famous discovery of what are now called Kepler's Laws, describing the motions of the planets round the sun.

—KENNETH LIBBRECHT, *The Snowflake: Winter's Secret Beauty*

Exercise 1

Below are five versions of a sentence. Decide which words receive more stress than the others in each version. Explain why.

1. The stunt double is essential to any action movie; that person may have to ride a horse backwards, jump from a tall building, or leap between speeding cars.

2. Essential to any action movie is the person riding a horse backwards, jumping from a tall building, or leaping between speeding cars: the stunt double.

3. The stunt double—essential to any action movie—may have to ride a horse backwards, jump from a tall building, or leap between speeding cars.

4. The stunt double, who may have to ride a horse backwards, jump from a tall building, or leap between speeding cars, is essential to any action movie.

5. In an action movie, a stunt double may have to leap between speeding cars, jump from a tall building, or ride a horse backwards.

31b | USING CUMULATIVE AND PERIODIC SENTENCES

In a **cumulative sentence**, the main idea (the independent clause) comes first; less important ideas or supplementary details follow.

> **The day was hot for June,** a pale sun burning in a cloudless sky, wilting the last of the irises, the rhododendron blossoms drooping.
>
> —ADAM HASLETT, "Devotion"

In a **periodic sentence**, however, the main idea comes last, just before the period.

> In a day when movies seem more and more predictable, when novels tend to be plotless, baggy monsters or minimalist exercises in interior emotion, **it's no surprise that sports has come to occupy an increasingly prominent place in the communal imagination.**
>
> —MICHIKO KAKUTANI, "Making Art of Sport"

Both of these types of sentences can be effective. Because cumulative sentences are more common, however, the infrequently encountered periodic sentence tends to provide emphasis.

31c | ORDERING IDEAS FROM LEAST TO MOST IMPORTANT

By arranging your ideas in **climactic order**—from least important to most important—you build up suspense. If you place your most important idea first, the sentence may seem to trail off. If you place it in the middle of the sentence, readers may not recognize its full significance. If, however, you place it at the end of the sentence, it will not only receive emphasis but also provide a springboard to the next sentence. In the following example, the writer emphasizes a doctor's desire to help the disadvantaged and then implies that this desire has been realized through work with young Haitian doctors:

> While he was in medical school, the soon-to-be doctor discovered his calling: to diagnose infectious diseases, to find ways of curing people with these diseases, and **to bring the lifesaving knowledge of modern medicine to the disadvantaged.** Most recently, he has been working with a small group of young doctors in Haiti.

❓ THINKING RHETORICALLY

CLIMACTIC ORDER

Placing the least important idea at the end of the sentence can be effective when you are trying to be humorous, as in the following example:

> Contemporary man, of course, has no such peace of mind. He finds himself in the midst of a crisis of faith. He is what we fashionably call "alienated." He has seen the ravages of war, he has known natural catastrophes, he has been to singles bars.
>
> —**WOODY ALLEN,** *Side Effects*

31d ‖ REPEATING IMPORTANT WORDS

Although effective writers avoid unnecessary repetition, they also understand that deliberate repetition emphasizes key words or ideas.

> We **forget** all too soon the things we thought we could never **forget.** We **forget** the loves and betrayals alike, **forget** what we whispered and what we screamed, **forget** who we are.   —**JOAN DIDION,** "On Keeping a Notebook"

In this case, the emphatic repetition of *forget* reinforces the author's point—that we do not remember many things that once seemed impossible to forget.

31e ‖ INVERTING WORD ORDER

Most sentences begin with a subject and end with a predicate. When you move words out of their normal order, you draw attention to them.

<u>At the back of the crowded room</u> sat a newspaper reporter.
[COMPARE: **A newspaper reporter** sat <u>**at the back of the crowded room**</u>.]

Notice the inverted word order in the second sentence of the following passage:

> [1]The Library Committee met with the City Council on several occasions to persuade them to fund the building of a library annex. [2]So successful were their efforts that a new wing will be added by next year. [3]This wing will contain archival materials that were previously stored in the basement.

The modifier *so successful* appears at the beginning of the sentence, rather than in its normal position, after the verb: *Their efforts were* so successful *that . . . .* The inverted word order emphasizes the committee's accomplishment.

ñ MULTILINGUAL WRITERS

INVERTING WORD ORDER

English sentences are inverted in various ways. Sometimes the main verb in the form of a participle is placed at the beginning of the sentence. The subject and the auxiliary verb(s) are then inverted.

part   aux s

Carved into the bench **were someone's initials.**
[COMPARE: Someone's initials were carved into the bench.]

For more information on English word order, see Chapter 47.

31f USING AN OCCASIONAL SHORT SENTENCE

In a paragraph of mostly long sentences, try using a short sentence for emphasis. To optimize the effect, lead up to the short sentence with an especially long sentence.

> After organizing the kitchen, buying the groceries, slicing the vegetables, mowing the lawn, weeding the garden, hanging the decorations, and setting up the grill, I was ready to have a good time when my guests arrived. **Then the phone rang.**

Exercise 2

Add emphasis to each of the following sentences by using the technique indicated at the beginning. You may have to add some words and/or delete others.

1. (climactic order) In the 1960 Olympics, Wilma Rudolph tied the world record in the 100-meter race, she tied the record in the 400-meter relay, she won the hearts of fans from around the world, and she broke the record in the 200-meter race.

2. (periodic sentence) Some sports reporters described Rudolph as a gazelle because of her beautiful stride.

3. (inversion) Rudolph's Olympic achievement is impressive, but her victory over a crippling disease is even more spectacular.

4. (final short sentence) Rudolph was born prematurely, weighing only four and one-half pounds. As a child, she suffered from double pneumonia, scarlet fever, and then polio.

5. (cumulative sentence) She received help from her family. Her brothers and sister massaged her legs. Her mother drove her to a hospital for therapy.

6. (inversion) Her siblings' willingness to help was essential to her recovery, as were her mother's vigilant care and her own determination.

7. (periodic sentence) Her passions became basketball and track after she recovered, built up her strength, and gained self-confidence.

8. (climactic order) Rudolph set a scoring record in basketball, she set the standard for future track and field stars, and she set an Olympic record in track.

32 | VARIETY

To make your writing lively and distinctive, include a variety of sentence types and lengths. Notice how the sentences in the following paragraph vary in length, form (simple, compound, and compound-complex), and function (statements, questions, and commands). The variety of sentences makes this paragraph about pleasure pleasurable to read.

> Start with the taste. Imagine a moment when the sensation of honey or sugar on the tongue was an astonishment, a kind of intoxication. The closest I've ever come to recovering such a sense of sweetness was secondhand, though it left a powerful impression on me even so. I'm thinking of my son's first experience with sugar: the icing on the cake at his first birthday. I have only the testimony of Isaac's face to go by (that, and his fierceness to repeat the experience), but it was plain that his first encounter with sugar had intoxicated him—was in fact an ecstasy, in the literal sense of the word. That is, he was beside himself with the pleasure of it, no longer here with me in space and time in quite the same way he had been just a moment before. Between bites Isaac gazed up at me in amazement (he was on my lap, and I was delivering the ambrosial forkfuls to his gaping mouth) as if to exclaim, "Your world contains *this?* From this day forward I shall dedicate my life to it." (Which he basically has done.) And I remember thinking, this is no minor desire, and then wondered: Could it be that sweetness is the prototype of *all* desire?   —**MICHAEL POLLAN**, *The Botany of Desire*

This chapter will help you

- revise sentence length and form (**32a**);
- vary sentence openings (**32b**); and
- use an occasional question, command, or exclamation (**32c**).

If you have difficulty distinguishing between various types of sentence structures, review the fundamentals in Chapters **20** and **21**.

32a REVISING SENTENCE LENGTH AND FORM

To avoid the choppiness of a series of short sentences, combine some
of them into longer sentences. You can combine sentences by using
a coordinating conjunction (such as *and, but,* or *or*), a subordinating
conjunction (such as *because, although,* or *when*), or a relative pronoun
(such as *who, that,* or *which*).

Short	Americans typically eat popcorn at movie theaters. They also eat it at sporting events.
Combined	Americans typically eat popcorn at movie theaters **and** sporting events. [coordinating conjunction (**20a(7)**)]
Short	Researchers have found thousand-year-old popcorn kernels. These kernels still pop.
Combined	Researchers have found thousand-year-old popcorn kernels **that** still pop. [relative pronoun (**25a(3)**)]
Short	Popcorn was in demand during the Great Depression. Impoverished families could afford it.
Combined	**Because** impoverished families could afford it, popcorn was in demand during the Great Depression. [subordinating conjunction (**20a(7)**)]

You may sometimes be able to use both a subordinating and a coordinating conjunction.

Short	Sugar was sent abroad during World War II. Little sugar was left for making candy. Americans started eating more popcorn.
Combined	**Because** sugar was sent abroad during World War II, little was left for making candy, **so** Americans started eating more popcorn. [subordinating and coordinating conjunctions (**20a(7)**)]

It is also possible to combine sentences by condensing one of them into
a phrase (**21a**).

Short	Some colonial families ate popcorn for breakfast. They ate it with sugar and cream.
Combined	Some colonial families ate popcorn **with sugar and cream** for breakfast. [prepositional phrase (21a(4))]
Short	The world's largest popcorn ball measured twelve feet in diameter. It took two thousand pounds of popcorn to create.
Combined	**Measuring twelve feet in diameter,** the world's largest popcorn ball took two thousand pounds of popcorn to create. [participial phrase (21a(3))]

❷ THINKING RHETORICALLY

SHORT SENTENCES

Occasionally, a series of brief sentences produces a special effect. The short sentences in the following passage capture the quick actions taking place as an accident is about to occur:

> "There's a truck in your lane!" my friend yelled. I swerved toward the shoulder. "Watch out!" she screamed. I hit the brakes. The wheel locked. The back of the car swerved to the right.

32b | VARYING SENTENCE OPENINGS

Most writers begin more than half of their sentences with a subject. Although this pattern is common, relying on it too heavily can make writing seem predictable. Experiment with the following alternatives for starting your sentences.

(1) Beginning with an adverb

Immediately, the dentist stopped drilling and asked me how I was doing.

(2) Beginning with a phrase

In the auditorium, voters waited in silence before casting their ballots. [prepositional phrase (**21a(4)**)]

A tight contest, the gubernatorial election was closely watched by election officials. [appositive phrase (**21a(5)**)]

To win, candidates need to convey a clear message to voters. [infinitive phrase (**21a(3)**)]

Appealing to their constituents, candidates stated their positions. [participial phrase (**21a(3)**)]

The election now over, we understood clearly how the incumbent defeated the challenger. [absolute phrase (**21a(6)**)]

(3) Beginning with a transitional word or phrase

In each of the following examples, the transitional word or phrase shows the relationship between the ideas in the pair of sentences. (See also **3d.**)

Many restaurants close within a few years of opening. **But** others, which offer good food at reasonable prices, become well established.

Difficulty in finding a place to park keeps some people from going out to lunch downtown. **However,** that problem may be alleviated with the construction of a new underground parking garage.

Independently owned restaurants struggle to get started for a number of reasons. **First of all,** they have to compete against successful restaurant chains.

(4) Beginning with a word that usually comes after the verb

I was an abysmal football player. **Soccer,** though, I could play well. [direct object]

Vital to any success I had were my mother's early lessons. [predicate adjective]

Exercise 1

Convert each set of short sentences into a single longer sentence.

1. On May 29, 1953, Edmund Hillary reached the summit of Mt. Everest. Hillary was a mountaineer from New Zealand. Tenzing Norgay was his Sherpa guide. Mt. Everest is the highest mountain in the world.

2. Hillary had been a member of a Swiss expedition. The Swiss expedition tried to reach the top of Mt. Everest in 1952. Bad weather stopped them eight hundred feet from the summit.

3. In March of 1953, Hillary joined an expedition from Great Britain. This expedition was led by John Hunt.

4. The expedition approached the peak. Conditions were worsening. Hunt directed Hillary and Norgay to continue to the summit.

5. Hillary thawed out his frozen boots on the morning of May 29. The two climbers then made the final ascent.

Exercise 2

Rewrite each sentence so that it does not begin with a subject.

1. John Spilsbury was an engraver and mapmaker from London who made the first jigsaw puzzle in about 1760.

2. He pasted a map onto a piece of wood and used a fine-bladed saw to cut around the borders of the countries.

3. The jigsaw puzzle was first an educational toy and has been a mainstay in households all over the world ever since its invention.

4. The original puzzles were quite expensive because the wooden pieces were cut by hand.

5. Most puzzles are made of cardboard today.

32c | USING QUESTIONS, EXCLAMATIONS, AND COMMANDS

You can vary sentences in a paragraph by introducing an occasional question, exclamation, or command (**21d**).

(1) Raising a question or two for variety

If people could realize that immigrant children are better off, and less scarred, by holding on to their first languages as they learn a second one, then perhaps Americans could accept a more drastic change. What if every English-speaking toddler were to start learning a foreign language at an early age, maybe in kindergarten? What if these children were to learn Spanish, for instance, the language already spoken by millions of American citizens, but also by so many neighbors to the South?

—ARIEL DORFMAN, "If Only We All Spoke Two Languages"

You can either answer the question you pose or let readers answer it for themselves, in which case it is called a **rhetorical question** (**21d**).

(2) Adding an exclamatory sentence for variety

But at other moments, the classroom is so lifeless or painful or confused— and I so powerless to do anything about it—that my claim to be a teacher seems a transparent sham. Then the enemy is everywhere: in those students from some alien planet, in the subject I thought I knew, and in the personal pathology that keeps me earning my living this way. What a fool I was to imagine that I had mastered this occult art—harder to divine than tea leaves and impossible for mortals to do even passably well!

—PARKER PALMER, *The Courage to Teach*

Although you can make sentences emphatic without using exclamation points (Chapter **31**), the introduction of an exclamatory sentence can break up a regular pattern of declarative sentences.

(3) Including a command for variety

Now I stare and stare at people shamelessly. Stare. It's the way to educate your eye.   —WALKER EVANS, *Unclassified*

In this case, a one-word command, "Stare," provides variety.

Exercise 3

Explain how questions and commands add variety to the following paragraph. Describe other ways in which this writer varies his sentences.

¹The gods, they say, give breath, and they take it away. ²But the same could be said—couldn't it?—of the humble comma. ³Add it to the present clause, and, of a sudden, the mind is, quite literally, given pause to think; take it out if you wish or forget it and the mind is deprived of a resting place. ⁴Yet still the comma gets no respect. ⁵It seems just a slip of a thing, a pedant's tick, a blip on the edge of our consciousness, a kind of printer's smudge almost. ⁶Small, we claim, is beautiful (especially in the age of the microchip). ⁷Yet what is so often used, and so rarely recalled, as the comma—unless it be breath itself?

—**PICO IYER, "In Praise of the Humble Comma"**

EFFECTIVE LANGUAGE

Dover Publications

33 ‖ GOOD USAGE

Using the right words at the right time can make the difference between having your ideas taken seriously and seeing them brushed aside. Keeping your readers in mind will help you choose words they understand and consider appropriate. This chapter will help you

- write in a clear, straightforward style (33a);
- choose words that are appropriate for your audience, purpose, and context (33b);
- use inclusive language (33c); and
- find information in dictionaries (33d) and thesauruses (33e).

33a ‖ CLEAR STYLE

Although different styles are appropriate for different situations, you should strive to make your writing easy to read. To achieve a clear style, first choose words that your audience understands and that are appropriate for the occasion.

Ornate   The majority believes that achievement derives primarily from the diligent pursuit of allocated tasks.

Clear   Most people believe that success results from hard work.

If you want readers to take your writing seriously, you must show them respect by not using obscure words when common words will do and by not using more words than necessary. Using words that are precise (34a) and sentences that are concise (Chapter 35) can also help you achieve a clear style.

Exercise 1

Revise the following sentences for an audience that prefers a clear, straightforward style.

1. Expert delineation of character in a job interview is a goal that is not always possible to achieve.

2. In an employment situation, social pleasantries may contribute to the successful functioning of job tasks, but such interactions should not distract attention from the need to complete all assignments in a timely manner.

3. Commitment to an ongoing and carefully programmed schedule of physical self-management can be a significant resource for stress reduction in the workplace.

33b   APPROPRIATE WORD CHOICE

Unless you are writing for a specialized audience and have good reason to believe that this audience will welcome slang, colloquial expressions, or jargon, the following advice can help you determine which words to use and which to avoid.

(1) Slang

The term **slang** covers a wide range of words or expressions that are used in informal situations or are considered fashionable by people in a particular age group, locality, or profession. Although such words are often used in private conversation or in writing intended to mimic conversation, they are usually out of place in academic or professional writing.

(2) Conversational (or colloquial) words

Words labeled *colloquial* in a dictionary are fine for casual conversation and for written dialogues or personal essays on a light topic. Such words are sometimes used for special effect in academic writing, but you should usually replace them with more appropriate words. For example, the conversational words *dumb* and *kid around* could be replaced by *illogical* and *tease.*

> **❶ CAUTION**
>
> Because contractions (such as *you'll* for "you will" and *she's* for "she is") reflect the sound of conversation, you can use them in certain types of writing to create a friendly tone. However, some of your instructors or supervisors may consider them too informal for academic or professional writing.

(3) Regionalisms

Regionalisms—such as *tank* for "pond" and *sweeper* for "vacuum cleaner"—can make writing lively and distinctive, but they are often considered too informal for academic and professional writing.

(4) Technical words or jargon

When writing for a diverse audience, an effective writer will not refer to the need for bifocals as *presbyopia.* However, technical language is appropriate when the audience can understand it (as when one physician writes to another) or when the audience would benefit by learning the terms in question. Sometimes, terms that originated as jargon enter mainstream usage. As computer use has grown, for example, technical terms such as *application (app)* and *cloud computing* have become commonly used and widely understood.

33C | INCLUSIVE LANGUAGE

By choosing words that are inclusive rather than exclusive, you invite readers into your writing. Prejudiced or derogatory language has no place in academic or professional writing; using it undermines your

Courtesy of Morrison

Photographs and statements on the websites of many companies indicate a commitment to an inclusive work environment.

authority and credibility. It is best to use language that will engage, not alienate, your readers.

(1) Nonsexist language

Effective writers show equal respect for men and women. For example, they avoid using *man* to refer to people in general because they understand that the word excludes women.

> Achievements [OR Human achievements]
> ~~Man's achievements~~ in science are impressive.

Women, like men, can be *firefighters* or *police officers*—words that have become gender-neutral alternatives to *firemen* and *policemen.* Use the following tips to ensure that your writing is respectful.

TIPS FOR AVOIDING SEXIST LANGUAGE

When reviewing drafts, check for and revise the following types of sexist language.

- **Generic *he*:** A doctor should listen to *his* patients.

  A doctor should listen to **his or her** patients. [use of the appropriate form of *he or she*]

  Doctors should listen to **their** patients. [use of plural forms]

  By listening to patients, **doctors obtain important diagnostic information**. [elimination of *his* by revising the sentence]

- **Occupational stereotype:** Glenda James, a *female* engineer at Howard Aviation, won the best-employee award.

  Glenda James, an engineer at Howard Aviation, won the best-employee award. [removal of the unnecessary gender reference]

- **Terms such as *man* and *mankind* or those with *-ess* or *-man* endings:** Labor laws benefit the common *man*. *Mankind* benefits from philanthropy. The *stewardess* brought me some orange juice.

  Labor laws benefit **working people.** [replacement of the stereotypical term with a gender-neutral term]

  Everyone benefits from philanthropy. [use of an indefinite pronoun]

  The **flight attendant** brought me some orange juice. [use of a gender-neutral term]

- **Stereotypical gender roles:** I was told that the university offers free tuition to faculty *wives*. The minister pronounced them *man* and *wife*.

  I was told that the university offers free tuition to faculty **spouses.** [replacement of the stereotypical term with a gender-neutral term]

  The minister pronounced them **husband** and wife. [use of a term equivalent to *wife*]

- **Inconsistent use of titles:** *Mr.* Holmes and his *wife,* Mary, took a long trip to China.

  Mr. and Mrs. [or Ms.] Holmes took a long trip to China. [consistent use of titles]

  Peter and Mary Holmes took a long trip to China. [removal of titles]

  Peter Holmes and **Mary Wolfe** took a long trip to China. [use of full names]

- **Unstated gender assumption:** Have your *mother make your costume* for the school pageant.

  Have your **parents provide you with a costume** for the school pageant. [replacement of the stereotypical words with gender-neutral ones]

Exercise 2

Make the following sentences inclusive by eliminating sexist language.

1. A special code of ethics guides a nurse in fulfilling her responsibilities.

2. According to the weatherman, this summer will be unseasonably cold.

3. Dr. William Avery and his wife donated money to the scholarship fund.

4. Professor Garcia mapped the journey of modern man.

5. While in college, she worked as a waitress in a diner.

(2) Nonracist language

Rarely is it necessary to identify anyone's race or ethnicity in academic or professional writing. However, you may need to use appropriate racial or ethnic terms if you are writing a demographic report, an argument against existing racial inequities, or a historical account of a particular event involving ethnic groups. Determining which terms a particular group prefers can be difficult because preferences sometimes vary within a group and change over time. One conventional way to refer to Americans of a specific descent is to include an adjective before the word *American*: *African American, Asian American, European American, Latin American, Mexican American, Native American.* These words are widely used; however, members of a particular group may identify themselves in more than one way. In addition to *African American* and *European American, Black* (or *black*) and *White* (or *white*) have long been used. People of Spanish-speaking descent may prefer *Chicano/Chicana, Hispanic, Latino/Latina, Puerto Rican,* or other terms. Members of cultures that are indigenous to North America may prefer a specific name such as *Cherokee* or *Haida,* though some also accept *American Indians* or *Native People.* An up-to-date dictionary that includes notes on usage can help you choose appropriate terms.

(3) Respectful language about differences

If a writing assignment requires you to distinguish people based on age, ability, geographical area, religion, or sexual orientation, show respect to the groups or individuals you discuss by using the terms they prefer.

(a) Referring to age

Although some people object to the term *senior citizen,* a better alternative has not emerged. When used respectfully, the term refers to a person who has reached the age of retirement (but may not have decided to retire) and is eligible for certain privileges granted by society. However, if you know your audience would object to this term, find out which alternative is preferred.

(b) Referring to disability or illness

In references to disabilities and illnesses, it is appropriate to put the person first. In this way, the focus is placed on the individual rather than on the limitation. Thus, *persons with disabilities* is preferred over *disabled persons.* You can find out whether such person-first expressions are preferred by noting whether they are used in the articles and books (or by the people) you consult. Be aware, though, that some writers and readers think that these types of expressions sound unnatural, and others maintain that they do not serve their intended purpose because the last word in a phrase can carry the greater weight, especially at the end of a sentence.

(c) Referring to geographical areas

Certain geographical terms need to be used with special care. Though most frequently used to refer to people from the United States, the term *American* may also refer to people from Canada, Mexico, Central America, or South America. If your audience may be confused by this term, use *people from the United States* or *US citizens* instead.

The term *Arab* refers to people who speak Arabic. If you cannot use specific terms such as *Iraqi* or *Saudi Arabian,* be sure you know that a country's people speak Arabic and not another language. Iranians, for example, are not Arabs because they speak Farsi.

British, rather than *English,* is the preferred term for referring to people from the island of Great Britain or from the United Kingdom.

(d) Referring to religion

Reference to a person's religion should be made only if it is relevant. If you must mention religious affiliation, use only those terms considered respectful. Because religions have both conservative and liberal followers, be careful not to make generalizations (7i(12)) about political stances.

(e) Referring to sexual orientation

If your rhetorical situation calls for identifying sexual orientation, choose terms used by the people you are discussing.

✔ **CHECKLIST** for Assessing Usage within a Rhetorical Situation

- Do your words convey the meaning you intend? Do they help you fulfill your purpose?
- Do any of your words make you sound too casual or too formal?
- Can your audience understand the words you have used? Do you explain any words your readers might not understand? Have you used any words that could offend readers?
- Are your words appropriate for the context in which they will be read?

33d   DICTIONARIES

A good dictionary is an indispensable tool for a writer. Desk dictionaries such as *The American Heritage Dictionary* and *Merriam-Webster's Collegiate Dictionary* do much more than provide the correct spellings of words; they also give meanings, parts of speech, plural forms, and verb tenses, as well as information about pronunciation and origin. In addition, a reliable dictionary includes labels that can help you decide whether words are appropriate for your purpose, audience, and context. Words labeled *dialect, slang, colloquial, nonstandard,* or *unconventional,* as well as those labeled *archaic* or *obsolete* (meaning that they are no longer in common use), are generally inappropriate for college and professional writing. If a word has no label, you can safely assume that it can be used in writing for school or work. Whether the word is appropriate, however, depends on the precise meaning a writer wants to convey (34a). Because meanings of words change and because new words are constantly introduced into English, it is important to choose a dictionary, whether print or electronic, that has a recent copyright date.

(1) Unabridged or specialized dictionaries

An **unabridged dictionary** provides a comprehensive survey of English words, including detailed information about their origins. A **specialized dictionary** presents words related to a specific discipline or to some aspect of usage.

Unabridged Dictionaries

The Oxford English Dictionary. 2nd ed. 20 vols. 1989–. CD-ROM. 2005.

Webster's Third New International Dictionary of the English Language. CD-ROM. 2002.

These dictionaries also have regularly updated online versions.

Specialized Dictionaries

The American Heritage Guide to Contemporary Usage and Style. 2005.

The Cambridge Guide to English Usage. 2004.

The New Fowler's Modern English Usage. 3rd ed. 2000.

The Oxford Dictionary of Idioms. 2004.

ñ MULTILINGUAL WRITERS

DICTIONARIES AND OTHER RESOURCES

The following dictionaries are recommended for nonnative speakers of English.

The American Heritage Dictionary of Phrasal Verbs. 2005.

Collins Cobuild Student's Dictionary plus Grammar. 2005.

Longman Advanced American English. 2007.

Merriam-Webster's Advanced Learner's English Dictionary. 2008.

Swan, Michael. *Practical English Usage.* 3rd ed. 2005. (This is a guide to problems encountered by multilingual writers.)

(2) Dictionary entries

Dictionary entries provide a range of information. Figure 33.1 shows sample entries from the eleventh edition of *Merriam-Webster's Collegiate Dictionary.* Notice that *cool* is listed four times: as an adjective, a verb, a noun, and an adverb. The types of information these entries provide can be found in almost all desk dictionaries, though sometimes in a different order.

TYPES OF INFORMATION PROVIDED BY DICTIONARY ENTRIES

- **Spelling, syllabication (word division), and pronunciation.** Dictionary entries begin with the correctly spelled word, divided into syllables, followed by the pronunciation.

- **Parts of speech and word forms.** Dictionaries identify parts of speech—for instance, with *n* for "noun" or *vi* for "intransitive verb." Meanings will vary depending on the part of speech identified. Dictionaries also indicate irregular forms of verbs, nouns, and adjectives: *fly, flew, flown, flying, flies; child, children; good, better, best.*

- **Word origin.** English has a rich heritage. A dictionary entry indicates whether a word has roots in an older version of English (Old English, roughly CE 700–1100, or Middle English, 1100–1500), has even deeper roots in another language (Latin, Greek, German, French, and so on), or has been added more recently from another language.

- **Date of first occurrence.** Most entries include the date when the use of the word (in the first sense listed in the entry) was initially recorded.

- **Definition(s).** Generally, the oldest meaning is given first. However, meanings can also be ordered according to frequency of usage, with the most common usage listed first.

- **Usage.** Quotations show how the word can be used in various contexts. Sometimes a comment on usage problems is placed at the end of an entry.

- **Idioms.** When the word is part of a common idiom (34c), the idiom is listed and defined, usually at the end of the entry.

- **Synonyms.** Some dictionaries provide explanations of subtle differences in meaning among a word's synonyms.

Pronunciation ——

Part of speech

Spelling ——

Origin

Usage for
second
definition
of word

¹cool \'kül\ *adj* [ME *col*, fr. OE *cōl*; akin to OHG *kuoli* cool, OE *ceald* cold — more at COLD] (bef. 12c) **1 :** moderately cold : lacking in warmth **2 a :** marked by steady dispassionate calmness and self-control ⟨a ~ and calculating administrator —*Current Biog.*⟩ **b :** lacking ardor or friendliness ⟨a ~ impersonal manner⟩ **c** *of jazz* : marked by restrained emotion and the frequent use of counterpoint **d :** free from tensions or violence ⟨meeting with minority groups in an attempt to keep the city ~⟩ **3** — used as an intensive ⟨a ~ million dollars⟩ **4 :** marked by deliberate effrontery or lack of due respect or discretion ⟨a ~ reply⟩ **5 :** facilitating or suggesting relief from heat ⟨a ~ dress⟩ **6 a** *of a color* : producing an impression of being cool; *specif* : of a hue in the range violet through blue to green **b** *of a musical tone* : relatively lacking in timbre or resonance **7** *slang* **a :** very good : EXCELLENT; *also* : ALL RIGHT **b :** FASHIONABLE, HIP ⟨not happy with the new shoes . . . because they were not ~ —Celestine Sibley⟩ — **cool·ish** \'kü-lish\ *adj* — **cool·ly** *also* **cooly** \'kü(l)-lē\ *adv* — **cool·ness** \'kül-nəs\ *n*

Related
word forms

syn COOL, COMPOSED, COLLECTED, UNRUFFLED, IMPERTURB-ABLE, NONCHALANT mean free from agitation or excitement. COOL may imply calmness, deliberateness, or dispassionateness ⟨kept a *cool* head⟩. COMPOSED implies freedom from agitation as a result of self-discipline or a sedate disposition ⟨the *composed* pianist gave a flawless concert⟩. COLLECTED implies a concentration of mind that eliminates distractions esp. in moments of crisis ⟨the nurse stayed calm and *collected*⟩. UNRUFFLED suggests apparent serenity and poise in the face of setbacks or in the midst of excitement ⟨harried but *unruffled*⟩. IMPERTURBABLE implies coolness or assurance even under severe provocation ⟨the speaker remained *imperturbable* despite the heckling⟩. NONCHALANT stresses an easy coolness of manner or casualness that suggests indifference or unconcern ⟨a *nonchalant* driver⟩.

Synonyms and
distinctions
with usage
examples

Entry for *cool*
used as a verb

²cool *vi* (bef. 12c) **1 :** to become cool : lose heat or warmth ⟨placed the pie in the window to ~⟩ — sometimes used with *off* or *down* **2 :** to lose ardor or passion ⟨his anger ~ed⟩ ~ *vt* **1 :** to make cool : impart a feeling of coolness to ⟨~ed the room with a fan⟩ — often used with *off* or *down* ⟨a swim ~ed us off a little⟩ **2 a :** to moderate the heat, excitement, or force of : CALM ⟨~ed her growing anger⟩ **b :** to slow or lessen the growth or activity of — usu. used with *off* or *down* ⟨wants to ~ off the economy without freezing it —*Newsweek*⟩ — **cool it :** to calm down : go easy ⟨the word went out to the young to *cool it* —W. M. Young⟩ — **cool one's heels :** to wait or be kept waiting for a long time esp. from or as if from disdain or discourtesy

Idiomatic
usage

³cool *n* (15c) **1 :** a cool time, place, or situation ⟨the ~ of the evening⟩ **2 a :** absence of excitement or emotional involvement : DETACHMENT ⟨must surrender his fine ~ and enter the closed crazy world of suicide —Wilfrid Sheed⟩ **b :** POISE, COMPOSURE ⟨press questions . . . seemed to rattle him and he lost his ~ —*New Republic*⟩ **3 :** HIPNESS
⁴cool *adv* (1841) : in a casual and nonchalant manner ⟨play it ~⟩

Figure 33.1. Examples of dictionary entries.

33e THESAURUSES

A **thesaurus** provides alternatives for frequently used words. Unlike a dictionary, which explains what a word means and how it evolved, a thesaurus provides only a list of words that serve as possible synonyms for each term it includes. A thesaurus can be useful, especially when you want to jog your memory about a word you know but cannot recall. You may, however, use a word incorrectly if you simply pick it from a list in a thesaurus. If you find an unfamiliar yet intriguing word, make sure that you are using it correctly by looking it up in a dictionary.

Exercise 3

Find definitions for the pairs of words in parentheses. Then choose the word you think best completes each sentence. Be prepared to explain your answers.

1. Sixteen prisoners on death row were granted (mercy/clemency).
2. The outcome of the election (excited/provoked) a riot.
3. The young couple was (covetous/greedy) of their neighbors' estate.
4. While she was traveling in Muslim countries, she wore (modest/chaste) clothing.
5. The president of the university (authorized/confirmed) the rumor that tuition would be increasing next year.

34 | PRECISE WORD CHOICE

Make words work for you. By choosing the right word and putting it in the right place, you can communicate exactly what you mean and make your writing distinctive. This chapter will help you

- choose words appropriate for your purpose, audience, and context (**34a**);
- create fresh, clear expressions (**34b**);
- use idioms and collocations (**34c**); and
- compose clear definitions (**34d**).

34a   ACCURATE AND PRECISE WORD CHOICE

(1) Denotations and connotations

Denotations are definitions of words, such as those that appear in dictionaries. For example, the noun *beach* denotes a sandy or pebbly shore. However, some words have more than one definition or one definition that can be interpreted in a number of ways. Select words whose denotations convey your point exactly.

Padre Island National Seashore ^is really great. ~~astounds even an indifferent tourist like me.~~

[Because *great* can mean "extremely large" as well as "outstanding" or "powerful," its use in this sentence is imprecise.]

Denotations of words can also sometimes be confused.

The park ranger~~inferred~~ ^implied^ that the Kemp's ridley sea turtle may become extinct.

[*Imply* means "to suggest," so *implied* is the exact word for this sentence. *Infer* means "to draw a conclusion from evidence": From the park ranger's comments, I *inferred* that the Kemp's ridley sea turtle may become extinct.]

The **Glossary of Usage** at the back of this book includes the definitions of many words that are commonly confused.

Connotations are the associations evoked by a word. *Beach,* for instance, may connote natural beauty, surf, shells, swimming, tanning, sunburn, and/or crowds. The context in which a word appears affects the associations it evokes. In a treatise on shoreline management, *beach* has scientific and geographic connotations; in a fashion magazine, this word is associated with bathing suits, sunglasses, and sunscreen. The challenge for writers is to choose the words that are most likely to spark the appropriate connotations in their readers' minds.

The ~~obstinacy~~ ^resilience^ of the Kemp's ridley sea turtle has delighted park rangers.

[*Obstinacy* has negative connotations, which make it an unlikely quality to cause delight.]

ñ MULTILINGUAL WRITERS

CONNOTATIONS

Your ability to recognize connotations will improve as your vocabulary increases. When you encounter a new word that seems to mean exactly what another word means, study the context in which each word is used. Then, to help yourself learn the new word and its context, create a phrase or a sentence that you can easily remember. If you are confused about the connotations of specific words, consult an ESL dictionary (see page 677).

(2) Specific, concrete words

A **general word** is all-inclusive, indefinite, and sweeping in scope. A **specific word** is precise, definite, and limited in scope.

General	Specific	More Specific/Concrete
food	fast food	cheeseburger
media	newspapers	*The Miami Herald*
place	city	Atlanta

An **abstract word** refers to a concept or idea, a quality or trait, or anything else that cannot be touched, heard, or seen. A **concrete word** signifies a particular object, a specific action, or anything that can be touched, heard, or seen.

Abstract	democracy, evil, strength, charity
Concrete	mosquito, hammer, plastic, fog

As you select words to fit your context, be as specific and concrete as you can. For example, instead of the word *bad,* consider using a more precise adjective.

bad neighbors: rowdy, snobby, nosy, fussy, sloppy, threatening

bad meat: tough, tainted, overcooked, undercooked, contaminated

bad wood: rotten, warped, scorched, knotty, termite-ridden

To test whether or not a word is specific, you can ask one or more of these questions about what you want to say: Exactly who? Exactly what? Exactly when? Exactly where? Exactly how? In the following examples, notice what a difference concrete words can make in expressing an idea and how adding details can expand or develop it.

Vague	She has kept no reminders of performing in her youth.
Specific	She has kept no sequined costume, no photographs, no fliers or posters from that part of her youth.

—LOUISE ERDRICH, "The Leap"

The word *thing* may refer to a task, an errand, an implement, a concept, an utterance, and so on. Because this word has so many referents, replace it with a specific word whenever possible.

We did not say a~~thing~~. [word]

Fear and horror are not the same~~thing~~. [emotion]

(3) Figurative language

Figurative language is the use of words in an imaginative rather than a literal sense. Similes and metaphors are the chief **figures of speech**. A **simile** is a comparison of dissimilar things using *like* or *as*. A **metaphor** is an implied comparison of dissimilar things, without *like* or *as*.

Similes

Norms live in the culture **like genes, manifesting themselves unexpectedly, the way a child's big ears appear from an ancestor of whom no picture or name remains.**

—CHARLES WOHLFORTH, "Conservation and Eugenics:
The Environmental Movement's Dirty Secret"

When **her body was hairless as a baby's,** she adjusted the showerhead so that the water burst forth in pelting streams.

—LOIDA MARITZA PÉREZ, *Geographies of Home*

Metaphors

His **money was a sharp pair of scissors** that snipped rapidly through tangles of red tape.   —HISAYE YAMAMOTO, "The Brown House"

Making tacos is a graceful dance.   —DENISE CHÁVEZ, *A Taco Testimony*

Single words can be used metaphorically.

These roses must be **planted** in good soil. [literal]

Keep your life **planted** wherever you can put down the most roots. [metaphorical]

Similes and metaphors are especially valuable when they are concrete and describe or evoke essential relationships that cannot otherwise be communicated. Similes or metaphors can be extended throughout a paragraph of comparison, but be careful not to mix them (27b).

Exercise 1

Study the passage below, and prepare to discuss the author's use of exact and figurative language to communicate her ideas.

[1]The kitchen where I'm making dinner is a New York kitchen. [2]Nice light, way too small, nowhere to put anything unless the stove goes. [3]My stove is huge, but it will never go. [4]My stove is where my head clears, my impressions settle, my reporter's life gets folded into my life, and whatever I've just learned, or think I've learned—whatever it was, out there in the world, that had seemed so different and surprising—bubbles away in the very small pot of what I think I know and, if I'm lucky, produces something like perspective.   —JANE KRAMER, "The Reporter's Kitchen"

Exercise 2

Use figurative language to provide details about each of the following topics.

1. the look on someone's face
2. a cold rainy day
3. studying for an exam
4. your favorite food
5. buying textbooks
6. a busy street
7. waiting in a long line to see a movie
8. the way someone talks

34b   CLICHÉS AND EUPHEMISMS

When forced or overused, certain expressions lose their impact. For example, the expressions *bite the dust, breath of fresh air,* and *smooth as silk* were once striking and thus effective. Excessive use, though, has drained them of their original force and made them **clichés**. Newer expressions such as *put a spin on something* and *think outside the box* have also lost their vitality because of overuse. Nonetheless, clichés are so much a part of the language, especially the spoken language, that nearly every writer uses them from time to time. But effective writers often give a fresh twist to an old saying.

> I seek a narrative, a fiction, to order days like the one I spent several years ago, on a gray June Saturday in Chicago, when I took a roller-coaster ride on the bell curve of my experience.
>
> —GAYLE PEMBERTON, "The Zen of Bigger Thomas"

[Notice how much more effective this expression is than a reference to "being on an emotional roller coaster."]

Variations on familiar expressions from literature and history, many of which have become part of everyday language, can often be used to good effect.

> We have met the enemy and he is us.   —WALT KELLY, Earth Day Poster, 1970

[This statement is a variation on one made by American naval officer Oliver Hazard Perry during the War of 1812: "We have met the enemy and they are ours."]

Good writers, however, do not rely too heavily on the words of others; they choose their own words to communicate their ideas.

Sometimes writers coin new expressions to substitute for words that have coarse or unpleasant connotations. These expressions, called **euphemisms**, occasionally become standardized. To avoid the word *dying*, for example, a writer might say that someone was *terminally ill*. Although euphemisms sound more pleasant than the words they replace, they can sometimes obscure facts. Euphemisms such as *revenue* *enhancement* for *tax hike* and *pre-owned* for *used* are considered insincere or deceitful.

Exercise 3

Replace the following overused expressions with carefully chosen words. Then use the replacements in sentences.

EXAMPLE

beyond the shadow of a doubt
undoubtedly   OR   with total certainty

1. reality check
2. global village
3. shout-out
4. face time
5. in your face

6. bottom line
7. in the loop
8. over the top
9. win by a landslide
10. call the shots

34C | IDIOMS AND COLLOCATIONS

Idioms are fixed expressions whose meanings cannot be entirely determined by knowing the meanings of their parts—examples are *bear in mind, fall in love,* and *stand a chance.* **Collocations** are combinations of words that frequently occur together. Unlike idioms, they have meanings that *can* be determined by knowing the meanings of their parts—think of *depend on, fond of, little while,* or *right now.* Regardless of whether you are using an idiom or a collocation, if you make even a small change to the expected wording, you may distract or confuse your readers.

She tried to keep a low ~~small~~ profile.

They had a vested ~~an invested~~ interest in the project.

As you edit your writing, keep an eye out for idioms or collocations that might not be worded correctly. Then check a general dictionary, a dictionary of idioms (see page 677), or the **Glossary of Usage** at the end of this book to ensure that your usage is appropriate. Use idioms with care, though. If overused, they may be considered clichés.

Because prepositions are often small, unstressed words, writers sometimes confuse them. The following is a list of common collocations containing prepositions.

CHOOSING THE RIGHT PREPOSITION

according **to** the source	intend **to** finish his degree
accused **of** the crime	opposition **to** the idea
based **on** the novel	parallel **to** the road
bored **by** it	perspective **on** the topic
conform **to/with** standards	plan **to** attend
connected **to** each other	prior **to** the ruling
consists **of** cards and letters	relevant **to** the discussion
different **from** the first draft	substitute beans **for** meat
happened **by** accident	superior **to** others
in accordance **with** policy	sure **to** see the movie
independent **of** his family	try **to** be on time
insist **on** repayment	typical **of** that period

ⓝ *MULTILINGUAL WRITERS*

UNDERSTANDING AND USING IDIOMS

The context in which an idiom appears can often help you understand the meaning. For example, if you read "When they learned that she had accepted illegal campaign contributions, several political commentators raked her over the coals," you would probably understand that *to rake over the coals* means "to criticize severely." As you learn new idioms from your reading, make a list of those you might want to use in your own writing. If you are confused about the meaning of a particular idiom, check a dictionary of idioms (see page 677).

Exercise 4

Write a sentence using each idiom or collocation correctly.

1. pass muster, pass the time
2. do one's best, do one's part, do one's duty
3. in a pinch, in a rut, in a way
4. cut down, cut back, cut corners
5. make time, make sure, make sense

34d   CLEAR DEFINITIONS

When words have more than one meaning, establish which meaning you have in mind. A definition can set the terms of the discussion.

> In this paper, I use the word *communism* **in the Marxist sense of social organization based on the holding of all property in common.**

A **formal definition** first states the term to be defined, then puts it into a class, and finally differentiates it from other members of that class.

> A *phosphene* [term] is **a luminous visual image** [class] that **results from applying pressure to the eyeball** [differentiation].

A short dictionary definition may be adequate when you need to convey the meaning of a word unfamiliar to readers.

> Here, *galvanic* means **"produced as if by electric shock."**

Giving a synonym may also clarify the meaning of a term. Such synonyms are often used as appositives (**21a(5)**).

> *Machismo,* **confidence with an attitude,** can be a pose rather than a reality.

Writers frequently show—rather than tell—what a word means by giving examples.

> Many homophones (**such as *be* and *bee* or *see* and *sea***) **are not spelling problems.**

Sometimes, your own definition can clarify a concept.

> *Clichés* could be defined as **thoughts that have hardened.**

When writing definitions, do not confuse readers by placing a predicate with a subject that is not logically connected to it (**27d(3)**). Constructions that combine *is* or *are* with *when*, *where*, or *because* are often illogical because forms of *be* signify identity or equality between the subject and what follows.

> The Internet~~is when~~ ^allows you ^to look at text and images from across the
> world.

Exercise 5

Using your own words, define each of the following terms in full sentences.

1. audacity
2. professionalism
3. dilemma
4. indifference
5. ambiguity
6. equal opportunity

35 | CONCISENESS

To facilitate readers' understanding, effective writers convey their thoughts clearly and efficiently. This does not mean that they always write short sentences; rather, they use each word wisely. This chapter will help you

- make each word count (**35a**) and
- use elliptical constructions (**35b**).

35a ELIMINATING REDUNDANCY AND WORDINESS

After writing a first draft, review your sentences to make sure that they contain only the words necessary to make your point.

(1) Redundancy

Restating a key point in different words can help readers understand it. But if you rephrase readily understood terms, your work will suffer from **redundancy**—repetition for no good reason.

Ballerinas auditioned ~~in the tryouts~~ for *The Nutcracker*.

Each student had a unique talent ~~and ability that he or she used in his or her~~ acting.

You should also avoid grammatical redundancy, as in double subjects (*my sister [she] is*), double comparisons (*[more] easier than*), and double negatives (*could[n't] hardly*).

(2) Wordiness

As you edit a draft, look for ways to rewrite sentences in fewer words, without risking the loss of important details. One exact word often says as much as several inexact ones.

spoke in a low and hard-to-hear voice   **mumbled**

a person who gives expert advice   **consultant**

Some unscrupulous brokers are ~~taking money and savings from~~ elderly
[cheating]

people ~~who need that money because they planned to use it as a retirement pension.~~
[out of their pensions.]

~~In the event that~~ taxes are raised, ~~expect complaints on the part of the voters.~~
[If]   [voters will complain.]

In addition, watch for vague words such as *area, aspect, factor, feature, kind, situation, thing,* and *type.* They may signal wordiness.

~~In an employment situation, effective~~ communication is essential at work.
[Effective]

REPLACEMENTS FOR WORDY EXPRESSIONS

Instead of	Use
at this moment (point) in time	now, today
due to the fact that	because
in view of the fact that	because
for the purpose of	for
it is clear (obvious) that	clearly (obviously)
there is no question that	unquestionably, certainly
without a doubt	undoubtedly
beyond the shadow of a doubt	certainly, surely
it is my opinion that	I think (believe) that
in this day and age	today
in the final analysis	finally

WORDINESS IN COMMON PHRASES

yellow [in color]	circular [in shape]
at 9:45 a.m. [in the morning]	return [back]
[basic] essentials	rich [and wealthy] nations
bitter[-tasting] salad	small[-size] potatoes
connect [up together]	[true] facts
because [of the fact that]	was [more or less] hinting
[really and truly] fearless	by [virtue of] his authority

---

(3) *There are* and *it is*

There or *it* may function as an **expletive**—a word that signals that the subject of the sentence will follow the verb, usually a form of *be* (**20b**). Writers use expletives to emphasize words that would not be emphasized in the typical subject-verb order. Notice the difference in rhythm between the following sentences:

Two children were playing in the yard. [typical order]

There were two children playing in the yard. [use of expletive]

However, expletives are easily overused. If you find that you have drafted several sentences that begin with expletives, revise a few of them.

Hundreds
~~There were hundreds~~ of fans~were~crowding onto the field.

Joining the crowd
~~It~~ was frightening ~~to join the crowd~~.

(4) Relative pronouns

The relative pronoun *who*, *which*, or *that* can frequently be deleted without affecting the meaning of a sentence. If one of these pronouns is followed by a form of the verb *be* (*am, is, are, was,* or *were*), you can often omit the pronoun and sometimes the verb as well.

The change ~~that~~ the young senator proposed yesterday angered most legislators.

The Endangered Species Act, ~~which was~~ passed in 1973, protects the habitat of endangered plants and animals.

When deleting a relative pronoun, you might have to make other changes to a sentence as well.

Nations ~~that provide~~ providing protection for endangered species often create preserves and forbid hunting of these species.

ⓝ MULTILINGUAL WRITERS

USING RELATIVE PRONOUNS

Review your sentences to make sure that no clause includes both a personal pronoun (**25a(1)**) and a relative pronoun (**25a(3)**) referring to the same antecedent (**25c**).

The drug **that** we were testing ~~it~~ has not been approved by the Food and Drug Administration.

The principal investigator, **whom** we depended on ~~her~~ for guidance, had to take a medical leave before the project was completed.

For more information on relative (adjectival) clauses, see Chapter 47.

35b   USING ELLIPTICAL CONSTRUCTIONS

An **elliptical construction** is one that deliberately omits words that can be understood from the context.

Speed is the goal for some swimmers, endurance ~~is the goal~~ for others, and relaxation ~~is the goal~~ for still others.

Sometimes, as an aid to clarity, commas mark omissions in elliptical constructions.

My family functioned like a baseball team: my mom was the coach; my brother, the pitcher; and my sister, the shortstop. [Use semicolons to separate items with internal commas (**37a**).]

Exercise 1

Revise this paragraph to eliminate wordiness and needless repetition.

¹Founded in the year 1967, *Rolling Stone* has become well known for covering culture and politics considered popular. ²Back in the day, the *Rolling Stone's* magazine's original focus was rock and roll. ³In its first year, I think it helped popularize musicians such as John Lennon, Mick Jagger, and also the guitarist Pete Townshend. ⁴Cover photographs featured the Beatles, Jimi Hendrix, Tina Turner, and the vocalist Jim Morrison, among others. ⁵The magazine also carried news reports related to the music of the 1960s period. ⁶The cost of the Monterey Pop Festival and additionally a raid at the Grateful Dead's house were two of the breaking news stories in 1967. ⁷Since that day and age, the magazine has become a mainstay on newsstands everywhere all over the world. ⁸Writers, as well as musicians, have gained nationwide recognition: in the early days, Hunter S. Thompson gained recognition for "Fear and Loathing in Las Vegas," and Tom Wolfe gained recognition for presenting the inner world of the Mercury astronauts; more recently, Michael Hastings gained recognition for reporting on military leadership. ⁹Though articles and interviews on topics related to music and politics continue to attract readers, reviews of films, books, and other types of entertainment have now become standard fare also. ¹⁰Always eye-catching and really impressive, the cover of the magazine now spotlights all kinds of people in the news, not just musicians: politicians, actors, actresses, models, comedians, movie directors, and even fictional characters (Darth Vader and Waldo) have appeared under the distinctive and colorful letters of the name *Rolling Stone*.

PUNCTUATION

Kate Derrick

36 ‖ THE COMMA

Punctuation lends to written language the same flexibility that facial expressions, pauses, and variations in voice pitch offer spoken language. The following sentences illustrate that flexibility:

When the recruiter called, Kenneth Martin answered.

When the recruiter called Kenneth, Martin answered.

When the first sentence is spoken, a pause after *called* makes it clear that the sentence refers to only two people: the recruiter and Kenneth Martin. In the second example, a pause after *Kenneth* lets the listener know that the sentence refers to three people: the recruiter, Kenneth, and Martin. In written text, the same intended meanings can be established by commas.

Pauses and commas are not always paired, however. Pauses are not a reliable guide for comma placement: commas are often called for where speakers do not pause, and pauses can occur where no comma is necessary. Thus, it is important to understand the basic principles of comma usage. This chapter will help you use commas to

- separate independent clauses joined by coordinating conjunctions (**36a**),
- set off introductory clauses and phrases (**36b**),
- separate items in a series (**36c**),
- set off nonessential (nonrestrictive) elements (**36d**),
- set off geographical names and items in dates and addresses (**36e**), and
- set off direct quotations (**36f**),

as well as help you to

- recognize unnecessary or misplaced commas (**36g**).

36a	BEFORE A COORDINATING CONJUNCTION LINKING INDEPENDENT CLAUSES

Use a comma before a coordinating conjunction (*and, but, for, nor, or, so,* or *yet*) that links two independent clauses. (Some people use *fanboys*, a made-up word formed of the first letters of the coordinating conjunctions, as an aid to remembering them; see **20a(7)**.) An **independent clause** is a group of words that can stand as a sentence (**21b(1)**).

INDEPENDENT CLAUSE**,** **COORDINATING CONJUNCTION**
INDEPENDENT CLAUSE.

	and	
	but	
	for	
Subject + predicate,	**nor**	subject + predicate.
	or	
	so	
	yet	

The Iditarod Trail Sled Dog Race begins in March**, but** training starts much sooner.

In the 1960s, Dorothy Page wanted to spark interest in the role of dog sledding in Alaskan history**, so** she proposed staging a long race.

No matter how many clauses are in a sentence, a comma comes before each coordinating conjunction.

The race takes several days to complete**, and** training is a year-round activity**, but** the mushers do not complain.

When the independent clauses are short, the comma is often omitted before *and, but,* or *or.*

My friend races **but** I don't.

If a coordinating conjunction joins two parts of a compound predicate (which means there is only one subject), a comma is not normally used before the conjunction. (See **20b** and **36g(3)**.)

The race starts in Anchorage⌃and ends in Nome.

A semicolon, instead of a comma, precedes a conjunction joining two independent clauses when at least one of the clauses already contains a comma. (See also **37a**.)

When running long distances, sled dogs burn more than ten thousand calories a day⁏ **so** they must be fed well.

Exercise 1

Combine each of the following pairs of sentences by using coordinating conjunctions and inserting commas where appropriate. (Remember that not all coordinating conjunctions link independent clauses and that *but, for, so,* and *yet* do not always function as coordinating conjunctions.) Explain why you used each of the conjunctions you inserted.

1. Dinosaurs lived for 165 million years. Then they became extinct.

2. No one knows why dinosaurs became extinct. Several theories have been proposed.

3. Some theorists believe that a huge meteor hit the earth. The climate may have changed dramatically.

4. Another theory suggests that dinosaurs did not actually become extinct. They simply evolved into lizards and birds.

5. Yet another theory suggests that they just grew too big. Not all of the dinosaurs were huge.

36b AFTER INTRODUCTORY CLAUSES, PHRASES, OR WORDS

(1) Following an introductory dependent clause

If you begin a sentence with a dependent (subordinate) clause (**21b(2)**), place a comma after it to set it off from the independent (main) clause (**21b(1)**).

INTRODUCTORY CLAUSE**,** INDEPENDENT CLAUSE.

Although the safest automobile on the road is expensive, the protection it offers justifies the cost.

(2) Following an introductory phrase

Place a comma after an introductory phrase to set it off from the independent clause.

INTRODUCTORY PHRASE**,** INDEPENDENT CLAUSE.

(a) Introductory prepositional phrases

Despite a downturn in the national economy, the number of students enrolled in this university has increased.

If you begin a sentence with a short introductory prepositional phrase (**21a(4)**), you may omit the comma as long as the resulting sentence is not difficult to read.

In 2009 the enrollment at the university increased.

BUT

In 2009, 625 new students enrolled in courses.
[A comma separates two numbers.]

A comma is not used after a prepositional phrase that begins a sentence in which the subject and predicate (**20b**) are inverted.

With children came responsibilities.
[The subject of the sentence is *responsibilities*: Responsibilities came with children.]

(b) Other types of introductory phrases

If you begin a sentence with a participial phrase (**21a(3)**) or an absolute phrase (**21a(6)**), place a comma after the phrase.

Having never left home, she imagined the outside world to be fantastic, almost magical. [participial phrase]

The language difference aside, life in Germany did not seem much different from life in the United States. [absolute phrase]

(3) Following an introductory word

> **INTRODUCTORY WORD,** INDEPENDENT CLAUSE.

Use a comma to set off an interjection, a **vocative** (a word used to address someone directly), or a transitional word that begins a sentence.

Yikes, I forgot to pick him up from the airport. [interjection]

Bob, I want you to know how very sorry I am. [vocative]

Moreover, I insist on paying for your taxi. [transitional word]

When there is no risk of misunderstanding, some introductory adverbs and transitional words do not need to be set off by a comma (see also **37a(1)**).

Sometimes even a good design is rejected by the board.

Exercise 2

Insert commas where necessary in the following paragraph. Explain why each comma is needed. Some sentences may not require editing.

¹If you had to describe sound would you call it a wave? ²Although sound cannot be seen people have described it this way for long time. ³In fact the Greek philosopher Aristotle believed that sound traveling through air was like waves in the sea. ⁴Envisioning waves in the air he hypothesized that sound would not be able to pass through a vacuum because there would be no

(continued on page 704)

(continued from page 703)

air to transmit it. [5]Aristotle's hypothesis was not tested until nearly two thousand years later. [6]In 1654 Otto von Guericke found that he could not hear a bell ringing inside the vacuum he had created. [7]Thus Guericke established the necessity of air for sound transmission. [8]However although most sound reaches us through the air it travels faster through liquids and solids.

36c SEPARATING ELEMENTS IN A SERIES OR COORDINATE ADJECTIVES

A **series** contains three or more parallel elements. To be parallel, elements must be grammatically equal; all of them must be words, phrases, or clauses. (See Chapter 30.)

(1) Words, phrases, or clauses in a series

A comma appears after each item in a series except the last one.

Ethics are based on **moral, social,** or **cultural values.** [words in a series]

The company's code of ethics encourages **seeking criticism of work, correcting mistakes,** and **acknowledging the contributions of everyone.** [phrases in a series]

Several circumstances can lead to unethical behavior: **people are tempted by a desire to succeed, they are pressured by others into acting inappropriately,** or **they are simply trying to survive.** [clauses in a series]

If elements in a series contain internal commas, you can prevent misreading by separating the items with semicolons.

According to their code of ethics, researchers must disclose all results, without omitting any data; indicate various interpretations of the data; and make the data and methodology available to other researchers, some of whom may choose to replicate the study.

❓ THINKING RHETORICALLY

SERIES COMMAS VERSUS CONJUNCTIONS

How do the following sentences differ?

We discussed them all: life, liberty, **and** the pursuit of happiness.

We discussed them all: life **and** liberty **and** the pursuit of happiness.

We discussed them all: life, liberty, the pursuit of happiness.

The first sentence follows conventional guidelines; that is, a comma and a conjunction precede the last element in the series. The less conventional second and third sentences do more than convey information. With two conjunctions and no commas, the second sentence slows down the pace of the reading, causing stress to be placed on each of the three elements in the series. In contrast, the third sentence, with commas but no conjunctions, speeds up the reading, as if to suggest that the rights listed do not need to be stressed because they are so familiar. To get a sense of how your sentences will be read and understood, try reading them aloud.

(2) Coordinate adjectives

Two or more adjectives that precede the same noun are called **coordinate adjectives**. To test whether adjectives are coordinate, either interchange them or put *and* between them. If the altered version of the adjectives-and-noun combination is acceptable, the adjectives are coordinate and should be separated by a comma or commas.

Crossing the **rushing, shallow** creek, I slipped off a rock and fell into the water.
[COMPARE: a rushing and shallow creek OR a shallow, rushing creek]

The adjectives in the following sentence are not separated by a comma. Notice that they cannot be interchanged or joined by *and*.

Sitting in the water, I saw an **old wooden** bridge.
[NOT a wooden old bridge OR an old and wooden bridge]

36d   WITH NONESSENTIAL ELEMENTS

Nonessential (nonrestrictive) elements provide supplemental information, that is, information a reader does not need in order to identify who or what is being discussed (see also **21b(2)**). Use commas to set off a nonessential word or word group: one comma precedes a nonessential element at the end of a sentence; two commas set off a nonessential element in the middle of a sentence.

The Annual Hilltop Folk Festival**,** **planned for late July,** should attract many tourists.

In the preceding sentence, the phrase placed between commas, *planned for late July*, conveys nonessential information: the reader knows which festival will attract tourists without being told when it will be held. When a phrase follows a proper noun (**20a(2)**), such as *The Annual Hilltop Folk Festival,* it is usually nonessential. Note, however, that in the following sentence, the phrase *planned for late July* is necessary for the reader to identify the festival as the one scheduled to occur in late July, not another time:

The festival **planned for late July** should attract many tourists.

In the preceding sentence, the phrase is an **essential (restrictive) element** because, without it, the reader will not know which festival the writer has in mind. Essential elements are not set off by commas; they are integrated into sentences (**21b(2)**).

(1) Setting off nonessential elements used as modifiers

(a) Adjectival clauses

Nonessential modifiers are often **adjectival (relative) clauses**, which are usually introduced by a relative pronoun, *who, which,* or *that* (**21b(2)**). In the following sentence, a comma sets off the adjectival clause because the reader does not need the content of that clause in order to identify the mountain:

We climbed Mt. McKinley**,** **which is over 15,000 feet high.**

(b) Participial phrases

Nonessential modifiers also include **participial phrases** (phrases that begin with a present or past participle of a verb) (**21a(3)**).

> Mt. McKinley**,** **towering above us,** brought to mind our abandoned plan for climbing it. [participial phrase beginning with a present participle]

> My sister**,** **slowed by a knee injury,** rarely hikes anymore. [participial phrase beginning with a past participle]

(c) Adverbial clauses

An **adverbial clause** (**21b(2)**) begins with a subordinating conjunction that signals cause (*because*), purpose (*so that*), or time (*when, after, before*). This type of clause is usually considered essential and thus is not set off by a comma when it appears at the end of a sentence.

> Dinosaurs may have become extinct **because their habitat was destroyed.**

In contrast, an adverbial clause that provides nonessential information, such as an aside or a comment, should be set off from the main clause.

> Dinosaurs are extinct**,** **though they are alive in many people's imaginations.**

(2) Setting off nonessential appositives

Appositives refer to the same person, place, object, idea, or event as a nearby noun or noun phrase but in different words (**21a(5)**). Nonessential appositives provide extra details about nouns or noun phrases (**21a(1)**) and are set off by commas; essential appositives are not. In the following sentence, the title of the article is mentioned, so the reader does not need the information provided by the appositive in order to identify the article. The appositive is thus set off by commas.

> "Living on the Line**,**" **Joanne Hart's most recent article,** describes the lives of factory workers in China.

In the next sentence, *Joanne Hart's article* is nonspecific, so an essential appositive containing the specific title of the article is integrated into the sentence. It is not set off by commas. Without the appositive, the reader would not know which of Hart's articles describes the lives of factory workers in China.

> Joanne Hart's article "Living on the Line" describes the lives of factory workers in China.

If Hart had written only this one article, the title would be set off by commas. The reader would not need the information in the appositive to identify the article.

Abbreviations of titles or degrees after names are treated as nonessential appositives.

> Was the letter from Frances Evans, PhD, or from Francis Evans, MD?

Increasingly, however, *Jr., Sr., II,* and *III* are considered part of a name, and the comma is thus often omitted.

> William Homer Barton, Jr.   OR   William Homer Barton Jr.

Exercise 3

Set off nonessential clauses, phrases, and appositives with commas.

1. Maine Coons long-haired cats with bushy tails have adapted to a harsh climate.
2. These animals which are extremely gentle despite their large size often weigh twenty pounds.
3. Most Maine Coons have exceptionally high intelligence for cats which enables them to recognize language and even to open doors.
4. Unlike most cats Maine Coons will play fetch with their owners.
5. According to a legend later proven to be false Maine Coons developed from interbreeding between wildcats and domestic cats.

(3) Setting off absolute phrases

An **absolute phrase** (the combination of a noun and a modifying word or phrase; see **21a(6)**) provides nonessential details and so should always be set off by a comma or commas.

The actor, **his hair wet and slicked back,** began his audition.

The director stared at him, **her mind flipping through the photographs she had viewed earlier.**

(4) Setting off transitional expressions and other parenthetical elements

Commas customarily set off transitional words and phrases such as *for example, that is,* and *namely.*

An airline ticket, **for example,** can be delivered electronically.

Some transitional words and short phrases such as *also, too, at least,* and *thus* need not be set off by commas.

Traveling has **thus** become easier in recent years.

Use commas to set off other parenthetical elements, such as words or phrases that provide commentary you wish to stress.

Over the past year, my flights have, **miraculously,** been on time.

(5) Setting off contrasted elements

Commas set off sentence elements in which words such as *never* and *unlike* express contrast.

A planet, **unlike** a star, reflects rather than generates light.

In sentences in which contrasted elements are introduced by *not only . . . but also,* place a comma before *but* if you want to emphasize what follows it. Otherwise, leave the comma out.

Planets **not only** vary in size, **but also** travel at different speeds.
[Comma added for emphasis.]

36e   WITH GEOGRAPHICAL NAMES AND ITEMS IN DATES AND ADDRESSES

Use commas to make geographical names, dates, and addresses easy to read.

(1) City and state

Nashville, Tennessee, is the capital of country-and-western music in the United States.

(2) Day and date

Martha left for Peru on **Wednesday, February 12, 2009,** and returned on March 12.

OR

Martha left for Peru on **Wednesday, 12 February 2009,** and returned on 12 March.

In the style used in the second sentence (which is not as common in the United States as the style in the first example), one comma is omitted because *12* precedes *February* and is thus clearly separate from *2009*.

(3) Addresses

In a sentence containing an address, the name of the person or organization, the street address, and the name of the town or city are all followed by commas, but the abbreviation for the state is not.

I had to write to **Ms. Melanie Hobson, Senior Analyst, Hobson Computing, 2873 Central Avenue, Orange Park, FL 32065.**

36f   WITH DIRECT QUOTATIONS

Many sentences containing direct quotations also contain signal phrases (or attributive tags) such as *The author claims* or *According to the author* (10d(2)). Use commas to set off these phrases whether they occur at the beginning, in the middle, or at the end of a sentence.

(1) Signal phrase at the beginning of a sentence

Place the comma directly after the signal phrase, before the quotation marks.

As Jacques Barzun claims, "It is a false analogy with science that makes one think latest is best."

(2) Signal phrase in the middle of a sentence

Place the first comma inside the quotation marks that precede the signal phrase; place the second comma directly after the phrase, before the next set of quotation marks.

"It is a false analogy with science," claims Jacques Barzun, "that makes one think latest is best."

(3) Signal phrase at the end of a sentence

Place the comma inside the quotation marks before the signal phrase.

"It is a false analogy with science that makes one think latest is best," claims Jacques Barzun.

36g   UNNECESSARY OR MISPLACED COMMAS

Although a comma may signal a pause, not every pause calls for a comma. As you read the following sentence aloud, you may pause naturally at several places, but no commas are necessary.

Heroic deeds done by ordinary people inspire others to act in ways that are not only moral but courageous.

(1) No comma between a subject and its verb or a verb and its object

Although speakers often pause after the subject (20b) or before the object (20c) of a sentence, such a pause should not be indicated by a comma.

In this climate, rain at frequent intervals⌇produces mosquitoes. [no separation between the subject (*rain*) and the verb (*produces*)]

The forecaster said⌇that rain was likely. [no separation between the verb (*said*) and the direct object (the noun clause *that rain was likely*)]

(2) No comma following a coordinating conjunction

Avoid using a comma after a coordinating conjunction (*and, but, for, nor, or, so,* or *yet*).

We worked very hard on her campaign for state representative**,**but⌇ the incumbent was too strong to defeat in the northern districts.

(3) No comma separating elements in a compound predicate

In general, avoid using a comma between two elements of a compound predicate (**20b**).

I read the comments carefully⌇and then started my revision.

However, if you want to place stress on the second element in a compound predicate, you may place a comma after the first element. Use this option sparingly, or it will lose its effect.

I read the comments word by word**,** and despaired.

(4) No comma setting off essential words, phrases, and clauses

In the following sentences, the elements in boldface are essential and so should not be set off by commas (**36d**).

Zoe was born⌇**in Chicago during the Great Depression.**

Perhaps⌇the thermostat is broken.

Everyone⌇**who has a mortgage**⌇is required to have fire insurance.

Someone⌇**wearing an orange wig**⌇greeted us at the door.

(5) No comma preceding the first item of a series or following the last

Make sure that you place commas only between elements in a series, not before or after the series.

She was known for⸲ her photographs⸲ sketches⸲ and engravings.

The exhibit included her most exuberant⸲ exciting⸲ and expensive⸲ photographs.

Exercise 4

Explain the use of each comma in the following paragraph.

[1]There is some evidence that musical training may enhance performance on some tests of mental abilities, but the effects are not great. [2]To some extent, this is another chicken-and-egg problem. [3]Does musical training enhance performance on the tests, or do children who take musical training exhibit enhanced performance on tests because of their particular interests and abilities? [4]But early musical training perhaps increases the possibility the child will have perfect pitch, as we noted, presumably enhancing later musical capabilities. [5]Actually, one recent and carefully done study found a greater increase in the IQ scores of children after taking music lessons than after taking drama or no lessons.

—RICHARD F. THOMPSON AND STEPHEN A. MADIGAN,
Memory: The Key to Consciousness

37 ‖ THE SEMICOLON AND THE COLON

Although semicolons and colons can both link independent clauses, the use of these punctuation marks in this way is determined by the purpose of the second clause and the relation between the two clauses. In addition, semicolons and colons each have unique uses. This chapter will help you

- use semicolons correctly (**37a**) and
- use colons correctly (**37b**).

37a ‖ THE SEMICOLON

The semicolon indicates that the phrases or clauses on either side of it are closely related. It most frequently connects two independent clauses when the second clause supports or contrasts with the first, but it can be used for other purposes as well.

(1) Connecting independent clauses

A semicolon placed between two independent clauses indicates that they are closely related. The second of the two clauses generally supports or contrasts with the first.

> For many cooks, basil is a key ingredient; it appears in recipes worldwide. [support]

> Sweet basil is used in many Mediterranean dishes; Thai basil is used in Asian and East Indian recipes. [contrast]

Although *and, but,* and similar words can signal these kinds of relationships, consider using an occasional semicolon for variety.

Sometimes, a transitional expression such as *for example* or *however* (23c(5)) accompanies a semicolon and further establishes the exact relationship between the ideas in the linked clauses.

Basil is omnipresent in the cuisine of some countries; **for example,** Italians use basil in salads, soups, and many vegetable dishes.

The culinary uses of basil are well known; **however,** this herb also has medicinal uses.

A comma is usually inserted after a transitional word, but it can be omitted if doing so will not lead to a misreading.

Because *basil* comes from a Greek word meaning "king," it suggests royalty; **indeed** some cooks accord basil royal status among herbs and spices.

(2) Separating elements that contain commas

In a series of phrases or clauses (Chapter 21) that contain commas, semicolons indicate where each phrase or clause ends and the next begins. In the following sentence, the semicolons help the reader distinguish three separate phrases.

To survive, mountain lions need a large area in which to range; a steady supply of deer, skunks, raccoons, foxes, and opossums; and the opportunity to find a mate, establish a den, and raise a litter.

Exercise 1

Revise the following sentences, using semicolons to separate independent clauses or elements that contain internal commas.

1. Soccer is a game played by two opposing teams on a rectangular field, each team tries to knock a ball, roughly twenty-eight inches in circumference, through the opponent's goal.

(continued on page 716)

(continued from page 715)

2. The game is called *soccer* only in Canada and the United States, elsewhere it is known as *football*.

3. Generally, a team consists of eleven players: defenders (or fullbacks), who defend the goal by trying to win control of the ball, midfielders (or halfbacks), who play both defense and offense, attackers (or forwards), whose primary responsibility is scoring goals; and a goalkeeper (or goalie), who guards the goal.

4. In amateur matches, players can be substituted frequently, however, in professional matches, the number of substitutions is limited.

5. Soccer players depend on five skills: kicking, which entails striking the ball powerfully with the top of the foot, dribbling, which requires tapping or rolling the ball while running, passing, which is similar to kicking but with less power and more control, heading, which involves striking the ball with the forehead, and trapping, which is the momentary stopping of the ball.

(3) Revising common semicolon errors

Semicolons do not set off phrases (**21a**) or dependent clauses (**21b(2)**) unless those elements contain commas. Use commas to set off a phrase or a dependent clause.

We consulted Alinka Kibukian;, the local horticulturalist.
 ^

Needing summer shade;, we planted two of the largest trees we could afford.
 ^

We learned that young trees need care;, which meant we had to do some extra chores after dinner each night.
 ^

Our trees have survived;, even though we live in a harsh climate.
 ^

Exercise 2

Use a comma to replace any semicolon that sets off a phrase or a dependent clause in the following sentences. Do not change properly used semicolons.

1. The Vice President of the United States walks along the fenced-in crowd; regularly stopping to shake a hand, pose for the camera, or hold a baby; a man who has held elected office for over forty years, he relishes being in the public eye.

2. Joe Biden has gone into the Grange Hall, where he sits with a small group of family farmers; peppering them with questions about the future of the farm, whether the corporate farm, the family farm, or some combination of the two bodes best for our nation's future; he leaves the hall, thanks his hosts, and makes his way to Air Force Two and his next commitment.

37b ‖ THE COLON

A colon calls attention to what follows, whether the grammatical unit is a clause, a phrase, or words in a series. It also separates numbers in parts of scriptural references and titles from subtitles. Leave only one space after a colon.

(1) Directing attention to an explanation, a summary, or a quotation

When a colon appears between two independent clauses, it signals that the second clause will explain or expand on the first.

No one expected the game to end as it did: after seven extra innings, the favored team collapsed.

A colon is also used after an independent clause to introduce a direct quotation.

The Fourteenth Dalai Lama explained the importance of forgiveness: "When other beings, especially those who hold a grudge against you, abuse and harm you out of envy, you should not abandon them, but hold them as objects of your greatest compassion and take care of them."

> ❶ **CAUTION**
>
> The rules for using an uppercase or a lowercase letter to begin the first word of an independent clause that follows a colon vary across style manuals.
>
> **MLA**   The first letter should be lowercase unless (1) it begins a word that is normally capitalized, (2) the independent clause is a quotation, or (3) the clause expresses a rule or principle.
>
> **APA**   The first letter should be uppercase.
>
> **CMS**   The first letter should be lowercase unless (1) it begins a word that is normally capitalized, (2) the independent clause is a quotation or a direct question, or (3) two or more sentences follow the colon.

A colon at the end of an independent clause is sometimes followed by a phrase rather than another clause. This use of the colon puts emphasis on the phrase.

I was finally confronted with what I had dreaded for months: the due date for the final balloon payment on my car loan.

All the style manuals advise using a lowercase letter to begin a phrase following a colon.

(2) Signaling that a list follows

Writers frequently use colons to introduce lists (which add to or clarify the information preceding the colon).

Three students received internships: Asa, Vanna, and Jack.

Avoid placing a colon between a verb and its complement (**20c**) or after the words *including* and *such as*.

> The winners were⌇Asa, Vanna, and Jack.

> Many vegetarians do not eat dairy products such as⌇butter and cheese.

(3) Separating a title and a subtitle

Use a colon between a work's title and its subtitle.

> *Collapse*: *How Societies Choose to Fail or Succeed*

(4) In reference numbers

Colons are often used between numbers in scriptural references.

> Ps. 3:5   Gen. 1:1

However, MLA prefers periods instead of colons in such references.

> Ps. 3.5   Gen. 1.1

(5) Specialized uses in business correspondence

A colon follows the salutation of a business letter and any notations.

> Dear Dr. Hodges: Dear Imogen: Encl:

A colon introduces the headings in a memo.

> To: From: Subject: Date:

Exercise 3

Insert colons where they are needed in the following sentences.

1. Before we discuss marketing, we need to outline the behavior of consumers consumer behavior is the process individuals go through as they select, buy, or use products or services to satisfy their needs and desires.

2. The process consists of six stages recognizing a need or desire, finding information, evaluating options, deciding to purchase, purchasing, and assessing purchases.

3. Many consumers rely on one popular publication for product information *Consumer Reports*.

4. When evaluating alternatives, a consumer uses criteria; for example, a house hunter might use some of the following price, location, size, age, style, and landscaping design.

5. The post-purchase assessment has one of two results satisfaction or dissatisfaction with the product or service.

38 THE APOSTROPHE

Apostrophes serve a number of purposes. You can use them to show that someone owns something *(my neighbor's television),* that someone has a specific relationship with someone else *(my neighbor's children),* or that someone has produced or created something *(my neighbor's recipe).* Apostrophes are also used in contractions *(can't, don't)* and in a few plural forms *(x's and y's).* This chapter will help you use apostrophes to

- indicate ownership and other relationships (**38a**),
- mark omissions of letters or numbers (**38b**), and
- form certain plurals (**38c**).

38a INDICATING OWNERSHIP AND OTHER RELATIONSHIPS

An apostrophe, often followed by an *s*, signals the possessive case of nouns. (For information on case, see **25a(1)** and **25b**.) Possessive nouns are used to express a variety of meanings.

Ownership	**Dyson's** sermon, the **minister's** robe
Origin	**Leakey's** research findings, the **guide's** decision
Human relationships	**Helen's** sister, the **teacher's** students
Possession of physical or psychological traits	**Mona Lisa's** smile, the **team's** spirit
Association between abstractions and attributes	**democracy's** struggles, **tyranny's** influence
Identification of documents and credentials	**driver's** license, **bachelor's** degree
Identification of things named after people	**St. John's** Cathedral, **Valentine's** Day
Specification of amounts	a **day's** wages, an **hour's** delay

> **ñ** *MULTILINGUAL WRITERS*
>
> ### WORD WITH APOSTROPHE AND S VERSUS PHRASE BEGINNING WITH *OF*
>
> In many cases, to indicate ownership, origin, and other meanings discussed in this chapter, you can use either a word with an apostrophe and an *s* or a prepositional phrase beginning with *of.*
>
> Henning Mankell**'s** novels   OR   the novels **of** Henning Mankell
>
> the plane**'s** arrival   OR   the arrival **of** the plane
>
> However, the ending -*'s* is more commonly used with nouns referring to people, and a phrase beginning with *of* is used with most nouns referring to location.
>
> my **uncle's** workshop, **Edward's** truck, the **student's** paper [nouns referring to people]
>
> the **end of** the movie, the **middle of** the day, the **front of** the building [nouns referring to location]

(1) Forming the possessive of singular nouns, indefinite pronouns, acronyms, and abbreviations

Add -*'s* to form the possessive case of most singular nouns, indefinite pronouns, acronyms (words formed by letters or initial word parts of phrases), and abbreviations.

the instructor**'s** office [noun]   Dickinson**'s** poems [noun]

someone**'s** billfold [indefinite pronoun]

sonar**'s** strength [an acronym of *sound, navigation, ranging*]
FAQ**'s** usefulness [an acronym for *frequently asked question*]

Luther Liggett Jr.**'s** letter [Notice that no comma precedes the abbreviation *Jr.* here, although *Jr.* is sometimes set off by a comma (**36d(2)**).]

To form the possessive of most singular proper nouns, add an apostrophe and an *s: Iowa's governor.* When a singular proper noun ends in -s, though, you will have to consult the style guide for the discipline in which you are writing. The *MLA Handbook for Writers of Research Papers* recommends always using -'s, as in *Illinois's legislature, Dickens's novels, Ms. Jones's address,* and *Descartes's reasoning.* The *Chicago Manual of Style,* however, notes some exceptions to this rule. An apostrophe without an *s* is appropriate when a singular common noun ends in -s *(physics' contribution)* and when the name of a place or an organization ends in -s but refers to a single entity *(United States' foreign aid).*

Possessive pronouns *(my, mine, our, ours, your, yours, his, her, hers, its, their, theirs,* and *whose)* are not written with apostrophes (**25b(3)**).

South Africa's democracy differs from **ours.**

The committee concluded **its** discussion.

> ❶ **CAUTION**
>
> Be careful not to confuse possessive pronouns with contractions. Confusing *its* and *it's* is a very common mistake. Keep in mind that whenever you write a contraction, you should be able to substitute the complete words for it without changing the meaning.
>
> | Possessive pronoun | Contraction |
> |---|---|
> | **Its** motor is small. | **It's** [It is] a small motor. |
> | **Whose** turn is it? | **Who's** [Who is] representing us? |
>
> *Its* is the possessive form of *it. It's* is a contraction for *it is* or *it has.*

(2) Forming the possessive of plural nouns ending in -s

Plural nouns ending in -s require only an apostrophe to form the possessive.

| the boys' game | the babies' toys | the Joneses' house |

Plural nouns that do not end in -s need both an apostrophe and an *s.*

| men's lives | women's health | children's projects |

> ## ❶ CAUTION
>
> An apostrophe is not needed to make a noun plural. To make most nouns plural, add -s or -es. Add an apostrophe only to signal ownership, origin, and other similar relationships.
>
> protesters
> The∧~~protesters'~~ swarmed the conference center.
>
> The protesters' gathering was on Wednesday.
>
> Likewise, to form the plural of a family name, use -s or -es, not an apostrophe.
>
> Johnsons
> The∧~~Johnson's~~ participated in the study.
>
> [COMPARE: The Johnsons' participation in the study was crucial.]
>
> Jameses
> The∧~~James's~~ live in the yellow house on the corner.
>
> [COMPARE: The Jameses' house is the yellow one on the corner.]

(3) Showing collaboration or joint ownership

In the first example below, the ending -'s has been added to the second singular noun (*plumber*). In the second example, just an apostrophe has been added to the second plural noun (*Lopezes*), which already ends in *s*.

the carpenter and the **plumber's** decision [They made the decision collaboratively.]

the Becks and the **Lopezes'** cabin [They own one cabin jointly.]

(4) Showing separate ownership or individual contributions

In the examples below, the possessive form of each plural noun ends with an apostrophe, and that of each singular noun has the ending -'s.

the **Becks'** and the **Lopezes'** cars [Each family owns a car.]

the **carpenter's** and the **plumber's** proposals [They each made a proposal.]

(5) Forming the possessive of a compound noun

Add -'s to the last word of a compound noun.

> my brother-in-**law's** friends, the attorney **general's** statements [singular]

> my brothers-in-**law's** friends, the attorneys **general's** statements [plural]

To avoid awkward constructions such as the last two, consider using a prepositional phrase beginning with *of* instead: *a friend of my brothers-in-law* and *the statements of the attorneys general.*

(6) Forming the possessive of a noun preceding a gerund

Depending on its number, a noun that precedes a gerund takes either -'s or just an apostrophe.

> Lucy**'s having** to be there seemed unnecessary. [singular noun preceding a gerund]

> The family appreciated the lawyers' **handling** of the matter. [plural noun preceding a gerund]

ñ MULTILINGUAL WRITERS

GERUND PHRASES

When a gerund appears after a possessive noun, the noun is the subject of the gerund phrase.

> **Lucy's having to be there** [COMPARE: **Lucy** has to be there.]

> **The lawyers' handling of the matter** [COMPARE: **The lawyers** handled the matter.]

A gerund phrase may serve as the subject or the object in a sentence (**21a(3)**).

> **Lucy's having to be there** seemed unnecessary. [s]

> The family appreciated **the lawyers' handling of the matter.** [obj]

Sometimes you may find it difficult to distinguish between a gerund and a present participle (21a(3)). A good way to tell the difference is to note whether the emphasis is on an action or on a person. In a sentence containing a gerund, the emphasis is on the action; in a sentence containing a participle, the emphasis is on the person.

Our successful completion of the project depends on **Terry's providing** the illustrations. [gerund; the emphasis is on the action, *providing*]

I remember **my brother telling** me the same joke last year. [participle; the emphasis is on the person, *my brother*]

(7) Naming products and geographical locations

Follow an organization's preference for the use of an apostrophe in its name or the name of a product. Follow local conventions for an apostrophe in the name of a geographical location.

Consumers Union   Actors' Equity   Shoppers Choice   Taster's Choice

Devil's Island   Devils Tower   Devils Mountain

© N. Reed of QEDImages/Alamy

REUTERS/Joe Skipper/Landov

Whether an apostrophe is used in a brand name is determined by the organization that owns that name.

Exercise 1

Following the pattern of the examples, change the modifier after each noun to a possessive form that precedes the noun.

EXAMPLES

proposals made by the committee   the committee's proposals
poems written by Keats   Keats's poems

1. the day named after St. Patrick
2. a leave of absence lasting six months
3. the position taken by HMOs
4. the report given by the eyewitness
5. the generosity of the Lees
6. a new book coauthored by Pat and Alan
7. the weights of the children
8. the spying done by the neighbors
9. the restaurants in Santa Fe
10. coffee roasted by Peet

38b   MARKING OMISSIONS OF LETTERS OR NUMBERS

Apostrophes signal contractions and other omissions in numbers and in words representing speech.

they're [they are]   class of '11 [class of 2011]

y'all [you all]   singin' [singing]

Contractions are not always appropriate for formal contexts. Your audience may expect you to use full words instead (for example, *cannot* instead of *can't* and *will not* instead of *won't*).

38c FORMING CERTAIN PLURALS

In the past, an apostrophe and an *s* were used to form the plural of a number, an abbreviation, or a word referred to as a term. Today, the apostrophe is rarely used in plural forms except for those of abbreviations that take periods or that contain lowercase letters or symbols.

The following plurals are generally formed by simply adding an *s:*

1990s   fours and fives   YWCAs   two *and*s   the three Rs

A few plural forms still include an apostrophe:

D.D.S.'s   *x*'s and *y*'s   +'s and –'s

The MLA also recommends that an apostrophe be used to form the plural of an uppercase letter (*A*'s and *B*'s).

Exercise 2

Insert apostrophes where needed in the following sentences. Be prepared to explain why they are necessary.

1. Whos in charge here?
2. Hansons book was published in the early 1920s.
3. They hired a rock n roll band for their engagement party.
4. NPRs fund drive begins this weekend.
5. Youll have to include the ISBNs of the books youre going to purchase.
6. Only three of the proposals are still being considered: yours, ours, and the Wilbers.
7. Its always a big deal when your children leave for college.
8. Not enough students enrolled in the summer 11 course.
9. The students formed groups of twos and threes.
10. Laquisha earned two As and two Bs this semester.

39 ‖ QUOTATION MARKS

Quotation marks enclose sentences or parts of sentences that play a special role. They can indicate that the words between them were first written or spoken by someone else or that they are being used in an unconventional way. This chapter will help you use quotation marks

- with direct quotations (**39a**),
- with titles of short works (**39b**),
- to indicate that words or phrases are used ironically or unconventionally (**39c**), and
- in combination with other punctuation marks (**39d**).

39a ‖ DIRECT QUOTATIONS

Double quotation marks set off direct quotations, including those in dialogue. Single quotation marks set off a quotation within a quotation.

(1) Double quotation marks with direct quotations

Quotation marks enclose only a direct quotation, not any accompanying signal phrase such as *she said* or *he replied*. When a sentence ends with quoted material, place the period inside the quotation marks. For guidelines on comma placement, see **39d(1)**.

> **"**I believe that we learn by practice,**"** writes Martha Graham in "An Athlete of God." **"**Whether it means to learn to dance by practicing dancing or to learn to live by practicing living, the principles are the same.**"**

When using direct quotations, reproduce all quoted material exactly as it appears in the original, including capitalization and punctuation. To learn how to set off long quotations as indented blocks, see **12a(2)**.

(2) No quotation marks for indirect quotations or paraphrases

Indirect quotations and paraphrases (**10d(3)**) are restatements of what someone else has said or written.

> Martha Graham believes that practice is necessary for learning, regardless of what we are trying to learn.

(3) Single quotation marks for quotations within quotations

If the quotation you are using includes another direct quotation, use single quotation marks with the embedded quotation.

> According to Anita Erickson, "when the narrator says, 'I have the right to my own opinion,' he means that he has the right to his own delusion."

However, if an embedded quotation appears within a block quotation, it should be enclosed in double quotation marks. (Keep in mind that double quotation marks are not used at the beginning or the end of a block quotation.)

> Anita Erickson claims that the narrator uses the word *opinion* deceptively.

> > Later in the chapter, when the narrator says, "I have the right to my own opinion," he means that he has the right to his own delusion. Although it is tempting to believe that the narrator is making decisions based on a rational belief system, his behavior suggests that he is more interested in deception. With poisonous lies, he has already deceived his business partner, his wife, and his children.

(4) Dialogue in quotation marks

When creating or reporting a dialogue, enclose in quotation marks what each person says, no matter how short. Use a separate paragraph for each speaker, beginning a new paragraph whenever the speaker changes. Narrative details can be included in the same paragraph as a direct quotation.

> Farmer looked up, smiling, and in a chirpy-sounding voice he said, "But that feeling has the disadvantage of being … " He paused a beat. "Wrong."
> "Well," I retorted, "it depends on how you look at it."
>
> —TRACY KIDDER, *Mountains Beyond Mountains*

When quoting more than one paragraph by a single speaker, put quotation marks at the beginning of each paragraph. However, do not place closing quotation marks at the end of each paragraph—only at the end of the last paragraph.

(5) Thoughts in quotation marks

Quotation marks set off thoughts that resemble speech.

> "He's already sulking about the outcome of the vote," I thought, as I watched the committee chair work through the agenda.

Thoughts are usually marked by such phrases as *I thought, he felt*, and *she believed*. Remember, though, that quotation marks are not used with thoughts that are reported indirectly (**39a(2)**).

> I wondered why he had not responded to my memo.

(6) Short excerpts of poetry within a sentence in quotation marks

When quoting fewer than four lines of poetry, enclose them in quotation marks and use a slash (**40h**) to indicate the line division.

> Together, mother and daughter recited their favorite lines: "Shall I compare thee to a summer's day? / Thou art more lovely and more temperate."

To learn how to format longer quotations of poetry, see **11e(4)**.

39b	TITLES OF SHORT WORKS

Quotation marks enclose the title of a short work, such as a story, an essay, a poem, or a song. The title of a longer work, such as a book, a magazine, a newspaper, or a play, should be italicized.

> "The Girls of Summer" first appeared in the *New Yorker*.

Short story	"The Lottery"	"A Good Man Is Hard to Find"
Essay	"Walden"	"A Modest Proposal"

Article	"Small World"	"Arabia's Empty Quarter"
Book chapter	"Rain"	"Cutting a Dash"
Short poem	"Orion"	"Where the Sidewalk Ends"
Song	"Lazy River"	"Like a Rolling Stone"
TV episode	"Show Down!"	"The Last Time"

Use double quotation marks around the title of a short work embedded in a longer italicized title.

Interpretations of "*Young Goodman Brown*" [book about a short story]

Use single quotation marks for a title within a longer title that is enclosed in double quotation marks.

"Irony in 'The Road Not Taken' " [article about a poem]

39c | FOR IRONIC TONE OR UNUSUAL USAGE

Writers sometimes use quotation marks to indicate that they are using a word or phrase ironically. The word *gourmet* is used ironically in the following sentence.

His "gourmet" dinner turned out to be processed turkey and instant mashed potatoes.

> ⚠ **CAUTION**
>
> Avoid using quotation marks around words that may not be appropriate for your rhetorical situation. Instead, take the time to choose suitable words. The revised sentence in the following pair is more effective than the first.
>
> | **Ineffective** | He is too much of a "wimp" to be a good leader. |
> | **Revised** | He is too indecisive to be a good leader. |
>
> Similarly, putting a cliché (34b) in quotation marks may make readers conclude that you do not care enough about conveying your meaning to think of a fresh expression.

39d | WITH OTHER PUNCTUATION MARKS

To decide whether to place some other punctuation mark inside or outside quotation marks, determine whether the particular mark functions as part of the quotation or part of the surrounding context.

(1) With commas and periods

Quoted material is usually accompanied by a signal phrase such as *she said* or *he replied*. When a sentence starts with such an expression, place a comma after it to separate the signal phrase from the quotation.

She replied, "There's more than one way to slice a pie."

If the sentence starts with the quotation instead, place the comma inside the closing quotation marks.

"There's more than one way to slice a pie," she replied.

Place a period inside closing quotation marks, whether single or double, if a quotation ends a sentence.

> Jeff responded, "I didn't understand 'An Algorithm for Life.'"

When quoting material from a source, provide the relevant page number(s). If you are following MLA guidelines, note the page number(s) in parentheses after the final quotation marks. Place the period that ends the sentence after the final parenthesis, unless the quotation is a block quotation (**12a(2)**).

> According to Diane Ackerman, "Love is a demanding sport involving all the muscle groups, including the brain" (86).

❶ CAUTION

Do not put a comma after *that* when it precedes a quotation.

> Diane Ackerman claims that "[l]ove is a demanding sport involving all the muscle groups, including the brain" (86).

(2) With semicolons and colons

Place semicolons and colons outside quotation marks.

> His favorite song was "Cyprus Avenue"; mine was "Astral Weeks."

> Because it is repeated, one line stands out in "The Conductor": "We are never as beautiful as now."

(3) With question marks, exclamation points, and dashes

If the direct quotation includes a question mark, an exclamation point, or a dash, place that punctuation *inside* the closing quotation marks.

> Jeremy asked, "What is truth?"

> Gordon shouted "Congratulations!"

> Laura said, "Let me tell—" Before she could finish her sentence, Dan walked into the room.

Use just one question mark inside the quotation marks when a question you write ends with a quoted question.

Why does the protagonist ask, "Where are we headed?"

If the punctuation is not part of the quoted material, place it *outside* the closing quotation marks.

Who wrote "The Figure a Sentence Makes"?

You have to read "Awareness and Freedom"!

She called me a "toaster head"—perhaps justifiably under the circumstances.

Exercise 1

Revise sentences in which quotation marks are used incorrectly and insert quotation marks where they are needed. Do not alter sentences that are written correctly. (The numbers in parentheses are page numbers, placed according to MLA guidelines.)

1. Have you read Susan B. Anthony's essay On Women's Right to Vote?

2. Anthony states, [I] exercised my citizen's rights (2).

3. However, she realizes that she has been indicted for "the alleged crime of having voted in the last presidential election" (2).

4. Anthony suggests that not allowing women to vote is a violation of 'the supreme law of the land' (3).

5. According to the author, "We, the whole people, . . . formed the Union."

6. She goes on to argue that Webster, Worcester, and Bouvier all define a citizen to be a person in the United States, entitled to vote and hold office.

7. Anthony maintains, Being persons, then, women are citizens; and no state has a right to make any law . . . that shall abridge their privileges or immunities (3).

40 THE PERIOD AND OTHER PUNCTUATION MARKS

To indicate the end of a sentence, you can use one of three punctuation marks: the period, the question mark, or the exclamation point. Which one you use depends on your meaning: do you want to make a statement, ask a question, or express an exclamation?

Everyone passed the exam.

Everyone passed the exam? [informal usage]

Everyone passed the exam!

Within sentences, you can use colons, dashes, parentheses, square brackets, ellipsis points, and slashes to emphasize, downplay, or clarify the information you want to convey. (For use of the colon, see **37b**; for use of the hyphen, see **41f**.) This chapter will help you use

- end punctuation marks (the period (**40a**), the question mark (**40b**), and the exclamation point (**40c**)),
- the dash (**40d**),
- parentheses (**40e**),
- square brackets (**40f**),
- ellipsis points (**40g**), and
- the slash (**40h**).

To accommodate computerized typesetting, both CMS and APA guidelines call for only one space after a period, a question mark, an exclamation point, and a colon. According to these manuals, there should be no space preceding or following a hyphen or a dash. The MLA style manual recommends using only one space after end punctuation marks but allows two spaces if they are used consistently.

40a THE PERIOD

(1) Marking the end of a sentence

Use a period at the end of a declarative sentence.

Many adults in the United States are overfed yet undernourished.

Soft drinks account for 7 percent of their average daily caloric intake.

In addition, place a period at the end of an instruction or recommendation written as an imperative sentence (**21d**).

Eat plenty of fruits and vegetables. Drink six to eight glasses of water a day.

Indirect questions are phrased as statements, so be sure to use a period, rather than a question mark, at the end of such a sentence.

The researcher explained why people eat so much junk food.
[COMPARE: Why do people eat so much junk food?]

(2) Following some abbreviations

Dr. Jr. a.m. p.m. vs. etc. et al.

Only one period follows an abbreviation that ends a sentence.

The tour begins at 1:00 p.m.

Periods are not used with many common abbreviations (for example, *MVP, mph,* and *FM*). (See Chapter **44**.) A dictionary lists the conventional form of an abbreviation as well as any alternatives.

40b THE QUESTION MARK

Place a question mark after a direct question.

How does the new atomic clock work? Who invented this clock?

Use a period, instead of a question mark, after an indirect question—that is, a question embedded in a statement.

I asked whether the new atomic clock could be used in cell phones.
[COMPARE: Can the new atomic clock be used in cell phones?]

ñ MULTILINGUAL WRITERS

INDIRECT QUESTIONS

In English, indirect questions are written as declarative sentences. The subject and verb are not inverted as they would be in the related direct question.

We do not know when ~~will~~ the meeting ^will^ end.

[COMPARE: When will the meeting end?]

For more on word order and questions, see Chapter 47.

Place a question mark after each question in a series of related questions, even when they are not full sentences.

Will the new atomic clock be used in cell phones? word processors? car navigation systems?

If a direct quotation is a question, place the question mark inside the final quotation marks.

Tony asked, "How small is this new clock?"

In contrast, if you include quoted material in a question of your own, place the question mark outside the final quotation marks.

Is the clock really "no larger than a sugar cube"?

If you embed in the middle of a sentence a question not attributable to anyone in particular, place a comma before it and a question mark after it.

When the question, how does the clock work? arose, the researchers described a technique used by manufacturers of computer chips.

The first letter of such a question should not be capitalized unless the question is extremely long or contains internal punctuation.

To indicate uncertainty about a fact such as a date of birth, place a question mark inside parentheses directly after the fact in question.

Chaucer was born in 1340 (?) and died in 1400.

| **40C** | THE EXCLAMATION POINT |

An exclamation point often marks the end of a sentence, but its primary purpose is rhetorical—to create emphasis.

Wow! What a game!

When a direct quotation ends with an exclamation point, no comma or period is placed immediately after it.

"Get a new pitcher!" he yelled.

He yelled, "Get a new pitcher!"

Use the exclamation point sparingly so that you do not diminish its impact. If you do not intend to signal strong emotion, place a comma after an interjection and a period at the end of the sentence.

Well, no one seriously expected this victory.

Exercise 1

Compose and punctuate brief sentences of the following types.

1. a declarative sentence containing a quoted exclamation
2. a sentence beginning with an interjection
3. a direct question
4. a declarative sentence containing an indirect question
5. a declarative sentence containing a direct question

40d   THE DASH

A dash (or em dash) marks a break in thought, sets off a nonessential element for emphasis or clarity, or follows an introductory list or series. The short dash (or en dash) is used mainly in number ranges (**44g(2)**).

> **TECH SAVVY**
>
> To use your keyboard to create a dash, type two hyphens with no spaces between, before, or after them. Most word-processing programs can be set to convert these hyphens automatically to an em dash. In Microsoft Word, you can also hold down the Option and Shift keys while typing a hyphen.

(1) To mark a break in the normal flow of a sentence

Use a dash to indicate a shift in thought or tone.

> I was awed by the almost superhuman effort Stonehenge represents—but who wouldn't be?

(2) To set off a nonessential element

A dash or a pair of dashes sets off a nonessential element for emphasis or clarity.

> Dr. Kruger's specialty is mycology—the study of fungi.

> The trail we took into the Grand Canyon—steep, narrow, winding, and lacking guardrails—made me wonder whether we could call a helicopter to fly us out.

(3) To set off an introductory list or series

If you decide to place a list or series at the beginning of a sentence in order to emphasize it, the main part of the sentence (after the dash) should sum up the meaning of the list or series.

> Eager, determined to succeed, and scared to death—all of these describe how I felt on the first day at work.

❷ *THINKING RHETORICALLY*

COMMAS, DASHES, AND COLONS

Although a comma, a dash, or a colon may be followed by an explanation, an example, or an illustration, the rhetorical impact of each of these punctuation marks differs.

He never failed to mention what was most important to him, the bottom line.

He never failed to mention what was most important to him— the bottom line.

He never failed to mention what was most important to him: the bottom line.

The comma, one of the most common punctuation marks, barely draws attention to what follows it. The dash, in contrast, signals a longer pause and so causes more emphasis to be placed on the information that follows. The colon is more direct and formal than either of the other two punctuation marks. (See **37b** for more about the colon.)

40e   PARENTHESES

Use parentheses to set off information that is not closely related to the main point of a sentence or paragraph but that provides an interesting detail, an explanation, or an illustration.

One of the most striking peculiarities of the human brain is the great development of the frontal lobes—they are much less developed in other primates and hardly evident at all in other mammals. They are the part of the brain that grows and develops most after birth (and their development is not complete until about the age of seven).

—OLIVER SACKS, *An Anthropologist on Mars*

Place parentheses around an acronym or an abbreviation when introducing it after its full form.

The Search for Extraterrestrial Intelligence (SETI) uses the Very Large Array (VLA) outside Sicorro, New Mexico, to scan the sky.

If you use numbers or letters in a list within a sentence, set them off by placing them within parentheses.

Your application should include (1) a current résumé, (2) a statement of purpose, and (3) two letters of recommendation.

For information on the use of parentheses in bibliographies and in-text citations, see Chapters **12**, **14**, **16**, and **18**.

❓ *THINKING RHETORICALLY*

DASHES AND PARENTHESES

Dashes and parentheses are both used to set off part of a sentence, but they differ in the amount of emphasis they signal. Whereas dashes call attention to the material that is set off, parentheses usually deemphasize such material.

Her grandfather—born during the Great Depression—was appointed by the president to the Securities and Exchange Commission.

Her grandfather (born in 1930) was appointed by the president to the Securities and Exchange Commission.

40f SQUARE BRACKETS

Square brackets set off additions or alterations that clarify direct quotations. In the following example, the bracketed noun specifies what is meant by the pronoun *They*:

"They [hyperlinks] are what turn the Web from a library of pages into a web" (Weinberger 170).

Square brackets also indicate that a letter at the beginning of a quotation has been changed from uppercase to lowercase, or vice versa.

David Weinberger claims that "[e]ven our notion of self as a continuous body moving through a continuous map of space and time is beginning to seem wrong on the Web" (10).

To avoid the awkwardness of using brackets in this way, you may be able to quote only part of a sentence and thus not need to change the capitalization.

David Weinberger claims that "our notion of self as a continuous body moving through a continuous map of space and time is beginning to seem wrong on the Web" (10).

Within parentheses, square brackets are used because having two sets of parentheses could be confusing.

People frequently provide personal information online. (See, for example, David Weinberger's *Small Pieces Loosely Joined* [Cambridge: Perseus, 2002].)

Angle brackets (< >) are used to enclose any web address included in an MLA works-cited list (**12b**) so that the period at the end of an entry is not confused with the dot(s) in the URL: <http://www.mla.org>.

40g ELLIPSIS POINTS

Ellipsis points indicate an omission from a quoted passage or a reflective pause or hesitation.

(1) To mark an omission within a quoted passage

Whenever you omit anything from material you quote, replace the omitted material with ellipsis points—three equally spaced periods. Be sure to compare your quoted sentence to the original, checking to see that your omission does not change the meaning of the original.

To avoid excessive use of ellipses, replace some direct quotations with paraphrases (**10d(3)**).

The following examples illustrate how to use ellipsis points in quotations from a passage by Patricia Gadsby.

Original

Cacao doesn't flower, as most plants do, at the tips of its outer and uppermost branches. Instead, its sweet white buds hang from the trunk and along a few fat branches, popping out of patches of bark called cushions, which form where leaves drop off. They're tiny, these flowers. Yet once pollinated by midges, no-see-ums that flit in the leafy detritus below, they'll make pulp-filled pods almost the size of rugby balls.

—PATRICIA GADSBY, "Endangered Chocolate"

(a) Omission within a quoted sentence

Patricia Gadsby notes that cacao flowers "once pollinated by midges . . . make pulp-filled pods almost the size of rugby balls."

Retain a comma, colon, or semicolon that appears in the original text if it makes a quoted sentence easier to read. If no misreading will occur, the punctuation mark can be omitted.

Patricia Gadsby describes the outcome of pollinating the cacao flowers: "Yet once pollinated by midges, . . . they'll make pulp-filled pods almost the size of rugby balls." [The comma after "midges" is retained.]

According to Gadsby, "Cacao doesn't flower . . . at the tips of its outer and uppermost branches." [The comma after "flower" is omitted]

(b) Omission at the beginning of a quoted sentence

Do not use ellipsis points to indicate that you have deleted words from the beginning of a quotation, whether it is run into the text or set off in a block. The opening part of the original sentence has been omitted in the following quotation.

According to Patricia Gadsby, cacao flowers will become "pulp-filled pods almost the size of rugby balls."

Note that the first letter of the integrated quotation is not capitalized.

(c) Omission at the end of a quoted sentence

To indicate that you have omitted words from the end of a sentence, put a single space between the last word and the set of three spaced ellipsis points. Then add the end punctuation mark (a period, a question mark, or an exclamation point). If the quoted material is followed by a parenthetical source or page reference, the end punctuation comes after the second parenthesis.

> Claiming that cacao flowers differ from those of most plants, Patricia Gadsby describes how "the sweet white buds hang from the trunk and along a few fat branches . . . ."
>
> OR ". . . a few fat branches . . . " (2).

(d) Omission of a sentence or more

To signal the omission of a sentence or more (even a paragraph or more), place an end punctuation mark (usually a period) before the ellipsis points.

> Patricia Gadsby describes the flowering of the cacao plant: "Its sweet white buds hang from the trunk and along a few fat branches, popping out of patches of bark called cushions, which form where leaves drop off. . . . Yet once pollinated by midges, no-see-ums that flit in the leafy detritus below, they'll make pulp-filled pods almost the size of rugby balls."

(e) Omission of a line or more of a poem

To signal the omission of a full line or more in quoted poetry, use spaced periods extending the length of either the line above it or the omitted line.

> The yellow fog that rubs its back upon the window-panes,
>
> . . . .
>
> Curled once about the house, and fell asleep.
>
> —T. S. ELIOT, "The Love Song of J. Alfred Prufrock"

(2) To mark an incomplete sentence

Ellipsis points show that a sentence has been intentionally left incomplete.

> Read aloud the passage that begins "The yellow fog . . . " and explain the imagery.

(3) To mark hesitation in a sentence

Ellipsis points can mark a reflective pause or a hesitation.

Keith saw four menacing youths coming toward him . . . and ran.

A dash can also be used to indicate this type of a pause.

40h   THE SLASH

A slash between words, as in *and/or*, *young/old*, and *heaven/hell*, indicates that either word is applicable in the given context. There are no spaces before and after a slash used in this way. Because extensive use of the slash can make writing choppy, use it judiciously and sparingly. (If you are following APA or MLA guidelines, avoid using *he/she, him/her,* and so on.)

A slash is also used to mark line divisions in quoted poetry. A slash used in this way is preceded and followed by a space.

Wallace Stevens refers to the listener who, "nothing himself, beholds **/** Nothing that is not there and the nothing that is."

Exercise 2

Add appropriate dashes, parentheses, square brackets, and slashes to the following sentences. Be ready to explain the reason for each mark you add.

1. The three recognized autism spectrum disorders ASDs are autism, Asperger syndrome, and pervasive developmental disorder–not otherwise specified PDD-NOS.

2. Disagreement concerning the causes of autism environmental, medical, and or genetic continues to flourish.

3. The rise in diagnoses of autism might be due to better diagnostic practices or an increase in the disorder itself.

Exercise 3

Punctuate the following sentences with appropriate end marks, commas, colons (**37b**), dashes, and parentheses. Do not use unnecessary punctuation. Give a justification for each mark you add, especially where more than one type of mark (for example, commas, dashes, or parentheses) is acceptable.

1. Many small country towns are very similar a truck stop a gas station a crowded diner and three bars

2. The simple life a nonexistent crime rate and down-home values these are some of the advantages these little towns offer

3. Why do we never see these quaint examples of pure Americana when we travel around the country on the interstates

4. Rolling across America on one of the big interstates I-20 I-40 I-70 I-80 or I-90 you are likely to pass within a few miles of a number of these towns

5. Such towns almost certainly will have a regional or perhaps an ethnic flavor Hispanic in the southwest Scandinavian in the north

6. When I visit one of these out-of-the-way places I always have a sense of well really a feeling of safety

7. There's one thing I can tell you small-town life is not boring

8. My one big question however is what do you do to earn a living in these towns

MECHANICS

© Gisuke Hagiwara/amanaimages/Corbis

41 | SPELLING, THE SPELL CHECKER, AND HYPHENATION

When you first draft a paper, you might not pay close attention to spelling words correctly. After all, the point of drafting is to generate and organize ideas. However, proofreading for spelling mistakes is essential as you near the end of the writing process. You want to submit the kind of writing your teacher, employer, or supervisor expects to read: polished work that is as nearly perfect as you can make it.

You can train yourself to be a good proofreader by checking a dictionary every time you question the spelling of a word. If two spellings are listed, such as *fulfill* and *fulfil*, either form is correct, although the first option provided is generally considered more common. Once you choose between such options, be sure to use the spelling you pick consistently. You can also learn to be a better speller by studying a few basic strategies. This chapter will help you

- use a spell checker (**41a**),
- spell words according to pronunciation (**41b**),
- spell words that sound alike (**41c**),
- understand how prefixes and suffixes affect spelling (**41d**),
- use *ei* and *ie* correctly (**41e**), and
- use hyphens to link and divide words (**41f**).

41a SPELL CHECKER

The spell checker is a wonderful invention, but only when you use it with care. A spell checker will usually flag

- misspellings of common words,
- some commonly confused words (such as *affect* and *effect*), and
- obvious typographical errors (such as *tge* for *the*).

However, a spell checker generally will *not* detect

- specialized vocabulary or foreign words not in its dictionary,

- typographical errors that are still correctly spelled words (such as *was* for *saw*), and
- misuses of words that sound alike but are not on the spell checker's list of commonly confused words.

The following strategies can help you use a spell checker effectively.

TIPS FOR USING A SPELL CHECKER

- If a spell checker regularly flags a word that is not in its dictionary but is spelled correctly, add that word to its dictionary by clicking on the Add button. From that point on, the spell checker will accept the word.

- Reject any offers the spell checker makes to correct all instances of a particular error.

- Use a dictionary to evaluate the alternative spellings the spell checker provides; some of them may be erroneous.

41b   SPELLING AND PRONUNCIATION

Many words in English are not spelled the way they are pronounced, so pronunciation is not a reliable guide to correct spelling. Sometimes, people skip over an unstressed syllable, as when *February* is pronounced "Febuary," or they slide over a sound that is hard to articulate, as when *library* is pronounced "libary." Other times, people add a sound—for instance, when they pronounce *athlete* as "athalete." And people may switch sounds around, as in "irrevelant" for *irrelevant.* Such mispronunciations can lead to misspellings.

You can help yourself remember the spellings of some words by considering the spellings of their root words—for example, the root word for *irrelevant* is *relevant.* You can also teach yourself the correct spellings of words by pronouncing them the way they are spelled, that is, by pronouncing each letter mentally so that you "hear" even silent letters. You are more likely to remember the *b* in *subtle* if you pronounce it when spelling that word. Here are a few words typically misspelled because they include unpronounced letters:

condem*n*   fore*i*gn   lab*o*ratory   mus*c*le   solem*n*

Here are a few more that include letters that are often not heard in rapid speech, though they can be heard when carefully pronounced:

can*d*idate   diffe*r*ent   enviro*n*ment   gove*rn*ment   sep*a*rate

❶ CAUTION

The words *and, have,* and *than* are often not stressed in speech and are thus likely misspelled.

           have   *than*   *and*
They would rather~~of~~ written two papers~~then~~ taken midterm~~an~~ final exams.

Watch for these misspellings when you proofread your papers.

41c   WORDS THAT SOUND ALIKE

Pairs of words such as *forth* and *fourth* or *sole* and *soul* are **homophones**: they sound alike but have different meanings and spellings. Some words that have different meanings sound exactly alike (*break/brake*); others sound alike in certain dialects (*marry/merry*). If you are unsure about the difference in meaning between any two words that sound alike, consult a dictionary. A number of frequently confused words are listed with explanations in this handbook's **Glossary of Usage**.

Also troublesome are two-word sequences that can be written as compound words or as separate words. The following are examples:

Everyday life was grueling.	She attended class **every day.**
They do not fight **anymore.**	They could not find **any more** evidence.

Other examples are *awhile/a while, everyone/every one, maybe/may be,* and *sometime/some time.*

A lot and *all right* are still spelled as two words. *Alot* is always considered incorrect; *alright* is also considered incorrect except in some newspapers and magazines. (See the **Glossary of Usage**.)

Singular nouns ending in *-nce* and plural nouns ending in *-nts* are easily confused.

Assistance is available.   I have two **assistants.**

His **patience** wore thin.   Some **patients** waited for hours.

Contractions and possessive pronouns are also often confused. In contractions, an apostrophe indicates an omitted letter (or letters). In possessive pronouns, there is no apostrophe. (See also **25b** and **38a(1)**.)

Contraction   **Possessive**

It's my turn next.   Each group waited **its** turn.

You're next.   **Your** turn is next.

There's no difference.   **Theirs** is no different.

TIPS FOR SPELLING WORDS THAT SOUND ALIKE

- Be alert for words that are commonly confused (*accept/except*).
- Distinguish between two-word sequences and single words that sound similar (*may be/maybe*).
- Use *-nts*, not *-nce*, for plural words (*instants/instance*).
- Mark contractions, but not possessive pronouns, with apostrophes (*who's/whose*).

41d   PREFIXES AND SUFFIXES

When a prefix is added to a base word (often called the **root**), the spelling of the base word is unaffected.

necessary, **un**necessary   moral, **im**moral

However, adding a suffix to the end of a base word often changes the spelling.

beauty, beauti**ful**   describe, descri**ption**   BUT   resist, resist**ance**

Although spellings of words with suffixes are irregular, they follow certain conventions.

(1) Dropping or retaining a final *e*

- If a suffix begins with a vowel, the final *e* of the base word is dropped: bride, brid**al**; come, com**ing**; combine, combin**ation**; prime, prim**ary**. However, to keep the /s/ sound of *ce* or the /j/ sound of *ge*, retain the final *e* before *-able* or *-ous*: courage**ous**, manage**able**, notice**able**.
- If a suffix begins with a consonant, the final *e* of the base word is usually retained: entire, entire**ly**; rude, rude**ness**; place, place**ment**; sure, sure**ly**. Exceptions include *argument, awful, ninth, truly,* and *wholly.*

(2) Doubling a final consonant when a suffix begins with a vowel

- If a one-syllable word with a single vowel or a stressed syllable with a single vowel ends with a consonant, double the final consonant: stop, sto**pped**, sto**pping**; omit, omi**tted**, omi**tting**.
- If there are two vowels before the consonant, the consonant is not doubled: seat, seat**ed**, seat**ing**; remain, remain**ed**, remain**ing**.
- If the final syllable is not stressed, the consonant is not doubled: edit, edit**ed**, edit**ing**; picket, picket**ed**, picket**ing**.

(3) Changing or retaining a final *y*

- Change a final *y* following a consonant to *i* when adding a suffix (except *-ing*): lazy, laz**ily**; defy, def**ies**, def**ied**, def**iance** BUT defy**ing**; modify, modif**ies**, modif**ied**, modif**ier** BUT modify**ing**.
- Retain the final *y* when it follows a vowel: gray, gray**ish**; stay, stay**s**, stay**ed**; obey, obey**s**, obey**ed**.
- Some verb forms are irregular and thus can cause difficulties: *lays, laid; pays, paid.* For a list of irregular verbs, see pages 562–64.

(4) Retaining a final *l* when *-ly* is added

cool, coo**lly**   formal, forma**lly**   real, rea**lly**   usual, usua**lly**

Exercise 1

Add the specified suffixes to the words that follow. Be prepared to explain the reason for the spelling of each resulting word.

EXAMPLE

-ly: late, casual, psychological   *lately   casually   psychologically*

1. -ing: put, admit, write, use, try, play
2. -ment: manage, commit, require, argue
3. -ous: continue, joy, acrimony, libel
4. -ed: race, tip, permit, carry, pray
5. -able: desire, read, trace, knowledge
6. -ly: true, sincere, normal, general

(5) Making a noun plural by adding -s or -es to the singular form

- If the sound in the plural form of a noun ending in *f* or *fe* changes from /f/ to /v/, change the ending to *-ve* before adding *-s:* thie**f**, thie**ves**; li**fe**, li**ves** BUT roo**f**, roo**fs**.

- Add *-es* to most nouns ending in *s, z, ch, sh,* or *x:* box, box**es**; peach, peach**es**.

- If a noun ends in a consonant and *y,* change the *y* to *i* and add *-es:* company, compan**ies**; ninety, ninet**ies**; territory, territor**ies**. (See also **41d(3)**.)

- If a noun ends in a consonant and *o,* add *-es:* hero, hero**es**; potato, potato**es**. However, note that sometimes just *-s* is added (photo, photo**s**; memo, memo**s**) and other times either an *-s* or *-es* suffix can be added (motto**s**, motto**es**; zero**s**, zero**es**).

- Certain nouns have irregular plural forms: woman, wom**en**; child, child**ren**; foot, f**eet**.

- Add *-s* to most proper nouns: the Lee**s**; the Kennedy**s**. Add *-es* to most proper nouns ending in *s, z, ch, sh,* or *x:* the Rodriguez**es**, the Jones**es** BUT the Bach**s** (in which *ch* is pronounced /k/).

❶ CAUTION

Words borrowed from Latin or Greek generally form their plurals as they did in the original language.

Singular	criterion	alumnus, alumna	analysis	datum	species
Plural	criteria	alumni, alumnae	analyses	data	species

Many words with such origins gradually come to be considered part of the English language, and during this process, two plural forms will be listed in dictionaries as acceptable: *syllabus/syllabuses, syllabi*. Be sure to use only one of the acceptable plural forms in a paper you write.

Exercise 2

Provide the plural forms for the following words. If you need extra help, check a dictionary.

1. virus
2. committee
3. phenomenon
4. copy
5. hero
6. embargo
7. shelf
8. belief
9. foot
10. portfolio
11. cactus
12. census

41e CONFUSION OF *EI* AND *IE*

An old rhyme will help you remember the order of letters in most words containing *e* and *i*:

Put *i* before *e*

Except after *c*

Or when sounded like *a*

As in *neighbor* and *weigh*.

Words with *i* before *e:* bel**ie**ve, ch**ie**f, pr**ie**st, y**ie**ld

Words with *e* before *i*, after *c:* conc**ei**t, perc**ei**ve, rec**ei**ve

Words with *ei* sounding like *a* in *cake:* **ei**ght, r**ei**n, th**ei**r, h**ei**r

Words that are exceptions to the rules in the rhyme include *either, neither, species, foreign*, and *weird*.

ñ **MULTILINGUAL WRITERS**

AMERICAN AND BRITISH SPELLING DIFFERENCES

Although most words are spelled the same in both the United States and Great Britain, some are spelled differently, including the following.

American	check	realize	color	connection
British	cheque	realise	colour	connexion

Use the American spellings when writing for an audience in the United States.

41f | HYPHENS

Hyphens link two or more words functioning as a single word and separate word parts to clarify meaning. They also have many conventional uses in numbers, fractions, and measurements. (Do not confuse the hyphen with a dash; see **40d** and **44g(2)**.)

(1) Between two or more words that form a compound

Some compounds are listed in the dictionary with hyphens (*eye-opener, cross-examination*), others are written as two words (*eye chart, cross fire*), and still others appear as one word (*eyewitness, crossbreed*). If you have questions about the spelling of a compound word, a dictionary is a good resource. However, it is also helpful to learn a few basic patterns.

- If two or more words serve as a single adjective before a noun, they should be hyphenated. If the words follow the noun, they are not hyphenated.

You submitted an **up-to-date** report. The report was **up to date.**

A **well-known** musician is performing tonight. The musician is **well known.**

- When the second word in a hyphenated expression is omitted, the first word is still followed by a hyphen.

They discussed both **private-** and **public-sector** partnerships.

- A hyphen is not used after adverbs ending in *-ly* (*poorly planned event*), in names of chemical compounds (*sodium chloride solution*), or in modifiers with a letter or numeral as the second element (*group C homes, type IV virus*).

(2) Between a prefix and a word to clarify meaning

- To avoid ambiguity or an awkward combination of letters or syllables, place a hyphen between the base word and its prefix: *anti-intellectual, de-emphasize, re-sign the petition* [COMPARE: *resign the position*].
- Place a hyphen between a prefix and a word beginning with a capital letter and between a prefix and a word already containing a hyphen: *anti-American, non-self-promoting.*
- Place a hyphen after the prefix *all-, e-, ex-,* or *self-: all-inclusive, e-commerce, ex-husband, self-esteem.* Otherwise, most words with prefixes are not hyphenated. (The use of the unhyphenated *email* has become very common, but *e-mail* is the spelling preferred by APA, CMS, and MLA. The prefix *e-* is sometimes used without a hyphen in trade names, such as eBay.)

(3) In numbers, fractions, and units of measure

- Place a hyphen between two numbers when they are spelled out: *thirty-two, ninety-nine.* However, no hyphen is used before or after the words *hundred, thousand,* and *million: five hundred sixty-three, forty-one million.*
- Hyphenate fractions that are spelled out: *three-fourths, one-half.*
- When you form a compound modifier that includes a number and a unit of measurement, place a hyphen between them: *twenty-first-century literature, twelve-year-old boy, ten-year project.*

Exercise 3

Convert the following groups of words into hyphenated compounds.

EXAMPLE

a movie lasting two hours   *a two-hour movie*

1. a boss who is well liked
2. a television screen that is forty-eight inches across
3. a highway with eight lanes
4. a painting from the seventeenth century
5. a chemist who won the Nobel Prize
6. a virus that is food borne

42 | CAPITALS

When you look at an advertisement, an e-mail message, or a paragraph in this book, you can easily pick out capital letters. These beacons draw your attention to significant details—for example, the beginnings of sentences or the names of particular people, places, and products. Although most capitalization conventions apply to any rhetorical situation, others are specific to a discipline or a profession. In this chapter, you will learn the conventions that are followed in most academic and professional settings. This chapter will help you

- use capitals for proper names (**42a**);
- capitalize words in titles and subtitles of works (**42b**);
- capitalize the first letter of a sentence (**42c**);
- use capitals for computer keys, menu items, and icon names (**42d**); and
- avoid unnecessary capitalization (**42e**).

❶ CAUTION

You may have noticed that capitalization styles differ in various types of publications. For instance, the word *president* is always capitalized in documents published by the US Government Printing Office, but it is capitalized in most newspapers only when it is followed by a specific name:

The delegates met with **P**resident Truman.

The delegates met with the **p**resident.

Be careful to use an appropriate capitalization style for your rhetorical situation.

Advertisers often highlight important words by capitalizing them.

42a PROPER NAMES

When you capitalize a word, you emphasize it. That is why names of people and places are capitalized, even when they are used as modifiers (*Mexico, Mexican government*). Some words, such as *college, company, park,* and *street,* are capitalized only if they are part of a name (*a university* but *University of Pennsylvania*). The following names and titles should be capitalized.

(1) Names of specific persons or things

Zora Neale Hurston	Flight 224	Honda Accord
John Paul II	Academy Award	USS *Cole*
Skylab	Nike	Microsoft Windows

For a brand name such as eBay or iPod that begins with a lowercase letter, do not change that letter to a capital when the name begins a sentence.

Many people like to shop on eBay.

eBay attracts many shoppers.

A word denoting a family relationship is capitalized only when it substitutes for the person's proper name.

I told **Mom** about the event. [I told Virginia about the event.]

I told my **mom** about the event. [NOT I told my Virginia about the event.]

(2) Titles accompanying proper names

A title is capitalized when it precedes the name of a person but not when it follows the name or stands alone.

Governor Bill Haslam	Bill Haslam, the governor
Captain Ray Machado	Ray Machado, our captain
Aunt Helen	Helen, my aunt
President Lincoln	Abraham Lincoln, the president of the United States

(3) Names of ethnic or cultural groups and languages

Asians	African Americans	Latinos/Latinas	Poles
Arabic	English	Korean	Spanish

(4) Names of bridges, buildings, monuments, and geographical features

Golden Gate Bridge	Empire State Building	Lincoln Memorial
Arctic Circle	Mississippi River	Grand Canyon

When referring to two or more geographical features, do not capitalize the generic term: *Lincoln and Jefferson memorials, Yellowstone and Olympic national parks.*

(5) Names of organizations, government agencies, institutions, and companies

B'nai B'rith	National Endowment for the Humanities
Phi Beta Kappa	Internal Revenue Service
Howard University	Ford Motor Company

When used as common nouns, *service, company,* and *university* are not capitalized. However, universities and other organizations often capitalize these words when they are used as shortened forms of the institutions' full names.

The policies of Hanson **U**niversity promote the rights of all individuals to equal opportunity in education. The **U**niversity complies with all applicable federal, state, and local laws.

(6) Names of days of the week, months, and holidays

Wednesday	August	Fourth of July

The names of the seasons—spring, summer, fall, winter—are not capitalized.

ñ MULTILINGUAL WRITERS

CAPITALIZING DAYS OF THE WEEK

Capitalization rules vary according to language. For example, in English, the names of days and months are capitalized, but in some other languages, such as Spanish and Italian, they are not.

(7) Designations for historical documents, periods, events, movements, and styles

Declaration of Independence   Renaissance   Industrial Revolution

A historical period that includes a number is not capitalized unless it is considered a proper name.

twentieth century   the Roaring Twenties

the seventies   the Gay Nineties

The name of a cultural movement or style is capitalized if it is derived from a person's name or if capitalization distinguishes the name of the movement or style from the ordinary use of the word or phrase.

Platonism   Reaganomics   New Criticism

Most names of cultural movements and styles are not capitalized.

art deco   impressionism   realism   deconstruction

(8) Names of religions, their adherents, holy days, titles of holy books, and words denoting the Supreme Being

Buddhism, Christianity, Islam, Judaism

Buddhist, Christian, Muslim, Jew

Bodhi Day, Easter, Ramadan, Yom Kippur

Sutras, Bible, Koran, Talmud BUT biblical, talmudic

Buddha, God, Allah, Yahweh

Some writers always capitalize personal pronouns (25a(1)) that refer to the Supreme Being; others capitalize such words only when capitalization is needed to prevent ambiguity:

The Lord commanded the prophet to warn His people.

(9) Words derived from proper names

Americanize [verb]   Orwellian [adjective]   Marxism [noun]

When a proper name becomes the name of a general class of objects or ideas, it is no longer capitalized. For example, the word *zipper* was originally the trademarked name of the fastening device and was capitalized;

it now refers to the class of such devices and is written with a lowercase letter. A word derived from a brand name, such as *Xerox* or *Kleenex*, should be capitalized. If possible, avoid using brand names and choose generic terms such as *photocopy* and *tissue* instead. If you are not sure whether a proper name or derivative has come to stand for a general class, look up the word in a dictionary.

(10) Abbreviations and acronyms

These forms are derived from the initial letters of capitalized word groups:

AMEX   AT&T   CBS   CST   NFL   OPEC   UNESCO   YMCA

(See also **40a(2)** and Chapter **44**.)

(11) Military terms

Names of forces and special units are capitalized, as are names of wars, battles, revolutions, and military awards.

United States Army   Marine Corps   Secret Service   Green Berets

Russian Revolution   Gulf War   Operation Overlord   Purple Heart

Military words such as *army, navy,* and *war* are not capitalized when they stand alone.

My sister joined the navy in 2008.

STYLE SHEET FOR CAPITALIZATION

Capitals	No capitals
the West [geographical region]	driving west [compass point]
a Chihuahua [a breed of dog named after a state in Mexico]	a poodle [a breed of dog]
Washington State University [a specific institution]	a state university
Revolutionary War [a specific war]	an eighteenth-century war
US Army [a specific army]	a peacetime army

Declaration of Independence [title of a document]	a declaration of independence
May [specific month]	spring [general season]
Memorial Day [specific day]	a holiday
two Democratic candidates [refers to a political party]	democratic procedures [refers to a form of government]
a Ford tractor [brand name]	a farm tractor
Parkinson's disease [a disease named for a person]	flu, asthma, leukemia
Governor Clay [a person's title]	the governor of this state

42b TITLES AND SUBTITLES

The first and last words in titles and subtitles are capitalized, as are major words—that is, all words other than articles (*a, an,* and *the*), coordinating conjunctions (*and, but, for, nor, or, so,* and *yet*), prepositions (see the list on page 508), and the infinitive marker *to.* (For more information on titles, see **39b** and **43a**.)

> *From Here to Eternity*

> "To Be a Student or Not to Be a Student"

APA guidelines differ slightly from other style guidelines: APA recommends capitalizing any word in a title, including a preposition, that has four or more letters.

> *Southwestern Pottery from Anasazi to Zuni* [MLA and CMS]

> *Southwestern Pottery From Anasazi to Zuni* [APA]

MLA, APA, and CMS advise capitalizing all words in a hyphenated compound, except for articles, coordinating conjunctions, and prepositions.

> "The Arab-Israeli Dilemma" [compound proper adjective]

> "Stop-and-Go Signals" [lowercase for the coordinating conjunction]

When a hyphenated word containing a prefix appears in a title or subtitle, capitalize both elements when the second element is a proper noun (**20a(2)**) or adjective (*Pre-Columbian*). However, if the word following the prefix is a common noun (as in *anti-independence*), capitalize it only if you are following APA guidelines.

"Pre-Columbian Artifacts in Peruvian Museums" [MLA, APA, and CMS]

"Anti-Independence Behavior in Adolescents" [APA]

"Anti-independence Behavior in Adolescents" [MLA and CMS]

42C   BEGINNING A SENTENCE

It is not difficult to remember that a sentence begins with a capital letter, but there are certain types of sentences that deserve special note.

(1) A quoted sentence

If a direct quotation is a full sentence, the first word should be capitalized.

> When asked to name the books she found most influential, Nadine Gordimer responded, "**In** general, the works that mean most to one—change one's thinking and therefore maybe one's life—are those read in youth."

Even if you interrupt a quoted sentence with commentary, only the first letter should be capitalized.

> "**O**ddly," states Ved Mehta, "**l**ike my earliest memories, the books that made the greatest impression on me were the ones I encountered as a small child."

However, if you integrate someone else's sentence into a sentence of your own, the first letter should be lowercase—and placed in brackets if you are following MLA guidelines.

Nadine Gordimer believes that "[i]n general, the works that mean most to one—change one's thinking and therefore maybe one's life—are those read in youth" (102).

(2) A freestanding parenthetical sentence

If you place a full sentence inside parentheses, and it is not embedded in a sentence of your own, be sure to capitalize the first word.

Lance Armstrong won the Tour de France a record-breaking seven times. (**P**revious record holders include Jacques Anquetil, Bernard Hinault, Eddy Merckx, and Miguel Indurain.)

If the sentence inside the parentheses occurs within a sentence of your own, the first word should not be capitalized.

Lance Armstrong won the Tour de France a record-breaking seven times (**p**reviously, he shared the record with four other cyclists).

(3) An independent clause following a colon

According to *The Chicago Manual of Style*, if there is only one independent clause (**21b(1)**) following a colon, the first word should be lower-cased. However, if two or more independent clauses follow the colon, the first word of each clause is capitalized.

The ear thermometer is used quite frequently now: **t**his type of thermometer records a temperature more accurately than a glass thermometer.

Two new thermometers are replacing the old thermometers filled with mercury: **T**he digital thermometer uses a heat sensor to determine body temperature. **T**he ear thermometer is actually an infrared thermometer that detects the temperature of the eardrum.

The APA manual recommends capitalizing the first word of any independent clause following a colon. The MLA manual advises capitalizing the first word only if the independent clause is a rule or principle.

Think of fever as a symptom, not as an illness: **I**t is the body's response to infection. [APA]

He has two basic rules for healthy living: **E**at sensibly and exercise strenuously at least three times a week. [APA and MLA]

A grammar checker will flag a word at the beginning of a sentence that should be capitalized, but it will not be able to determine whether a word following a colon should be capitalized.

(4) Abbreviated questions

In a series of abbreviated questions, the first words of all the questions are capitalized when the intent is to draw attention to the individual questions. Otherwise, questions in a series begin with lowercase letters.

How do we distinguish the legal codes for families? For individuals? For genetic research?

Did you remember to include your application? résumé? letters of recommendation?

42d COMPUTER KEYS, MENU ITEMS, AND ICON NAMES

When referring to a specific computer key, menu item, or icon name, capitalize the first letter.

To find the thesaurus, press Shift and the function key F7.

Instead of choosing Copy from the Edit menu, you can press Ctrl+C.

For additional information, click on Resources.

42e UNNECESSARY CAPITALS

(1) Capitalizing common nouns

Many nouns can be either common or proper, depending on the context. A **proper noun** (20a(2)), also called a *proper name*, identifies a specific entity. A **common noun** (20a(2)), which is usually preceded by a word such as *the, a, an, this,* or *that,* is not capitalized.

a speech course in theater and television [COMPARE: Speech 324: Theater and Television]

a university, this high school [COMPARE: University of Michigan, Elgin High School]

(2) Overusing capitalization to signal emphasis

Occasionally, a common noun is capitalized for emphasis.

Some politicians will do anything they can for Power.

If you use capitals for emphasis, do so sparingly; overuse will weaken the effect. For other ways to achieve emphasis, see Chapter 31.

(3) Signaling emphasis online

For online writing in academic and professional contexts, capitalize as you normally do. Be careful not to capitalize whole words for emphasis because your reader may feel as though you are SHOUTING (which is the term used for this rude and undesirable practice).

Exercise 1

Write a sentence using each of the following words correctly.

1. first lady
2. First Lady
3. mountains
4. Mountains
5. west
6. West
7. avenue
8. Avenue
9. independent
10. Independent
11. doctor
12. Doctor

Exercise 2

Edit the capitalization errors in the following paragraph. Be prepared to explain any changes that you make.

[1]Diana taurasi (Her teammates call her dee) plays basketball for the Phoenix mercury. [2]She has all the skills she needs to be a Star Player: She can pass and shoot, as well as rebound, block, and steal. [3]While playing for the university of connecticut huskies, she won the Naismith award twice and ranked in the majority of the big east's statistical categories. [4]Shortly after the huskies won their third straight ncaa title, taurasi was drafted first overall by the Phoenix mercury. [5]In april of 2004, taurasi played on the american national team against japan, and, in the Summer of 2004, she made her olympic debut in Athens.

43 ‖ ITALICS

Italics indicate that a word or a group of words is being used in a special way. For example, the use of italics can clear up the ambiguity in the following sentence:

The linguistics students discussed the word stress.

Does this sentence mean that the students discussed a particular word or that they discussed the correct pronunciation of words? By italicizing *stress,* the writer indicates that it was the word itself, not an accent pattern, that the students discussed.

The linguistics students discussed the word *stress.*

This chapter will help you use italics for

- the titles of separate works (**43a**);
- foreign words (**43b**);
- the names of legal cases (**43c**);
- the names of ships, submarines, aircraft, spacecraft, and satellites (**43d**);
- words, letters, or numerals used as such or letters used in mathematical expressions (**43e**); and
- words receiving emphasis (**43f**).

Word-processing programs make it easy to use italics. In handwritten documents, you can indicate italics by underlining.

Paul Harding's novel <u>Tinkers</u> won the 2010 Pulitzer Prize for literature.

The use of italics instead of underlining is now widely accepted in business writing and academic writing. MLA, APA, and CMS all call for italics.

⊡ TECH SAVVY

Remember that in e-mail messages and on web pages, an underlined word or phrase often indicates a hyperlink. If you are not able to format your e-mails or other electronic text with italics, use an underscore before and after words you would normally italicize.

Paul Harding's novel _Tinkers_ won the 2010 Pulitzer Prize for literature.

43a	TITLES OF WORKS PUBLISHED OR PRODUCED SEPARATELY

By convention, italics indicate the title of a longer work, while quotation marks indicate the title of a shorter work. For instance, the title of a collection of poetry published as a book (a longer work) is italicized (or underlined), and the title of any poem (shorter work) included in the book is enclosed in quotation marks (**39b**). These conventions help readers recognize the nature of a work and sometimes its relationship to another work.

Walt Whitman's "I Sing the Body Electric" first appeared in 1855 in the collection *Leaves of Grass*.

The titles of the following kinds of works are italicized:

Books	*The Little Prince*	*Huck Finn*
Magazines	*Wired*	*Rolling Stone*
Newspapers	*USA Today*	*Wall Street Journal*
Plays, films, DVDs	*The Lion King*	*Akeelah and the Bee*
Television and radio shows	*Mad Men*	*A Prairie Home Companion*
Recordings	*Can't Be Tamed*	*Great Verdi Overtures*
Works of art	*American Gothic*	*David*

Long poems	*Paradise Lost*	*The Divine Comedy*
Pamphlets	*Saving Energy*	*Tips for Gardeners*
Comic strips	*Peanuts*	*Doonesbury*

According to MLA guidelines, titles of websites are also italicized.

When an italicized title includes the title of a longer work within it, the embedded title is not italicized.

Modern Interpretations of Paradise Lost

If the italicized title includes the title of a short work within it, both titles are italicized, and the short work is also enclosed in quotation marks.

Willa Cather's "Paul's Case"

Titles are not placed in italics or between quotation marks when they stand alone on a title page, a book cover, or a newspaper page. Furthermore, neither italics nor quotation marks are necessary for titles of major historical documents and religious texts.

The Bill of Rights contains the first ten amendments to the US Constitution.

The Bible, a sacred text just as the Koran or the Torah is, begins with the Book of Genesis.

According to MLA and CMS guidelines, an initial *the* in a newspaper or periodical title is not italicized. Nor is it capitalized, unless it begins a sentence.

The story was published in the *New York Times.*

Also recommended is the omission of an article (*a, an,* or *the*) at the beginning of such a title when it would make a sentence awkward.

The report will appear in Thursday's ~~the~~ *Wall Street Journal.*

43b　FOREIGN WORDS

Use italics to indicate foreign words.

> Japan has a rich store of traditional folktales, *mukashibanashi,* "tales of long ago." —**GARY SNYDER,** *Back on the Fire*

A foreign word used frequently in a text should be italicized only once—at its first occurrence.

The Latin words used to classify plants and animals according to genus and species are italicized.

Homo sapiens　　　*Rosa setigera*　　　*Ixodes scapularis*

Countless words borrowed from other languages have become part of English and are therefore not italicized.

bayou (Choctaw)　　　karate (Japanese)　　　arroyo (Spanish)

If you are not sure whether a word has been accepted into English, look for it in a standard dictionary (**33d**).

43c　LEGAL CASES

Italics identify the names of legal cases.

Miranda v. Arizona　　　*Roe v. Wade*

The abbreviation *v.* (for "versus") may appear in either italic or nonitalic type, as long as the style is used consistently. Italics are also used for the shortened name of a well-known legal case.

> According to the *Miranda* decision, suspects must be informed of their right to remain silent and their right to legal advice.

Italics are not used to refer to a case by other than its official name.

> All the major networks covered the O. J. Simpson trial.

43d | NAMES OF SHIPS, SUBMARINES, AIRCRAFT, SPACECRAFT, AND SATELLITES

Italicize the names of specific ships, submarines, aircraft, spacecraft, and satellites.

USS *Enterprise*   USS *Hawkbill*   *Enola Gay*   *Atlantis*   *Aqua*

The names of trains, the models of vehicles, and the trade names of aircraft are not italicized.

Orient Express   Ford Mustang   Boeing 747

43e | WORDS, LETTERS, OR NUMERALS REFERRED TO AS SUCH AND LETTERS USED IN MATHEMATICAL EXPRESSIONS

When you refer to a specific word, letter, or numeral as itself, you should italicize it.

The word *love* is hard to define. [COMPARE: They were in love.]

The *b* in *bat* is not aspirated. [COMPARE: He earned a B+.]

The *2* on the sign has faded, and the *5* has disappeared. [COMPARE: She sent 250 cards.]

Statistical symbols and variables in algebraic expressions are also italicized.

The Pythagorean theorem is expressed as $a^2 + b^2 = c^2$.

43f | WORDS RECEIVING EMPHASIS

Used sparingly, italics can signal readers to stress certain words.

These *are* the right files. [The verb *are* receives more emphasis than it normally would.]

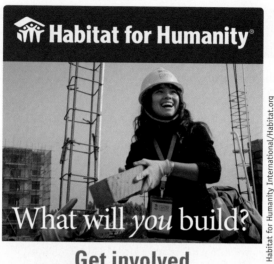

© Habitat for Humanity International/Habitat.org

This web banner uses italics to emphasize the importance of the individual in effecting change.

Italics can also emphasize emotional content.

> We have to go *now.* [The italicized word signals urgency.]

If overused, italics will lose their impact. Instead of italicizing words, substitute more specific words (Chapter **34**) or vary sentence structures (Chapter **32**).

Exercise 1

Identify all words that should be italicized in the following sentences. Explain why italics are necessary in each case.

1. Information about museum collections and exhibits can be found in art books, museum websites, and special sections of magazines and newspapers such as Smithsonian Magazine and the New York Times.

2. The website for the Metropolitan Museum of Art has pictures of Anthony Caro's sculpture Odalisque and Charles Demuth's painting The Figure 5 in Gold.

3. The title page of William Blake's Songs of Innocence is included in Masterpieces of the Metropolitan Museum of Art.

4. This book includes a photograph of a beautiful script used in the Koran; the script is known as the maghribi, or Western, style.

5. The large Tyrannosaurus rex discovered by Sue Hendrickson in South Dakota is on display at the Field Museum.

6. The International Museum of Cartoon Art provides information about the designers of such comic strips as Blondie, Peanuts, Mutt and Jeff, and Li'l Abner.

7. The Great Train Robbery, It Happened One Night, and Grand Illusion are in the collection at the Celeste Bartos Film Preservation Center.

8. In 1998, the Songwriters Hall of Fame honored John Williams, who has written music for such movies as Jaws, Star Wars, and E.T.

9. The Smithsonian Institution's National Air and Space Museum houses an impressive collection of aircraft and spacecraft, including Spirit of St. Louis and Gemini 4.

10. The digital collection listed on the website Experience Music Project includes music from the albums Fresh Cream and Bluesbreakers with Eric Clapton.

44 | ABBREVIATIONS, ACRONYMS, AND NUMBERS

Abbreviations, acronyms, and numbers facilitate easy recognition and effective communication in both academic papers and business documents. An **abbreviation** is a shortened version of a word or phrase: *assn.* (association), *dept.* (department), *et al.* (*et alii,* or "and others"). An **acronym** is a word formed by combining the initial letters and/or syllables of a series of words: *AIDS* (**a**cquired **i**mmune **d**eficiency **s**yndrome), *sonar* (**so**und **na**vigation **r**anging). This chapter will help you learn

- how and when to abbreviate (44a–d),
- when to explain an acronym (44e), and
- whether to spell out a number or use numerals (44f and 44g).

Courtesy of UPS Worldwide, Inc.

Abbreviated brand names create instant recognition for products or services.

44a ABBREVIATIONS WITH NAMES

The abbreviations *Ms., Mr., Mrs.,* and *Dr.* appear before names, whether given as full names or only surnames.

Ms. Sandy Scharnhorst   **Mrs.** Campbell

Mr. Alfredo Luján   **Dr.** Bollinger

Civil or military titles should not be abbreviated in academic writing.

Senator Bob Corker   Captain Derrick   Professor Kirsten Benson

Abbreviations such as *Jr., Sr.,* and *MD* appear after names.

Samuel Levy **Jr.**   Imogen Hickey, **MD**

Mark Ngo **Sr.**   Joan Richtsmeier, **PhD**

In the past, periods were customarily used in abbreviations for academic degrees, but MLA and CMS now recommend omitting periods from abbreviations such as *MA, PhD,* and *MD.* Although MLA still follows the convention calling for commas to set off *Jr.* or *Sr.,* these abbreviations are increasingly considered part of the names they follow and thus need not be set off by commas unless you are following MLA style.

Note that when two designations are possible, only one should be used.

Dr. Kristin Grine OR Kristin Grine, **MD** [NOT Dr. Kristin Grine, MD]

Abbreviations of plural proper nouns are often formed by simply adding *s* before the period: *Drs.* Grine and Hickey. But there are exceptions: the plural of *Mr.* is *Messrs.,* and the plural of *Mrs.* is *Mesdames,* for which there is no abbreviated form.

44b ADDRESSES IN CORRESPONDENCE

The names of states and words such as *Street, Road, Company,* and *Corporation* are usually written out when they appear in a letter, including in the address at the top of the page. However, they may be abbreviated when used in the address on an envelope.

| Sentence | Derson Manufacturing Company is located on Madison Street in Watertown, Minnesota. |

| Address | Derson Manufacturing Co.
200 Madison St.
Watertown, MN 55388 |

When addressing correspondence within the United States, use the two-letter state abbreviations established by the US Postal Service. (No period follows these abbreviations.) If you do not know an appropriate state abbreviation or zip code, you can find it on the Postal Service's website.

44C ABBREVIATIONS IN SOURCE DOCUMENTATION

Abbreviations are commonly used when citing research sources in bibliographies, footnotes, and endnotes. Common abbreviations include the following (not all citation styles accept all of these abbreviations).

Bibliographies and Notes

anon., Anon.	anonymous, Anonymous
biog.	biography, biographer, biographical
bull.	bulletin
c. or ca.	circa, about (for example, *c. 1920*)
col., cols.	column, columns
cont.	contents OR continues, continued
et al.	*et alii* ("and others")
fig.	figure
fwd.	foreword, foreword by
illus.	illustrated by, illustrator, illustration
inc., Inc.	including, Incorporated
intl.	international
introd.	introduction, introduction by
ms., mss.	manuscript, manuscripts
natl.	national

n.d.	no date, no date of publication
n.p.	no place of publication, no publisher
n. pag.	no pagination
no., nos.	number, numbers
p., pp.	page, pages
P, Pr.	Press
pref.	preface
pt., pts.	part, parts
trans. or tr.	translation, translated by
U, Univ.	University

Computer Terms

FTP	file transfer protocol
HTML	hypertext markup language
http	hypertext transfer protocol
KB	kilobyte
MB	megabyte
MOO	multiuser domain, object-oriented
PDF	portable document format
URL	uniform resource locator

Divisions of Government

Cong.	Congress
dept.	department
div.	division
govt.	government
GPO	Government Printing Office
HR	House of Representatives

44d   ACCEPTABLE ABBREVIATIONS IN ACADEMIC AND PROFESSIONAL WRITING

Abbreviations are usually too informal for use in sentences, although some have become so familiar that they are considered acceptable substitutes for full words.

(1) Abbreviations for special purposes

The names of months, days of the week, and units of measurement are usually written out (not abbreviated) when they are included in sentences, as are words such as *Street* and *Corporation.*

> On a Tuesday in September, we drove ninety-nine miles to San Francisco, California, where we stayed in a hotel on Market Street.

Words such as *volume, chapter,* and *page* are abbreviated (*vol., ch.,* and *p.*) in bibliographies and in citations of research sources, but they are written out within sentences.

> I read the introductory chapter and the three final pages in the first volume of the committee's report.

(2) Clipped forms

A word shortened by common usage, a **clipped form,** does not end with a period. Some clipped forms—such as *rep* (for *representative*), *exec* (for *executive*), and *info* (for *information*)—are too informal for use in college writing. Others—such as *exam, lab*, and *math*—have become acceptable because they have been used so frequently that they no longer seem like shortened forms.

(3) Abbreviations for time periods and zones

> 82 BC for *before Christ* [OR 82 BCE for *before the Common Era*]
>
> AD 95 for *anno Domini,* "in the year of our Lord" [OR 95 CE for *of the Common Era*]
>
> 7:40 a.m. for *ante meridiem,* "before noon"
>
> 4:52 EST for *Eastern Standard Time*

Words designating units of time, such as *minute* and *month,* are written out when they appear in sentences. They can be abbreviated in tables or charts.

> sec.   min.   hr.   wk.   mo.   yr.

(4) The abbreviation U.S. or US as an adjective

the U.S. Navy, the US economy
[COMPARE: They moved to the United States in 1990.]

The abbreviation *U.S.* or *US* should be used only as an adjective in academic and professional writing. When using *United States* as a noun, spell it out. The choice of *U.S.* or *US* will depend on the discipline in which you are writing: MLA lists US as the preferred form, but APA uses U.S., and CMS accepts either form.

(5) Individuals known by their initials

JFK   LBJ   E. B. White   B. B. King

In most cases, however, first and last names should be written out in full.

Oprah Winfrey   Peyton Manning   Donald Trump

(6) Some abbreviations for Latin expressions

Certain abbreviations for Latin expressions are common in academic writing.

cf. [compare]	et al. [and others]	i.e. [that is]
e.g. [for example]	etc. [and so forth]	vs. OR v. [versus]

44e   ACRONYMS

The ability to identify a particular acronym will vary from one audience to another. Some readers will know that NAFTA stands for the North American Free Trade Agreement; others may not. By spelling out acronyms the first time you use them, you are being courteous and clear. Introduce the acronym by placing it in parentheses after the group of words it stands for.

The Federal Emergency Management Administration (FEMA) was criticized by many after Hurricane Katrina.

ñ *MULTILINGUAL WRITERS*

USING ARTICLES WITH ABBREVIATIONS, ACRONYMS, OR NUMBERS

When you use an abbreviation, an acronym, or a number, you sometimes need an indefinite article. Choose *a* or *an* based on the pronunciation of the initial sound of the abbreviation, acronym, or number: use *a* before a consonant sound and *an* before a vowel sound.

A picture of **a UN** delegation is on the front page of today's newspaper. [*UN* begins with a consonant sound.]

I have **an IBM** computer. [*IBM* begins with a vowel sound.]

The reporter interviewed **a NASA** engineer. [*NASA* begins with a consonant sound.]

My friend drives **a 1964** Mustang. [*1964* begins with a consonant sound.]

Exercise 1

Decide whether the following sentences use forms apropriate for college essays. Correct any usage that is not appropriate.

1. I always wake up before 6 a.m.
2. The pope was buried in 670 *anno Domini.*
3. The Walkers live on Sandy Ridge Rd.
4. We live six blocks from Sunset Lane.
5. My parents always go to Florida in Feb.
6. Easter is sometimes celebrated during the third month of the yr.
7. Knoxville is in TN.
8. We can meet at the UPS shipping store.
9. She prefers to be addressed as Ms. Terry Campbell.
10. He is not very impressive as a state rep.

44f GENERAL USES OF NUMBERS

Depending on their uses, numbers are treated in different ways. MLA recommends spelling out numbers that are expressed in one or two words (*nine, ninety-one, nine hundred, nine million*). A numeral is used for any other number ($9\frac{1}{2}$, *9.9, 999*), unless it begins a sentence. CMS advises spelling out whole numbers from zero through one hundred and any number followed by the word *hundred, thousand, hundred thousand,* or *million.*

The register recorded 164 names.

APA advises spelling out numbers below ten, common fractions, and numbers that are spelled out in universally accepted usage (for example, the Twelve Apostles). All three of these style manuals recommend using words rather than numerals at the beginning of a sentence.

One hundred sixty-four names were recorded in the register.
[Notice that *and* is not used in numbers greater than one hundred. NOT One hundred and sixty-four names . . . .]

When numbers or amounts refer to the same entities throughout a passage, use numerals when any of the numbers would be more than two words long if spelled out.

Only 5 of the 134 delegates attended the final meeting. The remaining 129 delegates will be informed by e-mail.

In scientific or technical writing, numerals are used before abbreviations of units of measurements (*2 L, 30 cc*).

44g SPECIAL USES OF NUMBERS

(1) Expressing specific times of day in either numerals or words

Numerals or words can be used to express times of day. They should be used consistently.

4 p.m. OR four o'clock in the afternoon

9:30 a.m. OR half-past nine in the morning OR nine-thirty in the morning [Notice the use of hyphens.]

(2) Using numerals and words for dates

Months are written as words, years as numerals, and days and decades as either words or numerals. However, 9/11 is an acceptable alternative to September 11, 2001.

May 20, 1976 OR 20 May 1976 [NOT May 20th, 1976]

the fourth of December OR December 4

the fifties OR the 1950s

from 1999 to 2003 OR 1999–2003 [Use an en dash, not a hyphen, in number ranges.]

▣ *TECH SAVVY*

To create an en dash, press Option and the hyphen key simultaneously.

ñ *MULTILINGUAL WRITERS*

DIFFERENT WAYS OF WRITING DATES

Many cultures invert the numerals for the month and the day: *14/2/2009* or *14 February 2009*. In publications from the United States, the month generally precedes the day: *2/14/2009* or *February 14, 2009*.

(3) Using numerals in addresses

Numerals are commonly used in street addresses and for zip codes.

25 Arrow Drive, Apartment 1, Columbia, MO 78209

OR, for a mailing envelope, 25 Arrow Dr., Apt. 1, Columbia, MO 78209

(4) Using numerals for identification

A numeral may be used as part of a proper noun (20a(2)).

Channel 10   Edward III   Interstate 40   Room 311

(5) Referring to pages and divisions of books and plays

Numerals are used to designate pages and other divisions of books and plays.

page 15   Chapter 8   Part 2   in act 2, scene 1 OR in Act II, Scene I

(6) Expressing decimals and percentages numerically

Numerals are used to express decimals and percentages.

a 2.5 average   12 percent   0.853 metric ton

(7) Using numerals for large fractional numbers

Numerals with decimal points can be used to express large fractional numbers.

5.2 million inhabitants   1.6 billion years

ñ MULTILINGUAL WRITERS

COMMAS AND PERIODS WITH NUMERALS

Cultures differ in their use of the period and the comma with numerals. In American usage, a decimal point (period) indicates a number or part of a number that is smaller than one, and a comma divides large numbers into units of three digits.

7.65 (seven and sixty-five one-hundredths)   10,000 (ten thousand)

In some other cultures, these usages of the decimal point and the comma are reversed.

7,65 (seven and sixty-five one-hundredths)   10.000 (ten thousand)

(8) Different ways of writing monetary amounts

Monetary amounts should be spelled out if they occur infrequently in a piece of writing. Otherwise, numerals and symbols can be used.

two million dollars	$2,000,000
ninety-nine cents	99¢ OR $0.99

Exercise 2

Edit the following sentences to correct the usage of abbreviations and numbers.

1. A Natl. Historic Landmark, Hoover Dam is located about 30 miles s.e. of Las Vegas, Nev.

2. The dam is named after Herbert Hoover, the 31st pres. of the U.S.

3. It is administered by the U.S. Dept. of the Interior.

4. Built by the fed. gov. between nineteen thirty-three and 1935, this dam is still considered one of the greatest achievements in the history of civ. engineering.

5. Construction of the dam became possible after several states in the Southwest (namely, AZ, CA, CO, NV, NM, UT, and WY) agreed on a plan to share water from the river.

6. The concrete used in the dam would have built a highway 16 ft. wide, stretching all the way from San Francisco to NYC.

7. 3,500 men worked on the dam during an average month of construction; this work translated into a monthly payroll of $500,000.

8. Spanning the Colorado River, Hoover Dam created Lake Mead—a reservoir covering 247 sq. miles.

9. A popular tourist attraction, Hoover Dam was closed to the public after terrorists attacked the U.S. on 9/11/01.

10. Today, certain pts. of the dam remain closed to the public as part of the effort to improve U.S. security.

A

ADVICE for MULTILINGUAL WRITERS

© Ocean/Corbis

45 | DETERMINERS, NOUNS, AND ADJECTIVES

If you grew up speaking a language other than English, consider yourself fortunate: knowing two languages provides many cultural and linguistic resources. You may, however, encounter difficulties as you write in English, because it is impossible to translate word for word from one language to another. Studying the topics in this chapter and in Chapters **46** and **47** may help you overcome typical challenges faced by multilingual writers. This chapter will help you

- use determiners with proper nouns (**45a**),
- use determiners with count nouns (**45b**),
- use determiners with noncount nouns (**45c**),
- use determiners with adjectives (**45d**), and
- shift from nonspecific to specific references (**45e**).

45a | DETERMINERS AND PROPER NOUNS

A **proper noun** is the specific name of someone or something (for example, *Benito, Mexico,* or *Museum of Popular Art*). Proper nouns are capitalized (**42a**). A **determiner** is a noun marker—a word that comes *before* a noun. The most common determiners are **articles** (*a, an,* and *the*), **demonstratives** (*this, that, these,* and *those*), **possessives** (*my, your, his, her, its, our,* and *their*), and **quantifiers** (*many, few, much,* and *less*). Choosing the right determiner may be difficult for you if your primary language does not have determiners or if its determiners function differently than those in English.

Proper nouns are preceded either by *the* or by no article at all. To decide whether to use *the* with a proper noun, first ask yourself this question: **Is the proper noun singular or plural?** If the proper noun is plural, use *the* (*the Browns, the United States*). If the proper noun is singular, you can usually omit the article (*Jeff, Mr. Brown, Atlanta, China*). However, there are some singular proper nouns that *are* preceded by *the*.

SINGULAR PROPER NOUNS PRECEDED BY *THE*

- **Historical documents, periods, and events:** *the* Magna Carta, *the* Renaissance, *the* Velvet Revolution
- **Buildings, hotels, museums, and some bridges:** *the* Burj Khalifa, *the* Sheraton, *the* Prado, *the* Brooklyn Bridge
- **Oceans, seas, rivers, and deserts:** *the* Pacific Ocean, *the* Aegean Sea, *the* Amazon River, *the* Sahara Desert
- **Names that include *of:*** *the* Gulf of Mexico, *the* Statue of Liberty, *the* University of Tennessee, *the* Fourth of July

45b | DETERMINERS AND COUNT NOUNS

A **common noun** is a general label (such as *president, country, museum).* Common nouns are not capitalized. A common noun may or may not be preceded by a determiner (45a). To decide whether to use a determiner with a common noun, begin by asking yourself this question: **Is the noun a count noun or a noncount noun?** A **count noun** names something that can be counted and has a singular and a plural form (one *car,* two *cars*). If the common noun is a count noun, ask yourself another question: **Is the count noun referring to someone or something specific?** If so, the following guidelines indicate appropriate determiners to use with the noun.

DETERMINERS WITH COUNT NOUNS: SPECIFIC REFERENCES

- A singular count noun is preceded by *the, this, that,* or a possessive.

    The/This/That/My book is heavy.
- A plural count noun is preceded by *the, these, those,* or a possessive.

    The/These/Those/My books are heavy.
- Count nouns that refer to unique individuals or entities (that have only one possible referent) are preceded by *the.*

    The president of the organization will arrive soon.

    The sun sets in the west.

If a count noun does not refer to someone or something specific, but instead to a type of individual or entity, use the following guidelines.

DETERMINERS WITH COUNT NOUNS: NONSPECIFIC REFERENCES

- The article *a* is used before a singular count noun beginning with a consonant *sound* (not necessarily the letter representing the sound).

    We went to *a* **c**afe.

    He is attending *a* **u**niversity.

- The article *an* is used before a singular count noun beginning with a vowel *sound* (not necessarily the letter representing the sound).

    They had *an* **a**rgument.

    The presentation lasted *an* **h**our.

- The article *a* is used before an adjective that begins with a consonant sound.

    We went to *a* **s**mall cafe.

- The article *an* is used before an adjective that begins with a vowel sound.

    We went to *an* **o**utdoor cafe.

- Plural count nouns are preceded by *some, many,* or *few* when the quantity is a consideration.

    Some/Many/Few students have volunteered.

- Plural count nouns take no determiner at all when quantity is not a consideration.

    Students have volunteered.

    Potatoes are grown in Idaho.

45C   DETERMINERS AND NONCOUNT NOUNS

A **noncount noun** names something that cannot be counted; it has neither a singular nor a plural form. Some noncount nouns never take determiners.

TYPES OF NONCOUNT NOUNS THAT TAKE NO DETERMINERS

- **Games and sports:** baseball, basketball, chess, football, poker, tennis, soccer

  Soccer is my favorite sport.

- **Subjects of study:** biology, chemistry, economics, English, history, mathematics, psychology, sociology

  English is my favorite subject.

Other types of noncount nouns may or may not take determiners.

TYPES OF NONCOUNT NOUNS THAT MAY OR MAY NOT TAKE DETERMINERS

- **Abstractions:** confidence, democracy, education, happiness, health, honesty, importance, knowledge, love, news, wisdom

  An **education** is of utmost importance.

  Education is crucial to economic security.

- **Groups of things:** clothing, equipment, garbage, homework, money, scenery, traffic, transportation, vocabulary

  The **homework** for French class is time-consuming.

  I spend a lot of time doing **homework.**

- **Substances:** air, blood, coffee, ice, rice, tea, water, wood

  This **tea** is watery.

  She prefers **tea** for breakfast.

To decide which determiner to use with a noun referring to an abstraction, a group, or a substance, begin with the question you asked about count nouns: **Is the noncount noun referring to something specific?** If it is, use the determiners in the following list.

DETERMINERS WITH NONCOUNT NOUNS THAT REFER TO SPECIFIC ABSTRACTIONS, GROUPS OF THINGS, OR SUBSTANCES

Use *the, this, that,* or a possessive before a noncount noun making a specific reference.

The/This/That/Our information is important.

If the noncount noun is *not* referring to something specific, use the following guidelines.

> **DETERMINERS WITH NONCOUNT NOUNS THAT DO NOT REFER TO SPECIFIC ABSTRACTIONS, GROUPS OF THINGS, OR SUBSTANCES**
>
> A noncount noun is preceded by the determiner *some, much,* or *little* when quantity is a consideration.
>
>> We drank *some/much/little* water.
>
> A noncount noun takes no determiner at all when quantity is not a consideration.
>
>> We drank only water.

Because noncount nouns do not have singular and plural forms, sentences like the following should be edited:

We learned to use a lot of equipments. [An *s* is not added to a noncount noun.]

I finished two homeworks~assignments~today. [Numbers are not used with noncount nouns.]

The job requires ~a~ special machinery. [*A* and *an* are not used with noncount nouns.]

The vocabulary ~are~ is difficult. [Use a singular verb with a noncount noun.]

Some words can be used as either a count noun or a noncount noun.

They believed **life** was sacred. [noncount noun]

He led *an* interesting **life.** [count noun]

45d   DETERMINERS AND ADJECTIVES

Some adjectives add specificity to nouns. Use *the* before the following types of adjectives.

ADJECTIVES AND DETERMINERS: SPECIFIC REFERENCES

- Adjectives indicating sequence, such as *first, next, last,* and so forth

  The **first/next/last** person in line will win a prize.

- Adjectives indicating a single person or item, such as *right, only,* and so forth

  She had *the* **right/only** answer.

When describing how one of two individuals or entities differs from or surpasses the other, use the comparative form of an adjective (**26b**). The comparative form has the suffix *-er* or the word *more* or *less*:

Cars are cheap*er* here. Cars are *more* expensive there.

Use the article *the* before the comparative form in this phrase: *the* [comparative form] *of the two* [plural noun].

The older *of the two* sons is now a doctor.

She bought *the* less expensive *of the two* cars.

When describing how one of three or more individuals or entities surpasses all the others, use the superlative form of an adjective (**26b**). There are two superlative forms: (1) the adjective has the suffix *-est* and is preceded by the article *the,* or (2) the adjective does not have that suffix and is preceded by *the most* or *the least.*

Cars are *the* cheap*est* here. Cars are *the most* expensive there.

Use the following guidelines to help you choose which form to use.

GUIDELINES FOR FORMING COMPARATIVES AND SUPERLATIVES

- One-syllable words generally take the ending *-er* or *-est: fast, faster, fastest.*
- Two-syllable words ending in a consonant and *-y* also generally take the ending *-er* or *-est,* with the *y* changed to an *i: noisy, noisier, noisiest.*
- Two-syllable adjectives ending in *-ct, -nt,* or *-st* are preceded by *more/less* or *most/least: less exact, least exact; more recent, most recent; more honest,*

most honest. Two-syllable adjectives with a suffix such as *-ous, -ish, -ful, -ing,* or *-ed* are also preceded by *more/less* or *most/least*: *more/most famous; more/most squeamish; less/least careful; more/most lasting, less/least depressed.*

- Two-syllable adjectives ending in *-er, -ow,* or *-some* either take the ending *-er* or *-est* or are preceded by *more/less* or *most/least: narrower, more narrow, less narrow, narrowest, most narrow, least narrow.*

- Words of three or more syllables are preceded by *more/less* or *most/least: less/least fortunate; more/most intelligent.*

- Some modifiers have irregular comparative and superlative forms:

> *little, less, least*
> *good/well, better, best*
> *bad, worse, worst*

45e SHIFTING FROM NONSPECIFIC TO SPECIFIC REFERENCES

In writing, you usually introduce an individual or an entity with a nonspecific reference. After you have mentioned the individual or entity, you can use specific references.

First mention

A tsunami <u>warning</u> was issued last night.

Subsequent mention

This <u>warning</u> affected all low-lying areas.

A subsequent mention does not have to repeat the word used in the first mention. However, the word chosen must be closely related to the one introduced first.

The weather service <u>warned</u> people about possible flooding. **The** <u>warning</u> included possible evacuation routes.

Exercise 1

Edit the following common sayings so that determiners are used correctly.

1. The absence makes a heart grow fonder.
2. The actions speak louder than the words.
3. The bad news travels fast.
4. Best things come in the small packages.
5. The blood is thicker than the water.
6. Don't cry over the spilled milk.

46 | VERBS AND VERB FORMS

Learning how to use verbs effectively involves more than looking up their meanings in a dictionary. You must also understand how the *form* of a verb affects its meaning. Building on the discussion in Chapter 24, this chapter gives more information about

- verb tenses (46a),
- auxiliary verbs (46b),
- prepositional and phrasal verbs (46c), and
- participles used as adjectives (46d).

46a | VERB TENSES

English verbs are either regular verbs (24a(1)) or irregular verbs (24a(2)). This distinction is based on the forms of a verb. The forms of irregular verbs do not follow the set pattern that the forms of regular verbs do. If you have trouble choosing the right verb forms, study the charts on pages 561 and 562–64. As you become more familiar with English verb forms, you will understand how they provide information about time. Keep in mind that, although the words *present, past,* and *future* may lead you to think that these tenses refer to actions or events occurring now, in the past, and in the future, respectively, this strict separation is not always the case.

(1) Simple tenses

Simple tenses have many uses, which are not limited to indicating specific times. The conjugation of the **simple present tense** of a regular verb includes two forms of the verb: the base form and the *-s* form. Notice that the third-person singular form is the only form with the *-s* ending.

Simple Present Tense		
	Singular	Plural
First person	I **work**	We **work**
Second person	You **work**	You **work**
Third person	He, she, it **works**	They **work**

Use the simple present tense for the following purposes.

USES OF THE SIMPLE PRESENT TENSE

- To indicate a current state: We **are** ready.
- To report a general fact: The sun **rises** in the east.
- To describe a habitual action: Dana **uses** common sense.
- To add a sense of immediacy to a description of a historical event: In 1939, Hitler's armies **attack** Poland.
- To discuss literary and artistic works: Joseph Conrad **writes** about what he sees in the human heart.
- To refer to future events: The festival **begins** next month.

The simple past tense of a regular verb has only one form: the base form with the *-ed* ending. The past tense forms of irregular verbs vary (see **24a(2)**).

Simple Past Tense
I, you, he, she, it, we, they **worked**

The simple past tense is used to refer to completed actions or past events.

USES OF THE SIMPLE PAST TENSE

- To indicate a completed action: He **traveled** to the Philippines.
- To report a past event: The accident **occurred** several weeks ago.

The simple future tense of a regular verb also has only one form: the base form accompanied by the auxiliary *will*.

Simple Future Tense
I, you, he, she, it, we, they **will work**

The simple future tense refers to future actions or states.

USES OF THE SIMPLE FUTURE TENSE

- To promise to perform an action: I **will call** you tonight.
- To predict a future action: They **will finish** the project soon.
- To predict a future state of being: Everyone **will be** weary.

It is also possible to use a form of *be going to* when referring to the future (**46b(2)**).

I **am going to** study in Russia next year.

(2) Progressive tenses

Progressive tenses indicate that actions or events are repetitive, ongoing, or temporary. The present progressive tense consists of a present-tense form of the auxiliary verb *be* and the present participle (*-ing* form) of the main verb, whether that verb is regular or irregular. Notice that the present participle remains the same regardless of person and number, but the auxiliary *be* appears in three forms: *am* for first-person singular, *is* for third-person singular, and *are* for other person-number combinations.

Present Progressive Tense		
	Singular	Plural
First person	I am working	We are working
Second person	You are working	You are working
Third person	He, she, it is working	They are working

The present progressive tense signals an activity in progress or a temporary situation.

USES OF THE PRESENT PROGRESSIVE TENSE

- To show that an activity is in progress: The doctor **is attending** a conference in Nebraska.
- To indicate that a situation is temporary: We **are living** in a yurt right now.
- To refer to an action that will occur at a specific time in the future: They **are leaving** for Alaska next week.

Like the present progressive, the past progressive tense is a combination of the auxiliary verb *be* and the present participle (*-ing* form) of the main verb. However, the auxiliary verb is in the past tense, rather than in the present tense.

Past Progressive Tense		
	Singular	Plural
First person	I **was working**	We **were working**
Second person	You **were working**	You **were working**
Third person	He, she, it **was working**	They **were working**

The past progressive tense signals that an action or event occurred in the past and was repeated or ongoing.

USES OF THE PAST PROGRESSIVE TENSE

- To indicate that a past action was repetitive: The new member **was** constantly **interrupting** the discussion.
- To signal that a past action was occurring when something else happened: We **were eating** dinner when we heard the news.

A verb in the future progressive tense has only one form. Two auxiliaries, *will* and *be*, are used with the *-ing* form of the main verb.

Future Progressive Tense
I, you, he, she, it, we, they **will be working**

The future progressive tense indicates that actions will occur over some period of time in the future.

> **USE OF THE FUTURE PROGRESSIVE TENSE**
>
> ■ To indicate that an action will occur over a span of time in the future: She **will be giving** her report at the end of the meeting.

> ❶ *CAUTION*
>
> Some verbs do not express actions but rather mental states, emotions, conditions, or relationships. These verbs are not used in progressive forms; they include *believe, belong, contain, cost, know, like, own, prefer,* and *want.*
>
> contains
> The book∧ is containing many Central American folktales.
>
> knows
> He∧ is knowing many old myths.

(3) Perfect tenses

Perfect tenses indicate actions that were performed or events that occurred before a particular time. The present perfect tense is formed by combining the auxiliary *have* with the past participle of the main verb. The participle remains the same regardless of person and number; however, the auxiliary has two forms: *has* for third-person singular and *have* for the other person-number combinations.

Present Perfect Tense		
	Singular	Plural
First person	I **have worked**	We **have worked**
Second person	You **have worked**	You **have worked**
Third person	He, she, it **has worked**	They **have worked**

The present perfect tense is used for the following purposes.

USES OF THE PRESENT PERFECT TENSE

- To signal that a situation originating in the past is continuing into the present: They **have lived** in New Zealand for twenty years.

- To refer to a past action that has current relevance: I **have read** that book already, but I could certainly read it again.

The past perfect tense is also formed by combining the auxiliary *have* with the past participle. However, the auxiliary is in the past tense. There is only one form of the past perfect.

Past Perfect Tense

I, you, he, she, it, we, they **had worked**

The past perfect tense specifies that an action was completed at a time in the past prior to another time or before another past action.

USES OF THE PAST PERFECT TENSE

- To indicate that a past action occurred prior to a given time in the past: By the time he turned forty, he **had earned** enough money for retirement.

- To indicate that a past action occurred prior to another past action: She **had** already **mailed** the letter when she realized her mistake.

- To emphasize the point of preceding discourse: I spent the morning in my office. I shelved all my books, arranged the furniture, hung a few photographs, and learned to use the computer. My new job **had begun.**

The future perfect tense consists of two auxiliaries, *will* and *have*, along with the past participle of the main verb. There is only one form of the future perfect tense.

Future Perfect Tense

I, you, he, she, it, we, they **will have worked**

The future perfect tense refers to an action that is to be completed prior to a future time.

> **USE OF THE FUTURE PERFECT TENSE**
>
> ■ To refer to future completion of an action: By this time next year, I **will have finished** medical school.

(4) Perfect progressive tenses

Perfect progressive tenses combine the forms and meanings of the progressive and the perfect tenses. The present perfect progressive form consists of two auxiliaries, *have* and *be,* plus the present participle (*-ing* form) of the main verb. The form of the auxiliary *have* varies with person and number. The auxiliary *be* appears as the past participle, *been.*

Present Perfect Progressive Tense		
	Singular	Plural
First person	I have been working	We have been working
Second person	You have been working	You have been working
Third person	He, she, it has been working	They have been working

The present perfect progressive signals that an action, state, or event originating in the past is ongoing or incomplete.

> **USES OF THE PRESENT PERFECT PROGRESSIVE TENSE**
>
> ■ To signal that a state of being is ongoing: I **have been feeling** tired for a week.
>
> ■ To indicate that an action is incomplete: We **have been organizing** the conference since April.

The past perfect progressive tense follows the pattern *had* + *been* + present participle (*-ing* form) of the main verb. (The auxiliary *have* is in the past tense.)

Past Perfect Progressive Tense
I, you, he, she, it, we, they **had been working**

The past perfect progressive tense refers to a situation or an action occurring over a period of time in the past and prior to another past action.

> **USE OF THE PAST PERFECT PROGRESSIVE TENSE**
>
> ■ To indicate that an ongoing action occurred prior to a past action: She **had been living** so frugally all year that she saved enough money for a new car.

The future perfect progressive form has the pattern *will* + *have* + *been* + present participle (*-ing* form) of the main verb.

> **Future Perfect Progressive Tense**
>
> I, you, he, she, it, we, they **will have been working**

The future perfect progressive tense refers to an action that is occurring in the present and will continue to occur for a specific amount of time.

> **USE OF THE FUTURE PERFECT PROGRESSIVE TENSE**
>
> ■ To indicate that an action will continue until a specified time:
> In one month, I **will have been working** on this project for five years.

Exercise 1

Explain how the meaning of each sentence changes when the verb tense changes.

1. In "Fiji's Rainbow Reef," Les Kaufman (describes/described) the coral reefs of Fiji and (discusses/discussed) the factors affecting their health.
2. Rising water temperatures (damaged/have damaged/did damage) the reefs.
3. The algae that (provide/provided) color (do not survive/did not survive) in the warmer water.
4. The lack of algae (has left/had left) the coral "bleached."
5. Strangely, though, new life (is flourishing/was flourishing/has been flourishing) in some of these areas.
6. Scientists (study/will study) this area to understand its resilience.

(5) Using verb tenses to convey the duration or time sequence of actions and events

When you use more than one tense in a single sentence, you give readers information about how actions or events are related in time and duration.

Whenever the teacher **calls** on me, I **stutter** nervously.
[Verbs in the present tense indicate habitual actions.]

When the speaker **had finished,** everyone **applauded.**
[The past perfect tense *had finished* indicates a time before the action expressed by *applauded.*]

Infinitives and participles can be used to express time relations within a sentence. The present infinitive (*to* + base form) of a verb expresses action occurring later than the action expressed by the main verb.

They <u>**want to design**</u> a new museum. [The action of designing will take place in the future.]

The perfect infinitive (*to* + *have* + past participle) signals that an action, state, or event is potential or hypothetical or that it did not occur.

She <u>**hopes to have earned**</u> her degree by the end of next year.
[Earning the degree has the potential to occur.]

The governor <u>**would like to have postponed**</u> the vote.
[The postponement did not occur.]

The present participle (*-ing* form) indicates simultaneous or previous action.

Laughing loudly, the old friends **left** the restaurant arm in arm.
[The friends were laughing as they were leaving.]

Hearing that she was ill, I **rushed** right over.
[The action of hearing occurred first.]

The perfect participle (*having* + past participle) expresses action completed before the action conveyed by the main verb.

Having learned Spanish at an early age, she **spoke** to the Mexican diplomats in their native language.

The past participle can be used to express either simultaneous action or previous action.

Led by a former Peace Corps worker, the volunteers **provided** medical assistance. [The two actions occurred simultaneously.]

Encouraged by job prospects, he **moved** to Atlanta. [The encouragement preceded the move.]

Exercise 2

Revise the following sentences so that all verbs express logical time sequences.

1. We expected the storm to have bypassed our town, but it made a direct hit.
2. We would like to have prior notice; however, even the police officers were taken by surprise.
3. Not having known much about flooding, the emergency crew was at a disadvantage.
4. Having thrown sandbags all day, the volunteers had been exhausted by 5 p.m.
5. They went home, succeeding in preventing a major disaster.

46b   AUXILIARY VERBS

Auxiliary verbs add nuances of meaning to main verbs (24a(4)). Some provide information about time (46a), while others are used to provide emphasis, to form questions, or to indicate ability, certainty, obligation, and so on.

(1) The auxiliary verb *do*

Unlike *be* and *have*, the auxiliary verb *do* does not occur with other verbs to indicate tense. Instead, it is used in questions, negations, and emphatic sentences.

> **Do** you have any questions? [question]
>
> I **do** not have any questions. [negation]
>
> I **do** have a few comments. [emphatic sentence]

The auxiliary *do* is used only in the simple present (*do, does*) and the simple past (*did*).

(2) Modal verbs

The modal auxiliary verbs in English are *can, could, may, might, must, shall, should, will,* and *would* (24a(4)). English also has **phrasal modals**, which are modal auxiliaries consisting of more than one word. They have meanings similar to those of one-word modals.

> *be able to* (ability): We **were able to** find the original document.
>
> *have to* (obligation): You **have to** report your test results.

Other common phrasal modals are *be going to, be supposed to, had better, need to,* and *used to*. Modal auxiliaries and phrasal modals can sometimes be combined. The modal precedes the phrasal modal.

> I <u>**should**</u> be able to finish the project by Tuesday.
>
> He <u>**may**</u> have to move to another city.

Both modal auxiliaries and phrasal modals indicate a variety of meanings, including obligation, permission, and probability. Modal auxiliaries have only two forms: the base form and the perfective form (base form + *have* + past participle). Most phrasal modals have more than two forms (*am able to, is able to, were able to, has been able to*). Only *had better* and *used to* have a single form. The following box shows the most common uses of modal verbs in academic writing.

USING MODAL VERBS

Modal Auxiliaries

Verb	Meaning	Example(s)
can	Ability or possibility	New legislation **can** change tax rates. Anything **can** happen.
could	Possibility	The announcement **could** cause unrest.
may	Possibility	Funding **may** be the problem.
must	Obligation or necessity	Judges **must** be neutral. There **must** be a better answer.
should	Obligation or advice	Dissent **should** be acknowledged. You **should** pay off your credit-card balance.
will	Prediction or certainty	She **will** perform the experiment herself. A statistical analysis **will** be performed.
would	Prediction	All **would** benefit from fewer obligations.

Modal Auxiliaries with *Have* + Past Participle

Verb	Meaning	Example
may have	Conjecture	The tank **may have** leaked.
might have	Conjecture	The accident **might have** caused the delay.
must have	Conjecture	The police **must have** known about the protest.
should have	Criticism	Monitors **should have** reported the incident.

Phrasal Modals in the Present Tense

Verb	Meaning	Example(s)
be able to	Ability	They **are able to** respond quickly to emergencies.
have to	Obligation or necessity	The president **has to** attend the meeting. The water for the experiment **has to** be cold.
need to	Obligation or necessity	Students **need to** register for class this week. A good summary **needs to** be objective.

Phrasal Modals in the Past Tense

Verb	Meaning	Example
was/were able to	Ability	They **were able to** finish on time.
had to	Obligation	The journalist **had to** divulge his sources.

❶ CAUTION

Although English verbs are often followed by the infinitive marker *to* (as in *want to go* and *plan to leave*), modal auxiliaries are not.

We **should ~~to~~** finish our report by Friday.

Exercise 3

Fill in the blank with a modal auxiliary or a phrasal modal and describe the meaning it conveys.

1. Nations at war _____ follow the Geneva Conventions.

2. Everyone _____ be treated humanely.

3. In various wars, humanitarian groups _____ protect innocent victims.

4. Without humanitarian groups, many more people _____ lost their lives.

5. Critics of past wars state that more aid _____ been provided.

46c   PREPOSITIONAL VERBS AND PHRASAL VERBS

Prepositional verbs and phrasal verbs are both combinations of verbs with other words. A prepositional verb consists of a verb followed by a preposition; a phrasal verb consists of a verb followed by a particle.

(1) Prepositional verbs

Some verbs are typically followed by prepositions. Such verbs can be used in either the active voice or the passive voice (**24c**). Following are ten prepositional verbs that commonly occur in academic writing. Some are more often used in the active voice; others are more often used in the passive voice.

TEN PREPOSITIONAL VERBS COMMON IN ACADEMIC WRITING	
Active Voice	**Passive Voice**
depend on	be applied to
lead to	be derived from
look at	be divided into
refer to	be known as
result in	be used in

When you are reading, take note of prepositions that are combined with specific verbs.

(2) Phrasal verbs

A **phrasal verb** consists of a verb and a particle such as *up, out,* or *on.* A phrasal verb is often idiomatic, conveying a meaning that differs from the common meanings of the individual words. For example, the definitions that first come to mind for the words *blow* and *up* are not likely to help you understand the phrasal verb *blow up* when it means "to enlarge."

She **blew up** the photograph so that she could see the faces better.

Like verbs in general, phrasal verbs may have more than one meaning. *To blow up* means not only "to enlarge" but also "to inflate" or "to explode."

It is also important to note that a given verb can combine with several different particles. *Take* occurs with various particles to form the phrasal verbs *take in* ("understand"), *take on* ("undertake"), *take out* ("remove"), *take up* ("consume"), and *take down* ("dismantle"). In addition to *take*, the following verbs often appear in academic writing as phrasal verbs: *go, come, get, set, carry, turn, bring, look,* and *put.* The meanings of the phrasal verbs depend on the specific particle they include.

A small group of phrasal verbs have meanings that are similar to common definitions of the verbs themselves; their particles just add a sense of completion or emphasis.

They **wrote up** the report by six o'clock.

The particle *up* in *wrote up* does not refer to a direction; instead, it emphasizes the completion of the report. Still other phrasal verbs retain the common meanings of the verb and the particle.

The protesters **hung up** a banner.

The verb and particle in most phrasal verbs may be separated by a short noun phrase (**21a(1)**).

She **called** the meeting **off.** OR She **called off** the meeting.

If you use a pronoun with a phrasal verb, always place it between the verb and the particle.

The student **turned** <u>it</u> **in** yesterday.

Some phrasal verbs are not separable, however.

The group **went over** the proposal.

I **came across** an interesting fact.

You should be able to find the definitions of phrasal verbs in a conventional dictionary; however, a specialized dictionary will also provide information about the separability of these verbs. (See **33d** for a list of dictionaries.)

Exercise 4

Insert an appropriate preposition or particle after the verb in each sentence.

1. Overpopulation has brought _____ great changes on earth.

2. Deforestation often leads _____ extinctions.

3. High levels of carbon dioxide result _____ increased global temperatures.

4. Proposals for curbing emissions should be looked _____ closely.

5. Scientists have taken _____ the challenge of slowing the destruction.

46d PARTICIPLES USED AS ADJECTIVES

Both present participles (such as *amazing* and *interesting*) and past participles (*amazed* and *interested*) can be used as adjectives; however, they are not interchangeable. For example, when you want to indicate an emotion, use a present participle with a noun referring to someone or something that is the cause of the emotion. In the phrase *the exciting tennis match,* the tennis match is the cause of the excitement. Use the past participle with a noun referring to someone who experiences an emotion. In the phrase *the excited crowd,* the crowd is experiencing the excitement.

The following participles are commonly used as adjectives describing emotions.

PRESENT AND PAST PARTICIPLES USED AS ADJECTIVES

Causing the emotion	Experiencing the emotion
amazing	amazed
annoying	annoyed
boring	bored
confusing	confused
embarrassing	embarrassed
exciting	excited
interesting	interested
surprising	surprised
tiring	tired

Exercise 5

Choose the correct form of each participle.

1. My uncle is interesting/interested in most but not all sports.
2. He was exciting/excited by the World Cup matches in South Africa.
3. However, he did not like the annoying/annoyed sound of the vuvuzelas.
4. Soccer is his favorite sport; baseball he finds boring/bored.
5. He jokes that being a sports fan is a tiring/tired job.

47 ‖ WORD ORDER

The general order in an English sentence is subject-verb-object; however, few sentences consist of just three words. To help you understand and write sentences that are longer and more varied, this chapter discusses

- the appropriate sequence for adjectives (**47a**),
- the placement of adverbs of frequency (**47b**),
- the order of adverbs and direct objects (**47c**), and
- the order of words within certain clauses (**47d**).

47a   ORDERING ADJECTIVES

In English, two or three adjectives modifying the same noun are used in a particular order based on their meanings. (The use of more than two consecutive adjectives is rare.) The following list shows the usual order for adjectives of different types and gives examples of each type:

Evaluator	*fascinating, painful, content*
Size	*large, long, small, short*
Shape	*square, round, triangular*
Age	*young, old, aged, newborn, antique*
Color	*black, white, green, brown*
Origin	*Arabian, Cuban, Peruvian, Slavic*
Material	*silk, paper, pine, rubber*

We visited a **fascinating Italian** village. [evaluator, origin]

An **old black** dog stared at us. [age, color]

47b   PLACING ADVERBS OF FREQUENCY

Adverbs of frequency (such as *always, never, sometimes,* and *often*) appear before one-word verbs.

He **rarely** <u>goes</u> to horror movies.

However, these adverbs appear after a form of *be* when it is the main verb.

Novels written by Stephen King <u>are</u> **always** popular.

When a sentence contains more than one verb in a verb phrase, the adverb of frequency is placed after the first auxiliary verb.

My friends <u>have</u> **never** <u>read</u> *The Shining*.

47c   PLACING ADVERBS AND DIRECT OBJECTS

An adverb may be placed after a verb when the verb has no direct object (**20c**).

They worked **efficiently.**

Revise any sentence that includes an adverb before a direct object.

I read ~~quickly~~ the letter_∧ quickly.   OR   I_∧ quickly read ~~quickly~~ the letter.

Exercise 1

Correct the misplaced words in the following sentences.

1. Sam made a short amazing video.
2. He never has made a better video than this one.
3. He posted immediately it on his blog.
4. He used green strange lighting in all the action scenes.
5. Sam uses always a handheld camera.

47d ORDERING WORDS WITHIN CLAUSES

The word order of embedded questions and adjectival clauses (21b) differs from the standard subject-verb-object order of clauses.

(1) Embedded questions

The word order of questions and embedded questions is not the same. Notice the difference in each of the following pairs of sentences:

Is the source reliable? [question]

I do not know whether **the source is** reliable. [embedded question]

How **was the source evaluated?** [question]

He explained how **the source was evaluated.** [embedded question]

Does the author make a good argument? [question]

We should decide whether **the author makes** a good argument. [embedded question]

In the question in each pair, the subject and the verb (or the auxiliary verb if there is one) are inverted; in the embedded question, they are not. The auxiliary verb *do* is not used in embedded questions.

If a question begins with an interrogative pronoun such as *who* or *what* as the subject, the order of the question and the embedded question are the same.

Who worked on the project? [question]

They did not mention **who worked on the project.** [embedded question]

(2) Adjectival clauses

When a clause is used to modify a noun or pronoun, it is an adjectival clause. An adjectival clauses begins with a relative pronoun such as *that, which,* or *who* (**21b**). If the relative pronoun is the subject of the clause, the word order of the clause is standard.

$$\overset{\text{s}}{\underline{\text{Twitter}}} \overset{\text{v}}{\underline{\text{is based}}}$$ in San Francisco, California.

Twitter, $\overset{\text{s}}{\underline{\text{which}}}$ $\overset{\text{v}}{\underline{\text{is based}}}$ in San Francisco, California, has users from around the world.

If the relative pronoun is *not* the subject of the adjectival clause, the word that is the subject will not be the first word in the clause.

Protestors sent $\overset{do}{\underline{\textbf{tweets.}}}$

$\overset{do}{\underline{\text{Tweets}}}$ $\overset{}{\underline{\textbf{that}}}$ $\overset{\text{s}}{\underline{\textbf{protestors}}}$ $\overset{\text{v}}{\underline{\textbf{sent}}}$ to journalists were highly effective.

Notice in the preceding sentence that the adjectival clause "that protestors sent" begins with the direct object, so no direct object follows the verb *sent*.

Tweets **that** protestors sent ~~them~~ to journalists were highly effective.

Exercise 2

Revise the word order of each sentence.

1. The Human Genome Project, which Francis Collins initiated it, turned into an international effort.

2. Prior to 1953, scientists did not know for certain was the structure of DNA a double helix.

3. The discovery of the double helix, which James D. Watson and Francis Crick described it in 1953, eventually led to the study of human genetics.

4. Without an understanding of gene sequences, scientists would not know how do people inherit traits.

5. No one can predict with certainty how will people in the future use this knowledge.

GLOSSARY OF USAGE

The term *usage* refers to the ways words are used in specific contexts. As you know from speaking and writing every day, the words you choose depend on your audience and your purpose. By consulting the entries in this glossary, you will increase your ability to use words effectively. Many of the entries describe the contexts in which words are used; others distinguish between words that sound or look similar.

The labels below will help you choose appropriate words for your rhetorical situation. Be aware that the idea of standard usage may carry with it the assumption that words not considered standard are inferior. Words labeled "nonstandard" are commonly condemned, even though they may be words some people have grown up hearing and using. A better way to describe usage is to identify what is conventional, or accepted practice, for a specific rhetorical situation.

Conventional Words or phrases listed in dictionaries without special usage labels; generally considered appropriate in academic and professional writing.

Conversational Words or phrases that dictionaries label *informal, slang,* or *colloquial;* although often used in informal speech and writing, not generally appropriate for formal writing assignments.

Unconventional Words or phrases not generally considered appropriate in academic or professional writing and often labeled *nonstandard* in dictionaries; best avoided in formal contexts.

Agreement on usage occurs slowly, often after a period of debate. In this glossary, entries are marked with an asterisk (*) when new usages have been reported by dictionary editors but may not yet be accepted by everyone.

a lot of   *A lot of* is conversational for *many, much,* or *a great deal of:* They do not have ~~a lot of~~ **much** time. *A lot* is sometimes misspelled as *alot.*

a while, awhile   *A while* means "a period of time." It is often used with the prepositions *after, for,* and *in:* We rested for **a while.** *Awhile* means "a short time." It is not preceded by a preposition: We rested **awhile.**

accept, except   The verb *accept* means "to receive": I **accept** your apology. The verb *except* means "to exclude": The policy was to have everyone wait in line, but parents with mothers and small children were **excepted.** The preposition *except* means "other than": All **except** Joe will attend the conference.

advice, advise   *Advice* is a noun: They asked their attorney for **advice.** *Advise* is a verb: The attorney **advised** us to save all relevant documents.

affect, effect   *Affect* is a verb that means "to influence": The lobbyist's pleas did not **affect** the politician's decision. The noun *effect* means "a result": The **effect** of his decision on the staff's morale was positive and long lasting. When used as a verb, *effect* means "to produce" or "to cause": The activists believed that they could **effect** real political change.

agree on, agree to, agree with   *Agree on* means "to be in accord with others about something": We **agreed on** a date for the conference. *Agree to* means "to accept something" or "to consent to do something": The customer **agreed to** our terms. The negotiators **agreed to** conclude talks by midnight. *Agree with* means "to share an opinion with someone" or "to approve of something": I **agree with** you on this issue. No one **agreed with** his position.

all ready, already   *All ready* means "completely prepared": The rooms are **all ready** for the conference. *Already* means "by or before the time specified": She has **already** taken her final exams.

*all right   *All right* means "acceptable": The students asked whether it was **all right** to use dictionaries during the exam. *Alright* is not yet a generally accepted spelling of *all right,* although it is becoming more common in journalistic writing.

all together, altogether   *All together* means "as a group": The cast reviewed the script **all together.** *Altogether* means "wholly, thoroughly": That game is **altogether** too difficult.

allude, elude   *Allude* means "to refer to indirectly": The professor **alluded** to a medieval text. *Elude* means "to evade" or "to escape from": For the moment, his name **eludes** me.

allusion, illusion   An *allusion* is a casual or indirect reference: The **allusion** was to Shakespeare's *Twelfth Night.* An *illusion* is a false idea or an unreal image: His idea of college is an **illusion.**

alot See **a lot of.**

already See **all ready, already.**

alright See **all right.**

altogether See **all together, altogether.**

a.m., p.m. Use these abbreviations only with numerals: The show will begin at 7:00 **p.m.** [COMPARE: The show will begin at seven *in the evening.*]

*__among, between__ To follow traditional usage, use *among* with three or more entities (a group): The snorkelers swam **among** the fish. Use *between* when referring to only two entities: The rivalry **between** the two teams is intense. Current dictionaries also note the possibility of using *between* to refer to more than two entities, especially when these entities are considered distinct: We have strengthened the lines of communication **between** the various departments.

amount of, number of Use *amount of* before nouns that cannot be counted: The **amount of** rain that fell last year was insufficient. Use *number of* with nouns that can be counted: The **number of** students attending college has increased.

and/or This combination denotes three options: one, the other, or both. These options can also be presented separately with *or:* The student's application should be signed by a parent **and/or** a teacher. The student's application should be signed by a parent, a teacher, **or** both.

*__angry at, angry with__ Both *at* and *with* are commonly used after *angry*, although according to traditional guidelines, *with* should be used when a person is the cause of the anger: She was **angry with** me because I was late. Many voters were **angry at** the newspaper's coverage of the debate.

another, other, the other *Another* is followed by a singular noun: **another** book. *Other* is followed by a plural noun: **other** books. *The other* is followed by either a singular or a plural noun: **the other book, the other books.**

anymore, any more *Anymore* meaning "any longer" or "now" most frequently occurs in negative sentences: Sarah doesn't work here **anymore.** Its use in positive sentences is considered conversational; *now* is generally used instead: All he ever does ~~anymore~~ **now** is watch television. As two words, *any more* appears with *not* to mean "no more": We do not have **any more** time.

anyone, any one *Anyone* means "any person at all": We did not know **anyone.** *Any one* refers to one of a group: **Any one** of the options is better than the current situation.

*anyplace, everyplace, someplace These words are becoming increasingly common in academic writing. However, according to traditional usage rules, they should be replaced by *anywhere, everywhere,* and *somewhere.*

as Conversational when used after such verbs as *know, say,* and *see.* Use *that, if,* or *whether* instead: I do not know ~~as~~ **whether** my application is complete. Also considered conversational is the use of *as* instead of *who, which,* or *that:* Many of the performers ~~as~~ **who** have appeared on our program will be giving a concert this evening.

as, because The use of *as* to signal a cause may be vague; if it is, use *because* instead: ~~As~~ **Because** we were running out of gas, we turned around.

*as, like According to traditional usage, *as* begins either a phrase or a clause; *like* begins only a phrase: My brother drives too fast, just ~~like~~ **as** my father did. Current dictionaries note the informal use of *like* to begin clauses, especially after verbs such as *look, feel,* and *sound.*

assure, ensure, insure *Assure* means "to state with confidence, alleviating any doubt": The flight attendant **assured** us that our flight would arrive on time. *Ensure* and *insure* are usually interchangeable to mean "make certain," but only *insure* means "to protect against loss": The editor **ensured** [OR **insured**] that the reporter's facts were accurate. Physicians must **insure** themselves against malpractice suits.

awhile See **a while, awhile.**

bad Unconventional as an adverb; use *badly* instead. The team played **badly.** However, the adjective *bad* is used after sensory verbs such as *feel, look,* and *smell:* I feel **bad** that I forgot to return your book yesterday.

because See **as, because.**

being as, being that Unconventional; use *because* instead. ~~Being as~~ **Because** the road was closed, traffic was diverted to another route.

*beside, besides According to traditional usage, these two words have different meanings. *Beside* means "next to": The president sat **beside** the prime minister. *Besides* means "in addition to" or "other than": She has written many articles **besides** those on political reform. Current dictionaries report that professional writers regularly use *beside* to convey this meaning, as long as there is no risk of ambiguity.

better, had better *Better* is conversational. Use *had better* instead: We ~~better~~ **had better** finish the report by five o'clock.

between See **among, between.**

*bring, take Both words describe the same action but from different standpoints. *Bring* indicates movement toward the writer: She **brought** me some flowers. *Take* implies movement away from the writer: He **took** my overdue books to the library. Dictionaries report that this distinction is often blurred when the writer's position is ambiguous or irrelevant: He **brought** [OR **took**] her some flowers.

bunch Conversational to refer to a group: A ~~bunch~~ **group** of students participated in the experiment.

*****can, may** *Can* refers to ability, and *may* refers to permission: You **can** [are able to] drive seventy miles an hour, but you **may** not [are not permitted to] exceed the speed limit. Current dictionaries report that in contemporary usage *can* and *may* are used interchangeably to denote possibility or permission, although *may* is used more frequently in formal contexts.

can't hardly, can't scarcely Unconventional. Use *can hardly* or *can scarcely:* The students **can't hardly** wait for summer vacation.

capital, capitol As a noun, *capital* means either "a governing city" or "funds": The **capital** of Minnesota is St. Paul. An anonymous donor provided the **capital** for the project. As a modifier, *capital* means "chief" or "principal": This year's election is of **capital** importance. It may also refer to the death penalty: **Capital** punishment is legal in some states. A *capitol* is a statehouse; the *Capitol* is the U.S. congressional building in Washington, DC.

censor, censure, sensor As a verb, *censor* means "to remove or suppress because of immoral or otherwise objectionable ideas": Do you think a ratings board should **censor** films? As a noun, *censor* refers to a person who is authorized to remove material considered objectionable: The **censor** recommended that the book be banned. The verb *censure* means "to blame or criticize"; the noun *censure* is an expression of disapproval or blame. The Senate **censured** Joseph McCarthy. He received a **censure** from the Senate. A *sensor* is a device that responds to a stimulus: The **sensor** detects changes in light.

center around Conversational for "to center on" or "to revolve around": The discussion **centered** ~~around~~ **on** the public's response to tax-reform initiatives.

cite, site, sight *Cite* means "to mention": Be sure to **cite** your sources. *Site* is a location: The president visited the **site** for the new library. As a verb, *site* also means "to situate": The builder **sited** the factory near the freeway. The verb *sight* means "to see": The crew **sighted** land. As a noun, *sight* refers to the ability to see or to a view: Her **sight** worsened as she aged. What an incredible **sight!**

climactic, climatic *Climactic* refers to a climax, or high point: The actors rehearsed the **climactic** scene. *Climatic* refers to the *climate:* Many environmentalists are worried about the recent **climatic** changes.

coarse, course *Coarse* refers to roughness: The jacket was made of **coarse** linen. *Course* refers to a route: Our **course** to the island was indirect. *Course* may also refer to a plan of study: I want to take a **course** in nutrition.

compare to, compare with *Compare to* means "to regard as similar," and *compare with* means "to examine for similarities and/or differences": She **compared** her mind **to** a dusty attic. The student **compared** the first draft **with** the second.

complement, complementary, compliment, complimentary *Complement* means "to complete" or "to balance": Their personalities **complement** each other. They have **complementary** personalities. *Compliment* means "to express praise": The professor **complimented** the students on their first drafts. Her remarks were **complimentary.** *Complimentary* may also mean "provided free of charge": We received **complimentary** tickets.

***compose, comprise** *Compose* means "to make up": That collection **is composed** of medieval manuscripts. *Comprise* means "to consist of": The anthology **comprises** many famous essays. Dictionary editors have noted the increasing use of *comprise* in the passive voice to mean "to be composed of."

conscience, conscious, consciousness *Conscience* means "the sense of right and wrong": He examined his **conscience** before deciding whether to join the protest. *Conscious* means "awake": After an hour, the patient was fully **conscious.** After an hour, the patient regained **consciousness.** *Conscious* may also mean "aware": We were **conscious** of the possible consequences.

continual, continually, continuous, continuously *Continual* means "constantly recurring": **Continual** interruptions kept us from completing the project. Telephone calls **continually** interrupted us. *Continuous* means "uninterrupted": The job applicant had a record of ten years' **continuous** employment. The job applicant worked **continuously** from 2000 to 2009.

***convince, persuade** *Convince* means "to make someone believe something": His passionate speech **convinced** us that school reform was necessary. *Persuade* means "to motivate someone to act": She **persuaded** us to stop smoking. Dictionary editors note that many speakers now use *convince* as a synonym for *persuade.*

could of *Of* is often mistaken for the sound of the unstressed *have:* They **could of have** [OR might **have,** should **have,** would **have**] gone home.

couldn't care less *Couldn't care less* expresses complete lack of concern: She **couldn't care less** about her reputation. *Could care less* is considered unconventional in academic writing.

council, counsel A *council* is an advisory or decision-making group: The student **council** supported the new regulations. A *counsel* is a legal adviser: The defense **counsel** conferred with the judge. As a verb, *counsel* means "to give advice": She **counsels** people with eating disorders.

criteria, criterion *Criteria* is a plural noun meaning "a set of standards for judgment": The teachers explained the **criteria** for the assignment. The singular form is *criterion:* Their judgment was based on only one **criterion.**

*data *Data* is the plural form of *datum,* which means "piece of information" or "fact": When the **data are** complete, we will know the true cost. However, current dictionaries also note that *data* is frequently used as a mass entity (like the word *furniture*), appearing with a singular verb.

desert, dessert *Desert* can mean "a barren land": Gila monsters live in the **deserts** of the Southwest. As a verb, *desert* means "to leave": I thought my friends had **deserted** me. *Dessert* refers to something sweet eaten at the end of a meal: They ordered apple pie for **dessert.**

device, devise *Device* is a noun: She invented a **device** that measures extremely small quantities of liquid. *Devise* is a verb: We **devised** a plan for work distribution.

dialogue Many readers consider the use of *dialogue* as a verb to be an example of unnecessary jargon. Use *discuss* or *exchange views* instead: The committee members ~~dialogued about~~ discussed the issues.

differ from, differ with *Differ from* means "to be different": A bull snake **differs from** a rattlesnake in a number of ways. *Differ with* means "to disagree": Senator Brown has **differed with** Senator Owen on several issues.

different from, different than *Different from* is generally used with nouns, pronouns, noun phrases, and noun clauses: This school was **different from** most others. The school was **different from** what we had expected. *Different than* is used with adverbial clauses; *than* is the conjunction: We are no **different than** they are.

discreet, discrete *Discreet* means "showing good judgment or self-restraint": His friends complained openly, but his comments were quite **discreet.** *Discrete* means "distinct": The participants in the study came from three **discrete** groups.

disinterested, uninterested *Disinterested* means "impartial": A **disinterested** observer will give a fair opinion. *Uninterested* means "lacking interest": She was **uninterested** in the outcome of the game.

distinct, distinctive *Distinct* means "easily distinguished or perceived": Each proposal has **distinct** advantages. *Distinctive* means "characteristic" or "serving to distinguish": We studied the **distinctive** features of hawks.

****due to** Traditionally, *due to* was not synonymous with *because of:* ~~Due to~~ **Because of** holiday traffic, we arrived an hour late. However, dictionary editors now consider this usage of *due to* acceptable.

dyeing, dying *Dyeing* comes from *dye,* meaning "to color something, usually by soaking it": As a sign of solidarity, the students are **dyeing** their shirts the same color. *Dying* refers to the loss of life: Because of the drought, the plants are **dying.**

effect See **affect, effect.**

e.g. Abbreviation of *exempli gratia,* meaning "for example." Use only within parentheses: Digestive problems may be treated with herbs (**e.g.,** peppermint and fennel). Otherwise, replace *e.g.* with the English equivalent, *for example:* Social media differ from traditional media, ~~e.g.,~~ **for example,** television and newspapers. Do not confuse *e.g.* with *i.e.,* meaning "that is."

elicit, illicit *Elicit* means "to draw forth": He is **eliciting** contributions for a new playground. *Illicit* means "unlawful": The newspaper reported their **illicit** mishandling of public funds.

elude See **allude, elude.**

emigrate from, immigrate to *Emigrate* means "to leave one's own country": My ancestors **emigrated from** Ireland. *Immigrate* means "to arrive in a different country to settle": The Ulster Scots **immigrated to** the southern United States.

eminent, imminent *Eminent* means "distinguished": An **eminent** scholar in physics will be giving a public lecture tomorrow. *Imminent* means "about to happen": The merger of the two companies is **imminent.**

ensure See **assure, ensure, insure.**

enthuse Many readers object to the use of *enthuse.* Use *enthusiastic* or *enthusiastically* instead: Students ~~enthused~~ **spoke enthusiastically** about the new climbing wall. They were ~~enthused~~ **enthusiastic** about the new climbing wall.

especially, specially *Especially* emphasizes a characteristic or quality: Some people are **especially** sensitive to the sun. *Especially* also means "particularly": Wildflowers are abundant in this area, **especially** during May. *Specially* means "for a particular purpose": The classroom was **specially** designed for music students.

etc. Abbreviation of *et cetera,* meaning "and others of the same kind." Use only within parentheses: Be sure to bring appropriate camping gear (tent, sleeping bag, mess kit, **etc.**). Because *and* is part of the meaning of *etc.,* avoid using the combination *and etc.*

eventually, ultimately *Eventually* refers to some future time: She has made so many valuable contributions that I am sure she will **eventually** become the store supervisor. *Ultimately* refers to the final outcome after a series of events: The course was difficult but **ultimately** worthwhile.

everyday, every day *Everyday* means "routine" or "ordinary": These are **everyday** problems. *Every day* means "each day": I read the newspaper **every day.**

everyone, every one *Everyone* means "all": **Everyone** should attend. *Every one* refers to each person or item in a group: **Every one** of you should attend.

everyplace See **anyplace, everyplace, someplace.**

except See **accept, except.**

explicit, implicit *Explicit* means "expressed clearly and directly": Given his **explicit** directions, we knew how to proceed. *Implicit* means "implied or expressed indirectly": I mistakenly understood his silence to be his **implicit** approval of the project.

farther, further Generally, *farther* refers to geographic distance: We will have to drive **farther** tomorrow. *Further* means "more": If you need **further** assistance, please let me know.

****feel** Traditionally, *feel* was not synonymous with "think" or "believe": I **feel think** that more should be done to protect local habitat. Dictionary editors now consider this use of *feel* to be a standard alternative.

fewer, less *Fewer* occurs before nouns that can be counted: **fewer** technicians, **fewer** pencils. *Less* occurs before nouns that cannot be counted: **less** milk, **less** support. *Less than* may be used with measurements of time or distance: **less than** three months, **less than** twenty miles.

****first, firstly; second, secondly** Many college instructors prefer the use of *first* and *second*. However, dictionary editors state that *firstly* and *secondly* are also well-established forms.

foreword, forward A *foreword* is an introduction: The **foreword** to the book provided useful background information. *Forward* refers to a frontward direction: To get a closer look, we moved **forward** slowly.

former, latter Used together, *former* refers to the first of two; *latter* to the second of two. John and Ian are both English. The **former** is from Manchester; the **latter** is from Birmingham.

further See **farther, further.**

get Considered conversational in many common expressions: The weather ~~got better~~ **improved** overnight. I did not know what he ~~was getting at~~ **meant.**

good, well *Good* is an adjective, not an adverb: He pitched ~~good~~ **well** last night. *Good* in the sense of "in good health" may be used interchangeably with *well:* I feel **good** [OR **well**] this morning.

had better See **better, had better.**

half *A half a* or *a half an* is unconventional; use *half a/an* or *a half:* You should be able to complete the questionnaire in **a half ~~an~~** hour.

hanged, hung *Hanged* means "put to death by hanging": The prisoner was **hanged** at dawn. For all other meanings, use *hung:* He **hung** the picture above his desk.

hardly See **can't hardly, can't scarcely.**

has got, have got Conversational; omit *got:* I **have ~~got~~** a meeting tomorrow.

he/she, his/her As a solution to the problem of sexist language, these combinations are not universally accepted. Consider using *he or she* and *his or her.* See **33c.**

herself, himself, myself, yourself Unconventional as subjects in a sentence. Joe and ~~myself~~ **I** will lead the discussion. See **25a(2).**

hopefully According to traditional usage, *hopefully* means "with hope," not "it is hoped": **Hopefully,** the negotiators discussed the proposed treaty. However, dictionary editors have accepted the use of *hopefully* as a sentence modifier: **Hopefully,** the treaty will be ratified. If your instructor prefers you to follow traditional usage, use *I hope* in such a sentence: **I hope** the treaty will be ratified.

hung See **hanged, hung.**

i.e. Abbreviation of *id est,* meaning "that is." Use only within parentheses: All participants in the study ran the same distance (**i.e.,** six kilometers). Otherwise, replace *i.e.* with the English equivalent, *that is:* Assistance was offered to those who might have difficulty boarding, ~~i.e.,~~ **that is,** the elderly, the disabled, and parents with small children. Do not confuse *i.e.* with *e.g.,* meaning "for example."

illicit See **elicit, illicit.**

illusion See **allusion, illusion.**

immigrate See **emigrate from, immigrate to.**

imminent See **eminent, imminent.**

*****impact** Though *impact* is commonly used as a verb in business writing, many college teachers still use it as a noun only: The new tax ~~impacts~~ **affects** everyone.

implicit See **explicit, implicit.**

imply, infer *Imply* means "to suggest without actually stating": Though he never mentioned the statistics, he **implied** that they were questionable. *Infer* means "to draw a conclusion based on evidence": Given the tone of his voice, I **inferred** that he found the work substandard.

in regards to Unconventional; see **regard, regarding, regards.**

inside of, outside of Drop *of* when unnecessary: Security guards stood **out-side ~~of~~** the front door.

insure See **assure, ensure, insure.**

irregardless Unconventional; use *regardless* instead.

its, it's *Its* is a possessive form: The committee forwarded **its** recommendation. *It's* is a contraction of *it is* or *it has*: **It's** a beautiful day. **It's** been sunny for days.

-ize Some readers object to using this ending to create new verbs: *enronize*. Some of these new verbs, however, have already entered into common usage: *computerize*.

kind of a, sort of a The word *a* is unnecessary: This **kind of ~~a~~** book sells well. *Kind of* and *sort of* are not conventionally used to mean "somewhat": The report was ~~kind of~~ **somewhat** difficult to read.

later, latter *Later* means "after a specific time" or "a time after now": The concert ended **later** than we had expected. *Latter* refers to the second of two items: Of the two versions described, I prefer the **latter.**

lay, lie *Lay* (*laid, laying*) means "to put" or "to place": He **laid** the book aside. *Lie* (*lay, lain, lying*) means "to rest" or "to recline": I had just **lain** down when the alarm went off. *Lay* takes an object (to lay something); *lie* does not. These verbs may be confused because the present tense of *lay* and the past tense of *lie* are spelled the same way.

lead, led As a noun, *lead* means "a kind of metal": The paint had **lead** in it. As a verb, *lead* means "to conduct": A guide will **lead** a tour of the ruins. *Led* is the past tense of the verb *lead*: He **led** the country from 1949 to 1960.

less, less than See **fewer, less.**

lie See **lay, lie.**

like See **as, like.**

literally Conversational when used to emphasize the meaning of another word: I was ~~literally~~ **nearly** frozen after I finished shoveling the sidewalk. *Literally* is conventionally used to indicate that an expression is not being used figuratively: My friend **literally** climbs the walls after work; his fellow rock climbers join him at the local gym.

lose, loose *Lose* is a verb: She does not **lose** her patience often. *Loose* is chiefly used as an adjective: A few of the tiles are **loose.**

lots, lots of Conversational for *many* or *much:* He has ~~lots of~~ **many** friends. We have ~~lots~~ **much** to do before the end of the quarter.

mankind Considered sexist because it excludes women: All ~~mankind~~ **humanity** will benefit from this new discovery.

many, much *Many* is used with nouns that can be counted: **many** stores, too **many** assignments. *Much* is used with nouns that cannot be counted: **much** courage, not **much** time.

may See **can, may.**

may of, might of See **could of.**

maybe, may be *Maybe* is an adverb: **Maybe** the negotiators will succeed this time. *May* and *be* are verbs: The rumor **may be** true.

*****media, medium** According to traditional definitions, *media* is a plural word: The **media** have sometimes created the news in addition to reporting it. The singular form is *medium:* The newspaper is one **medium** that people seem to trust. Dictionary editors note the frequent use of *media* as a collective noun taking a singular verb, but this usage is still considered conversational.

might could Conversational for "might be able to": The director **might** ~~could~~ **be able to** review your application next week.

most Unconventional to mean "almost": We watch the news ~~most~~ **almost** every day.

much See **many, much.**

myself See **herself, himself, myself, yourself.**

neither . . . or *Nor,* not *or,* follows *neither:* The book is **neither** as funny ~~or~~ **nor** as original as critics have reported.

nothing like, nowhere near Unconventional; use *not nearly* instead: Her new book is ~~nowhere near~~ **not nearly** as mysterious as her previous novel.

number of When the expression *a number of* is used, the reference is plural: **A number of** positions **are** open. When *the number of* is used, the reference is singular: **The number of** possibilities **is** limited. See also **amount of, number of.**

off of Conversational; omit *of:* He walked **off ~~of~~** the field.

on account of Conversational; use *because of:* The singer canceled her engagement ~~**on account of**~~ **because of** a sore throat.

on the other hand Use *however* instead or make sure that the sentence or independent clause beginning with this transitional phrase is preceded by one starting with *on the one hand.*

other See **another, other, the other.**

passed, past *Passed* is the past tense of the verb *pass:* Deb **passed** the other runners right before the finish line. *Past* means "beyond a time or location": We walked **past** the high school.

per In ordinary contexts, use *a* or *an:* You should drink at least six glasses of water ~~**per**~~ **a** day.

percent, percentage *Percent* (also spelled *per cent*) is used with a specific number: **Sixty percent** of the students attended the ceremony. *Percentage* refers to an unspecified portion: The **percentage** of high school graduates attending college has increased in recent years.

perspective, prospective *Perspective* means "point of view": We discussed the issue from various **perspectives.** *Prospective* means "likely to become": **Prospective** journalists interviewed the editor in chief.

persuade See **convince, persuade.**

phenomena, phenomenon *Phenomena* is the plural form of *phenomenon:* Natural **phenomena** were given scientific explanations.

plus *Plus* joins nouns or noun phrases to make a sentence seem like an equation: Her endless curiosity **plus** her boundless energy makes her the perfect camp counselor. Note that a singular form of the verb is required (e.g., *makes*). *Plus* is not used to join clauses: I telephoned ~~**plus**~~ **and** I sent flowers.

p.m. See **a.m., p.m.**

precede, proceed To *precede* is to "go before": A moment of silence **preceded** the applause. To *proceed* is to "go forward": After stopping for a short rest, we **proceeded** to our destination.

prejudice, prejudiced *Prejudice* is a noun: They were unaware of their **prejudice.** *Prejudiced* is an adjective: She accused me of being **prejudiced.**

pretty *Pretty* means "attractive," not "rather" or "fairly": We were ~~**pretty**~~ **fairly** tired after cooking all day.

principal, principle As a noun, *principal* means "chief official": The **principal** greeted the students every day. It also means "capital": The loan's **principal** was still quite high. As an adjective, *principal* means "main": Tourism is the country's **principal** source of income. The noun *principle* refers to a rule, standard, or belief: She explained the three **principles** supporting the theory.

proceed See **precede, proceed.**

prospective See **perspective, prospective.**

quotation, quote In academic writing, *quotation,* rather than *quote,* refers to a sentence or passage repeated or copied from another source: She began her speech with a ~~quote~~ quotation from *Othello. Quote* expresses an action: My friend sometimes **quotes** lines from television commercials.

raise, rise *Raise* (*raised, raising*) means "to lift or cause to move upward, to bring up or increase": Retailers **raised** prices. *Rise* (*rose, risen, rising*) means "to get up" or "to ascend": The cost of living **rose** sharply. *Raise* takes an object (to **raise** something); *rise* does not.

real, really *Really* rather than *real* is used to mean "very": He is from a ~~real~~ **really** small town. To ensure this word's effectiveness, use it sparingly.

*****reason why** Traditionally, this combination was considered redundant: No one explained the reason ~~why~~ the negotiations failed. [OR No one explained ~~the reason~~ why the negotiations failed.] However, dictionary editors report its use by highly regarded writers.

regard, regarding, regards These forms are used in the following expressions: *in regard to, with regard to, as regards,* and *regarding* [NOT *in regards to, with regards to,* or *as regarding*].

*****relation, relationship** According to traditional definitions, *relation* is used to link abstractions: We studied the **relation** between language and social change. *Relationship* is used to link people: The **relationship** between the two friends grew strong. However, dictionary editors now label as standard the use of *relationship* to connect abstractions.

respectfully, respectively *Respectfully* means "showing respect": The children learned to treat one another **respectfully.** *Respectively* means "in the order designated": We discussed the issue with the chair, the dean, and the provost, **respectively.**

rise See **raise, rise.**

sensor See **censor, censure, sensor.**

sensual, sensuous *Sensual* refers to gratification of the physical senses, often those associated with sexual pleasure: Frequently found in this music are

sensual dance rhythms. *Sensuous* refers to gratification of the senses in response to art, music, nature, and so on: **Sensuous** landscape paintings lined the walls of the gallery.

shall, will Traditionally, *shall* was used with *I* or *we* to express future tense, and *will* was used with the other personal pronouns, but *shall* has almost disappeared in contemporary American English. *Shall* is still used in legal writing to indicate an obligation.

should of See **could of.**

sight See **cite, site, sight.**

sit, set *Sit* means "to be seated": Jonathan **sat** in the front row. *Set* means "to place something": The research assistant **set** the chemicals on the counter. *Set* takes an object (to **set** something); *sit* does not.

site See **cite, site, sight.**

so *So* intensifies another word when it is used with *that:* He was **so** nervous **that** he had trouble sleeping. Instead of using *so* alone, find a precise modifier: She was **so intensely** focused on her career. See **26f.**

someplace See **anyplace, everyplace, someplace.**

sometime, sometimes, some time *Sometime* means "at an unspecified time": They will meet **sometime** next month. *Sometimes* means "at times": **Sometimes** laws are unfair. *Some time* means "a span of time": They agreed to allow **some time** to pass before voting on the measure.

sort of a See **kind of a, sort of a.**

specially See **especially, specially.**

stationary, stationery *Stationary* means "in a fixed position": Traffic was **stationary** for an hour. *Stationery* means "writing paper and envelopes": The director ordered new department **stationery.**

supposed to, used to Be sure to include the frequently unsounded *d* at the end of the verb form: We are **supposed to** leave at 9:30 a.m. We **used to** leave earlier.

take See **bring, take.**

than, then *Than* is used in comparisons: The tape recorder is smaller **than** the radio. *Then* refers to a time sequence: Go straight ahead for three blocks; **then** turn left.

***that, which** *Which* occurs in nonessential (nonrestrictive) clauses: Myanmar, **which** borders Thailand, was formerly called Burma. Both *that* and *which* occur in essential (restrictive) clauses, although traditionally only *that* was considered acceptable: I am looking for an atlas **that** [OR **which**] includes demographic information. (For more information on essential and nonessential clauses, see **36d** and **36g**.)

*__that, which, who__ In essential (restrictive) clauses, *who* and *that* refer to people. We want to hire someone **who** [OR **that**] has had experience programming. Traditionally, only *who* was used to refer to people. *That,* as well as *which,* refers to things: He proposed a design **that** [OR **which**] will take advantage of solar energy.

their, there, they're *Their* is the possessive form of *they:* They will give **their** presentation tomorrow. *There* refers to location: I lived **there** for six years. *There* is also used as an expletive (see **35a(3)**): **There** is no explanation for the phenomenon. *They're* is a contraction of *they are:* **They're** leaving in the morning.

theirself, theirselves Unconventional; use *themselves.* The students finished the project by ~~theirself~~ **themselves.**

then See **than, then.**

thru *Through* is preferred in academic and professional writing: We drove ~~thru~~ **through** the whole state of South Dakota in one day.

thusly Unconventional; use *thus, in this way,* or *as follows* instead: He accompanied his father on archeological digs and ~~thusly~~ discovered his interest in ancient cultures.

time period Readers are likely to consider this combination redundant; use one word or the other, but not both: During this ~~time~~ **period,** the economy was strong.

to, too, two *To* is an infinitive marker: She wanted **to** become an actress. *To* is also used as a preposition, usually indicating direction: They walked **to** the memorial. *Too* means either "also" or "excessively": I voted for her **too.** They are **too** busy this year. *Two* is a number: She studied abroad for **two** years.

toward, towards Although both are acceptable, *toward* is preferred in American English.

try and Conversational for *try to:* The staff will **try ~~and~~ to** finish the project by Friday.

ultimately See **eventually, ultimately.**

uninterested See **disinterested, uninterested.**

*__unique__ Traditionally, *unique* meant "one of a kind" and thus was not preceded by a qualifier such as *more, most, quite,* or *very:* Her prose style is ~~quite~~

unique. However, dictionary editors note that *unique* is also widely used to mean "extraordinary."

use, utilize In most contexts, *use* is preferred to *utilize:* We ~~utilized~~ used a special dye in the experiment. However, *utilize* may suggest an effort to employ something for a purpose: We discussed how to **utilize** the resources we had been given.

used to See **supposed to, used to.**

very To ensure this word's effectiveness, use it sparingly. Whenever possible, choose a stronger word: She was ~~very satisfied~~ delighted with her new digital camera.

ways Conversational when referring to distance; use *way* instead: It's a long ~~ways~~ way from home.

well See **good, well.**

where Conversational for *that:* I noticed ~~where~~ that she had been elected.

where . . . at, where . . . to Conversational; omit *at* and *to:* **Where** is the library ~~at~~? **Where** are you moving ~~to~~?

which See **that, which** and **that, which, who.**

*****who, whom** *Who* is used as the subject or subject complement in a clause: We have decided to hire Marian Wright, ~~whom~~ who I believe is currently finishing her degree in business administration. [*Who* is the subject in *who is currently finishing her degree in business administration.*] See also **that, which, who.** *Whom* is used as an object: Jeff Kruger, ~~who~~ whom we hired in 2007, is now our top sales representative. [*Whom* is the object in *whom we hired.*] Dictionary editors note that in conversation *who* is commonly used as an object as long as it does not follow a preposition. See **25b(5).**

whose, who's *Whose* is a possessive form: **Whose** book is this? The book was written by a young Mexican-American woman **whose** family still lives in Chiapas. *Who's* is the contraction of *who is:* **Who's** going to run in the election? See **25b(3).**

will See **shall, will.**

with regards to Unconventional; see **regard, regarding, regards.**

would of See **could of.**

your, you're *Your* is a possessive form: Let's meet in **your** office. *You're* is a contraction of *you are:* **You're** gaining strength.

yourself See **herself, himself, myself, yourself.**

GLOSSARY OF TERMS

This glossary provides brief definitions of frequently used terms. Consult the index for references to terms not listed here.

absolute phrase A sentencelike structure containing a subject and its modifiers. Unlike a sentence, an absolute phrase has no verb marked for person, number, or tense: *The ceremony finally over,* the graduates tossed their mortarboards in the air. See **21a(6)**.

acronym A word formed by combining the initial letters or syllables of a series of words and pronounced as a word rather than as a series of letters: *NATO* for North Atlantic Treaty Organization. See **44e**.

active voice See **voice.**

adjectival clause A dependent clause, also called a **relative clause,** that modifies a noun or a pronoun. See **21b(2)**.

adjectival phrase A phrase that modifies a noun or a pronoun.

adjective A word that modifies a noun or a pronoun. Adjectives typically end in suffixes such as *-al, -able, -ant, -ative, -ic, -ish, -less, -ous,* and *-y.* See **20a(4)** and **26a. Coordinate adjectives** are two or more adjectives modifying the same noun and separated by a comma: a *brisk, cold* walk. See **36c(2)**.

adverb A word that modifies a verb, a verbal, an adjective, or another adverb. Adverbs commonly end in *-ly.* Some adverbs modify entire sentences: *Perhaps* the meeting could be postponed. See **20a(5)** and **26a**.

adverbial clause A dependent clause that modifies a verb, an adjective, or an adverb. See **21b(2)**.

adverbial conjunction A word such as *however* or *thus* that joins one independent clause to another; also known as a **conjunctive adverb.** See **21c(4)**. COMPARE: **conjunction.**

alt tags Descriptive lines of text for each visual image in an electronic document. Because these lines can be read by screen-reading software, they can assist visually impaired users. See **5d(3)**.

antecedent A word or group of words referred to by a pronoun. See **20a(3)** and **25c.**

appositive A pronoun, noun, or noun phrase that identifies, describes, or explains an adjacent pronoun, noun, or noun phrase. See **21a(5)** and **25b(4).**

article A word used to signal a noun. *The* is a definite article; *a* and *an* are indefinite articles. See **20a(4).**

asynchronous forum Online means of communication in which a period of time elapses between the sending and the receiving of a message. Blogs, listservs, and discussion forums are examples of asynchronous forums. See **5b.** COMPARE: **synchronous forum.**

auxiliary verb, auxiliary A verb that combines with a main verb. *Be, do,* and *have* are auxiliary verbs when they are used with main verbs. Also called **helping verbs. Modal auxiliaries** include *could, should,* and *may* and are used for such purposes as expressing doubt or obligation and making a request. See **20a(1)** and **24a(4).**

Boolean operators See **logical operators.**

case The form of a noun or a pronoun that indicates its relationship to other words in a sentence. Nouns and pronouns can be subjects or subject complements (**subjective case**), objects (**objective case**), or markers of possession and other relations (**possessive case**). See **25b.**

claim A statement that a writer wants readers to accept; also called a **proposition.** See **7d.**

clause A sequence of related words forming an independent unit (**independent clause,** or **main clause**) or an embedded unit (**dependent clause** used as an adverb, adjective, or noun). A clause has both a subject and a predicate. See **21b.**

cliché An expression that has lost its power to interest readers because of overuse. See **34b.**

clipped form A word that is a shortened form of another word: *bike* for *bicycle.* See **44d(2).**

collective noun A noun that refers to a group: *team, faculty, committee.* See **20a(2).**

collocation Common word combination such as *add to, adept at,* or *admiration for.* See **34c.**

colloquial A label for any word or phrase that is characteristic of informal speech. *Kid* is colloquial; *child* is used in formal contexts. See **33b.**

common noun A noun referring to any or all members of a class or group (*woman, city, holiday*) rather than to specific members (*Susan, Reno, New Year's Day*). COMPARE: **proper noun.** See **20a(2).**

complement A word or words used to complete the meaning of a verb. A **subject complement** is a word or phrase that follows a linking verb and categorizes or describes the subject. An **object complement** is a word or phrase that categorizes or describes a direct object when it follows such verbs as *make, paint, elect,* and *consider.* See **20c.**

complete predicate See **predicate.**

complete subject See **subject.**

complex sentence A sentence containing one independent clause and at least one dependent clause. See **21c(3).**

compound-complex sentence A sentence containing at least two independent clauses and one or more dependent clauses. See **21c(4).**

compound predicate A predicate that has two parts joined by a connecting word such as *and, or,* or *but;* each part contains a verb: Clara Barton *nursed the injured during the Civil War* and *later founded the American Red Cross.* See **20b.**

compound sentence A sentence containing at least two independent clauses and no dependent clauses. See **21c(2).**

compound subject Two subjects joined by a connecting word such as *and, or,* or *but: Students* and *faculty* are discussing the issue of grade inflation. See **20b.**

compound word Two or more words functioning as a single word: *ice cream, double-check.* See **41f(1).**

conditional clause An adverbial clause (**21b(2)**), usually beginning with *if,* that expresses a condition: *If it rains,* the outdoor concert will be postponed.

conjunction A word used to connect other words, phrases, clauses, or sentences. **Coordinating conjunctions** (*and, but, or, nor, for, so,* and *yet*) connect and relate words and word groups of equal grammatical rank. See **20a(7)** and **21c.** A **subordinating conjunction** such as *although, if,* or *when* begins a dependent clause and connects it to an independent clause. See **20a(7)** and **21c.** COMPARE: **adverbial conjunction.**

conjunctive adverb See **adverbial conjunction.**

convention, conventional Refers to language or behavior that follows the customs of a community such as the academic, medical, or business community.

coordinate adjective See **adjective.**

coordinating conjunction See **conjunction.**

coordination The use of grammatically equivalent constructions to link or balance ideas. See Chapter **29.**

correlative conjunctions, correlatives Two-part connecting words such as *either … or* and *not only … but also.* See **20a(7)** and **21c.**

count nouns Nouns naming things that can be counted (*word, student, remark*). See **20a(2).** COMPARE: **noncount nouns.**

dangling modifier A word or phrase that does not clearly modify another word or word group. See **26e.** COMPARE: **misplaced modifier.**

dangling participial phrase A verbal phrase that does not clearly modify another word or word group.

deductive reasoning A form of logical reasoning in which a conclusion is formed after relating a specific fact (minor premise) to a generalization (major premise). See **7h(2).** COMPARE: **inductive reasoning.**

demonstratives Four words (*this, that, these,* and *those*) that distinguish one individual, thing, event, or idea from another. Demonstratives may occur with or without nouns: *This* [demonstrative determiner] *law* will go into effect in two years. *This* [demonstrative pronoun] will go into effect in two years. See **25a(5).**

dependent clause See **clause.**

determiner A word that signals the approach of a noun. A determiner may be an article, a demonstrative, a possessive, or a quantifier: *a reason, this reason, his reason, three reasons.*

direct address See **vocative.**

direct object See **object.**

direct quotation See **quotation.**

ellipsis points Three spaced periods that indicate either a pause or the omission of material from a direct quotation. See **40g.**

elliptical clause A clause missing one or more words that are assumed to be understood. See **21b(2).**

essential element A word or word group that modifies another word or word group, providing information that is essential for identification. Essential elements are not set off by commas, parentheses, or dashes: The woman *who witnessed the accident* was called to testify. Also called a **restrictive element.** COMPARE: **nonessential element.** See **21b(2)** and **36d.**

ethos One of the three classical appeals; the use of language to demonstrate the writer's trustworthy character, good intentions, and substantial knowledge of a subject. Also called an **ethical appeal.** See **7f(1).** See also **logos** and **pathos.**

expletive A word signaling a structural change in a sentence, usually used so that new or important information is given at the end of the sentence: *There* were over four thousand runners in the marathon. See **20b(1).**

faulty predication A sentence error in which the predicate does not logically belong with the given subject. See **27d(2).**

figurative language The use of words in an imaginative rather than in a literal sense. See **34a(3).**

first person See **person.**

flaming A personal attack that occurs in an online exchange. See **5c.**

gender The grammatical label that distinguishes nouns or pronouns as masculine, feminine, or neuter. In English, grammatical gender usually corresponds to biological gender. Gender also describes how people see themselves, or are seen by others, as either male or female. See **25c(2)** and **33c(1).**

generic noun See **common noun.**

genre A literary category, such as drama or poetry, identified by its own conventions. See **11a.**

gerund A verbal that ends in *-ing* and functions as a noun: *Snowboarding* is a popular winter sport. See **21a(3).**

gerund phrase A verbal phrase that employs the *-ing* form of a verb and functions as a noun: Some students prefer *studying in the library.* See **21a(3).**

helping verb See **auxiliary verb.**

homophones Words that have the same sound and sometimes the same spelling but differ in meaning: *their, there,* and *they're* or *capital* meaning "funds" and *capital* meaning "the top of a pillar." See **41c.**

idiom An expression whose meaning often cannot be derived from its elements. *Burning the midnight oil* means "staying up late studying." See **34c.**

imperative mood See **mood.**

indefinite article See **article.**

indefinite pronoun A pronoun such as *everyone* or *anything* that does not refer to a specific person, place, thing, or idea. See **25c(1).**

independent clause See **clause.**

indicative mood See **mood.**

indirect object See **object.**

indirect question A sentence that includes an embedded question, punctuated with a period instead of a question mark: My friends asked me *why I left the party early.* See **40a(1).**

indirect quotation See **quotation.**

inductive reasoning The reasoning process that begins with facts or observations and moves to general principles that account for those facts or observations. See **7h(1).** COMPARE: **deductive reasoning.**

infinitive A verbal that consists of the base form of the verb, usually preceded by the infinitive marker *to.* An infinitive is used chiefly as a noun, less frequently as an adjective or adverb: My father likes *to golf.* See **21a(3)** and **24b(6).**

infinitive phrase A verbal phrase that contains the infinitive form of a verb: They volunteered *to work at the local hospital.* See **21a(3).**

inflection A change in the form of a word that indicates a grammatical feature such as number, person, tense, or degree. For example, *-ed* added to a verb indicates the past tense, and *-er* indicates the comparative degree of an adjective or adverb.

intensifier See **qualifier.**

intensive pronoun See **reflexive pronoun.**

interjection A word expressing a simple exclamation: *Hey! Oops!* When used at the beginnings of sentences, mild interjections are set off by commas. See **20a(8).**

intransitive verb A verb that does not take an object: Everyone *laughed.* See **20d.** COMPARE: **transitive verb.**

invention Using strategies to generate ideas for writing.

inversion A change in the usual subject-verb order of a sentence: *Are you* ready? See **20d.**

keywords Specific words used with a search tool (such as Google) to find information. See **8b.**

linking verb A verb that relates a subject to a subject complement. Examples of linking verbs are *be, become, seem, appear, feel, look, taste, smell,* and *sound.* See **20a(1)** and **24a(4).**

logical operators Words used to broaden or narrow electronic database searches. These include *or, and, not,* and *near.* Also called **Boolean operators.** See **8c.**

logos One of the three classical appeals; the use of language to show clear reasoning. Also called a **logical appeal**. See **7f(2)**. See also **ethos** and **pathos**.

major premise See **premise**.

main clause Also called **independent clause**. See **clause**.

minor premise See **premise**.

misplaced modifier A descriptive or qualifying word or phrase placed in a position that confuses the reader: I read about a wildfire that was out of control *in yesterday's paper*. [The modifier belongs after *read*.] See **26d**.

mixed construction A confusing sentence that is the result of an unintentional shift from one grammatical pattern to another: When police appeared who were supposed to calm the crowds showed up, most people had already gone home. [The sentence should be recast with either *appeared* or *showed up*, not with both.] See **27d(1)**.

mixed metaphor A construction that includes parts of two or more unrelated metaphors: Her *fiery* personality *dampened* our hopes of a compromise. See **27b**.

modal auxiliary See **auxiliary verb**.

modifier A word or word group that describes, limits, or qualifies another. See Chapter **26**.

mood A set of verb forms or inflections used to indicate how a speaker or writer regards an assertion: as a fact or opinion (**indicative mood**); as a command or instruction (**imperative mood**); or as a wish, hypothesis, request, or condition contrary to fact (**subjunctive mood**). See **24d**.

netiquette Word formed from *Internet* and *etiquette* to refer to guidelines for writing e-mail messages and other online postings and for online behavior in general. See **5c**.

nominalization Formation of a noun by adding a suffix to a verb or an adjective: *require, requirement; sad, sadness*.

nominative case Also called **subjective case**. See **case**.

noncount nouns Nouns naming things that cannot be counted (*architecture, water*). See **20a(2)**. COMPARE: **count nouns**.

nonessential element A word or word group that modifies another word or word group but does not provide information essential for identification. Nonessential elements are set off by commas, parentheses, or dashes: Carol Murphy, *president of the university*, plans to meet with alumni representatives. Also called a **nonrestrictive element**. See **21b(2)** and **36d**. COMPARE: **essential element**.

nonrestrictive element See **nonessential element.**

nonstandard, nonstandardized Refers to speech forms that are not considered conventional in many academic and professional settings. See the **Glossary of Usage.**

noun A word that names a person, place, thing, idea, animal, quality, event, and so on: *Alanis, America, desk, justice, dog, strength, departure.* See **20a(2).** See also **collective noun, common noun, count noun, noncount noun,** and **proper noun.**

noun clause A dependent clause used as a noun. See **21b(2).**

noun phrase A noun and its modifiers. See **21a(1).**

number The property of a word that indicates whether it refers to one (**singular**) or to more than one (**plural**). Number is reflected in the word's form: *river/rivers, this/those, he sees/they see.* See **25c(4)** and **24f.**

object A noun, pronoun, noun phrase, or noun clause that follows a preposition or a transitive verb or verbal. A **direct object** names the person or thing that receives the action of the verb: I sent the *package.* An **indirect object** usually indicates to whom the action was directed or for whom the action was performed: I sent *you* the package. See **20c(1)** and **20c(2).** The **object of a preposition** follows a preposition: I sent the package to *you.* See **21a(4).**

object complement See **complement.**

object of a preposition See **object.**

objective case See **case.**

parenthetical element Any word, phrase, or clause that adds detail to a sentence or any sentence that adds detail to a paragraph but is not essential for understanding the core meaning. Commas, dashes, or parentheses separate these elements from the rest of the sentence or paragraph. See **35d, 40d,** and **40e.**

participial phrase A verbal phrase that includes a participle: The stagehand *carrying the trunk* fell over the threshold. See **21a(3).** See also **participle** and **phrase.**

participle A verb form that may function as part of a verb phrase (had *determined,* was *thinking*) or as a modifier (a *determined* effort; the couple, *thinking* about their past). A **present participle** is formed by adding *-ing* to the base form of a verb. A **past participle** is usually formed by adding *-ed* to the base form of a verb (*walked, passed*); however, many verbs have irregular past-participle forms (*written, bought, gone*). See **24a(1)** and **24a(2).**

particle A word such as *across, away, down, for, in, off, out, up, on,* or *with* that combines with a main verb to form a phrasal verb: *write down, look up.* See **24a(3)**.

parts of speech The classes into which words may be grouped according to their forms and grammatical relationships. The traditional parts of speech are verbs, nouns, pronouns, adjectives, adverbs, prepositions, conjunctions, and interjections.

passive voice See **voice.**

past participle See **participle.**

pathos One of the three classical appeals; the use of language to stir the feelings of an audience. Also called an **emotional appeal** or a **pathetic appeal.** See **7f(3)**. See also **ethos** and **logos.**

person The property of nouns, pronouns, and their corresponding verbs that distinguishes the speaker or writer **(first person)**, the individuals addressed **(second person)**, and the individuals or things referred to **(third person)**. See **24b.**

personal pronoun A pronoun that refers to a specific person, place, thing, and so on. Pronoun forms correspond to three cases: subjective, objective, and possessive. See **25a(1)**.

phrasal verb A grammatical unit consisting of a verb and a particle such as *after, in, up, off,* or *out: fill in, sort out.* See **24a(3)**.

phrase A sequence of grammatically related words that functions as a unit in a sentence but lacks a subject, a predicate, or both: *in front of the stage.* See **21a.**

point of view The vantage point from which a topic is viewed; also, the stance a writer takes: objective or impartial (third person), directive (second person), or personal (first person). See **28b.**

possessive case See **case.**

predicate The part of a sentence that expresses what a subject is, does, or experiences. It consists of the main verb, its auxiliaries, and any complements and modifiers. The **simple predicate** consists of only the main verb and any accompanying auxiliaries. See **20b** and **20c.** COMPARE: **subject.**

premise An assumption or a proposition on which an argument or explanation is based. In logic, premises are either **major** (general) or **minor** (specific); when combined correctly, they lead to a conclusion. See **7h(2)**. See also **syllogism.**

preposition A word such as *at, in, by,* or *of* that relates a pronoun, noun, noun phrase, or noun clause to other words in the sentence. See **20a(6)**.

prepositional phrase A preposition with its object and any modifiers: *at* the nearby airport, *by* the sea. See **21a(4)**.

present participle See **participle**.

primary source A source that provides firsthand information. See **8a(3)**. COMPARE: **secondary source**.

pronoun A word that takes the position of a noun, noun phrase, or noun clause and functions as that word or word group does: *it, that, he, them.* See **20a(3)** and Chapter **25**.

proper adjective An adjective that is derived from the name of a person or place: *Marxist* theories. See **41a(9)**.

proper noun The name of a specific person, place, organization, and so on: *Dr. Pimomo, Fargo, National Education Association.* Proper nouns are capitalized. See **20a(2)**. COMPARE: **common noun**.

proposition See **claim**.

qualifier A word that intensifies or moderates the meaning of an adverb or adjective: *quite* pleased, *somewhat* reluctant. Words that intensify are sometimes called **intensifiers**.

quotation A **direct quotation** (also called **direct discourse**) is the exact repetition of someone's spoken or written words. An **indirect quotation** is a report of someone's written or spoken words not stated in the exact words of the writer or speaker. See **10d(2)** and Chapter **39**.

reflexive pronoun A pronoun that ends in *-self* or *-selves* (*myself* or *themselves*) and refers to a preceding noun or pronoun in the sentence: *He* added a picture of *himself* to his web page. When used to provide emphasis, such a pronoun is called an **intensive pronoun**: The president *herself* awarded the scholarships. See **25a(2)**.

refutation A strategy for addressing opposing points of view by discussing those views and explaining why they are unsatisfactory. See **7e(2)** and **7g(3)**.

relative clause See **adjectival clause**.

relative pronoun A word (*who, whom, that, which,* or *whose*) used to introduce an **adjectival clause**, also called a **relative clause**. An antecedent for the relative pronoun can be found in the main clause. See **21b(2)**.

restrictive element See **essential element**.

rhetorical appeal The means of persuasion in argumentative writing, relying on reason, authority, or emotion. See **7f**.

rhetorical opportunity A chance for a writer to resolve an issue or problem with the purposeful use of language. See **1b**.

Rogerian argument An approach to argumentation that is based on the work of psychologist Carl R. Rogers and that emphasizes the importance of withholding judgment of others' ideas until they are fully understood. See **7g(2)**.

secondary source A source that analyzes or interprets firsthand information. See **8a(3)**. COMPARE: **primary source.**

sentence modifier A modifier related to a whole sentence, not to a specific word or word group within it: *All things considered,* the committee acted appropriately when it approved the amendment to the bylaws. See **26a(4)**.

signal phrase A short phrase that identifies the source of a quotation: *according to Jones, Jones claims.* See **10d**.

simple predicate See **predicate.**

simple subject See **subject.**

split infinitive The separation of the two parts of an infinitive form by at least one word: *to completely cover.* See **21a(3)**.

squinting modifier A modifier that is unclear because it can refer to words either preceding it or following it: Proofreading *quickly* results in missed spelling errors. See **26d(3)**.

Standardized English The usage expected in most academic and business settings. See the **Glossary of Usage.**

subject The general idea addressed in a piece of writing. See **2a**. COMPARE: **topic.** Also, the pronoun, noun, or noun phrase that carries out the action or assumes the state described in the predicate of a sentence. Usually preceding the predicate, the subject includes the main noun or pronoun and all modifiers. A **simple subject** consists of only the main noun or pronoun. See **20b** and **20d**. COMPARE: **predicate.**

subject complement See **complement.**

subjective case See **case.**

subjunctive mood See **mood.**

subordinating conjunction See **conjunction.**

subordination The connection of a grammatical structure to another, usually a dependent clause to an independent clause: *Even though customers were satisfied with the product,* the company wanted to improve it. See Chapter **29**.

syllogism Method for deductive reasoning consisting of two premises and a conclusion. See **7h(2)**. See also **premise.**

synchronous forum Online means of communication in which messages are exchanged in real time; that is, the receiver of a message sees it on the screen right after the sender completes it. See **5b**. COMPARE: **asynchronous forum.**

tense The form of a verb that indicates when and for how long an action or state occurs. See **24b** and **24c**.

theme The main idea of a literary work. See **11c(7)**.

thesis The central point or main idea of an essay. See **2c**.

tone The writer's attitude toward the subject and the audience, usually conveyed through word choice and sentence structure. See **3a(3)**.

topic The specific, narrowed main idea of an essay. See **2b**. COMPARE: **subject.**

topic sentence A statement of the main idea of a paragraph. See **3c(1)**.

Toulmin model A system of argumentation developed by philosopher Stephen Toulmin in which a claim and supporting reasons or evidence depend on a shared assumption. See **7g(3)**.

transitions Words, phrases, sentences, or paragraphs that relate ideas by linking sentences, paragraphs, or larger segments of writing. See **3d** and **23c(5)**.

transitive verb A verb that takes an object. The researchers *reported* their findings. See **20d**. COMPARE: **intransitive verb.**

usability testing The process of soliciting reactions from potential users of a website or other complex electronic document in order to improve the content or design of the document. See **5d(3)**.

verb A word denoting action, occurrence, or existence (state of being). See **20a(1)** and Chapter **24**.

verb phrase A main verb and any auxiliaries. See **21a(2)** and **24a(4)**.

verbal A verb form functioning as a noun, an adjective, or an adverb. See **21a(3)**. See also **gerund, infinitive,** and **participle.**

vocative Set off by commas, the name of or the descriptive term for a person or persons being addressed. See **36b(3)**.

voice A property of a verb that indicates the relationship between the verb and its subject. The **active voice** is used to show that the subject performs the action expressed by the verb; the **passive voice** is used to show that the subject receives the action. See **24d**.

warrant According to the Toulmin model, the underlying assumption connecting a claim and data. See **7g(3)**.

CREDITS

These pages constitute an extension of the copyright page. We have made every effort to trace the ownership of all copyrighted material and to secure permission from copyright holders. In the event of any question arising as to the use of any material, we will be pleased to make the necessary corrections in future printings.

pp. 11–12: Kathleen Dean Moore, "The Happy Basket" in *Wild Comfort: The Solace of Nature* (Boston: Trumpeter, 2010), 21–22.

p. 12: Nina G. Jablonski, *Skin: A Natural History* (Berkeley: University of California Press, 2006), 3.

pp. 12–13: Rebecca Skloot, *The Immortal Life of Henrietta Lacks* (New York: Crown/Random House, 2010), 6–7.

p. 15: US Department of Education, Office of Innovation and Improvement, "Innovations in Education: Creating Strong District School Choice Programs," Washington DC (May 2004), http://www2.ed.gov/admins/comm/choice/choiceprograms/report.pdf.

p. 16: Atul Gawande, "Crimson Tide" in *Complications: A Surgeon's Notes on an Imperfect Science* (New York: Picador, 2002), 150.

pp. 23, 25, 27, 28, 32: Freewriting, thesis statements, and outline used by permission of Mary LeNoir.

p. 27: Frank McCourt, "Foreword," in *Eats, Shoots & Leaves* by Lynne Truss (New York: Gotham, 2003), xi.

p. 27: Richard Selzer, "Diary of an Infidel: Notes from a Monastery" in *Taking the World in for Repairs* (New York: Morrow, 1986), 13.

p. 27: Amnesty International, "Abolish the Death Penalty," http://www.amnesty.org/en/death-penalty.

p. 29: Deborah Tannen, "Gender in the Classroom," in *Across Cultures: A Reader for Writers*, 6th ed., edited by Sheena Gillespie and Robert Becker (New York: Longman, 2004), p. 165.

p. 29: Mary Pipher, "Growing Our Souls" in *Writing to Change the World* (New York: Riverhead-Penguin, 2006), 53.

p. 30: Sam Swope, "The Animal in Miguel" in *I Am a Pencil: A Teacher, His Kids, and Their Wonderful World of Stories* (New York: Holt/Owl, 2005), 114.

p. 30: Charles Seife, *Zero: The Biography of a Dangerous Idea* (New York: Penguin, 2000), 5.

p. 34: Brenda Jo Brueggemann, "American Sign Language and the Academy" in *Deaf Subjects: between Identities and Places* (New York: New York University Press, 2009), 29.

p. 35: Barbara Kingsolver, "Lily's Chickens," in *Small Wonder: Essays* (New York: HarperCollins, 2002), 110.

pp. 36–37: Jill Lepore, "Prologue: Party Like It's 1773" in *The Whites of Their Eyes: The Tea Party's Revolution and the Battle over American History* (Princeton, NJ: Princeton University Press, 2010), 2.

pp. 37–38: Ishmael Beah, *A Long Way Gone: Memoirs of a Boy Soldier* (New York: Crichton, 2007), 18.

pp. 38–39: Sam Swope, "The Case of the Missing Report Cards," in *I Am a Pencil: A Teacher, His Kids, and Their Wonderful World of Stories* (New York: Holt/Owl, 2005), 140.

pp. 39–40: From "Topic of Cancer" by Christopher Hitchens from *Vanity Fair*, September 2010, p. 204. Used by permission of the author.

p. 40: Mark Orwoll, "Revolution in the Skies," *Travel Leisure*, November 2010, 169.

pp. 40–41: Reprinted with the permission of Simon & Schuster, Inc. from AMERICAN GRACE by Robert D. Putnam and David E. Campbell, p. 2. Copyright © 2010 Robert D. Putnam and David E. Campbell.

p. 42: Jody M. Roy, "The Case of the Cowboy," in *Love to Hate: America's Obsession with Hatred and Violence* (New York: Columbia University Press, 2002).

p. 43: Joel Arem, *Rocks and Minerals* (Totnes, England: Geoscience Press, 1994).

p. 47: Dorothy Allison, *Two or Three Things I Know for Sure* (New York: Penguin/ Plume, 1996), 6.

p. 48: Rick Roth, "Snake Charmer," interview by Sara Martel, *Sierra,* January– February 2011, 11.

p. 49: Jennifer Howard, "Americans Are Closing the Book on Reading, Study Finds," *Chronicle of Higher Education* 54:14 (November 19, 2007), A12.

p. 50: Terry Tempest Williams, "The Clan of One-Breasted Women" in *Refuge* (New York: Random House/Vintage, 1992), 281.

p. 50: Eudora Welty, "A Sweet Devouring" first published in *Mademoiselle*, 1957. Collected in *The Eye of the Story* (New York: Penguin/Random House, 1977).

p. 50: Frederick Douglass, "What to the Slave Is the Fourth of July?" Reprinted in his 1855 autobiography, *My Bondage and My Freedom.*

p. 50: Patricia J. Williams, *Open House: Of Family, Friends, Food, Piano Lessons, and the Search for a Room of My Own* (New York: Farrar, 2004), 3.

p. 51: Melissa Gotthardt, "The Miracle Diet," *AARP,* January/February 2007, 26.

p. 51: Rebecca Traister, *Big Girls Don't Cry* (New York: Free Press, 2010), 15.

pp. 51–52: From "Not Seeing the Forest for the Dollar Bills" by Donella Meadows, *Valley News*, June 30, 1990. Reprinted by permission of Sustainability Institute.

p. 52: Zora Neale Hurston, *Dust Tracks on a Road: An Autobiography* (Philadelphia: Lippincott, 1942), 288.

p. 52: Kathy L. Glass, "'Tending to the Roots': Anna Julia Cooper's Sociopolitical Thought and Activism," *Meridians* 6.1 (2005): 23–55.

p. 52: Excerpt from "September 11, 2001 Somewhere over Pennsylvania" by Randall Sullivan from *Rolling Stone*, 4/11/02. © Rolling Stone LLC 2002. All Rights Reserved. Reprinted by permission.

p. 53: Debra Utacia Krol, "Peterson Yazzie," *Native Peoples: Arts and Lifeways*, January/February 2007, 45.

pp. 54–55: Malcolm Gladwell, *Blink: The Power of Thinking without Thinking* (Boston: Little, Brown, 2005), 13–14.

p. 55: Richard Lederer, "English Is a Crazy Language" in *Crazy English* (New York: Pocket Books, 1989), 3.

p. 55: Patricia Marx, "Dressin' Texan," *New Yorker*, March 19, 2007, 68.

p. 59: K. Bindas. "Re-remembering a Segregated Past: Race in American Memory." *History and Memory* 22.1 (2010): 113–35. Used by permission of Indiana University Press.

p. 59: Tal Birdsey, *A Room for Learning: The Making of a School in Vermont* (New York: St. Martin's, 2009), 34.

p. 60: Richard F. Thompson and Stephen A. Madigan, *Memory: The Key to Consciousness* (Washington, DC: Joseph Henry Press, 2005), 83.

p. 60: Mary E. Curtis and John R. Kruidenier, "Teaching Adults to Read: A Summer of Scientifically Based Research Principles" (Jessup, MD: National Institute for Literacy, 2005), 9, accessed October 27, 2010, http://www.eric.ed.gov/PDFS/ED493064.pdf.

p. 60: Amy Tan, "Two Kinds" in *The Joy Luck Club* (New York: Penguin, 2006), 142.

pp. 61–62: Constance Holden, "Identical Twins Reared Apart," *Science*, 207 (March 1980), 1323–25.

p. 62: "Spellings Addresses PTA Convention," *The Achiever* 4.10 (September 2005), n.p., accessed October 27, 2010, http://www2.ed.gov/news/newsletters.achiever.2005/090105.html.

pp. 67, 69–72: Writer's memo and first draft by Mary LeNoir. Used by permission of the author.

pp. 79–87: "How Student-Athletes Really Choose a College" by Mary Lenoir. Used by permission of the author.

p. 147: Cornel West, *Race Matters* (Boston: Beacon Press, 2001), 3.

pp. 151, 152–53, 154: "The Tucson Shootings: Words and Deeds" by Debra Hughes originally appeared in *Narrative* magazine. Reprinted by permission of *Narrative* magazine and the author.

p. 157: Mary Pipher, *Writing to Change the World* (New York: Riverhead-Penguin, 2006), 223–24.

pp. 171–76: "Naming Opportunities: Opportunities for Whom" by Anna Seitz. Used by permission of the author.

p. 184: Derek Bok, *The Politics of Happiness: What Government Can Learn from the New Research on Well-Being* (Princeton, NJ: Princeton University Press), 4.

p. 201: Natalie Angier, *Woman: An Intimate Geography* (New York: Anchor/Doubleday, 2000), 355.

p. 202: "Cocksure" by Malcolm Gladwell, *New Yorker*, July 27, 2009, 39.

p. 203: "Is Military Incompetence Adaptive?" by Richard Wrangham from *Evolution and Human Behavior*, 20:1 (January 1999).

p. 210: Marsha Orgeron, "'You Are Invited to Participate': Interactive Fandom in the Age of the Movie Magazine," *Journal of Film and Video* 61:3 (Fall 2009), 3–23.

p. 212: Brian Halweil, "Emperor's New Crops" in *Taking Sides: Clashing Views on Controversial Environmental Issues* (11th ed.), edited by Thomas A. Easton (Dubuque, IA: McGraw, 2005), 256.

p. 213: Andy Rees, *Genetically Modified Food: A Short Guide for the Confused* (Ann Arbor, MI: Pluto, 2006), 8.

p. 215: Oliver Sacks, "A Man of Letters," in *The Mind's Eye* (New York: Knopf, 2010), 75.

p. 216: Jim Cullen, *The American Dream: A Short History of an Idea That Shaped a Nation* (New York: Oxford University Press, 2004), 7.

p. 220: Carl Zimmer, *Soul Made Flesh: The Discovery of the Brain—and How It Changed the World* (New York: Free Press, 2004), 7.

pp. 220–21: Michael Hanlon, "Climate Apocalypse When?" *New Scientist,* November 17, 2007, 20.

p. 222: Joseph M. Marshall, III, "Tasunke Witko (His Crazy Horse)," *Native Peoples,* January/February 2007, 76–79.

p. 227: Patricia McConnell, *The Other End of the Leash* (New York: Ballantine, 2002), 142.

p. 229: Excerpt from "A Farm on Every Floor" by Dickson Despommier from *New York Times,* 23 Aug. 2009. Copyright © 2009 The New York Times. Reprinted by permission.

p. 238: "Prose Poems: Portrait" from GIRL AT THE WINDOW © 1991 by Pinkie Gordon Lane. Reprinted by permission of Louisiana State University Press.

pp. 250–56: "The Role of Storytelling in Fighting Nineteenth-Century Chauvinism" by Kristin Ford. Used by permission of the author.

p. 264: Barbara Ehrenreich, *Nickel and Dimed: On (Not) Getting By in America* (New York: Holt/Metropolitan, 2001), 214.

p. 274: From *English Journal: The Journal of the Secondary Section of the National Council of Teachers of English* 98.1 (September 2008). Used by permission of National Council of Teachers of English.

pp. 278, 279: From *SKIN: A Natural History,* by Nina G. Jablonski, © 2006 by Nina G. Jablonski. Published by the University of California Press. Used by permission.

pp. 300–311: "Genetically Modified Foods and Developing Countries" by Marianna Suslin. Used by permission of the author.

p. 314: Excerpt from "Gender Stereotypes and Perceptions of Occupational Status Among University Students" by Danielle Dezell. Used by permission of the author.

p. 318: Excerpt from abstract to Matthew Gervais and David Wilson's article "The Evolution and Functions of Laughter and Humor" from *Quarterly Review of Biology* 80:4 (December 2005), 395.

p. 319: Higher Education Academy Psychology Network (2008). Case study from *Improving Provision for Disabled Psychology Students.* Available from http://www.psychology.heacademy. ac.uk/ipdps.

pp. 321–39: "Gender Stereotypes and Perceptions of Occupational Status Among University Students" by Danielle Dezell. Used by permission of the author.

p. 344: F. J. Sulloway and R. L. Zweigenhaft, "Birth Order and Risk Taking in Athletics: A Meta-Analysis and Study of Major League Baseball," *Personality and Social Psychology Review* 14 (April 30, 2010), 412.

p. 353: Title page from HOW TO MAKE OPPORTUNITY EQUAL by Paul Gomberg. Used by permission of Blackwell Publishing Ltd.

p. 632–33: Paul K. Humiston, "Small World," in *I Thought My Father Was God* by Paul Auster (New York: Holt, 2001), 183.

p. 633: Jame Gorman, "Finding a Wild, Fearsome World beneath Every Fallen Leaf," in *The Best American Science and Nature Writing 2003*, edited by Richard Dawkins (Boston: Houghton, 2003), 67.

p. 634: Annie Dillard, "The Stunt Pilot," in *The Writing Life* (New York: Harper/Perennial, 1990), 93.

p. 636: Malcolm Gladwell, *Blink: The Power of Thinking without Thinking* (Boston: Little, Brown: 2005), 8–9.

pp. 636–37: Antoine Bechara, Hanna Damasio, Daniel Tranel, and Antonio R. Damasio, "Deciding Advantageously before Knowing the Advantageous Strategy," *Science* 275 (February 28, 1997), 1293.

p. 650: Letter from Birmingham Jail by Dr. Martin Luther King, Jr. Reprinted by arrangement with The Heirs to the Estate of Martin Luther King Jr., c/o Writers House as agent for the proprietor New York, NY. Copyright 1963 Dr. Martin Luther King Jr; copyright renewed 1991 Coretta Scott King.

p. 651: Jean Kilbourne, *Deadly Persuasion* (New York: Free Press, 1999).

p. 651: Gretel Ehrlich, "About Men," in *The Solace of Open Places* (New York: Viking/Penguin, 1986), 52–53.

p. 653: Leslie Marmon Silko, "Interior and Exterior Landscapes," in *Yellow Woman and a Beauty of the Spirit* (New York: Simon & Schuster, 1997), 27.

p. 654: Rebecca Solnit, Storming the Gates of Paradise: Landscapes for Politics (Berkeley, CA: University of California Press, 2008), 115.

p. 654: Kenneth Libbrecht, *The Snowflake: Winter's Secret Beauty* (Stillwater, MN: Voyageur Press, 2003), 35.

p. 655: Adam Haslett, "Devotion," in You Are Not a Stranger Here: Stories (New York: Doubleday/Anchor, 2003), 65.

p. 655: Michiko Kakutani, "Making Art of Sport," *New York Times Magazine*, December 15, 1997.

p. 656: Woody Allen, *Side Effects* (New York: Ballantine, 1986), 83.

p. 656: Joan Didion, "On Keeping a Notebook," in *Slouching towards Bethlehem* (New York: Farrar, Straus & Giroux, 2008), 139.

p. 659: Michael Pollan, *The Botany of Desire: A Plant's-Eye View of the World* (New York: Random House, 2002), 18.

p. 664: Ariel Dorfman, "If Only We All Spoke Two Languages," *New York Times*, June 24, 1998.

p. 664: Parker Palmer, *The Courage to Teach: Exploring the Inner Landscape of a Teacher's Life* (San Francisco: Jossey Bass, 2007).

p. 664: Walker Evans, *Unclassified* (Zurich, Switzerland: Scalo, 2000).

p. 665: Pico Iyer, "In Praise of the Humble Comma, *Time*, June 13, 1988.

p. 679: By permission. From *Merriam-Webster's Collegiate Dictionary*, 11th Edition © 2011 by Merriam-Webster, Incorporated (www.MerriamWebster.com).

p. 683: Louise Erdrich, "The Leap," in *The Red Convertible: Selected and New Stories 1978–2008* (New York: Harper Perennial, 2010), 205.

p. 684: Charles Wohlforth, "Conservation and Eugenics," *Orion*, July/August 2010, 28.

p. 684: Loida Maritza Pérez, *Geographies of Home* (New York: Penguin, 2000).

p. 684: Hisaye Yamamoto, "Las Vegas Charley," in *Seventeen Syllables* (San Diego, CA: Harcourt, 1994).

p. 684: Denise Chavez, *A Taco Testimony: Meditations on Family, Food and Culture* (Tuscon, AZ: Rio Nuevo, 2006).

p. 685: Jane Kramer, "The Reporter's Kitchen, *New Yorker,* August 19, 2002.

p. 686: Gayle Pemberton, "The Zen of Bigger Thomas, in *The Hottest Water in Chicago: Notes of a Native Daughter* (Middletown, CT: Weslyan University Press, 1998), 168.

p. 713: Richard F. Thompson and Stephen A. Madigan, *Memory: The Key to Consciousness* (Washington, DC: Joseph Henry Press, 2005), 83.

p. 730: Tracy Kidder, *Mountains beyond Mountains: The Quest of Dr. Paul Farmer, a Man Who Would Cure the World* (New York: Random House, 2009), 218.

p. 734: Diane Ackerman, *A Natural History of Love* (New York: Vintage/Random House, 1995), 86.

p. 741: Oliver Sacks, "The Last Hippie" in *An Anthropologist on Mars* (New York: Vintage/Random House, 1995), 59.

pp. 742, 743: David Weinberger, *Small Pieces Loosely Joined: A Unified Theory of the Web* (New York: Basic Books, 2003), 10, 170.

p. 744: Patricia Gadsby, "Endangered Chocolate," *Discover,* August 1, 2002.

p. 746: Wallace Stevens, "The Snow Man," in *The Collected Poems of Wallace Stevens* (New York: Random House/Vintage, 1990), 10.

p. 776: Gary Snyder, *Back on the Fire: Essays* (Berkeley, CA: Counterpoint Press, 2008), 107.

INDEX

Numbers and letters in color refer to chapters and sections in the handbook; other numbers refer to pages.

(cont.)

(cont.)

Index

911

wire service article, MLA
documentation style for, **12b**:
276
with regards to. See regard, regarding,
regards
Wohlforth, Charles, **34a**: 684
word choice, **10d**: 219, **33b**: 670–71,
34a: 681–85
word forms, dictionary information on,
33d: 678–79
word order, **47a–d**: 818–21
inverted, **20d**: 520, **31e**: 656–57,
47d: 820
of subject, verb, and object, **20d**:
519
word processor, **5a**: 99. *See also*
grammar checker; spell checker
for footnotes, **16a**: 399
and graphs, **13d**: 317
and italics, **43**: 773
for superscript numbers, **12a**: 258
for tables, **6c**: 128, **13c**: 317
tracking revisions using, **3a**: 45
for visual documents, **6d**: 133
wordiness, **35a**: 691–93
words
commas in series of, **36c**: 704
including necessary, **27e**: 628–29
versus numerals, **44f–g**: 787–90
placing for emphasis, **31a**: 653–54
referred to as such, **43e**: 777
repeating for emphasis, **31d**: 656
repeating for parallelism, **30a**:
647–48
useless, **35a**: 691
Wordsworth, William, **11c**: 237
wordy expressions, replacements for,
35a: 692
working bibliography, **10c**: 214
working thesis, **8a**: 183
works-cited list, **10c**: 214, **12a**: 257–58
examples of, **7j**: 176, **11f**: 256, **12c**:
310

world view, of author, **9a**: 200–201
WorldCat, **8c**: 191
would of. See could of
Wrangham, Richard, **9c**: 203
wrapping, of text, **6c**: 132
Wright, Richard, **11d**: 245
writer, in rhetorical situation, **1a**: 4
writer's memo, **3e**: 66–67
writing
argumentative, **1c**: 12–13
choosing subjects for, **2a**: 22–24
expository, **1c**: 12
expressive, **1c**: 11–12
about literature, **11**: 233
about reading, **1c**: 12
rhetorically, **1a**: 4–6
writing centers, **3e**: 64, 65, **4b**: 92
writing portfolio, **4d**: 97–98
writing process, **3a**: 45, 64, 77, **7**: 140
abbreviating, **4b**: 91–92
stages of, **3**: 44
WWW Virtual Library, **8b**: 185
WYSIWYG (What You See Is What
You Get), **5d**: 113

-y, changing to *i*, **41d**: 755
Yahoo!, **5d**: 113, **8b**: 185
Yamamoto, Hisaye, **34a**: 684
year of publication, in APA-style
citations, **14a**: 340, **14b**: 349,
352, 354, 356, 357, 359, 360
yes-or-no questions, **8e**: 196
you
addressing reader as, **25e**: 601, **28b**:
635
understood, **21d**: 540, **22a**: 542
your, you're, 839
yourself. See herself, himself, myself,
yourself

Zanjani, Sally, **15b**: 381

CHECKLICSTS